*I feel a sense of calm in the
greenhouse, a sense of well-being
—I'm not being suffocated.
It's a privilege to be here, to have
this space, not to have ceilings
and walls that are oppressive.
When we leave, we miss the light.
The greenhouse is a continuation
of the house; it's not quite the garden,
but a pre-opening to the garden.*

Florence Latapie

We felt comfortable, the sun warmed the air, half-closed shades on the roof created a soft light that changed with the clouds, a gentle current of fresh air flowed into the space, the plants were luxuriant, the relationship with the sky was infinite. The almost immaterial envelope created a feeling of well-being, a feeling of lightness and immense freedom ...

Visiting botanical gardens and greenhouses as students in the 1970s and 1980s, we were impressed by their beautiful, pleasant, and welcoming atmosphere, convinced that it might be a wonderful place in which to live. Close to the sky, to the environment and to the climate, sheltered from rain and wind, warmed by the sun, with a light curtain for protection, and air to cool you down—in greenhouses, we discovered a different, friendlier approach to our relationship with the climate and the pleasure of natural comfort. They showed us that we had to live with the climate, that we had to seek to engage with it rather than ignore it, that we had to open up rather than insulate, that we had to stop always seeing the outside climate as something we had to protect ourselves from.

It became clear to us that we had to look at the transition from the outside to the inside of a building in a different way, no longer as a rigid boundary, a barrier.

Instead, it was preferable to establish a fluid, shifting, adaptable relationship that delicately modifies the external climate to create a habitable interior, letting in as much sun, air, natural light, and vistas as possible, and intervening only when the climate alone no longer offers sufficient comfort.

Our history with winter gardens begins here.

How Winter Gardens Work

The winter garden is a space defined by four distinct vertical elements whose position—open or closed, depending on the season, moment, or use—ensures optimal functionality. Operated manually by inhabitants through familiar gestures such as opening sliding doors or drawing a curtain, these elements regulate the interior climate for thermal comfort. Their ease of operability encourages regular use, emphasizing the importance of the design.

(1) Thermal curtain: Made of sheep's wool, this element prevents heat loss in the insulated, heated interior on winter nights while keeping the interior cool on hot summer days. Its reflective exterior shields against direct solar exposure.

(2) Glazed facade of heated space: Large double-glazed aluminum-framed sliding panels separate the insulated and heated interior from the winter garden. They maximize daylight, provide generous outdoor views, and open for wide access to the winter garden. The combination of this element with the thermal curtain results in a higher performance of insulation than a conventional envelope with a 50% window to wall ratio.

(3) Solar curtain: The inner layer of the winter garden is a permeable textile on a curtain track that blocks direct sunlight to avoid overheating and controls privacy. The textile is composed of aluminum stripes that reflect solar radiation while facilitating air circulation through the gaps between the metallic pieces.

(4) Glazed facade of winter garden: The outer layer closes the winter garden with aluminum-framed sliding panels of polycarbonate or single-glazed fillings, or a combination. It allows air circulation through slits in the frame. Typically, two-thirds of the panels can be opened to maximize airflow.

The floor, ceiling, and interior walls of the winter garden are made of exposed concrete to take advantage of its thermal mass. A small balcony in front of the winter garden provides protection from the high summer sun and makes it easy to clean the winter garden facade.

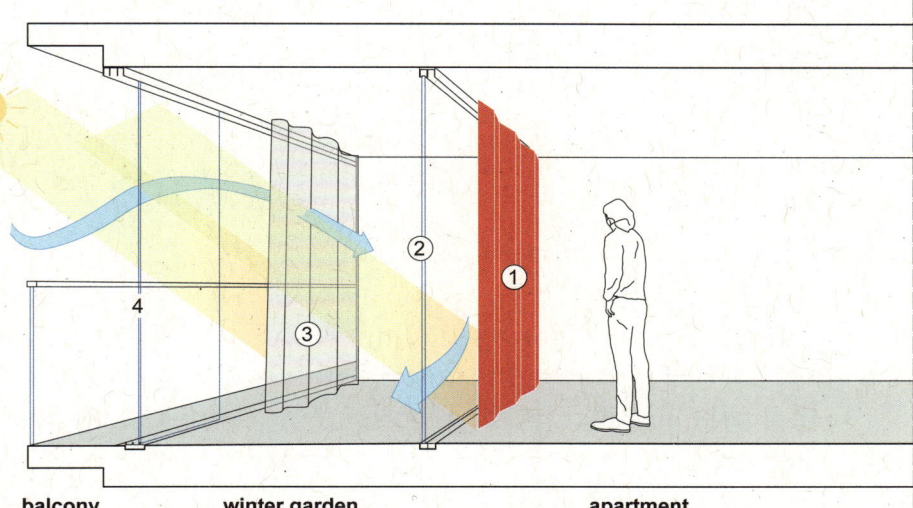

1. thermal curtain (U-value = 2.17 W/m²K)
2. sliding doors of heated space
   (U-value ≤ 1.4 W/m²K, visible light transmittance (VLT) ≥ 0.76, solar factor (SF) ≥ 0.55)
   ① + ② U-value ≈ 0.8 W/m²K
3. solar curtain
4. sliding doors of winter garden

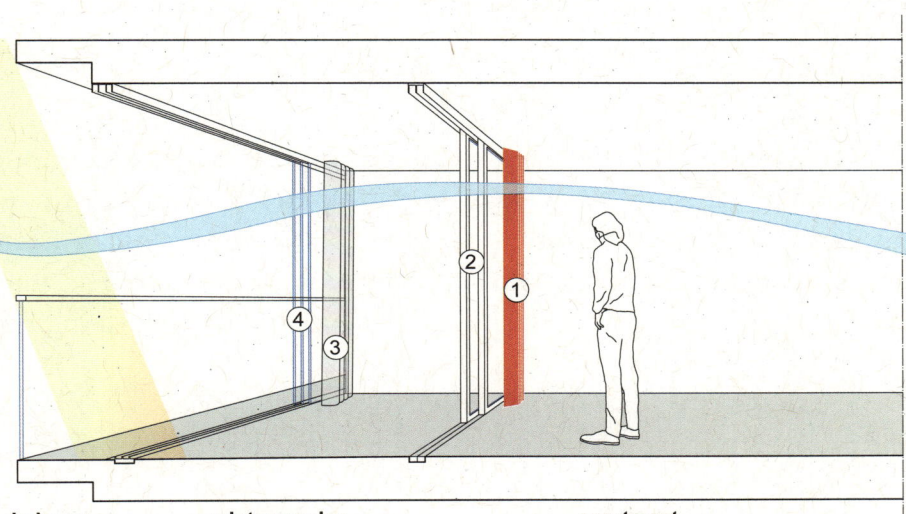

1. thermal curtain
2. sliding doors of heated space open
3. solar curtain
4. sliding doors of winter garden open, so the winter garden is an extension of the balcony and protected from direct sunlight

Scenario for Optimal Winter Comfort

In winter, both transparent facades are closed and winter gardens function as buffer spaces. During the daytime, solar and thermal curtains are kept open, allowing low solar angles to enter the envelope through both glass facades. The greenhouse effect heats the winter garden, creating a natural insulation so the temperature is warmer than outdoors. At night, the heat stored in the structure during the daytime due to solar radiation is released into the space. The thermal curtains are closed to further insulate against heat loss and keep the interior warm.

Scenario for Optimal Summer Comfort

Both facades are opened during the summer, and the winter garden system transforms into a well-ventilated and weatherproof loggia that shades the interior from the high sun. The occupants use the maximum surface area of the apartment. Heat evacuation and proper ventilation are guaranteed. Solar curtains are deployed to control sunlight and reduce temperatures. During peak days, when the sun is strong and outdoor temperatures too high, the interior facade with its reflective thermal curtain can be closed to keep the temperature indoors lower than outdoors. At night, all layers are opened for natural ventilation.

Mid-season Scenario

The operability of the elements depends on the weather, month, and time of day. During sunny days, gentle temperatures inside the winter garden allow the occupants to leave the sliding doors of the heated space open and use the area as an extension of the indoors. During colder nights, the thermal curtain can be closed to help to maintain the indoor temperature.

These systems offer numerous environmental benefits for both the parent building and its inhabitants. They control thermodynamic exchanges with the outdoors and allow users to take advantage of the climate through daily and seasonal adaptability. They mitigate heat loss through multiple layering, and unlike insulation they allow in maximum solar gains and daylight while preserving the surrounding views and contact with nature and the environment. During colder months, winter gardens reduce airflow infiltration in the parent building by reducing wind pressure on the facade, and they allow the renewal of fresh air from a naturally preconditioned space, which is more hygienic and healthier than using mechanical systems. This reduces the demand for heating and replaces the use of a mechanical supply and extract ventilation, as the preheating of the air happens naturally in the winter garden. During the mid-season, the winter garden helps to mitigate the climatic variations, and heating is avoided until later in the winter.

Low winter sunlight can enter the space

WINTER – DAYTIME
takes advantage of the solar gain through the large glazed facades
accumulation of heat in the structure
creates a climatic buffer space that provides preheated fresh air for ventilation
$T°_{wg} > T°_{ext}$

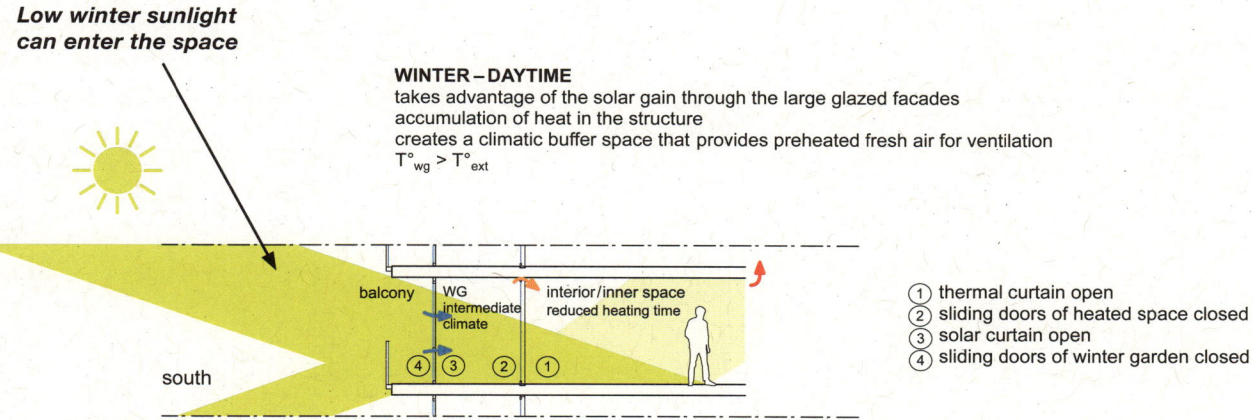

① thermal curtain open
② sliding doors of heated space closed
③ solar curtain open
④ sliding doors of winter garden closed

WINTER – NIGHTTIME
keeps the heat during the night and restores the heat stored during the day in the structure
winter garden: insulating buffer space
$T°_{wg} > T°_{ext}$

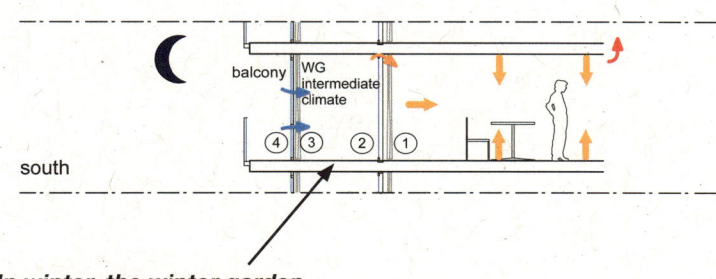

① thermal curtain closed
② sliding doors of heated space closed
③ solar curtain closed
④ sliding doors of winter garden closed

In winter, the winter garden acts as a buffer, keeping the heat in and the cold out

In summer, the balconies block the high sunlight

SUMMER – DAYTIME
protects from direct sunlight, circulates the air,
retains the coolness of the structure accumulated overnight
winter garden: deep terrace protecting the glass facade from direct sunlight, providing shading to create naturally comfortable spaces

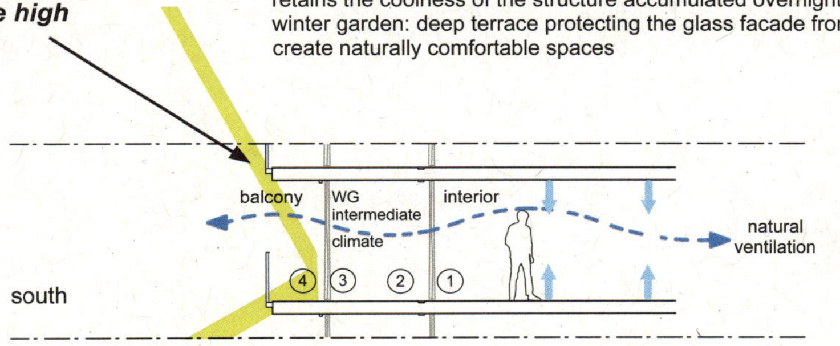

① thermal curtain closed
② sliding doors of inner space open
③ solar curtain closed
④ sliding doors of winter garden open

SUMMER – NIGHTTIME
allows night ventilation to cool the air and the structure

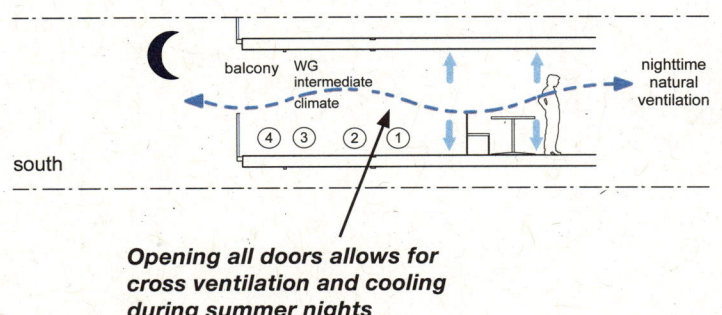

① thermal curtain open
② slidings doors of inner space open
③ solar curtain open
④ sliding doors of winter garden open

Opening all doors allows for cross ventilation and cooling during summer nights

1. On Climate, Comfort, and
the Pleasure of Inhabiting

Projects with Winter Gardens

Individual Housing

House V, Bordeaux (1988)
(Transformation)
– Size: 124 m²
– Size existing: 75 m²
– Greenhouse: 45 m² / 36%

House Latapie, Bordeaux (1993)
– Size: 185 m²
– Greenhouse: 62 m² / 33%
– Cost: 55,275 € excl. tax

House M, Dordogne (1997)
– Size: 242 m²
– Greenhouse: 51 m² / 21%
– Cost: 115,000 € excl. tax

House Floquet, Bordeaux (1999)
(Transformation)
– Size: 340 m²
– Greenhouse: 90 m² / 26%
– Cost: 138,000 € excl. tax

House S, Coutras (2000)
– Size: 282 m²
– Greenhouse: 145 m² / 51%
– Cost: 64,800 € excl. tax

House R, Keremma (2005)
– Size: 316 m²
– 65 m² / 21%

Collective Housing

Cité Manifeste, Mulhouse (2005)
– Size: 2,260 m²
– Greenhouse: 389 m² / 17%
– Client: SA HLM SOMCO
– Cost: 1.05 M€ excl. tax

23 dwellings, Trignac (2010)
– Size: 2,850 m²
– Greenhouse: 446 m² / 16%
– Client: SILENE Saint-Nazaire
– Cost: 2.3 M€ excl. tax

Tour Bois-le-Prêtre, Paris (2011) with Frédéric Druot (Transformation)
– Size: 12,460 m²
– Size existing: 8,900 m²
– Winter garden: 3,616 m² / 29%
– Client: Paris Habitat
– Cost: 11.25 M€ excl. tax

53 semi-collective dwellings, Saint-Nazaire (2011)
– Size: 6,010 m²
– Winter garden: 1,201 m² / 20%
– Client: SILENE OPAC Saint-Nazaire
– Cost: 5 M€ excl. tax

Social and student housing, Ourcq-Jaurès / Paris (2014)
– Size: 6,735 m²
– Winter garden: 720 m² / 11%
– Client: Société Immobilière d'Économie Mixte de la Ville de Paris
– Cost: 10.7 M€ excl. tax

La Chesnaie, Saint-Nazaire (2016) (Transformation)
– Size: 10,280 m²
– Size existing: 3,725 m²
– Winter garden: 3,547 m² / 34%
– Client: SILENE OPAC Saint-Nazaire
– Cost: 6.6 M€ excl. tax

59 dwellings, Neppert Gardens, Mulhouse (2015)
– Size: 8,820 m²
– Winter garden: 2,410 m² / 27%
– Client: SOMCO Mulhouse
– Cost: 5.75 M€ excl. tax

96 dwellings, Chalon-sur-Saône / Prés-Saint-Jean (2016)
– Size: 14,725 m²
– Winter garden: 2,617 m² / 18%
– Client: OPAC Saône-et-Loire
– Cost: 12 M€ excl. tax

530 dwellings G H I of Cité du Grand Parc, Bordeaux (2017) with Frédéric Druot and Christophe Hutin (Transformation)
– Size: 68,000 m²
– Size existing: 38,400 m²
– Winter garden: 23,500 m² / 35%
– Client: Aquitanis O.P.H. of the urban community of Bordeaux
– Cost: 27.2 M€ excl. tax for transformation and renovation + 1.2 M€ excl. tax for new dwellings

Office and housing tower, Chêne-Bourg / Geneva (2020)
– Size: 16,210 m²
– Winter garden: 3,656 m² / 23%
– Client: SBB Swiss Federal Railways
– Cost: 36.4 M CHF excl. tax

18 dwellings, Rixheim (2021)
– Size: 1,500 m²
– Winter garden: 402 m² / 27%
– Client: SA d'HLM SOMCO
– Cost: 1.4 M€ excl. tax

Public Buildings

University of Arts and Human Sciences, Grenoble (1995 and 2001)
– Size: 5,060 m²
– Client: University Pierre Mendès-France, Grenoble
– Cost: 3.08 M€ excl. tax

School of Architecture, Nantes (2009)
– Size: 15,150 m² + 4,430 m² extra space + 5,305 m² accessible outdoor terraces
– Client: Federal Ministry of Culture and Communication – DRAC Pays de la Loire
– Cost: 17.75 M€ excl. tax

Polyvalent Theatre, Lille (2013)
– Size: 3,790 m²
– Client: City of Lille
– Cost: 6.9 M€ excl. tax + 1.2 M€ excl. tax for scenography

FRAC Grand Large – Hauts-de-France, contemporary art center, Dunkerque (2015)
– Size: 11,130 m²
– Size existing: 1,972 m²
– Client: Community of Dunkerque
– Cost: 12 M€ excl. tax

House Latapie, Bordeaux

Climate, Comfort, and Use

A Conversation between
Anne Lacaton, Jean-Philippe Vassal,
Ilka Ruby, and Andreas Ruby

Paris
France

Ilka Ruby: There are a number of monographic publications about your work published by different magazines, but you have never really made a book about your work so far. This book is the first one edited by yourselves, and it is dedicated to a very specific topic: the use of the winter garden in your work. Why was it important for you to make this book?

Anne Lacaton (AL): The winter garden is a central element in many of our projects, because it helps us to free architecture from a lot of confining conditions. It liberates the act of dwelling from the straightjacket of the ground plan by expanding it with an extra space without a program. We are fascinated by the winter garden because it replaces the classical facade as a two-dimensional boundary between inside and outside with a three-dimensional space that allows for a soft and gradual transition between the house and its surroundings.

Almost all of our projects, starting with the Latapie house thirty years ago, have included some elements of a winter garden, of a double envelope, but it has always been very difficult to prove that this created real climate efficiency that could be accounted for in the regulations, as all these projects have demonstrated.

When we literally replaced the facade of an existing apartment building like the Tour Bois-le-Prêtre with a winter garden, we had difficulty proving that the winter garden would generate the same insulation effect as a classical facade. In the latter case, you insulate with different materials, which have a U-value (a measure of insulation performance). The winter garden also has an insulation effect, but it is based on passive solar gain. It heats air by capturing solar energy within the envelope of the winter garden. You can't calculate this effect because air does not have a U-value. You can only assess the insulating performance by precise temperature measurements once the building is in use. Even though all the projects we have done prove the effectiveness, this principle still raises questions and suspicions. So we decided to do a study that measures the thermal performance of winter gardens in a number of our projects over a significant period of time, and then scientifically analyze the actual thermal behavior of our buildings.

The design concepts we show in this book are not the result of engineering.

If the projects had been calculated at the very beginning according to conventional engineering methods, none would probably have been done—or at least not in the way they were realized. But, as architects, we had a strong intuition—nurtured by very close observation and a precise analysis of the functioning of agricultural greenhouses—that these concepts worked. Based on this intuition, observation, and painstaking studies, we developed the argument of how we want to use the winter garden.

Andreas Ruby: Did engineering play a role in the development of your approach to the winter garden?

Jean-Philippe Vassal: Indirectly, yes. We understood quite quickly that the architecture we wanted to make—open, transparent, with an easy flow between the indoor spaces and the natural climate outside—wouldn't stand up under conventional thermal regulations. These are written for standard buildings that are not very open and wrapped in insulating materials. Engineering in general applies these standard calculations, and we always faced this problem.

We were convinced of the interest and efficiency of the winter garden, so we had to demonstrate that what we were proposing was as good as, or better than, standard construction.

We knew our approach was correct, based on observation, relevant comparisons, and intuition. But it had to be done through calculations to prove it meets the objectives required by regulations so the projects could obtain a building permit and be built. For this, we turned to the engineering of agricultural structures; their approach, very different from that of buildings, supported our aims.

When we built our first projects with standard greenhouses, a private home in Coutras and collective housing in Mulhouse, we noticed that there are two approaches to the engineering of saving energy. We went to the Agence de la Transition Écologique, a public agency that deals with questions of energy savings. Inside that organization, one group of engineers was working on agriculture and greenhouses and another focused on housing. The greenhouse and agriculture group considered only energy from the sun, and since that's practically limitless, it's no big deal if some of it is lost. The engineers working on housing, by contrast, focused entirely on heat loss. So they concentrated on insulation, heating systems, and window size—completely ignoring potential gains from the sun. Official calculations of energy efficiency didn't take solar into account until 2012.

The contrast between these approaches could not have been greater. We thought it would be interesting to use the approach of the greenhouse engineers to design housing.

IR: You had to work with the other group of engineers as well at some point. How did they react when you proposed adopting the ideas of their colleagues from the greenhouse department?

Jean-Philippe Vassal: In general, they agreed that the winter garden reduces energy consumption in winter, but they didn't really know how to calculate the value using their standard software. And they were suspicious about comfort in summer.

They didn't take into account that in our projects there is no winter garden in summer; in the warmer months, it's entirely opened up and simply provides shade.

The winter garden is basically a transparent facade at the edge of the building that in colder months admits the rays of the sun to the interior and provides an insulating space. In summer, the winter garden is opened up and simply transforms into a covered open area (like a loggia) that provides shade and keeps the interior cool. In winter it's a winter garden, and in summer it's just a garden.

The other issue is that the principle of the winter garden, which is a bioclimatic design, involves "active" inhabitants who manage the elements to create the best thermal and comfort efficiency. Regulations and engineers don't take this into account because they think residents can't be relied on to actually open or close the windows or curtains as needed.

AL: As an architect, you have to combine observation and imagination. If you understand how a greenhouse works, and if you understand how a garage or a darker space works, then you can imagine how the two of them combined will work. Our approach is to observe many different situations of climatic conditions and to combine them in new ways. So if someone says people can't live all year in a greenhouse, we totally agree—and that's not what we're suggesting. But people can live in a greenhouse when it's an extra space that's combined with other spaces. Clearly none of our projects proposes just a greenhouse to live in; we always use it as an extension of domestic space. But it's habitable a very large part of the time, so it augments and enriches the entire house.

AR: When did your interest in greenhouses actually start? Where did it come from?

JPV: During our studies, we already grew interested in greenhouses, both the larger ones in botanical gardens and the more commonplace horticultural ones used for growing crops. In 1979, I completed my final thesis on the relation between nature and the city. I needed photographs of greenhouses and went to the Jardin fleuriste municipal, the beautiful botanical gardens in Paris with stunning greenhouses. It was amazing to visit, especially in winter, because you could see old ladies who went there during the day to meet and talk. While it was two or three degrees Celsius outside, inside it was eighteen degrees with 80% humidity—so warm that they'd take off their winter coats. We found it very interesting how these people could appropriate this space in this domestic way, even bringing their knitting.

AL: It felt like a living room with exotic plants and a lot of birds. For us, the climate inside these glazed greenhouses created an extraordinary sensation of comfort and well-being. It was impressive for us that one could have this very direct relationship with nature by virtue of the plants inside, but also with the surrounding, due to the structures' extreme transparency. We were enchanted by the lightness of the construction, the elegance, the immateriality. At that time, we didn't look at greenhouses with regard to questions of energy savings, even though the solar architecture of that era aroused our curiosity. We fell in love with the botanical greenhouses because of the strong sensation we felt inside, the perception of the climate, which was not technological but physical and sensual.

JPV: For me the temperature and the humidity in a greenhouse are a very welcoming sensation. They seem to protect you. It is as if something envelopes your body, almost like a hug. Even the very

House V, Bordeaux

16 On Climate, Comfort, and the Pleasure of Inhabiting

House M, Dordogne

concept of the botanical garden exudes a sense of kindness to me. You bring plants from far away and take care of them by purposefully creating the climatic conditions they need in order to thrive in a climate where they normally couldn't survive. For me this is an act of kindness.

AL: What struck us particularly was that the climate and the sensations we felt inside these greenhouses were equally pleasant in both summer and winter. So we started to wonder whether we could also create this feeling of comfort and well-being in a house.

IR: *You started to do that in your first projects, but you did not work with botanical greenhouses. Instead, you worked with industrially made agricultural greenhouse typologies. Why?*

AL: We realized the potential of agricultural greenhouses to be integrated in an architectural project, both in terms of their flexibility as a modular system and in terms of their economy. Their cost is about one-tenth of that of conventional building systems. To better understand agricultural greenhouses, we contacted some manufacturers. And we went to the professional agricultural fair SIFEL (Salon Interprofessionnel de Fruits et Légumes) in Agen, a small town between Bordeaux and Toulouse, an area that's famous for its tomatoes, salad, and other vegetables and fruits sold in markets across France.

JPV: This fair was very interesting, with exhibits of all kinds of agricultural machines but also the latest models and technologies of greenhouses. We were amazed by their combination of simplicity and efficiency. They were strikingly simple in terms of their construction and incredibly efficient in maximizing light, but also allowed precise management of the climate via very simple systems: natural ventilation and shade. We went to this fair year after year to see how the various elements of the greenhouse, such as the inflatable plastic envelope, the metal frame, etc., underwent regular improvement based on a highly pragmatic and experimental approach. The engineers grew so adept at working these systems that they could eventually keep the interior temperature within a half-degree centigrade of the target, or direct any condensation away from the plants, where it might leave spots.

It's really incredible what greenhouses can do these days. For example, you have some where the roof can open up completely during rainstorms to water the plants. They have systems to control the pressure inside to minimize the air that escapes when you open a door—allowing you to maintain a constant temperature. There are special fabrics to control mosquitos and other insects, and to create varying degrees of shade, all the way to the complete darkness needed by chrysanthemums.

AR: *Apart from the botanical greenhouses, another major influence was your experience living and working in Africa after you graduated from architecture school. Jean-Philippe, you stayed there five years, with Anne joining you for extended periods of time. How did this experience shape your approach to architecture, and housing in particular?*

JPV: Africa made us understand the notion of habitat in a much more profound way than whatever we may have learned in architecture school. In Africa, we discovered a notion of habitat that also included a part of nature or unbuilt space, and that a house could be something that is not simply limited to its walls. In the African desert we learned from nomads that their home is not their tent. Their home is the desert. They only spend maybe five hours in the tent, to sleep. When they get up in the morning, they go to a little bush or a tree to find shade. When the shade moves, they move as well and go to another tree. And they always bring a carpet with them. One place is for the morning, while another is better for the afternoon because it has more fresh air. And it's only very late in the night that they go back to the tent. So their habitat is clearly larger than their tent—evidence of the perfectly natural relationship the nomads have with their environment.

AL: The nomads' living space isn't determined by rooms. It can be formal or informal, inside or outside, or both at once without being defined by materials or limits. This was a totally new discovery for us, because in our education as architects there was the inside and the outside. The idea that a space for living could also be beyond the walls of a building seemed utterly impossible.

We also learned what it really means to "live with your climate." This is a question that we don't experience here in France. When we talk about the climate, it stems from an approach of protection or under a technical view of energy savings and global warming. But we rarely take the more natural and fundamental approach of "how to create a friendly and positive relationship with our climate." When you live in hot countries, with little technology at your disposal, you're forced to see things differently, to find a way to adapt.

IR: *You lived in Niamey, the capital of Niger. Did you find this inclusion of outdoor domestic space also in urban housing?*

JPV: Yes, just in different typologies. In the urban areas you find these traditional houses that are organized around patios. When people build on a plot, they always leave a space in the middle where they can have a tree. It's a place that is empty, and it's where most of domestic life happens. The inhabitants cook there, their children play there, and like in the nomadic tent, there is always the relation between shaded areas (mostly the inside of the house) and the patio as a kind of open-air living room. Also here, the house isn't limited by its walls.

AR: Did you see this expanded habitat as a purely "exotic" phenomenon, or could you see relationships to the Western tradition of housing?

JPV: In the modern tradition of housing not so much, but in the vernacular architecture of certain regions, yes. For instance in the Landes, a large pine-tree forest landscape south of Bordeaux, you find the *maison landaise*. It's a house that stands on a clearing in the forest, and about fifteen meters away from the house there is a single tree. When it's hot you go and have lunch in its shadow. So we can find this notion of a domestic space beyond the walls of a house also in Europe, but it's more marginal.

AL: Compared to the open living spaces of the African habitat, European housing felt very conventional and constraining to us. Everything has its dedicated place; every room is defined by a function. When designing, we wanted to change that typology to give greater liberty and create more generous spaces. It was not a matter of expanding everything a little, but rather providing something extra, to allow another kind of experience of inhabiting space. An extra space that would also extend the time you can spend outside—in a protected way. And we found that the greenhouse does all of this perfectly. It protects you with a transparent envelope that generates a different climate between the interior of the house and what's happening outside. From our very first projects, we added greenhouses to more traditional spaces.

IR: When you started to use the greenhouse as a typological extension of residential buildings, it seems that some of its spatial properties also rubbed off on the more conventional parts of these projects. Would you say that the greenhouse transformed your thinking about space in general?

JPV: Yes, absolutely. Working with the greenhouse especially in our early projects helped us understand that space should really be defined by qualities rather than functions. Qualities like large or narrow, shady or bright, quiet or loud, inside or outside—or something in between. It's very important for us to find a diversity of ambiences within a house, which can change depending on conditions outside such as sunlight, climate, or geography. The inhabitants will use different spaces at different times for different activities, creating mobility within the house. For instance, in the loft: you put your bed in one place, but you might move it when the season, the climate, or the direction of the sun changes. Industrial spaces such as lofts often present closed conditions. But it is interesting to open them up to create a combination of very intimate indoor spaces with the bright light from outside, and the exterior itself. The winter garden is clearly a tool to connect indoor and outdoor space. It creates possibilities for your body to find its best comfort quite easily—similar to the way the nomads in the desert negotiate their spaces depending on the time of day and activities such as eating or sleeping. We consider it a kind of architectural luxury for inhabitants to be able to migrate through their house in this way.

AR: Your architectural imagination was long nurtured by a fascination with botanical greenhouses and a notion of habitat that was larger than a house, but those interests were still disconnected. When did you manage to combine them for the first time?

AL: Our first project with a greenhouse was in Bordeaux, in 1988. We wanted to connect two small houses, and we placed a standard eighty-square-meter glass greenhouse between them, allowing us to expand and reconfigure the houses and create new relationships between the existing spaces. It is a very pleasant place, still in use today. And now, more than thirty years later, the greenhouse is full of vegetation.

At that time, we were still studying glass greenhouses. The simpler agricultural greenhouse with plastic cladding came a bit later, in 1991, in the first design for House Latapie, which never got built. That's the first time we really studied, in depth, the use of a greenhouse for housing. The next year we did a revised design for the Latapies that built on those principles. A few years later we used the idea in a house in Coutras, and then in Cité Manifeste in Mulhouse.

IR: What's the advantage of plastic over glass in greenhouses?

JPV: Plastic is much more economical because the structure is lighter and the material is cheaper. The most advanced

House Floquet, Bordeaux

House S, Coutras

greenhouses today have roofs made of a double layer of plastic, which is inflated to create a cushion of air. This improves the insulation immediately because it's better at keeping the heat inside, even during the night.

So far we haven't worked with these in housing, but at documenta (the art exhibition in Kassel, Germany), we built exhibition spaces entirely with that technology. And at the FRAC in Dunkerque, we used a double foil for the roof, though there it was a different product, PTFE, which is relatively common in architecture but much more expensive than agricultural products.

AL: But for housing, it's a question of insurance. Building codes typically call for materials with a warranty of at least ten years. Since the foils used in standard greenhouses aren't subject to those regulations, their manufacturers don't offer any particular guarantee—even though the materials are extremely durable. That's why we've used a single-layer polycarbonate in the vast majority of our projects.

AR: What about the durability and recyclability of polycarbonate? Would you say it's sustainable?

AL: Polycarbonate is recyclable and also pretty durable. After about ten years its transparency slowly decreases, but it doesn't lose its strength or impermeability. So perhaps every twenty years or so it would be good to replace it, not because it's getting too weak, but for transparency reasons. For instance, in the Latapie house, which was built in 1993, the owners only replaced it when they decided to sell the house almost thirty years after construction. Its strength hadn't degraded at all, but it was a little white, and they wanted to make it look new again. Mulhouse was completed in 2005—seventeen years ago—and they have no plans to exchange it.

IR: But isn't polycarbonate, with its relatively short lifespan, ecologically problematic?

JPV: The idea of recycling is really important, which is always true with plastics. But the problem is not the plastic itself. Only when it's thrown away and doesn't get recycled does it create an ecological problem. Manufacturers today are constantly working to extend its lifespan and make recycling easier.

AL: There's still a lot of work to be done to improve the sustainability of any material we might use. We are paying attention to this, but you have to consider the larger context. If you want to build today, you have to work with materials that are available and also respect the non-environmental requirements they face.

And remember that polycarbonate, at less than one millimeter thick, represents only a small quantity of what goes into a structure. Other more traditional materials used in much larger quantities are often more difficult to recycle than polycarbonate. Materials that can't be easily separated, such as plasterboard partitions or reinforced concrete, are tough to recycle. The lifespan of polycarbonate is much longer than that of many insulated claddings, which often degrade rapidly.

JPV: We always try to find the material that is most efficient, so we use as little as possible while creating the maximum possible volume. Depending on the specific task, you can do that with glass, with plastic, with steel, or sometimes with concrete. It is very important that these materials can be easily separated.

AR: What are the qualities of polycarbonate that make it so interesting to you?

AL: In all of our projects, we build transparent facades—for thermal reasons, for natural light, for views, and for better solar gain. If a winter garden's facade isn't transparent, it lacks thermal efficiency. Polycarbonate is light, transparent, and cost-efficient, allowing us to achieve these qualities on all projects, including economical ones. It's very suitable for winter gardens, for example, where there's no need for insulation. Glass can also fulfill this function, but it's much heavier and expensive, so it would have to be reserved for larger-budget projects. We use it because there's currently no alternative that offers those advantages.

JPV: We also like the specific type of transparency that you can achieve with polycarbonate. Personally, we prefer undulated panels. With the undulation you get transparency that's a bit blurred. Inhabitants often say it makes them feel more protected than glass because they feel less visually exposed to people outside. We also like that the facades of our winter gardens don't look like the glass-curtain facades found in many buildings. In this way we can create more intimacy and the profiles can also be thinner.

IR: Do you see transparency as an essential value in architecture?

AL: We see no reason to make any building not totally transparent. In a building that's transparent, you can create opacity where needed—but the inverse isn't true of walls made from brick or concrete. You can control or filter this transparency from totally closed to completely open. In traditional buildings, the size of the windows places a hard limit on the building's porosity, limiting the daylight and the view. It's an imposed reality. Transparency, by contrast, offers inhabitants the liberty to create the interior space they want.

IR: *The winter garden at House Latapie represents more than half the volume of the entire house. How did you arrive at this unusual typological solution? Did the clients influence this surprising choice?*

JPV: When Mr. and Mrs. Latapie came to us, they were strongly considering a standard catalog home, which, due to their budget, would have been about 65 to 70 square meters.

AL: But this house didn't really fit the plot they had bought, so they decided to consult an architect. From the beginning we believed that a house of 65 to 70 square meters wouldn't be comfortable or sufficient for their needs. When we started talking with them, we sought to quickly move the conversation far beyond a discussion of square meters and number of bedrooms.

We tried to understand their dreams, how they wanted to live. They had a camper van, and whenever they had time off they would drive south to Spain, to the beaches near Seville. They said the best moment was when they parked the vehicle and took out the table. It wasn't the camper that made the experience special. The magic kicked in when they served lunch or dinner at the seaside or slept under a starry sky. It was a beautiful understanding of living. And it reminded us immediately of the nomadic way of life we had discovered in Africa.

JPV: But since Bordeaux doesn't have the climate of Seville or Niger, we tried to generate a climatic condition similar to that of southern Spain—by using a greenhouse. And in a second step, we could implement a domestic volume within the envelope of the greenhouse. The project took off from that situation, with the intention of creating a big house and a nice climate.

AR: *The first design for House Latapie was very radical, in terms of both the living concept and its appearance. The Latapies had originally considered a standard catalog house. What made them go along with your proposal?*

JPV: The Latapies didn't particularly want a standard house, but they couldn't imagine anything else. When we started talking about other possibilities, they were immediately interested. We visited some greenhouses with them to help them appreciate the atmosphere inside. They began to understand how greenhouses can transform the climate, how the sun coming through the glass could warm up a winter day. And they saw how light the structure could be, nearly invisible, not much more than an envelope, much simpler and cheaper than a normal residential building. Ultimately, the combination of thermal performance and the low cost persuaded them to accept the idea.

IR: *But this first design for House Latapie didn't get built. Why?*

JPV: It exceeded their budget, even though we had planned to use very simple materials and a standard and economical greenhouse. We even had authorization from the municipality, which was rather extraordinary. But in the end it was a bit too expensive: 65,000 euros, and roughly 10,000 euros over their limit.

When we told them we could not lower the construction cost any further, they tried hard to raise more money because they really loved the project. But they were also very clear that they didn't want the house to constrain them all their lives. It was perfectly understandable and reasonable. They suggested building the house in phases, but we didn't want them to embark on a project that would take years to complete. When the first design exceeded their budget, they got very anxious but were still confident and decided to continue working with us. We suggested starting over, taking lessons from what we'd been through. And in the end, we found a solution that worked.

AR: *The second design looks different and is organized quite differently, but it sticks to the idea of a winter garden that doubles the living space. How did you convince them to embark, for a second time, on a journey that was anything but safe?*

AL: Their enthusiasm never flagged. They wanted to go all the way, and they had confidence in us. We found that touching, and it motivated us to keep moving forward. We told them that we would change the design to bring down the costs, but still stick to the ideas we had discussed before. We analyzed the reason our first design had been too expensive so we might reformulate it without abandoning the idea of creating a large winter garden. The original design had included a pair of boxes within a greenhouse for the various living spaces. But that idea required separate structures for the greenhouse and the boxes, creating redundancies that significantly increased costs. So we understood that our new design had to incorporate just one structure.

JPV: The realized design cost 55,275 euros—which was just

House R, Keremma

Cité Manifeste, Mulhouse

within their budget. And this time we didn't use a standard greenhouse. Although the new design was really different from the first one, it incorporated the same principles, and even radicalized them. The first design was much more original, more playful. The second is very straightforward and can even appear a bit austere. But they understood that the new design would offer them the same possibilities. And when it was clear it would be within their budget, they agreed. In the end, they've been really happy there.

IR: How did you imagine the Latapies would use the winter garden?

AL: Our thoughts were initially influenced by big greenhouses like the ones we had visited in botanical gardens. We imagined, somewhat naively, that the spaces would be filled with palm trees, rhododendrons, and flowers. But the Latapies filled it with furniture, a couch, tables, various armchairs and sometimes even an old motorbike in need of repair. It was always changing, from season to season, from year to year.

AR: What was your reaction when you saw the space like that?

JPV: It completely blew our minds. We felt the way the Latapies appropriated the space really taught us something; it was much more interesting than anything we had imagined. The family soon started spending most of their time in the winter garden. They even celebrated Christmas there. The living room in the enclosed part of the house was often deserted because the winter garden had become their actual living room.

IR: What did you learn from their appropriation of the winter garden?

JPV: Despite all the domestic elements they placed in it, the space didn't feel domesticated. It radiated the atmosphere of a furnished exterior space. We realized that the Latapies had somehow projected their holiday camper experience onto their new home, with the only difference being that the space was housed inside a transparent envelope. In a winter garden you're protected from wind and rain, but you can still have the sensation of these elements. The children always said that what they liked most about the winter garden was hearing the rain on the roof while they stayed dry. Even if they had to wear their coats in the winter months, they still liked playing in the winter garden.

AR: You integrated winter gardens in many subsequent projects. Were the reactions of the inhabitants there similar?

AL: We are always surprised by the freedom with which people use the winter garden space. The extra space, without any designated function, liberates something in the way people live. It creates a freedom that's normally lacking in standard housing constrained by their small rooms and conventional layouts. The Latapies once said something that really touched us: "We never felt limited by the space of the greenhouse." That was very nice to hear.

IR: Unlike with the Latapies, at House S in Coutras, your second project, you used a completely standardized greenhouse product. How did this decision play out economically?

AL: The boundaries of the Latapies' property presented us with certain constraints. There, we had to raise the greenhouse, putting it on top of a wall, to create more interior living space. This required an adaptation of the standard greenhouse, which increased the cost. That's why we had to modify the initial project by using more common construction elements that were more appropriate.

In Coutras, there were no site constraints, so we could build a single-story house using two greenhouses that we got almost off the shelf, without any adaptations.

JPV: The Coutras house was very inexpensive. It's 280 square meters and cost around 65,000 euros in 2000 (about what the first design of House Latapie would have cost, eight years earlier, for a house that was about two-thirds the size). If you build a greenhouse from a catalog today, it's around 200 to 300 euros per square meter, whereas a regular house costs at least 1,000 to 2,000 euros per square meter. So by using a greenhouse to provide a waterproof envelope, then placing a simple insulated volume inside, you can realize large dimensions and still be extremely economical.

AR: Were you ever tempted to "optimize" the greenhouse, to adapt so it might work better as a residential house?

AL: We carefully studied standard agricultural greenhouses. It was remarkable to see how every element was precisely designed to maximize efficiency and economy. Filclair, the manufacturer we mostly work with, had an explanation for the design of every piece of the construction, every assemblage. We concluded that in terms of optimization of the design it is very difficult to do it better.

Since these greenhouses are mass-produced in vast quantities and massive sizes for agriculture, they are efficient and economical in their original configuration. And the manufacturer has no interest in modifying them for special cases like a house. So we understood that if we wanted to do projects with Filclair's greenhouses, we had to use them exactly as they were. The minor modifications we make for our projects are done by the independent company that installs the greenhouses.

JPV: As soon as you change one element of their product—say, removing every second column or changing the height—the greenhouse can lose its economical efficiency and structural integrity. But manufacturers also offer context-specific modifications. For example, they adapt the standard prototype for special environments where there's a lot of wind, snow, or heat.

The precision of their system is really remarkable. The roof braces, for instance, are only around 3–4 cm in diameter. They're precisely calculated to ensure the exact strength they need, with a minimum of material. This allows maximum sunlight to enter the greenhouse.

AL: This optimization and minimalism stands in opposition to what's done in "normal construction," where regulators typically overestimate risks and account for a large margin of error in any calculation. And that tends to make structures bigger and "fatter," and far from their optimal size.

It's really incredibly precise. We can learn from this rigor and transfer this kind of thinking to housing, which is far less exacting, especially when it comes to managing interior temperatures. Even with all the mechanics of standard construction, the precision is much less than that of greenhouses.

AR: Would it be fair to say your architectural contribution to the Coutras house was less a classical design act than a conceptual one, like Marcel Duchamp selecting an industrially produced urinal and declaring it to be a work of art?

AL: It is not a conceptual act; it is the result of a project that seeks to achieve a generously sized, comfortable living space on a budget by adopting passive solar systems. The clients came to us because they liked the principle of the Latapie house, and they could see themselves living in a similar house. The project follows the same principles but is adapted to the land we had, in the countryside.

At the end of our discussions, we agreed to use a standard greenhouse construction, but this time in glass, which they liked more than polycarbonate. The house would have been much smaller because glass greenhouses are more expensive. But we were denied a building permit because the inclination of the roof of the glass greenhouse didn't meet local regulations, so we had to revise the project. We then proposed a plastic greenhouse, which has a rounded roof.

The clients were initially reluctant because, as farmers, they saw plastic greenhouses all around them and they considered glass to be more chic. But they slowly came around. And when it became clear that for the same price they could get twice the house, they quickly agreed.

JPV: We took them to a professional greenhouse near Bordeaux where cucumbers are grown. Inside, we explained the climate and qualities and what we wanted to do. As we were talking, the owner overheard us, and as we were leaving we saw his house almost adjacent. It was a very standard and traditional house. Looking at both structures, he said, "Well, I guess I'm kind of dumb. It really would be so much nicer to live in the greenhouse."

IR: But then again, you can't really live in a greenhouse, can you?

JPV: Greenhouses get a lot of solar radiation during the day, which naturally heats the interior, but the energy and heat dissipate very quickly at night. In the winter, the interior temperature is higher than outside at night, but still not enough for a living space. So you can't live in a greenhouse all the time.

But when you place an insulated volume with its own heating system inside a greenhouse and combine these two systems, you can create something very interesting. The volume inside doesn't lose its energy as easily, and the greenhouse acts as an intermediate climatic space, which reduces the temperature difference between the heated volume and the outside. Even less so when you are in the city, since in the city it never gets as cold as in the countryside. The combination of the two systems—winter garden and insulated volume—creates a lot of possibilities. You always have the climate outside, which is different depending on the orientation, the weather, the season, etc. Then you have the greenhouse itself that reacts to that exterior climate. And then you have a part of the house that's insulated and heated in winter with normal radiators. In summer it works differently, because the greenhouse is opened up and ventilated and becomes almost an outdoor space. You have a lot of possibilities of interaction among the systems, and if you learn to control them you have more possibilities than with a single climate zone.

23 dwellings, Trignac

Tour Bois-le-Prêtre (transformation), Paris

AL: It's a question of heat exchange, which doesn't happen directly from inside to outside since the greenhouse creates a buffer space, and we use this a lot. None of the greenhouses in our housing projects are heated. And because the bedrooms or other rooms are not inside the greenhouse, but in insulated and heated adjoining spaces, you can adapt your life to this special space.

All the studies we've done, which are in this book, illustrate that. The graphs show day by day how the winter garden reacts, and how because of it the adjacent rooms remain, without heating, very close to twenty degrees Celsius (considered the optimal temperature for interior spaces), so you use a lot less energy to reach that level.

AR: *For the Latapies, you couldn't realize a two-story house with a standard greenhouse structure. But the Cité Manifeste in Mulhouse did just that. What made it possible?*

JPV: In Mulhouse we effectively used the same standard greenhouse as in Coutras, though on two levels, like in the first design for the Latapies. But in Mulhouse it was easier to fix the greenhouse atop the concrete ground-floor structure because it was a bigger, multifamily social housing development. The more greenhouse elements you use, the more stable the structure will be. And when you have a bigger number of flats, the building also gets more economical.

The biggest issue for the greenhouses is not their weight (they're superlight) but their wind resistance. If you place them at ground level, it's quite easy to anchor them. But in Mulhouse we had to find a solution for attaching them on top of the concrete ground-floor structure. This needed some extra calculations, and we had to reinforce the posts. But other than these minor adaptations, everything is standard, including the systems for sun protection and opening and closing the roof panels.

IR: *So would you say you turned a social housing project into an experimental project?*

AL: Cité Manifeste is often described as experimental. But that which is new doesn't necessarily have to be experimental. It was not the goal of the client to make an experimental project. The company wanted to create contemporary housing that would meet the expectations and needs of people today, and standard typologies, which are more and more constrained, no longer meet these needs. The client was open-minded and willing to consider nonstandard solutions. They trusted us to develop the project, but we had to prove that everything would be built according to the regulations in effect. The most difficult part was proving that the project would achieve the thermal efficiency required to receive public subsidies. The regulatory calculation models that applied to standard housing had no way of accounting for greenhouses, so their value could not be calculated. Regulations have since evolved, and projects like Cité Manifeste have certainly helped.

IR: *Can you describe that evolution in the regulations? And do you think your work in this field has helped change the methods of calculation, making it easier to build such projects today?*

AL: The thermal regulations in effect at the time we did Cité Manifeste didn't take into account either solar gains or the benefits of winter gardens. They ignored their effects, so the potential benefits had to be calculated as if they were an insulation material. In spite of this, we found solutions that allowed us to build our projects and demonstrate the effectiveness of the idea. All of these early works helped us gain experience and prove the "validity" of the concept, which gave us the confidence we needed to continue including winter gardens in our buildings and improving their design. In that way, they confirmed our approach despite the difficulty of showing they complied with regulations that didn't recognize what we were doing.

In the past twenty years, thermal regulations in France have evolved, with each new version allowing us to go a little further in accounting for winter gardens in the calculation of energy performance. By 2008, when we built a housing project on Rue de l'Ourcq in Paris, new regulations let us give a single, fixed value to the winter gardens, which was already a step forward. The housing we built in Chalon and the transformation of the Grand Parc in Bordeaux, in 2012 and 2013, were the first projects where more precise calculations could be made. That was due to the introduction of the RT 2012, which included the notion of solarized buffer spaces. On our latest projects, such as the tower in Geneva, finished in 2020, or apartments we're studying in Paris, at St. Vincent de Paul, very precise simulations allow us to get as close as possible to reality and to demonstrate the real day-to-day efficiency. Solar gain and winter gardens can now be integrated into the calculation. Without boasting, we think it's fair to say these projects served as case studies that questioned the regulations and undoubtedly helped spur their evolution.

AR: *Back to Cité Manifeste: Without a regulatory framework, what evidence did you use to convince your client?*

JPV: Clients usually want to have proof by calculations. But the thermal advantages of greenhouses couldn't be shown by prior calculations. Instead, we would have had to measure their performance once they were in use, or use the calculation models of agricultural greenhouses. But those aren't recognized for nonagricultural buildings. Even without formal proof in our hands, though, we were confident in the product and its properties because we had done detailed analyses of greenhouses. And that's what we used to build our case in favor of the idea.

We know that greenhouses are used in different climates. They work in Sweden, where they are covered with snow. They work in Kenya, where it is hot. They work in places where there's a lot of wind. The problem is that engineers and public institutions aren't willing to accept such empirical knowledge, much less validate it. They want an Excel sheet that shows data from known models.

AL: We brought Pierre Zemp, director of the client company, SOMCO Mulhouse, to the Coutras and Latapie houses. He was in favor of the project, but he wanted to understand how houses with greenhouses worked. It was amazing to see how the experience of both houses completely changed his attitude. We got to Coutras on a winter afternoon before the family had gotten home. When the owner arrived and we could enter the greenhouse, it was extremely hot inside. Mr. Zemp was somewhat shocked and said, "Well, it's clearly way too hot." The owner replied: "Wait a second!" Then she pressed a button to electrically open the roof a bit, and the space quickly cooled down. She explained that they kept the house closed while they were away during the day because that meant they didn't need to heat the insulated part of the house, which is inside the greenhouse. Their home needs heating two months less than neighboring houses. "OK, you architects are serious and I believe you," Mr. Zemp said.

IR: *You insist that this was not an experimental project, but it's still rather ambitious. Once you had the client's basic approval, did everything go smoothly?*

AL: There were a number of challenges, but they were mostly related to the regulatory framework and not the design and construction. Because the Cité Manifeste was a social housing project built with public subsidies, we needed to fulfill a number of requirements. One of them was a kind of certification of sustainability, which defines energy savings in a very simplistic way, oriented toward standard buildings. If you are outside this category, it is difficult to check the boxes.

The officials in charge didn't want to consider the specificity of this project. They simply compared it with their standard protocols, and of course it didn't fit. They concluded that the project did not comply with the regulation and wrote a negative report, which meant the project was ineligible for public subsidies. Mr. Zemp pressed on and asked the government for an exemption. A special commission examined our project and concluded that it didn't need any exemption, because it was perfectly in line with the spirit of the law and the performance objectives it laid out. The only problem was figuring out how to calculate its performance. That's when we met Christian Cardonnel, an engineer who studied the project and was able to vouch for its validity. In the end, the project's performance exceeded the standards in effect and the government approved the subsidies.

AR: *The Mulhouse project represented a significant change for you in terms of scale, typology, and ownership. Instead of working with a family, you had a public client building a multifamily social housing project with fourteen apartments. Did these new conditions lead to new architectural challenges?*

JPV: As with all of our houses, we were motivated to work on the dimensions of the flats and to make them much bigger than typical social housing standards. As usual in social housing, the budget was based on standard-sized, two- or three-bedroom flats. Mr. Zemp's concern was that if we made a flat two or three times bigger than usual, he would need to increase the rent accordingly, which he couldn't do for social housing. We replied that there was no reason to do that if he determined the rent of the flats based on the cost of the building rather than their size. He agreed to do this if we didn't exceed the budget. We came in under budget, and he kept the standard rents, even though each apartment was two to three times bigger than normal.

IR: *Why is it so important for you to make a space that is larger than the project brief calls for?*

AL: The space that client asks for in the functional program is often the result of compromises between what the users want and the budget, defined in a global and not very precise way. So the program rarely fulfills the users' expectations. And the spaces are regulated by standards or functional constraints. This leaves little room for other undefined uses, for greater freedom on the part of the users.

53 semi-collective dwellings, Saint-Nazaire

Social and student housing,
Ourcq-Jaurès / Paris

The extra space isn't included in the program, so it's not subject to many of the functional rules. It is a space of freedom, an unprogrammed place whose use must be negotiated by the users. When we built the Latapie house we started to think about the size of the extra space. We came to think that the ideal would be a 1:1 proportion between the extra space and the programmed. Since then, in every project we've done, we've included additional space in roughly this proportion.

JPV: We always try to build the maximum volume permitted under local rules, which is typically far more than what the building program calls for. We use this surplus to create the extra space. And sometimes we go even further. In the Architecture School of Nantes, we could only build up to 24 meters, but there was nothing that precluded activities on the roof. So we built a rooftop terrace, which is accessible to the public via a large ramp. We always try to extend not only the interior but also outside in spaces that aren't part of the volume.

AR: *Is the extra space fundamentally to be understood as a critique of minimum living standards (*Existenzminimum*)? Are you saying that the space mandated in such programs is too small and that such rules need to be reconsidered?*

JPV: The extra space is not only an extension of the inside space toward the outside, it is also a third space between the inside and the outside. This is a topic I explored in my master's thesis, *Vegetation in the City*. I was fascinated by the idea of the garden as a transitional space, and my design used vegetation as a sort of buffer zone in urban areas, where you are not immediately confronted with the city when you open the door. In cities, it's always surprising how abrupt the transition between your domestic interior and the city outside can be. And sometimes it barely exists at all. There's just a thin piece of wood or metal that separates the totally intimate from the totally public. In the countryside, the garden creates an intermediate space between private and public. Neighbors can each be on their side of the garden fence and talk about their tomatoes. The garden is a place to decompress. It's certainly one of the reasons why so many people dream of a house with a garden. But this dream has produced a sprawling suburbia around the world. It comes at the cost of excessive infrastructure, traffic jams, and social disintegration, while its original promise melts down to miniature gardens with a house in the middle. The question therefore is how we can address this dream in a meaningful way, in the context of the city. It's necessary to abandon the concept of minimum space for urban housing, which tends to result in a continual diminution of what's acceptable. And it leaves no freedom to offer a more generous level of space and fulfill the expectations of people who dream of living in a house.

AL: When we build winter gardens and balconies in new housing projects or in transformations like the Tour Bois-le-Prêtre in Paris or Grand Parc in Bordeaux, it's to create a "ground," even if it is small. Even if the balcony is only one meter deep and the winter garden another three meters, this extra space fundamentally is a spatial rematerialization of a terrain. It's a stacking of terrain, like in the famous project by Site called "Highrise of Homes." It's the idea that we can re-create the dream of a house with a garden, providing the feeling of liberty and independence typically only found outside of the city. Re-enacting this dream and the pleasure of inhabiting the city would be further enriched by all the qualities that you don't have in the countryside or the suburbs: proximity to public transport, culture, shopping, and all kinds of services.

IR: *The winter garden isn't just a buffer zone between domestic space and urban space, but also between two different climates, because the domestic space is heated and the winter garden isn't. To benefit from the thermal effect of the winter garden, which cools the apartment in summer and heats it in winter, the inhabitants have to manually adjust multiple layers of the facade. Is this entirely self-explanatory or do you have to train them?*

AL: It's very easy to understand how to use the various elements to control the climate in the winter gardens and the apartments. These are natural movements that anyone can manage. We give residents an instruction manual that explains how to get optimal efficiency by adjusting the four layers—the glass doors, the two different curtains, and the winter garden facade. It is clear that the inhabitants have to be actively engaged. That's the principle of passive buildings. But we think this is actually something positive. For us, talking about sustainability or about energy savings while ignoring the need for residents to take some level of action doesn't make a lot of sense. But if you want to involve the inhabitants, it's also important that they get some benefit in exchange. They have to find something that's in their interest or increases their pleasure in some way. And what they get in exchange is a larger home plus a nice space, like the winter garden, which they can use as a little garden.

JPV: Operating the winter garden is quite similar to dealing with different layers of clothing. If it's a bit cool, you pull something over your shoulders. When it gets too hot, you take it off. If there's too much sun, you seek out shade. These are very simple things that you do instinctively. The idea that your body reacts and you immediately do what's needed to make yourself comfortable is for us very interesting. We consider a house to be something like a big garment. If it's too hot, you open the roof to let the warm air out and draw the curtains to create shade. If it is too cold, you close the thermal curtains in the rooms to keep the warmth inside. The regulation of the climate in the winter garden is very intuitive, unlike many mechanized systems.

AR: *You've also used winter gardens in public buildings, often on a very large scale, such as at the FRAC in Dunkerque and the architecture school in Nantes. What role do winter gardens play in these very different situations?*

AL: The same functions as in housing: extra space and a climate buffer. The extra space offers a decompression zone that is useful and pleasant and distinct from the space called for in the brief. This is true not only of housing, but also in cultural or educational buildings such as schools or museums—really anything. Moreover, this intermediate climatic buffer helps save energy without having to block out light with walls covered in conventional insulation. In Nantes, the intermediate space is actually very similar to that in a house. The students and teachers are effectively the inhabitants of the school, and they use the extra space exactly like residents of a house, for all kinds of activities that can't take place in the classrooms—for studying, building models, relaxing, playing, etc. The school understood that the extra space is a place for sharing, so after you use it you have to fully free it up so others can also enjoy it. It cannot be permanently appropriated by any one group.

JPV: The extra space works well in Nantes because it's also used for circulation. Instead of making two-meter-wide corridors, we created giant spaces that stretch out to the facade. The constant movement there is one of their major assets. They're so wide that you can use them for classes or working spaces without impeding the circulation.

AL: In museums, the extra space works somewhat differently because there are no permanent users, just visitors who stay for a short time. For instance, the extra greenhouse space on the rooftop at the FRAC in Dunkerque gives people the chance to forge a connection to the landscape and the sky while offering the museum a place to show different kinds of exhibitions. The FRAC's exhibition spaces follow the classic museum model: climate-controlled, white-walled rooms. The greenhouse rooftop features artworks that visitors are meant to not merely look at but also interact with and spend time with—while enjoying the sea views.

IR: *It seems that the extra space in this project wasn't just the rooftop but the entire volume of the former shipyard building. The competition brief asked to reprogram it for use by the art center, but you decided to leave it completely empty. Were you not worried that the client might not make sufficient use of this giant space?*

JPV: In the beginning, it was indeed unclear how this extra space might be used, and by whom. It took a while for the museum to really come to grips with it. There was even a proposal to put another museum, disconnected from the FRAC, inside the space. That would have been totally contradictory to our project idea. But this plan wasn't implemented, and the entire space was given to the FRAC. Because it was so big, there was a search for special kinds of programs for its use. Some ideas were to create films for giant projection screens, or to reproduce large-scale art installations that had been shown at other big venues, or even to mix art with concerts and festivals. For instance, in 2019, the space was used for the first instance of an art triennial on the theme of gigantism. Everything is possible as long as the FRAC remains involved.

AR: *It seems as if the client was overwhelmed by the size of this void, and having it to fill it became something of a burden.*

JPV: Yes, but that was an unnecessary concern. There really is no need to fill it. For us, it was always clear that the void should remain a void. It can be temporarily used for a specific situation or need, but it must be emptied afterward to again become a void—so it can always offer limitless possibilities.

AL: When we created our proposal for the renovation of the Palais de Tokyo in Paris, we approached the building as a void that was repeatedly filled and emptied. After each exhibition, the space would be cleared to ready it for the next exhibition. This is very different from functional spaces that are always there for specific programs—a bedroom, a classroom, an office, etc. This is a really interesting condition for any building, be it a house, an architecture school, or an art center. If you have a space

On Climate, Comfort, and the Pleasure of Inhabiting

La Chesnaie (transformation), Saint-Nazaire

with no real specified use, it can reinvent itself constantly.

JPV: Early on, this void of the Palais de Tokyo was also expressed by the walls, which were rough, just as we found them. But step by step, with more and more exhibitions, they became more and more white. And some of the partitions also sometimes stayed. This created a creeping diminution of the freedom of the space and its ability to reinvent itself.

AL: They started filling the space step by step with a new restaurant, a new library, with new places for young artists, as if they were scared by the idea of non-defined spaces.

JPV: But luckily Palais de Tokyo is too big to be totally filled. There are so many passages and connections among the different levels. But it really doesn't make any sense to close off a part of the building permanently just to host a fashion show for three weeks a year. Instead, one could use it temporarily for fashion, but the rest of the time you leave it open. Rather than dividing the space and programming it for a specified purpose or event, create a schedule that would allow the entirety of the space to remain open as the default. It can be divided as needed, but should always be returned to its original state.

IR: *The Palais de Tokyo was ultimately more than an architectural project for you. When you moved to Paris from Bordeaux, it became the new home for your office. How did that influence your work?*

AL: Moving our office to the Palais for the duration of the project was truly liberating. It gave us a feeling of unlimited freedom. It was very spontaneous. After winning the competition, we decided to move to Paris for a while to do the project, and the next day we closed our office in Bordeaux. We ended up in this huge space and had it all to ourselves. It was really a magical moment.

JPV: We were just a few people working in a 30,000-square-meter building with ten-meter ceilings in the middle of Paris. We experienced the space as pioneers. It was very cold in winter and hot in summer, and we became nomads inside this immense structure, migrating up floor by floor as the project progressed and ending up just beneath the glass roof. We often ask ourselves how we might again create a situation of such unimaginable luxury.

We had some really great times there. It's incredible how such a place, with all that space, can influence your work. We prepared our proposal for Nantes in the Palais, and I think our design was strongly influenced by inhabiting that huge volume. The intimate, physical experience of that space shifted our approach to architecture into another dimension. Inside the Palais de Tokyo, we couldn't think small.

38 On Climate, Comfort, and the Pleasure of Inhabiting

96 dwellings,
Chalon-sur-Saône, Prés-Saint-Jean

A Bioclimatic Approach

A Conversation between
Anne Lacaton, Jean-Philippe Vassal,
and Christian Cardonnel

Paris
France

A committed and inexhaustible autodidact, the thermal engineer Christian Cardonnel has been involved in the majority of Lacaton & Vassal's projects. Their long-standing collaboration dates back to the early 2000s, when the Cité Manifeste project raised a whole new set of questions about thermal regulations applied to multifamily housing. The relationship between Lacaton & Vassal and Cardonnel is based on a shared vision of comfort and the relationship between a building and its climate. Below is a conversation in which the three look back at the foundations of their partnership and point out the shortcomings of validation systems based on calculations—to the detriment of observation, intuition, and life itself.

Anne Lacaton: When we met in 2003, you gave us your book Solaire actif et passif. *It's certainly the oldest thing we know about you. Can you put it in context, in terms of your interests at the time?*

Christian Cardonnel: I published the book in 1983 in collaboration with the technical magazine *Chaud Froid Performance*. I was 28 at the time, and had set up my own design office, Études Solaires, which has since become Cardonnel Ingénierie. Solar energy has always fascinated me, and I built my first solar water heater when I was eighteen. My aim with this very pragmatic book was to compile everything I knew about solar energy to disseminate it to professionals and foster a more structured dialogue with them. Indeed, I've always been bothered by this separation of approaches: on the one hand, architects defend a vernacular bioclimatic design—using bay windows, Trombe walls, buffer spaces, etc.—and on the other, specialists advocate the use of technical systems.

I thought we needed to strike a balance between the two visions, passive and active. They can intelligently complement each other. I took advantage of this publication to establish new links and, in particular, to use observation and calculation to look at bioclimatic winter gardens as used by you and Jean-Philippe. These are excellent objects for study: they are transitional spaces, heated by the sun and indirectly by heat loss from the building they're attached to. Depending on the opening of windows and the use of solar or thermal protection, they create a temperate atmosphere that changes with the day and the seasons, enriching the living space. After all, being in the sun is very pleasant. It's exciting to be able to create spaces that are balanced in this respect! And although solar energy can't solve everything, if a building is comfortable exclusively thanks to the sun for 3,000 to 4,000 hours out of the 8,760 hours in a year, that's already very good, as the need for additional heating is considerably reduced.

The book opened many doors for me. I was gradually recognized for the interest of my proposals on thermal balances, which enabled me to join the working groups of the Ministry of Housing to draw up the future thermal rules, now known as the RE 2020 energy and energy-efficiency regulations.

AL: What have been your influences in terms of travel or encounters? And how do you differentiate yourself from other engineers?

CC: In 1980, I made a decisive trip to Quebec, then consulted many books on solar buildings and houses by Quebecois and American architects. All these experiences inspired me. I also got in touch with the Association Française pour l'Etude et le Développement des Applications de l'Energie Solaire and analyzed numerous calculation methods. I also made friends with a number of architects in the south of France, including Robert Laignelot, Michel Franjus, and Michel Gerber. There were also Georges and Jeanne-Marie Alexandroff, Jean-Pierre Cordier, and, of course, the two of you as well as engineers like Roger Cadiergues, Jacques Giordano, and René Gilles.

As a thermal engineer, I didn't want my role to be reduced to calculating the power of radiators and boilers. That was no fun at all! In fact, I was an early campaigner against the direct use of electricity by the Joule effect. Spending kWh of this precious energy on electric convection heaters when it could be used in other ways has always seemed problematic to me. We can't just think in terms of losses or systems. I've always thought that getting heat via sun streaming through a window was better than a nuclear power plant. With the energy supplier Gaz de France in the 1990s with the RT 89 law, I led the fight against the electric convector, which was very inexpensive compared with a hot-water radiator installation, but so much more costly in terms of primary energy (1 kWh electric = 3 kWh primary energy at the time). We then developed a hydro-wired radiator at a more affordable price, followed by condensing generation. At the same time, improvements in insulation—both solid wall and glazing—helped bring the Uw coefficient down from 2.5/3.0 in 1983 to less than 1.3 in 2020.

Jean-Philippe Vassal: This bioclimatic approach, and the importance of personalities like Michel Gerber, coincides with our architecture studies in Bordeaux. We were very interested in this path at a time when no one was talking about the thermal performance of buildings. But since then, something seems to have been lost or forgotten. It seems to me that houses are becoming more and more closed in on themselves. Would you agree?

CC: Yes, of course! And strong lobbying by insulation manufacturers helps to explain this state of affairs. A typical 100 m² house requires around 200 m² and 20 to 30 m³ of glass wool, compared with barely 20 m² of glazed surface. Margins on insulation products are high, which partly explains why big insulation manufacturers have been reluctant to develop large windows. In 2003, when I worked on drafting the French thermal regulation RT 2005, I succeeded in imposing a minimum proportion of glazed surface equal to one-sixth of the habitable surface, whereas the promoters were going in the opposite direction. The ministry followed my lead, as did the glass and window industries.

AL: How do you achieve the balance you're seeking between the passive and active approaches?

CC: My working method consists of eight steps. First and foremost, you need to be familiar with the properties of the site you're working on, studying its climate, resources, and access to energy. Then I analyze the building's typology, with a view to its compactness. This is followed by a study of the project's thermal insulation, thermal mass, and thermal inertia to ensure the stability of its interior temperature. Fourth, I examine ventilation and exhaust requirements in relation to the desired indoor air quality. In the fifth stage, I look at free inputs, such as solar and light coming from bay windows, as well as internal inputs from occupants—artificial lighting and domestic uses. Taking into consideration all this information lets us draw up a bioclimatic balance sheet for the building, and determine any requirements for heating, cooling, daylighting, and hot water. And it's only at the end of the process, after measuring actual needs, that we can recommend systems, calculate requirements and losses, and determine energy consumption. This is summarized in kilowatt hours, but also in terms of CO_2 emissions and investment costs. These different stages enable us to raise or lower various parameters, to balance it and integrate adjustment and optimization logics, depending of course on the involvement of the architects.

JPV: So you study system requirements as a last resort. When we approach a project, we always think in terms of external inputs. This means first considering the climate, any heat sources—including the sun—to capture as much energy as possible. Only then can we determine a system that would best complement this comfort. As is often the case, starting with the logic of technical equipment leads to a completely different way of thinking: asking how to prevent the heat produced by the radiator from escaping into the outside world. So the hierarchy of thought is really decisive.

AL: I'd like to return to the context of our meeting in 2003, during the Cité Manifeste project in Mulhouse. We had already adapted the design of greenhouses for single-family homes. But applying this approach to the construction of collective housing was more complicated as there are all those regulatory boxes to tick! This was the first time we had to prove that it was possible to comply with the thermal regulations applied to collective housing (at the time, RT 2000) while using the bioclimatic principle of the horticultural greenhouse. Our intuition and pragmatic approach had always sufficed to bring our projects to fruition, but here we had to demonstrate that it would comply with thermal regulations. The engineering office we were working with at the time was very skeptical and declined to continue with the study. Our client, SOMCO, a social-housing property management, received very negative feedback from the certification organization Qualitel, which completely jeopardized

1   On Climate, Comfort, and the Pleasure of Inhabiting

Buildings G, H, and I of Cité du Grand
Parc, Bordeaux, with Frédéric Druot
and Christophe Hutin (transformation)

Office and housing tower,
Chêne-Bourg, Geneva

our chances of obtaining a subsidy. Against this backdrop of stalemate and disillusionment, we asked for an exception from the Title V commission at the Ministry of the Environment. Our client was nevertheless very pessimistic.

JPV: We presented our project to a dozen or so people: architects, technicians, industrialists, and engineers. And while we had just come to beg for an exception, the project was so well received that the course of history was reversed. Not only was no exemption required, allowing us to get the subsidy, but our customer's view of the project also completely changed.

CC: Yes, that's true. I was a member of the Title V commission at the time, and I argued for the inclusion of this major change. This presentation was the starting point for us first meeting.

JPV: The Cité Manifeste homes function like ecological houses in a dense environment. They feature two types of bioclimatic spaces: winter gardens and greenhouses. When we designed House Latapie (1993), we were already interested in the architecture of horticultural greenhouses and the climatic comfort they offered. At the time, we felt that the complementarity of an insulated space with an envelope functioning like a greenhouse could create a kind of intermediate climate of great interest to the occupant. But we still had to produce the calculations necessary to prove that our project met the standards of the collective, and we weren't equipped to do so.

CC: I didn't have the tools myself! Your project was of great interest to me, as it was an extension of my research. So I was very happy to get involved. We set up specific calculation models that let us integrate solarized buffer spaces such as conservatories into calculation methods and regulatory texts. These calculations were based on those I had already carried out for the study of winter gardens in my book *Solaire actif et passif*. On the basis of this work, I was able to align the thermal equations for buffer spaces to draw up a balance sheet showing that these spaces were calculable and therefore feasible.

AL: *How did you develop the calculations?*

CC: We took one typical day per month, observing the outside temperature hour by hour. I then calculated the solar-energy input and established the thermal balance of the conservatory based on what was gained in terms of solar-energy input and what was lost through its wall to the outside. This allowed me to estimate the ambient temperature of the conservatory. This was often higher than the outside temperature and close to the inside temperature. This was where space balancing came into play. We were able to determine when it was useful to open the large windows to let in energy, and when to close them. These calculations were further modulated according to the use of insulating curtains and solar shading. In this way, we developed an approach to indoor temperature, using European-standard formulas, of course.

One thing led to another, and these were taken up and validated by the Centre Scientifique et Technique du Bâtiment, an organization of great importance in France. Winter gardens are considered as solarized buffer spaces. In the calculation rule, it's easy to include the window-surface area, the inertia of floors, and solar and thermal protection. The winter garden is then associated with solar gains, heat and air exchanges, thermal mass and solar protection. The mathematical model is complete, but its functionality could be understood even more precisely if we were to use increments of even less than an hour. My approach to calculations is improving, but I still reason in terms of the users' ability to open or close the walls. In the Cité Manifeste, at mid-season, we manage to balance the spaces, but in summer it's a little more difficult. It's then that users have to take over and manage things themselves to control their own comfort.

AL: *This method, Christian, reveals the importance of taking the user into account, and opens up this very broad question of comfort. In the perpetual quest for balance between passive and active, what is your approach to thermal comfort?*

CC: Most engineers work with comfort standards based on an operative value. But occupants experience comfort very differently in the same space. The notion of comfort is very subtle and not an exact science. In my work, I rely a lot on intuition and I try to rely on actual practices, even if we can't take into account all the habits of users. It's not possible to "hand-tailor" every home. But the ways regulations consider various uses are very conventional, and that's problematic.

The issue of summer comfort in buildings is now of paramount importance. We're well on the way to achieving this thanks to improvements in solar protection, glazing properties, and ventilation. If photovoltaic energy is available, there's no reason fans can't be activated to move the air from inside to outside. In fact, the power of a natural thermal draft is low. The installation of a climatic or Provençal well can also significantly improve comfort, as can the integration of heated and cooled floors or ceilings. This is a complementary solution that I've been very interested in lately.

A building cannot claim to be exclusively active or passive. This brings us back to our initial objective: to imagine a balance that can be implemented. In passive houses, the user has to be active, opening windows at the right moment, lowering solar protection, etc. Conversely, in active houses, where everything relies on systems and sensors, people are too passive. We need to find an in-between solution. Home automation devices coupled with the integration of predictive data will enable us to go further and our smart phones to transmit the information to us. Wouldn't it be nice in the winter to know that we're going to get free heating from the sun the day after it rains!

AL: *But at the same time, passive architecture makes residents more competent because they have to get involved and try to understand how the space works vis-à-vis the climate. It seems that more and more people are motivated to do this. So when it comes to considering comfort and related calculations, we need to take the user more into account.*

JPV: *Conversely, in a building based on active systems, it's curious to consider the user as entirely passive. In thermal calculations, we don't take into account the fact that people come and go or open or close the windows. But if a window exists, we need to know that it can be opened! An active system leads to a completely airtight architecture, in much the same way as what's found in tertiary spaces, in which the user's gesture, however minimal, is invisible.*

CC: The scenarios used in the regulations assume that people are absent during the day, and that no one is going to open windows or activate solar protection. The assumption is that the dwelling will work by itself. In real life, however, there are "maybes," nuances, modulations. Admittedly, we're now trying to take better account of these variations, but the reasoning is still in its infancy.

AL: *In terms of thermal regulations, has there been an evolution in the way the winter garden is considered? Or must we still use roundabout calculations to get it taken into account?*

CC: The solarized buffer space is taken into account in the regulatory calculation. This method is complex, and the main concern is that design offices often don't have the right approach to conservatories. Very few of them have mastered the calculation. There's a lack of training on the subject, but it's not their priority. The evolution of these regulations is based on the consistency of estimates of ambient temperature in winter gardens. It's a question of analyzing a temperature ratio, the buffer space coefficient, the little b, which should make it possible to show the effects of the conservatory on the envelope and enhance its role and effectiveness as a climatic buffer space. If $b = 0$, the conservatory is at the same temperature as the surrounding space. If $b = 1$, it means that it is at the outside temperature, and therefore inefficient. We generally have b coefficients of around 0.5, but during the day the b can become negative, meaning that the conservatory is warmer than the surrounding space and can be opened. But in order to avoid a negative coefficient in summer, which could lead to overheating, calculations must be made by the hour and weighted by the day. This coefficient provides an indicator of how well the conservatory is functioning. It must therefore be calculated very precisely to define the value of a conservatory. We are delighted that the new regulations (RE 2020) emphasize the importance of the BBio—bioclimatic balance—and will even result in a BBio that's 30% lower than that required by RT 2012, the thermal regulation that was replaced by RE 2020. The efficiency of winter gardens will be accounted for with increasing accuracy.

AL: *The question of the b coefficient is interesting because it's part of the content of the regulations, which now allow winter gardens to be considered in calculations. But few thermal engineers take this into account in detail. They use a default value equal to 0.8 or 1, which is counterproductive for the energy calculation of the winter garden, giving it the value of a cellar or basement and not allowing the valorization of its true efficiency.*

CC: In fact, the efficiency of a winter garden is often incorrectly calculated, as the overall building performance, that is, without any mechanical systems, must also be taken into account in the calculations. By measuring the internal temperature of a building, we should be able to simplify our mathematical models. Today's regulations are too cumbersome.

JPV: *Yes, and our projects suffer because the actual utility of the winter garden is not taken into account. For example, the fact that the winter garden is fully open in fine weather is not considered in the regulatory calculations. In summer, however, it functions quite differently. The balcony overhang over the main window acts as a shade and the window receives no direct sunlight. The winter garden is transformed into an open terrace rather than a closed space that*

On Climate, Comfort, and the Pleasure of Inhabiting

18 dwellings, Rixheim

46 On Climate, Comfort, and the Pleasure of Inhabiting

University of Arts and Human Sciences,
Grenoble

catches the sun. And it's precisely this dual function that interests us. There are four layers—one facing outward, consisting of a polycarbonate sliding window and a sunshade, and 2.5 meters deeper, a double-glazed insulated sliding window with its thermal curtain. Moving these four elements independently creates a dynamic insulation that will be very different in winter and summer, so it's neither too cold nor too hot. Unlike triple glazing, which remains in the same position and can become problematic in summer, our system allows adjustments so you can very precisely achieve the comfort you want for each season.

CC: Absolutely, but this important variable linked to mobile and dynamic insulation isn't easy to take into account in regulatory calculations, and it's an obstacle to bioclimatic approaches. We absolutely need to make progress on this issue, and the Centre Scientifique et Technique du Bâtiment needs to do more about it. Here again, we come up against overly cumbersome mathematical models that require us to demonstrate everything, leaving little room for pragmatism and experience.

JPV: *Our way of working is based on observing phenomena. In Sweden and Denmark, many apartments have a lot of south-facing glazing, because it's necessary to capture solar gain and light. In Barcelona, buildings dating back to the 1970s feature large balconies with wooden sun shields. In designing the winter gardens, our idea is to combine these two situations and offer every possible combination to adapt to the daily and seasonal constraints of temperate climates. We realize that there's calculation and then there's life. But life is much more precise than calculation. It's interesting to put things in perspective. Calculations may improve, but life will always be more precise. Why should we trust calculations more than the gardens of the Alhambra in Granada or the wind towers of Yemen? Horticulturists have sometimes worked for decades to evolve their hanging systems, to capture more light by modifying the shape of their greenhouse profiles. This incredible sophistication is achieved over the very long term. We should learn much more from observation. Calculations that are not based on observation can quickly become erroneous.*

CC: Calculation times and the development of models that are unfortunately not very profitable for the teams working on them are the main stumbling blocks. Specialists prefer to spend time on a controlled ventilation system that requires several technical opinions. Our insulating wool curtains, for example, require complex technical assessments—but they don't bring in much money when compared to sophisticated machines or systems.

JPV: *On the other hand, current thermal regulations take into account the worst times of the year, in both the coldest periods of the winter and hottest days of summer. This certainly encourages us to avoid the worst, but it makes it very difficult to produce the best.*

AL: We're faced with a system that completely lacks common sense and has no confidence in the inhabitants' ability to operate a building autonomously. It even assumes that a user's intervention can foil the automation. We're realizing that more insulation or advanced technology won't be the way to improve energy efficiency. We'll have to rely on the individual and his or her interaction to change various parameters.

CC: At a time when our ways of working are undergoing major transformation, the regulations still make no provision for daytime occupation of the home, or for working from home. This is a mistake. The behavior of inhabitants is far too scripted, and that's problematic. By integrating the actual conduct of residents, energy balances change and become more interesting. Therein lies the paradox between conventional calculation and real life. To integrate parameters that include occupant behavior, as you rightly did with Atmos Lab in producing this book, we'd need to make a Title V–type application under the RE 2020 regulations to integrate active user management. Today, the Ministry of the Environment, the Centre Scientifique et Technique du Bâtiment, and even home-automation specialists are finding it very hard to integrate active building management into their thinking. We struggle to control energy needs according to time of day, climate, weather forecasts, and occupants' behavior. This is a major problem when it comes to designing tomorrow's apartments. The future application of the Elan law—a 2018 measure aimed at facilitating the construction of housing—should enable us to show that a building is comfortable and energy efficient thanks to its design and the behavior of its users. This will be helped by metering systems that allow occupants to see their energy consumption in real time.

AL: *That's why we felt it was so important, in the study we carried out with Atmos Lab on several of our projects, to incorporate actual observations of typical user behavior. Otherwise, there's no way of proving that winter gardens actually work, or that they are effective and efficient! Most important is following your intuition and observation when conceiving of a project. Calculations come next. They must not determine a project. On their own, the most powerful mathematical models would never produce the architecture we do.*

The current trend is to rely exclusively on calculations. Under pressure from people like you, regulations can evolve, even if we regret that at the same time, the ministry has changed the rules and included winter gardens in calculations of the gross floor area, which is a disincentive to building them. How absurd! Winter gardens are becoming almost impossible to create in new construction and in densely populated areas when the permitted build surface is limited. Developers prefer to create more living space, which allows them to charge more.

Winter gardens are also very interesting as a tool for improving existing housing. This makes them much more attractive than external thermal insulation, which is widely encouraged by the French government's thermal renovation incentive programs. This is what we've done at the Cité du Grand Parc in Bordeaux and on the Tour Bois-le-Prêtre in Paris. To fully appreciate their value, you need to link winter gardens directly to the issue of energy savings.

CC: Of course! The winter garden is a dynamic space that can be occupied 80% of the time, and which also significantly reduces a building's energy requirements. It's fantastic! It reduces heat loss on the facade by more than half and significantly increases user comfort. In the RE 2020, we're introducing a new methodology for calculating the energy performance of converted attic spaces less than 1.8 m high. And I'm working to include winter gardens or bioclimatic solarized spaces in calculations of BBio and Cep (primary energy consumption per year)—around half the bioclimatic surface area or living area.

JPV: There seem to be two contradictory movements. On the one hand, there's a desire to make the home as insulated and airtight as possible, with maximum impermeability. On the other hand, it should meet hygiene and comfort needs through good ventilation and aeration, because indoor air quality is recognized as very important. This implies mechanical ventilation systems, since natural ventilation by opening windows isn't accepted in the principle of maximum insulation of a dwelling.

CC: Yes, and the aeraulic balance of a building is not at all easy to calculate. We can use airflows to remove heat or restore it. You'd think air would follow a single direction, but that's not the case at all. Certain air currents can be beneficial in summer and create zones of discomfort in winter, even if they improve our hygiene. This complex balance is difficult to master, and mathematical models have a hard time translating into reality.

JPV: This means questions of aeration and ventilation are even more complex than those of thermal engineering!

CC: Yes, and we're just beginning to take an interest in indoor air quality! Today, installing sensors will make it possible to determine changes in temperature and humidity and detect the amount of CO_2 in a room. We'll be able to act according to the levels displayed. We're not fish. We live in the air, but with very little information or feedback on its quality.

AL: This raises the issue of outdoor pollution. Today, we expect buildings to protect us from the city's noise and air-quality problems. It would be smarter to address those issues at their source, but it's easier to simply say that buildings should bear that burden.

JPV: And to help spur an evolution of all these issues of living pleasure and comfort, I think it's worth going back to the question of the referent. When you look at books by thermal engineers dating from the modern era, including those about solar energy, you get the impression that the reference building is invariably the traditional house, with attic space, a pitched roof, closed rooms, a few windows, a main door, and sometimes a fireplace. But to change mindsets, we might need to try a paradigm shift. That's how we approached the Latapie house. We didn't use the traditional house as our starting point, but the horticultural greenhouse and industrial shed. Referring to greenhouses for housing created a very big gap. That's what made it so interesting: finding very different references and bringing them back into the project, recombining them to produce something truly astonishing. The dominant reference for comfort features—glazing and insulation—remains the traditional house, meaning we've come to a standstill in terms of the development of construction technologies.

CC: I couldn't agree more! The reference to the single-family home is omnipresent. It certainly prevents us from evolving. We need to break with this reference. I hope the ongoing transformation of our lifestyles—the integration of telecommuting, school, gardening, and sport into the domestic space—will lead us to question our references and draw inspiration from new archetypes.

On Climate, Comfort, and the Pleasure of Inhabiting

School of Architecture, Nantes

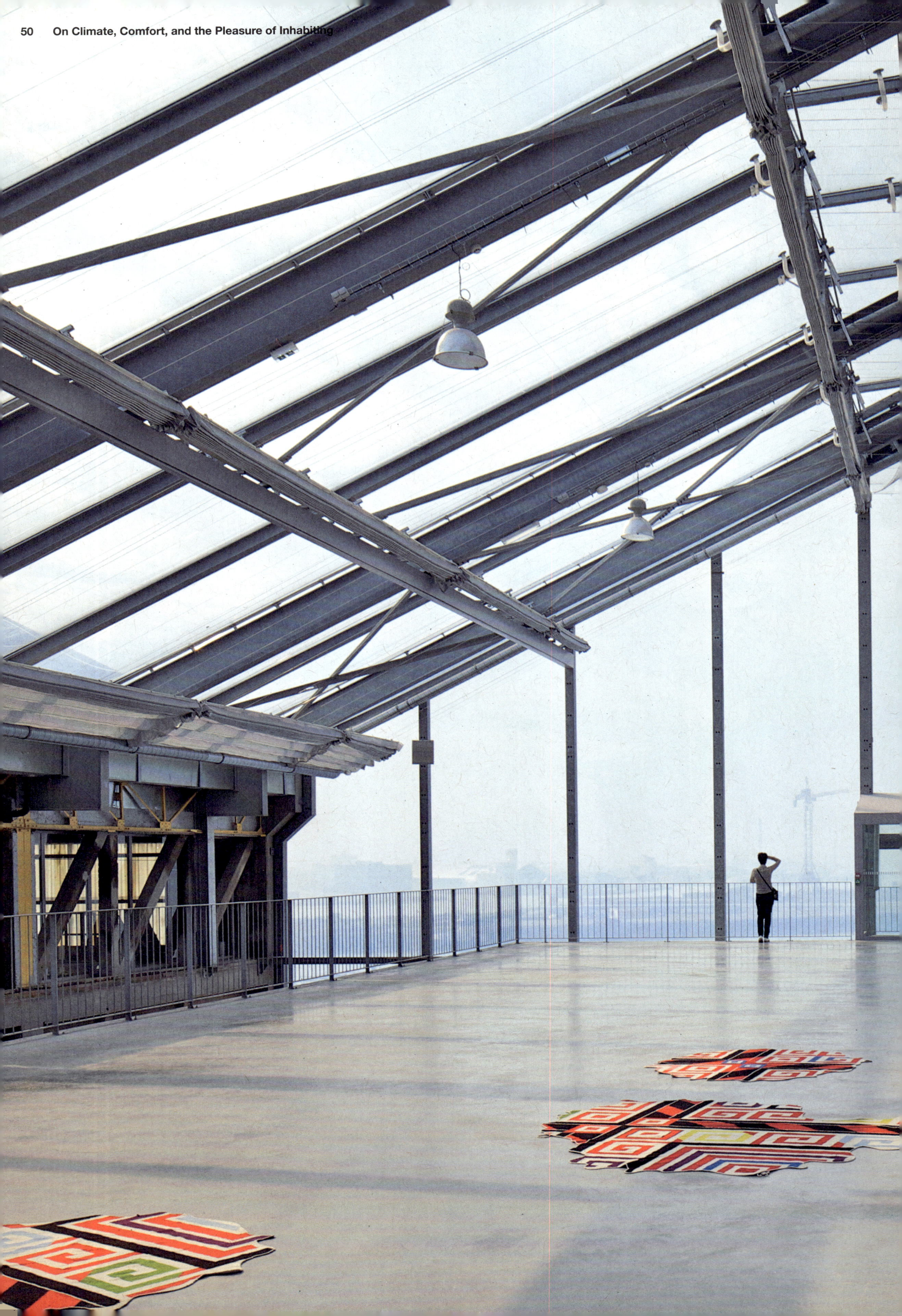

On Climate, Comfort, and the Pleasure of Inhabiting

FRAC Grand Large – Hauts-de-France,
contemporary art center, Dunkerque

Polyvalent Theatre, Lille

2. The Case Studies

Introduction

The objective of this work is to show the benefits of the bioclimatic design of buildings and the effectiveness of the winter gardens, which are a basic element of this design. To support this approach, we conducted a scientific examination of four projects built between 2005 and 2020—new constructions or transformations of existing structures—that include winter gardens. Between 2018 and 2021, a typical unit of each project was studied using state-of-the-art technology and best practices grounded in real monitoring. In particular, we wanted to highlight the effects of the winter gardens and accurately analyze their thermal behavior. We chose these four projects as case studies because they illustrate our approach and the evolution of our thinking over time, following the knowledge we gained from one project to another. And because they correspond to the evolution of thermal regulations, they constitute representative case studies.

The first step in the research was fieldwork, with temperature and humidity measurements and interviews with the occupants. Then computer models were created and calibrated. To maximize their accuracy, we used the actual performance of the building as determined by our measurements as a reference point. The aim was to mimic the actual measured temperature by adjusting building properties in the models that are often invisible and cannot be determined in advance or otherwise (such as air infiltration, air exchange, thermal inertia, and internal heat gains).

For each case study, we analyzed climate, solar incidence, potential for air movement, daylight levels, and thermal behavior. First simulations were carried out in "free-running" mode, meaning without the use of heating or cooling, to understand the natural conditions the building provides by itself. This particular method, rarely used in general practice, has been employed to put forward the qualities and the efficiency of the building itself with all its layers. This method demonstrates the performance of the building design independent from the use of mechanical systems, with the goal of their reduction.

Each of the four case studies is complemented by a comparison case that shows how an alternate option for the project, different in each instance, might have worked. These comparative studies and simulations, and their results, are developed in the following section.

The Case Studies

How to Read the Case Studies
Climate Diagrams

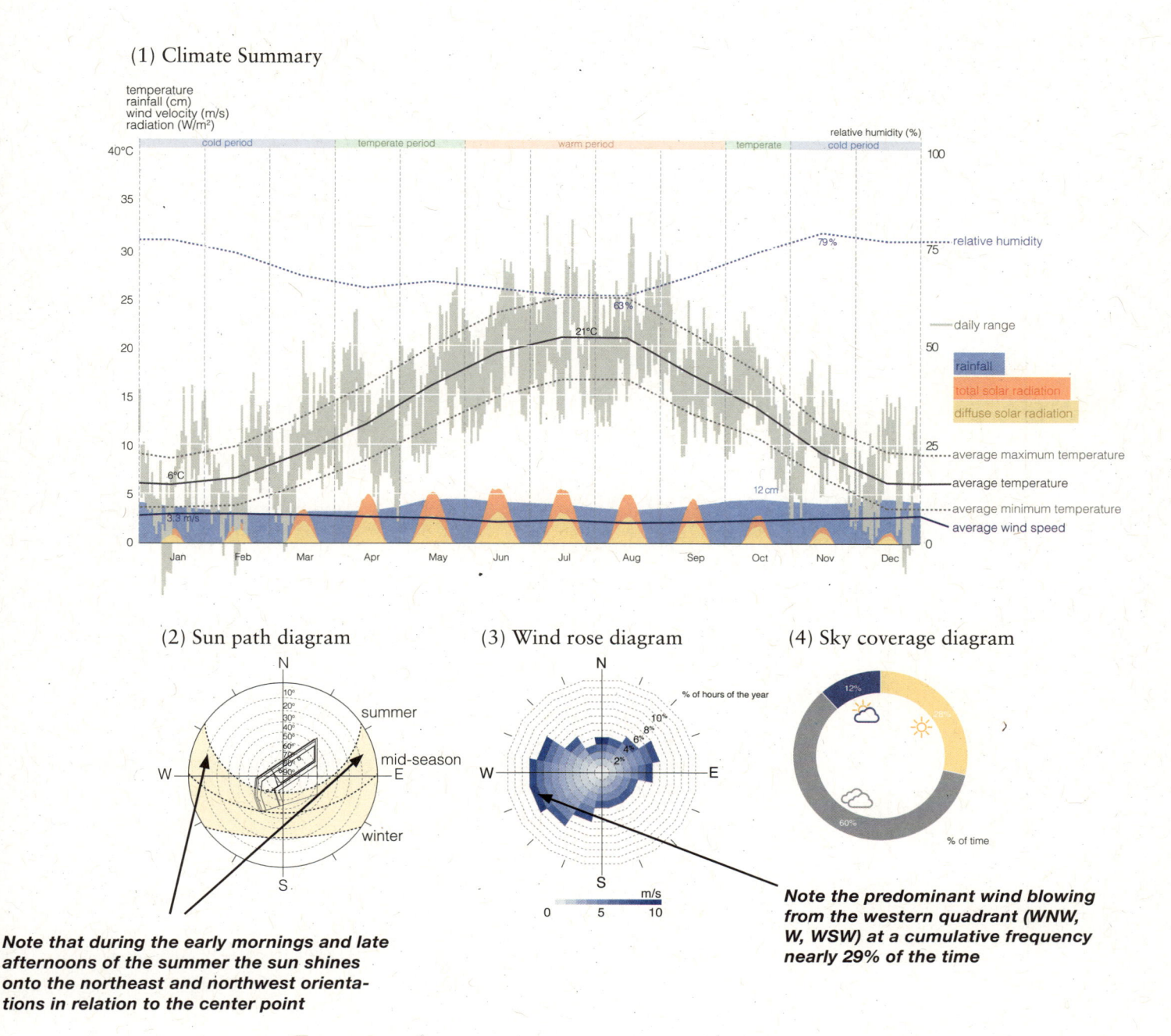

(1) Climate Summary

(2) Sun path diagram

Note that during the early mornings and late afternoons of the summer the sun shines onto the northeast and northwest orientations in relation to the center point

(3) Wind rose diagram

Note the predominant wind blowing from the western quadrant (WNW, W, WSW) at a cumulative frequency nearly 29% of the time

(4) Sky coverage diagram

(1) Climate summary: This chart displays the local weather data throughout the year: temperatures (in °C), solar radiation (in W/m²), wind speed (in m/s), rainfall (in mm), and relative humidity (secondary axis, in %). The variables are based on a local weather file (containing averaged hourly records from 2000 to 2009, the most recent at the time of the studies). The solid and dotted curves indicate the monthly averages of: temperatures (with averages of maximum and minimum), relative humidity, and wind speed. The gray pattern indicates the temperature range for each day of the year. The blue pattern indicates the total monthly rainfall. Solar radiation (hourly average) is represented across a day of each month. The orange part represents the total solar radiation, which includes both direct sunlight and the part diffused by the atmosphere, while the yellow part represents only the diffuse part.

(2) Sun path diagram: This diagram shows the stereographic path of the sun throughout the year relative to the center point. It represents the hemisphere of the celestial vault projected stereographically, which allows for measuring solar angles. The yellow pattern marks all locations of the sun throughout the year from sunrise to sunset. The dashed arcs mark the passage of the sun during the summer and winter solstices (June 21 and Dec. 21) and the mid-season equinoxes (March 21 and Sept. 21). The intersections of these arcs with the concentric dotted lines that run from the center of the diagram outward indicate the sun's altitude in the sky. Overlaying the site plan with the sun's path provides a quick way to see how the facades are exposed to the sun.

(3) Wind rose diagram: This diagram shows the wind rose throughout the year. It shows from where the winds blow, how fast, and how often. The triangles coming out of the center point to the wind direction, while the concentric white circles mark the frequencies with which the wind blows from each direction in percentage of hours of the year.

(4) Sky coverage diagram: This diagram shows the amount of cloud cover in the local sky in percentage of time of the season. The proportion of time with clear sunny skies is represented in yellow, with partially cloudy skies in blue and overcast skies in gray. These diagrams give a quick read of how sunny, cloudy, or overcast the skies are in summer and in winter.

56　The Case Studies

Color-Coded Spatial Maps

(1) Color-coded spatial map

Numbers mark the local average of calculated values (e.g., solar heat gains) in the room

The global averages are marked on the legend. These are calculated as area-weighted averages that include only spaces where local averages are marked and thus relevant.

kWh/(m²·winter period)
0　　25　　50
average 4 kWh/(m²·winter period)

(2) Solar heat gains in winter

kWh/(m²·period)

0　5　10　15　20　25　30　35　40　45　50

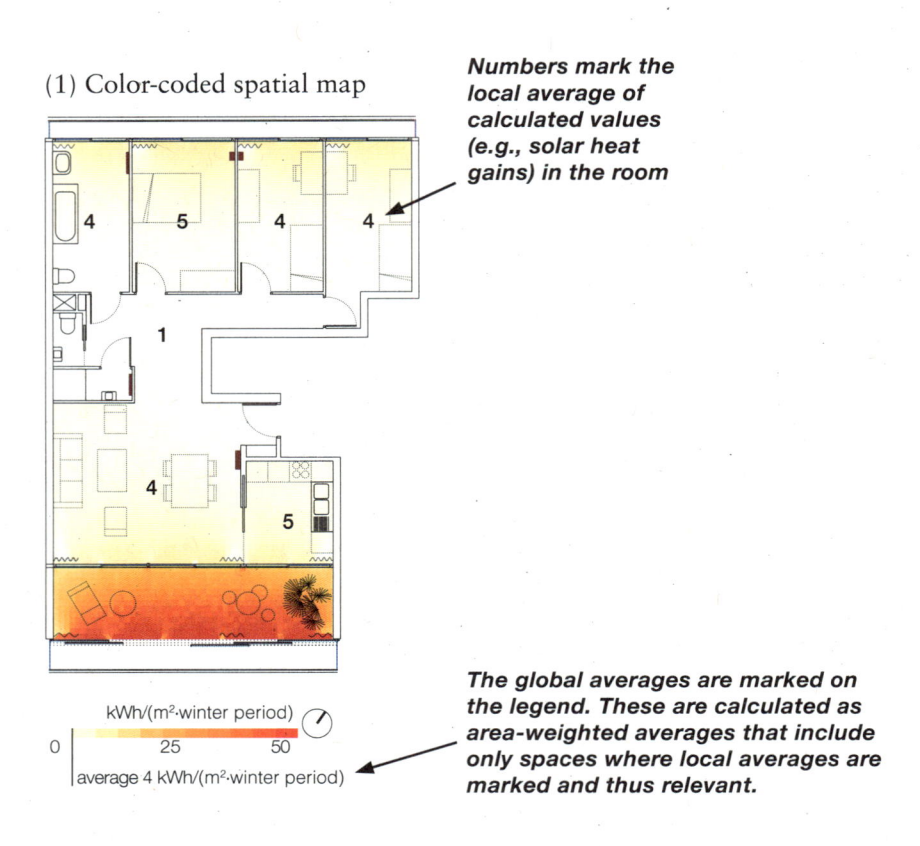

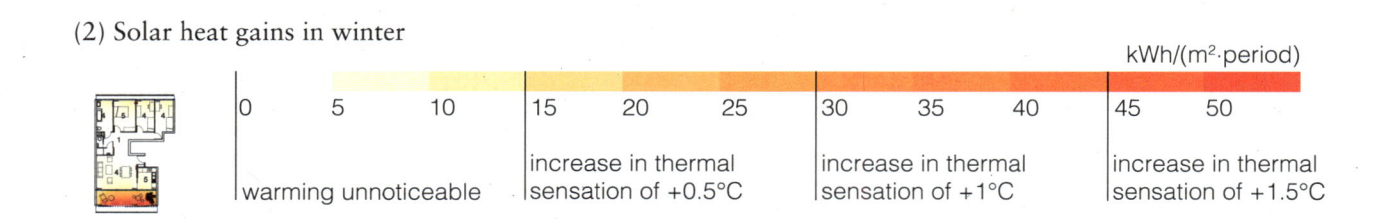

warming unnoticeable | increase in thermal sensation of +0.5°C | increase in thermal sensation of +1°C | increase in thermal sensation of +1.5°C

(1) Color-coded spatial map: These color-coded spatial maps show data calculated onto a test plane either placed horizontally at a specific height or in sections depending on the type of simulation. The plane is divided into a grid of 0.15 m by 0.15 m. These grids are used to visualize solar access, solar heat gains, natural airflow, and daylight autonomy. All graphs are defined by color-coded legends that specify the units of calculations.

(2) Solar heat gains in winter: This color-coded spatial map reports incident solar radiation data calculated on the floor. It quantifies the cumulative radiation reaching indoors in winter (Dec. 21–Mar. 21). Quantities of radiation in kilowatt hour per square meter (kWh/m²) are shown by value scale, progressing from white over yellow and orange to red. The more intense the radiation, the redder—serving as a visual metaphor for heat gain. The heat can also be translated into an average increase of felt temperature, if the sun hits the human body directly. The intense orange corresponds to an average increase of 1.5°C, according to CIBSE Guide A for Environmental Design (the premier reference source in the United Kingdom for designers of low-energy buildings).

(3) Solar access in summer or winter

hours of sun per day

0 1 2 3 4 5 6 7 8

(4) Natural airflow in summer under average wind conditions

m/s

0 | 0.2 0.4 | 0.6 0.8 1 | 1.2 1.4 1.6 1.8 2 |

calm | pleasant | air is moving | drafty
cooling unnoticeable | decrease in thermal sensation of -1.5°C | decrease in thermal sensation of -3°C | decrease in thermal sensation of -4.5°C

(5) Daylight autonomy (EN 17037)

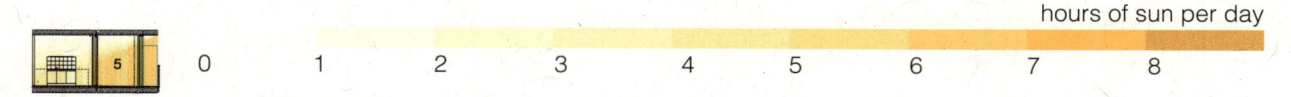

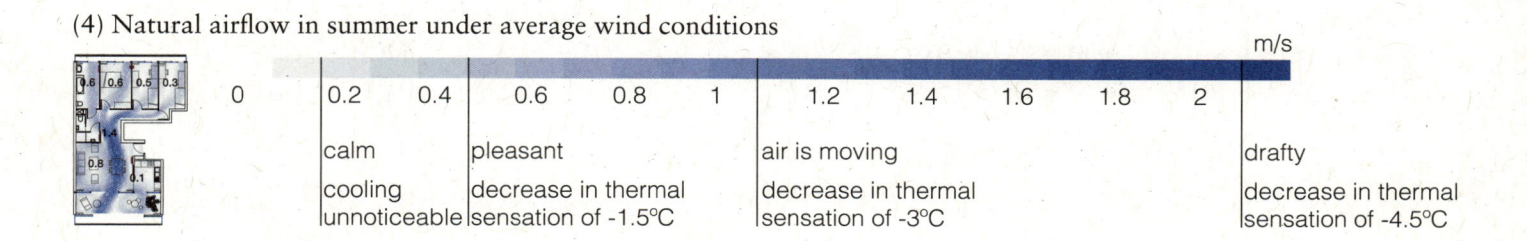

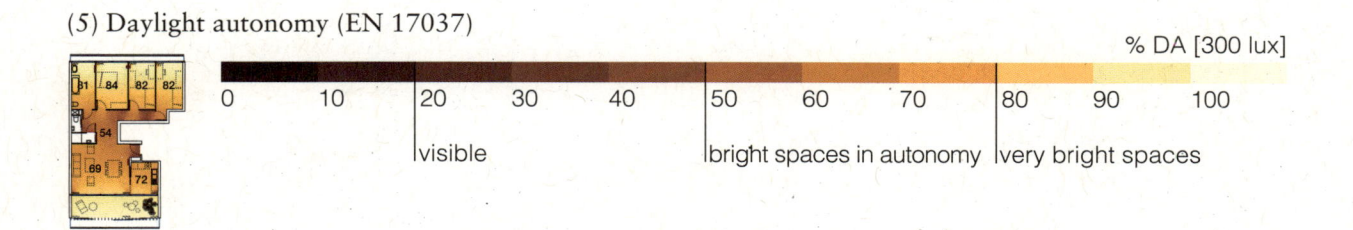

% DA [300 lux]

0 10 20 30 40 50 60 70 80 90 100

visible | bright spaces in autonomy | very bright spaces

(6) Space heating demand

kWh/(m²·year)

0 5 10 15 20 25 30 35 40 45 50

negligible energy demand | energy demand targeted by most standards today such as Passive House | high energy demand

(3) Solar access in summer or winter: The solar-access map reports sun-hours data calculated in a section. It quantifies the number of hours (h) that sunrays reach indoors on the summer solstice (June 21) or on the winter solstice (Dec. 21), assuming a clear sky. Number of hours is shown by a value scale, progressing from white to yellow. The more time the sun is available indoors, the more yellow—serving as a visual metaphor for catching more sunrays.

(4) Natural airflow in summer under average wind conditions: This color-coded spatial map reports natural airflow data calculated at a body height of 1.10 m with all panels open. It quantifies the air flowing through the unit during average wind conditions in summer. Air velocity values in meters per second (m/s) are shown by value scale, progressing from white to blue. The faster, the darker—serving as a visual metaphor for air blowing. Natural airflow patterns are revealed and further indicated by vectors.

(5) Daylight Autonomy (EN 17037): This color-coded spatial map reports daylight-autonomy data calculated on a plane at a table height of 0.80 m. It quantifies the annual percentage of daytime that each square receives at least 300 lux. This is the natural illuminance level that correlates with the actual perception of daylight, enough light to perform most tasks, and a near-zero probability that occupants will turn on electric lighting (design levels for artificial lighting also use a 300 lux threshold). Rooms in which daylight is not required by regulation are excluded from calculations. Daylight quality is shown by value scale, progressing from brown, over yellow to white: the greater the daylight autonomy, the whiter—serving as a visual metaphor for brightness.

(6) Space heating demand: This color-coded spatial map shows the heating demand data in kilowatt hour per square meter per year (kWh/[m²·year]). Each thermal zone represents a part of the space with similar thermal characteristics. A continuous space can be split into multiple zones if physical conditions vary (e.g., the part of the space that receives more solar gains may behave differently than the adjacent one). Connections between multiple zones of the same space are defined in such a way that air connections are maintained while radiant intensities differ. Heating consumption is shown by value scale, progressing from white to red: the higher the consumption, the redder—serving as a visual metaphor for heat.

The Case Studies

Thermal Graphs

(1) Operative temperatures during a typical year in free-running mode

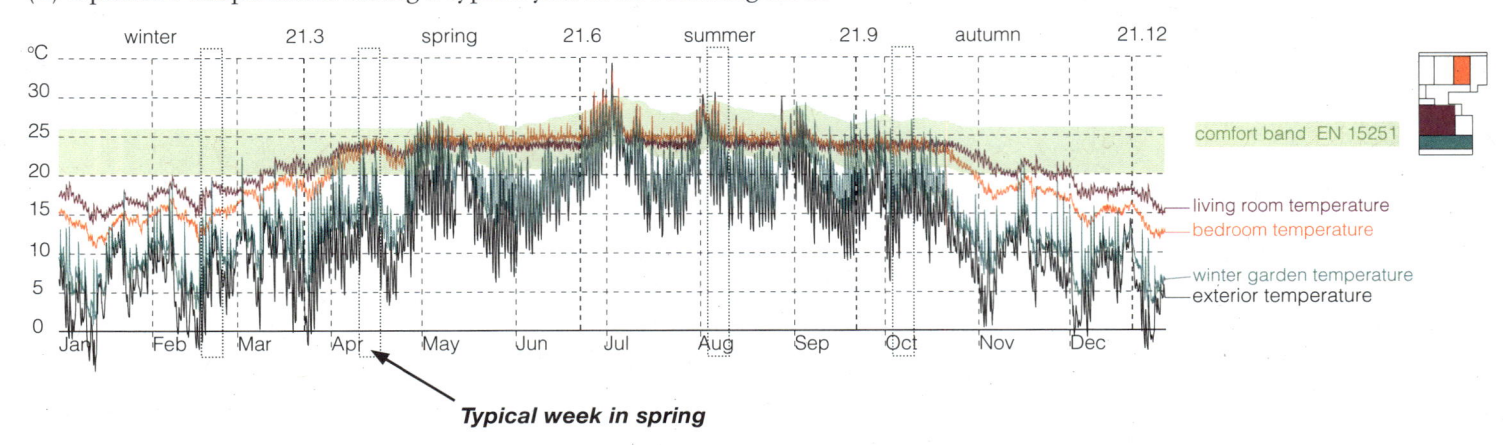

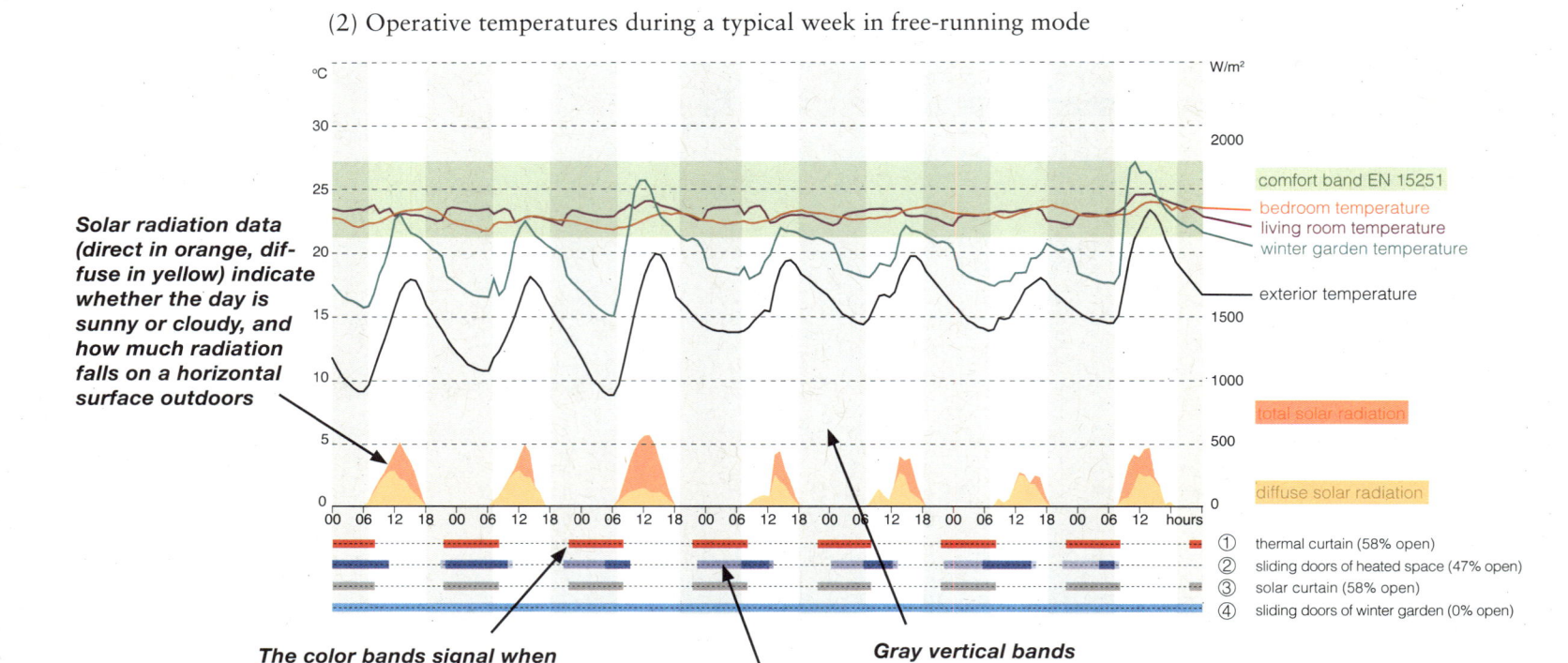

- comfort band EN 15251
- living room temperature
- bedroom temperature
- winter garden temperature
- exterior temperature

Typical week in spring

(2) Operative temperatures during a typical week in free-running mode

Solar radiation data (direct in orange, diffuse in yellow) indicate whether the day is sunny or cloudy, and how much radiation falls on a horizontal surface outdoors

- comfort band EN 15251
- bedroom temperature
- living room temperature
- winter garden temperature
- exterior temperature
- total solar radiation
- diffuse solar radiation

① thermal curtain (58% open)
② sliding doors of heated space (47% open)
③ solar curtain (58% open)
④ sliding doors of winter garden (0% open)

The color bands signal when occupants operate the four facade elements—when the band is visible, the element is also visible (blue: windows closed; red: curtains drawn)

Gray vertical bands signal nighttime

A more transparent blue indicates that the element is partially open

(1) Operative temperatures during a typical year in free-running mode: This chart displays data in parallel and over time with operative temperatures (in °C) on the left vertical axis and all hours of the year on the horizontal axis. The solid curves show calculated temperatures of the different spaces and the outdoor temperatures during a typical year in free-running mode. The green band indicates the comfort band of temperatures according to EN 15251 (Category II). This graph provides a global view of annual temperature fluctuations and marks typical weeks selected for the detailed zoom-in.

(2) Operative temperatures during a typical week in free-running mode:

This chart displays data in parallel and over time: operative temperatures (in °C) on the left vertical axis, outdoor solar radiation (in W/m²) on the right vertical axis, and below the graph is the occupant's operation of the four facade elements (sliding doors and curtains). The solid curves show calculated temperatures of the different spaces during a typical week in free-running mode. The vertical white band marks daytime, the vertical gray band nighttime. The horizontal green band indicates the comfort band of temperatures according to EN 15251 (Category II). The orange pattern indicates the total solar radiation available from the sky (composed of the direct and diffuse components of radiation), while the yellow patterns indicate solely the diffuse component. The colored lines below the graph are the operation bands (red, blue, gray, and light blue) that show when the occupants operate the different facade elements in percentage open. This graph reveals physical correlations such as the winter garden's temperature staying above the exterior one, the sky conditions that follow solar radiation levels, and the impact of closing the interior curtain at night, keeping indoor temperatures stable while the exterior one drops.

The Case Studies

(3) Operative temperatures during a typical day in free-running mode

Temperature naturally reached in the room

Temperatures
- comfort band EN 15251
- exterior
- winter garden
- living room
- bedroom

Solar radiation
- total radiation
- diffuse portion

Envelope operability
- 1. thermal curtain
- 2. sliding doors of heated space
- 3. solar curtain
- 4. sliding doors of winter garden
- element is closed
- --- element is open

(4) Winter air temperatures and heating load

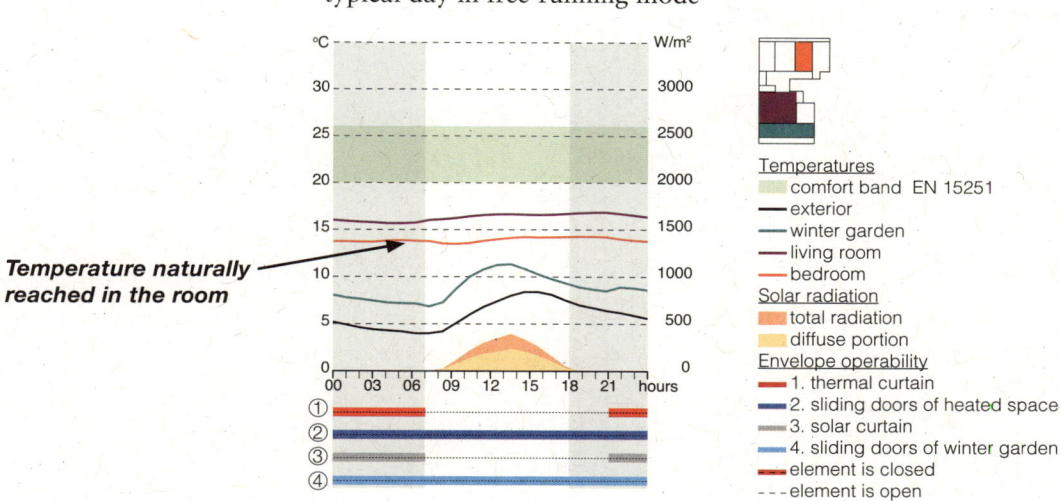

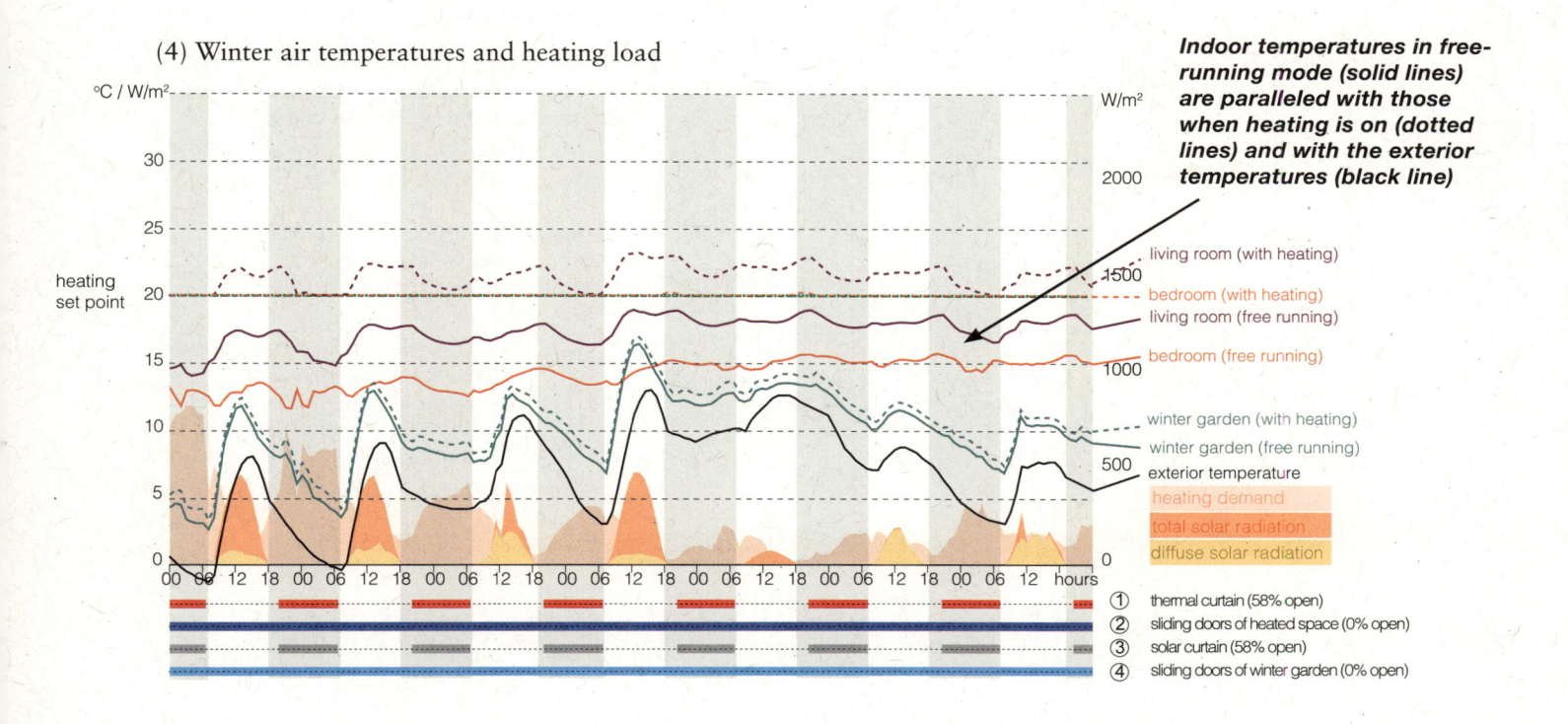

heating set point

Indoor temperatures in free-running mode (solid lines) are paralleled with those when heating is on (dotted lines) and with the exterior temperatures (black line)

- living room (with heating)
- bedroom (with heating)
- living room (free running)
- bedroom (free running)
- winter garden (with heating)
- winter garden (free running)
- exterior temperature
- heating demand
- total solar radiation
- diffuse solar radiation

① thermal curtain (58% open)
② sliding doors of heated space (0% open)
③ solar curtain (58% open)
④ sliding doors of winter garden (0% open)

(3) Operative temperatures during a typical day in free-running mode: This graph shows the same information as the typical week but averaged over a typical day of a month. All the climate parameters of a month are averaged hourly and input in the climate file, and the building is simulated under these conditions. The information displayed is therefore the average conditions of the month. As the diagram zooms in more, it is easier to see the relationship between the operability of the elements and the impact on the resulting temperature.

(4) Winter air temperatures and heating load: This chart shows air temperature as opposed to the rest, which show operative temperatures. This is because in thermal simulations, the heating is triggered based on air temperature, which better shows the correlation between temperatures and heating demand needed to compensate to reach 20°C. The following data is shown in parallel and over time: air temperatures (in °C) and total energy demand for heating (in W/m²) on the left vertical axis, aside from outdoor solar radiation, and the occupant's operation of the facade elements. The dashed and solid curves show calculated temperatures of the different spaces during a typical week and under different conditions, with and without heating. The red patterns indicate the heating demand when the heating system is on. This graph reveals physical correlations such as the drop in heating demand on sunny winter days as the winter garden captures heat, and the increase of the demand at nighttime.

60 The Case Studies

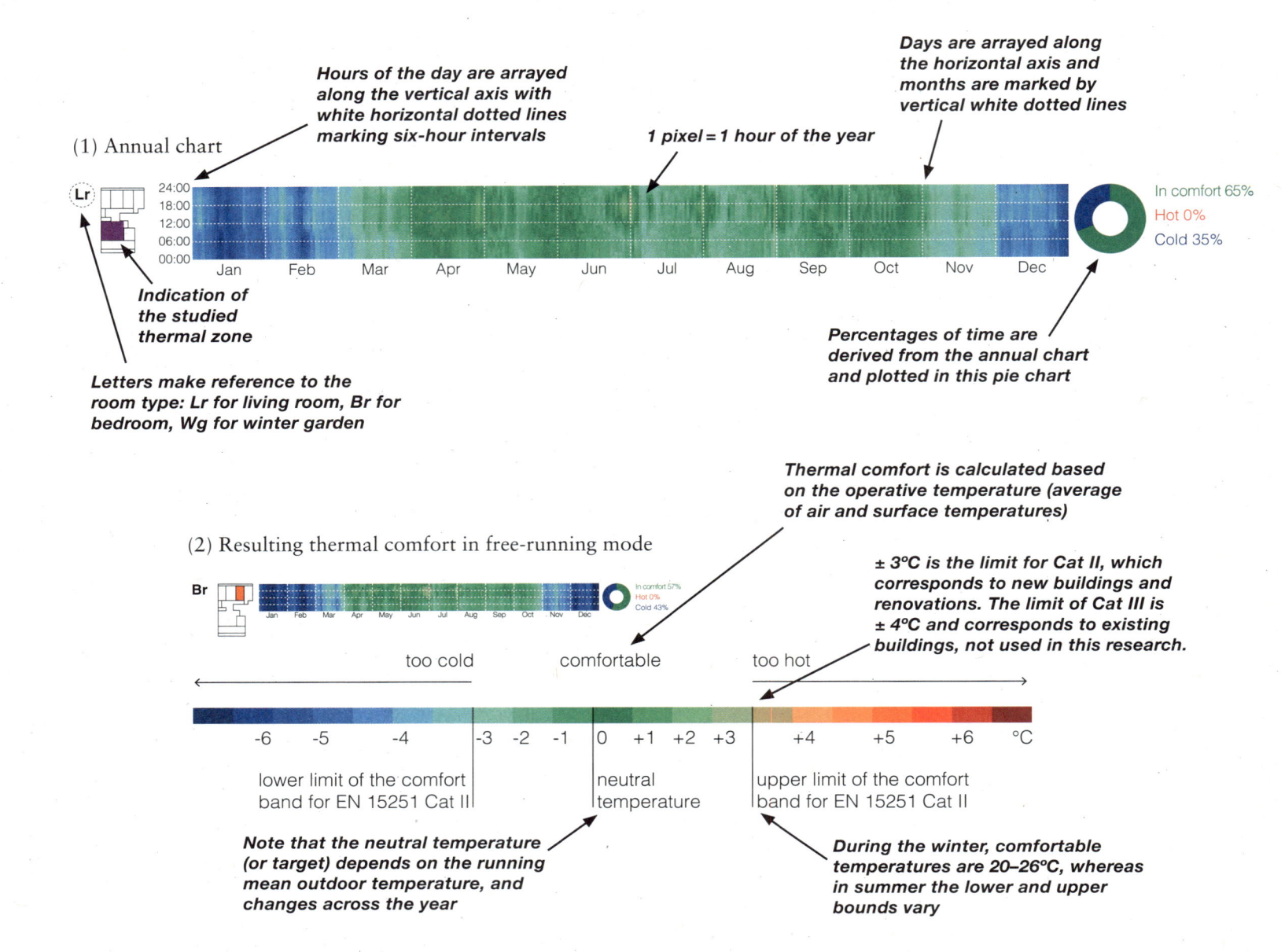

Color-Coded Temporal Charts

(1) Annual chart

Hours of the day are arrayed along the vertical axis with white horizontal dotted lines marking six-hour intervals

1 pixel = 1 hour of the year

Days are arrayed along the horizontal axis and months are marked by vertical white dotted lines

In comfort 65%
Hot 0%
Cold 35%

Indication of the studied thermal zone

Percentages of time are derived from the annual chart and plotted in this pie chart

Letters make reference to the room type: Lr for living room, Br for bedroom, Wg for winter garden

(2) Resulting thermal comfort in free-running mode

Thermal comfort is calculated based on the operative temperature (average of air and surface temperatures)

Br — In comfort 57% / Hot 0% / Cold 43%

± 3°C is the limit for Cat II, which corresponds to new buildings and renovations. The limit of Cat III is ± 4°C and corresponds to existing buildings, not used in this research.

too cold — comfortable — too hot

-6 -5 -4 -3 -2 -1 0 +1 +2 +3 +4 +5 +6 °C

lower limit of the comfort band for EN 15251 Cat II | neutral temperature | upper limit of the comfort band for EN 15251 Cat II

Note that the neutral temperature (or target) depends on the running mean outdoor temperature, and changes across the year

During the winter, comfortable temperatures are 20–26°C, whereas in summer the lower and upper bounds vary

(1) Annual chart: This color-coded temporal chart shows data calculated for every hour of the year. It is a table of colored pixels composed of 24 rows (hours) and 365 columns (days), marking the 8,760 hours of the year. Horizontal white dotted lines mark the six-hour time frame while the vertical ones mark the monthly. A pie chart on the side indicates the percentage of time during the year that each condition is met.

(2) Resulting thermal comfort in free-running mode: This color-coded temporal chart shows thermal comfort data calculated for a specific thermal zone according to EN 15251. It quantifies thermal satisfaction for each hour of the year and provides a visual insight into when conditions in the room studied are comfortable and when they are not, and how much the conditions deviate from comfort. Charts are always shown in free-running mode (without any heating or cooling). The temperature displayed is the operative temperature, which can be referred to as the felt temperature (calculated as the average of air temperature and of surrounding radiant temperature). Thermal comfort is evaluated based on the difference between the indoor operative temperature and the ideal comfort temperature determined by EN 15251 Category II (new buildings and renovations). Conditions are considered comfortable when the absolute difference is within ±3°C from the ideal comfort temperature (the center of the comfort band at 0°C). The bounds of the comfort band vary throughout the year and span from 20 to 26°C during the colder months, and rise as a function of outdoor temperature during the warmer months (the span is always of 6°C in the case of new buildings or renovations, according to EN 15251).

The Case Studies

(3) Outdoor temperatures

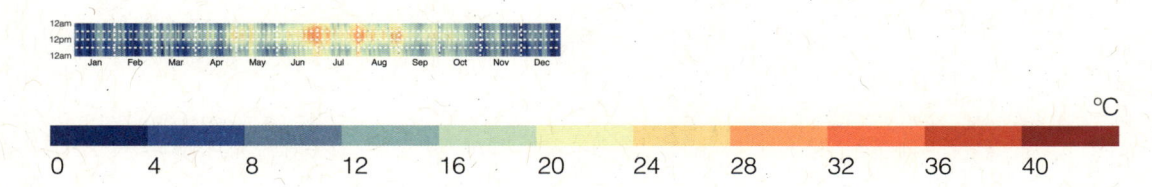

0 4 8 12 16 20 24 28 32 36 40 °C

(4) UTCI (Universal Thermal Climate Index)

Wg

← cold stress | comfortable | heat stress →
strong   moderate   slight   slight   strong   very strong   extreme

-13   0   9   26 28   32   38   46 °C

In an outdoor environment, comfortable temperatures are 9 to 26°C

UTCI is the resulting felt temperature outdoors, gathering air temperature, mean radiant temperature, wind speed, and humidity

(5) Hourly heating demand

All

33% time ON
1.6 kW peak

0   5   10   15   20   25   30   35   40   45   50   W/m²

peak demand targeted by Passive House

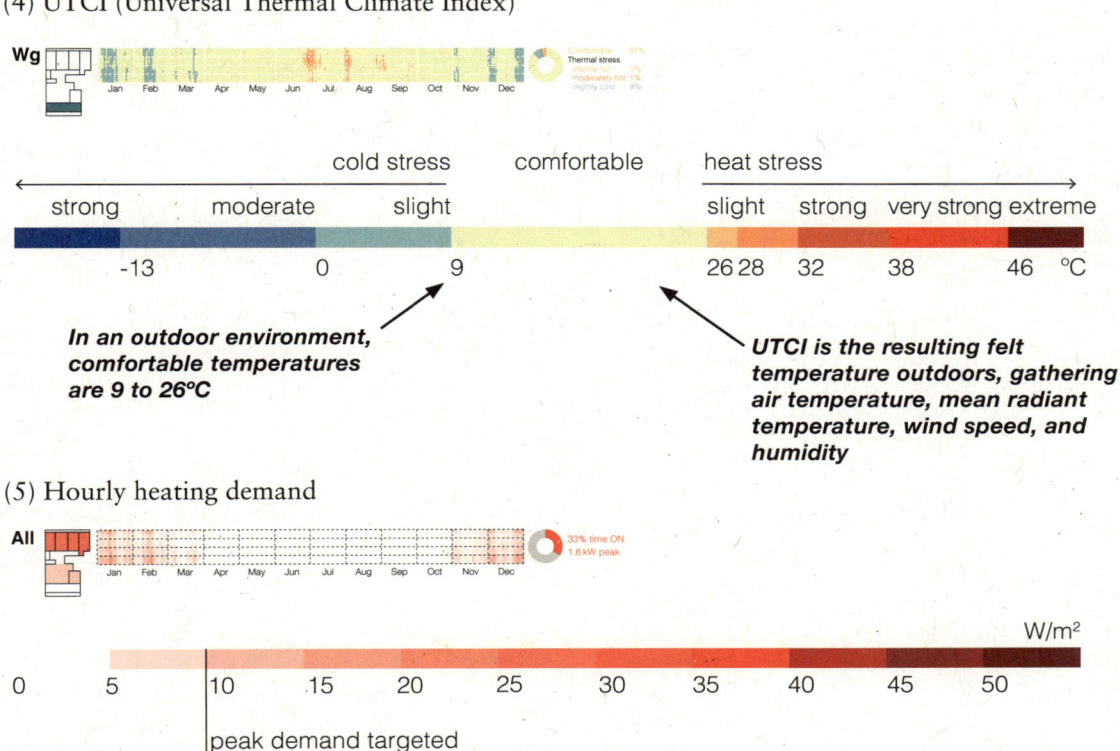

(3) Outdoor temperatures: This color-coded temporal chart shows outdoor temperatures as they appear in the climate file. The scale covers 0°C to 40°C, and blue represents cooler temperatures whereas red represents hotter temperatures.

(4) UTCI (Universal Thermal Climate Index): This color-coded temporal chart shows outdoor thermal comfort data calculated in the winter garden according to the UTCI metric. It quantifies thermal stress levels for each hour of the year by colored category and provides a visual insight of when conditions are thermally comfortable for an outdoor environment in the winter garden. Yellow is used to represent comfort (no thermal stress), red for stress by heat, blue for stress by cold, and darker yellow and lighter blue for slight stress.

(5) Hourly heating demand: This color-coded temporal chart shows heating-demand data calculated for all studied thermal zones considering a heating set point of 20°C. It quantifies heating demand of the residential unit for each hour of the year and provides a visual insight of when energy is needed to maintain indoor temperatures at the temperature set point. Heating demand is shown hourly by value scale, progressing from white to dark red: the redder, the higher the energy demand.

62   The Case Studies

Horizontal Bar Charts

(1) Heating demand variation

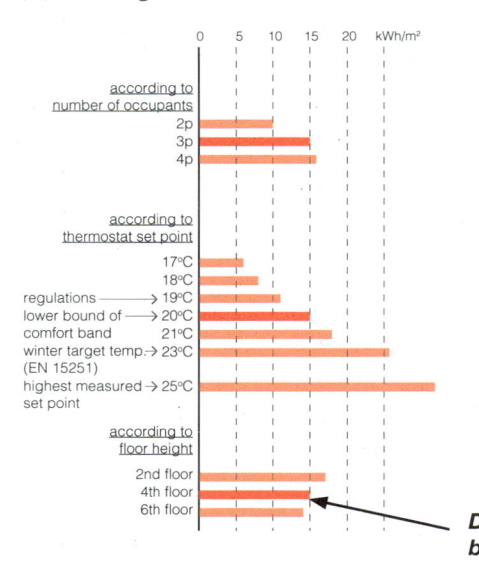

0   5   10   15   20   kWh/m²

according to number of occupants
- 2p
- 3p
- 4p

according to thermostat set point
- 17°C
- 18°C
- regulations → 19°C
- lower bound of → 20°C
- comfort band   21°C
- winter target temp.→ 23°C (EN 15251)
- highest measured → 25°C set point

according to floor height
- 2nd floor
- 4th floor
- 6th floor

Darker bars indicate calculation bases in the case studies

(2) Space exceeding 50% of time with DA [300] (EN 17037)

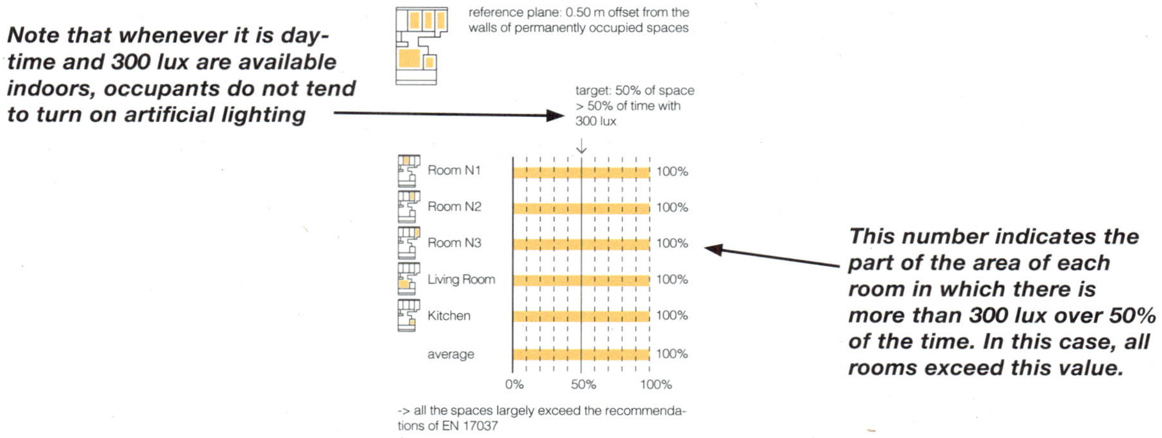

reference plane: 0.50 m offset from the walls of permanently occupied spaces

Note that whenever it is daytime and 300 lux are available indoors, occupants do not tend to turn on artificial lighting

target: 50% of space > 50% of time with 300 lux

- Room N1 — 100%
- Room N2 — 100%
- Room N3 — 100%
- Living Room — 100%
- Kitchen — 100%
- average — 100%

0%   50%   100%

→ all the spaces largely exceed the recommendations of EN 17037

This number indicates the part of the area of each room in which there is more than 300 lux over 50% of the time. In this case, all rooms exceed this value.

(3) Overheating evaluation

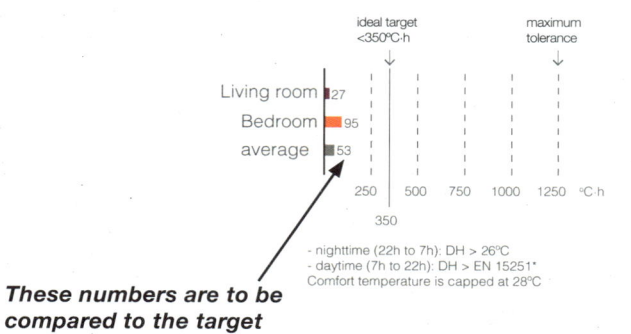

ideal target <350°C·h   maximum tolerance

- Living room — 27
- Bedroom — 95
- average — 53

250   500   750   1000   1250   °C·h
350

- nighttime (22h to 7h): DH > 26°C
- daytime (7h to 22h): DH > EN 15251*
Comfort temperature is capped at 28°C

These numbers are to be compared to the target

---

(1) Heating demand variation: This horizontal bar chart shows how the total heating demand per year (in kWh/m²·year) of the entire residential unit varies according to different parameters: the number of occupants (in number of people), the thermostat set point (in °C), and the floor height (per floor number). For each parameter tested, the bars colored in dark red indicate the calculation bases in the case studies. For example, whenever the number of occupants varies, the thermostat set point is kept at 20°C and the floor height to the fourth floor.

(2) Space exceeding 50% of time with DA [300] (EN 17037): This horizontal bar chart shows the space (in % of the area) within each permanently occupied room that meets the criteria for Daylight Autonomy. The graph displays the key information considered to calculate compliance with EN 17037. A room is considered daylit if it meets the target of receiving 300 lux across half of its space half of the time. The small plan shows the test surfaces considered for all permanently occupied spaces, which are placed at 0.80 m above the floor and 0.50 m offset from the walls. the apartment's compliance with the norm is indicated below the chart.

(3) Overheating evaluation: This horizontal bar chart shows the duration and intensity of periods of discomfort (in degree hours °C·h) caused by overheating in the studied rooms. According to RE 2020 (French regulations at the time of the studies), a room is deemed uncomfortable when its interior temperature exceeds the upper threshold of the comfort band EN 15251, capped at 28°C during the day and 26°C during the night. From these thresholds, each hour of temperature overrun is quantified, then accumulated to define the level of discomfort in the room. If, for example, a temperature of 28°C is calculated inside the dwelling at night for one hour, the sum of the differences in temperature with the reference temperature is multiplied by the number of hours of excess: $2°C·h = (28°C − 26°C) · 1h$.

The Case Studies

Scatter Plot Charts

(1) Winter garden operative temperatures as a function of outdoors

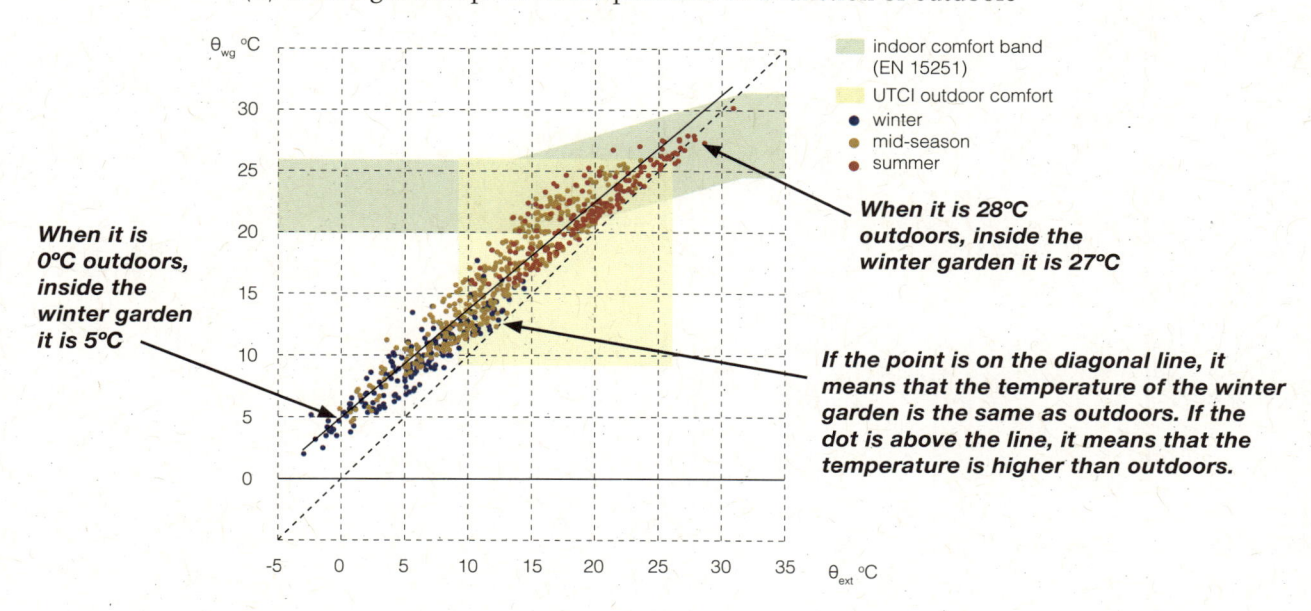

When it is 0°C outdoors, inside the winter garden it is 5°C

When it is 28°C outdoors, inside the winter garden it is 27°C

If the point is on the diagonal line, it means that the temperature of the winter garden is the same as outdoors. If the dot is above the line, it means that the temperature is higher than outdoors.

Legend:
- indoor comfort band (EN 15251)
- UTCI outdoor comfort
- winter
- mid-season
- summer

(2) Operative temperatures indoors as a function of outdoors

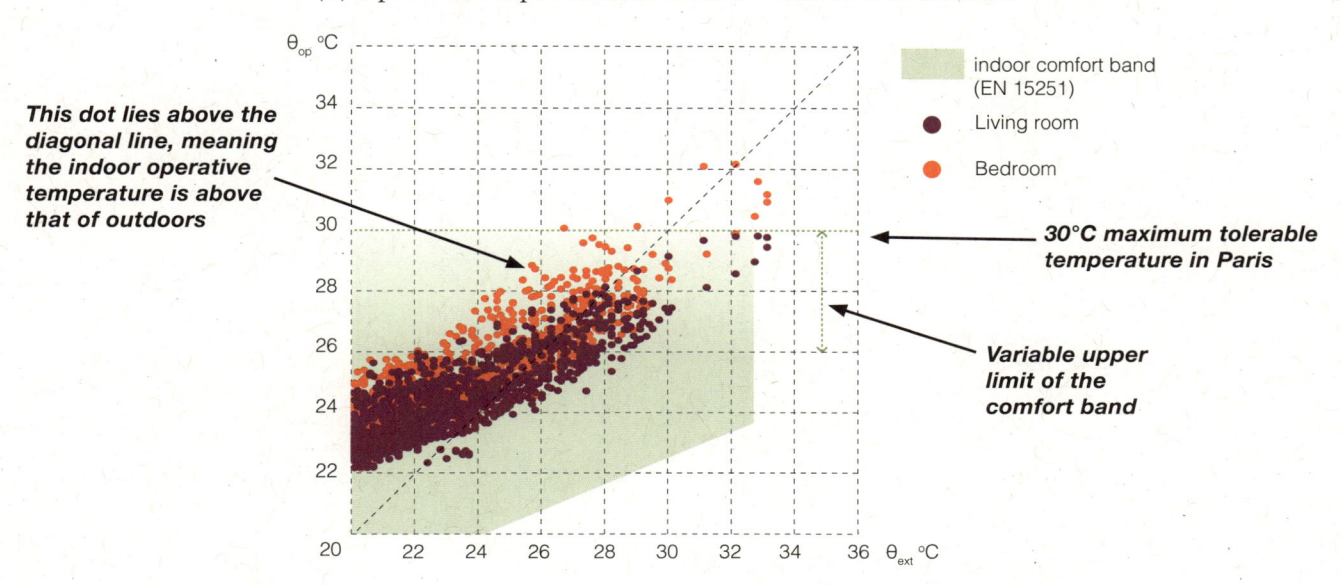

This dot lies above the diagonal line, meaning the indoor operative temperature is above that of outdoors

30°C maximum tolerable temperature in Paris

Variable upper limit of the comfort band

Legend:
- indoor comfort band (EN 15251)
- Living room
- Bedroom

---

(1) Winter garden operative temperatures as a function of outdoors: This scatter plot compares the winter gardens' temperatures with the exterior temperatures; it plots the daily averages of minimum and maximum operative temperatures calculated inside the winter gardens for the whole year (total of 730 temperatures). Each dot marks a calculated average temperature and is colored according to the season it represents: blue for winter, yellow for mid-season, orange for summer. The green pattern outlines the simplified comfort band for indoor conditions (as it does not account for the weighted average of the previous weeks). The dashed diagonal line indicates where the winter garden's temperature would equal the exterior one.

(2) Operative temperatures indoors as a function of outdoors: This scatter plot compares the bedroom and living room's operative temperatures with the exterior temperatures for every hour above 20°C. Each dot marks a calculated hourly operative temperature and is colored according to the room it represents: orange for bedroom and purple for living room. The green pattern outlines the adaptive comfort band for indoor conditions according to EN 15251. The dashed diagonal line indicates where the indoors operative temperatures would equal the exterior one. The further away from the diagonal, the greater the temperature difference between outdoors and indoors.

64 The Case Studies

Staggered Column, Custom Line, and Box Charts

(1) Solar heat gains and losses of the winter garden

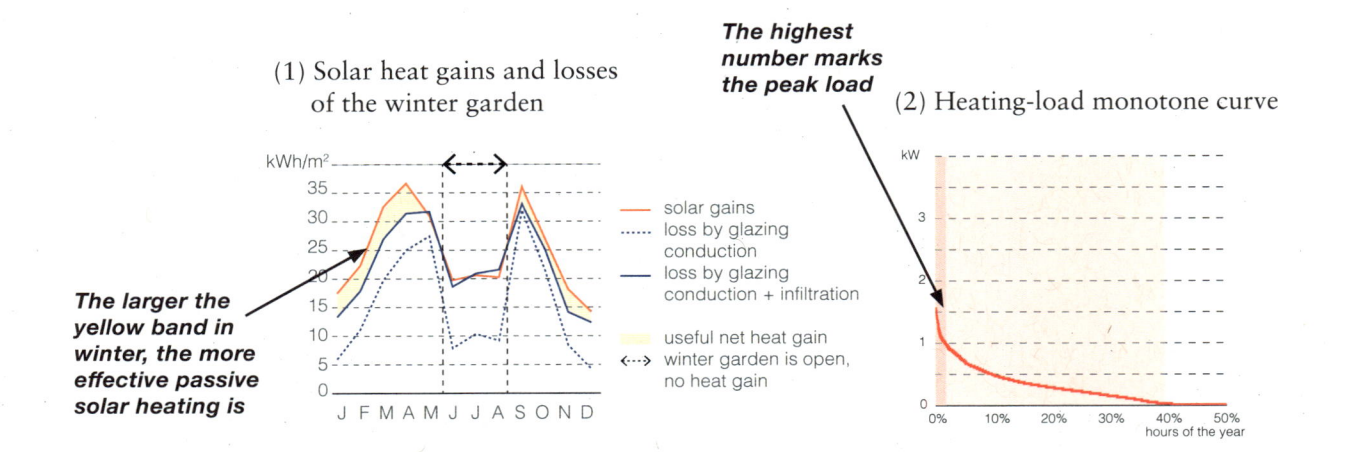

kWh/m²
- solar gains
- loss by glazing conduction
- loss by glazing conduction + infiltration
- useful net heat gain
- ⟵⋯⟶ winter garden is open, no heat gain

J F M A M J J A S O N D

The larger the yellow band in winter, the more effective passive solar heating is

(2) Heating-load monotone curve

kW — hours of the year (0% – 50%)

The highest number marks the peak load

(3) Thermodynamic balance

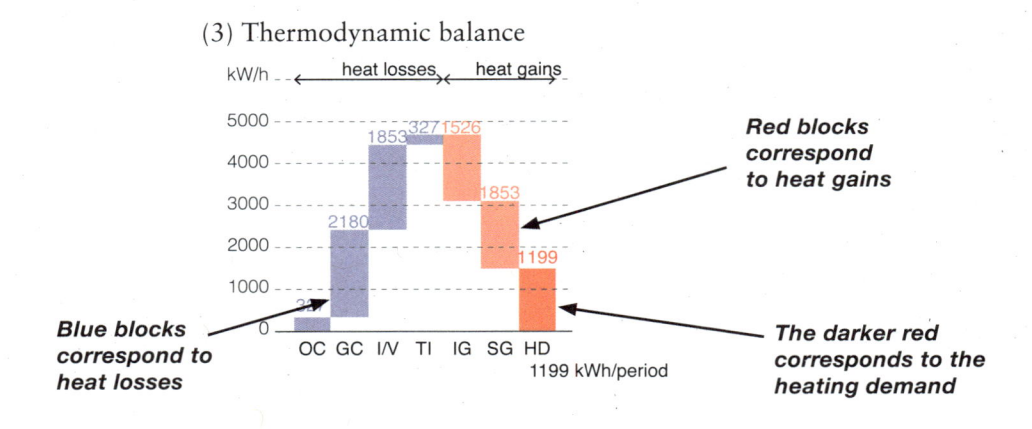

kW/h — heat losses ⟵ ⟶ heat gains

Values: 2180, 1853, 327, 1526, 1853, 1199

OC GC I/V TI IG SG HD
1199 kWh/period

Blue blocks correspond to heat losses

Red blocks correspond to heat gains

The darker red corresponds to the heating demand

(4) Winter garden air temperatures compared to outdoors

°C

- outdoor comfort band (UTCI)
- outdoors
- winter garden (b coefficient = 0.60)
- seasonal averages — 15.5°C
- annual averages — 12.5°C
- averages low, high
- extreme low, high

*in summer, winter garden sliding doors are open

winter   spring   summer*   autumn

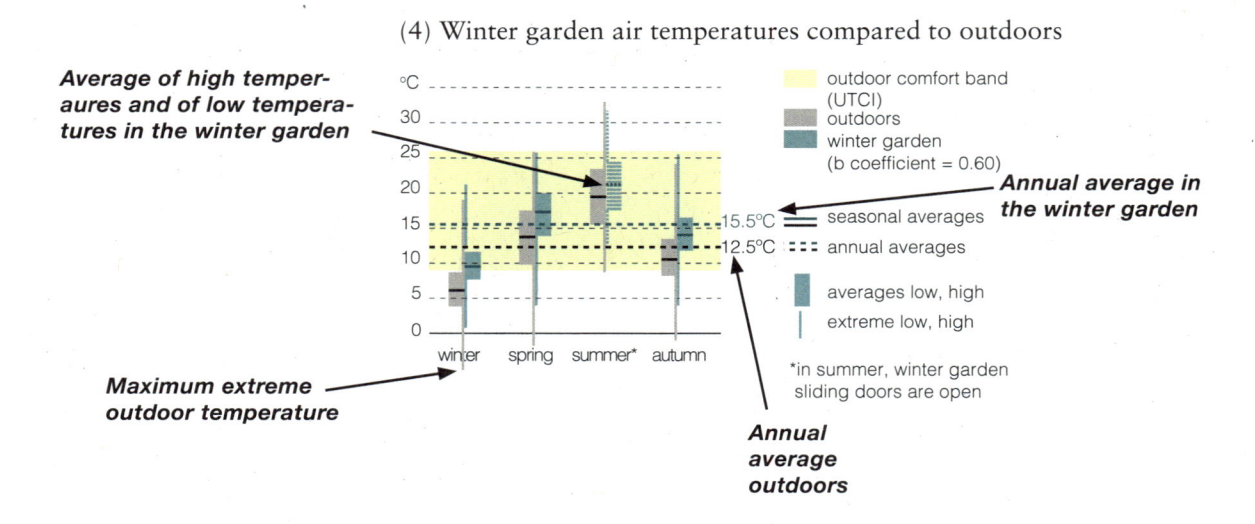

Average of high temperatures and of low temperatures in the winter garden

Annual average in the winter garden

Maximum extreme outdoor temperature

Annual average outdoors

---

(1) Solar heat gains and losses of the winter garden: This chart shows in parallel both the monthly solar heat gains and total heat loss in the winter garden to indicate whether their sum results in an overall heat loss or gain.

(2) Heating-load monotone curve: This chart sorts in decreasing order the hourly total heating demand (in kW). It shows how long peak demands occur. Such information often serves in the design of heating, ventilation, and air conditioning (HVAC) systems and allows to define the size of the equipment based on its utility.

(3) Thermodynamic balance: This chart arrays the physical factors that affect the thermodynamic balance of the spaces during the heating season from November to March and covers the thermodynamic exchanges of the entire house, including the winter garden. Colored blocks show their respective impact on the overall energy transfer (in kWh/period). Read from left to right, heat losses (in blue) cause energy demand while heat gains (in red) offset it. The actual heating demand is represented in darker red.

(4) Winter garden air temperatures compared to outdoors: This box plot shows seasonal temperature variations inside the winter garden next to that of outdoors. The thin bars indicate the extreme minimum and maximum temperatures reached per season. The boxes show the range of maximum and minimum average temperatures for each season, while the middle line shows the seasonal average. This plot conveys an effective insight of the temperature difference the winter garden produces with outdoors. The b coefficient is used in regulations to account for the winter garden as the "new outdoors" of the heated envelope. It measures the ratio between the delta indoors–outdoors and the delta indoors–winter garden.

Case Study 1: Cité Manifeste, Mulhouse, France

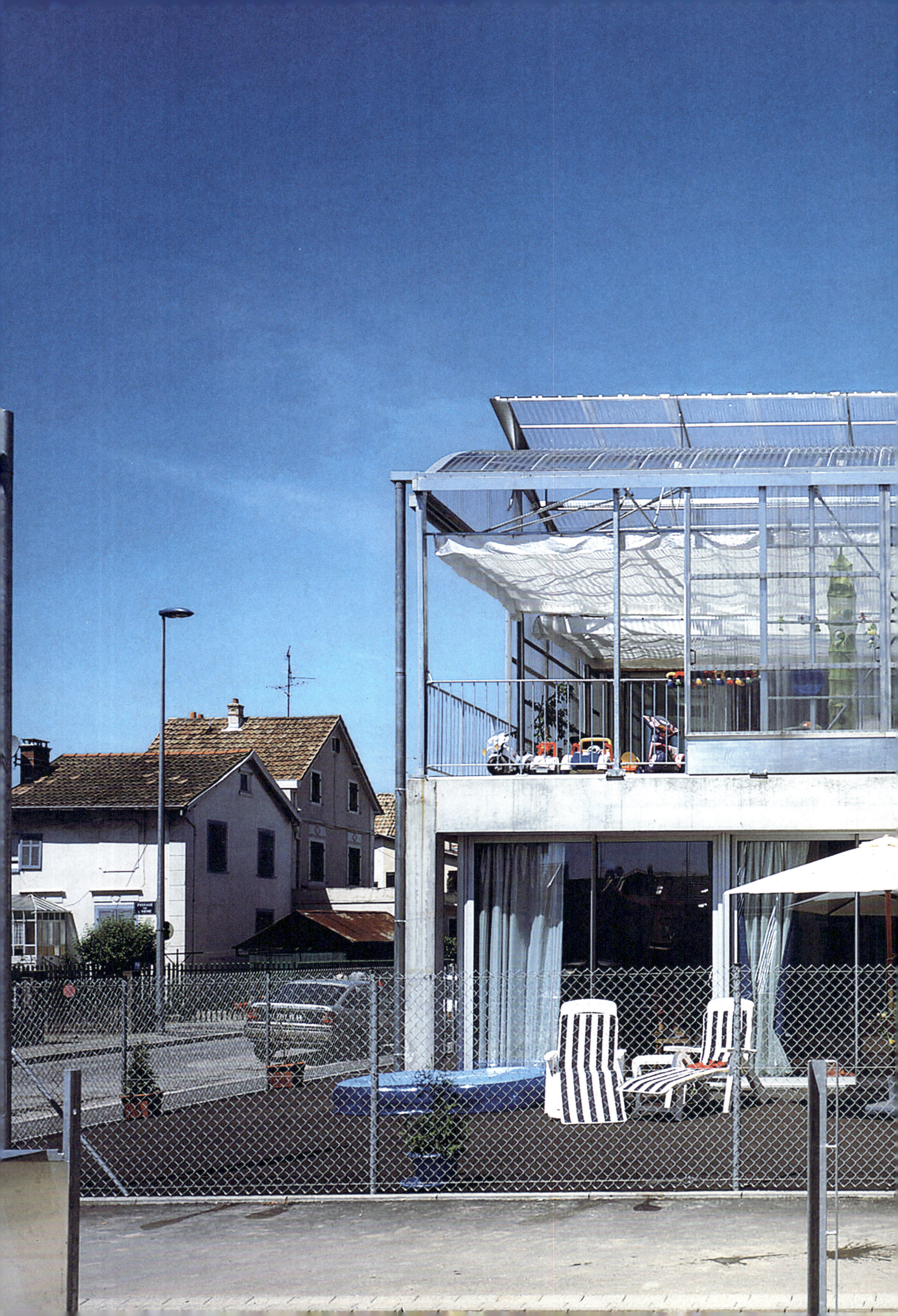

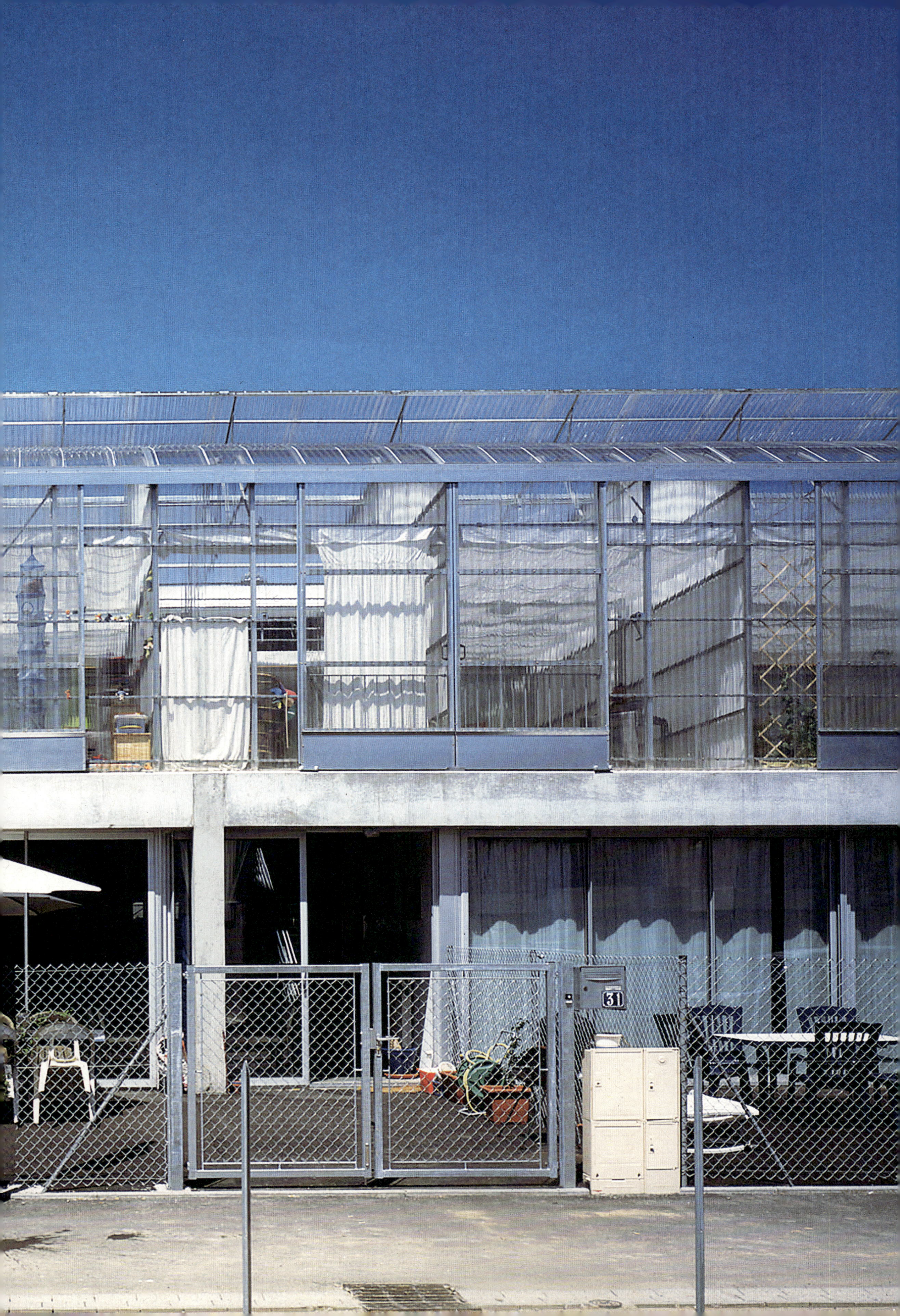
31

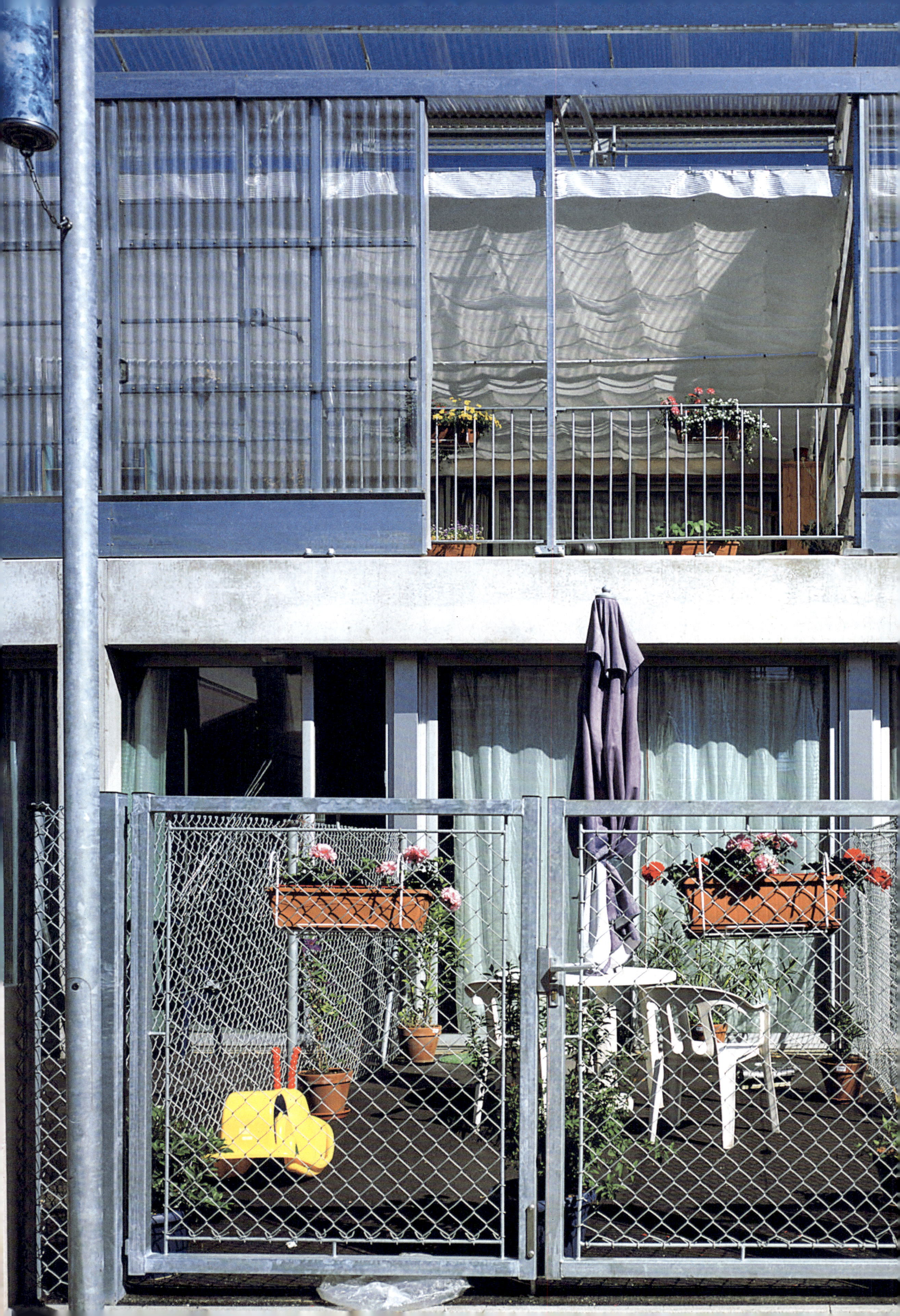

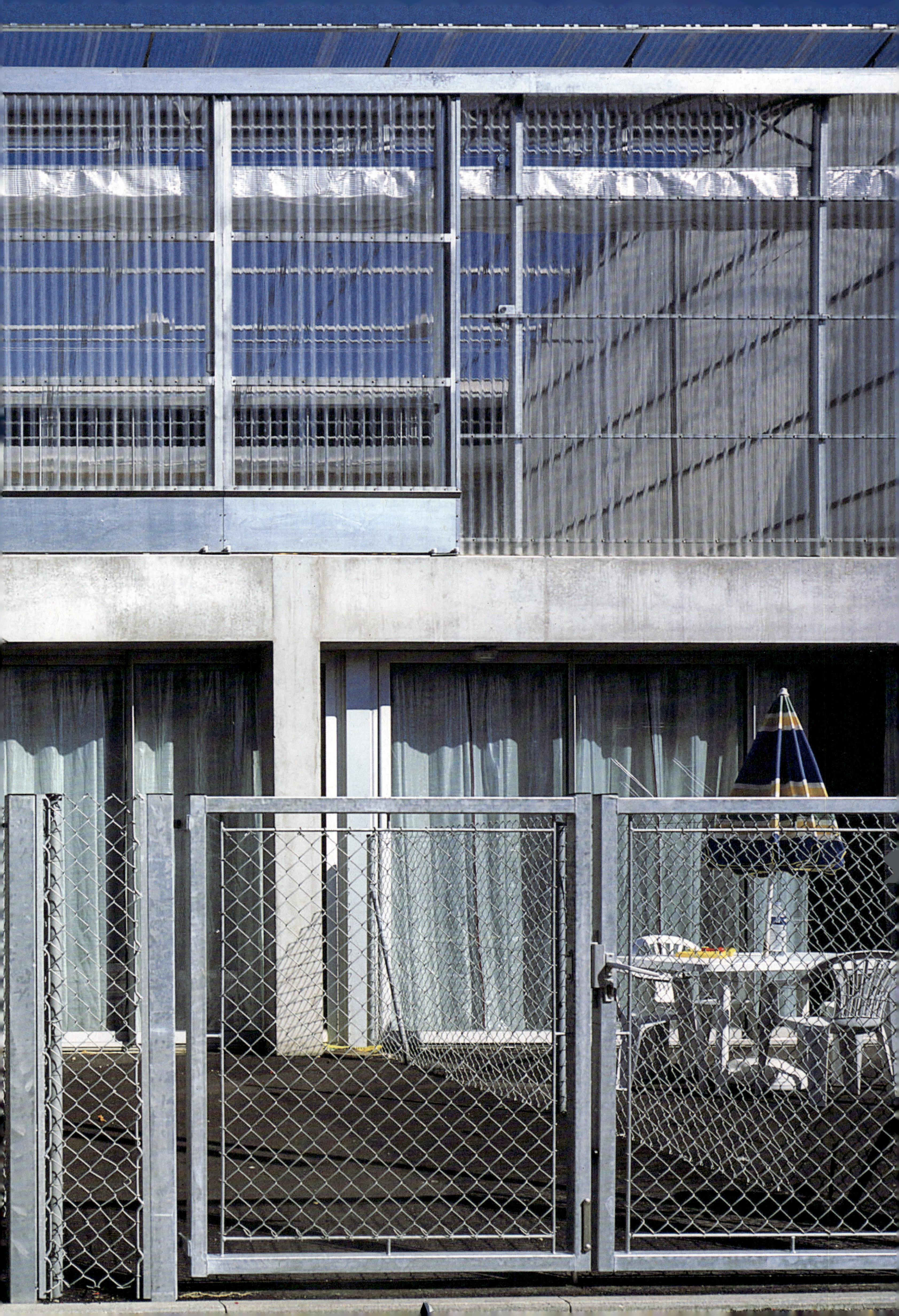

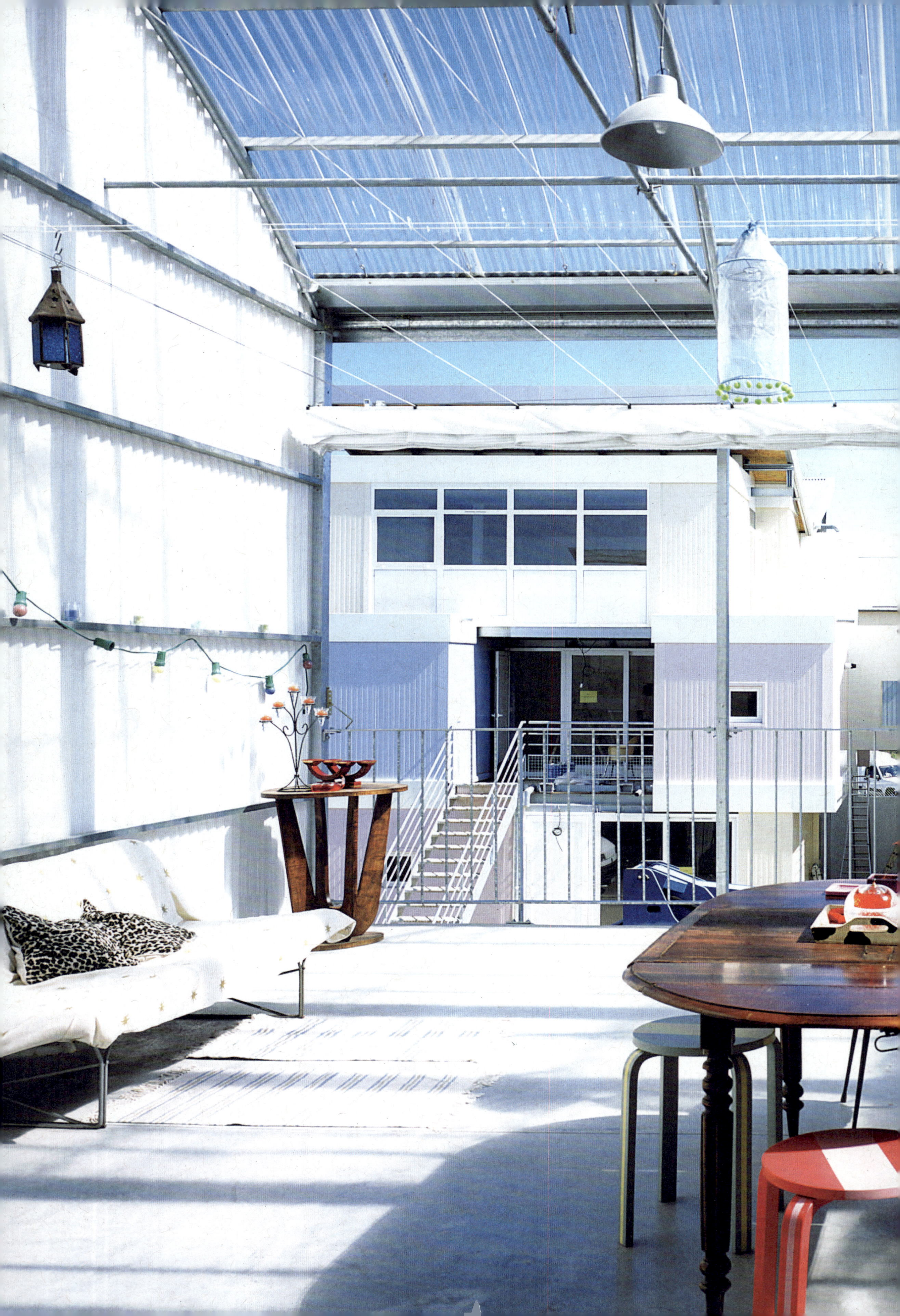

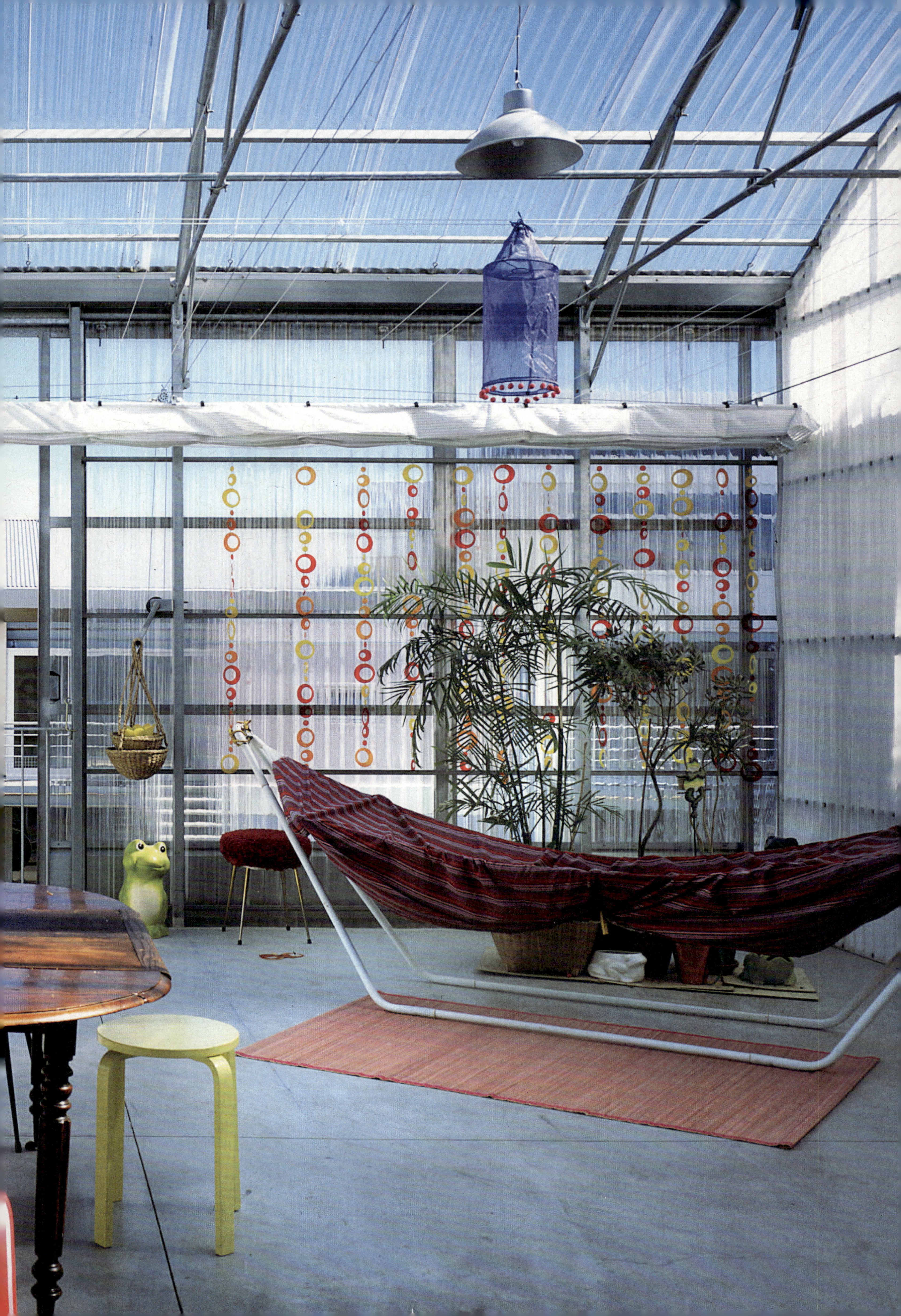

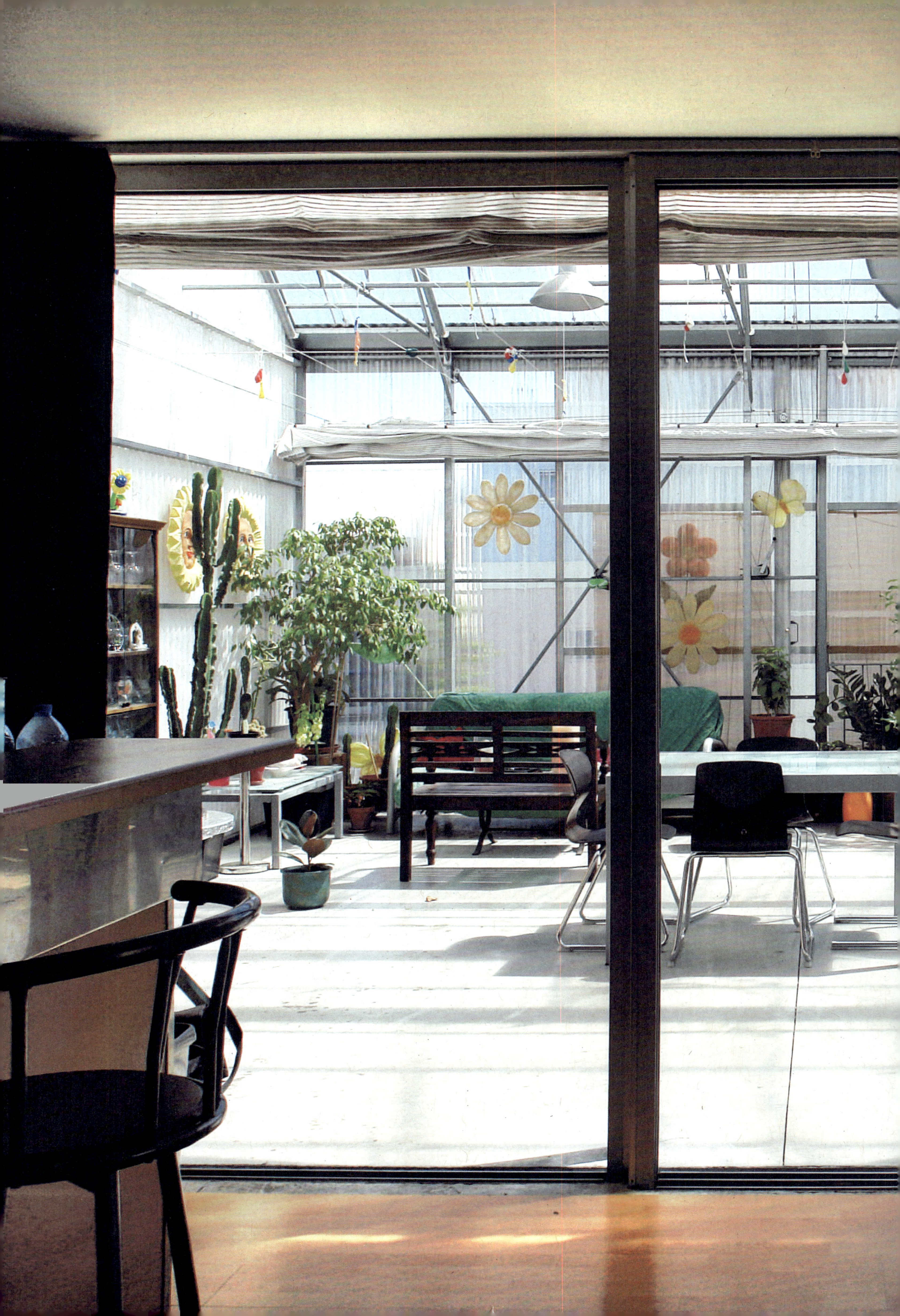

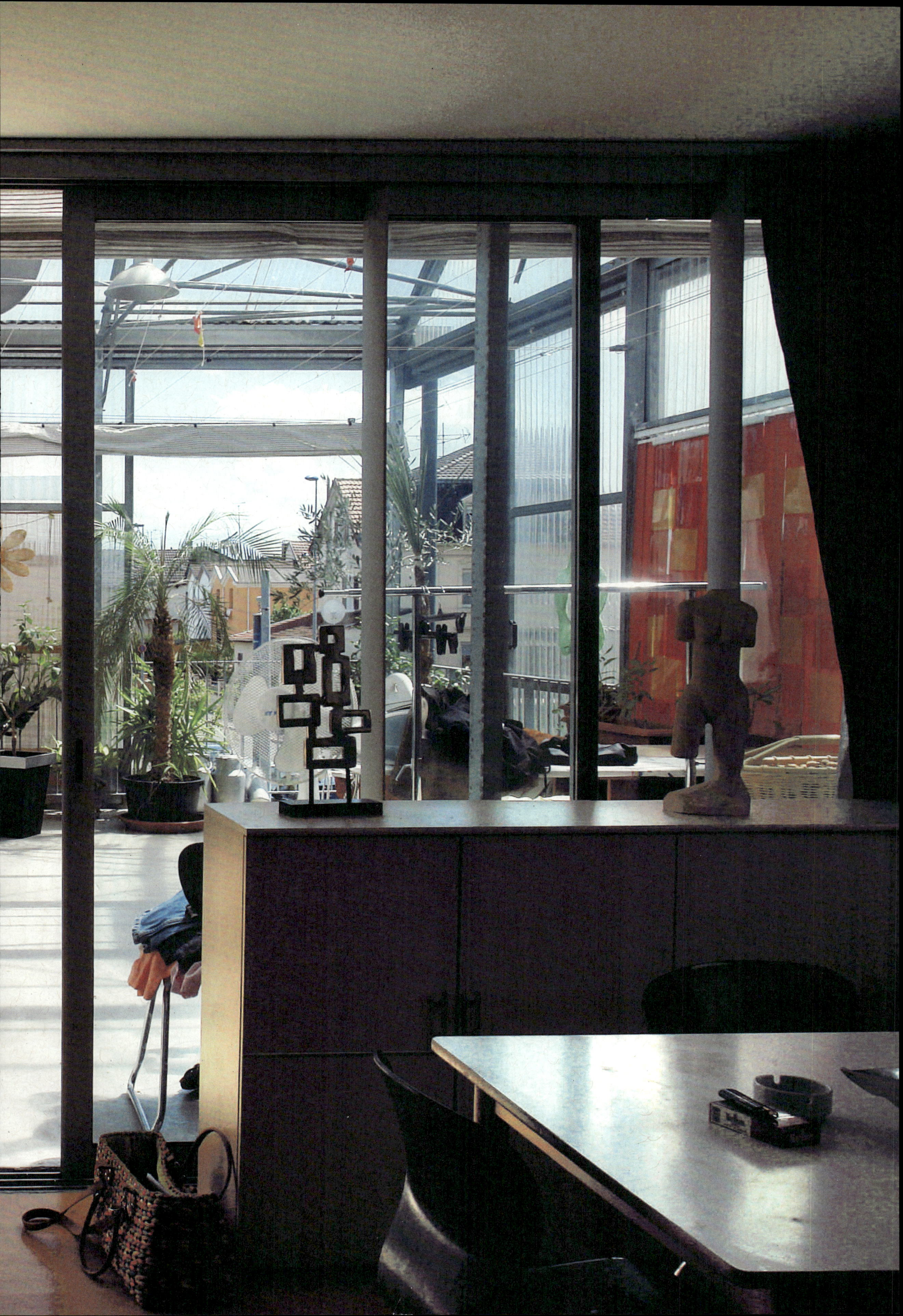

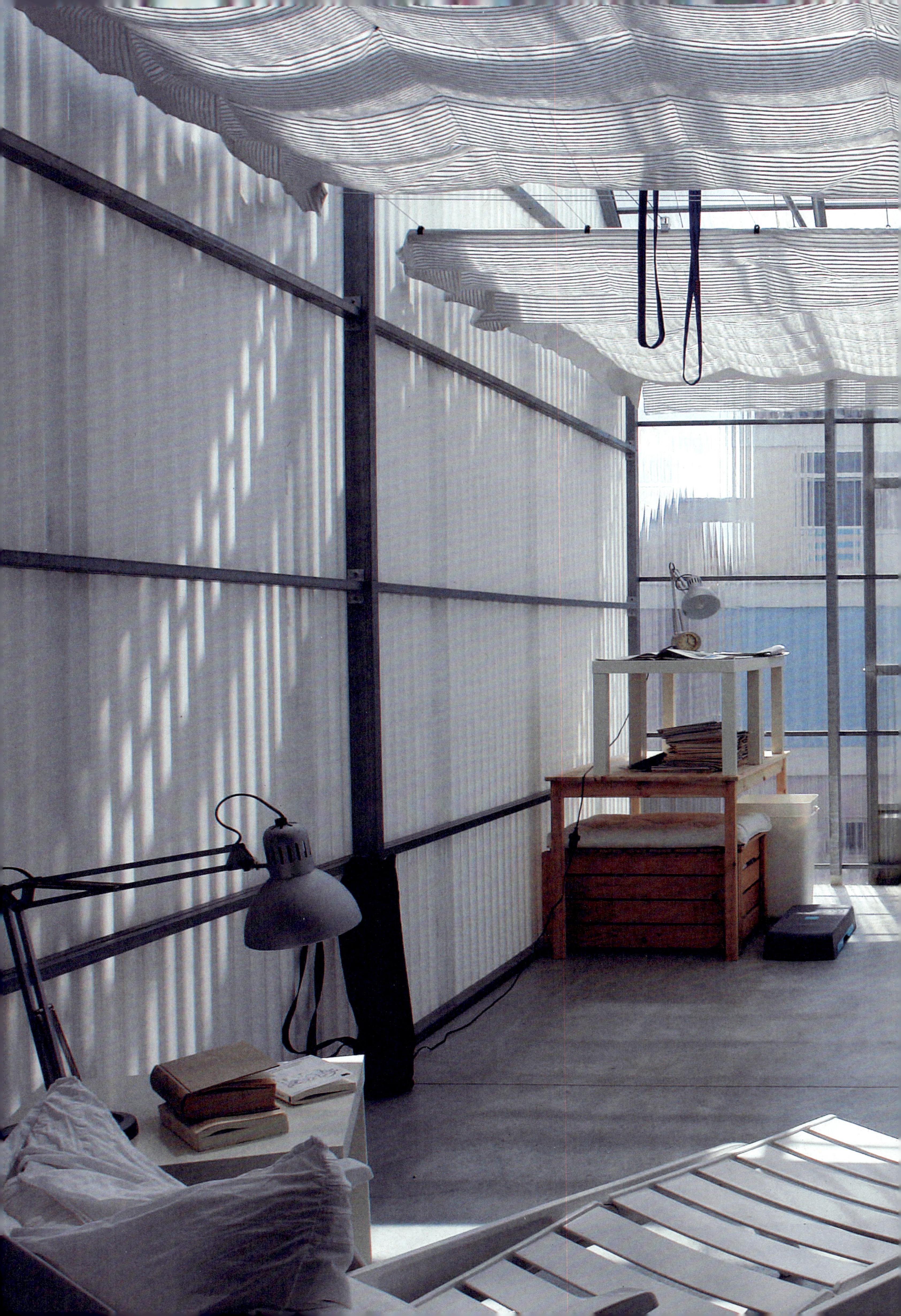

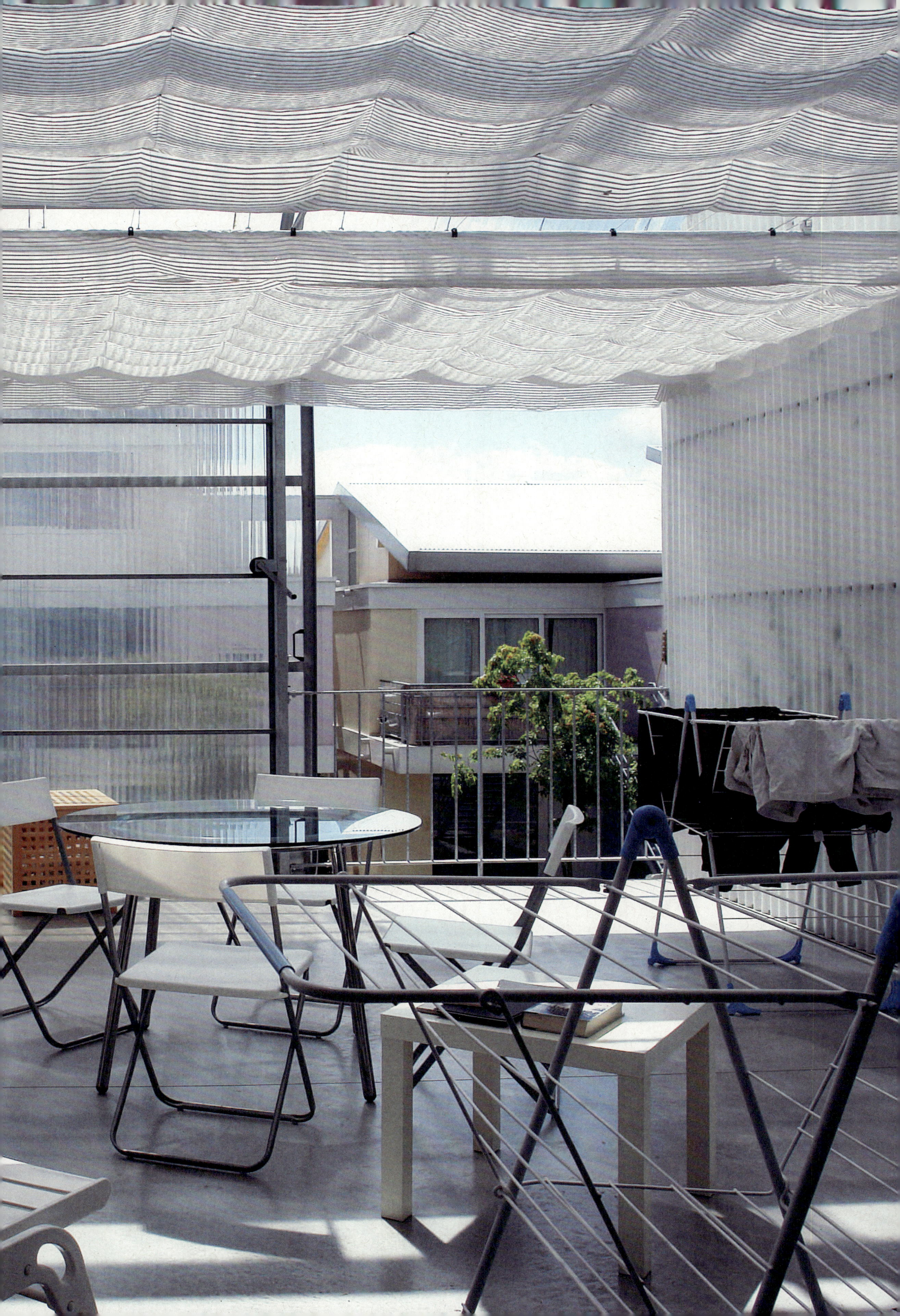

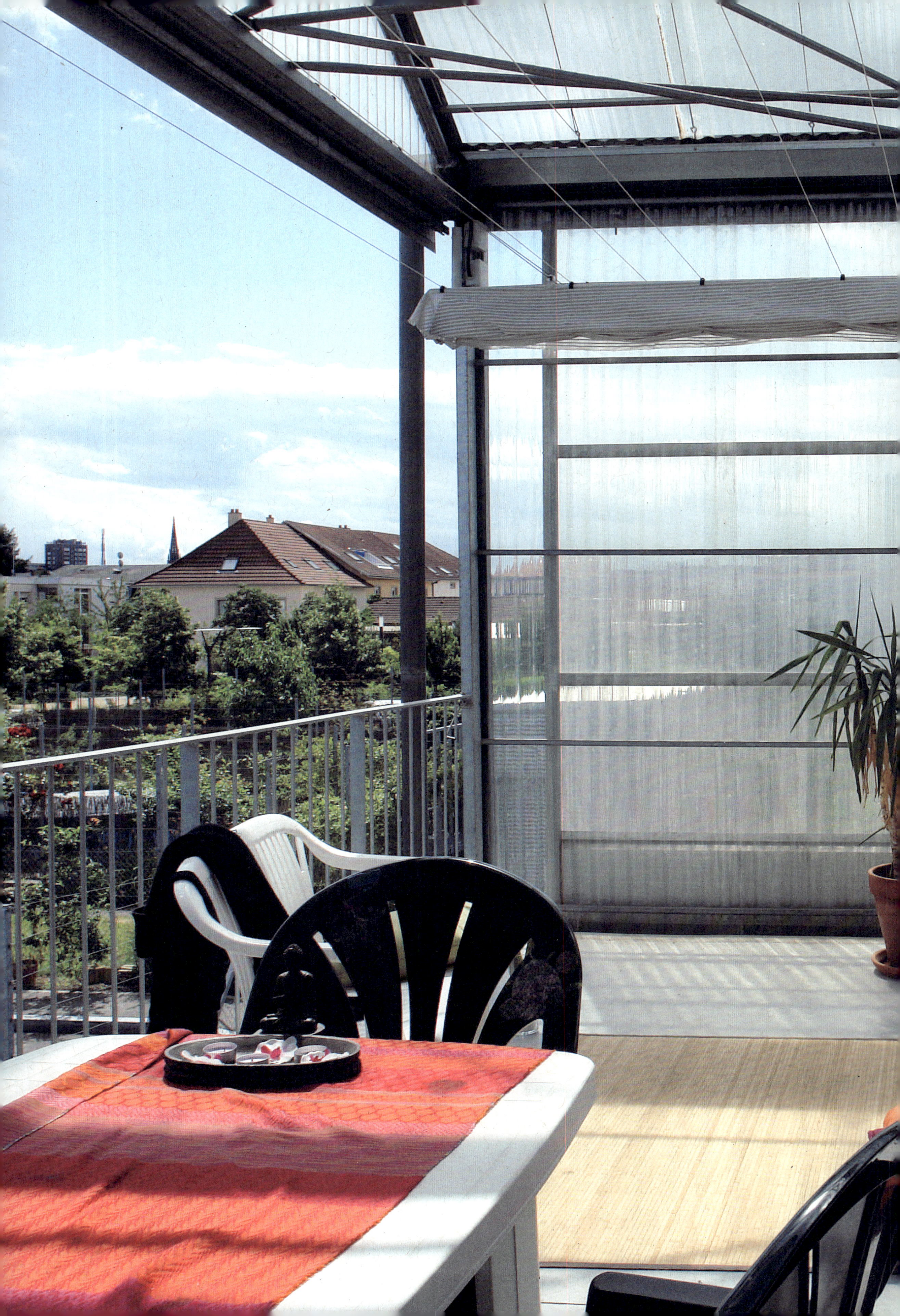

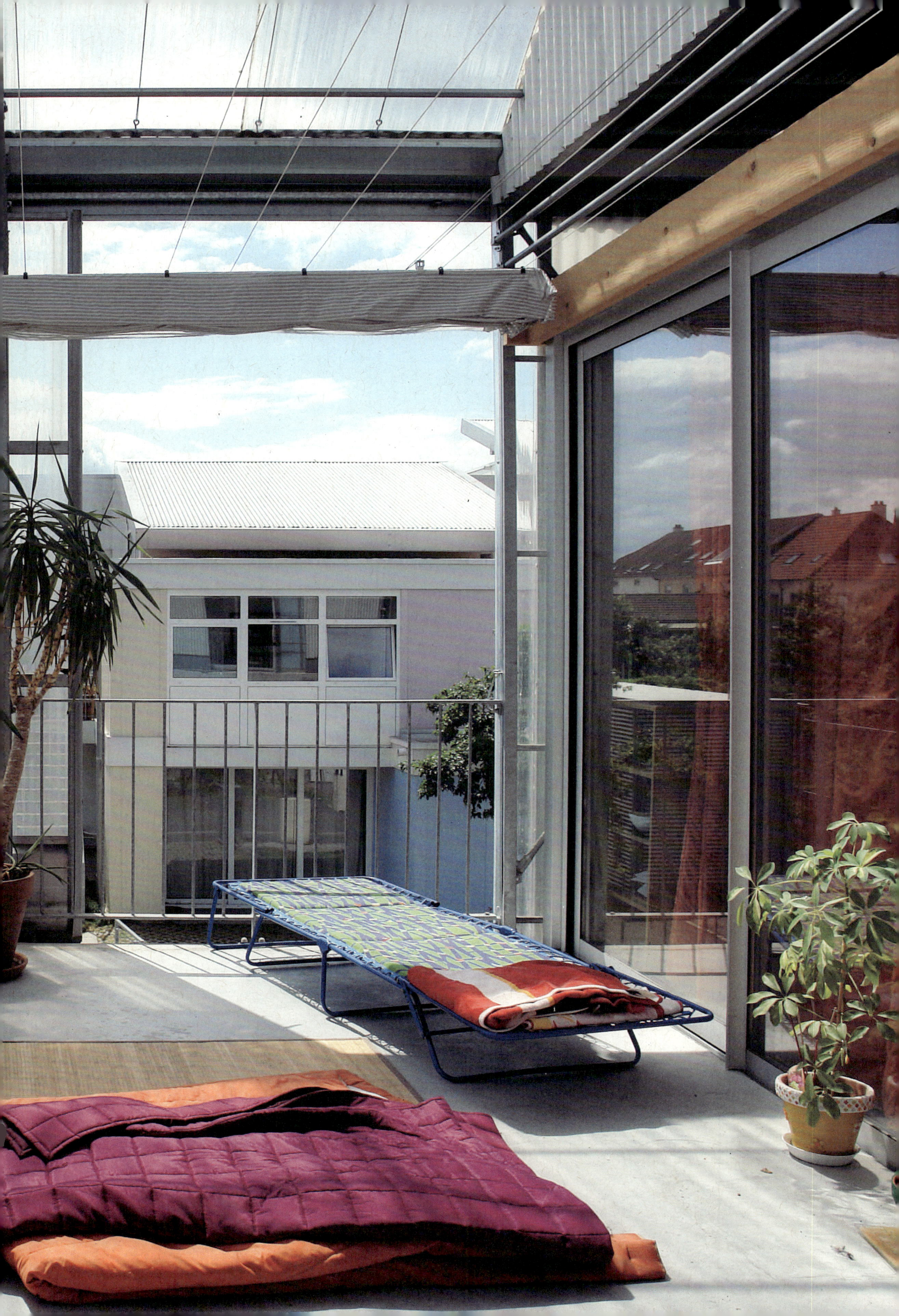

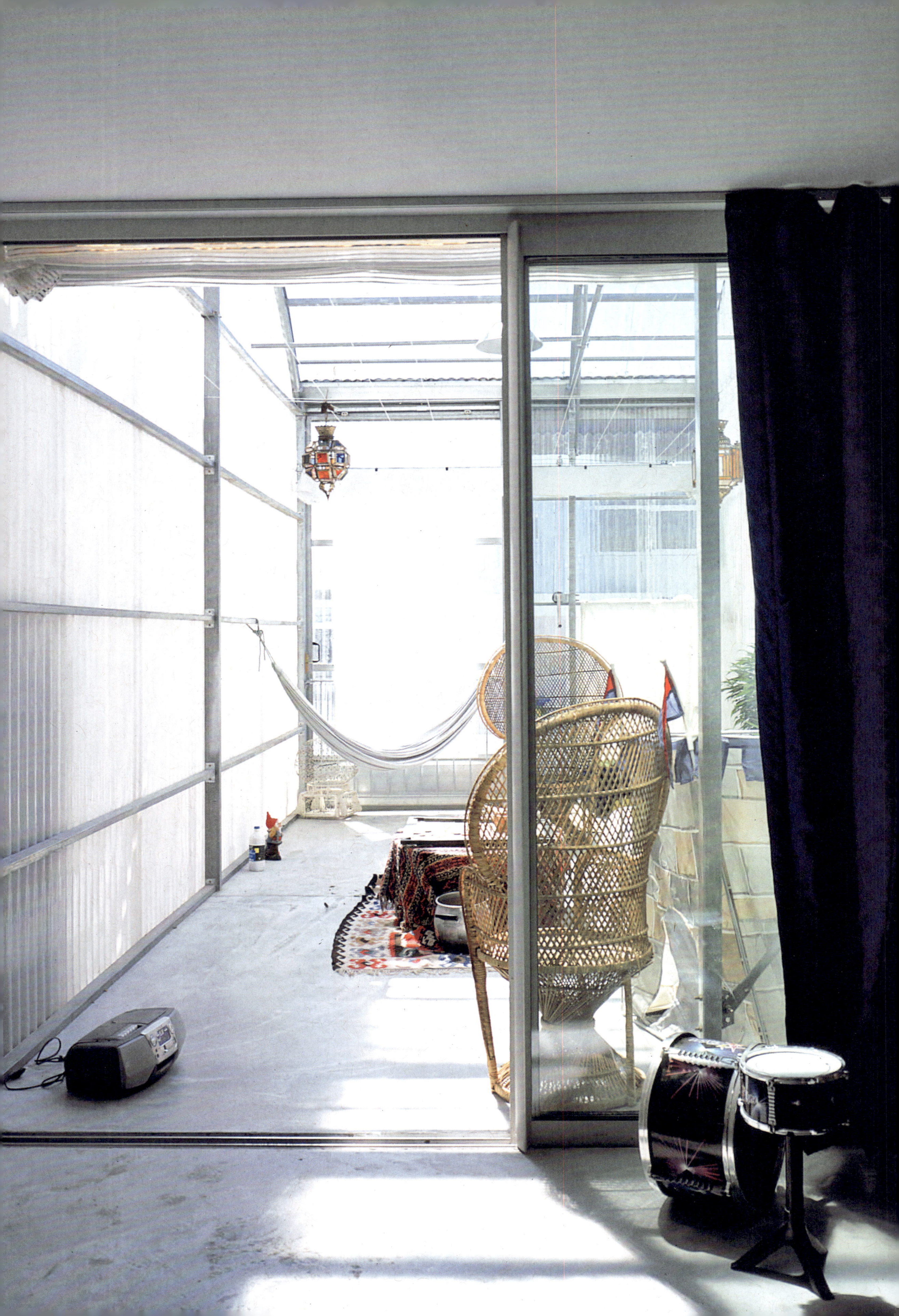

Case Study 1
Cité Manifeste

Mulhouse
France
2005

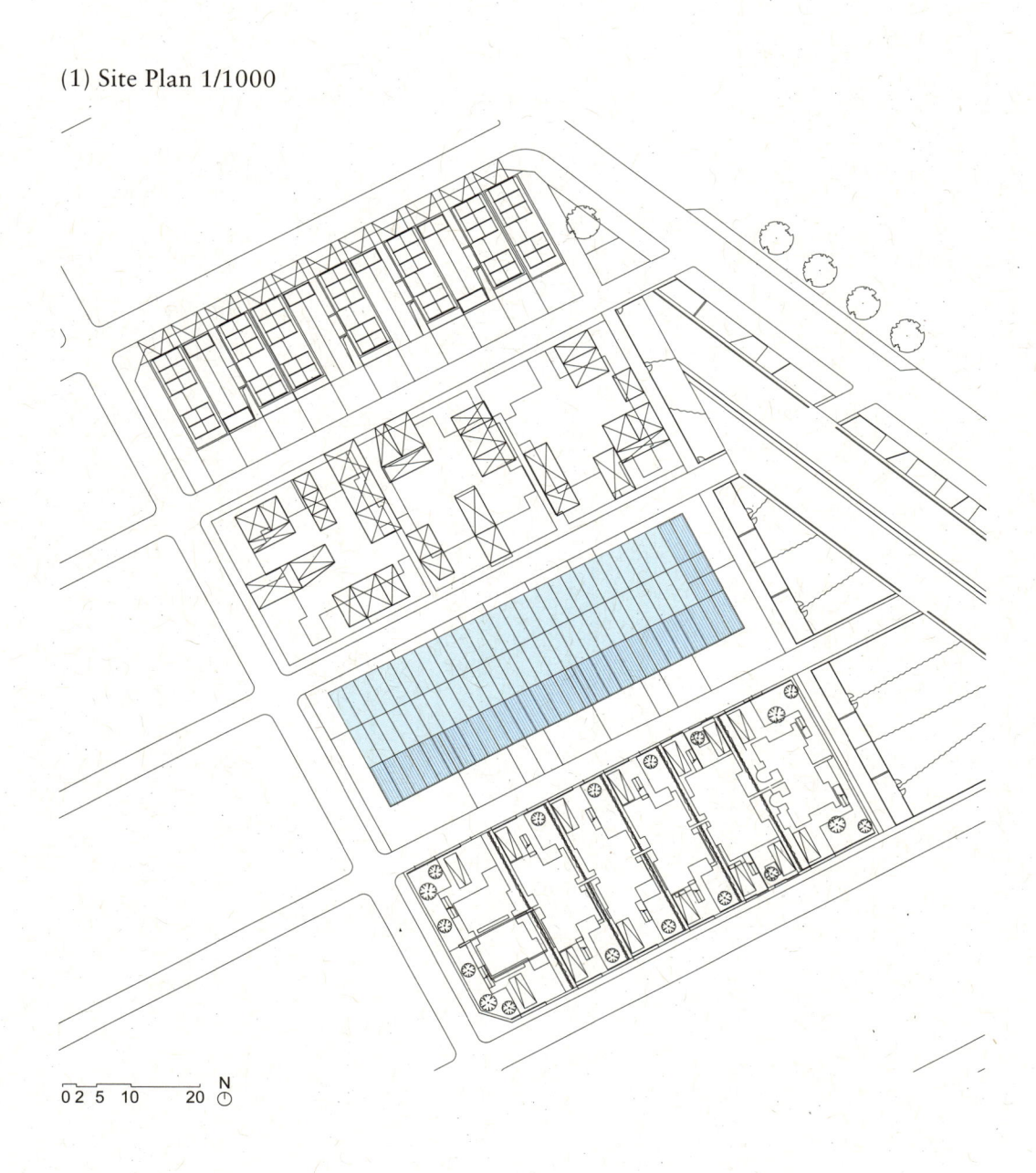

(1) Site Plan 1/1000

This fourteen-home project, a continuation of the Cité Ouvrière in Mulhouse, belongs to a social housing development of 61 rental units, created by five teams of architects. The rigid framework of minimum floor area and comfort standards for social housing often leads to a confined organization of rooms, perpetuating a classic and traditional housing model. Our objective was to produce quality housing that is, at equal cost, much larger than the dwellings that follow the norms. Following the Latapie house (1993) and the Coutras house (2000), we sought to achieve similar qualities but with a greater number of units. Our experience building those two—the observation of high-performance agricultural, industrial, and commercial buildings, the practice of lofts—confirmed that it is possible to build housing that is larger, more open, freer, lighter, more comfortable, less expensive.

Case Study 1

Project and Environmental Conditions
Building

(1) Plan 1/400

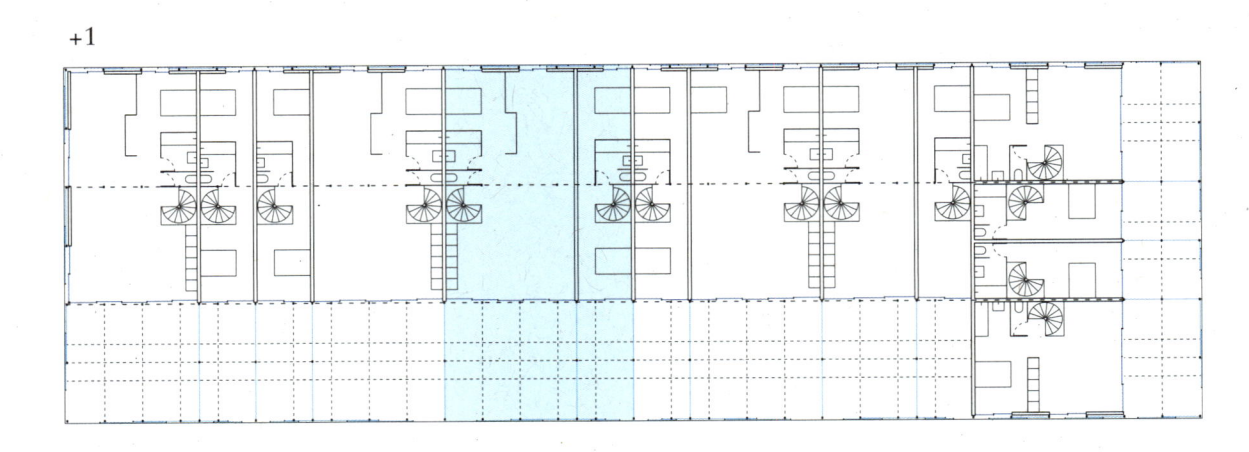

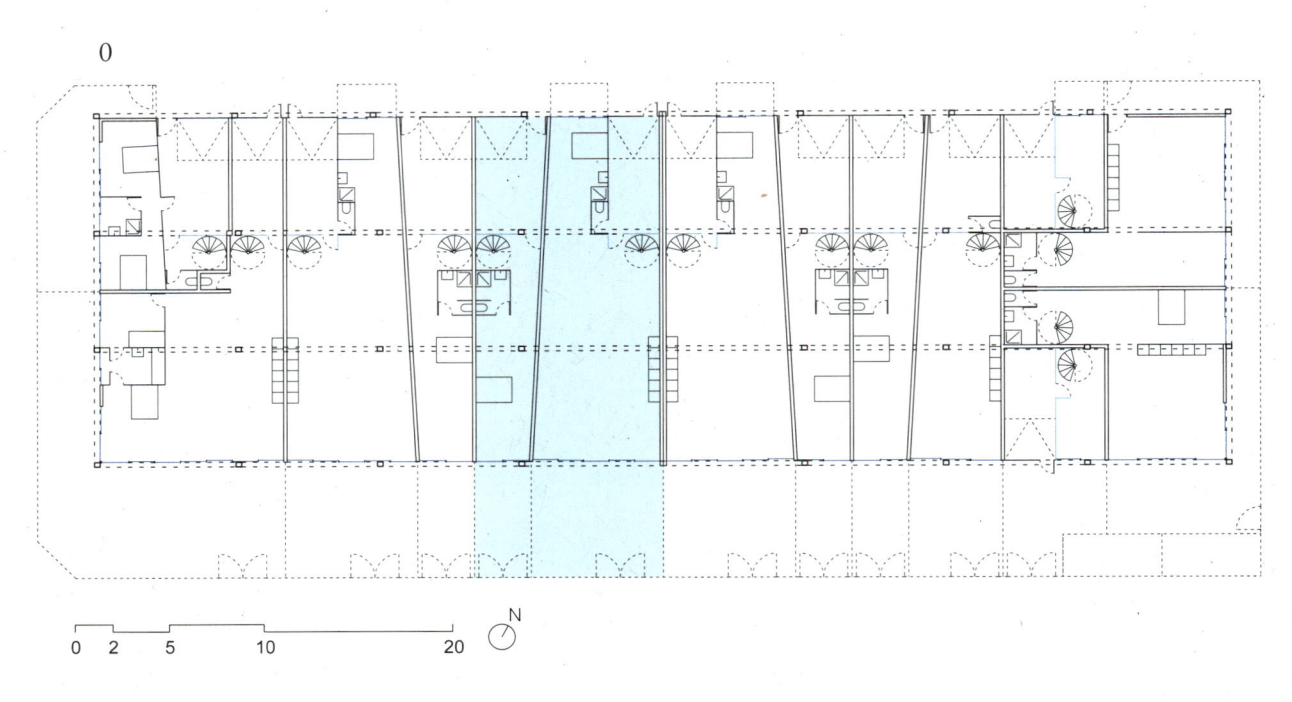

+1

0

The creation of a structure and a simple, economical, and efficient shell makes it possible to define, on the loft principle, an open-plan floor space and a maximum volume that have contrasting, complementary, and surprising spatial qualities. The column-beam structure of the ground floor forms a three-meter-high concrete platform, on which we could construct the horticulture greenhouses. The facades have many sliding glass panels, and part of the greenhouse is insulated and heated. The other part is a winter garden, well ventilated through the roof and facade. The intermediate interior facades open onto this winter garden via large floor-to-ceiling windows. A horizontal shade unwinds inside the greenhouse. The greenhouse principle, with its automatic climate-control systems, made it possible to develop bioclimatic comfort solutions. Afterward, the volume was divided up into fourteen housing units that extend all the way through the building. All of the apartments are duplexes, allowing residents to enjoy the qualities of two levels. The inhabitants have come to appreciate the possibilities offered by the units' depth, and they all have occupied it in their own way, adding furniture and curtains according to their needs.

Case Study 1

Project and Environmental Conditions
Unit

(1) Plan of analyzed unit 1/150

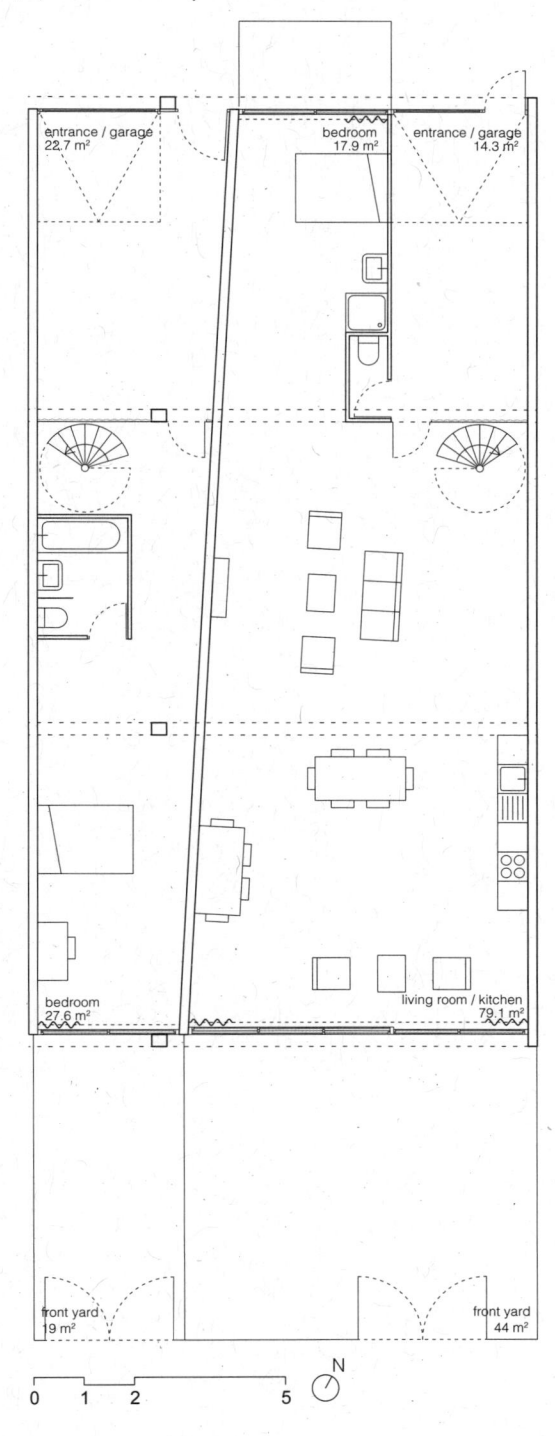

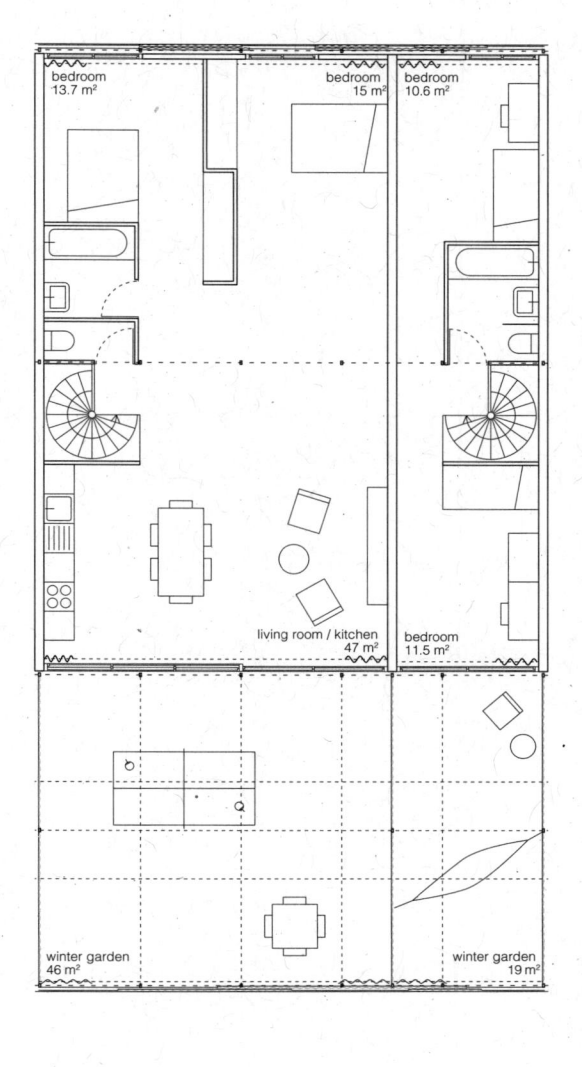

Throughout the year, the loftlike open layout offers a variety of light, comfort, and climatic ambience. This is due to the building depth, double orientation, and duplex composition. During hot summer days, this allows a retreat into the cooler interior, and on warm winter days and in the spring and fall, occupants can take advantage of the bright and sun-heated facades adjacent to the greenhouses. The generous apartment sizes, without predefined partitioning, allow for plentiful flexibility in the configuration of the interior space depending on the individual needs of the inhabitants.

Case Study 1

Project and Environmental Conditions
Climate

(1) Mulhouse climate summary

Mulhouse has the coldest winters of all four climates

(2) Sky coverage in winter and summer

(3) Solar radiation in the sky vault in winter and summer

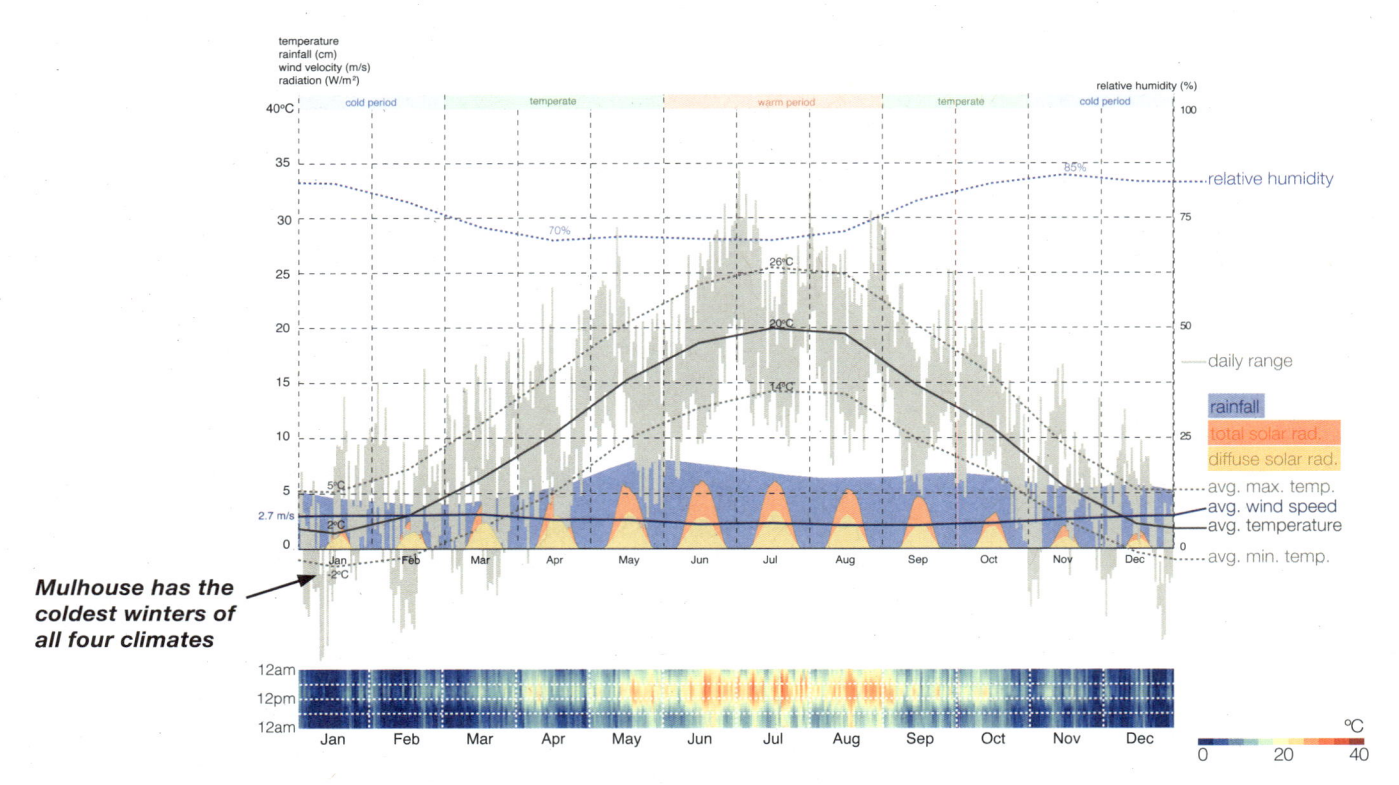

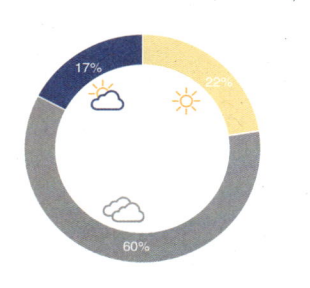

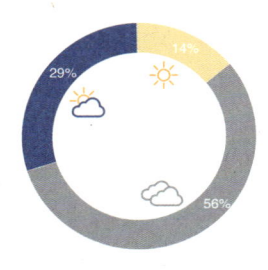

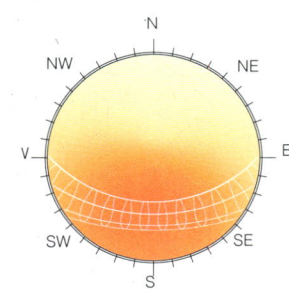

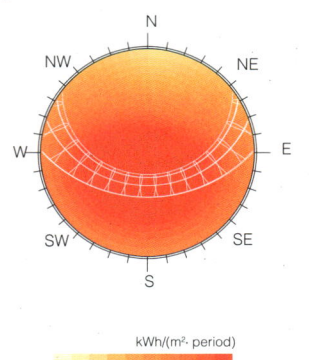

(3) Annual wind rose

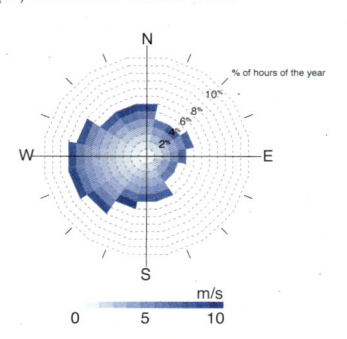

(1) Mulhouse climate summary: Mulhouse has the most extreme climate of the four studied as well as the largest daily variations in temperature. The sun is rather strong with a large proportion of diffuse radiation due to the considerable sky cover. During the hot period, the average high temperature is around 26°C, though it goes beyond 30°C about seven days a year. The amplitude is large (12°C a day), which calls for the use of thermal inertia to cool down the spaces naturally. During the cold period, the average high temperature is only around 5°C, and the average low is -2°C. Temperatures below zero happen from early November to the end of March, and many days can remain below zero throughout the day.

(2)/(3) Sky coverage and solar radiation in the sky vault in winter and summer: In winter, the sky is mostly covered, and radiation is higher on the south orientation, followed by the southeast and southwest. In summer, the sky is mostly cloudy, and radiation is higher on the horizontal surfaces. Among the vertical surfaces, the southwest and southeast receive the largest amount of radiation followed by the south, east, and west.

(4) Annual wind rose: Wind blows in a rather homogeneous way from all orientations, though predominantly from the west quadrant. The speed is low, with an annual average of 2.7 m/s.

Case Study 1

Project and Environmental Conditions
Environmental Features

BUILDING
Year of delivery	2005
Type of delivery	New build
Type of building	Row houses
Total amount of floors	2
Thermal regulation	RT 2000

SIMULATED UNIT
2 typical units
Heated surface	266 m²
Winter garden surface	62 m²
Balcony surface	0 m²
Ratio of extra space / heated surface	23%
Orientation	SE/NW
Ratio of exposed envelope that is winter garden	72%
Total air renewal	0.21 ach
Winter garden infiltration	120–90 m³/h, accounting 30 m³/(h·person)

TECHNICAL SYSTEMS
Ventilation typ	Individual, humidity controlled exhaust ventilation
Heating system type	Individual gas boiler per apartment
Heating regulation	Individual
Cep max	130 kWh/(m²·year)
Cep projet	95 kWh/(m²·year) < Cep max

Cep (Primary Energy Consumption in the French regulations): Cepmax is the allowed limit and Cep project is the project's calculated value with the compliance methodology → (Cep max, Cep projet)

WINTER GARDEN

Orientation	Depth	Volume	Exposed facade area	Exposed concrete area	Total inertia (of winter garden)
Southeast	6.3 m	394 m³	231 m²	62 m²	0.16 m²/m³
					19 kJ/(°K·m³)

m² of exposed concrete per m³ of air volume of the winter garden thermal capacity of the concrete

Winter garden's ability to store thermal energy considering 6 cm of active thermal mass

	Element	Material	U-value W/m²·K	SF	VLT	Reflectivity
①	Thermal curtain	Sheep's wool	2.17	0	0	0.9
②	Sliding doors of heated space	Double glazing	4.4	0.4	0.4	-
③	Solar curtain	Aluminum	-	0.65	0.65	0.33
④	Winter garden envelope	Transparent polycarbonate	5.7	0.85	0.85	-

* SF: Solar Factor, VLT: Visible Light Transmittance

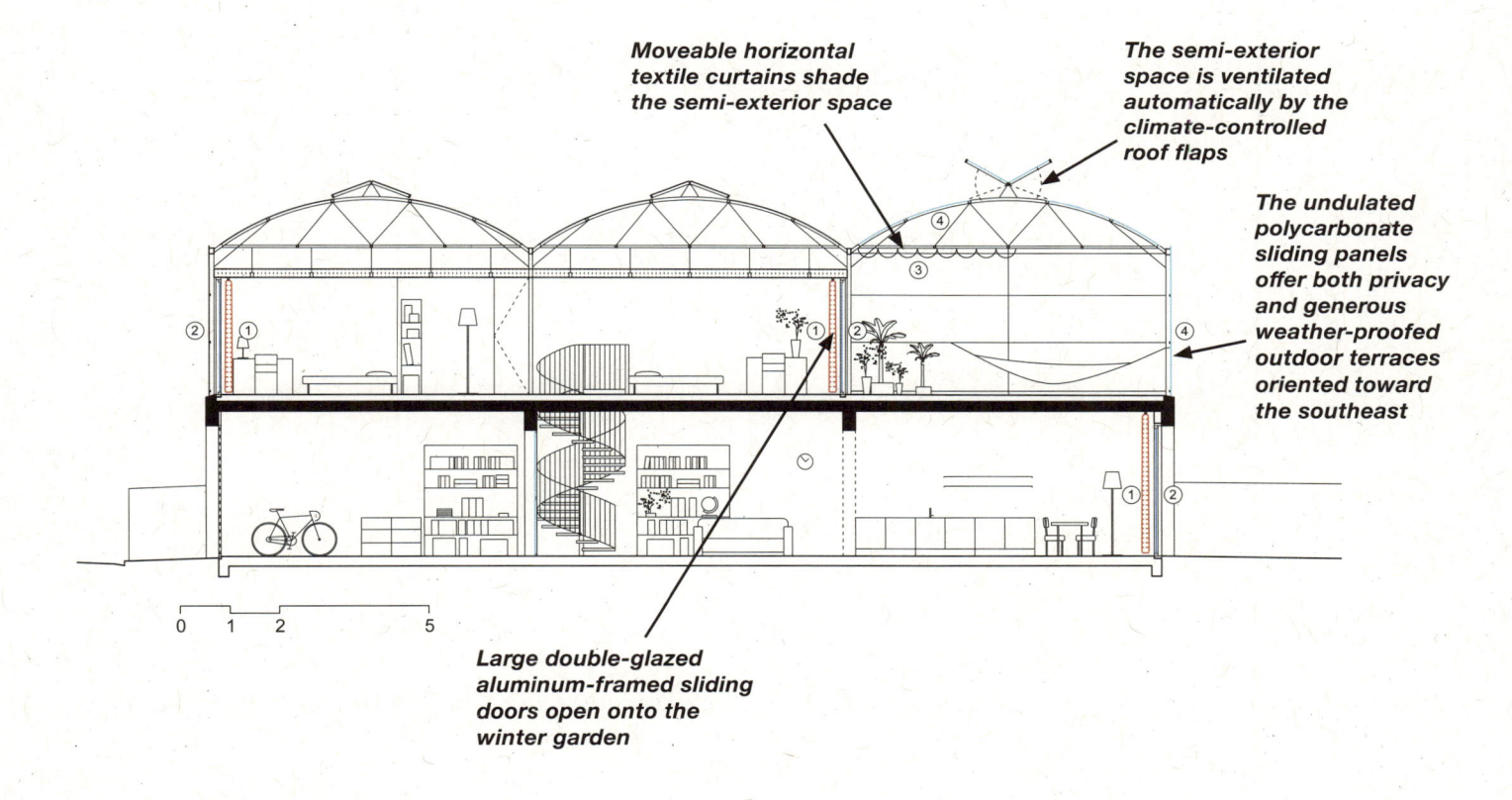

Moveable horizontal textile curtains shade the semi-exterior space

The semi-exterior space is ventilated automatically by the climate-controlled roof flaps

The undulated polycarbonate sliding panels offer both privacy and generous weather-proofed outdoor terraces oriented toward the southeast

Large double-glazed aluminum-framed sliding doors open onto the winter garden

The winter garden on the first floor is oriented toward the southeast. Its roof is made of transparent polycarbonate and has a shading that is 35% transmissive and an automated opening representing 23% of the roof surface. Vertical surfaces are also made of polycarbonate and do not have shading but are operable on 50% of their area. The unit is fully glazed on both floors in the southeast orientation and has a 50% window-to-wall ratio on the northwest one. U-values of the glazed elements are rather high (4.4 W/m²·K) since the building was planned in 2004, but they are complemented with the thermal curtain, which has a U-value of 2.17 W/m²·K.

Case Study 1

Project and Environmental Conditions
Sun and Wind

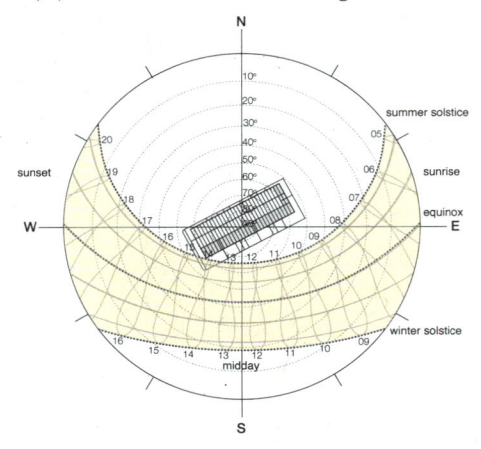

(1) Solar access at building scale

(2) Solar access at unit scale

(3) Solar heat gains in winter

(4) Natural airflow (summer)

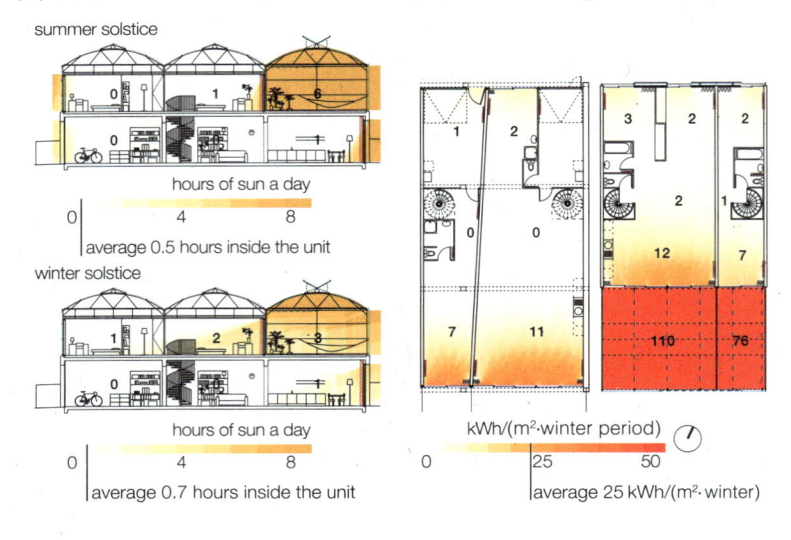

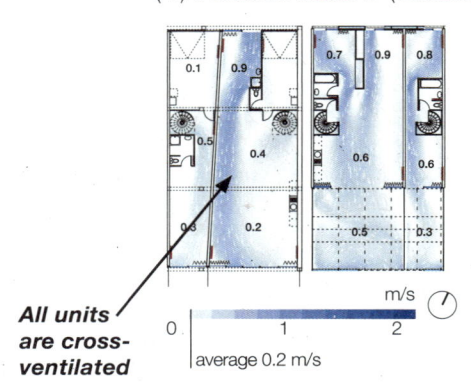

All units are cross-ventilated

(1) Solar access at building scale: The building is located in a suburban area with low buildings. The sun can reach all of the facades. Winter gardens are oriented toward the southeast, whereas the more opaque facade is oriented toward the northwest. The units receive at least nine hours of sun during the equinoxes, reaching the high solar access target of EN 17037.

(2) Solar access at unit scale: The winter garden is exposed to the sun all year round due to its glazed roof. The interior spaces of the houses receive more sun in winter than in summer. During the summer, the sun is high and can be blocked with the shading and curtains. In winter, due to its low angles the sun permeates the interior.

(3) Solar heat gains in winter: In the living rooms, the winter garden acts as a natural radiator, producing 12 kWh/m² of heat, which is equivalent to having a small radiator on during half of the day.

(4) Natural airflow in summer under average wind conditions: Under average conditions, a breeze flows effectively in both levels due to the large openings on both facades and the open plan. Maximum wind speed is below 1 m/s, which still represents a decrease in the felt temperature of -4°C.

Case Study 1

Project and Condition
Daylight

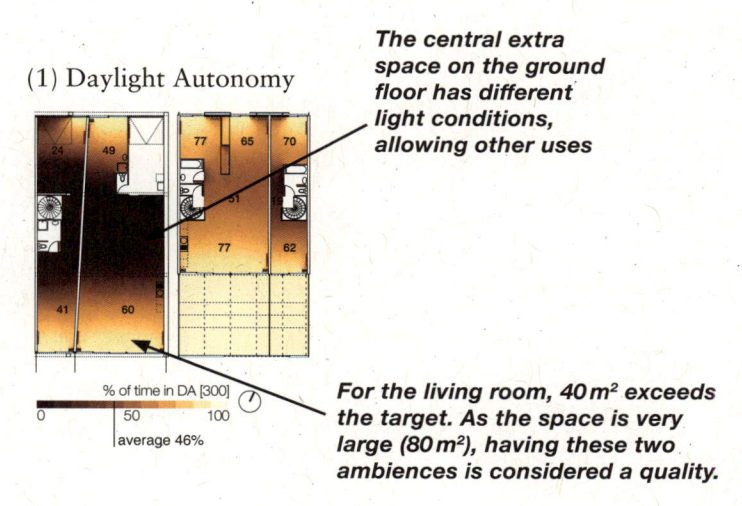

(1) Daylight Autonomy

% of time in DA [300]
0   50   100
average 46%

The central extra space on the ground floor has different light conditions, allowing other uses

For the living room, 40 m² exceeds the target. As the space is very large (80 m²), having these two ambiences is considered a quality.

(2) Space exceeding 50% of the time with DA [300] (EN 17037)

reference plane: 50 cm off the walls from permanently occupied spaces

target 50% of space > 50% of time with DA [300]

Upper Lr	100%
Room N1	100%
Room N2	99%
Room S1	78%
Room N3	100%
Room N4	57%
Room S2	43%
40 m² of Lr	70%
Lower Lr	35%
average	79%

All the spaces (considering the standard sizes) exceed the recommendations of EN 17037

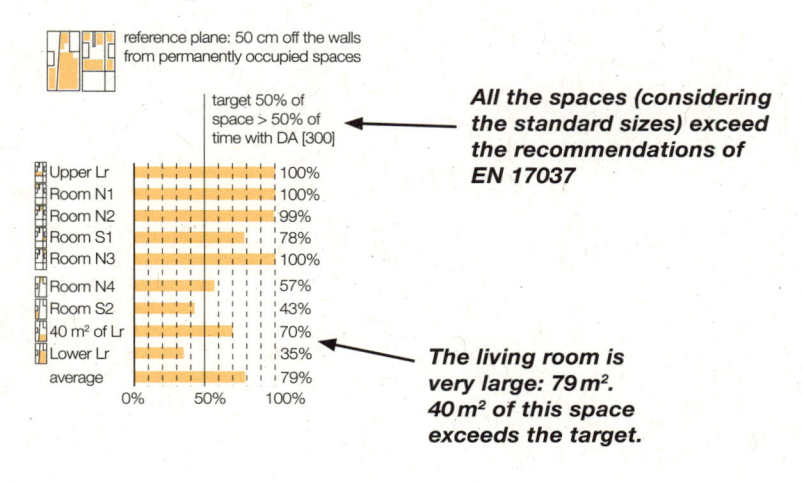

The living room is very large: 79 m². 40 m² of this space exceeds the target.

(1) Daylight Autonomy: Daylight levels are heterogeneous across the spaces. Whereas the first floor is in full daylight (DA ranging from 62 to 77%), the ground floor has more varied conditions. Living rooms are bright and in autonomy, with 60 and 77% DA respectively. Low visible transmittances of glazings moderate daylight levels inside.

(2) Space exceeding 50% of the time with DA [300] (EN 17037): All the spaces of the first floor largely exceed the EN target. On the ground floor, the large spaces near the glazed areas that correspond to the standard size of living areas are very bright and exceed the EN target. From the 40 m² that are close to the facade, 70% receive 300 lux naturally more than 50% of the time, which is far above the requirement of EN 17037. The central spaces of the plan are darker due to the depth of the building. Considering the generosity of space, this variation in intensity is an added quality.

Free-Running Mode
Seasonal Performance

(1) Operative temperatures across the year

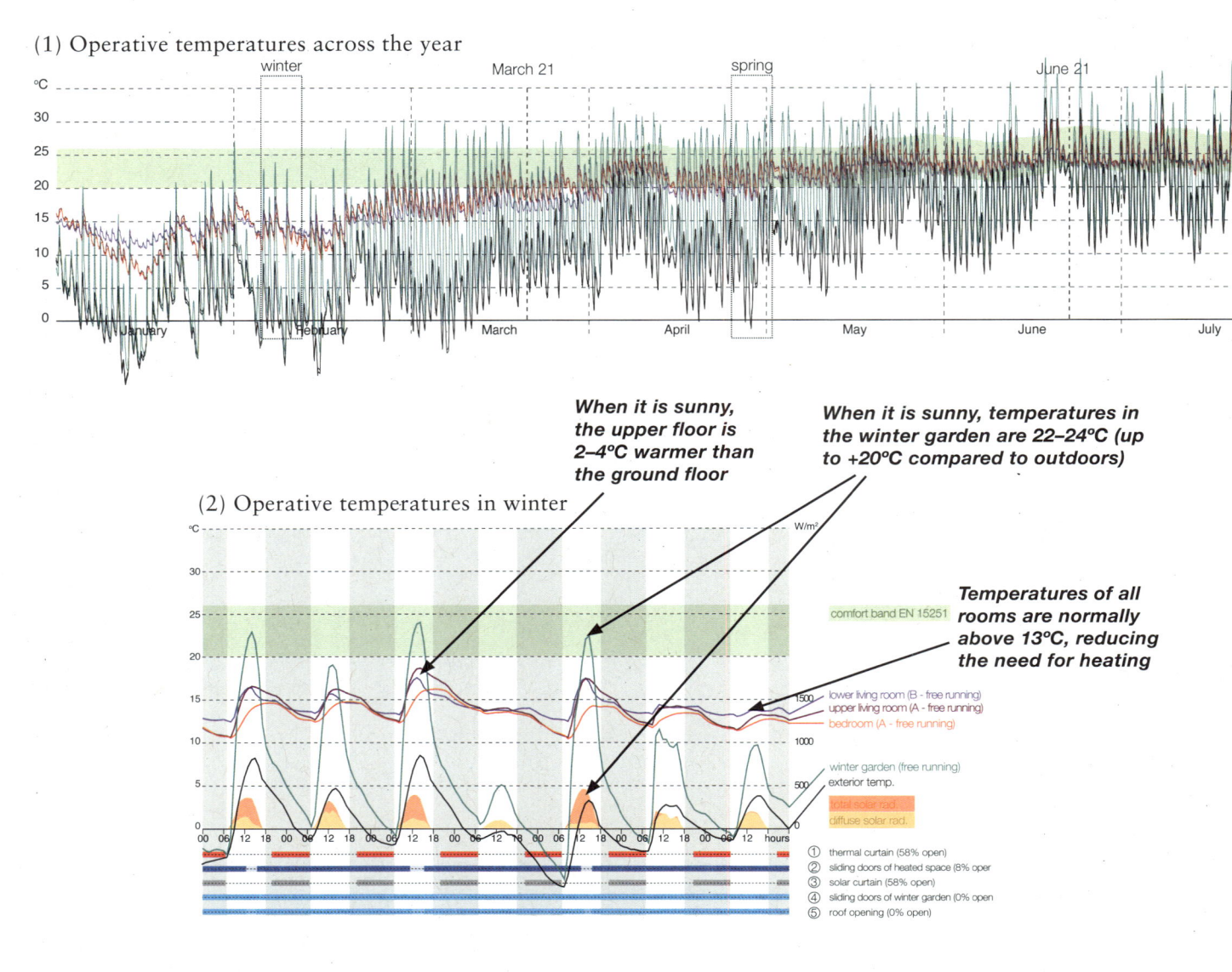

(2) Operative temperatures in winter

When it is sunny, the upper floor is 2–4°C warmer than the ground floor

When it is sunny, temperatures in the winter garden are 22–24°C (up to +20°C compared to outdoors)

Temperatures of all rooms are normally above 13°C, reducing the need for heating

- ① thermal curtain (58% open)
- ② sliding doors of heated space (8% open)
- ③ solar curtain (58% open)
- ④ sliding doors of winter garden (0% open)
- ⑤ roof opening (0% open)

(3) Operative temperatures in spring

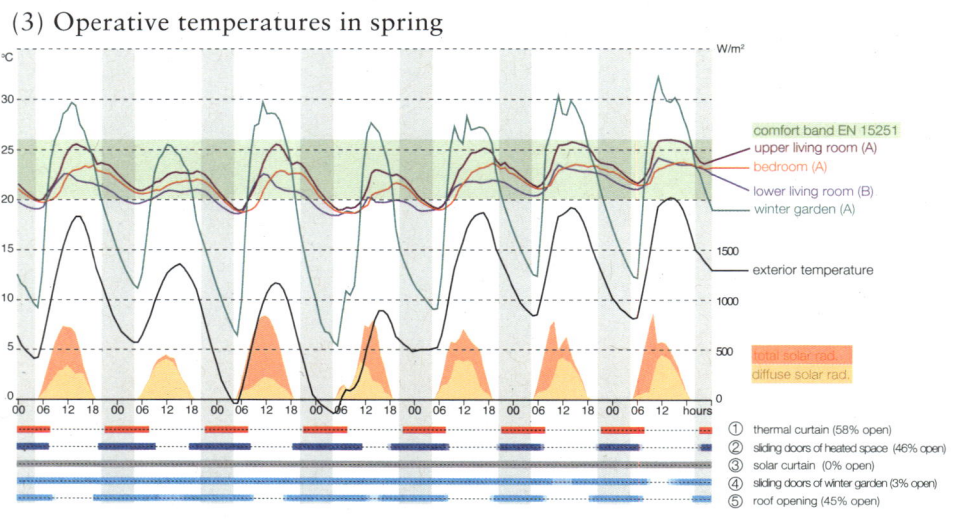

- ① thermal curtain (58% open)
- ② sliding doors of heated space (46% open)
- ③ solar curtain (0% open)
- ④ sliding doors of winter garden (3% open)
- ⑤ roof opening (45% open)

(1) Operative temperatures across the year: The simulation in free-running mode shows that indoor temperatures vary naturally from 7 to 31°C.

(2) Operative temperatures in winter: Temperatures in free-running mode remain around 12–17°C indoors. During sunny days, the winter garden heats up fast and living room temperatures reach 17–18°C whereas the bedroom reaches 14–16°C. During cloudy days, winter garden temperatures remain 5–7°C above outdoors, and on sunny days the difference can reach 20°C, bringing them inside the comfort band. The inertia of the winter garden maintains warmer temperatures during the night. However, by the early morning, the winter garden temperature is almost coupled with outdoors.

(3) Operative temperatures in spring: During the spring, indoor temperatures remain in comfort, oscillating between the lower and upper bounds of the comfort band. These variations are controlled with the operability of the elements toward the winter garden. Winter garden temperatures are 10–23°C higher than outdoors during daytime. If the temperature rises too high, the roof vents automatically open to bring the temperature back down, ensuring optimal performance. During nighttime, it remains 2–5°C warmer due to the inertia of the concrete. The upper living room has the highest temperatures, around 2°C more than the other rooms, due to the contact with the winter garden.

Case Study 1

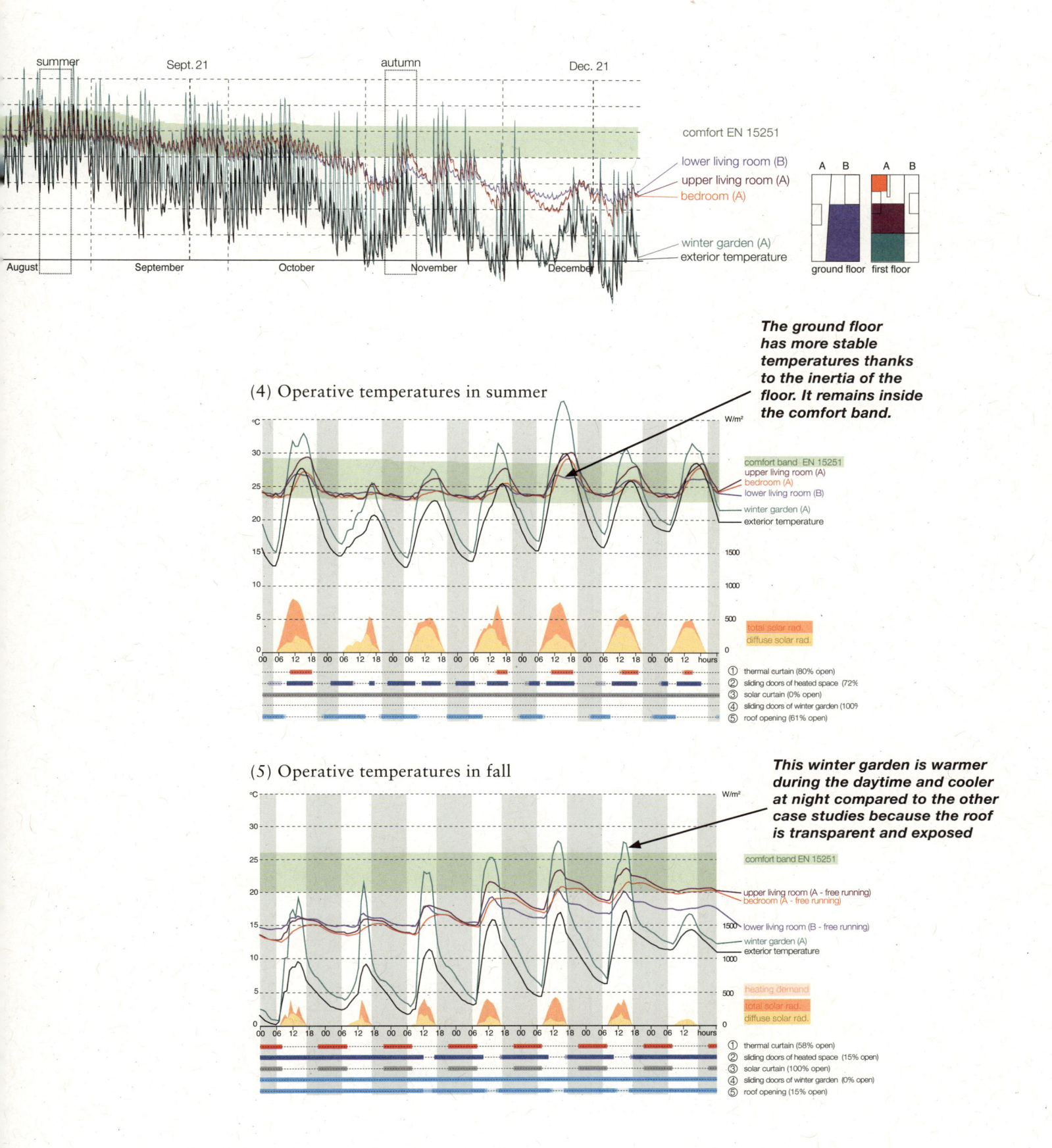

(4) Operative temperatures in summer

The ground floor has more stable temperatures thanks to the inertia of the floor. It remains inside the comfort band.

(5) Operative temperatures in fall

This winter garden is warmer during the daytime and cooler at night compared to the other case studies because the roof is transparent and exposed

(4) Operative temperatures in summer: During a typical summer week, all indoor operative temperatures are within comfort all the time thanks to the effectiveness of the cross ventilation—when all sliding panels are open—and thanks to the inertia of the concrete structure, which stabilizes temperatures. Winter garden operative temperatures are warmer than outdoors by 2–10°C. In general, the upper floor is warmer due to the ventilation via the winter garden, but the ground floor remains very stable and cool, as its temperature never rises above 27°C. All units have rooms on the ground floor where occupants can spend time during hot days. The temperature of the bedrooms in the northwest remains similar to that of the ground floor, but overheat slightly more during peak sunny days. Closing the reflective thermal curtain reduces indoor temperatures—note that the thermal curtain (red line) is closed in the afternoons as temperatures are high and the sun hits the facade. In reality, these could be closed for more time to further reduce temperatures.

(5) Operative temperatures in fall: During the fall, indoor operative temperatures vary between 13 and 23°C in free-running mode, depending on outdoor temperatures, sky coverage, and the conditions of the previous days. The difference between all indoor spaces is small. During the daytime and on sunny days, the winter garden's operative temperature is 10–12°C higher than outdoors, whereas at night the difference falls down to 1–2°C. On cloudy days, the difference is only 2–3°C.

Case Study 1

Free-Running Mode
Typical Days

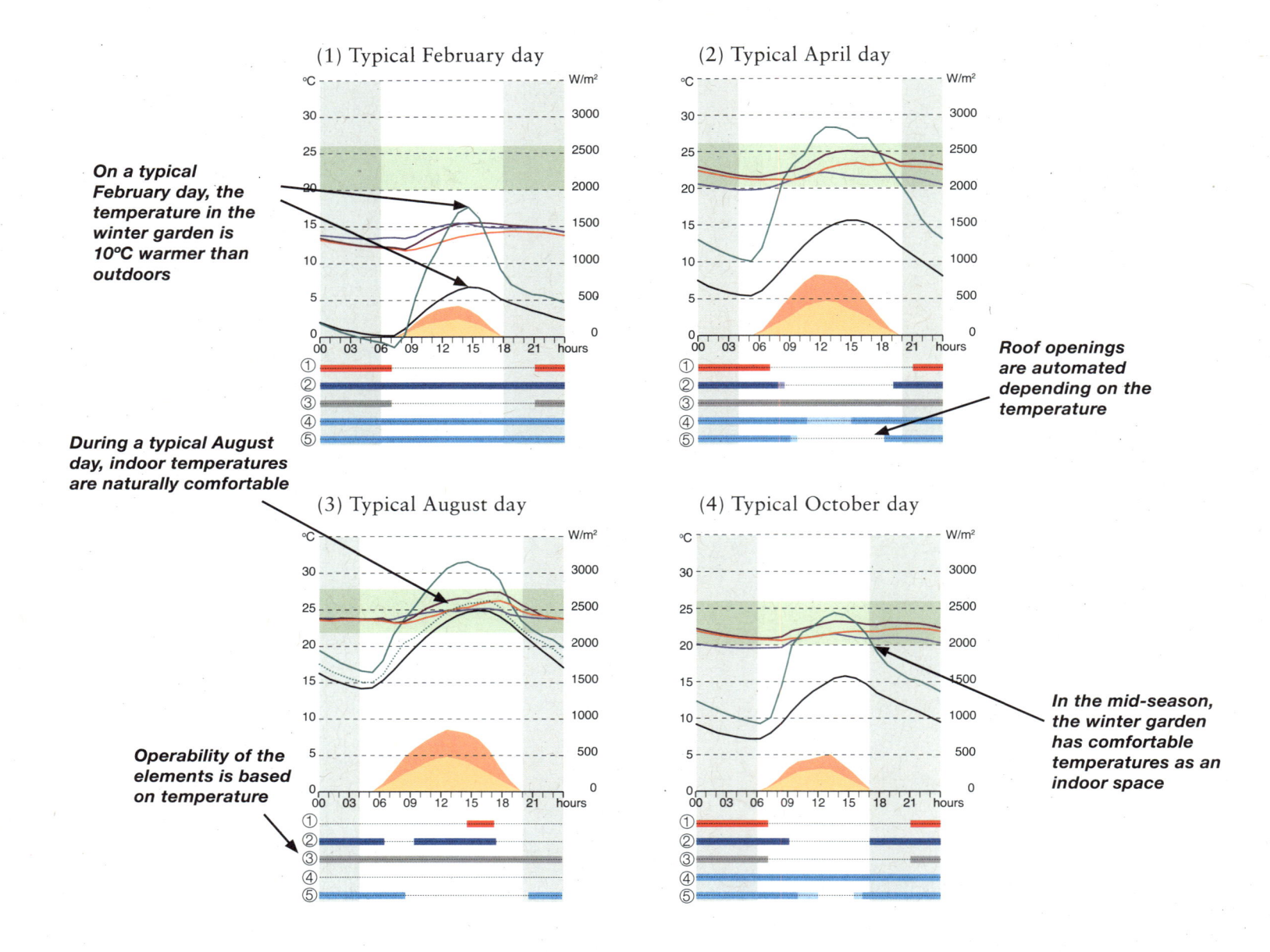

(1) Typical February day

On a typical February day, the temperature in the winter garden is 10°C warmer than outdoors

(2) Typical April day

Roof openings are automated depending on the temperature

(3) Typical August day

During a typical August day, indoor temperatures are naturally comfortable

Operability of the elements is based on temperature

(4) Typical October day

In the mid-season, the winter garden has comfortable temperatures as an indoor space

---

(1) Typical February day: In winter, all sliding doors remain closed and the thermal curtain is deployed at night. Operative temperatures in free-running mode remain relatively stable, varying from 12 to 15°C, depending on the room and time of day. The lowest floor in contact with the ground has the highest temperatures. The winter garden temperature follows outdoor patterns, but with more extreme values. During the night, the operative temperature is slightly under the exterior temperature due to the sky radiation (1–2°C) that cools down the polycarbonate, which reduces radiant temperatures, whereas during the day, even when there is little sun, temperatures can rise to 17°C, a difference of around 10°C with the outdoors.

(2) Typical April day: In spring, the exterior sliding doors of the winter garden are left closed during the day, but the roof opens from around noon until nighttime. The solar curtain of the winter garden is deployed day and night. Thermal curtains are only closed at night. Indoor operative temperatures vary from 20 to 25°C depending on the room and time of day. The living room in contact with the winter garden is also the warmest space, 1–1.5°C higher than the rest of the house, and the lower floor has the lowest temperatures. Winter garden operative temperatures follow outdoor temperatures, but are 5°C higher at night and about 12–13°C higher in the afternoon, reaching 28–29°C. These temperatures are perceived as too hot during this time of the year, but the sliding doors could be left open for longer periods if the occupants wanted lower temperatures.

(3) Typical August day: In summer, all winter garden openings and interior openings are left completely open. The solar protection under the roof is deployed across the day. The thermal curtain is closed for some hours during the afternoon to prevent temperature rise. Across the house, the temperature remains stable around 24–27°C, within the comfort band. The living room in contact with the winter garden has an operative temperature of 26°C during the afternoon. Inside the winter garden, operative temperatures follow outdoor temperatures, 2°C higher at night but about 6.5°C higher in the afternoon, reaching 31.5°C. This is due to the lack of more efficient solar protection on the vertical walls and not enough solar protection on the roof. The simulation is limited by how the shading is modeled (as it cannot model the gap with the roof). Real felt temperatures would be slightly closer to air temperature, which peaks at only 26°C.

(4) Typical October day: During the fall, the sliding doors are open to the winter garden during the daytime, and the roof vents are open during the central hours of the day. The solar curtain is fully open, and at night the thermal curtain is deployed. Operative temperatures in free-running mode vary from 20 to 24°C, depending on the room and time of day. The living room in contact with the winter garden has the higher operative temperatures, and the lower floor the lowest. The winter garden follows the variations from outdoors but with temperatures 3–9°C higher.

Case Study 1

Free-Running Mode
Extreme Days

(1) Extreme winter day

On extreme winter days, the winter garden temperature is 13°C above outdoors

(2) Extreme summer day

This level of heat is punctual. Note that the dwelling offers many spaces with various thermal conditions from which the occupants can choose.

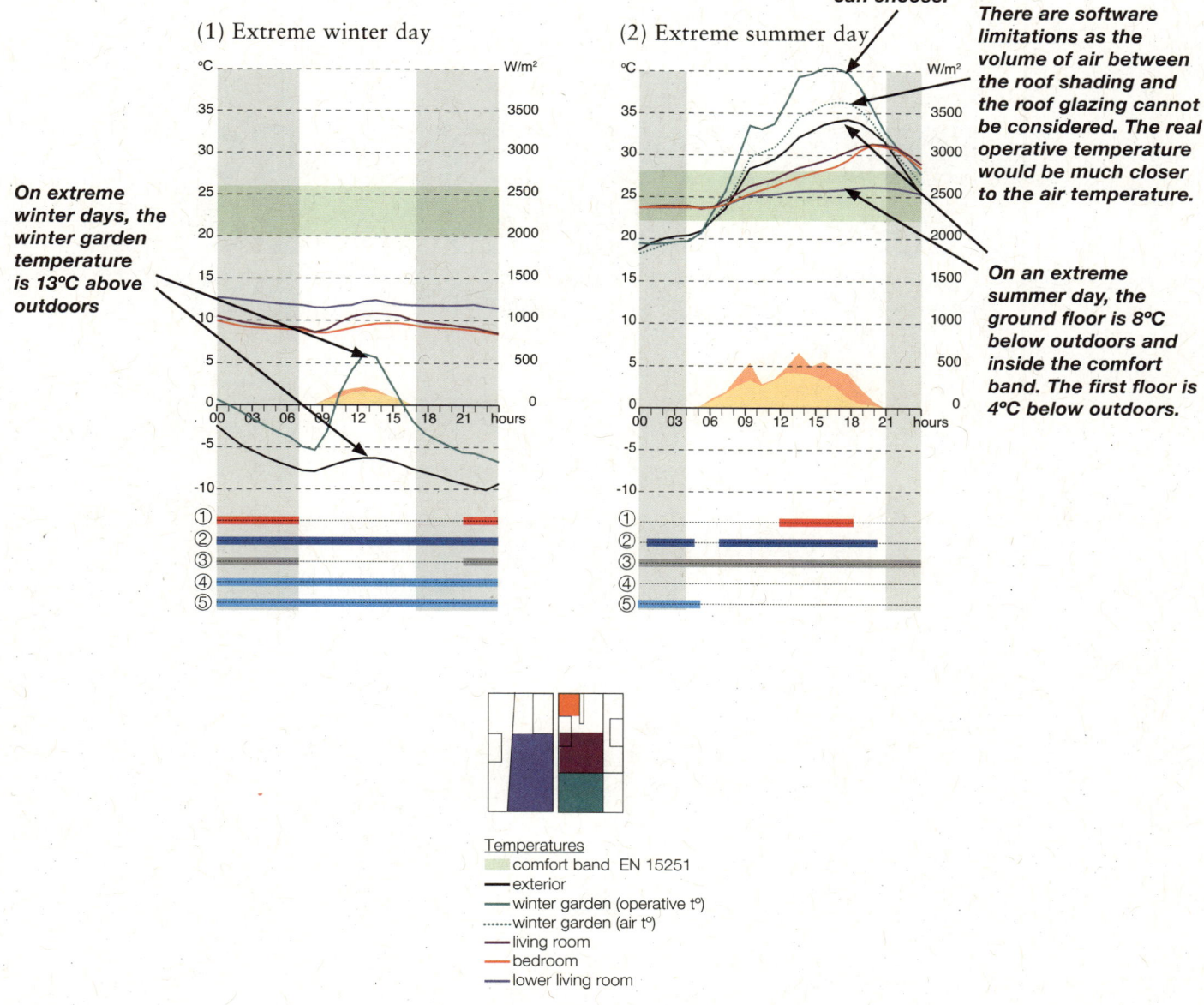

There are software limitations as the volume of air between the roof shading and the roof glazing cannot be considered. The real operative temperature would be much closer to the air temperature.

On an extreme summer day, the ground floor is 8°C below outdoors and inside the comfort band. The first floor is 4°C below outdoors.

Temperatures
- comfort band EN 15251
- exterior
- winter garden (operative t°)
- winter garden (air t°)
- living room
- bedroom
- lower living room

Solar radiation
- total radiation
- diffuse portion

Envelope operability
1. thermal curtain
2. sliding doors of heated space
3. solar curtain
4. sliding doors of winter garden
5. roof opening of winter garden
- element is closed
- element is open

(1) Extreme winter day: During an extreme winter day, when outdoor temperatures remain below zero all day and night, and can drop as low as -10°C, all sliding panels remain closed and both curtains are deployed at night. Operative temperatures in free-running mode in the upper level vary from 8.5 to 10.5°C, whereas in the lower level (in contact with the ground and with less heat loss through the roof) temperatures are about 2°C higher and remain around 12–13°C. It is to be noted that the coldest days are normally sunny. This enlarges the temperature difference between the winter garden and outdoors, which makes them particularly effective for extreme days. At night, the difference can be around 2–5°C, but during the day it is around 13°C: when it is -7°C outdoors, the winter garden has operative temperatures of around 6°C.

(2) Extreme summer day: During an extreme summer day, when outdoor temperatures can reach 34°C, all openings of the winter garden are left open day and night. During the peak hours, the sliding doors to the winter garden are closed to avoid warmer air from the winter garden coming in. The solar curtain is deployed the whole day, and the thermal curtain is also used to limit solar gains indoors during the afternoon. Interior operative temperatures of the upper level follow the variation of outdoors, but 2–5°C lower and with a time lag of 3–4 hours due to the effect of thermal inertia. Temperatures on the ground floor are much more stable, and vary from 24 to 26°C; even when the outdoor temperature reaches its peak, it is 8°C lower indoors. Inside the winter garden, operative temperatures reach 40°C in the afternoon due to the heat radiated from the transparent surfaces. This is equivalent to about 6°C more than outdoors. Due to the software limitations, the real felt temperature cannot be simulated, but would be slightly closer to air temperature that reaches 36°C (2°C more than outdoors).

Free-Running Mode
Thermal Comfort Conditions

(1) Resulting thermal comfort per room

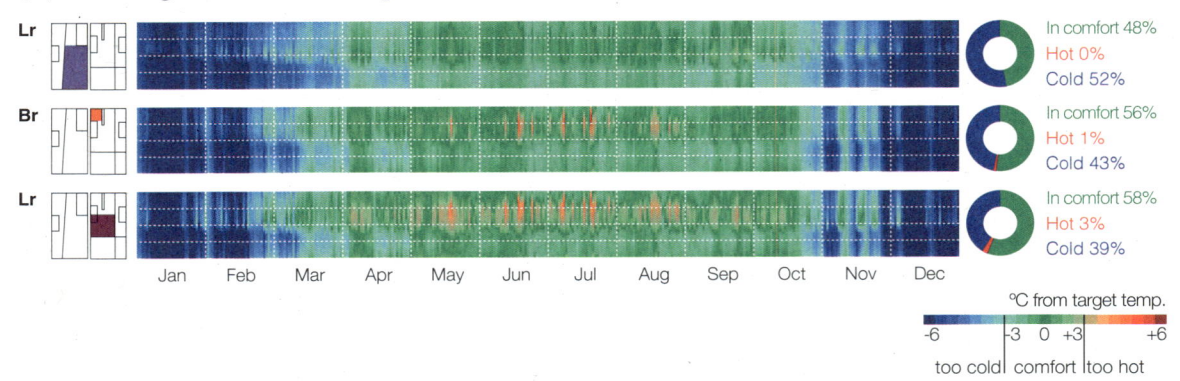

Lr — In comfort 48% / Hot 0% / Cold 52%
Br — In comfort 56% / Hot 1% / Cold 43%
Lr — In comfort 58% / Hot 3% / Cold 39%

°C from target temp.
-6 -3 0 +3 +6
too cold | comfort | too hot

(2) Operative temperatures indoors as a function of outdoors

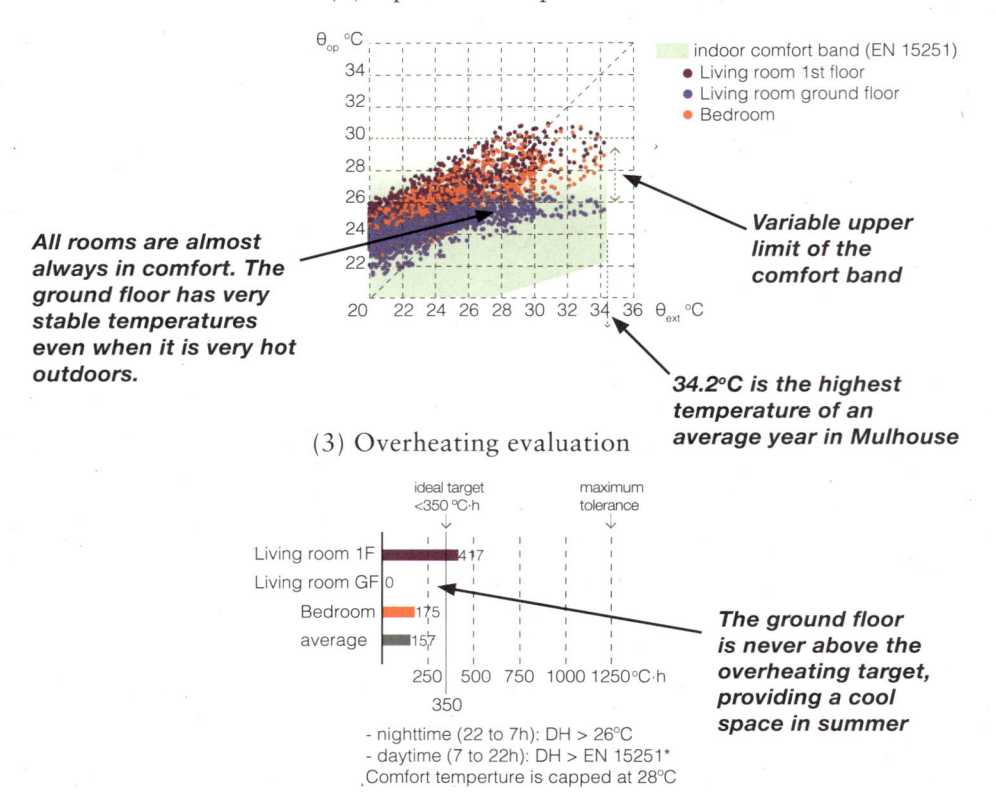

θ_{op} °C vs θ_{ext} °C

- indoor comfort band (EN 15251)
- Living room 1st floor
- Living room ground floor
- Bedroom

All rooms are almost always in comfort. The ground floor has very stable temperatures even when it is very hot outdoors.

Variable upper limit of the comfort band

34.2°C is the highest temperature of an average year in Mulhouse

(3) Overheating evaluation

ideal target <350 °C·h   maximum tolerance

Living room 1F — 417
Living room GF — 0
Bedroom — 175
average — 157

250 500 750 1000 1250 °C·h
350

- nighttime (22 to 7h): DH > 26°C
- daytime (7 to 22h): DH > EN 15251*
- Comfort temperture is capped at 28°C

The ground floor is never above the overheating target, providing a cool space in summer

(1) Resulting thermal comfort per room: Indoor spaces are comfortable around 48–58% of the time. Spaces on the ground floor do not overheat. Some rooms on the first floor have their operative temperatures above the comfort band 1–3% of the time, which is still within acceptable boundaries of today's way of measuring comfort.

(2) Operative temperatures indoors as a function of outdoors: The ground floor has very stable conditions, as its temperature never rises above 26°C, even when outdoors is 34.2°C, a difference of more than 8°C. On the first floor temperatures are higher, but remain within comfort most of the time. When the outdoor temperature peaks around 34°C, the temperature in these spaces is 28–31°C, as closing the thermal curtain helps reduce solar gains.

(3) Overheating evaluation: On average, the houses do not overheat, as the combined average of degree hours above comfort target is 57 (ideal target <350°C·h). The living room on the first floor has more degree hours than the ideal target above 26°C (417 > 350°C·h). However, the bedrooms oriented toward the north remain much cooler (175°C·h > comfort target), and the living room of the ground floor never gets above 26°C. Occupants can always choose to spend their time in cooler places.

Case Study 1

Free-Running Mode
Conditions in the Winter Garden

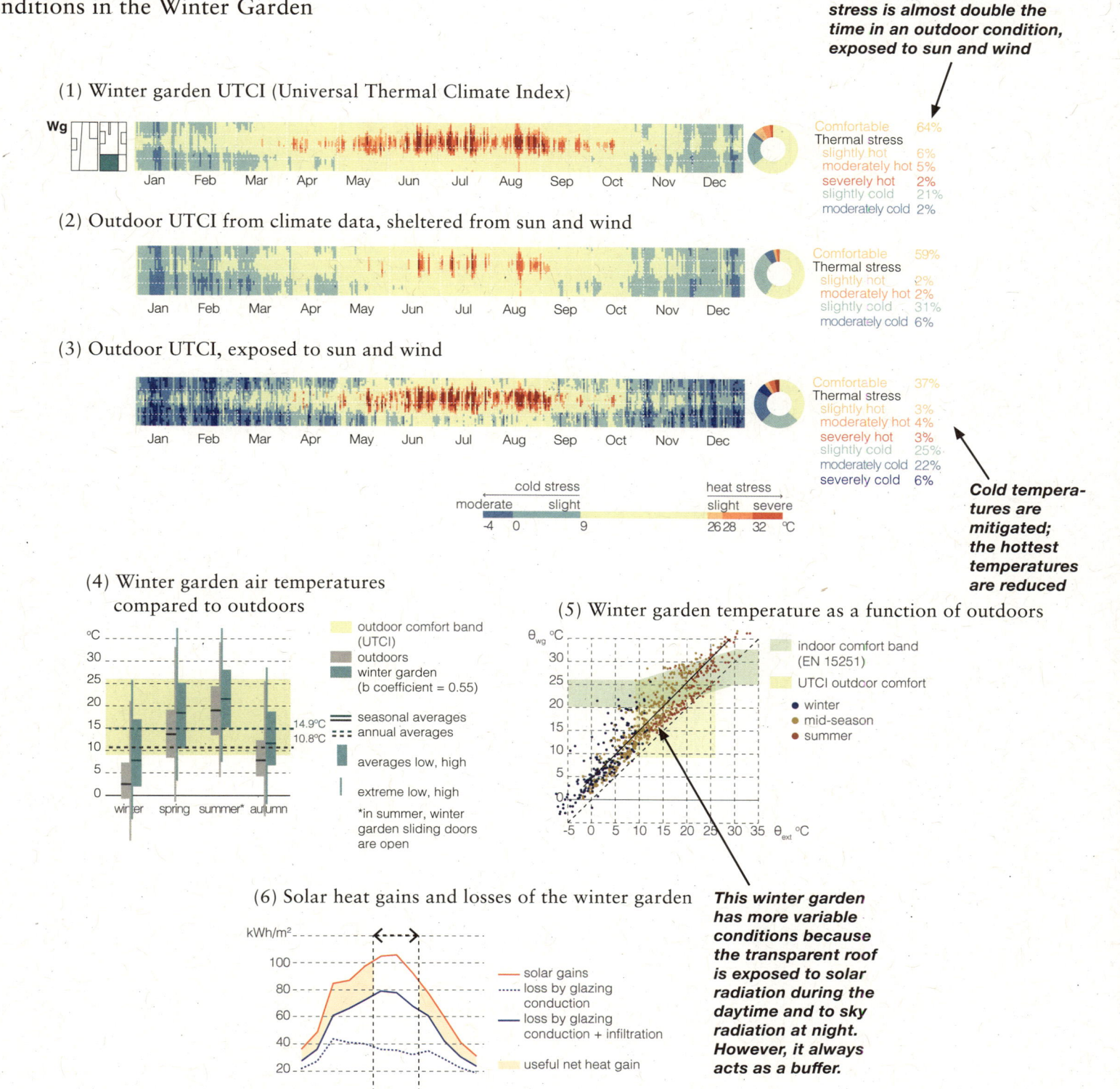

The time without thermal stress is almost double the time in an outdoor condition, exposed to sun and wind

(1) Winter garden UTCI (Universal Thermal Climate Index)

Comfortable 64%
Thermal stress
slightly hot 6%
moderately hot 5%
severely hot 2%
slightly cold 21%
moderately cold 2%

(2) Outdoor UTCI from climate data, sheltered from sun and wind

Comfortable 59%
Thermal stress
slightly hot 2%
moderately hot 2%
slightly cold 31%
moderately cold 6%

(3) Outdoor UTCI, exposed to sun and wind

Comfortable 37%
Thermal stress
slightly hot 3%
moderately hot 4%
severely hot 3%
slightly cold 25%
moderately cold 22%
severely cold 6%

Cold temperatures are mitigated; the hottest temperatures are reduced

cold stress / heat stress
moderate slight / slight severe
-4   0   9   26 28 32 °C

(4) Winter garden air temperatures compared to outdoors

- outdoor comfort band (UTCI)
- outdoors
- winter garden (b coefficient = 0.55)
- seasonal averages
- annual averages
- averages low, high
- extreme low, high

14.9°C
10.8°C

*in summer, winter garden sliding doors are open

(5) Winter garden temperature as a function of outdoors

- indoor comfort band (EN 15251)
- UTCI outdoor comfort
- winter
- mid-season
- summer

θ_{wg} °C / θ_{ext} °C

(6) Solar heat gains and losses of the winter garden

- solar gains
- loss by glazing conduction
- loss by glazing conduction + infiltration
- useful net heat gain

This winter garden has more variable conditions because the transparent roof is exposed to solar radiation during the daytime and to sky radiation at night. However, it always acts as a buffer.

(1)–(3) Winter garden and outdoor UTCI: These diagrams show the efficiency of the winter garden compared to being exposed directly to outdoor conditions with sun and wind, and in a sheltered situation. The winter garden is not in thermal stress (UTCI 9–26°C) 64% of the time. For 2% of the year, the heat is severe. The cold stress is only slight (0–9°C) 21% of the time, and on a few days it can be moderate (2% of the time). In an exposed situation outdoors, the time when there is cold stress is more than double, as it reaches 53%. Besides, the severity of the stress is much greater (22% of the time in moderate cold, and 6% in severe cold). Compared to a sheltered outdoors, the winter garden still has much milder conditions, as it spends 14% less time in cold stress. Regarding heat, the winter garden has slightly more heat stress than outdoors (13% of the time in total), both in an exposed situation (10%) and sheltered (4%). Improving the shading system would reduce the severe thermal stress caused by heat. The occupant can choose to be elsewhere.

(4) Winter garden air temperatures compared to outdoors: The winter garden is on average 4°C warmer than outdoors. During the winter, the difference is larger (about 6°C) than in summer (about 2.5°C). During the winter, outdoor temperatures are never comfortable, whereas the winter garden has comfortable temperatures during a large part of the winter. The b coefficient is calculated following the European Norm (EN 13789) to calculate the reduction of heat losses of the heated envelope thanks to the effect of the winter garden. Here the result is 0.6, meaning that the winter garden reduces heat loss by 40%.

(5) Winter garden temperature as a function of outdoors: Temperatures are always higher than outdoors, by an average of 4°C. When it is cloudy, temperatures are closer to outdoors, and when it is sunny the differences are greater.

(6) Solar heat gains and losses of the winter garden: The winter garden represents a net gain throughout the year. Whereas in the coldest month it represents about 8–10 kWh/m², in April it can reach 21 kWh/m² of heat gain. The difference between the winter garden and outdoors is larger during the summer and spring due to the larger solar gains, but smaller in fall and winter due to the amount of exposed surface.

Case Study 1

Active Mode
Winter Air Temperatures and Heating Load

(1) Winter air temperatures and heating demand

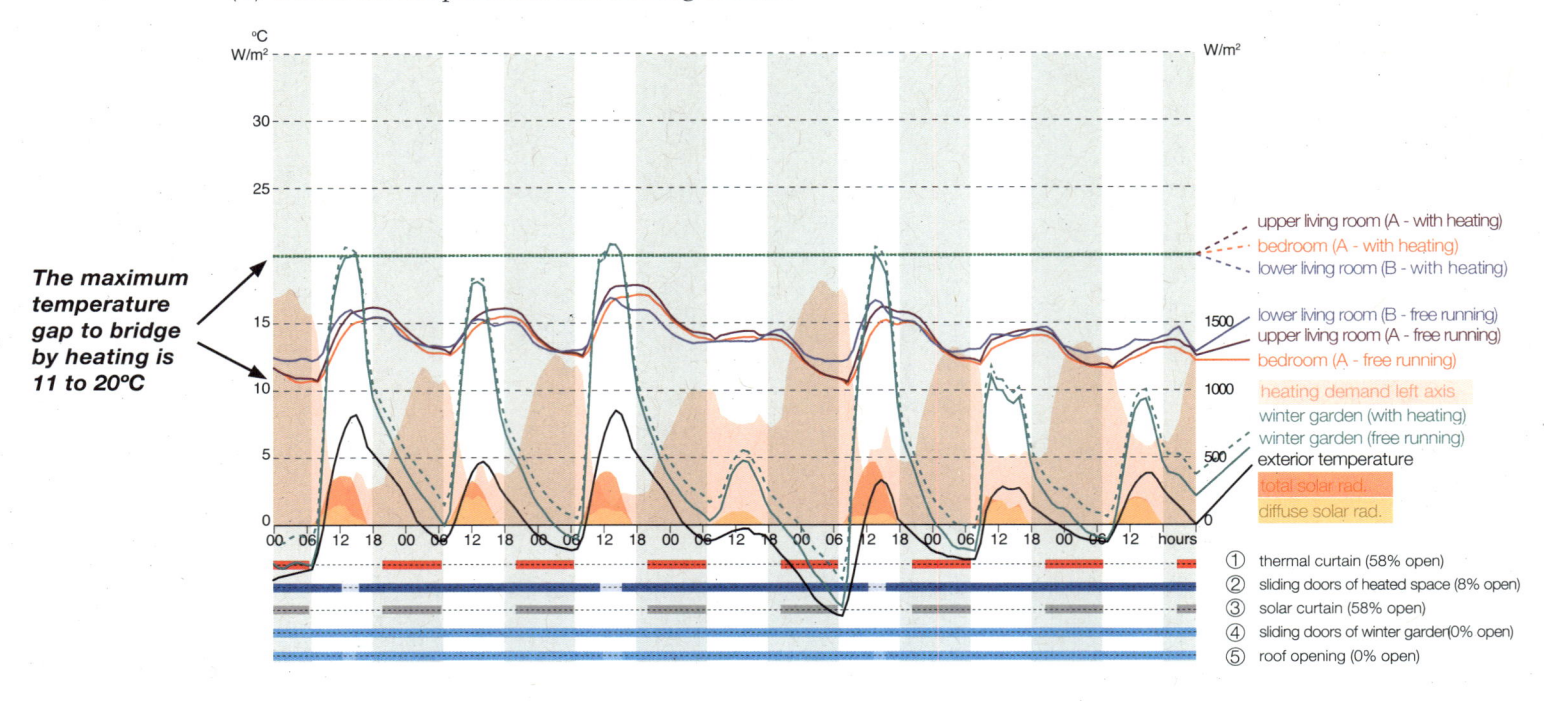

The maximum temperature gap to bridge by heating is 11 to 20°C

- upper living room (A - with heating)
- bedroom (A - with heating)
- lower living room (B - with heating)
- lower living room (B - free running)
- upper living room (A - free running)
- bedroom (A - free running)
- heating demand left axis
- winter garden (with heating)
- winter garden (free running)
- exterior temperature
- total solar rad.
- diffuse solar rad.

① thermal curtain (58% open)
② sliding doors of heated space (8% open)
③ solar curtain (58% open)
④ sliding doors of winter garden (0% open)
⑤ roof opening (0% open)

(1) Winter air temperatures and heating demand: This graphic shows air temperature rather than the operative temperature of previous graphics—for heat load evaluations. In free-running mode, temperature across the house varies from 11 to 17°C on average. The difference to be bridged by heating is 3 to 9°C depending on outdoor conditions. When heating is on indoors, temperatures in the winter garden are slightly higher at night (up to 2°C), as it collects the heat from indoors, further insulating the heated envelope.

Case Study 1

Active Mode Heating Demand

(1) Space heating demand

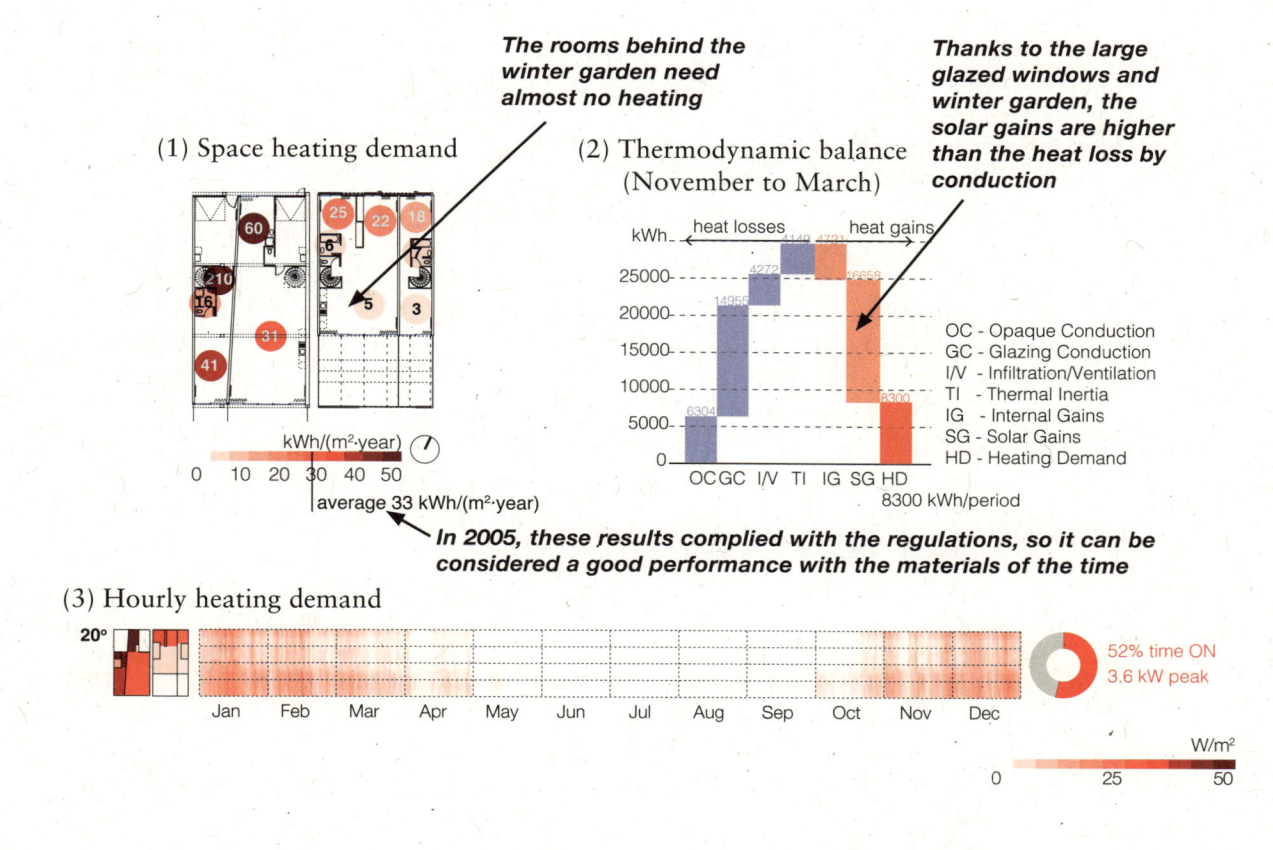

kWh/(m²·year)
0 10 20 30 40 50

average 33 kWh/(m²·year)

The rooms behind the winter garden need almost no heating

(2) Thermodynamic balance (November to March)

kWh — heat losses — heat gains

OC - Opaque Conduction
GC - Glazing Conduction
I/V - Infiltration/Ventilation
TI - Thermal Inertia
IG - Internal Gains
SG - Solar Gains
HD - Heating Demand

8300 kWh/period

Thanks to the large glazed windows and winter garden, the solar gains are higher than the heat loss by conduction

In 2005, these results complied with the regulations, so it can be considered a good performance with the materials of the time

(3) Hourly heating demand

20°

Jan Feb Mar Apr May Jun Jul Aug Sep Oct Nov Dec

52% time ON
3.6 kW peak

W/m²
0   25   50

(4) Heating load monotone curve

kW
0% 10% 20% 30% 40% 50%
hours of the year

98% of the time, the heating system works with less than 65% of the full power demand

(5) Heating demand variation

0 20 40 60 80 100

according to number of occupants
2p
3p
4p
5p
6p

according to thermostat set point
17°C
18°C
regulations → 19°C
lower bound of → 20°C
comfort band   21°C
winter target temp. → 23°C
(EN 15251)
highest measured → 25°C
setpoint

according to floor
1st floor
GF

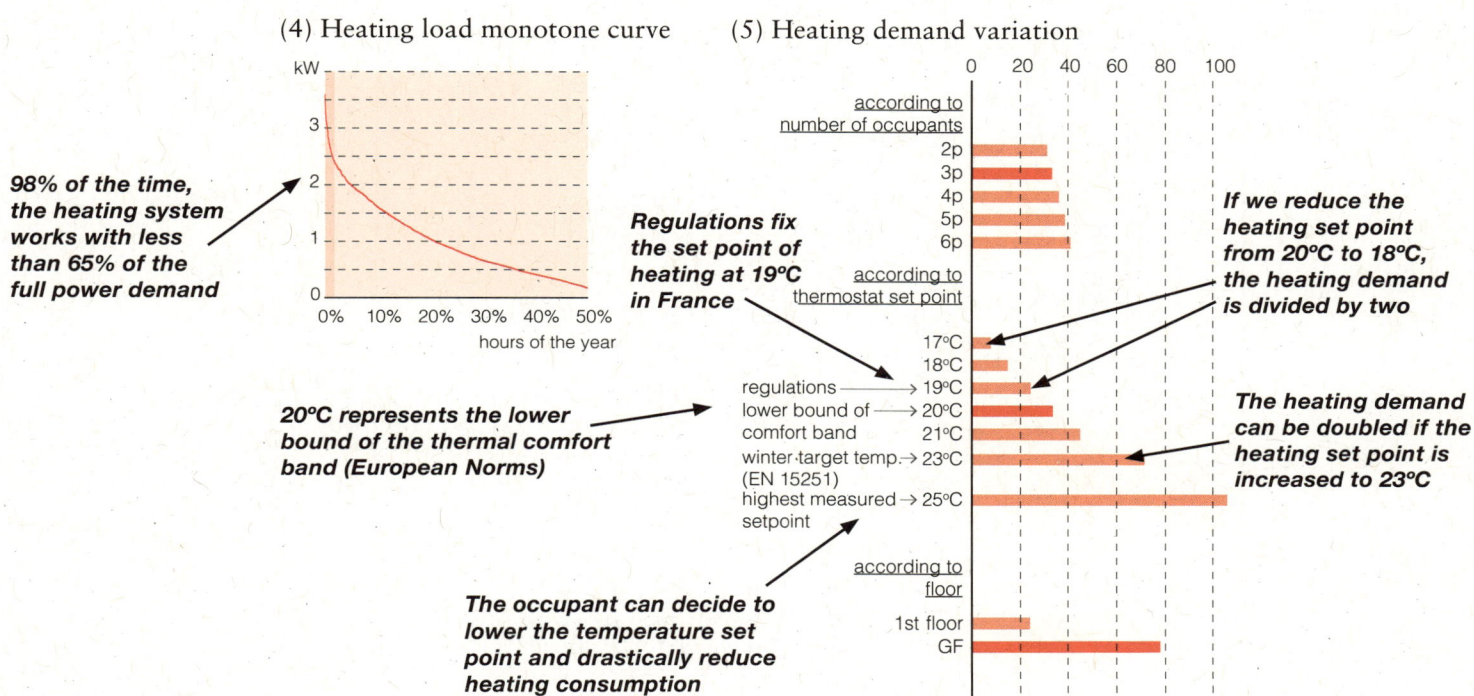

Regulations fix the set point of heating at 19°C in France

20°C represents the lower bound of the thermal comfort band (European Norms)

The occupant can decide to lower the temperature set point and drastically reduce heating consumption

If we reduce the heating set point from 20°C to 18°C, the heating demand is divided by two

The heating demand can be doubled if the heating set point is increased to 23°C

---

(1) Space heating demand: The total heating demand of the houses is 33 kWh/(m²·year), with most of the load happening on the ground floor due to the low insulation toward the ground and the garage. On the first floor the demand is very low, as the spaces behind the winter garden require very little heat input.

(2) Thermodynamic balance (November to March): Looking at the thermodynamic balance, solar gains represent the largest heat contribution, accounting for more than heating and internal gains combined. Overall, these are greater than the losses by glazing conduction.

(3) Hourly heating demand: From the beginning of November until mid-March, heating is necessary almost the entire day. In October and from March to the end of April, heating is required at night.

(4) Heating load monotone curve: Heating could be on for half of the year. However, if nights are not accounted for, that amount of time would be much less. Ninety-eight percent of the time, the heating system works with less than 65% of the full power demand. This allows us to question the size of the equipment.

(5) Heating demand variation: Variation in occupancy is not significant for the heating load. Increasing the set point from 20 to 22°C demands 50% more heating, whereas increasing it to 23°C can almost double the amount. On the other hand, reducing it to 18°C can cut heating requirements in half.

Case Summary
Main Values

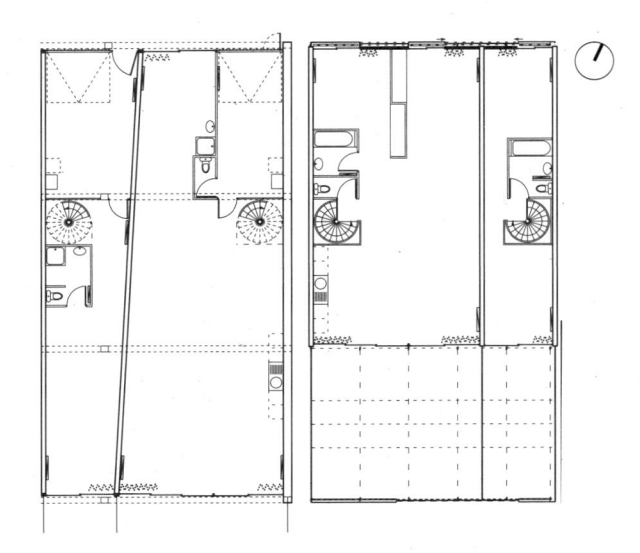

Daylight:
average Daylight Autonomy DA [300]: 46% of the time

all the spaces (considering the standard sizes) exceed the recommendations of EN 17037, except for room S2 where only 43% of the space exceeds 300 lux at least 50% of the time

Temperature and comfort in free-running mode:
above comfort: 1% of the time
within comfort: 49% of the time
below comfort: 50% of the time

average degree·hours
above comfort: 157°C·h

Solar gains and winter garden effect:
(temperature difference between the winter garden and outside)
winter: +1 to +20°C
mid-season: +5 to +17°C

Heating demand:
total: 33 kWh/(m²·year)
peak demand: 3.6 kW
Heating on:
4,604 / 8,760 hours per year
232 / 365 days per year

Cité Manifeste is one of the first projects to integrate greenhouses with collective housing. All units have standard-sized rooms that fulfill the traditional requirements of a house. In addition, the building has two extra spaces per unit, each with a different climatic condition. On the first floor, the greenhouse provides a protected outdoor space that is warmer than the exterior climate all year round (4°C more on average). When the weather is sunny, and during the winter, the greenhouse can be up to 20°C warmer than outdoors. On the ground floor, the extra space provides a darker indoor space toward the center that is particularly fresh in summer and helps cope with peak days. All the standard spaces have abundant daylight. In 2005, when the project was completed, the technical specifications of the materials were not that advanced and regulations were more permissive. The resulting heating demand is moderate, at 33 kWh/m², but represents a good performance for the time. In summer, whereas the first floor behind the winter garden surpasses the ideal overheating target, the ground floor is zero hours above the target. The occupant can choose between varied ambiences. The houses could benefit from several improvements, such as additional shading on the winter garden's south facade to reduce overheating during warmer days; additional operable elements on the winter garden; less transparent shading on the winter garden roof; more transmissive glazing for the rooms facing the winter garden to improve the transfer of the solar heat gains to the indoors; additional insulation on the ground floor, both to the garage and to the ground, would mitigate heat loss; and a fully opaque shading on the first meter of the winter garden to limit the very high summer radiation. The case comparisons of this project are Trignac, which has the same layout as Cité Manifeste, but with improved technical specifications, and a version of Cité Manifeste with up-to-date technical specifications.

Case Study 1

Case Comparison 1
Modification: Same Project in Trignac

(1) Case modification

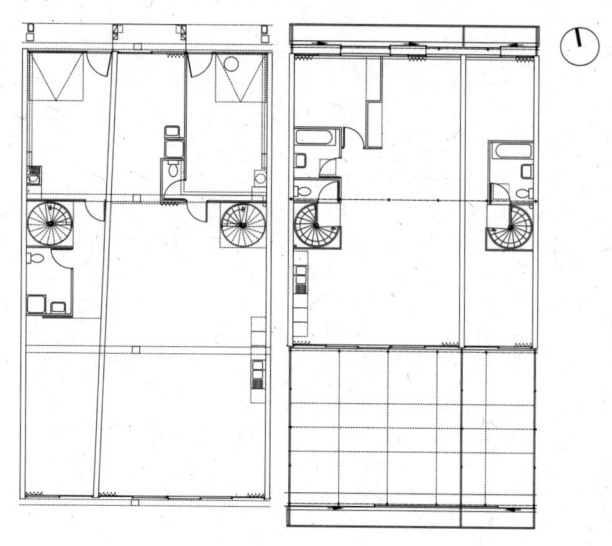

Daylight:
average daylight autonomy DA [300]: 59% of the time (**+13%**)

all the spaces (considering the standard sizes) exceed the recommendations of EN 17037

Temperature and comfort in free-running mode:
above comfort: 0% (**-1%**) of the time
within comfort: 56% (**+7%**) of the time
below comfort: 44% (**-6%**) of the time

The climate is slightly different (more oceanic) than that of Mulhouse (more continental), as it is more temperate

average degree·hours
above comfort: 123°C·h (**-34°C·h**)

Solar gains and winter garden effect:
(temperature difference between the winter garden and outside)
winter: +1 to +11°C
mid-season: +1 to +10°C

Heating demand:
total: 17 kWh/(m²·year) (**-16 kWh/(m²·year)**)
peak demand: 3.0 kW (**-0.6 kW**)
Heating on:
4,688 / 8,760 hours per year (**+84 h**)
234 / 365 days per year (**+2 d**)

Variation compared to the original project

Modifications in detail:
Full ground insulation, with more thermal resistance: U = 0.31 W/(m²·K)
Additional insulation below winter garden and garage: U = 0.31 W/(m²·K)
Additional insulation in all external walls: U = 0.42 W/(m²·K)
Better U-value for glazing and sliding panel frames: U = 2.20 W/(m²·K), SF = 0.43
Better performing winter garden shading: Opacity = 0.75
Additional balconies on south and north facades
The simulation was carried out with the climate of Trignac.

Five years after Cité Manifeste, a similar floor plan was realized in the Trignac district of Saint-Nazaire on the Atlantic coast. The housing estate consists of two buildings with two and three stories. All 23 social housing units are accessed on the ground floor and are either double-oriented or stretch through. The two-story building with thirteen duplexes is almost identical to the floor plan of Cité Manifeste, with one difference: the addition of one-meter-deep balconies on both sides to protect from direct sunlight. In addition, material characteristics have been improved. The double glazing's U-value was doubled from U = 4.4 (W/m²·K) in Cité Manifeste to U = 2.2 (W/m²·K), and the solar factor differs slightly (SF = 0.43 instead of 0.4). The floor slabs and walls were better insulated. In order to understand the impact of the materials used here, as well as the influence of the different climates—Atlantic versus Continental—the results presented from the Cité Manifeste case study are compared to the more recent project in Trignac. The project of Trignac, located in a milder climate, performs better during all seasons: The heating demand is divided in half, and overheating hours are reduced, meeting the ideal target. Inside the winter garden, temperatures are also milder.

96 Case Study 1

Case Comparison 1
Sun and Daylight

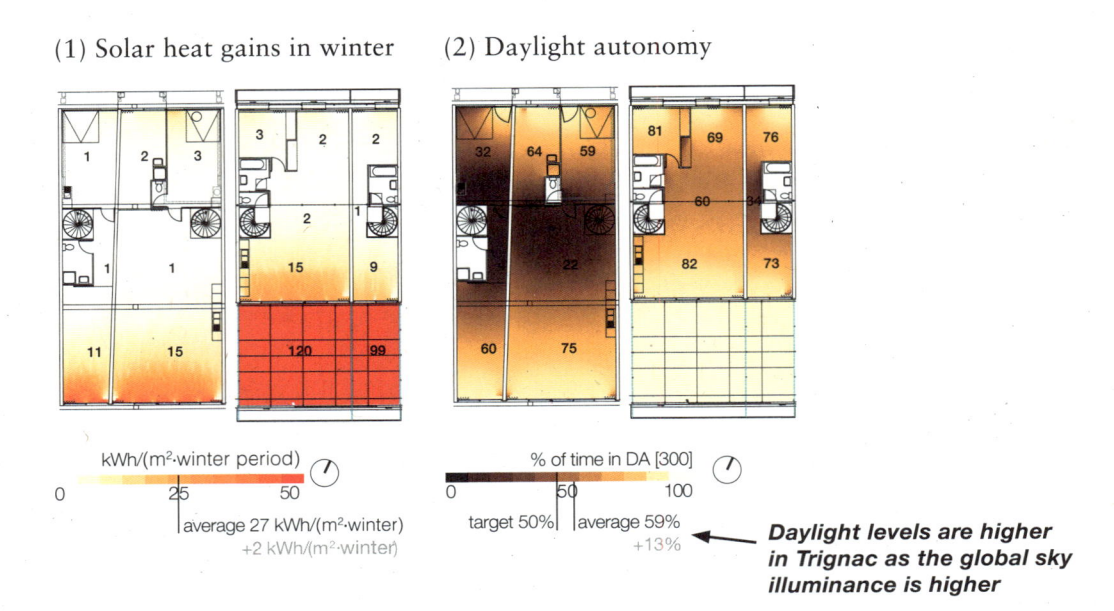

(1) Solar heat gains in winter

(2) Daylight autonomy

kWh/(m²·winter period)
0   25   50
average 27 kWh/(m²·winter)
+2 kWh/(m²·winter)

% of time in DA [300]
0   50   100
target 50% average 59%
+13%

Daylight levels are higher in Trignac as the global sky illuminance is higher

(1) Solar heat gains in winter: The solar radiation of Trignac is more intense than in Mulhouse, which is translated into slightly higher values indoors, both in winter and in summer.

(2) Daylight Autonomy: Daylight provision is also slightly higher in the climate of Trignac, as the average daylight autonomy is 13% higher. In this case, all the rooms exceed the recommendations of EN, even the entire living room on the ground floor.

Case Study 1

Case Comparison 1
Typical Days

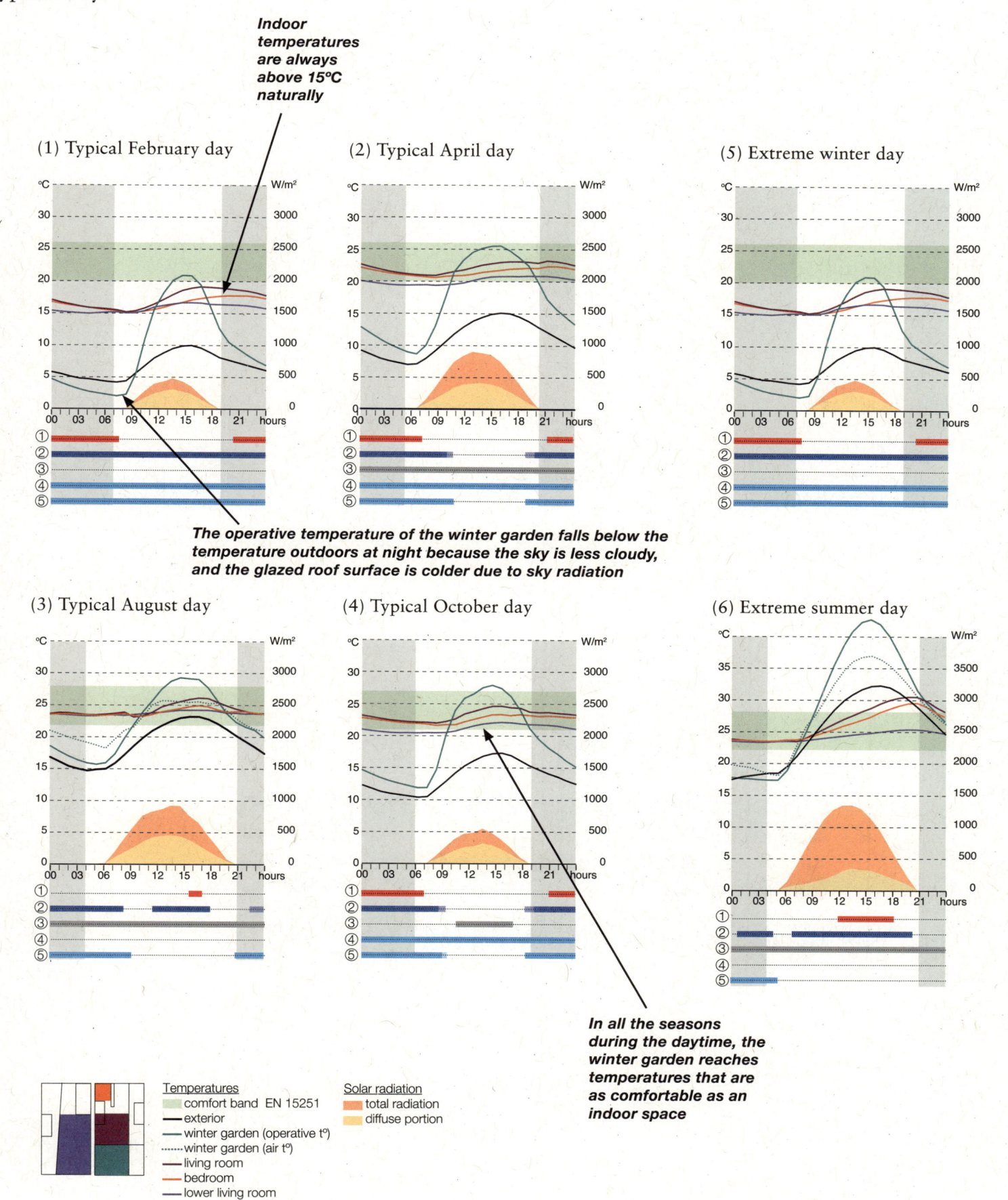

Indoor temperatures are always above 15°C naturally

(1) Typical February day

(2) Typical April day

(5) Extreme winter day

The operative temperature of the winter garden falls below the temperature outdoors at night because the sky is less cloudy, and the glazed roof surface is colder due to sky radiation

(3) Typical August day

(4) Typical October day

(6) Extreme summer day

In all the seasons during the daytime, the winter garden reaches temperatures that are as comfortable as an indoor space

Temperatures
- comfort band EN 15251
- exterior
- winter garden (operative t°)
- winter garden (air t°)
- living room
- bedroom
- lower living room

Solar radiation
- total radiation
- diffuse portion

(1)–(4) Typical days: In this case, temperatures of the built project in Mulhouse are not shown because outdoor temperatures are also different and a direct comparison does not make sense. Winter temperatures in free-running mode are on average 3–4°C higher than in Mulhouse. However, outdoor temperatures are also higher by the same amount. During the spring, conditions are very similar in both cases. During the summer, indoor temperatures are similar, but the winter garden in Trignac's climate is hotter during peak hours. Air temperature remains around 25–26°C, and the real operative temperature would be slightly closer to these values. During the fall, conditions in Trignac's climate are significantly better, as all indoor temperatures are in comfort naturally, and even the winter garden's temperatures are in comfort during the daytime.

(5)/(6) Extreme days: During an extreme summer day, the higher exterior radiation in Trignac translates into higher indoor operative temperatures (by 1–3°C). During an extreme winter day, indoor conditions are more favorable in Trignac as the first floor has about 5°C more than in Mulhouse, where the first floor has about 2–3°C more.

Case Comparison 1
Thermal Comfort Conditions

(1) Overheating evaluation

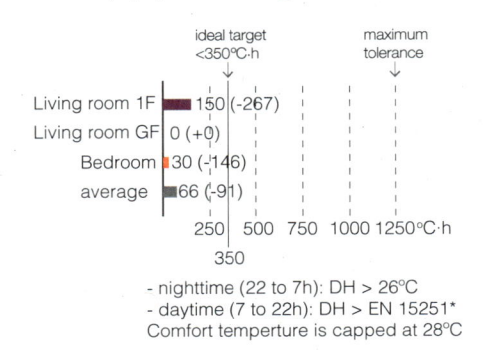

ideal target <350°C·h | maximum tolerance

Living room 1F 150 (-267)
Living room GF 0 (+0)
Bedroom 30 (-146)
average 66 (-91)

250 500 750 1000 1250 °C·h
350

- nighttime (22 to 7h): DH > 26°C
- daytime (7 to 22h): DH > EN 15251*
Comfort temperture is capped at 28°C

(2) Winter garden UTCI (Universal Thermal Climate Index)

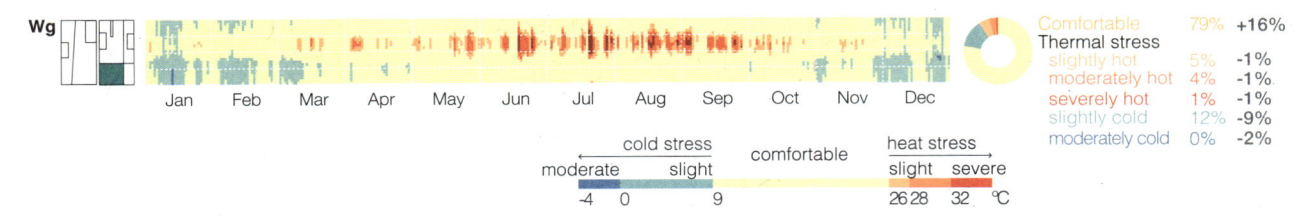

Wg

Jan Feb Mar Apr May Jun Jul Aug Sep Oct Nov Dec

cold stress | comfortable | heat stress
moderate slight | slight severe
-4 0 9 26 28 32 °C

Comfortable 79% +16%
Thermal stress
slightly hot 5% -1%
moderately hot 4% -1%
severely hot 1% -1%
slightly cold 12% -9%
moderately cold 0% -2%

(3) Resulting thermal comfort per room

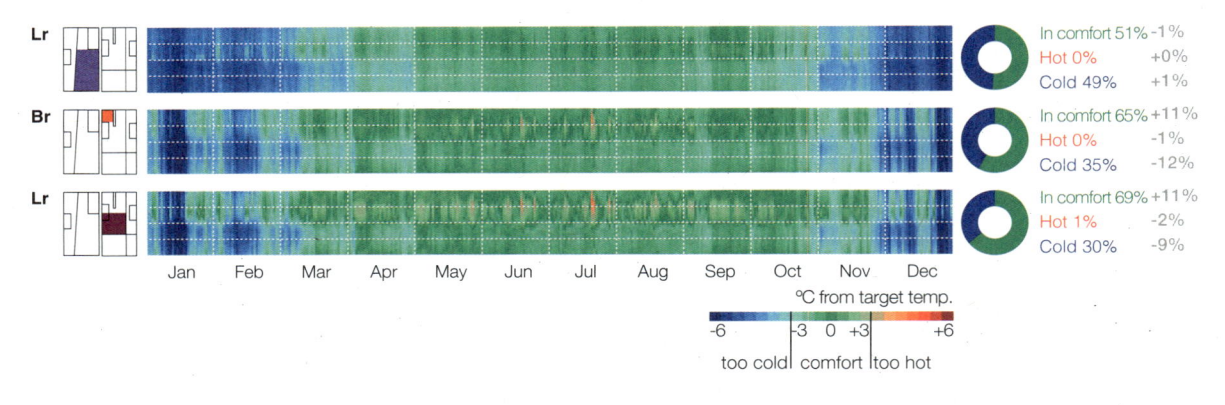

Lr

Br

Lr

Jan Feb Mar Apr May Jun Jul Aug Sep Oct Nov Dec

°C from target temp.
-6 -3 0 +3 +6
too cold | comfort | too hot

In comfort 51% -1%
Hot 0% +0%
Cold 49% +1%

In comfort 65% +11%
Hot 0% -1%
Cold 35% -12%

In comfort 69% +11%
Hot 1% -2%
Cold 30% -9%

(1) Overheating evaluation: The overheating conditions are also much better, as the degree hours are largely below the ideal target, even in the living room on the first floor. Only during extreme days is the indoor temperature slightly too hot.

(2) Winter garden UTCI (Universal Thermal Climate Index): The milder climate of Trignac combined with the improved shading also creates better conditions in the winter garden. The time when temperatures are comfortable for an outdoor space increase by 16%, as the thermal stress from both heat and cold is reduced.

(3) Resulting thermal comfort per room: Time in comfort on the upper floor increases by 11% compared to the case of Mulhouse, as the time with both hot and cold hours is reduced. Only the living room is 1% of the time above comfort—the rest of the spaces is 0% of the time—which is very low.

Case Study 1

Case Comparison 1
Active Mode

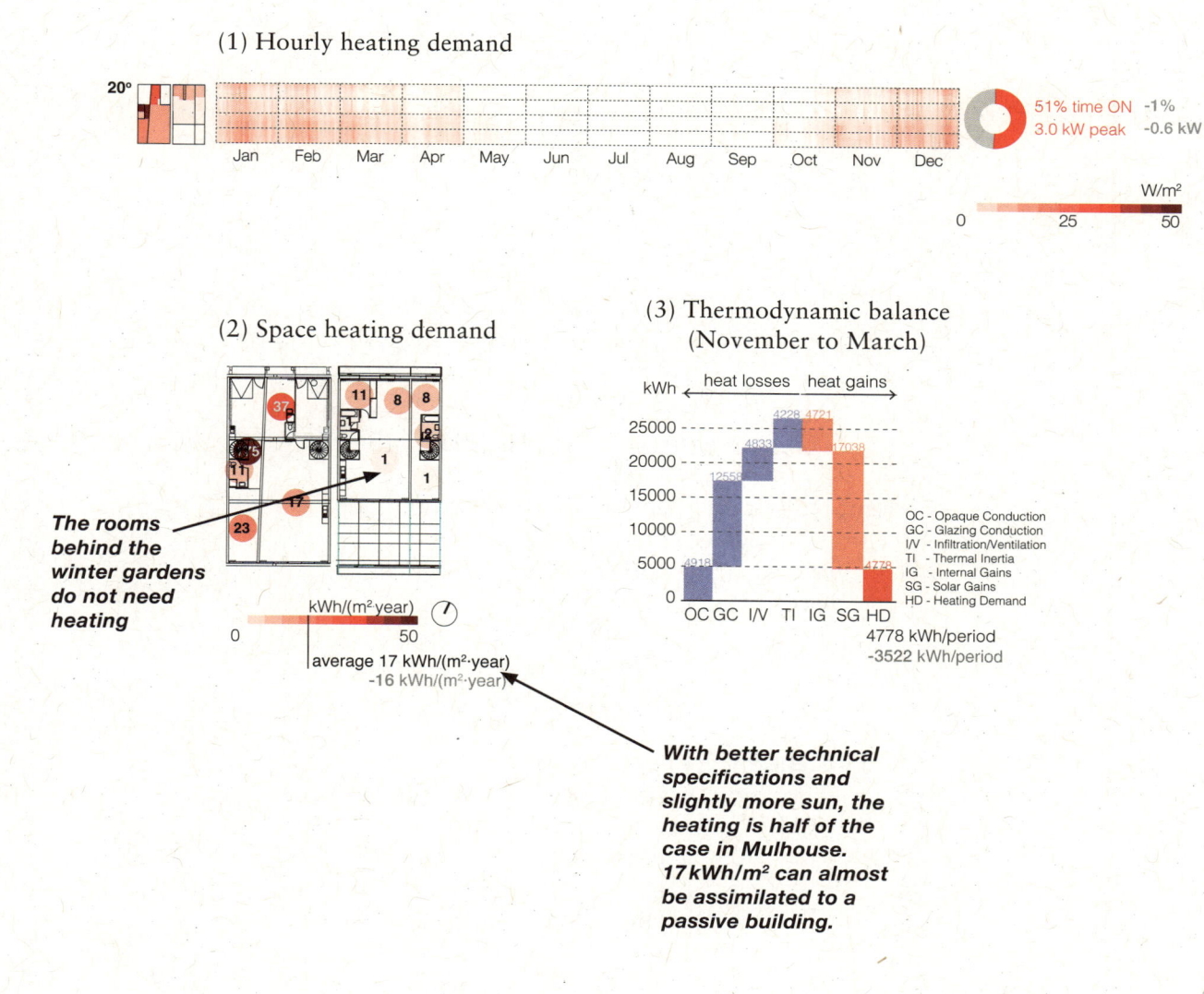

(1) Hourly heating demand

Jan Feb Mar Apr May Jun Jul Aug Sep Oct Nov Dec

51% time ON -1%
3.0 kW peak -0.6 kW

W/m²
0   25   50

(2) Space heating demand

(3) Thermodynamic balance
(November to March)

The rooms behind the winter gardens do not need heating

kWh/(m²·year)
0   50
average 17 kWh/(m²·year)
-16 kWh/(m²·year)

kWh   heat losses   heat gains
25000
20000
15000
10000
5000
0
    OC GC I/V TI IG SG HD

OC - Opaque Conduction
GC - Glazing Conduction
I/V - Infiltration/Ventilation
TI - Thermal Inertia
IG - Internal Gains
SG - Solar Gains
HD - Heating Demand

4778 kWh/period
-3522 kWh/period

With better technical specifications and slightly more sun, the heating is half of the case in Mulhouse. 17 kWh/m² can almost be assimilated to a passive building.

(1) Hourly heating demand: Demand is mainly from early November to late April. The period is similar to Mulhouse, but with much less intensity.

(2) Space heating demand: Heating demand is cut down to almost half compared to the original case. Peak demand is also slightly lower (14%). The reduction of the demand happens evenly across the house.

(3) Thermodynamic balance (November to March): All heat losses are lower and solar gains are higher than in Mulhouse, which explains the reduced heating demand. The heat gains largely depend on the solar input.

Case Comparison 2
Modification: Same Project with 2024 Specifications

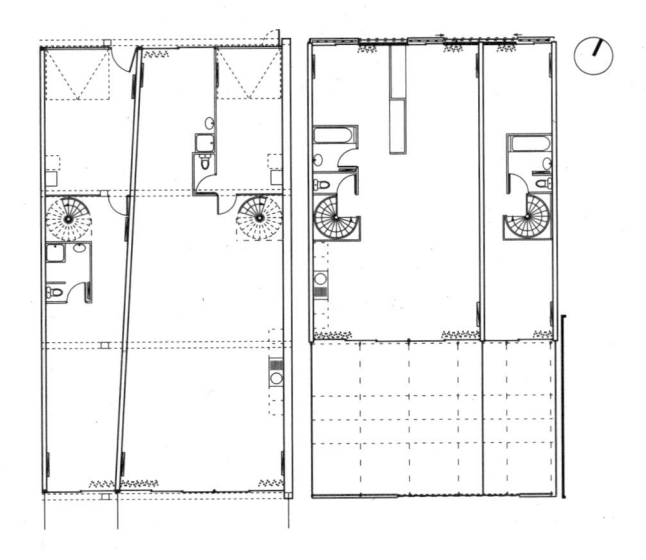

Daylight:
average daylight autonomy DA [300]: 54% (**+8%**) of the time

all the spaces (considering the standard sizes) exceed the recommendations of EN 17037

Temperature and comfort in free-running mode:
above comfort: 1% of the time
within comfort: 66% (**+17%**) of the time
below comfort: 33% (**-17%**) of the time

average degree·hours
above comfort: 66°C·h (**-91°C·h**)

Solar gains and winter garden effect:
(temperature difference between the winter garden and outside)
winter: +1 to +11°C
mid-season: +5 to +11°C

Heating demand:
total: 16 kWh/(m²·year) (**-17 kWh/(m²·year)**)
peak demand: 2.9 kW (**-0.7 kW**)
Heating on:
3,685 / 8,760 hours per year (**-919 h**)
210 / 365 days per year (**-22 d**)

Variation compared to the original project

Modifications in detail:
Ground insulation extended to the whole slab: U = 0.41 W/(m²·K)
Improved insulation on the whole heated envelope: U = 0.20 W/(m²·K)
Improved windows on the heated envelope: U = 1.40 W/(m²·K)
More transmissive glazing: SF = 0.65, VLT = 0.7
More opaque shading in the winter garden roof: Opacity = 0.75
Additional shading on the winter garden facade: Opacity = 0.75

In this scenario, the architectural project remains the same but the technical specifications were improved to meet up-to-date standards: insulation was improved with a higher thermal resistance in all opaque and glazed elements and added in places where it was missing (the ground and toward unheated spaces), the glazing was made more transmissive, and the shading more opaque. As a result, the increased insulation helped to cut the heating demand to less than half, meeting contemporary passive standards. As there are considerably less solar gains in summer, overheating is reduced both in the winter garden and in adjacent spaces, making overheating meet the ideal up-to-date target. Also, more daylight is transmitted through the glazing, bringing more light into the deeper spaces. The same improvements would be achieved in Trignac with the same update of specifications. These results show that the project itself is still efficient and it only needs an upgrade of materials to up-to-date standards to meet contemporary targets.

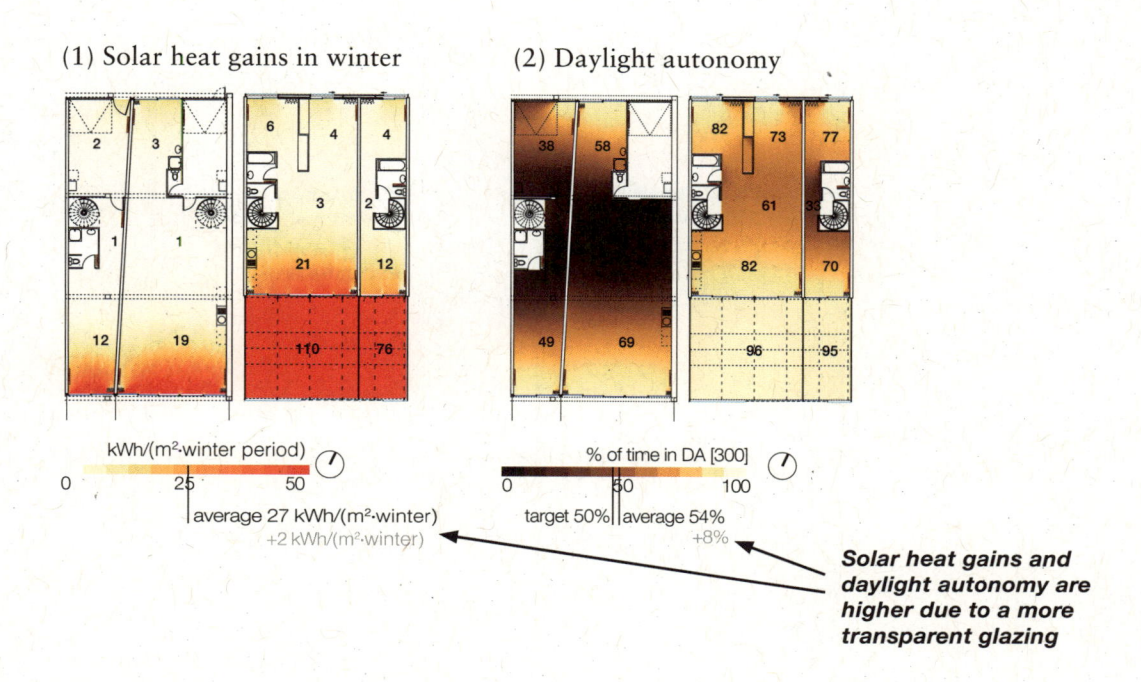

Case Comparison 2
Sun and Daylight

(1) Solar heat gains in winter

(2) Daylight autonomy

kWh/(m²·winter period)
0   25   50

% of time in DA [300]
0   50   100

average 27 kWh/(m²·winter)
+2 kWh/(m²·winter)

target 50% average 54%
+8%

Solar heat gains and daylight autonomy are higher due to a more transparent glazing

(1) Solar heat gains in winter: Glazings are 63% more transmissive of heat and 75% more transmissive of light, but the solar curtain is 23% less transmissive of heat as it now blocks 80% of the total incoming radiation. Overall, solar heat gains in summer are less, whereas there are slightly more in winter.

(2) Daylight Autonomy: Daylight levels are considerably higher (8% more daylight autonomy) due to the more transmissive glazing.

Case Comparison 2
Typical Days

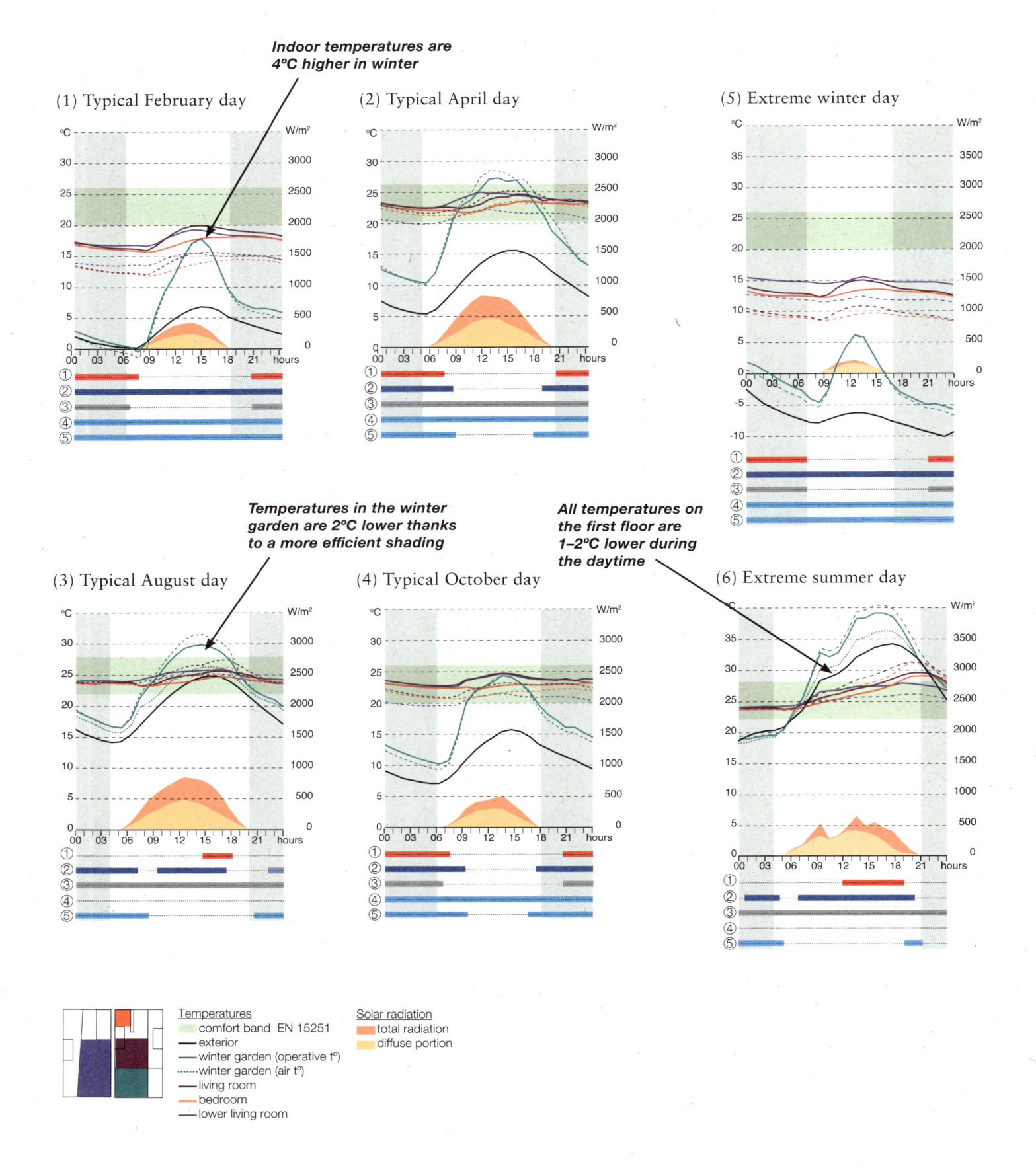

(1) Typical February day

Indoor temperatures are 4°C higher in winter

(2) Typical April day

(5) Extreme winter day

(3) Typical August day

Temperatures in the winter garden are 2°C lower thanks to a more efficient shading

(4) Typical October day

All temperatures on the first floor are 1–2°C lower during the daytime

(6) Extreme summer day

Temperatures
- comfort band EN 15251
- exterior
- winter garden (operative t°)
- winter garden (air t°)
- living room
- bedroom
- lower living room

Solar radiation
- total radiation
- diffuse portion

(1)–(4) Typical days: During the winter, indoor operative temperatures are 4°C higher on average both day and night, as the insulation and improved glazing better retain the heat gains. During the summer, in the daytime temperatures are 1–2°C lower on the upper floor and 0.5°C higher on the ground floor. In the winter garden, temperatures are 1–2°C lower thanks to a more performative shading. During the spring, temperatures on the ground floor are about 2°C higher due to the higher insulation. In the living room on the upper floor, temperatures are 1°C higher during the daytime due to the more transmissive glazing. During the fall, temperatures are 1–2°C higher on the first floor and 3°C higher on the ground floor.

(5)/(6) Extreme days: During an extreme summer day, the winter garden and the first floor are 1–2°C cooler during daytime, whereas the ground floor is 1°C warmer. The latter remains within comfort even when outdoor temperatures peak at 34°C. During an extreme winter day, indoor temperatures on the first floor are 4–5°C higher than in the realized project, and never drop below 12.5°C when the outdoors is between -10°C and -2°C. The ground floor has higher temperatures as it is less exposed to sky radiation, and is maintained at 15°C. In the winter garden, conditions are similar.

Case Comparison 2
Resulting Thermal Comfort and Active Mode

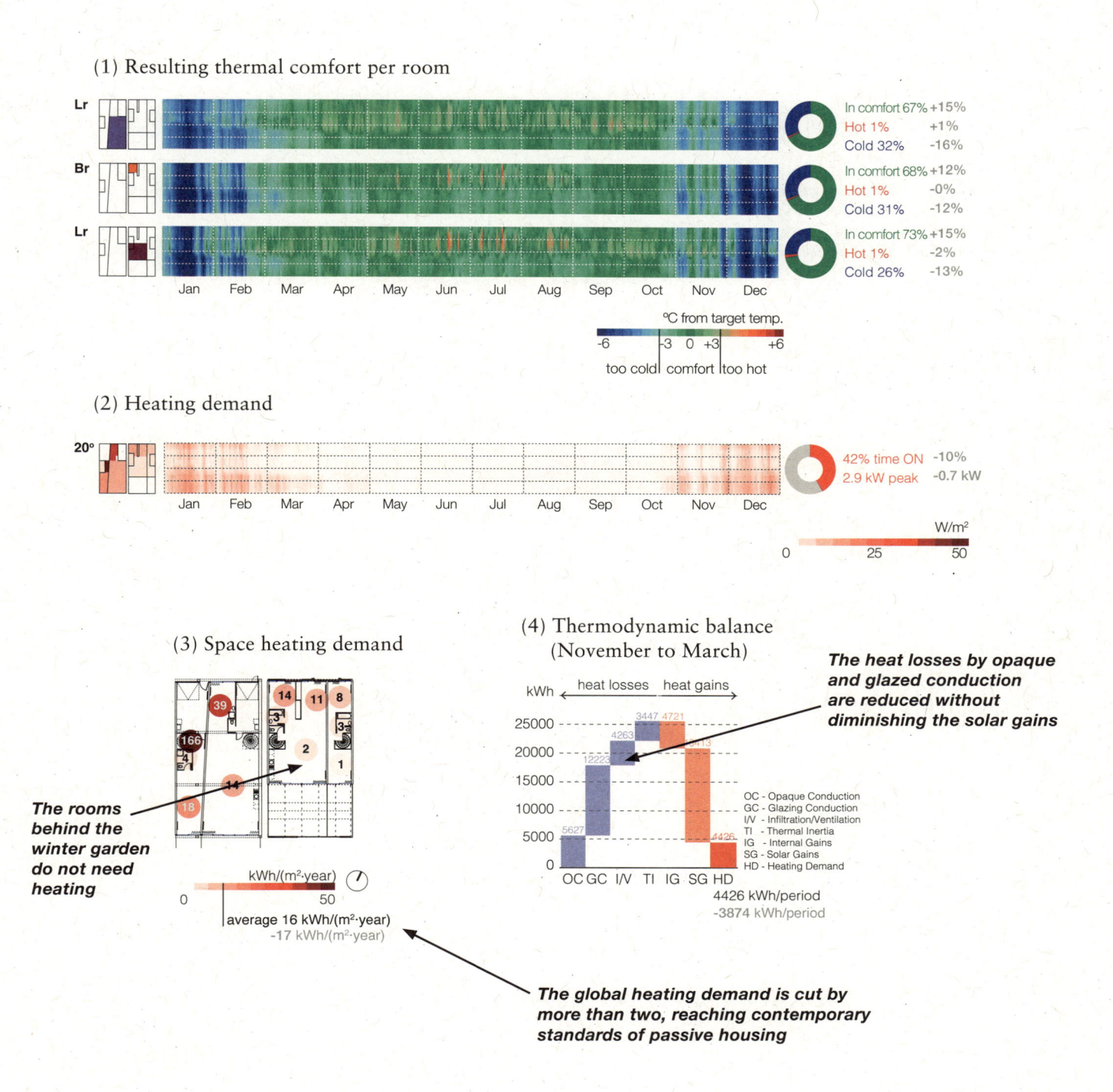

(1) Resulting thermal comfort per room

Lr — In comfort 67% +15% / Hot 1% +1% / Cold 32% -16%
Br — In comfort 68% +12% / Hot 1% -0% / Cold 31% -12%
Lr — In comfort 73% +15% / Hot 1% -2% / Cold 26% -13%

°C from target temp.
-6 -3 0 +3 +6
too cold | comfort | too hot

(2) Heating demand

20°

42% time ON -10%
2.9 kW peak -0.7 kW

W/m²
0   25   50

(3) Space heating demand

kWh/(m²·year)
0   50
average 16 kWh/(m²·year)
-17 kWh/(m²·year)

The rooms behind the winter garden do not need heating

(4) Thermodynamic balance (November to March)

kWh ← heat losses   heat gains →

OC - Opaque Conduction
GC - Glazing Conduction
I/V - Infiltration/Ventilation
TI - Thermal Inertia
IG - Internal Gains
SG - Solar Gains
HD - Heating Demand

OC GC I/V TI IG SG HD
4426 kWh/period
-3874 kWh/period

The heat losses by opaque and glazed conduction are reduced without diminishing the solar gains

The global heating demand is cut by more than two, reaching contemporary standards of passive housing

(1) Resulting thermal comfort per room: Overall, time in comfort is increased by 15% throughout the house, as the time below comfort is drastically reduced. Spaces are naturally comfortable 68–73% of the time. All the spaces in the house have temperatures above comfort only 1% of the time. However, the severity is more pronounced on the upper floor.

(2)–(3) Space heating demand: The overall heating demand is cut down to 48% reaching 16 kWh/m², which corresponds to today's standards for passive housing. This means that the design is very efficient, since we can achieve up-to-date standards just by improving the performance of the materials. The reduction of the demand happens evenly across the house.

(4) Thermodynamic balance (November to March): Adding insulation and improving the glazing specifications reduces all heat losses, without diminishing solar gains. This results in an overall reduction of the heating demand.

Case Comparison 2
Thermal Comfort Conditions

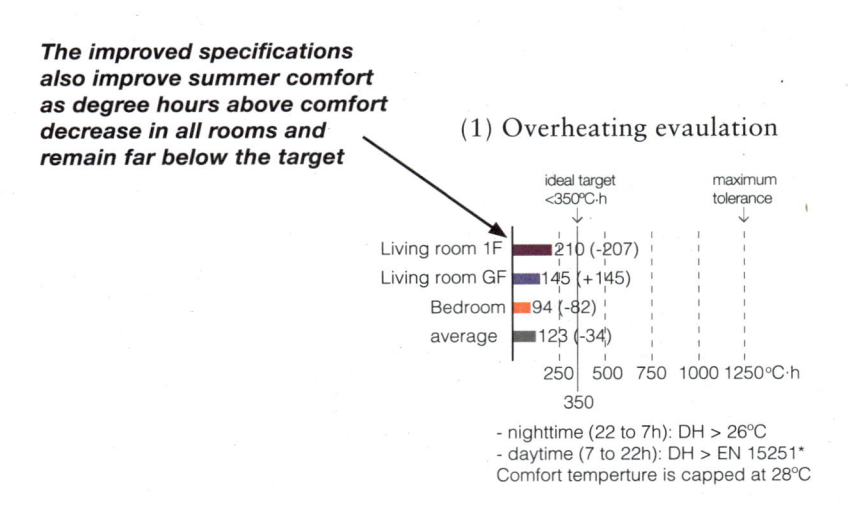

The improved specifications also improve summer comfort as degree hours above comfort decrease in all rooms and remain far below the target

(1) Overheating evaulation

	ideal target <350°C·h	maximum tolerance
Living room 1F	210 (-207)	
Living room GF	145 (+145)	
Bedroom	94 (-82)	
average	123 (-34)	

250 | 500 750 1000 1250 °C·h
350

- nighttime (22 to 7h): DH > 26°C
- daytime (7 to 22h): DH > EN 15251*
Comfort temperture is capped at 28°C

(2) Winter garden UTCI (Universal Thermal Climate Index)

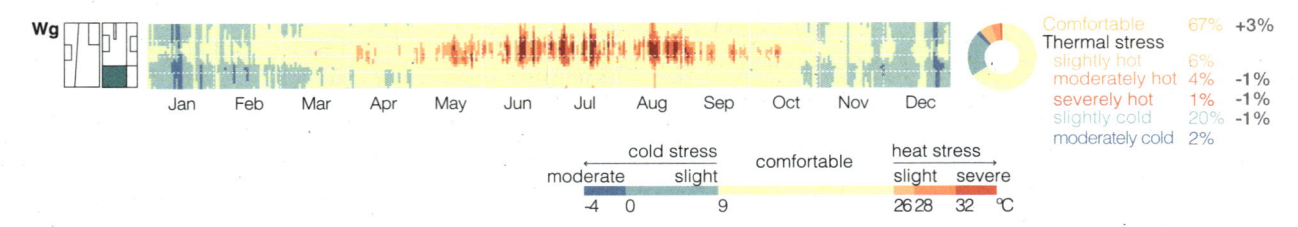

Wg

Jan Feb Mar Apr May Jun Jul Aug Sep Oct Nov Dec

cold stress — moderate slight — comfortable — heat stress slight severe
-4 0 9 26 28 32 °C

Comfortable 67% +3%
Thermal stress
slightly hot 6%
moderately hot 4% -1%
severely hot 1% -1%
slightly cold 20% -1%
moderately cold 2%

1) Overheating evaulation: Overheating across the house is improved as now all the rooms fall largely below the ideal target of 350°C·h above 26°C. On average, overheating hours were reduced by 22%.

(2) Winter garden UTCI (Universal Thermal Climate Index): Improving the shading specifications reduces heat stress 2% of the time, which is significant. Severe and moderate heat stress are both reduced by 1%.

05　Case Study 2: Student and Social Housing, Ourcq-Jaurès, Paris, France

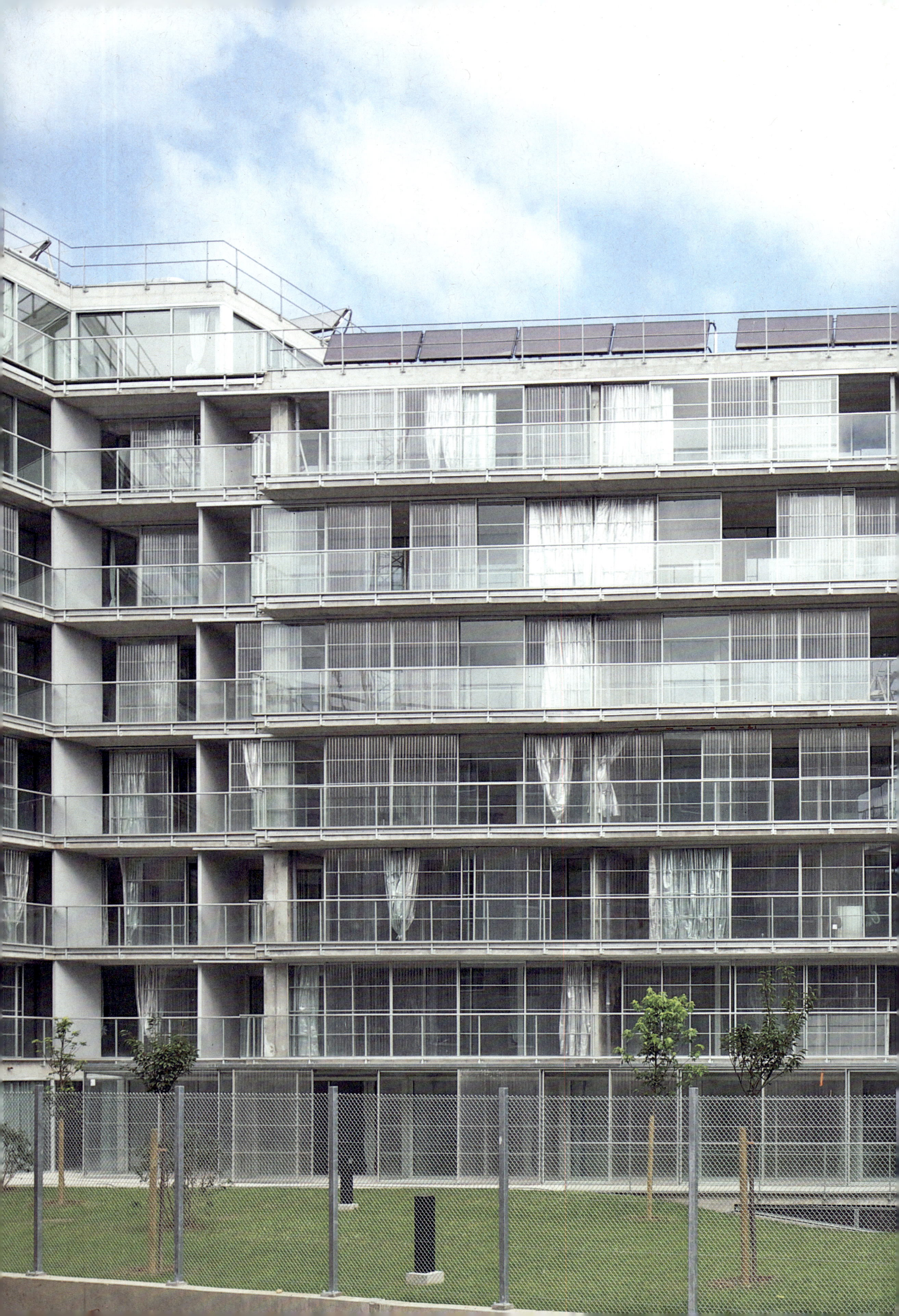

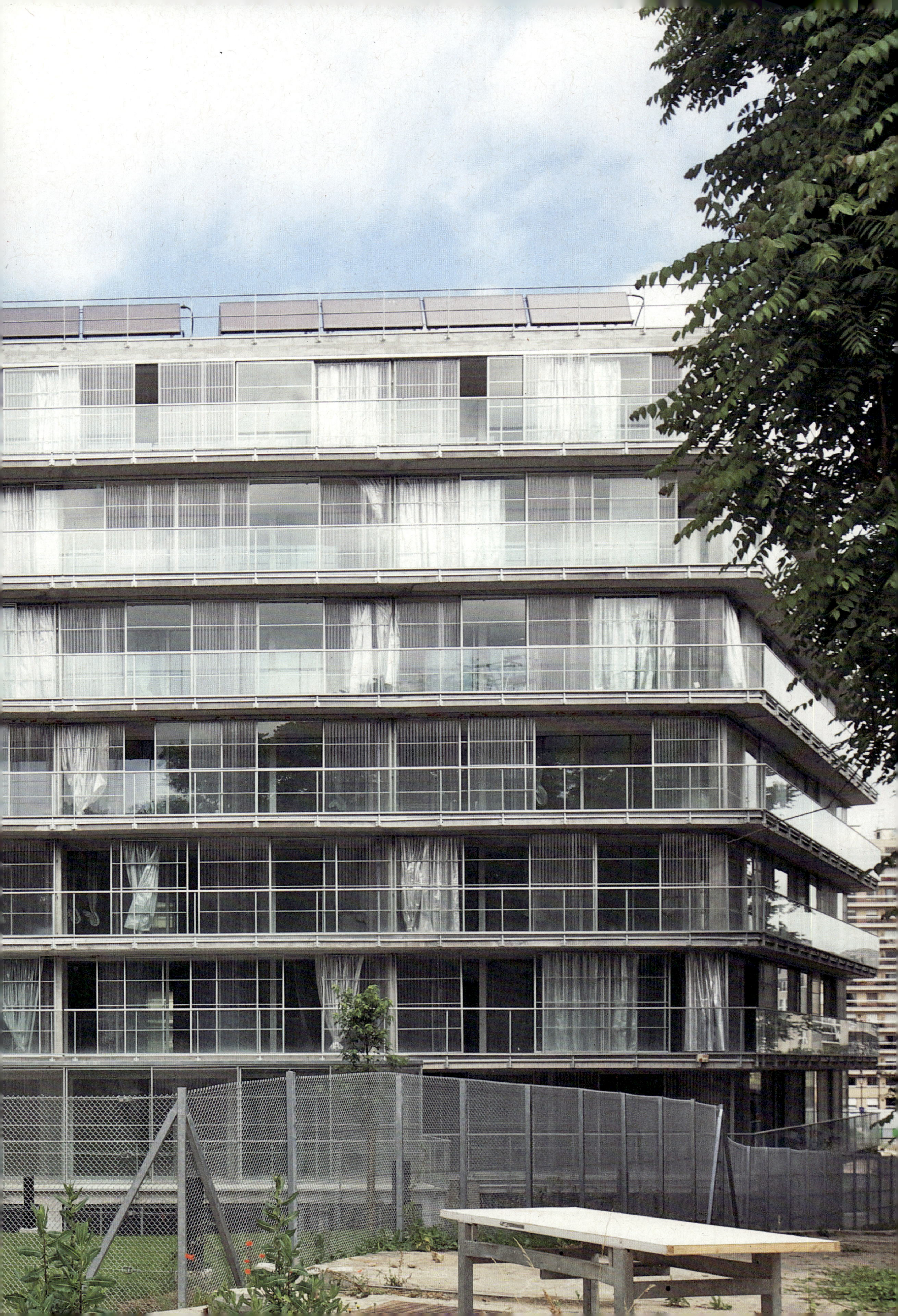

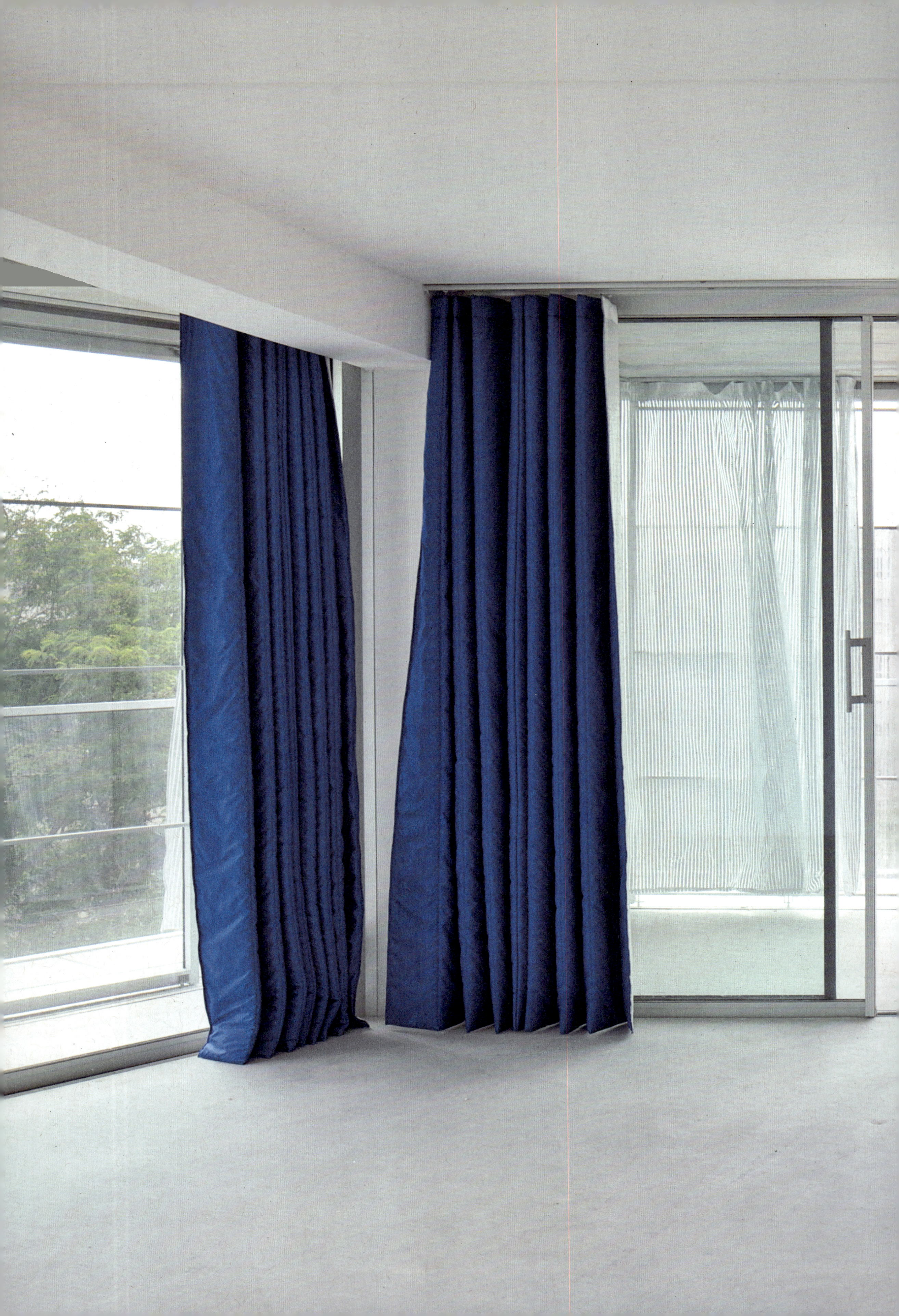

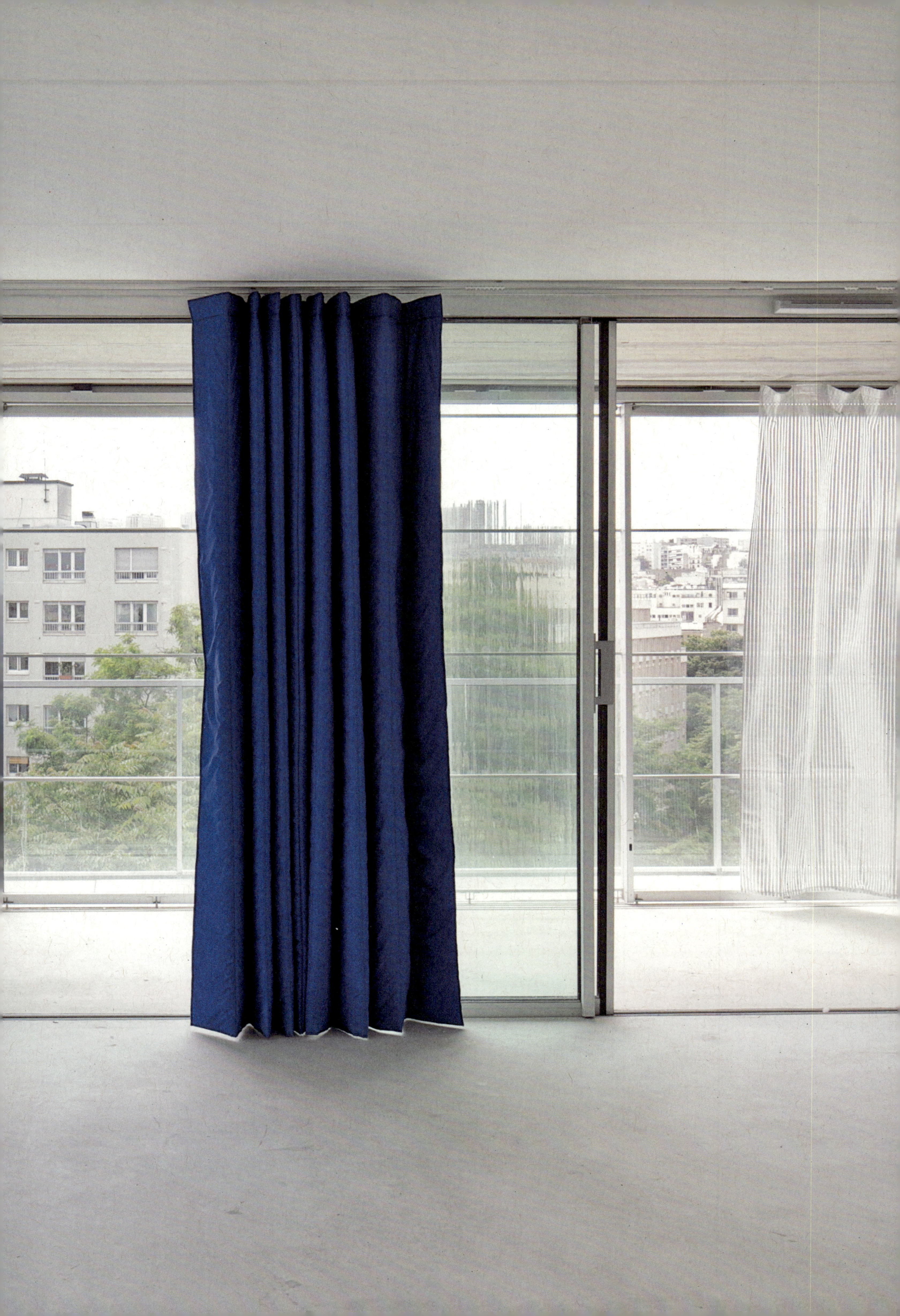

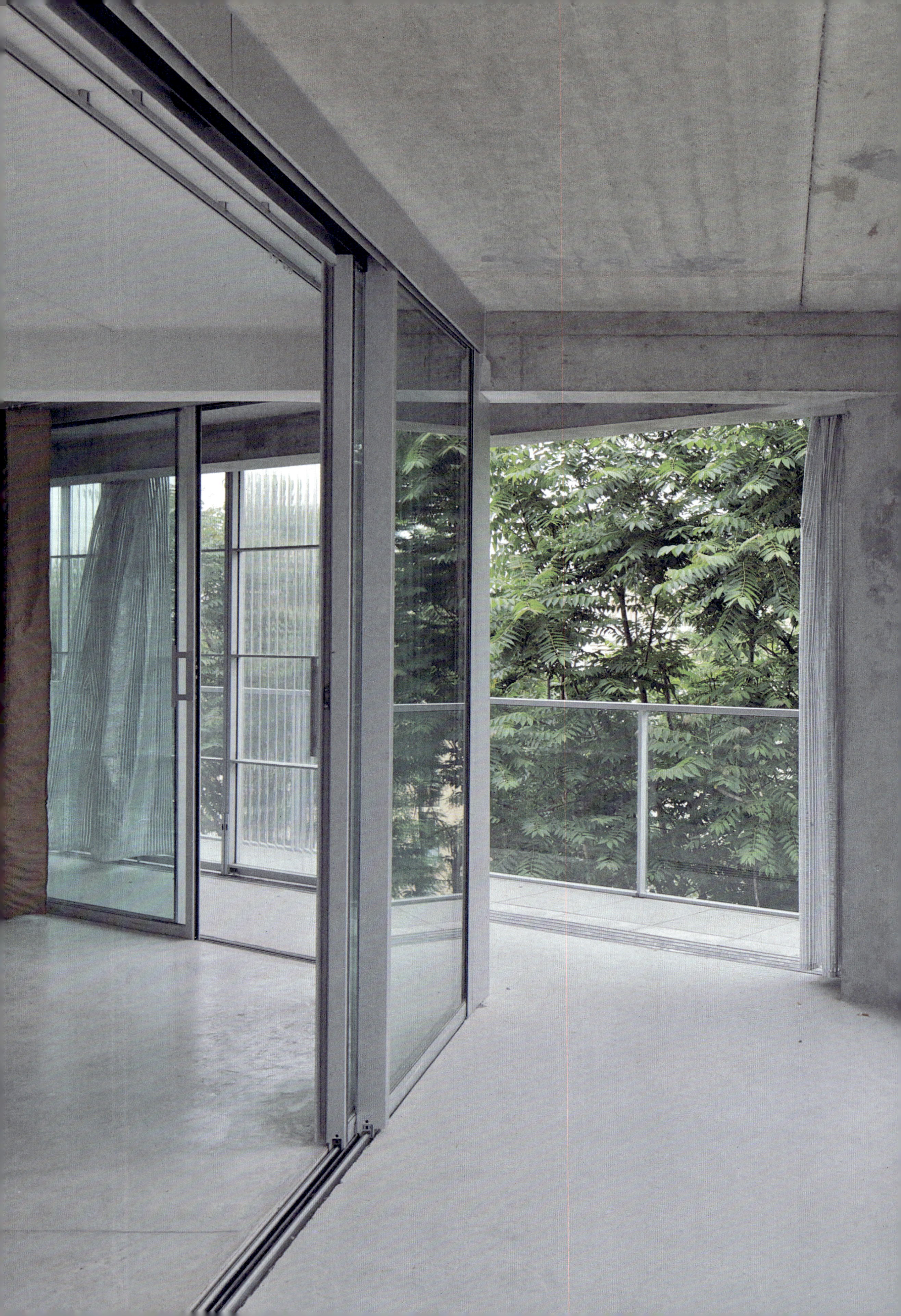

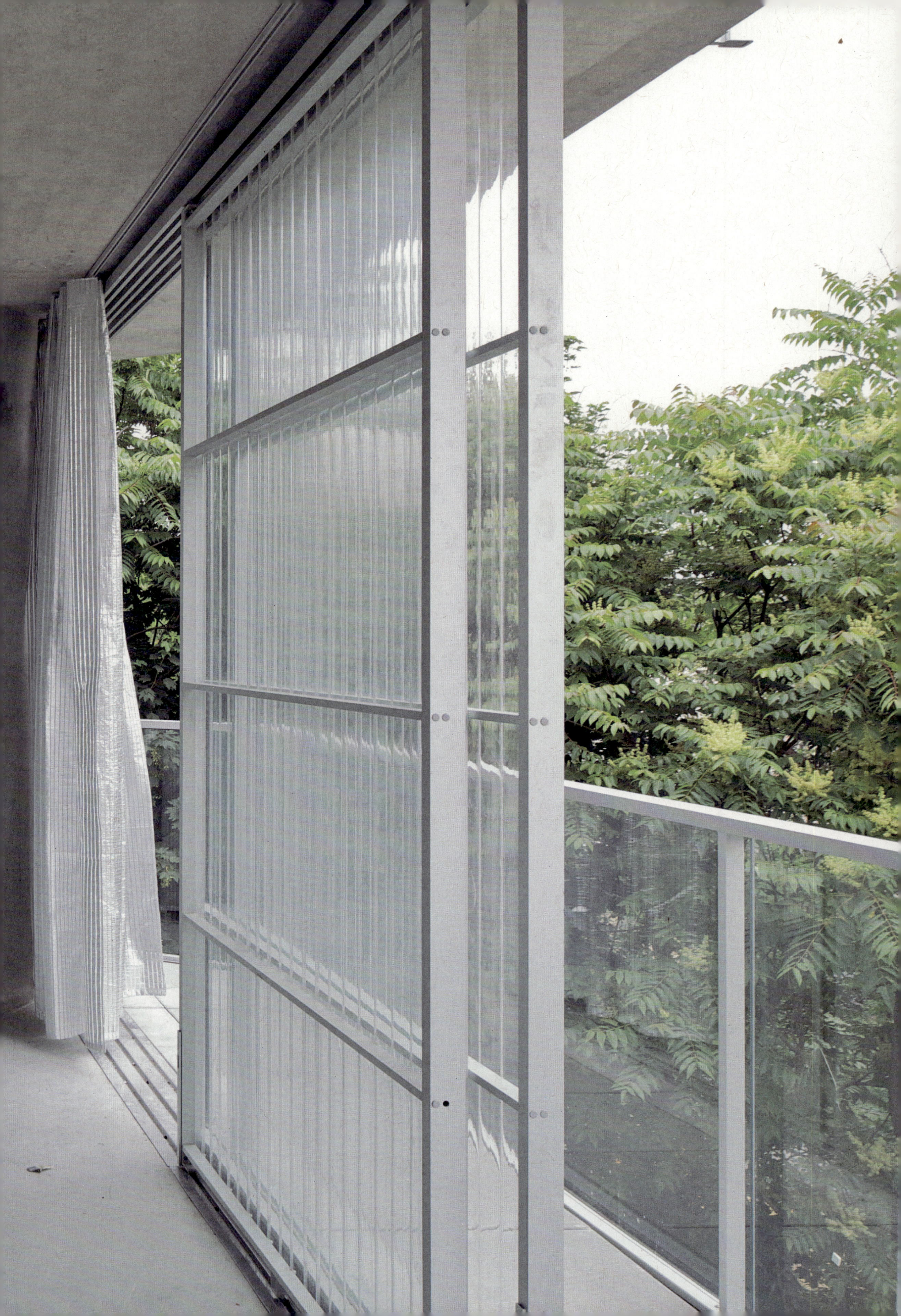

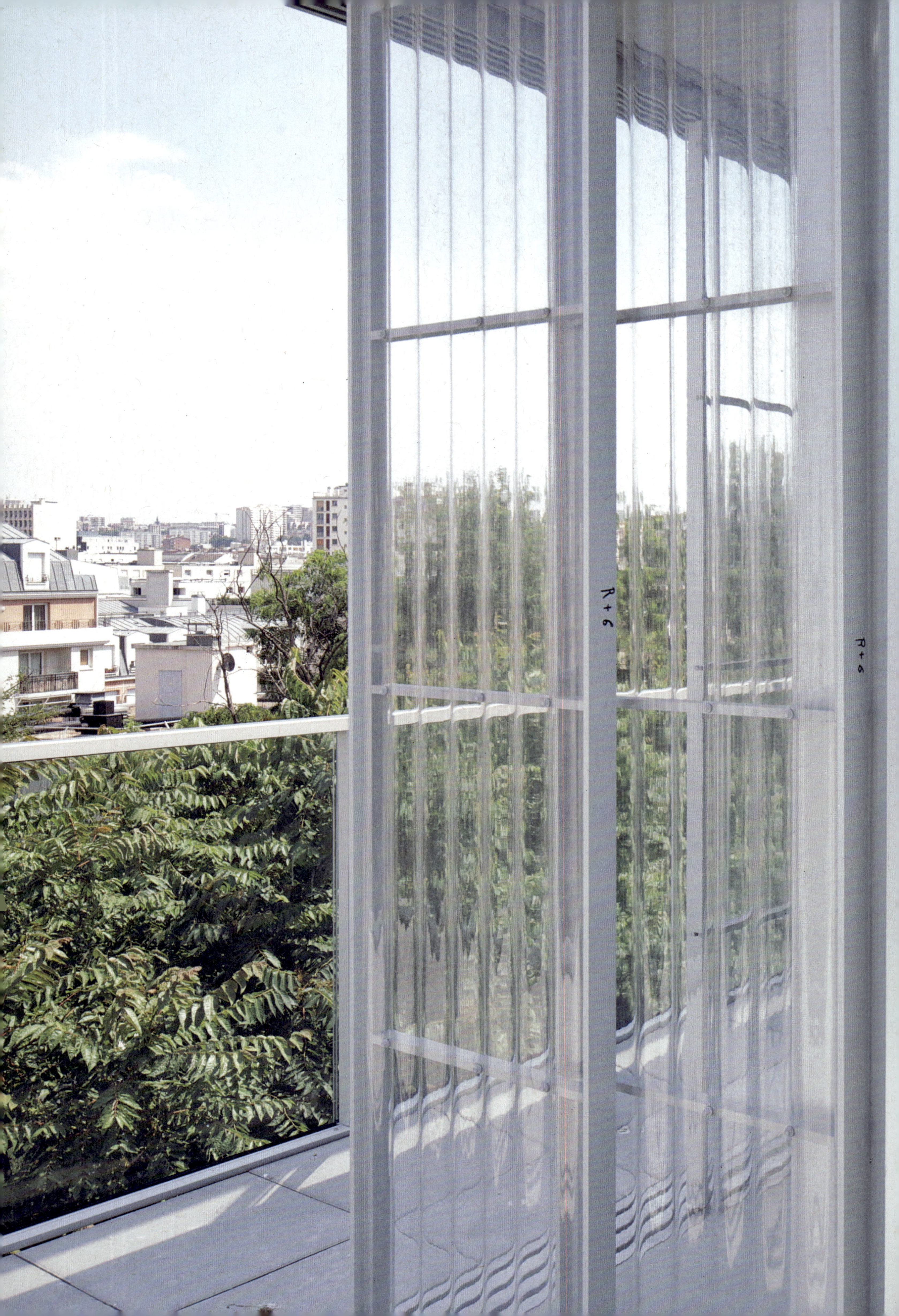
R + 6
R + 6

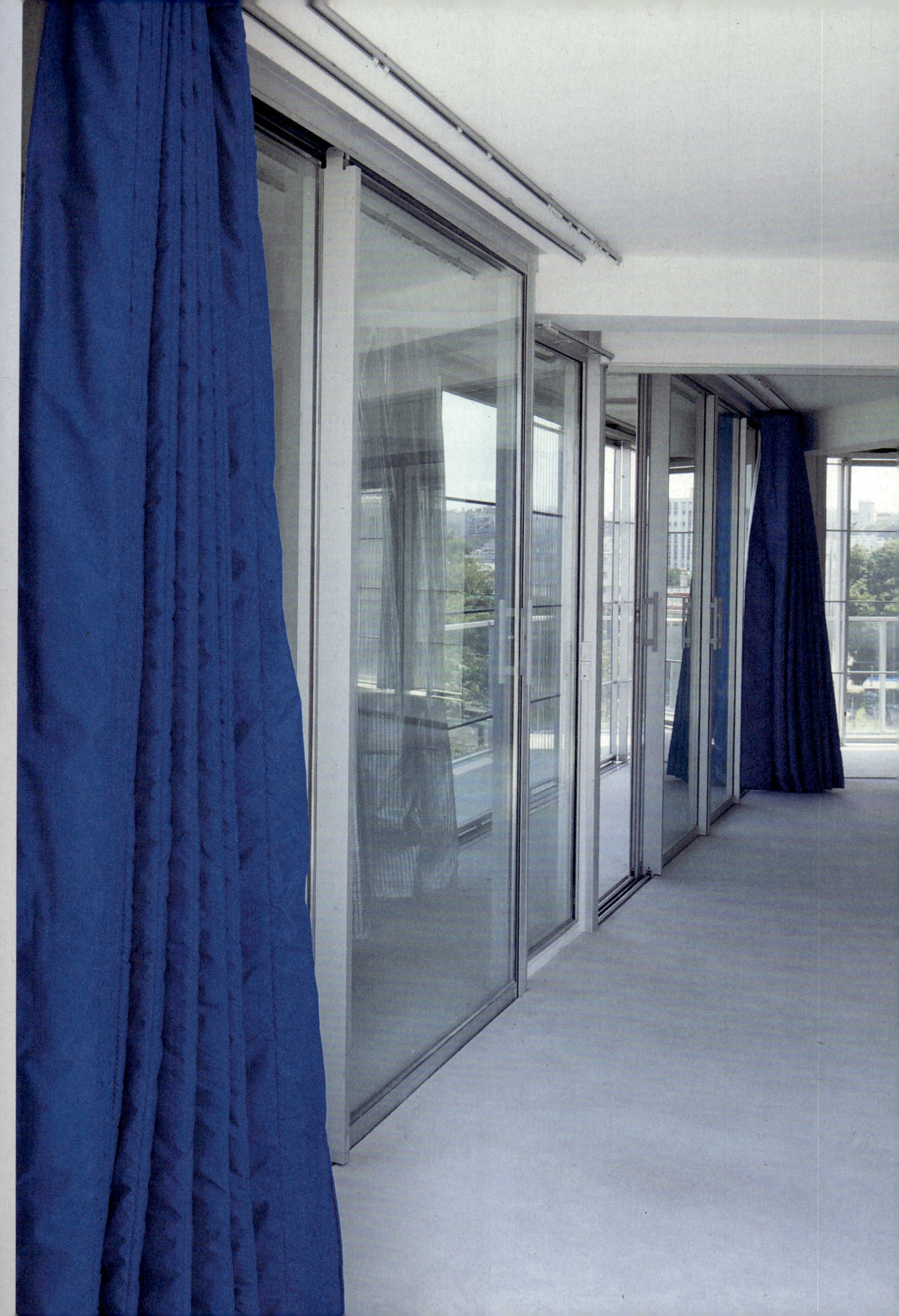

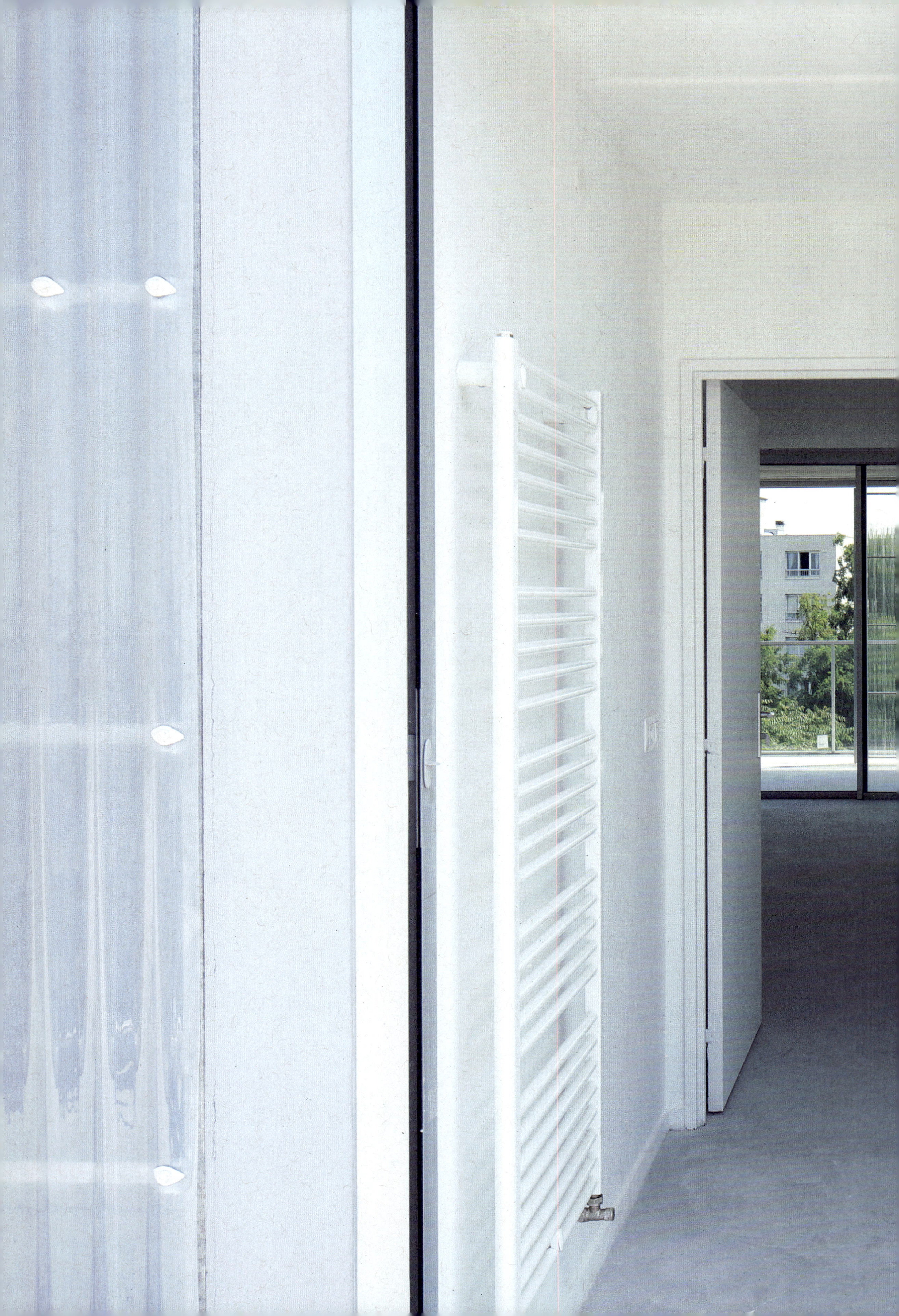

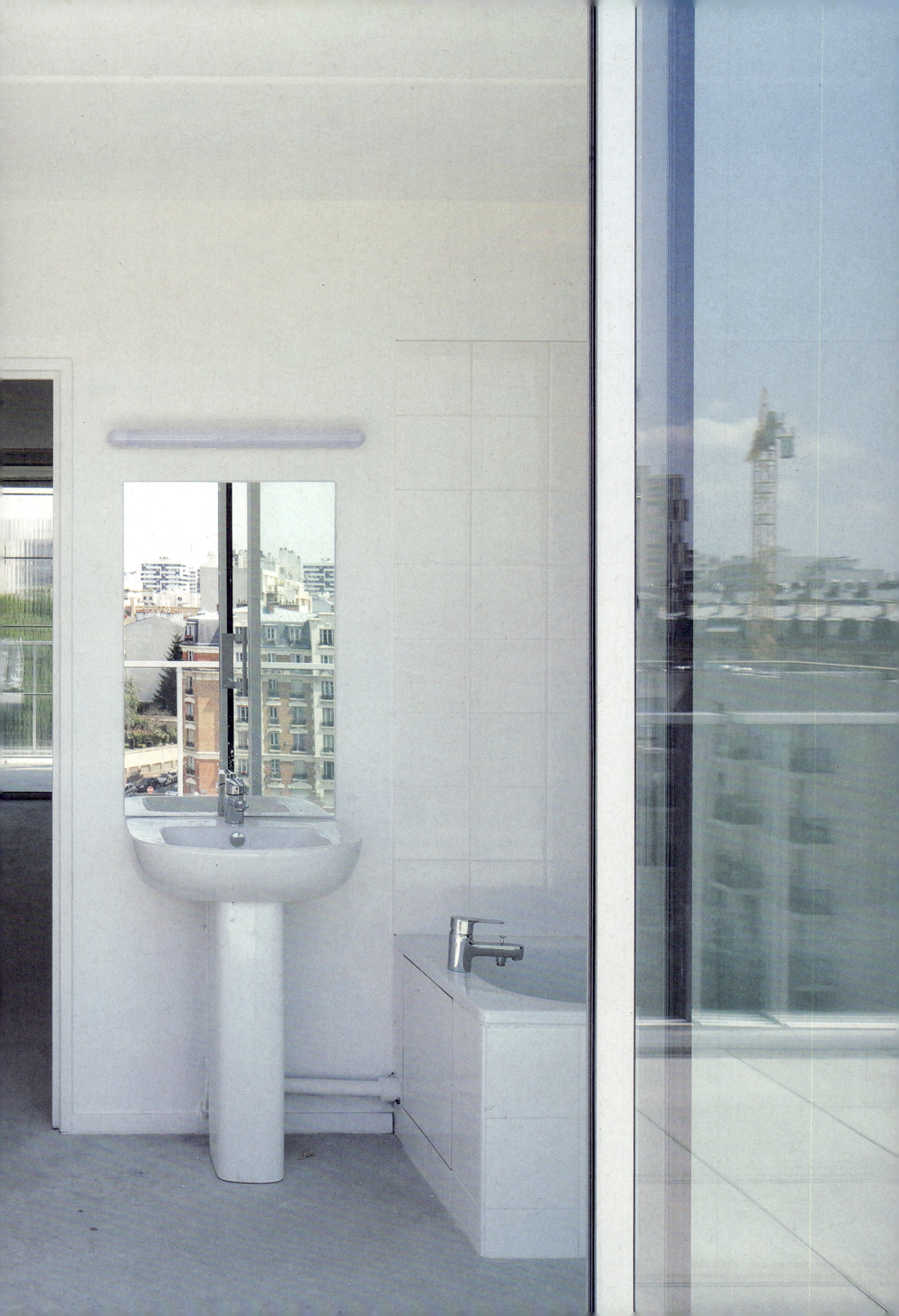

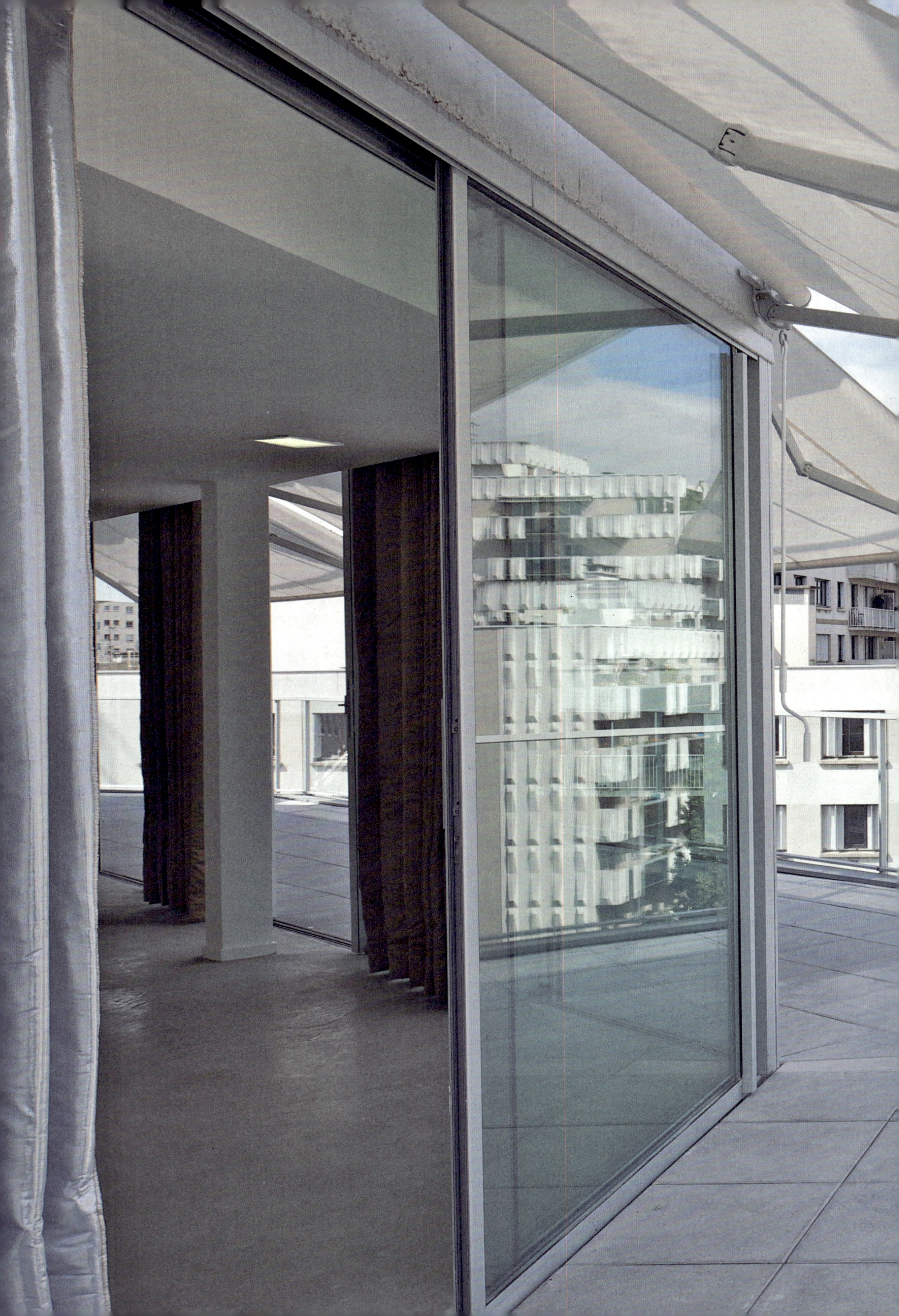

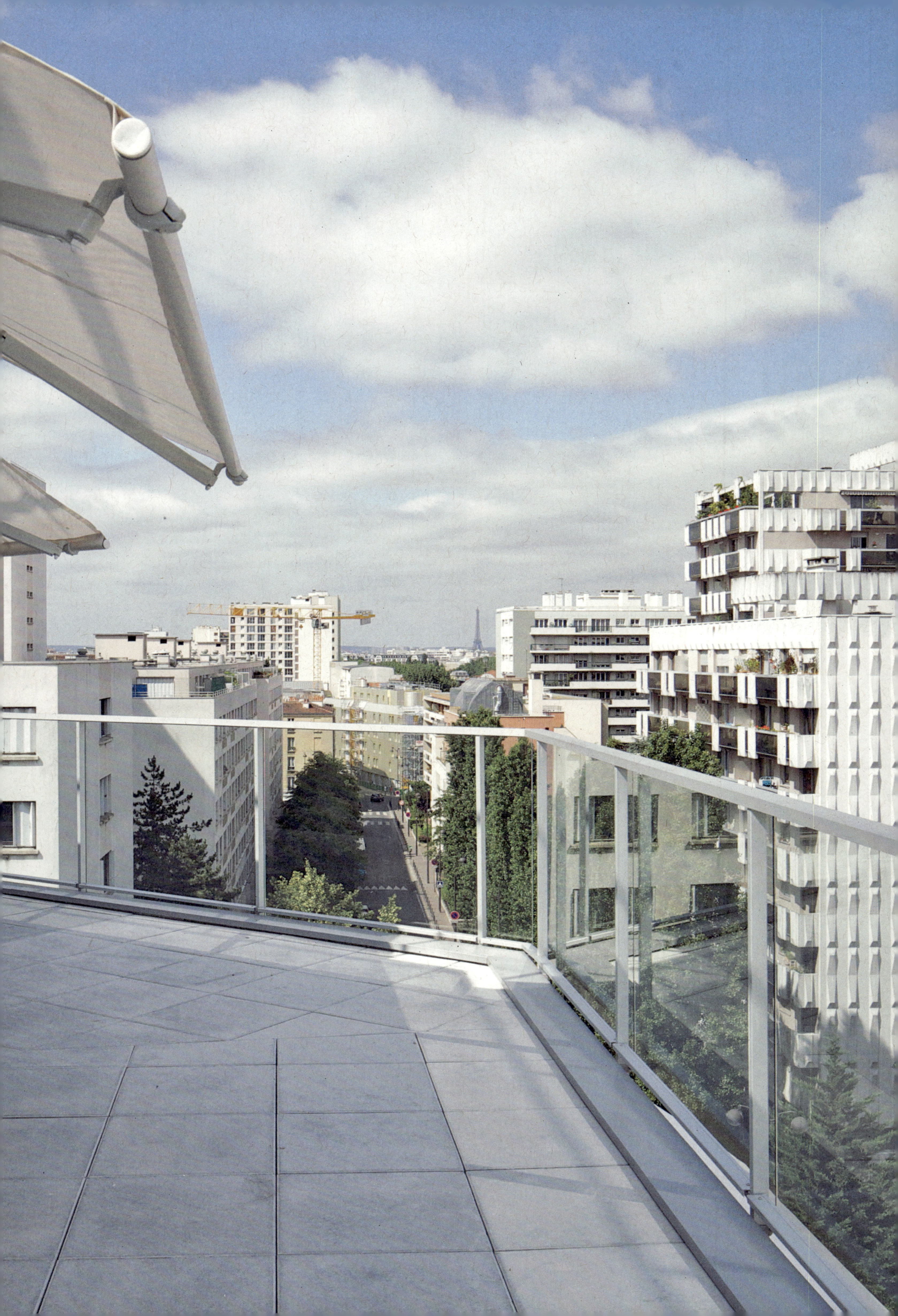

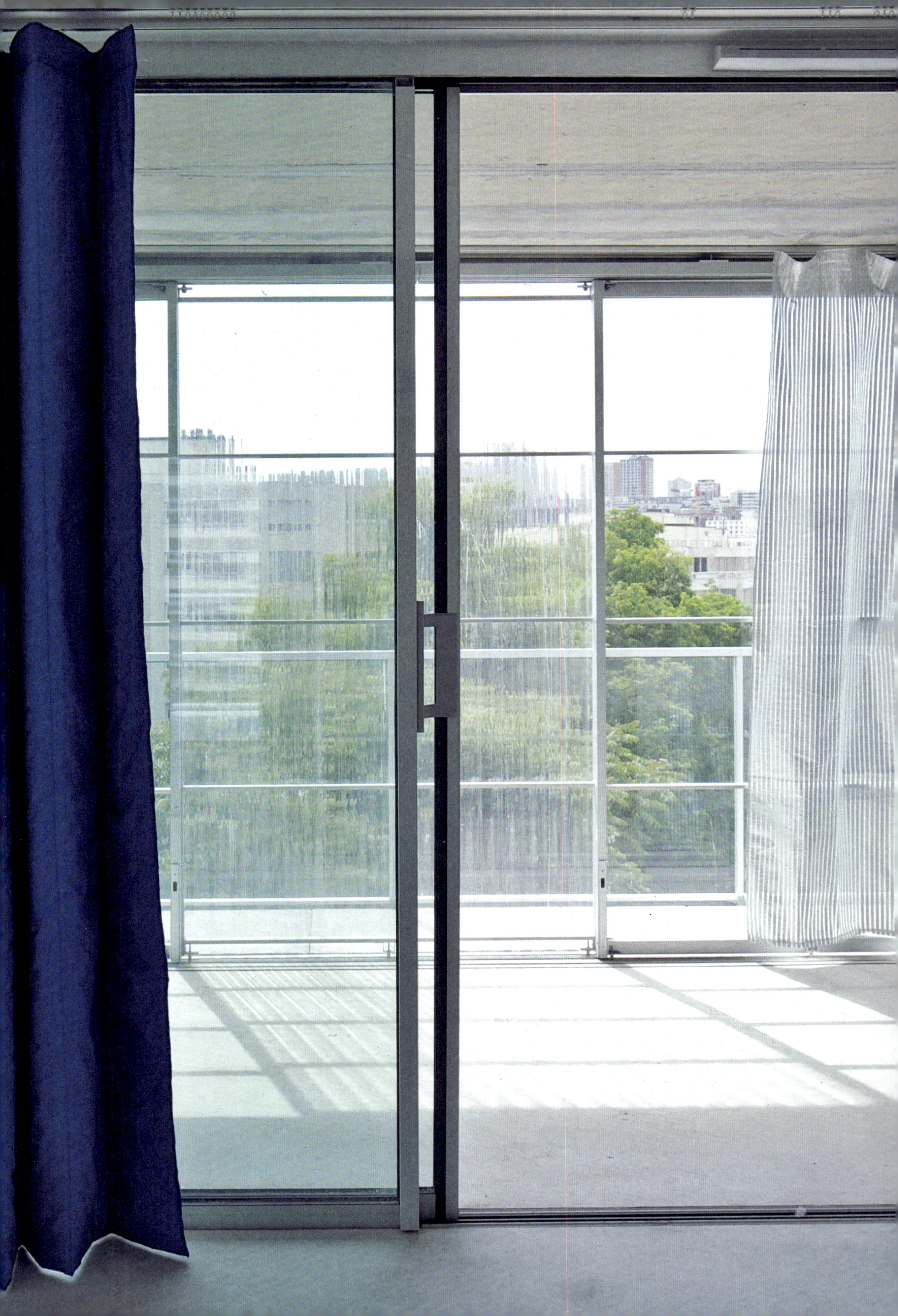

Student and Social Housing Ourcq-Jaurès

Paris
France
2014

(1) Site Plan 1/1000

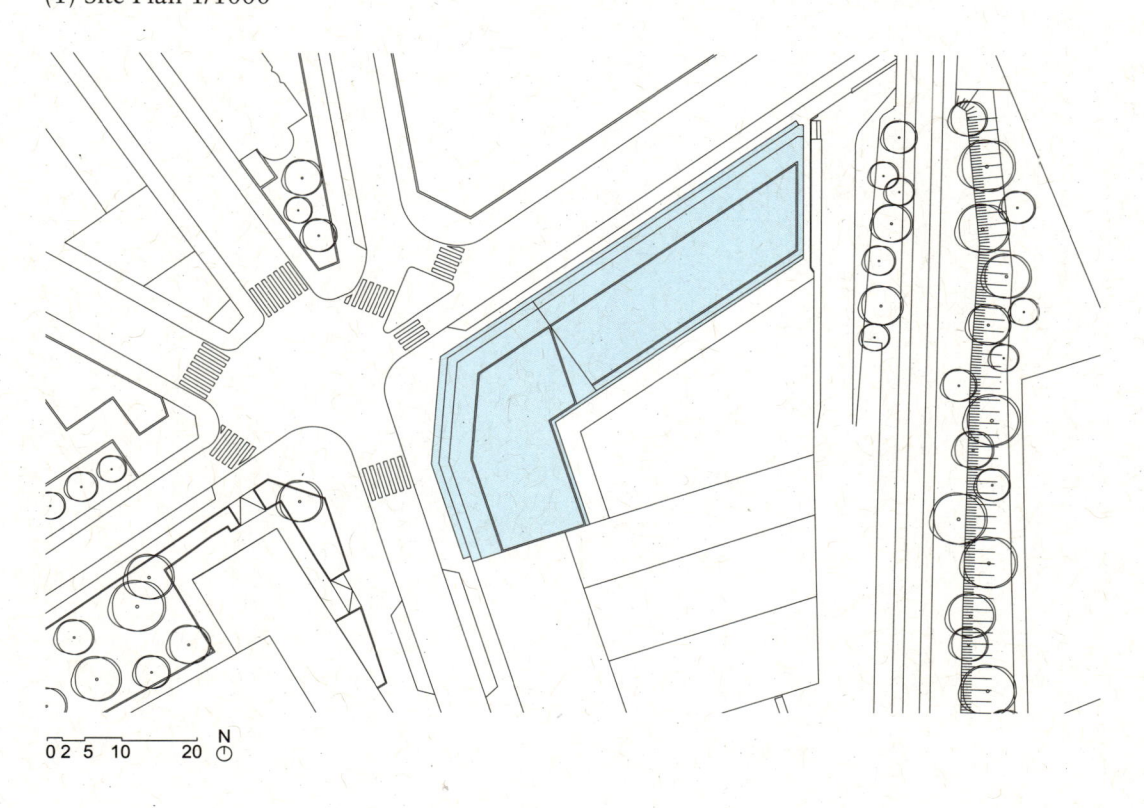

The building is located in the nineteenth arrondissement of Paris, in between the Ourcq Canal and the "Petite Ceinture" railroad tracks, today out of use. This northern district of Paris is in the process of being fully restructured, and many new dwellings are being built. The project includes 98 student dwellings and thirty social dwellings, as well as a specialized care home for disabled adults and three shops. The complex is completed by a garage for bicycles and cars in the basement and semi-basement, taking advantage of the two-meter height difference along the plot's side. The project provides spacious dwellings and gives the inhabitants the opportunity to enjoy the two orientations: the garden and the street. Each of the thirty social dwellings faces two sides. The living rooms and kitchens are on the garden side and open onto a 2.10 m deep winter garden of 9–28 m², facing south or southeast, extended by a one-meter-deep balcony. The bedrooms and main bathrooms, all well glazed, are on the north facade, and open onto a continuous balcony.

Case Study 2

Project and Environmental Conditions
Building

(1) Plan 1/400

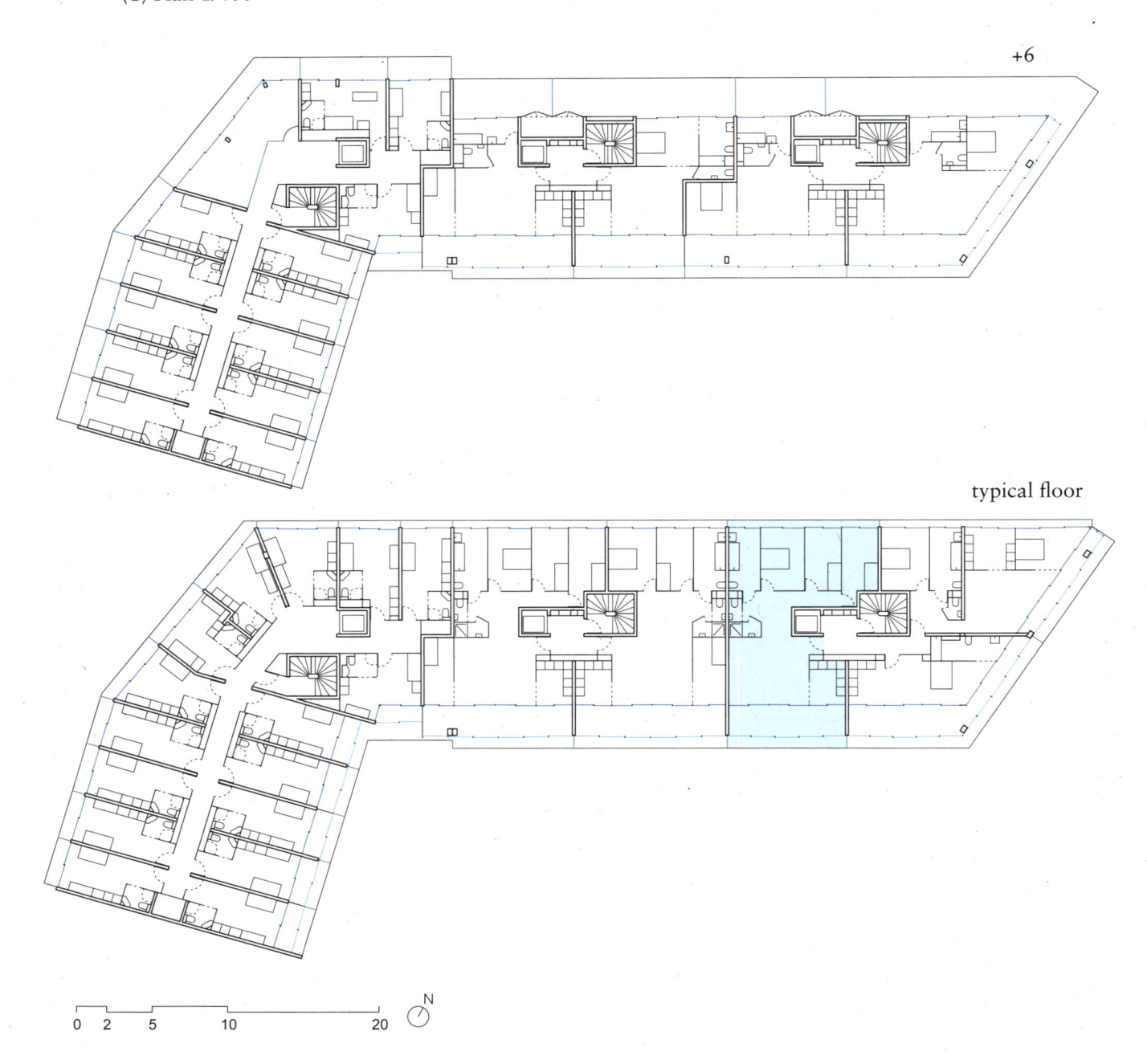

+6

typical floor

0 2 5 10 20   N

(1) Site plan: The student dwellings are between 19 and 23 m², all with large glazed sliding doors. Toward the street, they open onto a balcony. On the garden side, most have a 3.7 m² winter garden, extended by a balcony. Inside, the prefabricated bathrooms are optimized to offer more space to the living room. On the garden side, the ground floor is used by the specialized care home, hosting six disabled residents. The rooms and living spaces benefit from the southeast orientation, as well as the use of the garden and a lawn planted with trees and flowering bushes. The shops occupy the entire facade facing the street, interrupted only by the entrances of the residences. The winter gardens and balconies provide each apartment with a private outdoor space, offering the possibility to live outside, to have a little garden, like for a house. Combined with thermal and shading curtains, the winter gardens are also efficient for thermal comfort, in winter and in summer, by creating a buffer space with an intermediate climate. This bioclimatic approach, efficient in saving energy, provides at the same time an extra space for additional uses. Essential to the quality of life in an urban context, these private outdoor spaces bring the apartment closer to the living conditions and pleasure of an individual house.

21 Case Study 2

Project and Environmental Conditions
Unit

(1) Plan of analyzed unit 1/150

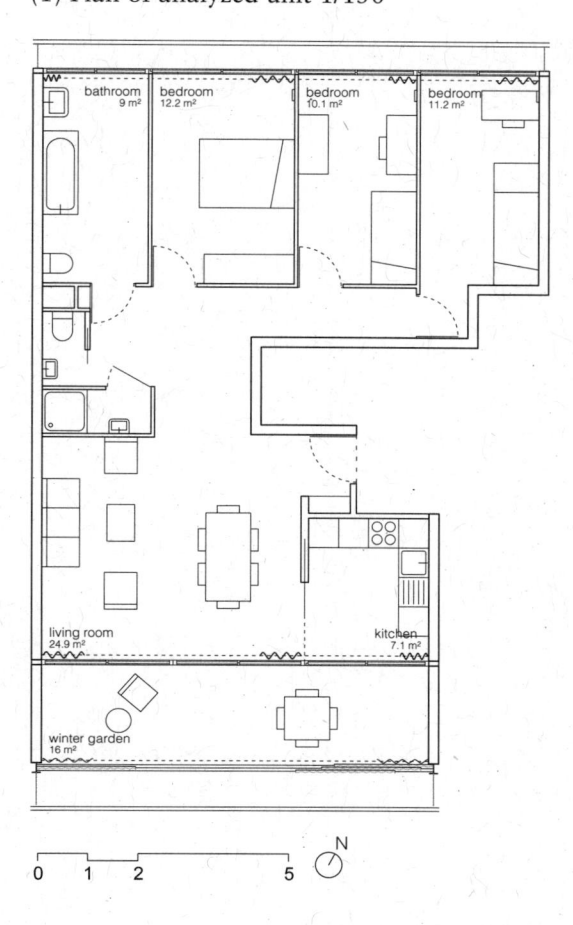

The double orientation provides the apartments with natural cross ventilation, controllable through the sliding doors. The bedrooms and the generous bathroom merge into the continuous one-meter-deep balcony facing the street. The living room and the kitchen open onto the 2.40 m deep winter garden with a surface of 16 m² and the one-meter-deep balcony facing the planted courtyard.

Case Study 2

Project and Environmental Conditions
Climate

(1) Paris climate summary

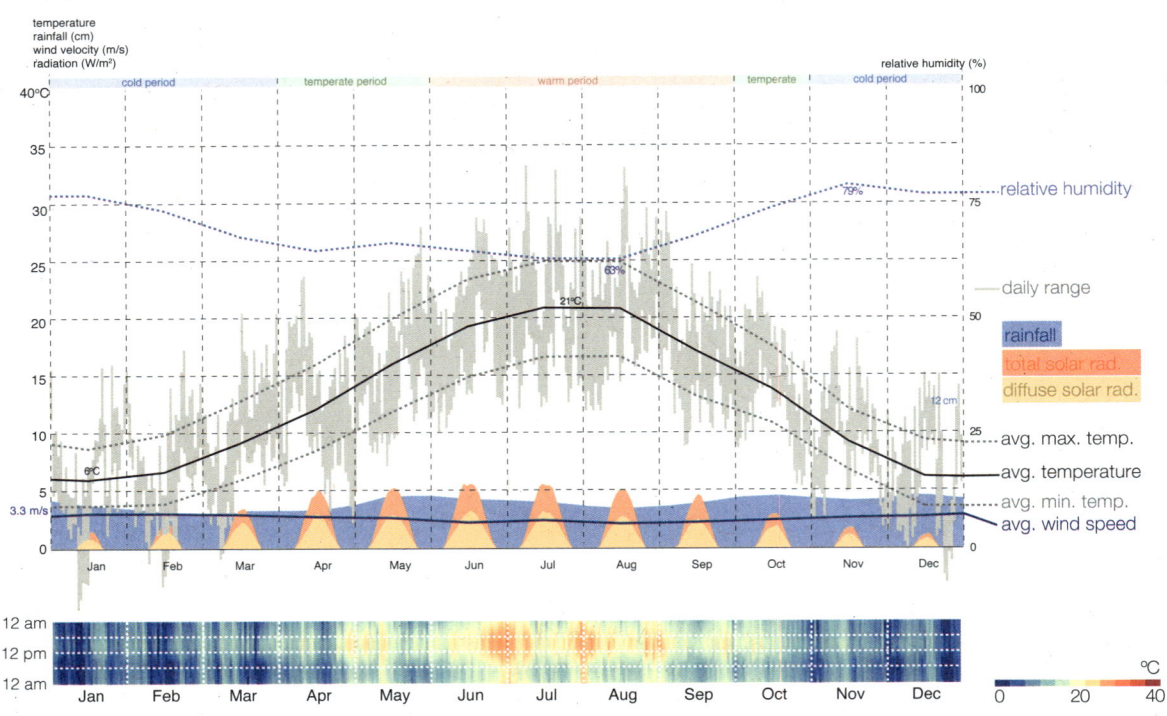

(2) Sky coverage in winter and summer

(3) Solar radiation in the sky vault in winter and summer

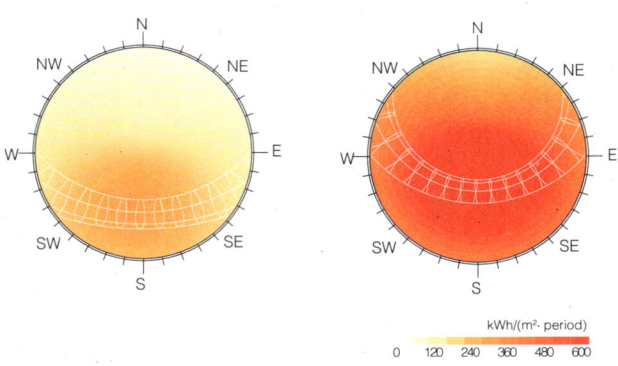

(4) Annual wind rose

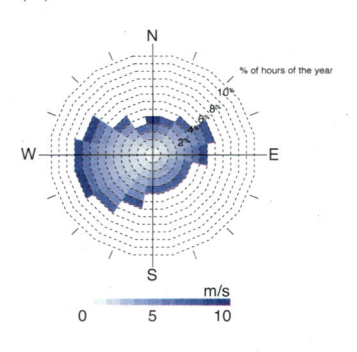

(1) Paris climate summary: Paris has a temperate climate, with the mildest summer of the four climates studied. Solar radiation is mostly diffuse due to the considerable cloud cover. During the hot period, the average high temperature is around 25°C, though it goes beyond 30°C about four days a year. The amplitude is large enough to use thermal inertia to cool down spaces naturally (around 8°C on average).

(2)/(3) Sky coverage and solar radiation in the sky vault in winter and summer: During the winter, the sky is mostly covered (74% of the time) and radiation is higher in the south quadrant. During the summer, the sky is sunny 28% of the time and solar radiation is higher on south-inclined roofs. Among the vertical surfaces, the south quadrant still receives the highest amount of heat.

(4) Annual wind rose: Wind blows mainly from the west-southwest quadrant, followed by the east-northeast, with an annual average speed of 2.7 m/s, which is rather low.

Project and Environmental Conditions
Environmental Features

BUILDING
Year of delivery	2014
Type of delivery	New build
Type of building	Urban building inside the urban tissue
Total amount of floors	7
Thermal regulation	RT 2005

SIMULATED UNIT
Floor	4th
Heated surface	93 m²
Winter garden surface	16 m²
Balcony surface	7 m²
Ratio of extra space/heated surface	24%
Orientation	NW/SE
Ratio of exposed envelope that is winter garden	50%
Total air renewal	90 m³/h, accounting 30 m³/(h·person)
Winter garden infiltration	5–10 air changes per hour

TECHNICAL SYSTEMS
Ventilation type	Extraction only hygro-adjustable CMV (Controlled Mechanical Ventilation)
Heating system type	Collective heat exchanger supplied by district heating
Heating regulation	Thermostatic radiator valves
Cep max	50 kWh/(m²·year)
Cep project	46 kWh/(m²·year) < Cep max

WINTER GARDEN

Orientation	Depth	Volume	Exposed facade area	Exposed concrete area	Total inertia (of winter garden)
Southeast	2.4 m	41 m³	19 m²	33 m²	0.80 489 kJ/m³K

	Element	Material	U-value W/(m²K)	SF	VLT	Reflectivity
①	Thermal curtain	Sheep's wool	2.17	0	0	0.9
②	Sliding doors of heated space	Double glazing	1.5	0.57	0.76	-
③	Solar curtain	Aluminum	-	0.38	0.4	0.6
④	Sliding doors of winter garden	2/3 transparent polycarbonate 1/3 single glazing	5.7	0.88	0.88	-

* SF: Solar Factor; VLT: Visible Light Transmittance

The winter garden is on the southeast side of the apartment

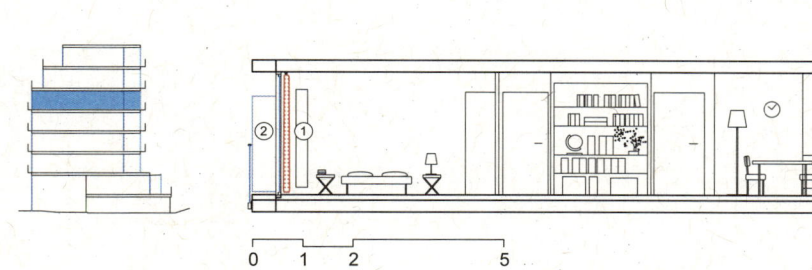

Floor-to-ceiling double-glazed sliding panels at the limits of the heated space, sliding doors of single glazing, and undulated polycarbonate for the winter gardens and glazed parapets with steel-frame railings allow unobstructed views in both directions, toward the city and the garden. The winter garden with an exposed facade of 19 m² represents 15% of the total apartment space. Air from the bathrooms and toilets is extracted by a simple installation of a extraction only hygro-adjustable controlled mechanical ventilation (CMV). The winter garden of Ourcq-Jaurès is oriented toward the southeast. It is 2.4 m deep, representing 24% of the total area, and is adjacent to the living room and kitchen. The exterior facade of the winter garden is made of sliding panels (or doors): generally two-fifths are clear glazing and three-fifths transparent corrugated polycarbonate.

Case Study 2

Project and Environmental Conditions
Sun and Wind

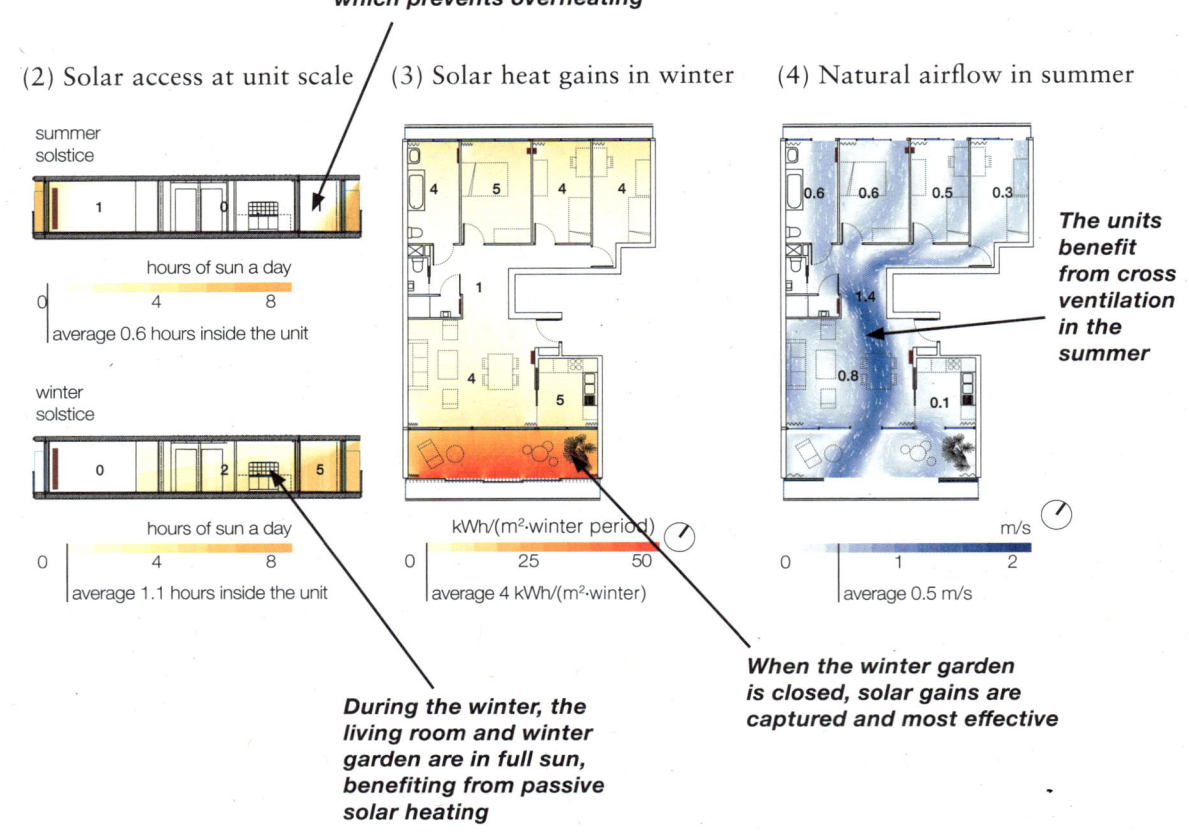

(1) Solar access at building scale

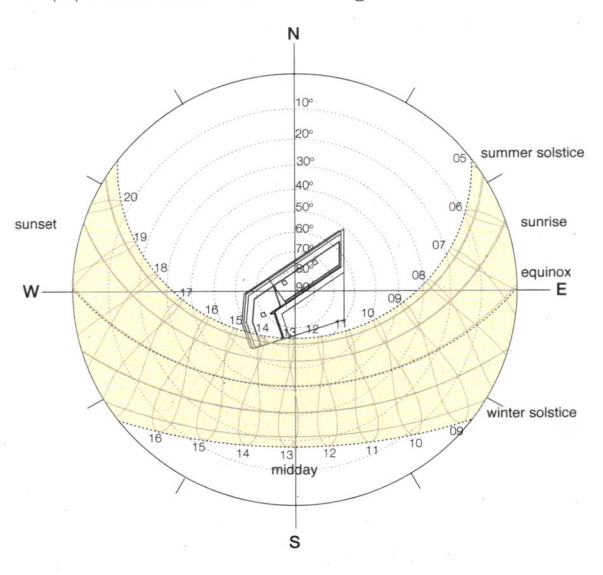

During the summer, the sun does not reach indoors, which prevents overheating

(2) Solar access at unit scale   (3) Solar heat gains in winter   (4) Natural airflow in summer

summer solstice

hours of sun a day
0   4   8
average 0.6 hours inside the unit

winter solstice

hours of sun a day
0   4   8
average 1.1 hours inside the unit

kWh/(m²·winter period)
0   25   50
average 4 kWh/(m²·winter)

m/s
0   1   2
average 0.5 m/s

The units benefit from cross ventilation in the summer

When the winter garden is closed, solar gains are captured and most effective

During the winter, the living room and winter garden are in full sun, benefiting from passive solar heating

---

(1) Solar access at building scale: The facades of the residential units face southeast and northwest. During the summer, all the levels of the residential units receive significant amounts of sun on the southeast side. The first three levels are partially covered by vegetation and neighboring buildings, whereas the upper three are more exposed. During winter, the southeast facade receives considerable amounts of sun. The northwest facade receives barely any sun. The units receive at least six hours of sun during the equinoxes, reaching the high solar access target of EN 17037.

(2) Solar access at unit scale: During the winter, the winter garden is in full sun, and the sun even permeates into the living room, raising the temperature both in the buffer space and indoors. During the summer, the depths of the balcony and the winter garden are properly calculated to limit the heat load through the glazed facades. On the northwest facade with no winter garden, the sun enters the bedroom and creates a relatively high heat load in the evening.

(3) Solar heat gains in winter: During the winter, the winter garden receives a heat gain from the sun of 41 kWh/m², whereas the living room and bedrooms receive 4 kWh/m². This contributes to the passive heating of the space.

(4) Natural airflow in summer: Under average wind conditions, and when all sliding doors are open, all the rooms of the apartment and the winter garden benefit from cross ventilation, as air velocity varies from 0 to 2 m/s. At 0.5 m/s, the breeze is perceived by the occupants, which occurs in most of the rooms.

Case Study 2

Project and Environmental Conditions
Daylight

(1) Daylight autonomy

% of time in DA [300]
0 — 50 — 100
target 50% | average 73%

Plenty of daylight reaches far into the living room (300 lux or more 69% of the time on average)

(2) Space exceeding 50% of time with DA [300] (EN 17037)

reference plane: 50 cm off the walls from permanently occupied spaces.

target 50% of space > 50% of time with DA [300]

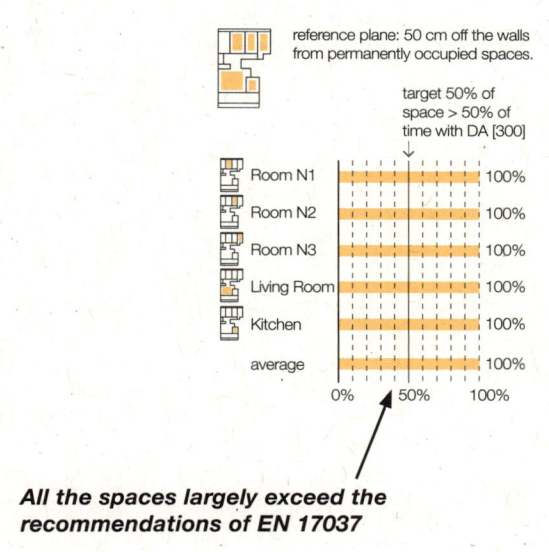

Room N1	100%
Room N2	100%
Room N3	100%
Living Room	100%
Kitchen	100%
average	100%

All the spaces largely exceed the recommendations of EN 17037

(1) Daylight Autonomy: The fully glazed facade and clear finishings provide abundant daylight levels inside, despite the depth of the plan. Median levels across the year are higher than 750 lux. The living room receives 300 lux naturally at least 69% of the time, and bedrooms 81–84%, which means they are fairly autonomous from electric lighting.

(2) Space exceeding 50% of time with DA [300] (EN 17037): All the apartment area receives 300 lux at least 50% of the time naturally, which is far above the daylight target recommendation of EN 17037. The winter garden is naturally the brightest space, with 300 lux naturally 92% of the time.

Case Study 2

Free-Runing Mode Seasonal Performance

(1) Operative temperatures across the year

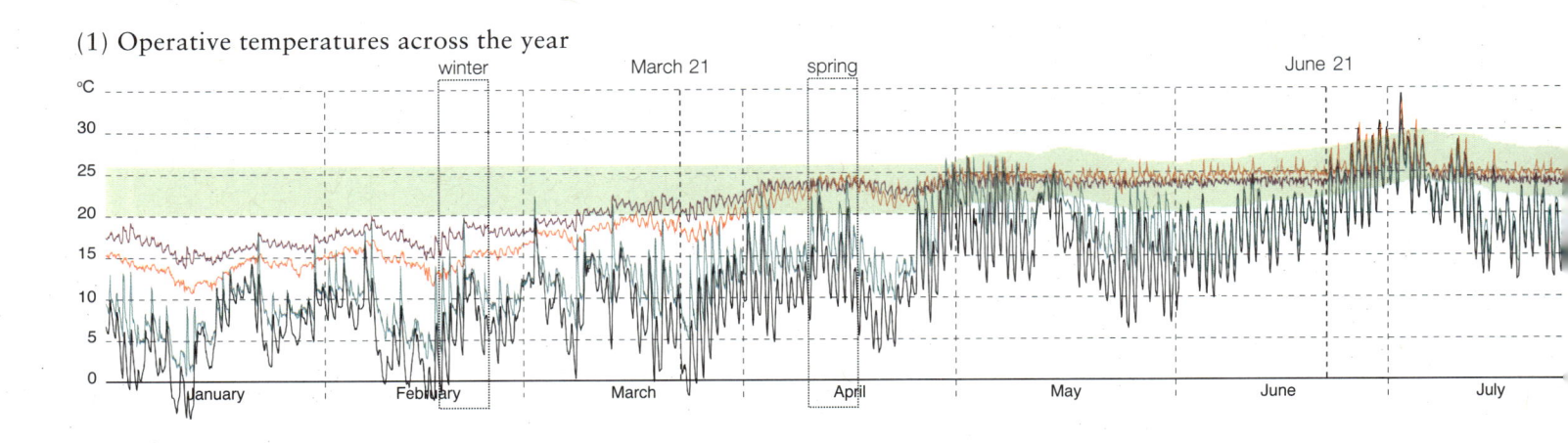

(2) Operative temperatures in winter

Winter garden operative temperatures are 5–7°C warmer than outdoors on sunny days, creating an effective thermal buffer

Winter gardens are 1–5°C warmer than outdoors on cloudy days

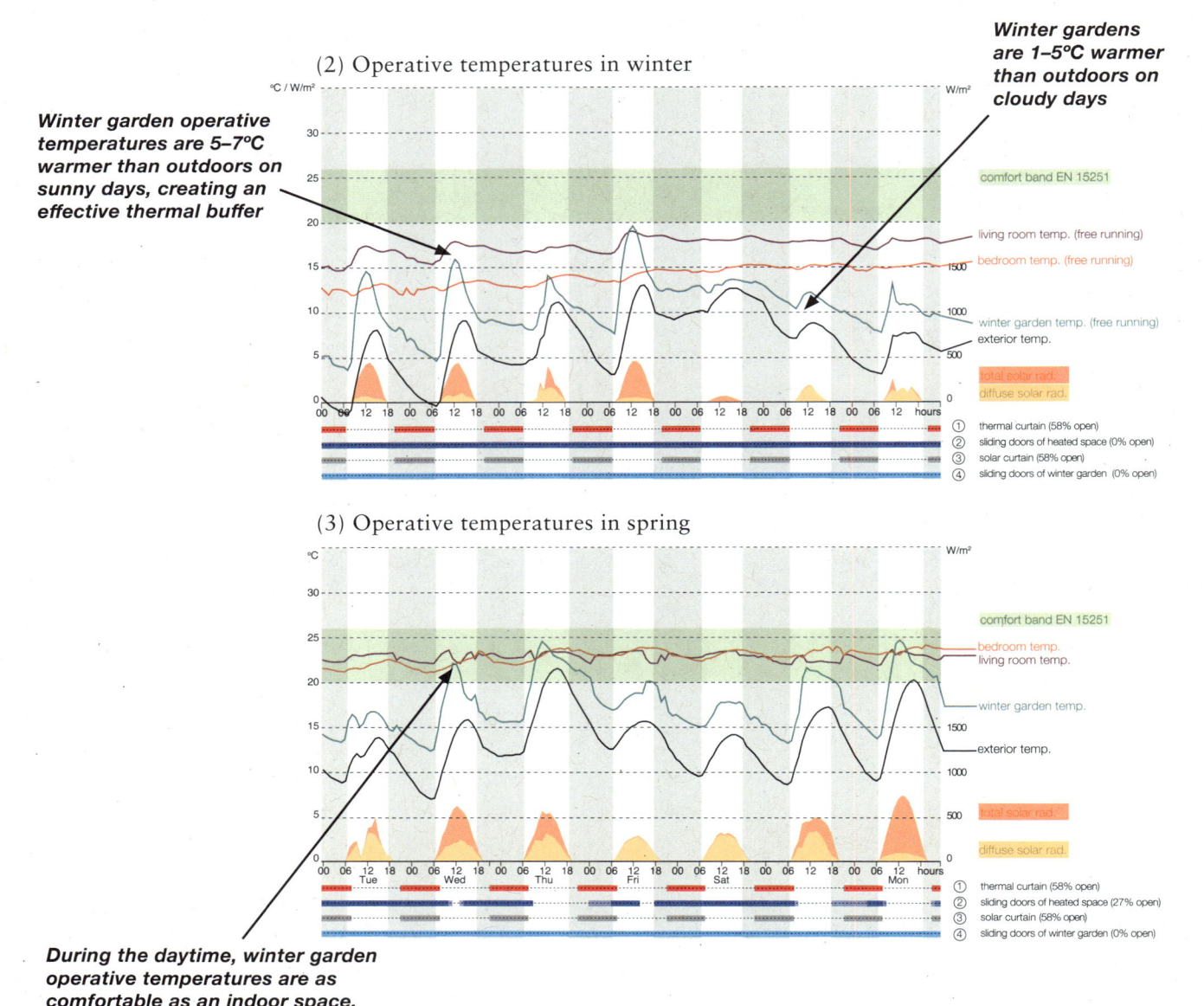

(3) Operative temperatures in spring

During the daytime, winter garden operative temperatures are as comfortable as an indoor space, extending the space for living

(1) Operative temperatures across the year: The simulation in free-running mode shows that spaces reach a good performance as indoor temperatures vary naturally from 12 to 30°C.

(2) Operative temperatures in winter: Indoor operative temperatures remain very stable and below the comfort band in free-running mode. While living room temperatures are near comfort, between 15 and 19°C thanks to the buffer effect of the winter garden, bedroom temperatures remain lower, between 13 and 16°C. Winter garden operative temperatures are 5–7°C warmer than outdoors during or after sunny days and 1–5°C on cloudy ones.

(3) Operative temperatures in spring: Indoor operative temperatures are very stable and within comfort naturally, between 21 and 24°C—even if the outdoor air temperature varies between 7 and 22°C—as the intuitive use of the various elements of the envelope helps to control interior conditions. Winter garden temperatures are consistently 2–5°C above outdoors. During sunny days, the winter garden heats up sufficiently to have comfortable temperatures as an indoor space. This allows one to open the sliding doors of the heated space to let the sun in and naturally heat up the interior space, enlarging it. During cloudy days, comfortable temperatures indoors are maintained due to the buffer effect of the winter garden.

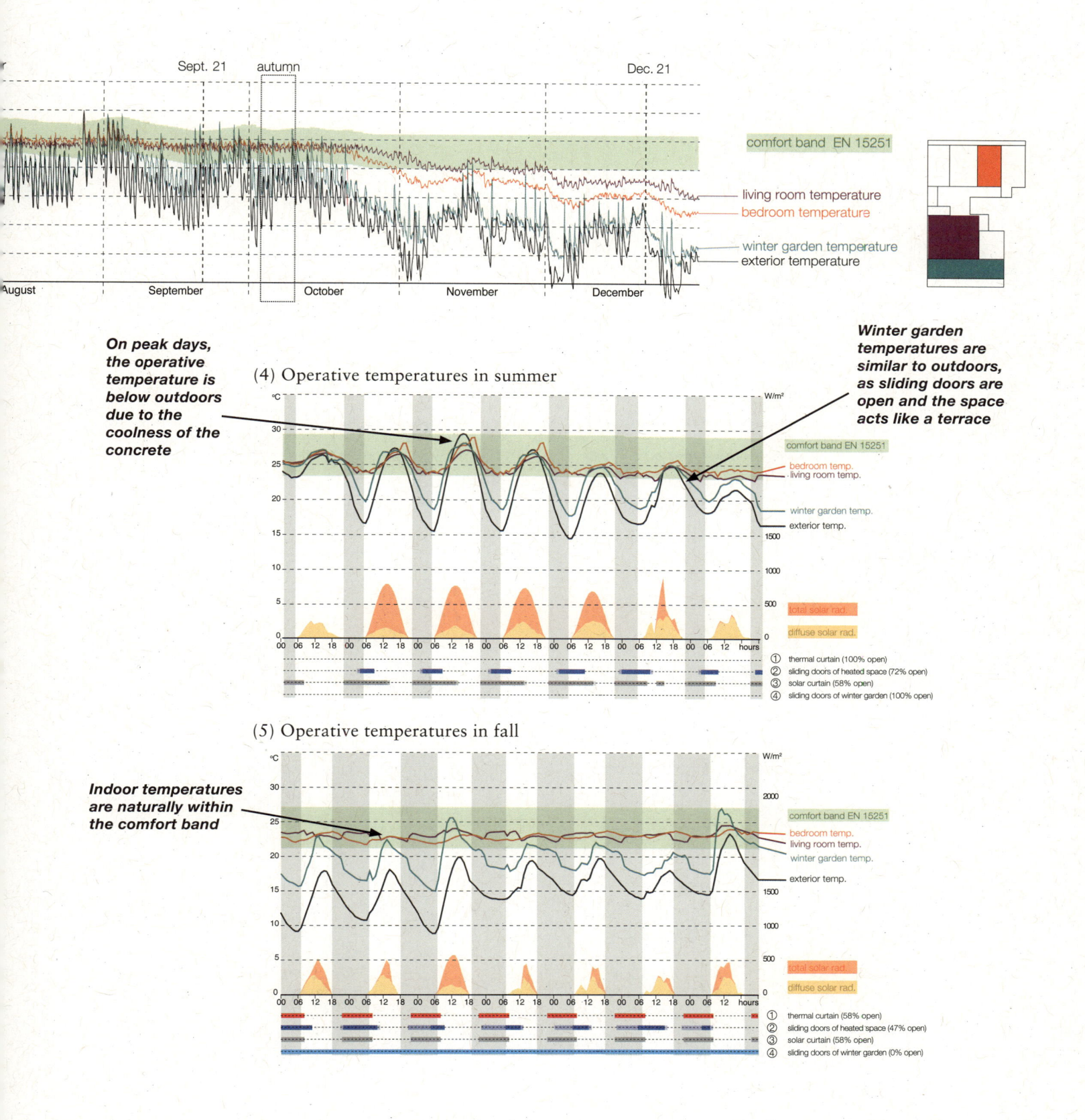

Case Study 2

Sept. 21 | autumn | Dec. 21

comfort band EN 15251
living room temperature
bedroom temperature
winter garden temperature
exterior temperature

August | September | October | November | December

On peak days, the operative temperature is below outdoors due to the coolness of the concrete

(4) Operative temperatures in summer

comfort band EN 15251
bedroom temp.
living room temp.
winter garden temp.
exterior temp.

total solar rad.
diffuse solar rad.

00 06 12 18 hours

① thermal curtain (100% open)
② sliding doors of heated space (72% open)
③ solar curtain (58% open)
④ sliding doors of winter garden (100% open)

Winter garden temperatures are similar to outdoors, as sliding doors are open and the space acts like a terrace

(5) Operative temperatures in fall

comfort band EN 15251
bedroom temp.
living room temp.
winter garden temp.
exterior temp.

total solar rad.
diffuse solar rad.

00 06 12 18 hours

① thermal curtain (58% open)
② sliding doors of heated space (47% open)
③ solar curtain (58% open)
④ sliding doors of winter garden (0% open)

Indoor temperatures are naturally within the comfort band

(4) Operative temperatures in summer: All the living spaces have operative temperatures inside the comfort band during both the day and the night, with no overheating thanks to the effectiveness of the shading, cross ventilation, and thermal inertia. The thermal inertia of the exposed concrete lowers indoor temperatures during peak days, as it remains about 2°C below outdoors (third day of the displayed week). Only bedroom operative temperatures peak in the sunny afternoons (+ 2°C) due to direct solar exposure of the glass facade with no outdoor shading. At least partially closing the thermal curtain in the evening would certainly contribute to reducing this effect.

(5) Operative temperatures in fall: Indoor operative temperatures are very stable and within the comfort range naturally, between 22 and 24°C—even if outdoors vary between 9 and 24°C—as the intuitive use of the envelope elements helps to control interior conditions. Winter garden temperatures are consistently 2–6°C above outdoors. During sunny days, the winter garden heats up sufficiently to have comfortable temperatures as an indoor space. It allows the opening of the sliding doors of the heated space to let the sun in and heat up the interior space, enlarging the living space. During cloudy days, the temperature of the winter garden reaches the lower level of the interior comfort band, and doors can still be left open. Indoors, comfortable temperatures are maintained due to the buffer effect of the winter garden.

Free-Running Mode Typical Days

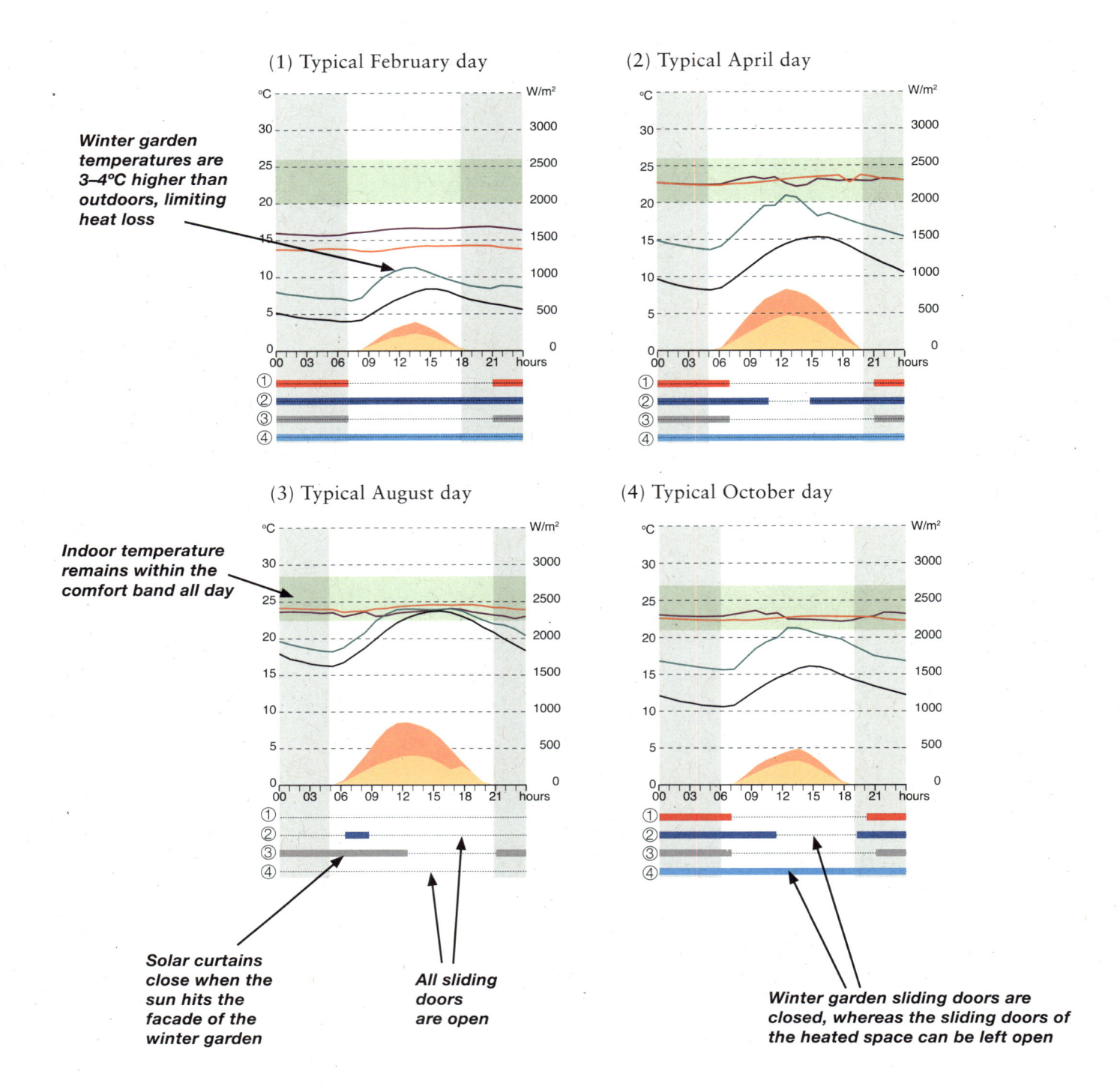

(1) Typical February day

Winter garden temperatures are 3–4°C higher than outdoors, limiting heat loss

(2) Typical April day

(3) Typical August day

Indoor temperature remains within the comfort band all day

**(4) Typical October day*

Solar curtains close when the sun hits the facade of the winter garden

All sliding doors are open

Winter garden sliding doors are closed, whereas the sliding doors of the heated space can be left open

(1) Typical February day: During a typical winter day, all openings remain closed and both curtains are deployed only at night. Operative temperatures in free-running mode remain very stable. The living room is about 16–17°C whereas the bedrooms are around 14°C. The winter garden is 2–3°C warmer than outdoors, especially during the daytime.

(2) Typical April day: During a typical spring day, the sliding doors of the winter garden remain closed, whereas the ones of the heated space are only opened for a few hours, enlarging the living space. Both curtains are deployed only at night. Indoor temperatures remain stable around 23–24°C, whereas the winter garden has a stable difference with outdoors of around 4–5°C.

(3) Typical August day: During a typical summer day, the winter garden becomes a covered terrace with sliding doors left fully open, whereas interior sliding doors are only closed during the morning. Operative temperature in the living room remains stable, around 23–24°C. Slabs of balconies and winter gardens protect the living rooms from direct sun, avoiding the increase of temperature. In the bedrooms, temperatures are around 24–25°C. Inside the winter garden, operative temperatures are 1–2°C higher than outdoors, except during the afternoon, when the temperature matches outdoors due to adequate solar protection and natural ventilation.

(4) Typical October day: During a typical fall day, the winter garden sliding doors remain closed, whereas those of the heated space are open all afternoon. Both curtains are deployed only at night. Indoor temperatures remain stable, around 22–24°C, whereas the winter garden has a stable difference with outdoors of around 3–4°C.

Case Study 2

Free-Running Mode
Extreme Days

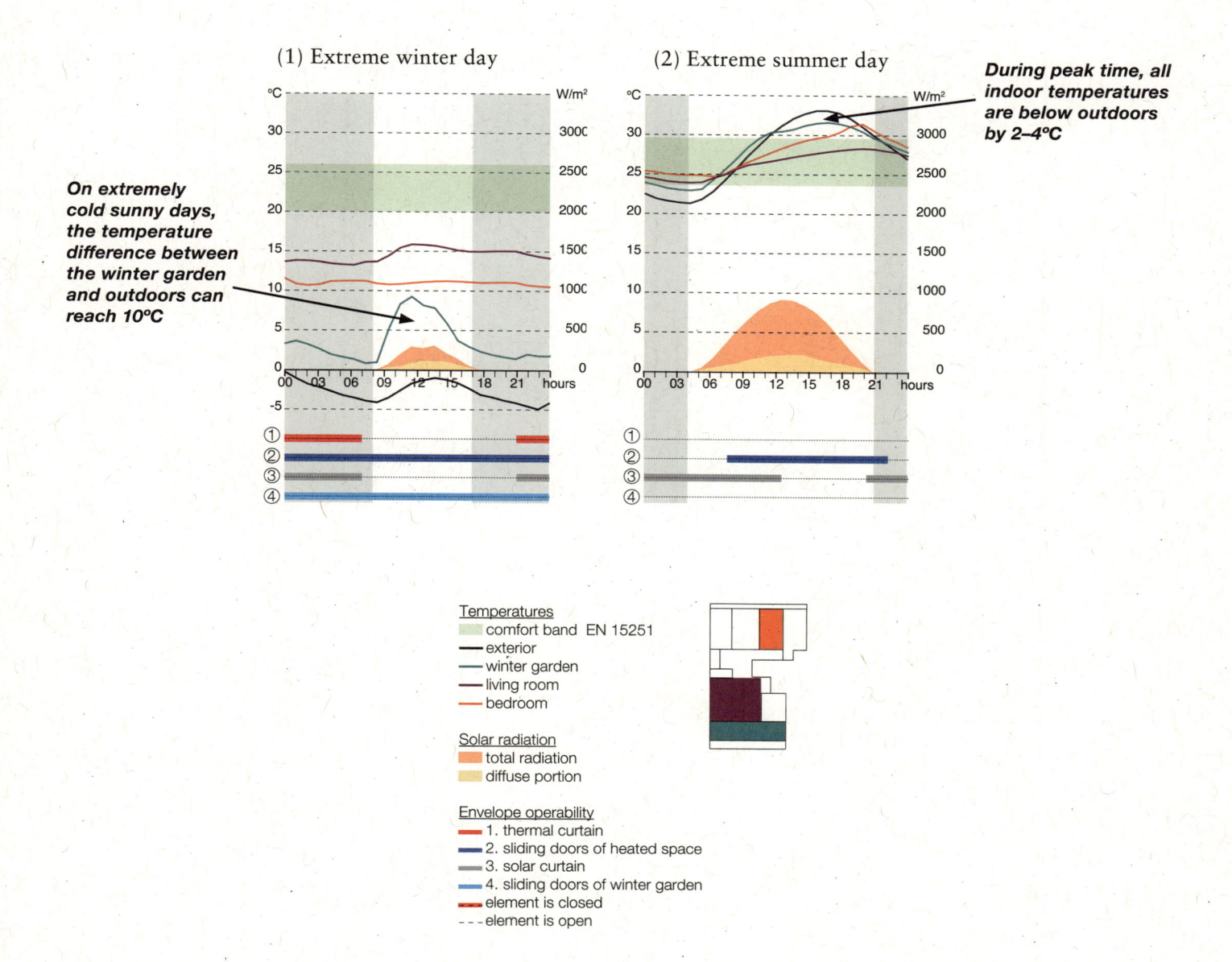

(1) Extreme winter day

On extremely cold sunny days, the temperature difference between the winter garden and outdoors can reach 10°C

(2) Extreme summer day

During peak time, all indoor temperatures are below outdoors by 2–4°C

Temperatures
- comfort band EN 15251
- exterior
- winter garden
- living room
- bedroom

Solar radiation
- total radiation
- diffuse portion

Envelope operability
- 1. thermal curtain
- 2. sliding doors of heated space
- 3. solar curtain
- 4. sliding doors of winter garden
- element is closed
- element is open

(1) Extreme winter day: During an extreme winter day, when outdoor temperatures remain below zero all day and night, both sliding doors remain closed and both curtains are deployed at night. Operative temperatures in free-running mode still remain stable, around 14–15°C for the living room and 11°C for the bedroom. It is to be noted that the coldest days are sunny. This increases the temperature difference between the winter garden and outdoors, which makes it particularly effective during extreme days. At night, the difference can be around 3–5°C, but during the day, the difference is above 10°C: when it is -2°C outdoors, the winter garden has operative temperatures of around 8–9°C.

(2) Extreme summer day: During an extreme summer day, when outdoor temperatures can reach 33–34°C, all openings are left open at night, and closed when outdoor temperature is higher than indoors. The solar curtain is deployed until noon, when the sun reaches the facade. Interior operative temperatures follow the fluctuation of outdoors, but are much more stable thanks to the thermal inertia present in the concrete slabs. Living room temperatures range from 23 to 28°C, which is still within the comfort band. The peak is lagged compared to outdoors due to the capture and release of the heat by the concrete, which happens between 5 pm and 9 pm. Bedroom temperatures follow the same pattern as the living room but with a higher peak around 7–8 pm, reaching 31°C. This happens when the sun directly hits the northwest facade. Closed thermal curtains in the evening would certainly contribute to reducing this peak. Additional exterior solar protection would also help (note that the elements shown only correspond to the winter garden elements and not to the north facade). Winter garden—fully open as a terrace—operative temperatures follow outdoors more closely, but remain 2–3°C lower in the afternoon due to the proper shading, the effect of thermal inertia, and adequate ventilation.

Free-Running Mode
Thermal Comfort Conditions

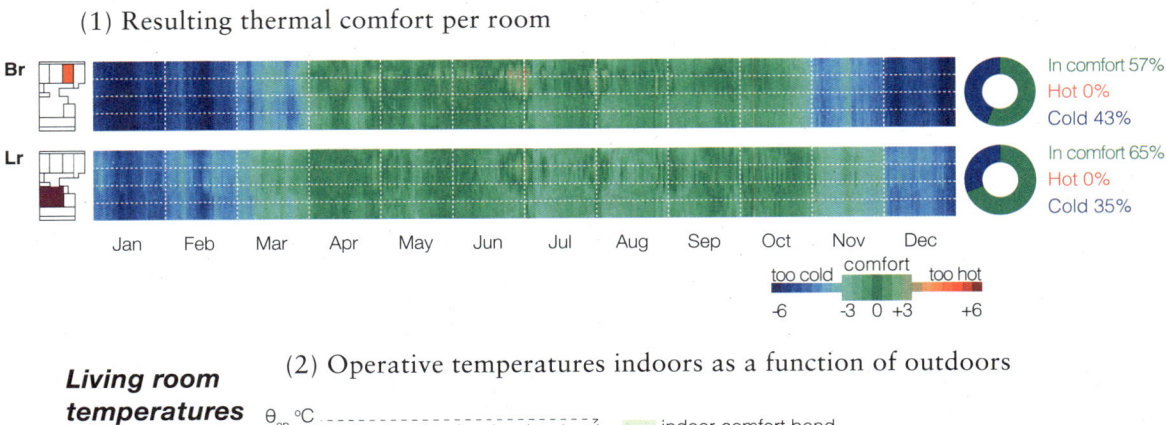

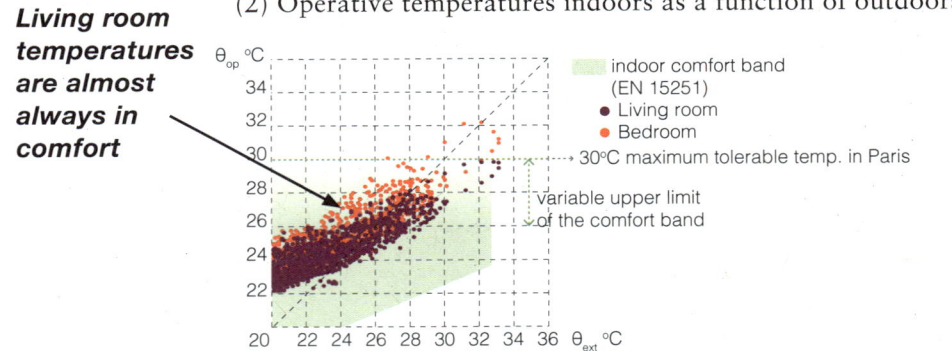

(1) Resulting thermal comfort per room

Br — In comfort 57% / Hot 0% / Cold 43%
Lr — In comfort 65% / Hot 0% / Cold 35%

Jan Feb Mar Apr May Jun Jul Aug Sep Oct Nov Dec

too cold — comfort — too hot
-6   -3 0 +3   +6

(2) Operative temperatures indoors as a function of outdoors

Living room temperatures are almost always in comfort

θ_{op} °C

- indoor comfort band (EN 15251)
- Living room
- Bedroom
- 30°C maximum tolerable temp. in Paris
- variable upper limit of the comfort band

θ_{ext} °C

(3) Overheating evaluation

ideal target <350 °C·h
maximum tolerance

Living room 27
Bedroom 95
average 53

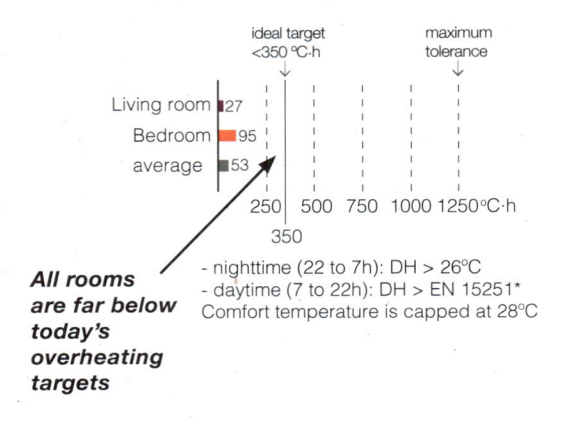

250 | 500 750 1000 1250 °C·h
350

- nighttime (22 to 7h): DH > 26°C
- daytime (7 to 22h): DH > EN 15251*
  Comfort temperature is capped at 28°C

All rooms are far below today's overheating targets

(1) Resulting thermal comfort per room: The unit is naturally in comfort most of the time: on average 61% of the year without heating. The living room is naturally in comfort 65% of the time, with only three months a year with temperatures that are below comfort by a small margin. Bedrooms are naturally in comfort without heating 57% of the time, with only five months a year with temperatures that are below comfort.

(2) Operative temperatures indoors as a function of outdoors: The unit has no overheating time. Whereas the living room is never above comfort, the bedroom has only some hours above the comfort band (26–32°C), which is an optimal summer performance. Hours with temperature above the comfort band are very sporadic and happen almost exclusively in the space without a winter garden. In the living room, the thermal inertia helps to cool down temperatures, even during peak summer days: the more the outdoor temperature rises, the more there is a difference between outdoors and the living room operative temperature. Bedrooms are hot in the evening, when the sun hits the facade. Closing the thermal curtains would help to reduce these hours. Even so, at night the space cools down sufficiently to avoid being too hot. The winter garden heats up the interior when temperatures are low in summer and also cools down the interior when the exterior temperature rises—due to the solar protection and the thermal inertia.

(3) Overheating evaluation: The degree hours above comfort are largely below contemporary targets.

Case Study 2

Free-Running Mode
Conditions inside the Winter Garden

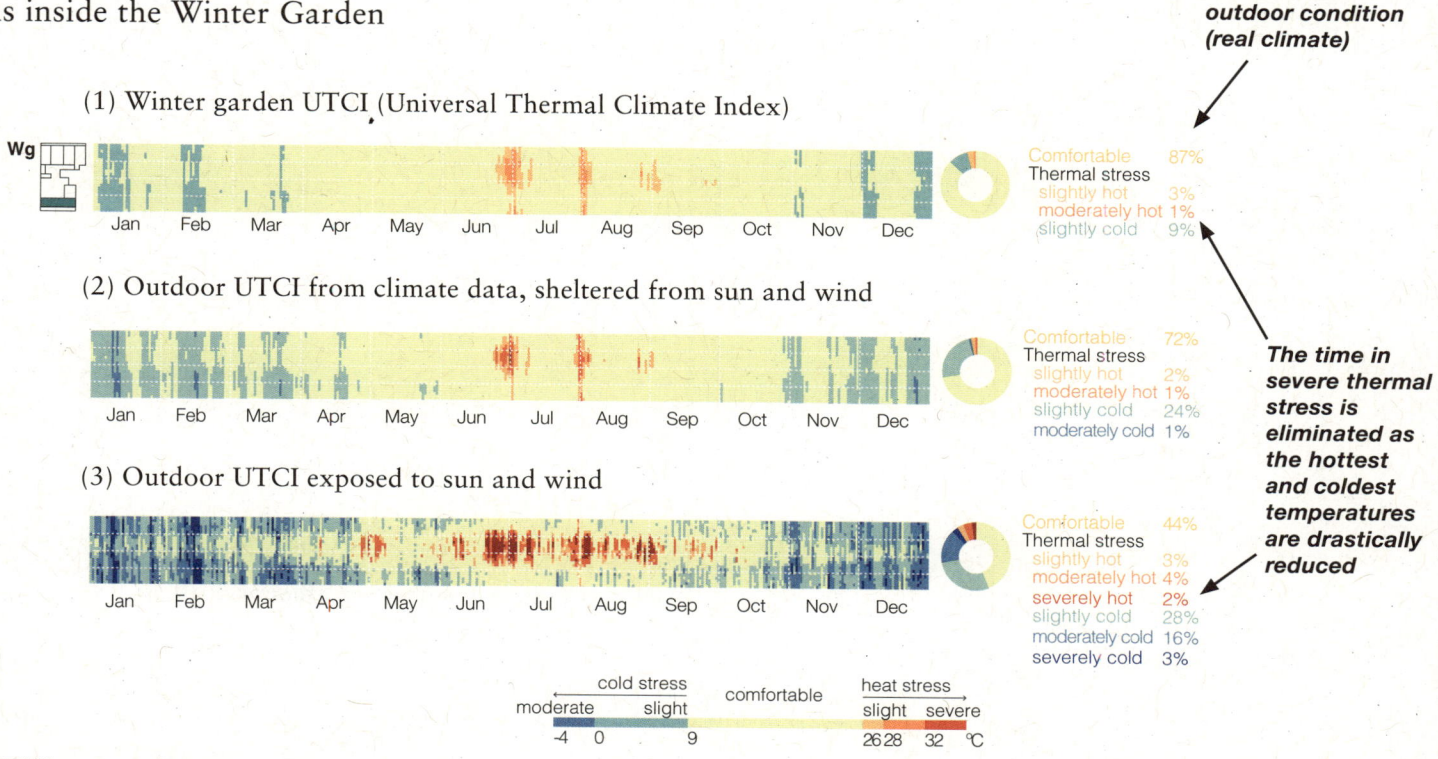

(1) Winter garden UTCI (Universal Thermal Climate Index)

Comfortable 87%
Thermal stress
slightly hot 3%
moderately hot 1%
slightly cold 9%

Time in comfort is doubled compared to an exposed outdoor condition (real climate)

(2) Outdoor UTCI from climate data, sheltered from sun and wind

Comfortable 72%
Thermal stress
slightly hot 2%
moderately hot 1%
slightly cold 24%
moderately cold 1%

The time in severe thermal stress is eliminated as the hottest and coldest temperatures are drastically reduced

(3) Outdoor UTCI exposed to sun and wind

Comfortable 44%
Thermal stress
slightly hot 3%
moderately hot 4%
severely hot 2%
slightly cold 28%
moderately cold 16%
severely cold 3%

cold stress — comfortable — heat stress
moderate | slight | | slight | severe
-4   0   9   26 28   32 °C

(4) Winter garden air temperatures compared to outdoors

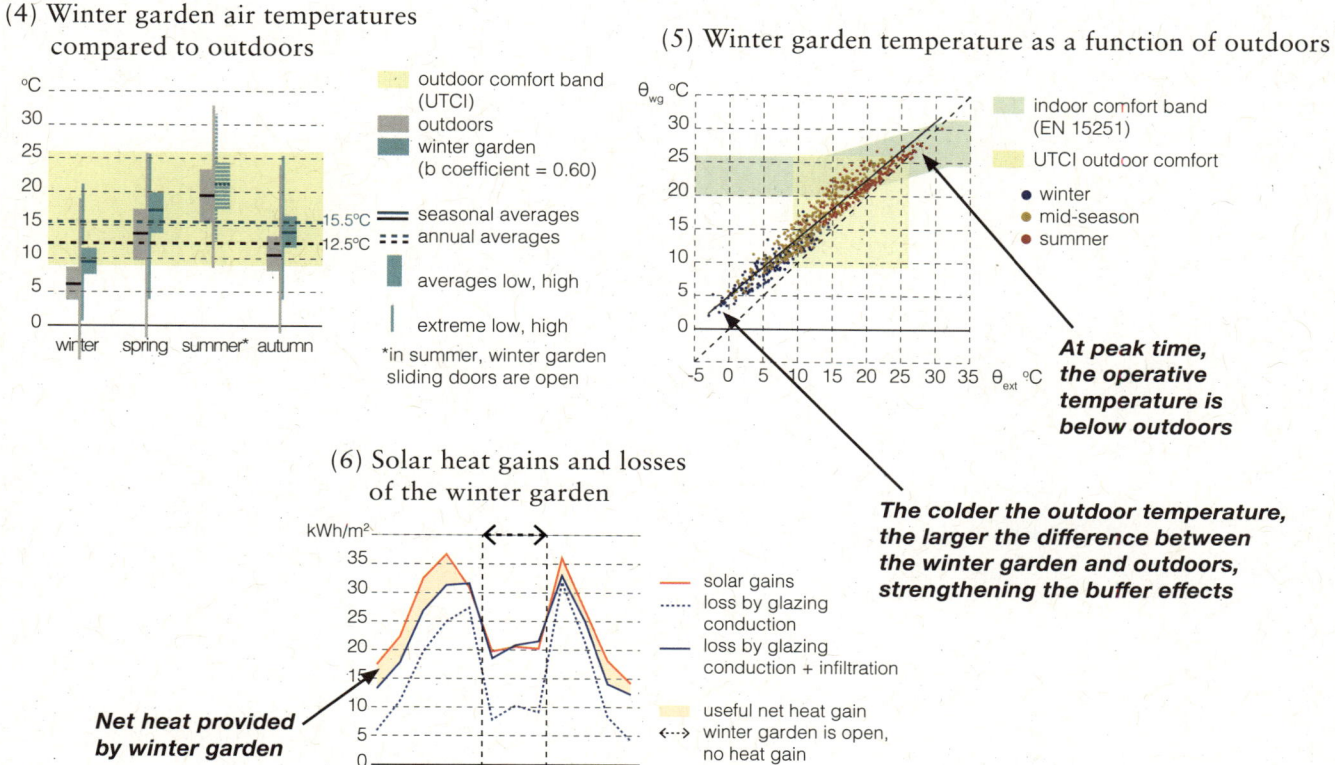

- outdoor comfort band (UTCI)
- outdoors
- winter garden (b coefficient = 0.60)
- 15.5°C seasonal averages
- 12.5°C annual averages
- averages low, high
- extreme low, high

*in summer, winter garden sliding doors are open

(5) Winter garden temperature as a function of outdoors

- indoor comfort band (EN 15251)
- UTCI outdoor comfort
- winter
- mid-season
- summer

At peak time, the operative temperature is below outdoors

The colder the outdoor temperature, the larger the difference between the winter garden and outdoors, strengthening the buffer effects

(6) Solar heat gains and losses of the winter garden

- solar gains
- loss by glazing conduction
- loss by glazing conduction + infiltration
- useful net heat gain
- winter garden is open, no heat gain

Net heat provided by winter garden

---

(1)–(3) Winter garden and outdoor UTCI: These diagrams show how the winter garden improves outdoor comfort by comparing the UTCI inside with an exposed situation to sun and wind and to a sheltered situation (climate data). The winter garden has comfortable temperatures 87% of the time, which is double the time compared to an exposed situation. There is slight thermal stress during the coldest and hottest days of the year, but it is mitigated compared to any situation outdoors.

(4) Winter garden air temperatures compared to outdoors: During the mid-season and winter, the winter garden has higher air temperatures than outdoors, from 1 to 8°C. During the summer, winter garden temperatures are closer to outdoors, as the average is around 1°C higher. However, peaks are lower as the extreme outdoor temperature is higher than the extreme of the winter garden. The b coefficient is calculated following the European Norm (EN 13789) to calculate the reduction of heat losses of the heated envelope thanks to the effect of the winter garden. Here the result is 0.60, meaning that the winter garden reduces heat loss by 40%.

(5) Winter garden temperature as a function of outdoors: During the winter, the winter garden works mostly as a buffer space: the colder the outdoor temperature, the larger the difference between the winter garden and outdoors, which strengthens the buffer effect. During the mid-season, conditions are variable according to climate, but the space is as comfortable as outdoors (UTCI) and indoors (EN 15251) for a large period of time. During the summer, the winter garden, when opened up as a terrace, is comfortable most of the time. During peak days, its operative temperature remains below outdoors, as the concrete stabilizes peaks.

(6) Solar heat gains and losses of the winter garden: The winter garden provides a net heat gain from September to June, as solar gains are higher than the sum of losses by glazing conduction and infiltration. In January, this gain is double the losses.

Active Mode
Winter Air Temperatures and Heating Load

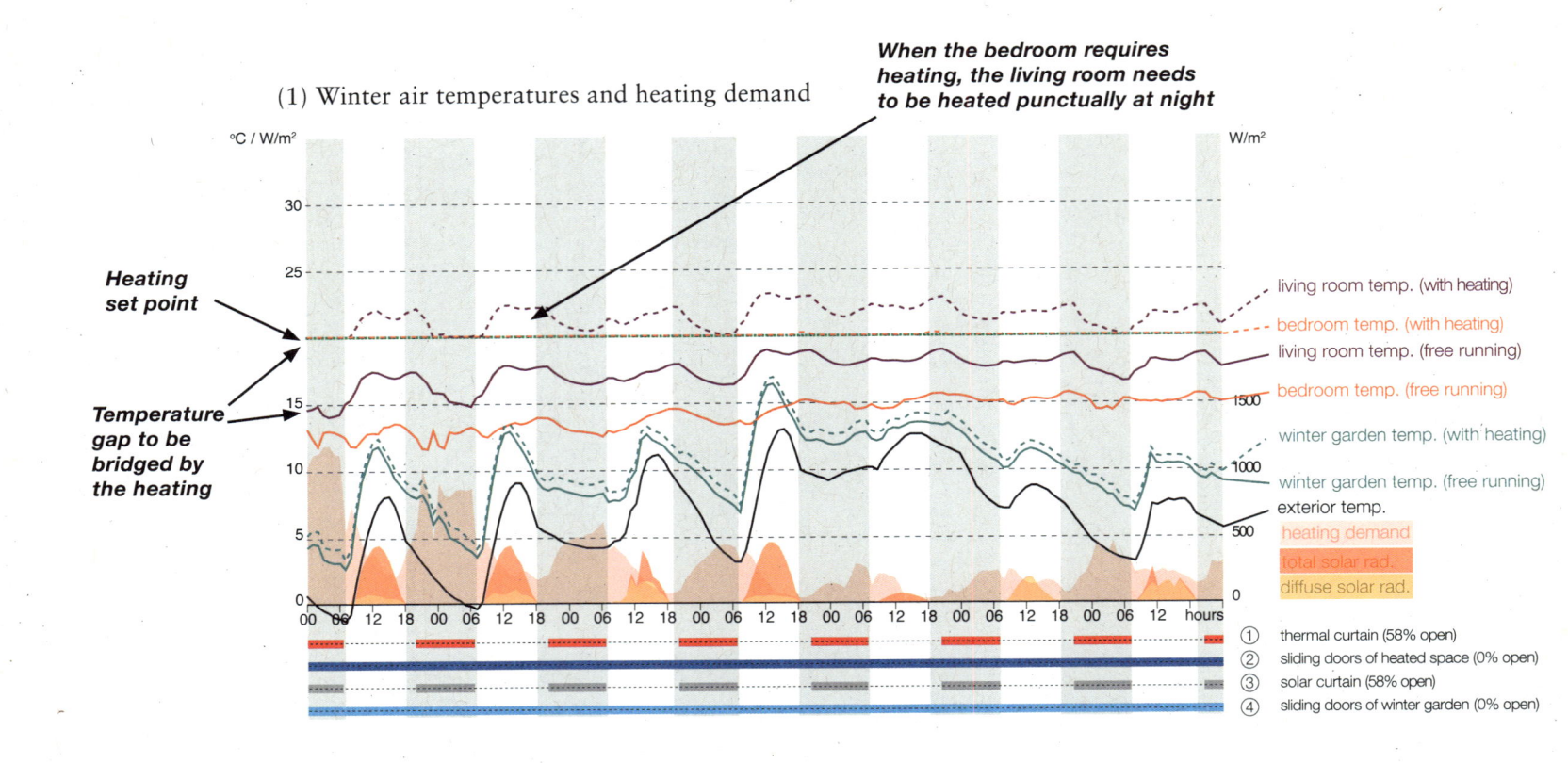

(1) Winter air temperatures and heating demand

When the bedroom requires heating, the living room needs to be heated punctually at night

Heating set point

Temperature gap to be bridged by the heating

living room temp. (with heating)
bedroom temp. (with heating)
living room temp. (free running)
bedroom temp. (free running)
winter garden temp. (with heating)
winter garden temp. (free running)
exterior temp.
heating demand
total solar rad.
diffuse solar rad.

① thermal curtain (58% open)
② sliding doors of heated space (0% open)
③ solar curtain (58% open)
④ sliding doors of winter garden (0% open)

(1) Winter air temperatures and heating demand: This graphic shows air temperature—rather than the operative temperature of previous graphics—for heat load evaluations. While living room air temperatures are near comfort naturally, between 15 and 19°C—thanks to the buffer effect of the winter garden—bedroom temperatures remain lower, between 13 and 16°C. When the bedrooms are heated, the living room is naturally above 20°C and does not require heating (20–23°C). This indicates that the living room in free-running mode is not in comfort because it passes some heat to the bedrooms. Most of the heating is used at night when occupants are actually sleeping and the set point could be lower, and in the morning. When the heating is turned on inside, winter garden temperatures can be similar or 1°C higher, as it collects the losses from inside.

Energy Demand
Heating Demand

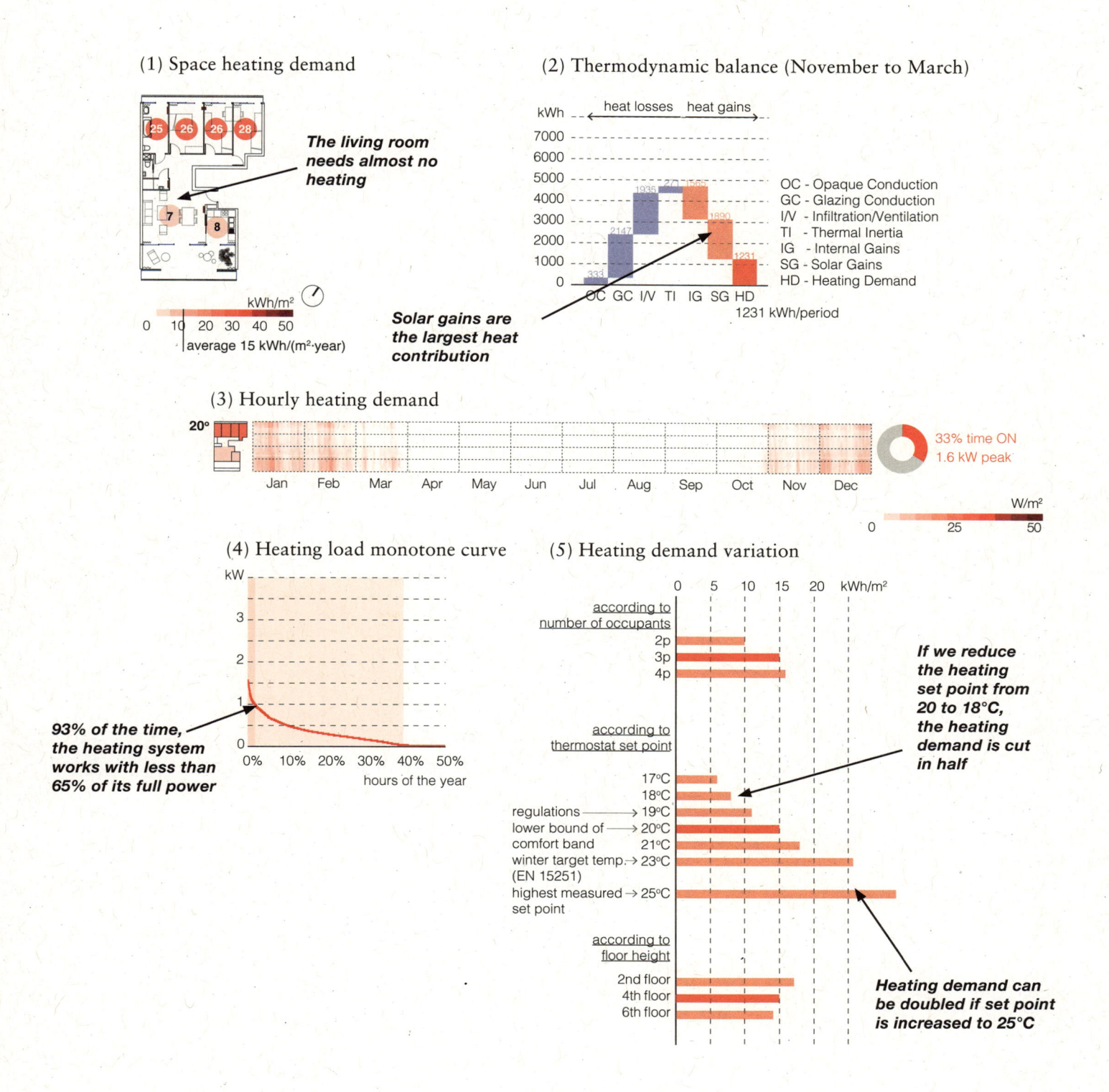

(1) Space heating demand

kWh/m²
0 10 20 30 40 50
average 15 kWh/(m²·year)

The living room needs almost no heating

(2) Thermodynamic balance (November to March)

kWh — heat losses ← → heat gains

OC - Opaque Conduction
GC - Glazing Conduction
I/V - Infiltration/Ventilation
TI - Thermal Inertia
IG - Internal Gains
SG - Solar Gains
HD - Heating Demand

1231 kWh/period

Solar gains are the largest heat contribution

(3) Hourly heating demand

20°
Jan Feb Mar Apr May Jun Jul Aug Sep Oct Nov Dec

33% time ON
1.6 kW peak

W/m²
0   25   50

(4) Heating load monotone curve

kW
0% 10% 20% 30% 40% 50%
hours of the year

93% of the time, the heating system works with less than 65% of its full power

(5) Heating demand variation

0 5 10 15 20 kWh/m²

according to number of occupants
2p
3p
4p

according to thermostat set point
17°C
18°C
regulations → 19°C
lower bound of → 20°C
comfort band   21°C
winter target temp. → 23°C
(EN 15251)
highest measured → 25°C
set point

according to floor height
2nd floor
4th floor
6th floor

If we reduce the heating set point from 20 to 18°C, the heating demand is cut in half

Heating demand can be doubled if set point is increased to 25°C

---

(1) Space heating demand: The heating demand of the living room and kitchen with winter garden is very low: 7–8 kWh/(m²·year). The northwest rooms without a winter garden on their facade demand three to four times more. The average remains very low, some 15 kWh/(m²·year).

(2) Thermodynamic balance (November to March): Solar gains due to the glazed facades with winter gardens provide the largest source of heat, representing almost double the energy of mechanical heating, and 30% more than internal gains. The winter gardens make it possible to compensate for the losses through glazing and benefiting from fully glazed facades.

(3) Hourly heating demand: Heating demand reaches a total of 15 kWh/m², which remains quite low. The demand is concentrated from the beginning of November until the end of March, which represents 33% of the year.

(4) Heating load monotone curve: Peak demand is 1.6 kW. As the intensive use is for a very short period of time, the equipment could be optimized and reduced.

(5) Heating demand variation: Varying occupation can have an impact on the heating demand, as more fresh air will be required. An apartment with two users would consume 30% less than an apartment with four occupants. Varying the floor height is also a source of higher heating consumption, as the lower floors would require 15% more energy. The thermostat has a large impact on energy demand: raising it from 20 to 23°C increases the demand by about 70%, whereas raising it to 25°C (as observed in measurements) can almost double the demand. Lowering it from 20 to 18°C cuts the demand by half, reaching only 8 kWh/(m²·year).

Case Summary
Main Values

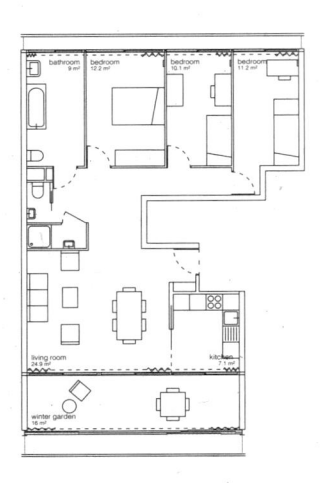

Daylight:
average daylight autonomy DA [300]: 73% of the time

all the spaces largely exceed the recommendations of EN 17037

Temperature and comfort in free-running mode:
above comfort: 0% of the time
within comfort: 61% of the time
below comfort: 39% of the time

average degree·hours
above comfort: 53°C·h

Solar gains and winter garden effect:
(temperature difference between the winter garden and outside)
winter: +3 to +8°C
mid-season: +3 to +7°C

Heating demand:
total: 15 kWh/(m²·year)
peak demand: 1.6 kW
Heating on:
2,918 / 8,760 hours per year
147 / 365 days per year

In Ourcq-Jaurès, the main living spaces with winter gardens are facing southeast; the bedrooms do not have a winter garden and are facing northwest. The plan is fairly open to effectively cross ventilate between the two opposite facades. Daylight levels in the apartment are high, with 73% of DA [300] on average. The living spaces behind the winter garden also have very high Daylight Autonomy: 69% for the living room and 72% for the kitchen. During 61% of the year, temperatures are thermally comfortable without any cooling or heating. In winter, temperatures never drop below 12°C in the bedrooms without the winter gardens, and they never drop below 15°C in the living room behind the winter garden. During the winter, temperatures in the winter garden are 3 to 8°C above outdoors. In this period, solar heat gains represent 50% more than the energy required to heat up the apartment, and solar gains are overall higher than losses by the glazed envelope. The heating demand is very low, only 15 kWh/m², which corresponds to what today is considered passive. In summer, high temperatures are rare in the apartment, as the spaces never surpass the overheating target of EN 15251, and rarely reach 29°C. Sometimes temperatures can be slightly hot at night (above 26°C), but the amount of hours is far below the ideal limit of 350°C·h (according to the contemporary French norms). During the mid-season, especially in spring, when it is sunny, the winter garden reaches comfortable temperatures indoors and can be used as an extra space. A north-facing winter garden could further reduce heat loss in that orientation and protect from the sun late in the afternoon during summer, reducing overheating. This scenario is evaluated as a case comparison.

Case Comparison
Modification: Additional Winter Garden

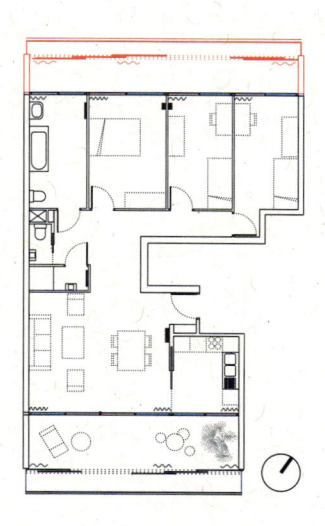

Daylight:
average daylight autonomy DA [300]: 65% of the time (**-8%**)

all the spaces largely exceed the recommendations of EN 17037

Temperature and comfort in free-running mode:
above comfort: 0% of the time
within comfort: 63% (**+2%**) of the time
below comfort: 37% (**-2%**) of the time

average degree·hours
above comfort: 31°C·h (**-22 °C·h**)

Solar gains and winter garden effect:
(temperature difference between the north winter garden and outside)
winter: +1 to +2°C
mid-season: +2 to +4°C

Heating demand:
total: 10 kWh/(m²·year) (**-5 kWh/(m²·year)**)
peak demand: 1.3 kW (**-0.3 kW**)
Heating on:
2,491 / 8,760 hours per year (**-427 h**)
141/ 365 days per year (**-6 d**)

Variation compared to the original project

Modifications in detail:
Winter garden is doubled on the bedroom side, depth: 1 m
same layers and operation conditions

A second winter garden one meter deep plus a balcony on the north facade reduces heating demand further to 10 kWh/m², which becomes negligible. During a typical February day, bedrooms are 2°C warmer due to the buffer effect of the winter garden, and infiltration losses are reduced even further, which explains the reduction in the heating demand. The presence of the winter garden also reduces solar radiation reaching the bedrooms, which further reduces the overheating of summer afternoons and increases future climate resiliency.

Case Comparison
Sun and Daylight

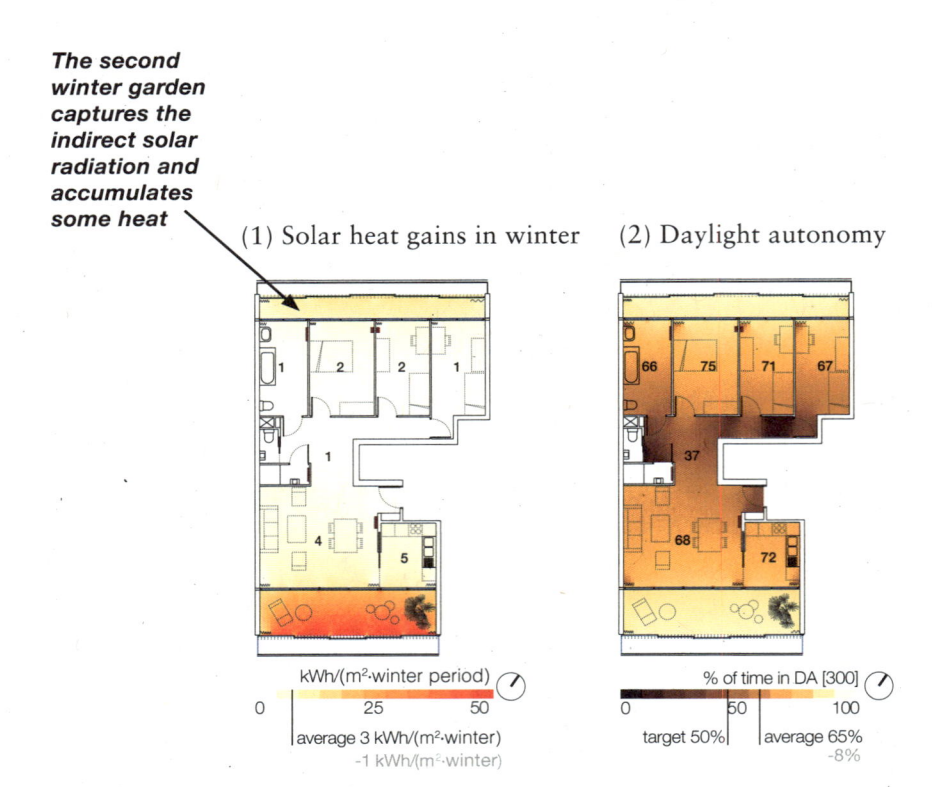

The second winter garden captures the indirect solar radiation and accumulates some heat

(1) Solar heat gains in winter

(2) Daylight autonomy

kWh/(m²·winter period)
0   25   50
average 3 kWh/(m²·winter)
-1 kWh/(m²·winter)

% of time in DA [300]
0   50   100
target 50%   average 65%
-8%

(1) Solar heat gains in winter: Adding a winter garden on the north side helps capture the solar heat in winter while blocking the intense sun of summer afternoons. During the summer, the apartment receives much less radiation than in the actual project thanks to the shading of the winter garden. During the winter, values are similar, but the winter garden creates an effective buffer toward the north.

(2) Daylight Autonomy: Daylight Autonomy is similar to the actual project though reduced in the bedrooms due to the presence of the winter garden. Still, 100% of each permanently occupied space exceeds the target of 50% DA [300].

Case Comparison
Typical Days

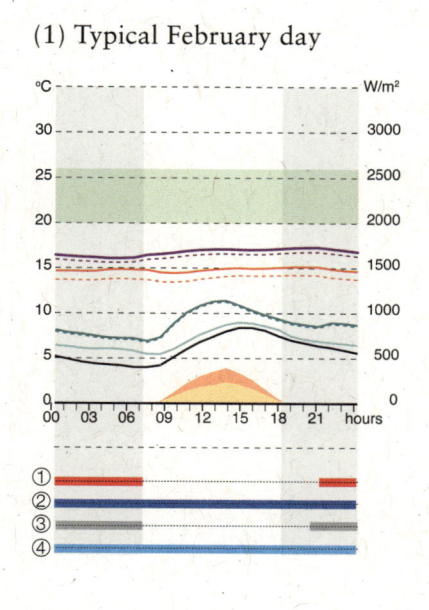

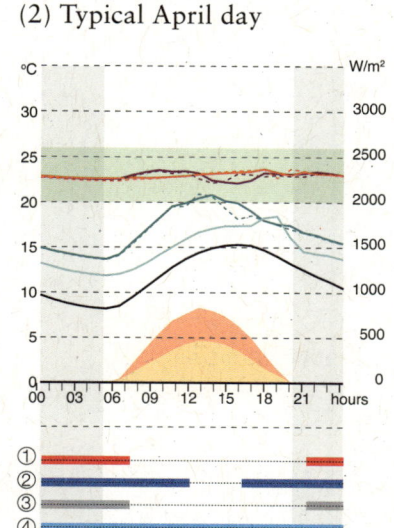

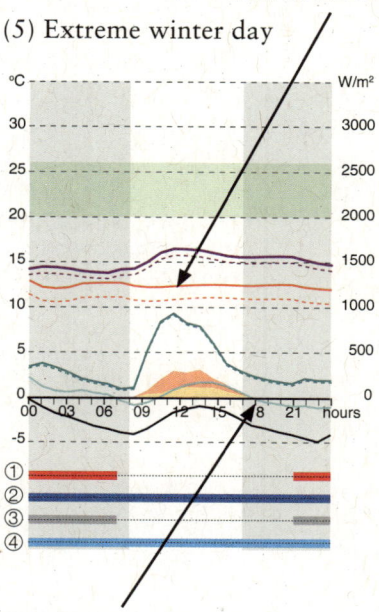

(1) Typical February day
(2) Typical April day
(5) Extreme winter day

Temperatures in the bedroom are 2°C warmer than in the real case

The north winter garden has 3 to 4°C higher temperatures than outdoors, which proves its effectiveness as a buffer

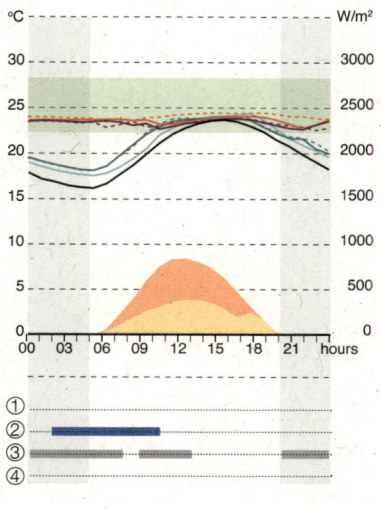

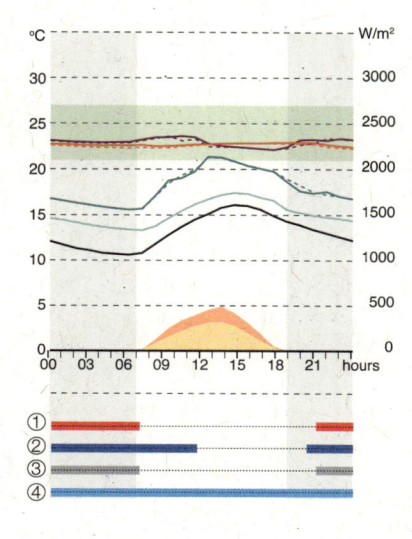

(3) Typical August day
(4) Typical October day
(5) Extreme summer day

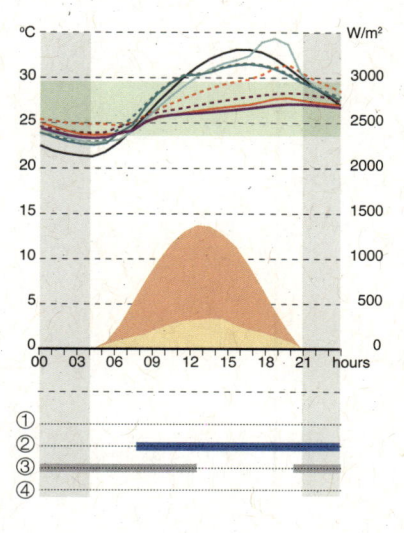

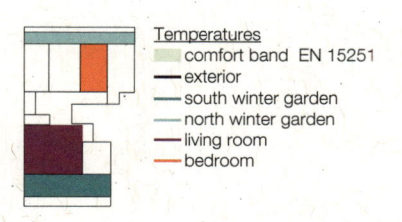

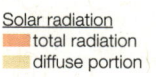

Temperatures
- comfort band EN 15251
- exterior
- south winter garden
- north winter garden
- living room
- bedroom

Solar radiation
- total radiation
- diffuse portion

(1) Typical February day: During a typical winter day, indoor temperatures remain very stable and higher than in the actual project, around 0.5–1°C. The difference between the rooms is reduced. The north winter garden has 1–3°C lower operative temperatures than the south one, depending on the sun. This proves that it is still useful as a buffer, even when it receives no sun.

(2) Typical April day: Indoor temperatures are similar across the apartment and stable around 23–24°C, which is again similar to the actual project. Temperature differences between the winter gardens are maintained.

(3) Typical August day: Temperatures are stable, around 23–24°C, across the apartment. The winter garden temperatures are very similar due to adequate solar protection and good natural ventilation.

(4) Typical October day: Indoor temperatures are similar across the apartment and stable, around 22–24°C, which is again similar to the actual project. Temperature differences between the winter gardens are also maintained.

(5) Extreme winter day: The temperature is around 1°C higher in the living room and about 3°C higher in the bedroom, which is significant. The north winter garden is 3 to 4°C warmer than outdoors, which proves its effectiveness as a buffer.

(6) Extreme summer day: The bedroom temperature is lower due to the shading provided by the winter garden, which acts as an awning. The temperature of the north winter garden is closer to outdoors, as it has less thermal inertia. In the evening, the sun warms it, moving the peak in temperature from the bedroom to the winter garden and improving indoor conditions.

Case Comparison
Thermal Comfort Conditions

The additional winter garden improves the summer comfort as degree hours above 26°C decrease in all rooms and remain far below the target

(1) Overheating evaluation

ideal target <350 °C·h
maximum tolerance

Living room 22 (-5)
Bedroom 42 (-53)
average 31 (-22)

250 500 750 1000 1250 °C·h
350

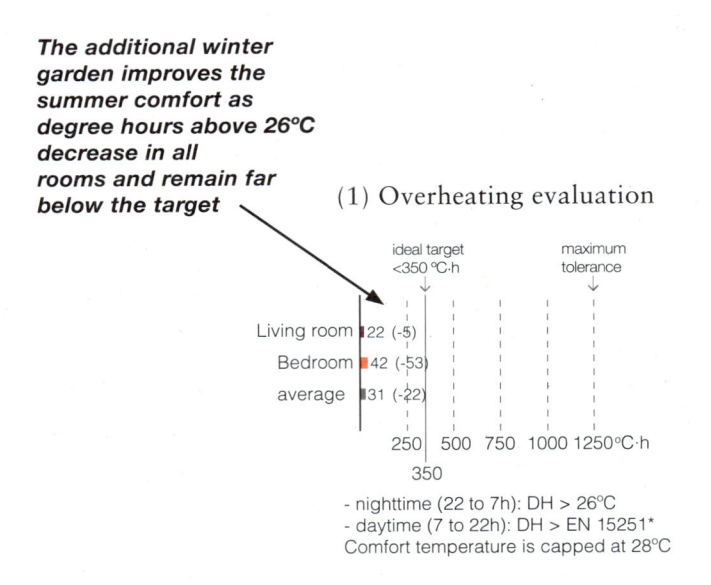

- nighttime (22 to 7h): DH > 26°C
- daytime (7 to 22h): DH > EN 15251*
Comfort temperature is capped at 28°C

(2) Winter garden UTCI (Universal Thermal Climate Index)

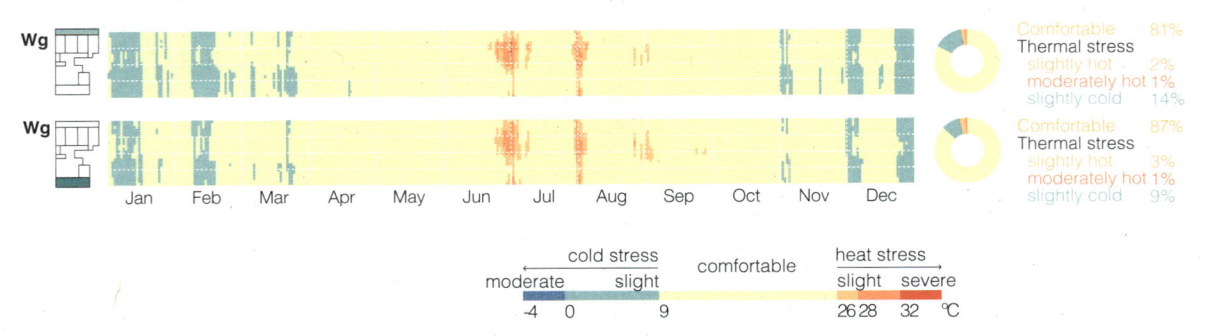

Wg
Comfortable 81%
Thermal stress
slightly hot 2%
moderately hot 1%
slightly cold 14%

Wg
Comfortable 87%
Thermal stress
slightly hot 3%
moderately hot 1%
slightly cold 9%

Jan Feb Mar Apr May Jun Jul Aug Sep Oct Nov Dec

cold stress — comfortable — heat stress
moderate slight   slight severe
-4   0   9   26 28 32 °C

(3) Resulting thermal comfort per room

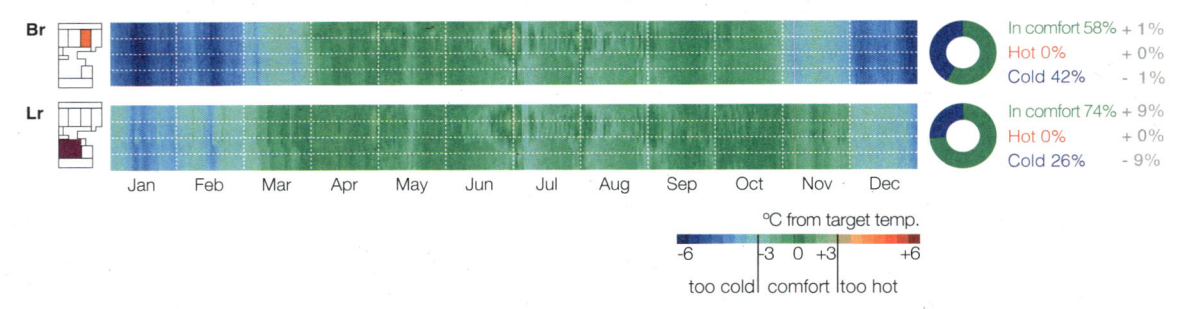

Br
In comfort 58% + 1%
Hot 0% + 0%
Cold 42% - 1%

Lr
In comfort 74% + 9%
Hot 0% + 0%
Cold 26% - 9%

Jan Feb Mar Apr May Jun Jul Aug Sep Oct Nov Dec

°C from target temp.
-6   -3 0 +3   +6
too cold comfort too hot

(1) Overheating evaluation: The unit has no overheating time, as the bedrooms are now shaded. They are also cooler at night, with half of the hours above 26°C.

(2) Winter garden UTCI (Universal Thermal Climate Index): The north-facing winter garden is comfortable for outdoor use 81% of the time, which is 9% better than a sheltered exterior. This proves its effectiveness even in the north orientation. In an exposed outdoor situation, no thermal stress is only achieved 44% of the time, which is almost half of the north winter garden. In winter, the north winter garden has 1–3°C lower temperatures than the south one, depending on the sun. This proves that it is still useful as a buffer, even when it receives no sun.

(3) Resulting thermal comfort per room: Time when the operative temperature of the bedrooms is in comfort is similar to the actual project, but the cold severity is reduced: during March and November, temperatures are almost comfortable naturally. This is reflected in the heating demand, which is cut in half.

Case Comparison
Heating Demand

(1) Space heating demand

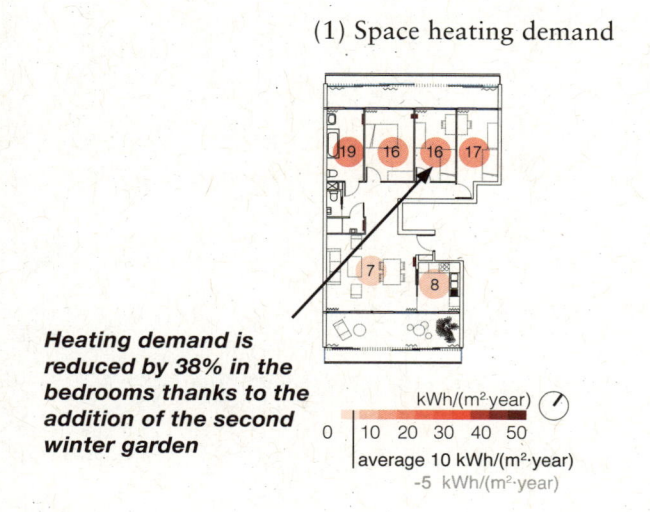

Heating demand is reduced by 38% in the bedrooms thanks to the addition of the second winter garden

kWh/(m²·year)
0 10 20 30 40 50
average 10 kWh/(m²·year)
-5 kWh/(m²·year)

(2) Thermodynamic balance (November to March)

kWh — heat losses — heat gains

1231 in the real case

OC - Opaque Conduction
GC - Glazing Conduction
I/V - Infiltration/Ventilation
TI - Thermal Inertia
IG - Internal Gains
SG - Solar Gains
HD - Heating Demand

924 kWh/period
-307 kWh/period

-307 kWh/period or -25% compared to built project

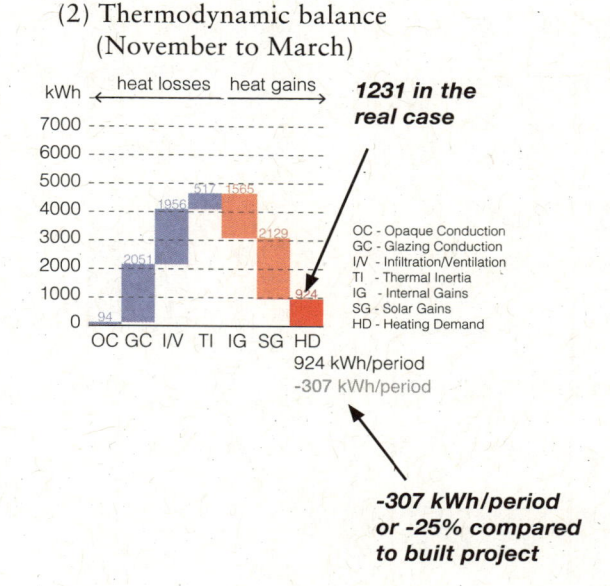

(1) Space heating demand: The heating demand is reduced from 15 to 10 kWh/(m²·year). The period of time when heating is needed is shorter, and peak demand is about 40% lower. The demand is still concentrated in the bedrooms and bathroom.

(2) Thermodynamic balance (November to March): Looking at the thermodynamic balance, exchange with the exterior is reduced, and solar gains remain the highest heat source, which now more than doubles the heating, and helps to reduce the overall heating demand.

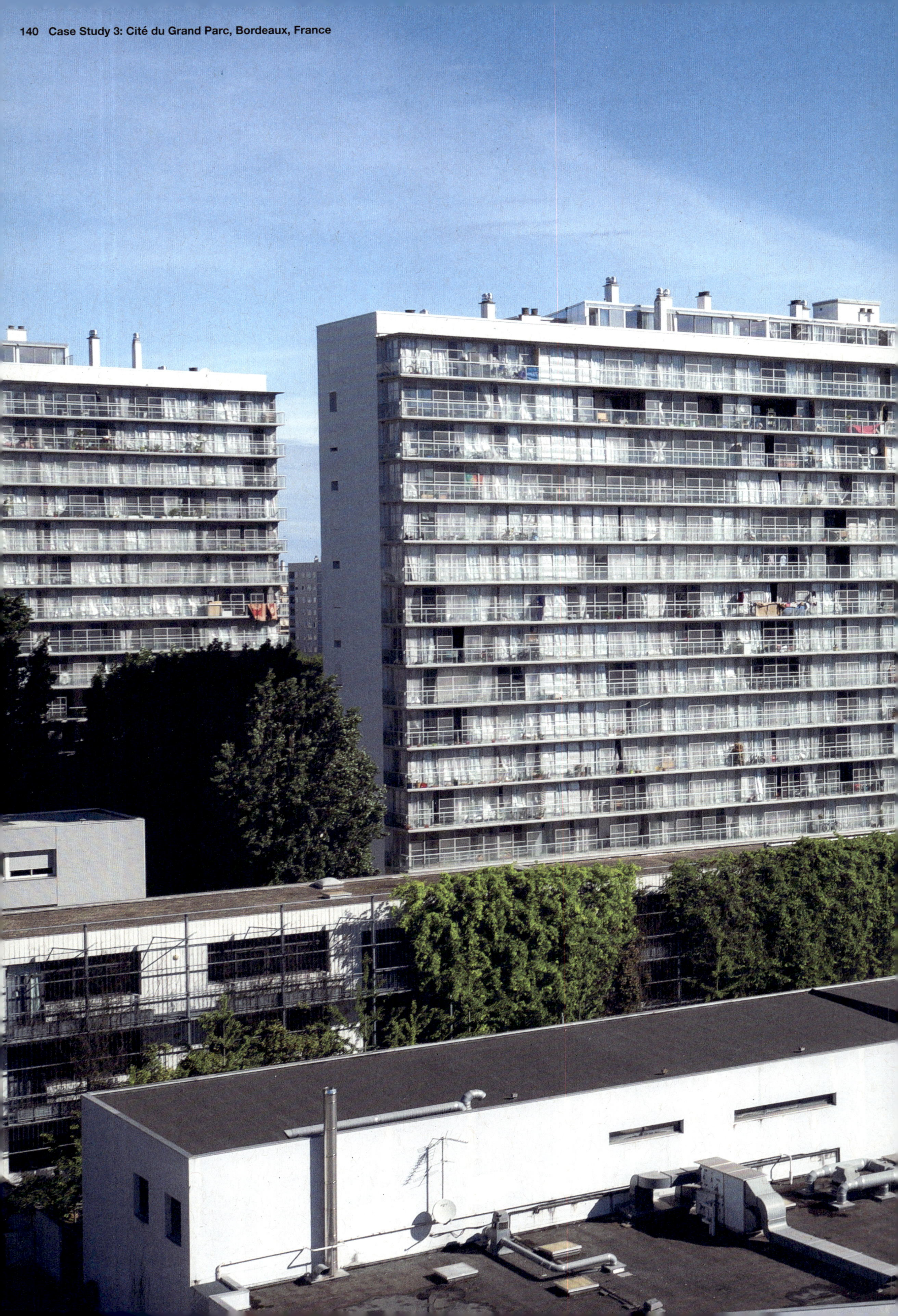

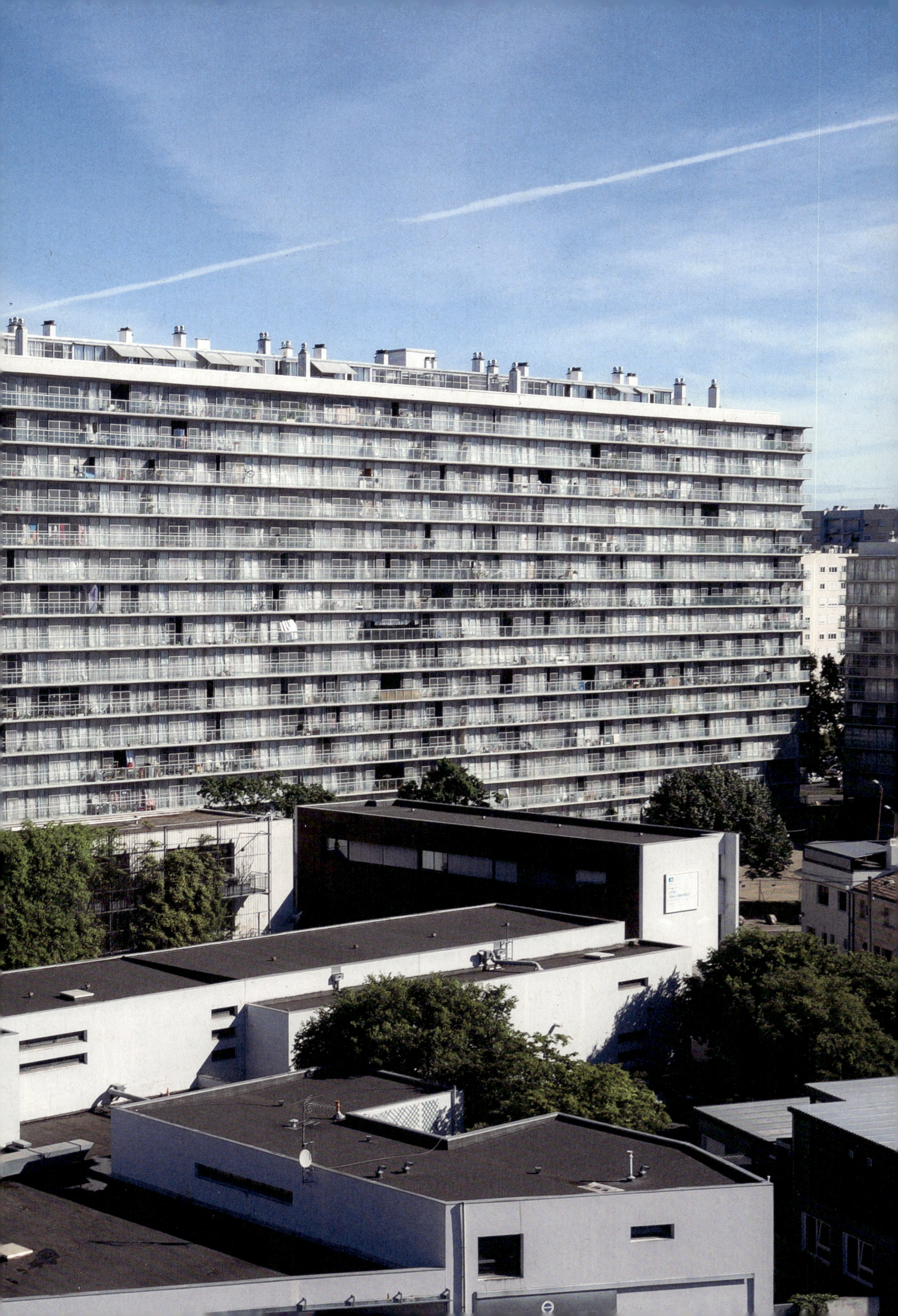

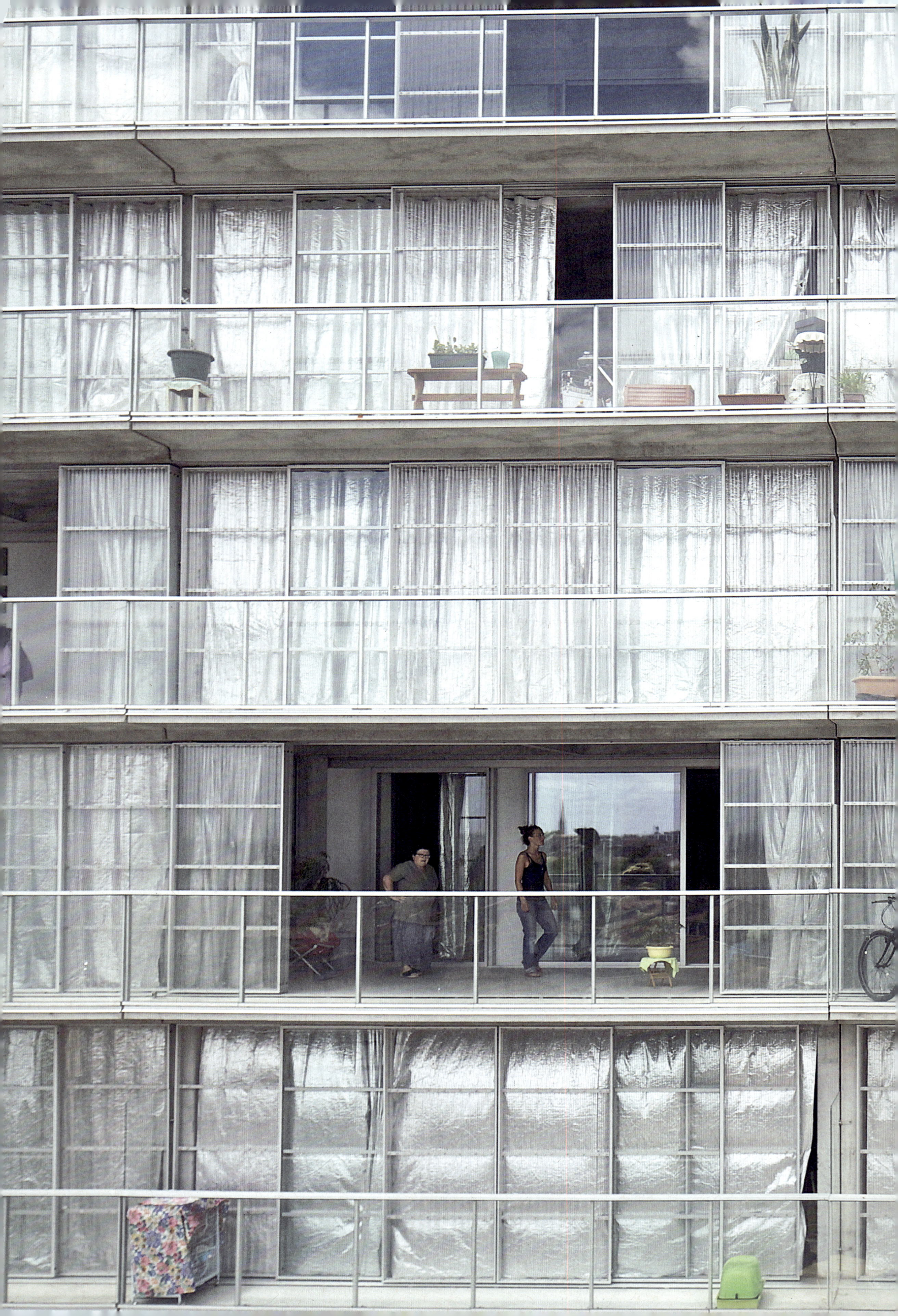

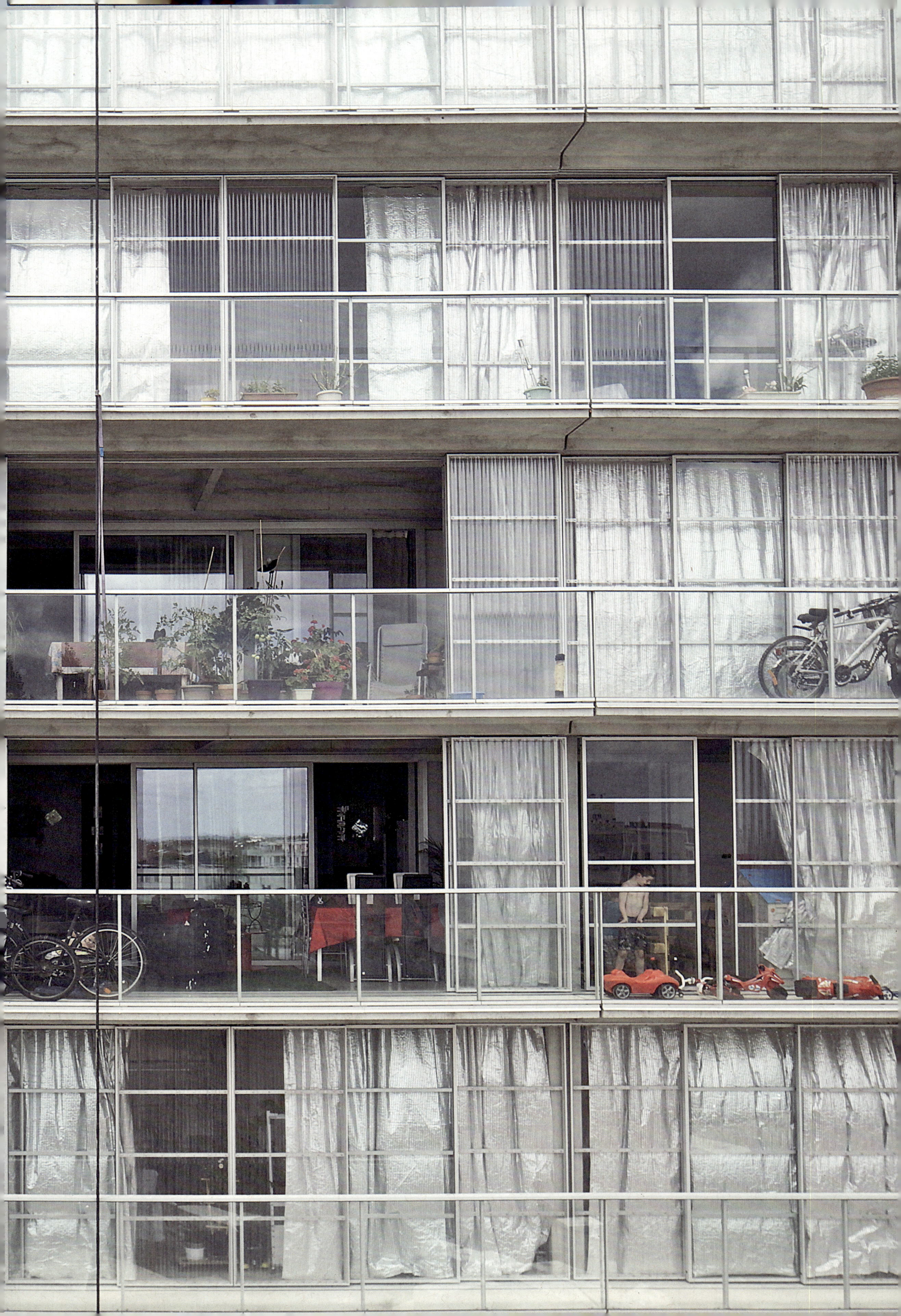

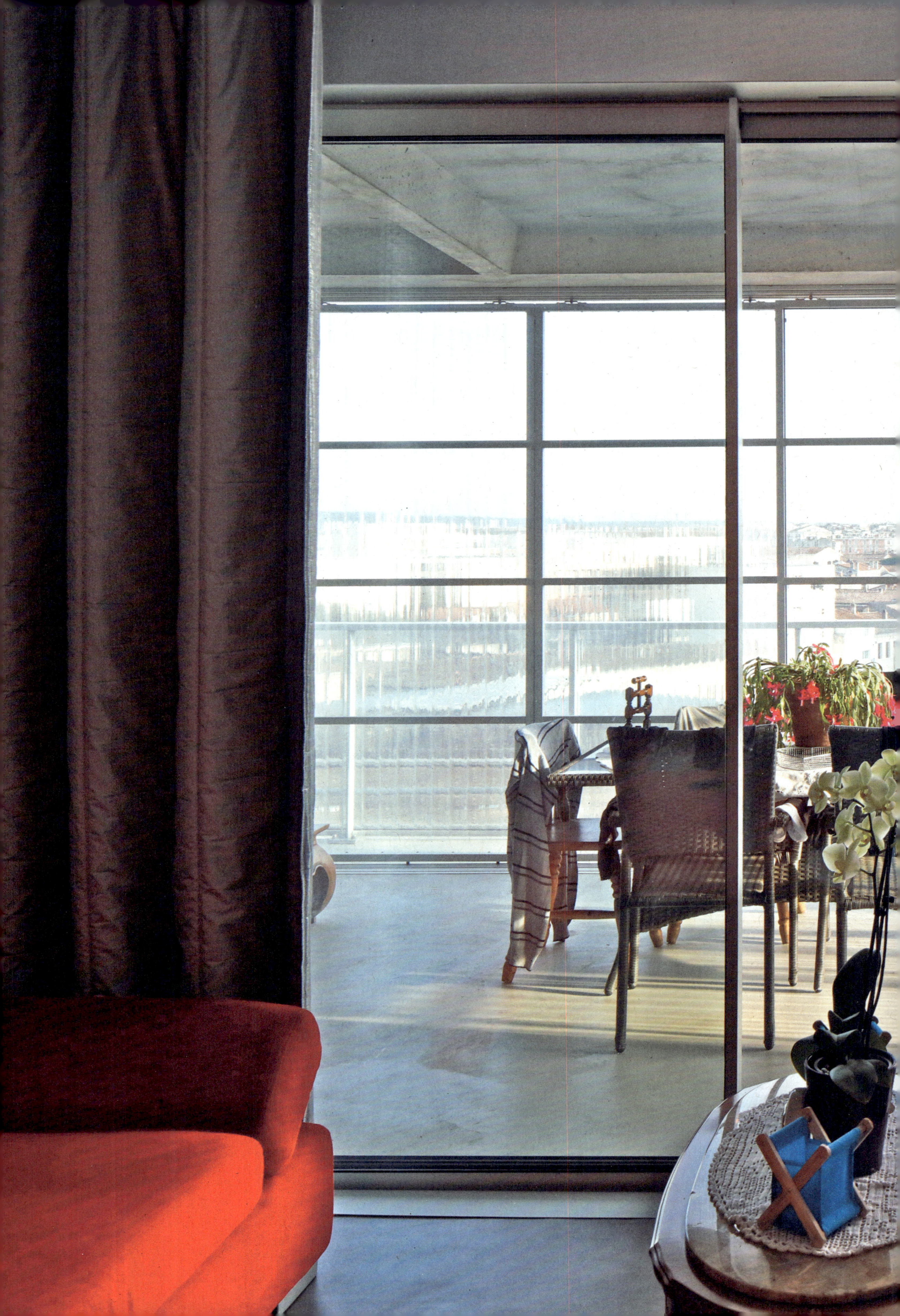

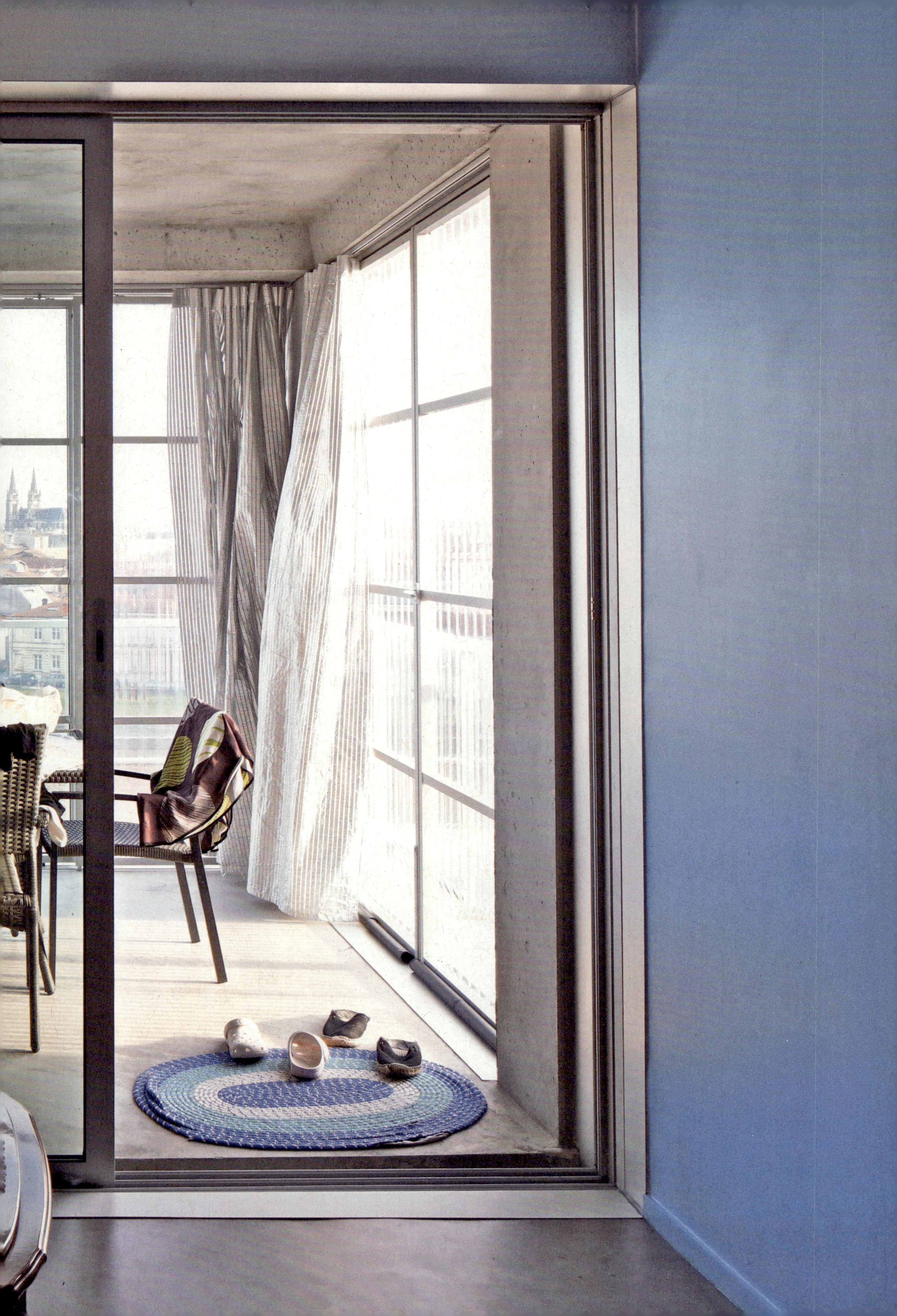

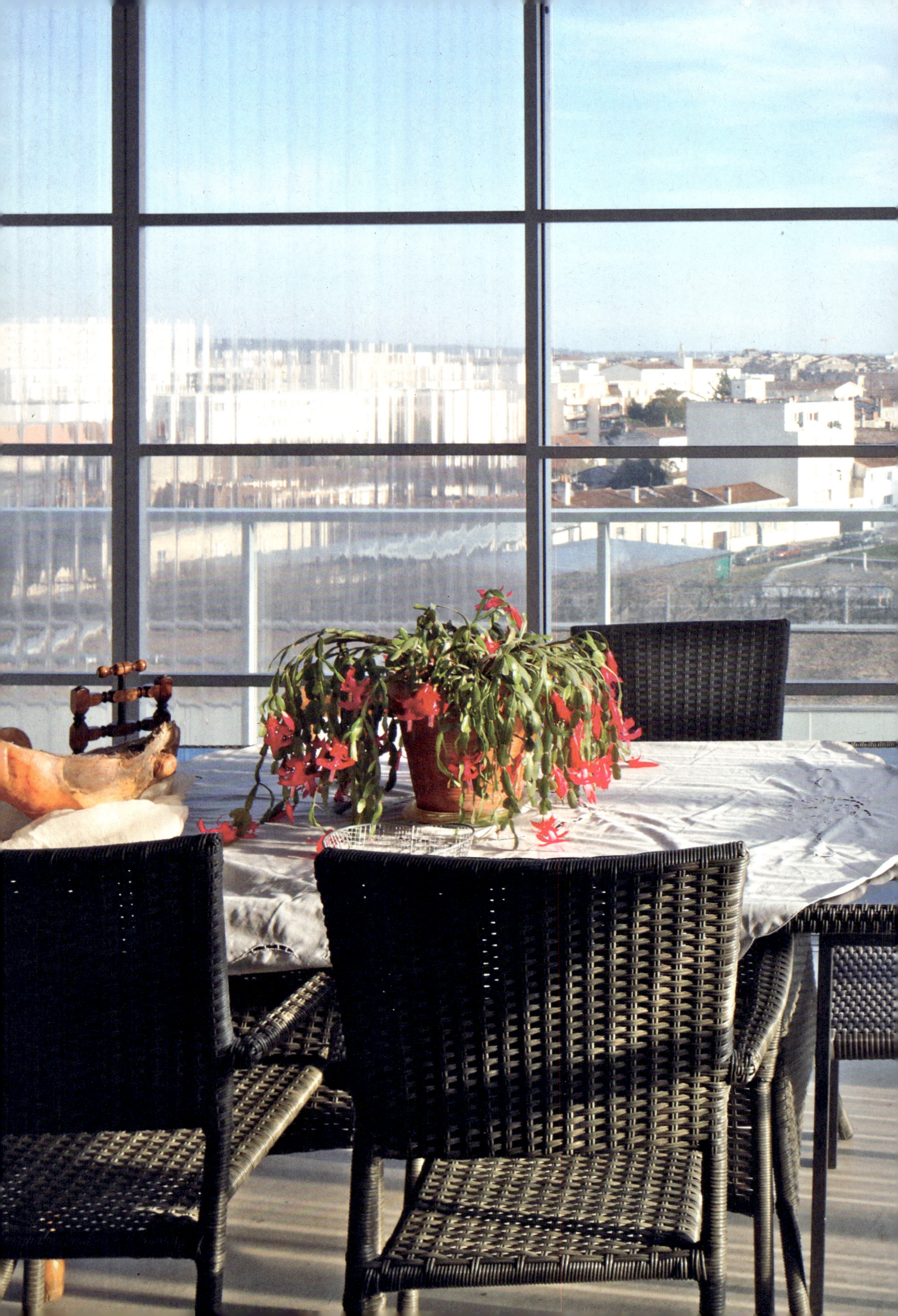

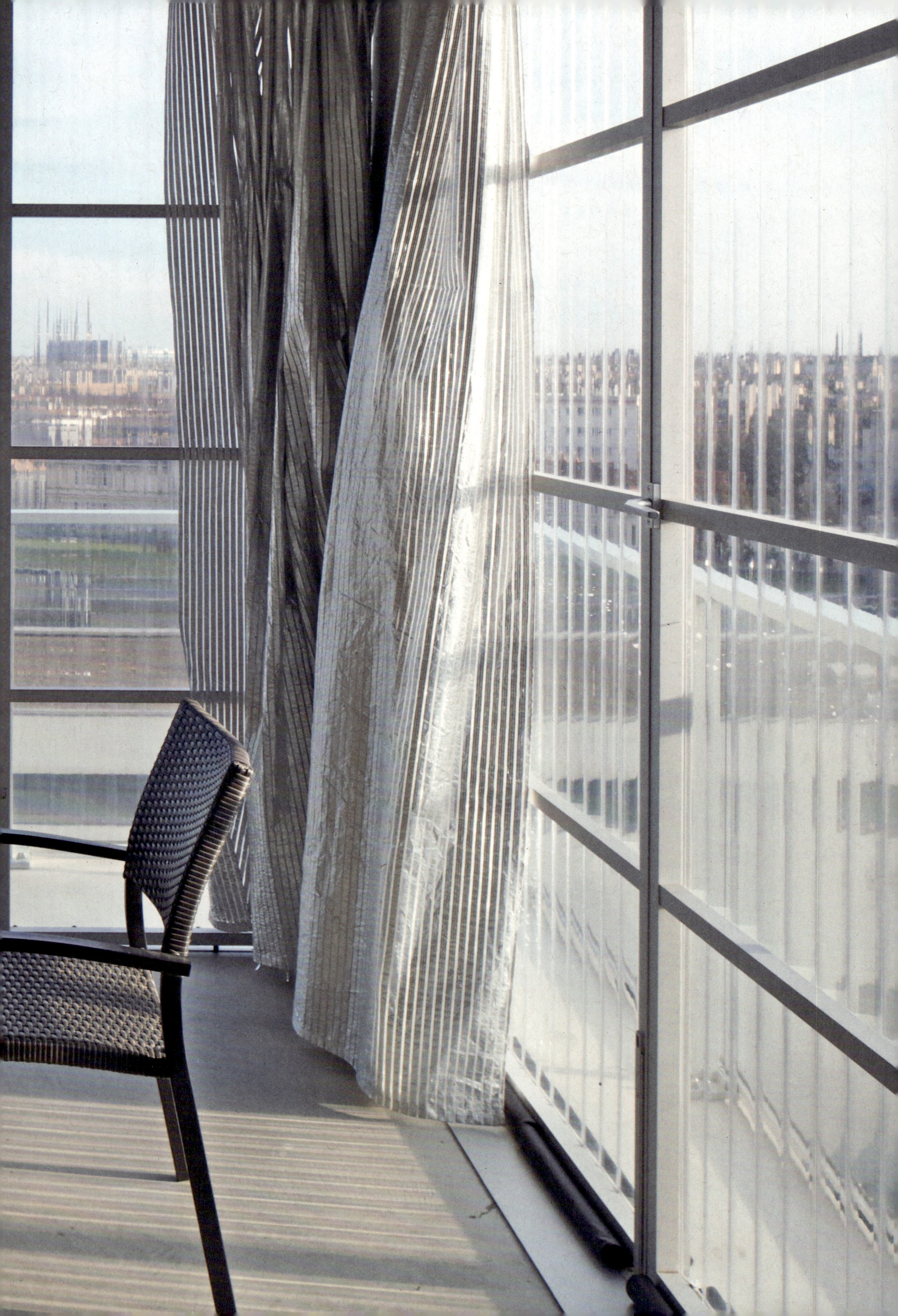

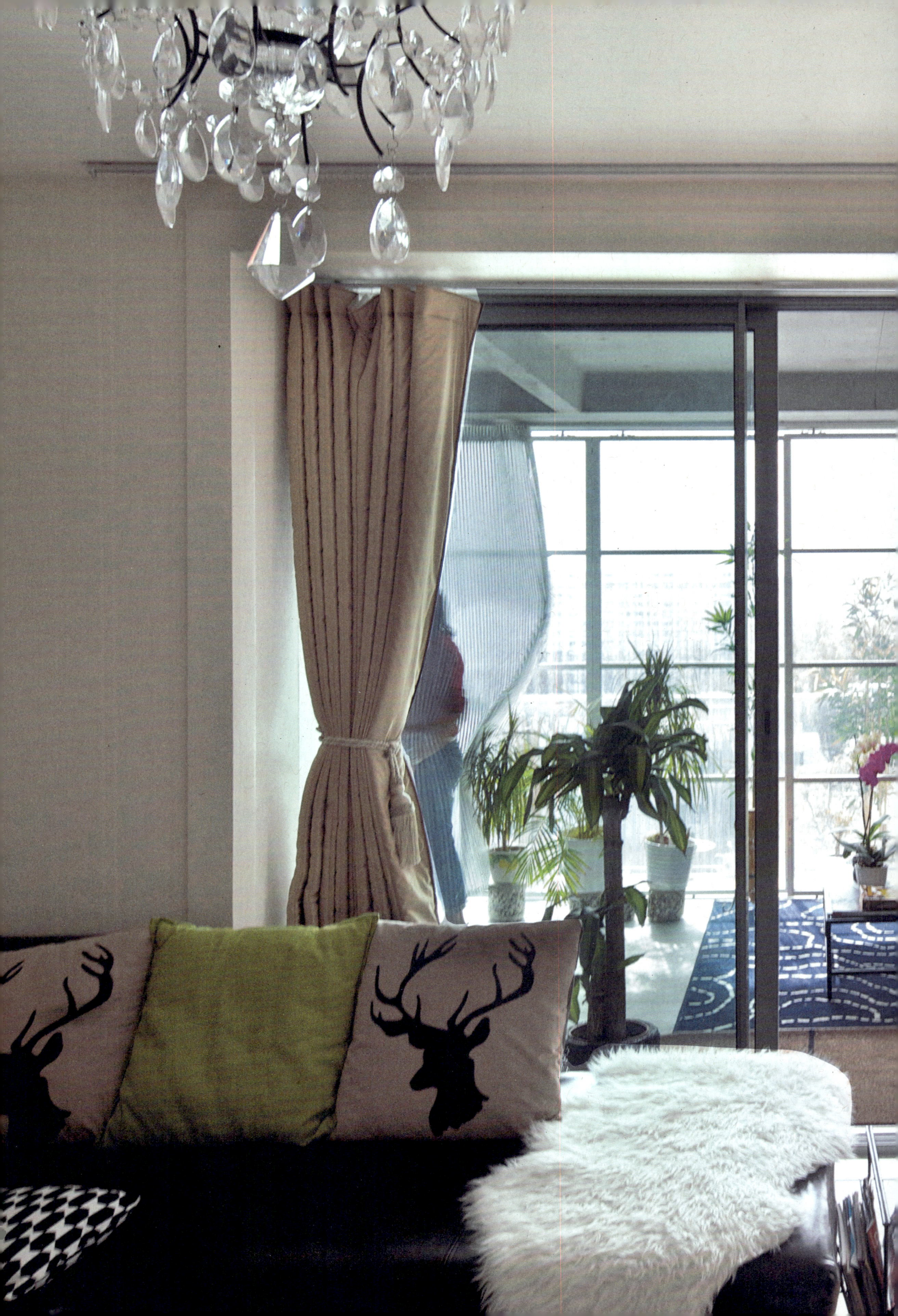

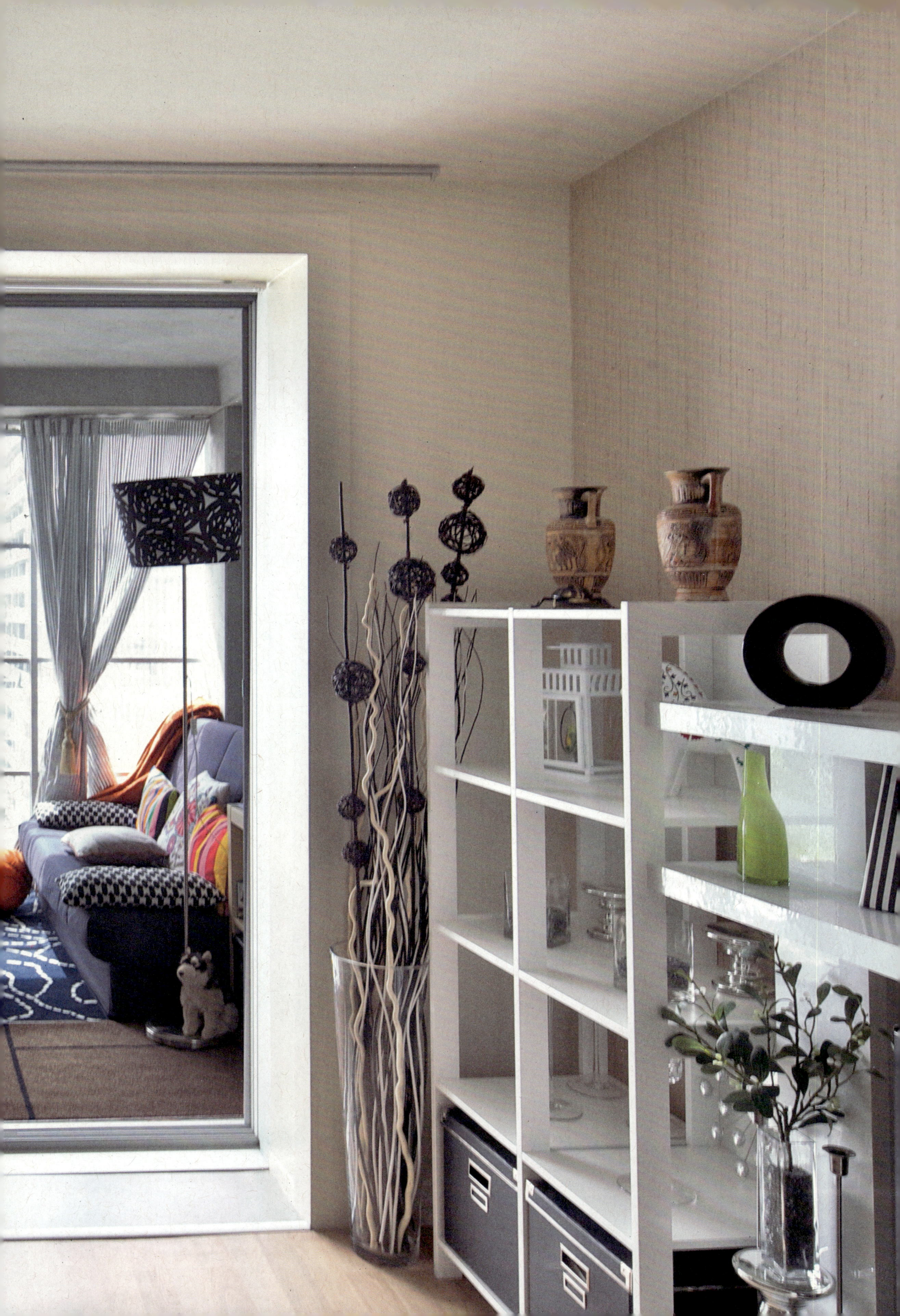

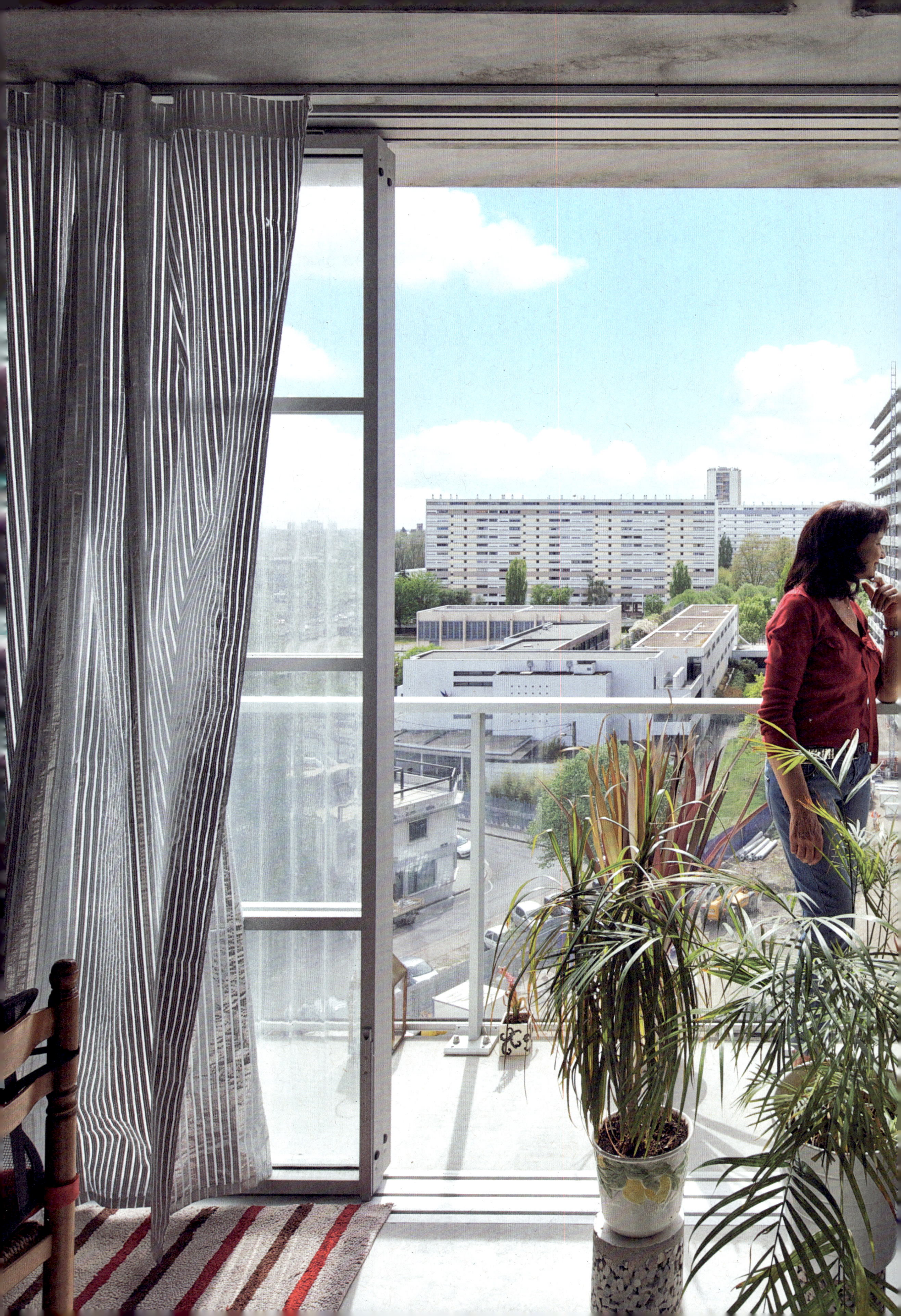

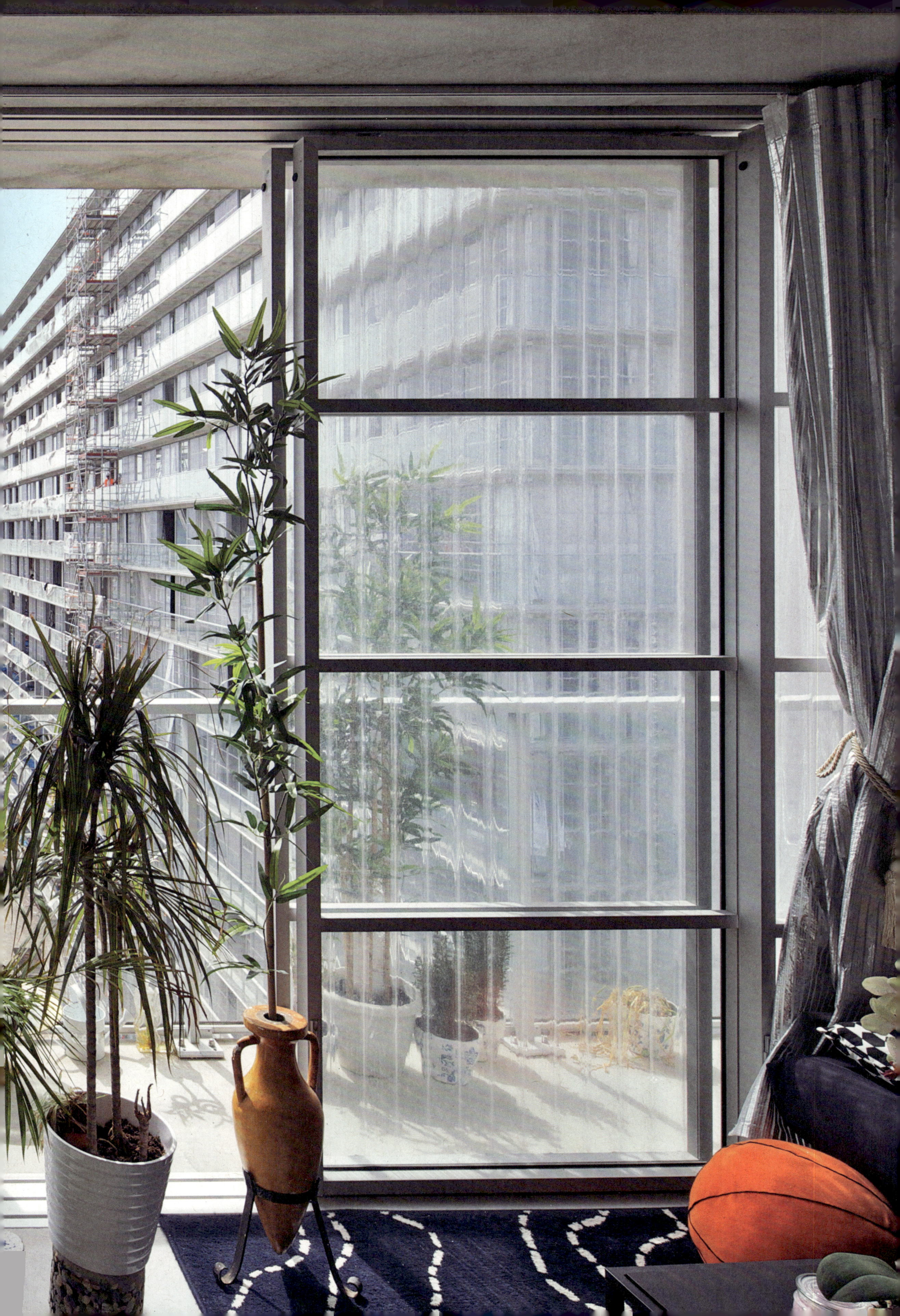

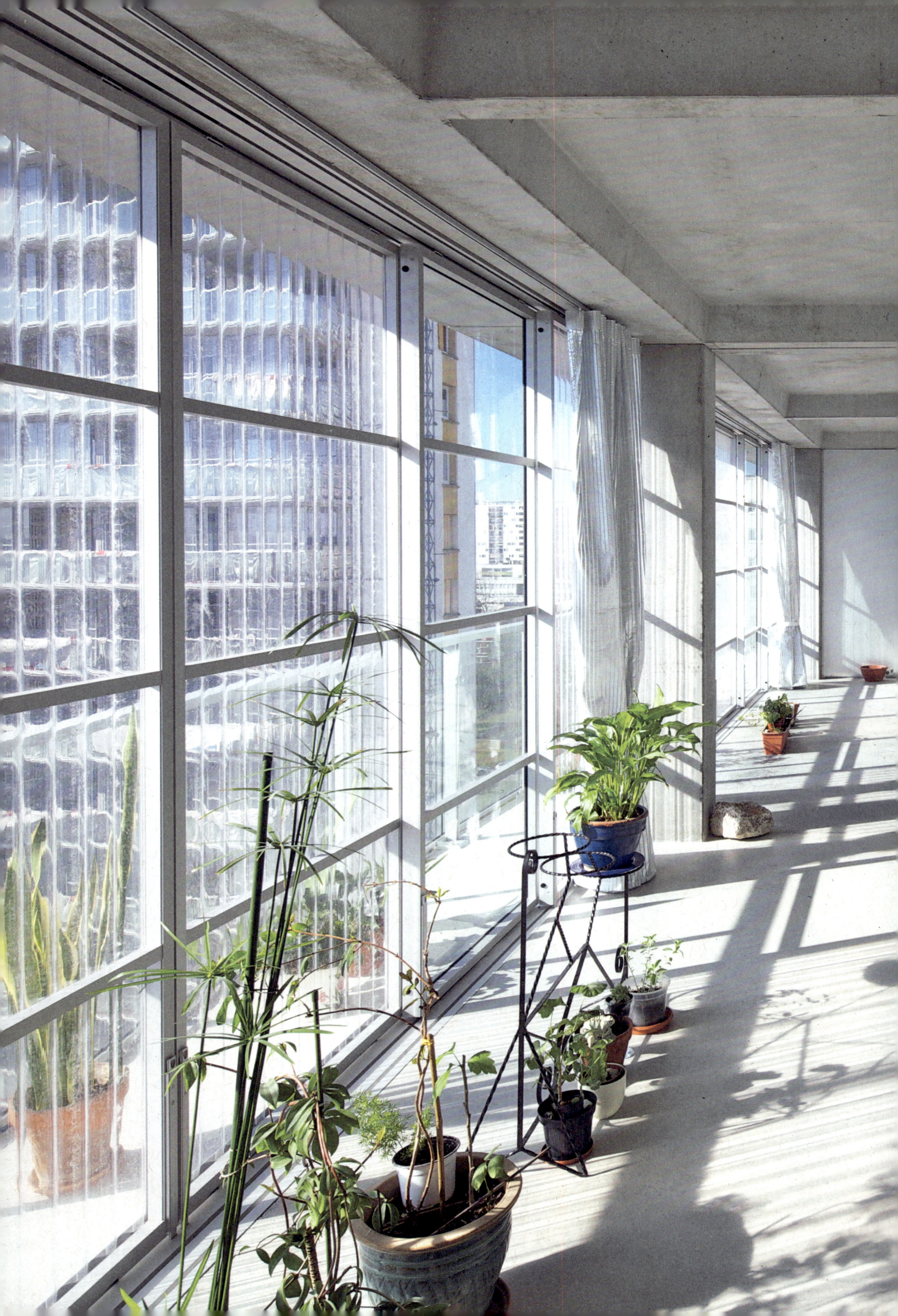

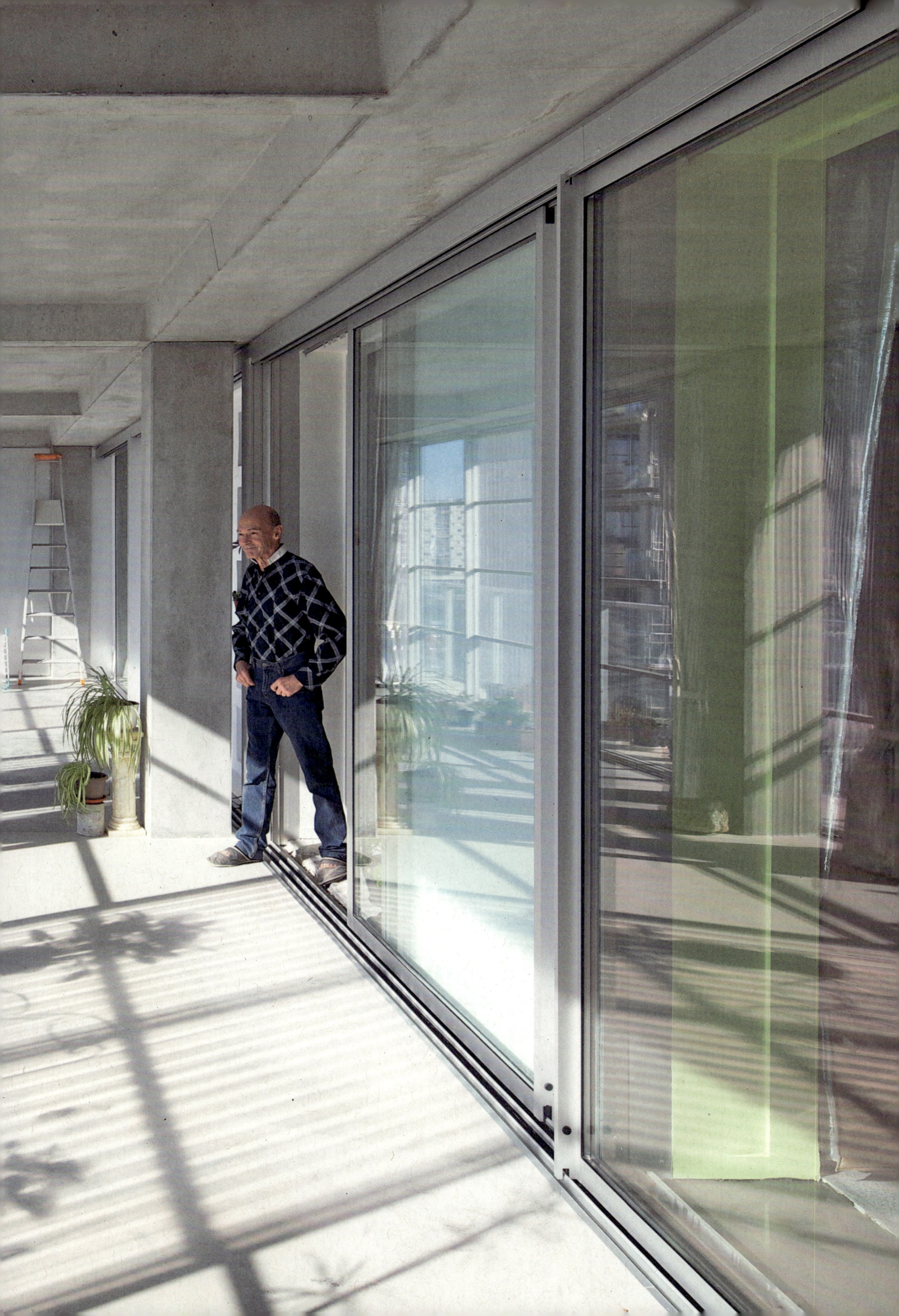

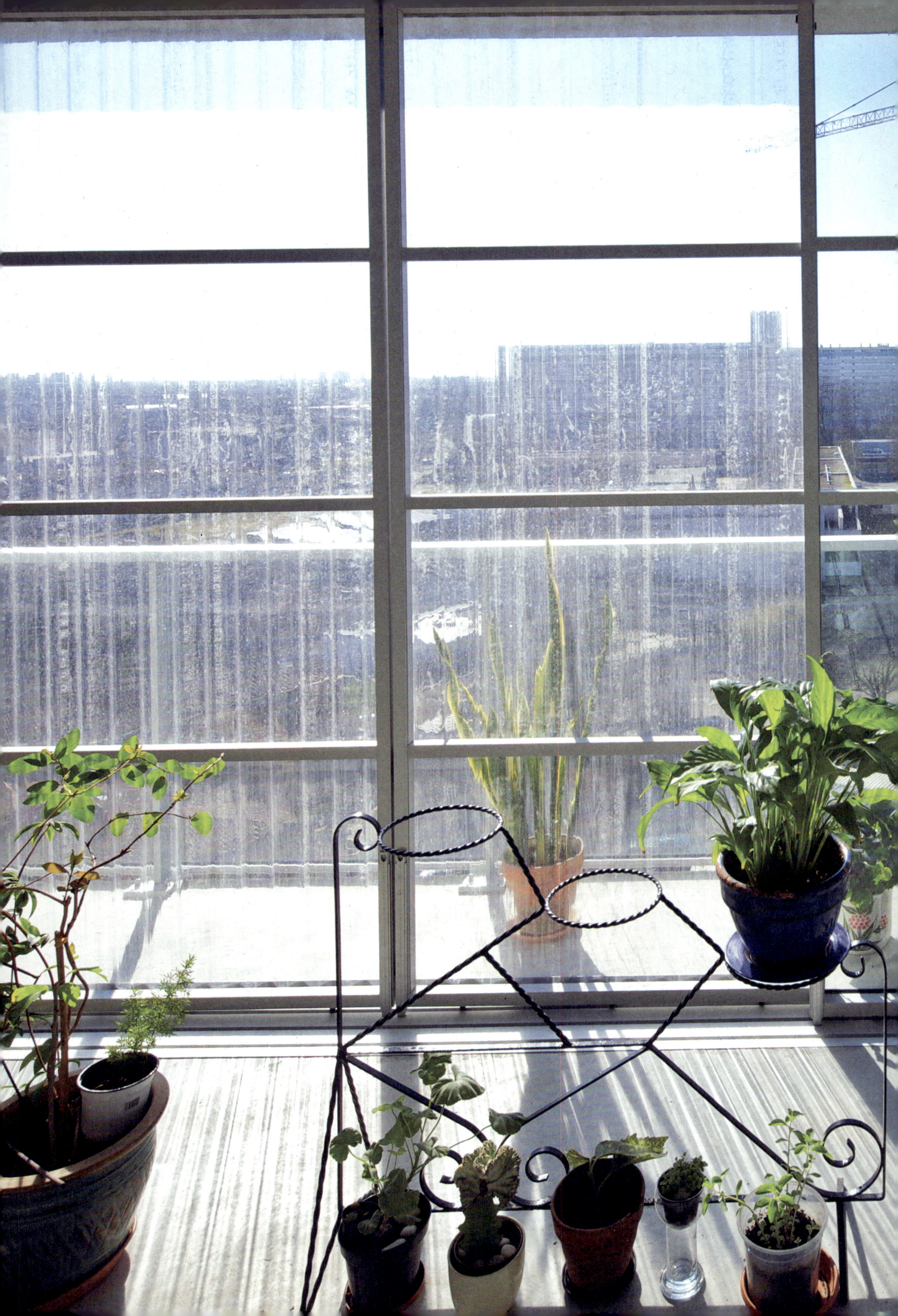

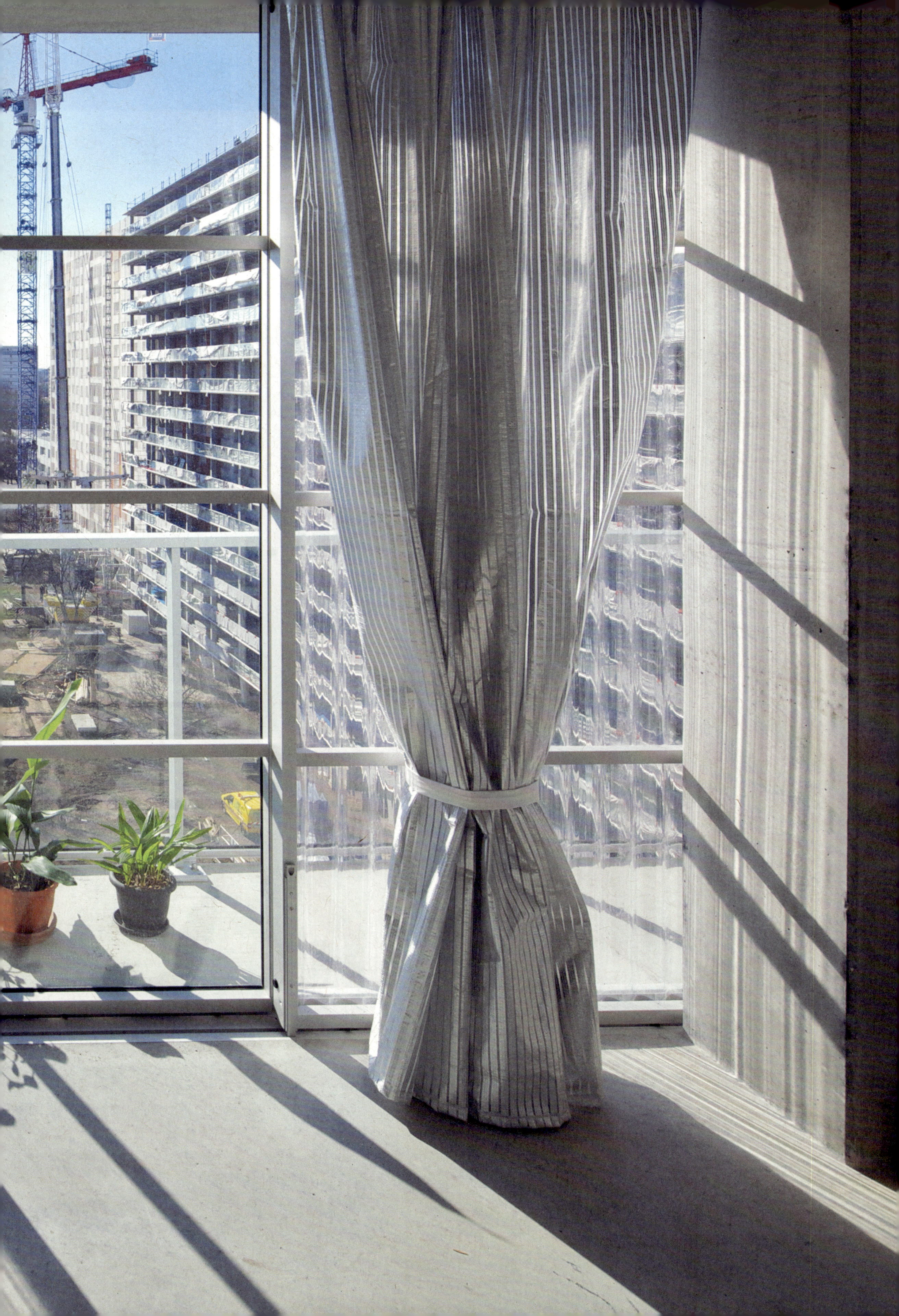

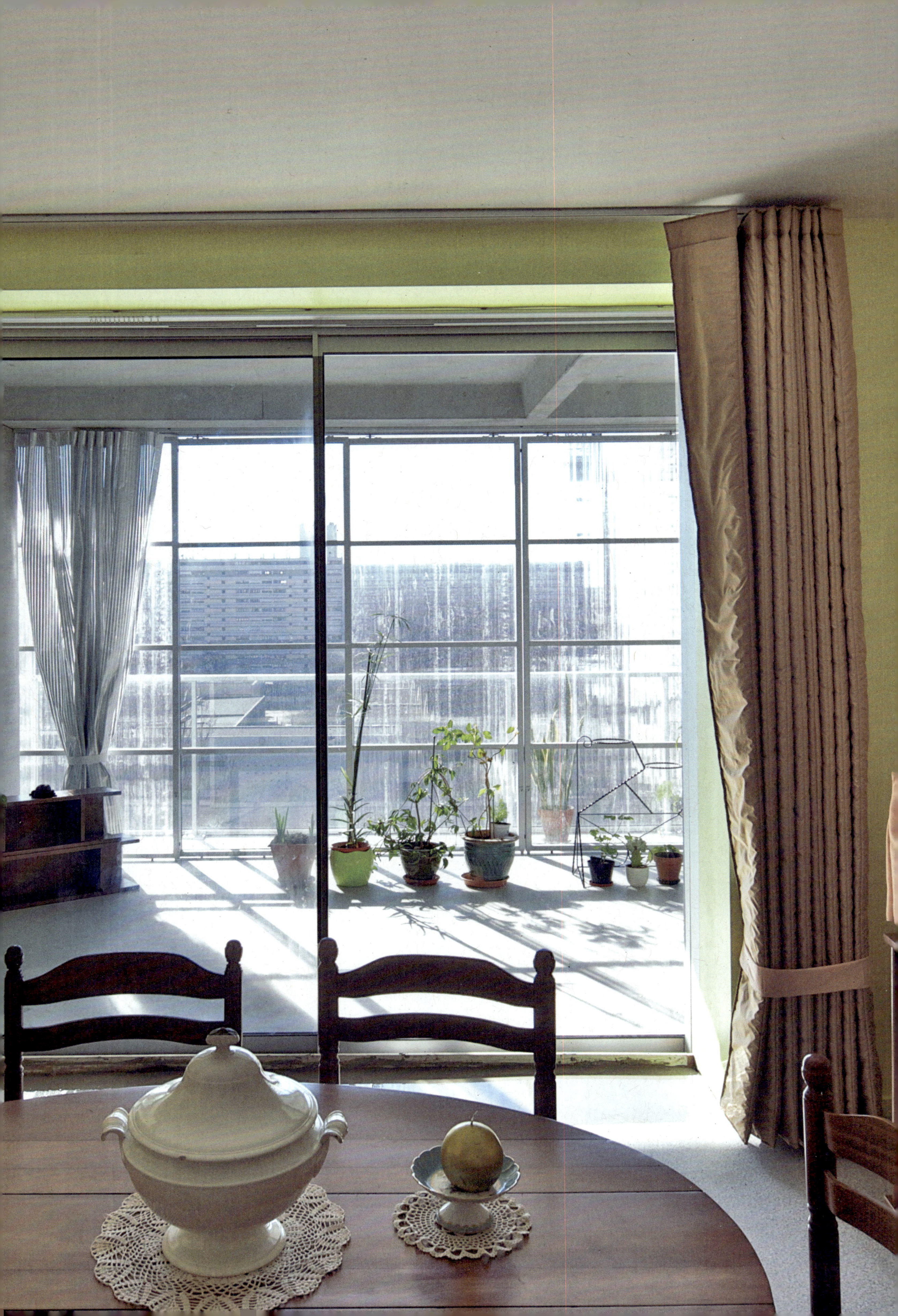

Case Study 3

Cité du Grand Parc

Bordeaux
France
2016

(1) Site Plan 1/2000

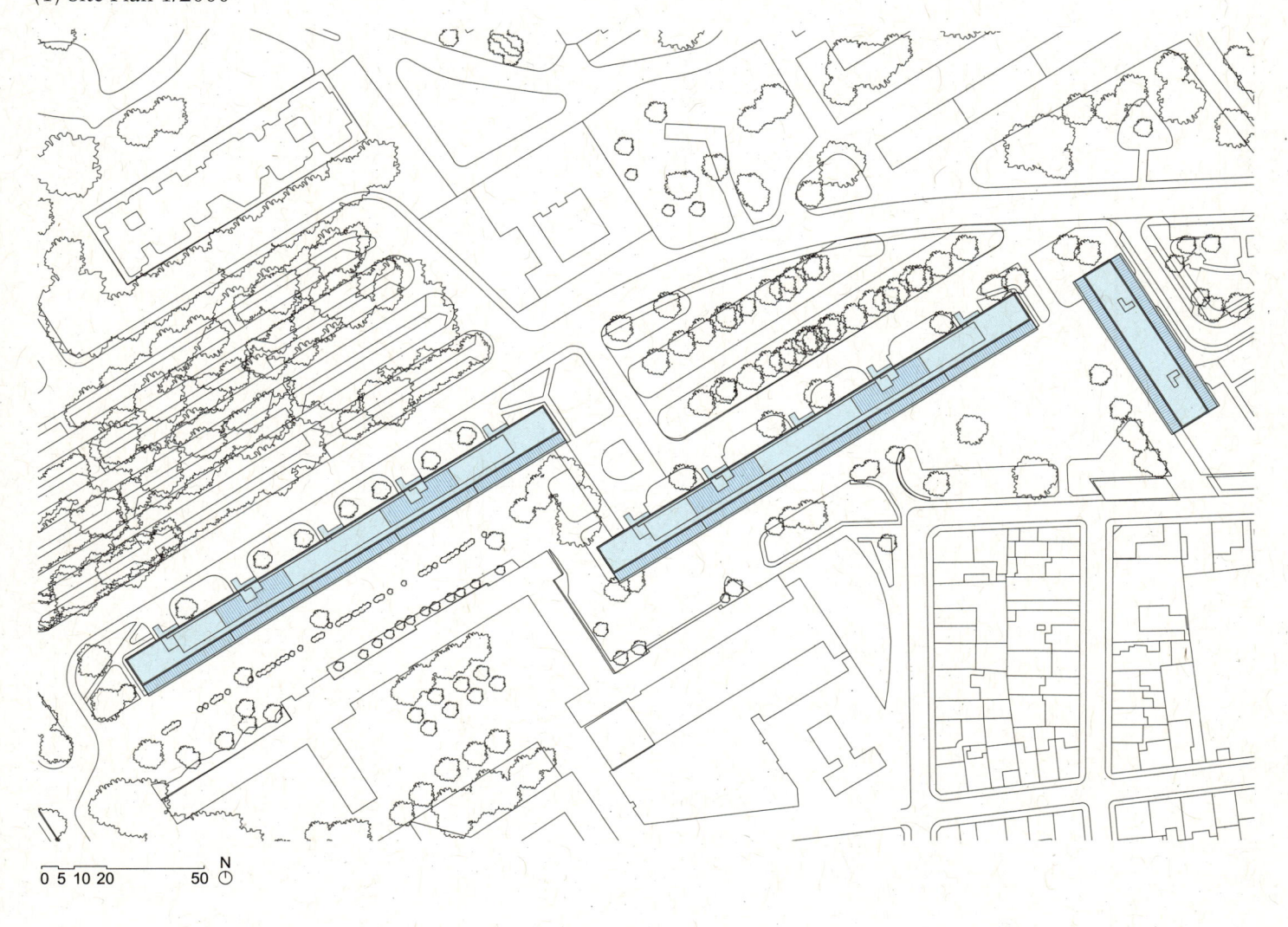

The project consists of the transformation of three fully occupied modernist social housing blocks in the Cité du Grand Parc in Bordeaux, a modernist district of 4,000 apartments built in the early 1960s. The three buildings, ten to fifteen floors high, contain 530 apartments. They had to be renovated after their demolition was ruled out. The project of transformation starts from the interior of the dwellings, giving new qualities to the apartments by creating a precise and careful inventory of the existing qualities that should be preserved and the shortcomings that should be supplemented. The project is based on the decision to transform the existing building without making significant interventions in the existing structure, stairs, or floors, and instead work with additions and extensions. This economical approach makes it possible to concentrate resources on generous extensions that improve the quality and the dimensions of the dwellings in a significant and sustainable way.

158 Case Study 3

Project and Environmental Conditions
Building

(1) Plans 1/400, Block H and I

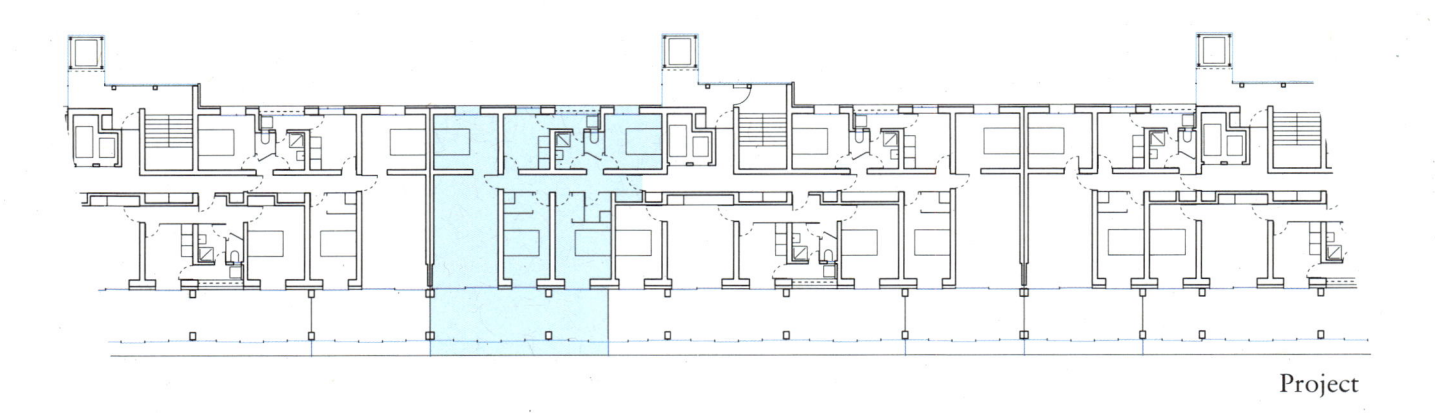

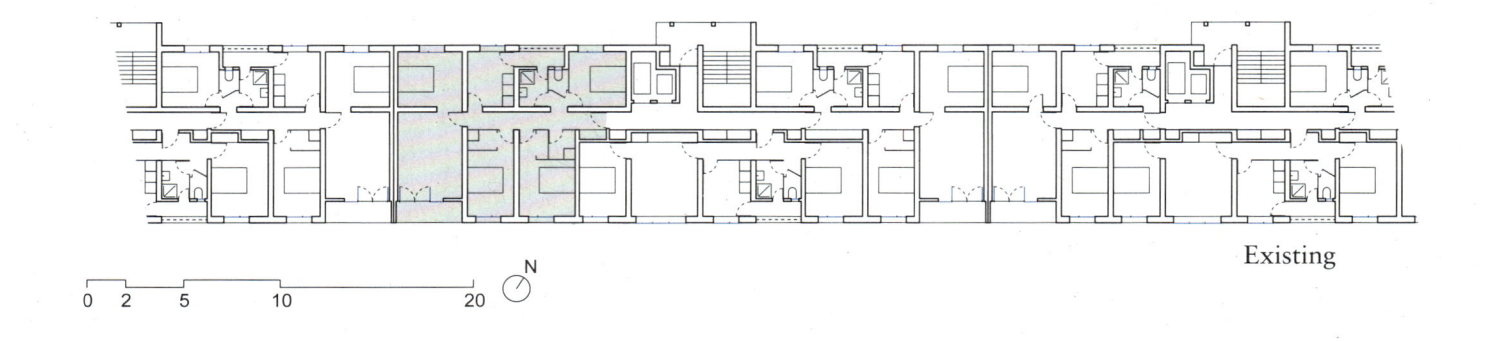

Project

Existing

0 2   5   10   20   N

(2) Oversight Plan 1/1000

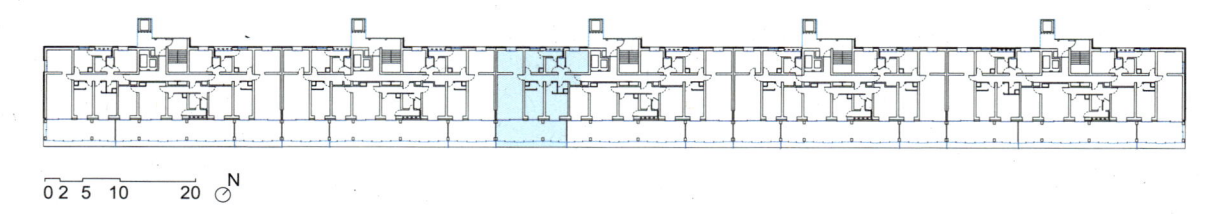

0 2 5 10   20   N

All apartments open onto large winter gardens and balconies, which provide the opportunity to enjoy more space, more natural light, more mobility of use, and better views. They offer pleasant extra spaces 3.8 m deep, which can be used to their fullest. The existing windows are replaced by large glass sliding doors that connect every room of the dwelling to the winter garden, offering more freedom of use and mobility, like in a house. It is an extraordinary living situation. The transformation was implemented while the building was occupied. All the inhabitants stayed in their dwellings without any increase in rent.

Case Study 3

Project and Environmental Conditions
Unit

(1) Analyzed unit 1:150

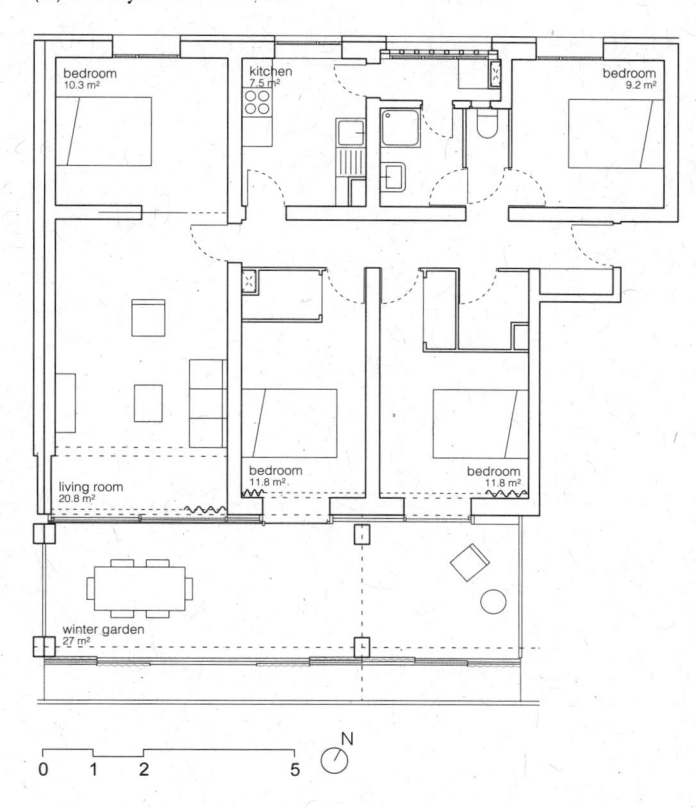

bedroom
10.3 m²

kitchen
7.5 m²

bedroom
9.2 m²

living room
20.8 m²

bedroom
11.8 m²

bedroom
11.8 m²

winter garden
27 m²

0 1 2   5   N

The unit's spatial extensions with fully glazed sliding doors add freedom of use and movement as well as appropriation, offering direct contact to the exterior along the full length of the sun-oriented facade. Living rooms, bedrooms, and, in part, bathrooms are now directly connected to the extra spaces that invite the invention of further uses.

Case Study 3

Project and Environmental Conditions
Climate

(1) Bordeaux climate summary

Bordeaux has the hottest summer and highest peaks of the four case studies

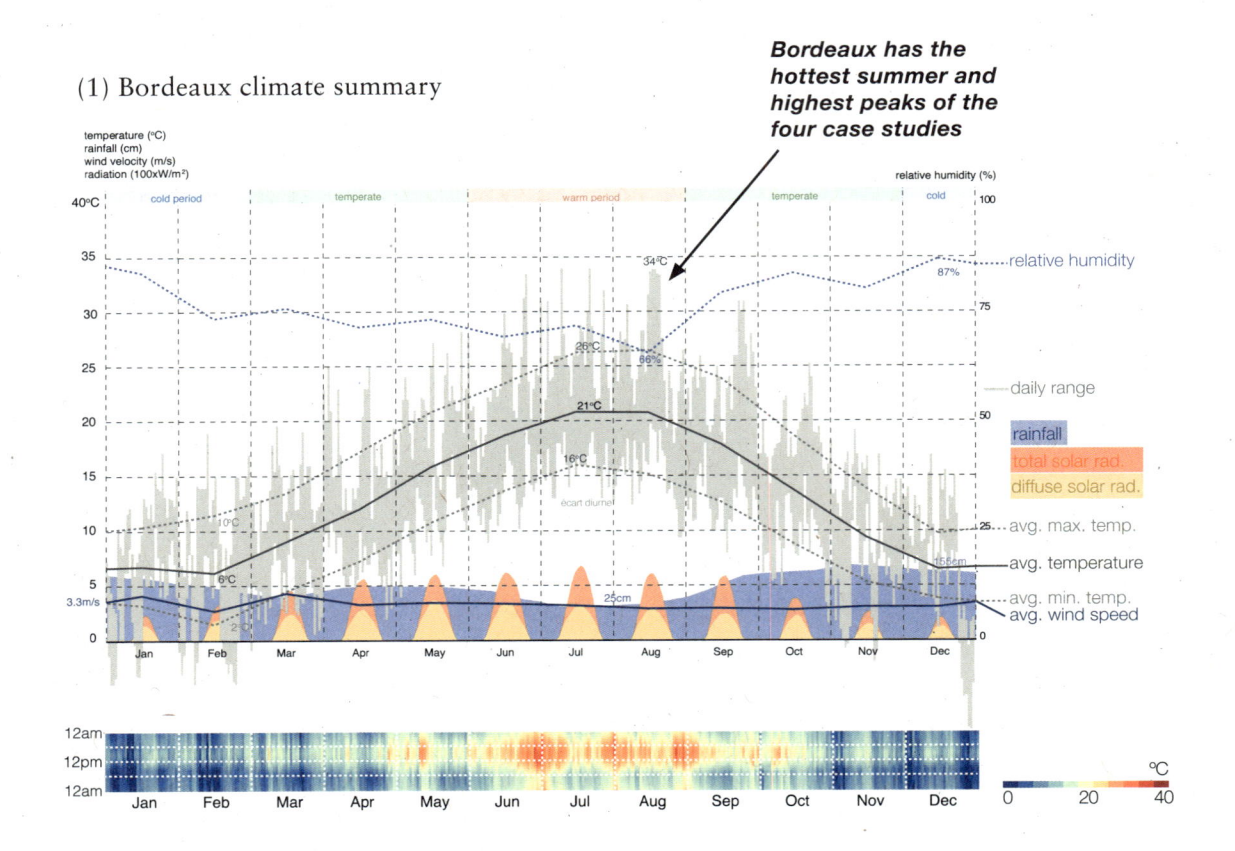

(2) Sky coverage in winter and summer

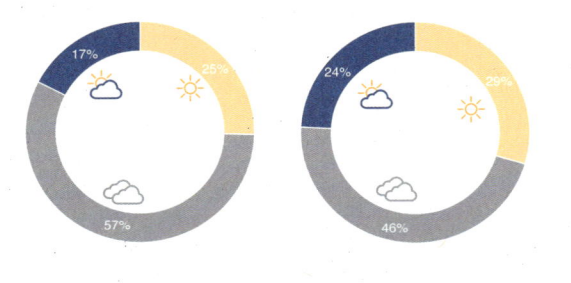

(3) Sky radiation in the sky vault in winter and summer

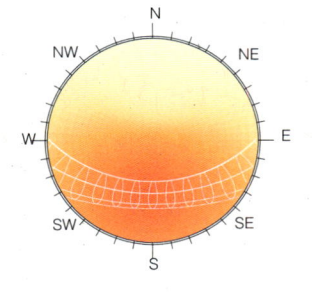

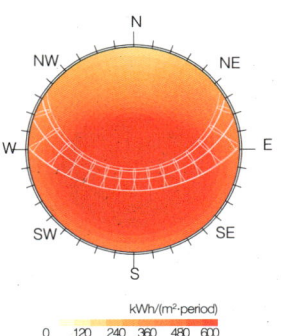

(4) Annual wind rose

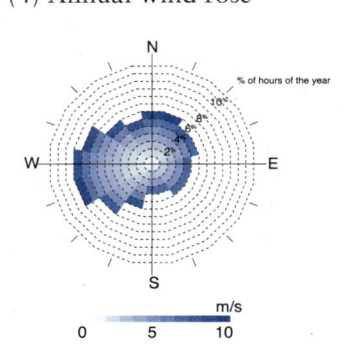

(1) Bordeaux climate summary: The climate is temperate with a large daily amplitude and has the hottest summer of all four case studies. The sun is strong and has a large proportion of direct radiation in summer. During the hot period, the average high temperature is around 26°C, which is similar to other climates, though it goes beyond 30°C much more often than in the other climates (about sixteen days a year) and can easily reach 34–35°C. During the cold period, the average high temperature reaches about 10°C, but the average low is around 2°C, and it drops below zero very often, about thirty days a year from late December to the end of February. During the summer, the amplitude is large (10°C a day), which calls for the use of thermal inertia to cool the spaces naturally.

(2)/(3) Sky coverage in winter and summer and sky radiation in the sky vault in winter and summer: During the summer, the sky is quite sunny and radiation is higher on the horizontal surfaces. Among the vertical surfaces, the southwest and south receive the largest amount of radiation, followed by the southeast, west, and east. During the coldest months, the sky is mostly cloudy and radiation is higher on the south orientation, followed by the southwest and southeast.

(4) Annual wind rose: Wind blows homogeneously from all orientations, though predominantly from the west, and with a modest average speed of 3.3 m/s. The southeast orientation is almost always sheltered.

Case Study 3

Project and Environmental Conditions
Project Data

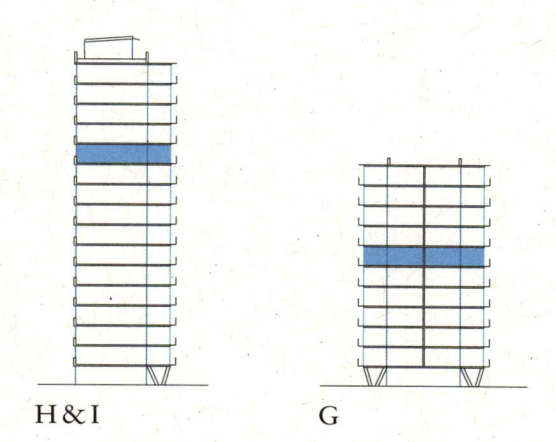

H & I   G

BUILDING
Year of delivery	2016
Type of delivery	Refurbishment and extension
Type of building	Free-standing blocks
Total amount of floors	16 (H & I), 11 (G)
Thermal regulation	RTexistant global

SIMULATED UNIT
Block	H
Floor	11th
Heated surface	97 m²
Winter garden surface	28 m²
Balcony surface	8 m²
Ratio of extra space / heated surface	30%
Orientation	SE/NW
Ratio of exposed envelope that is winter garden	50%
Unit infiltration	0.37 ach
Total air renewal	90 m³/h, accounting 30 m³/(h·person)
Winter garden infiltration	3.5–6.3 ach

TECHNICAL SYSTEMS
Ventilation type	Hybrid natural: assisted mechanical ventilation
Heating system type	Central
Heating regulation	Collective floor heating
Cep max	72 kWh/(m²·year)
Cep project	49 kWh/(m²·year) < Cep max

WINTER GARDEN

Orientation	Depth	Volume	Exposed facade area	Exposed concrete area	Total inertia (of winter garden)
Southeast	3.0 m	72 m³	24 m²	57 m²	0.79 144 kJ/m³K

	Element	Material	U-value W/(m²K)	SF	VLT	Reflectivity
①	Thermal curtain	Sheep's wool	2.17	0	0	0.71
②	Sliding doors of heated space	Double glazing	1.7	0.45	0.75	-
③	Solar curtain	Aluminum	-	0.38	0.38	0.6
④	Sliding doors of winter garden	2/3 transparent polycarbonate 1/3 single glazing	5.7	0.85	0.85	-

* SF: Solar Factor; VLT: Visible Light Transmittance

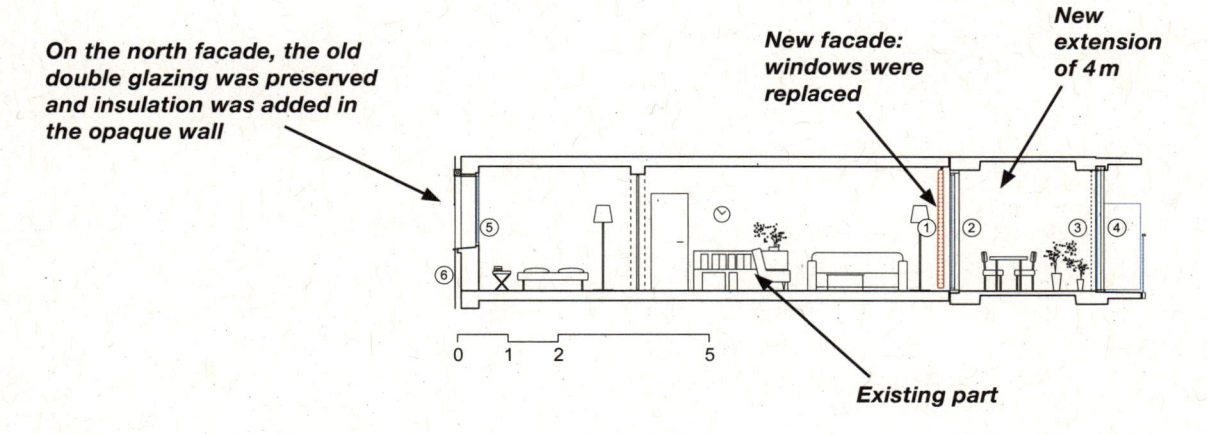

On the north facade, the old double glazing was preserved and insulation was added in the opaque wall

New facade: windows were replaced

New extension of 4 m

Existing part

The winter garden's facade of aluminum-framed sliding doors alternates with polycarbonate and single-glass fillings: one single glazing follows two polycarbonate panels. The former room height of 2.74 m defines the extension. In the context of the transformation, the northern facades and side walls were insulated.

The unit is very compact. The transformation included the addition of a deep winter garden of 3.0 m on the southeast facade. The extension was made with prefabricated concrete, whose inertia contributes to stabilizing temperatures, especially during peak days. The U-value of the exterior glazing on the southeast side was increased from a single glazing of 5.7 W/(m²·K) to a double glazing of 1.7 W/(m²·K). However, the addition of the winter garden and thermal curtains can be considered equivalent to a U-value of 0.95 W/(m²·K). The northwest facade has been insulated, reaching a U-value of 0.24 W/(m²·K).

Case Study 3

Project and Environmental Conditions
Sun and Wind

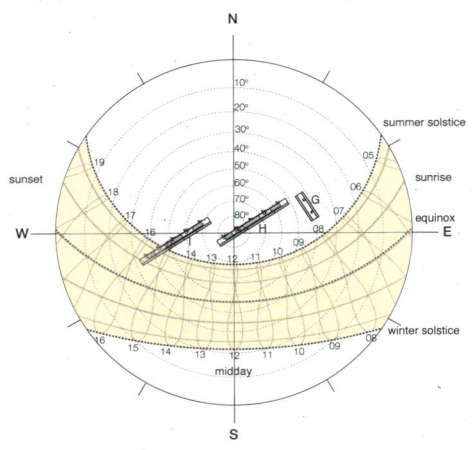

(1) Solar access at building scale

(2) Solar access at unit scale

(3) Solar heat gains in winter

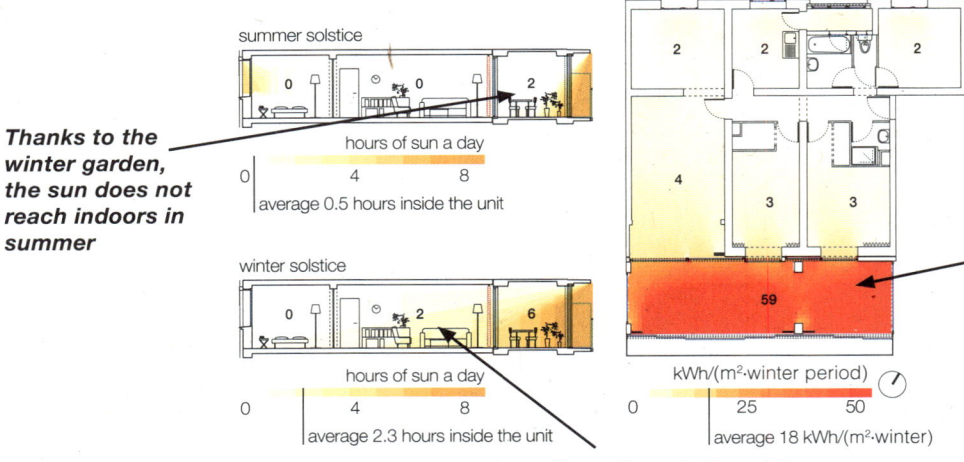

Thanks to the winter garden, the sun does not reach indoors in summer

average 0.5 hours inside the unit

average 2.3 hours inside the unit

average 18 kWh/(m²·winter)

The solar gains reaching the winter garden during the winter period are equivalent to the heat provided by a radiator

Even though the winter garden is deep, the sun reaches indoors in winter

(4) Natural airflow in summer

Wind speed from cross ventilation is equivalent to the air speed of a fan

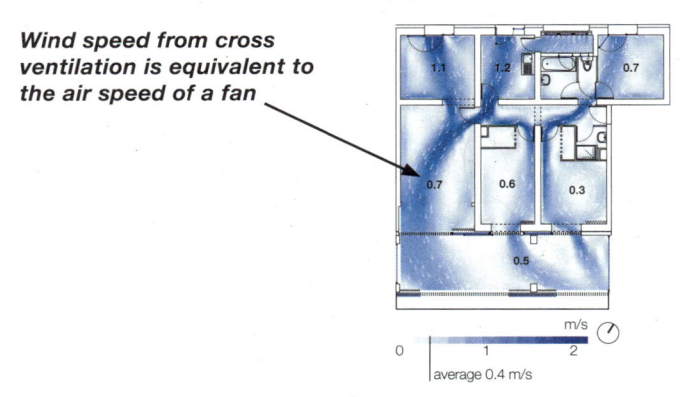

average 0.4 m/s

(1) Solar access at building scale: The main facades of the long buildings H and I are oriented toward the southeast and northwest. The shorter G building is rotated 90° compared to the others. The context is low, as neighboring buildings do not overshadow any of the units. The southeast facade receives the sun throughout the year, whereas the northwest facade only does during summer afternoons. The units receive at least eight hours of sun during the equinoxes, reaching the high solar access target of EN 17037.

(2)/(3) Solar access at unit scale and solar heat gains in winter: Solar access is concentrated in the winter garden throughout the year and reaches the interior during the winter, when heating is needed. In winter, the space receives much more sun than in summer, as during the shortest days of the year the winter garden receives some six hours of sun a day. During the summer, both the winter garden and balcony act as solar protection and reduce the gains inside. The use of the solar curtain reduces them further.

(4) Natural airflow in summer: Under average conditions and with all sliding panels open, all rooms benefit from cross ventilation and refreshment at occupant height. Wind speed inside the apartment is 0.4 m/s, an air speed that can be perceived by the body. In the living room, it can reach 2 m/s, which reduces the felt temperature by about 4°C, and is equivalent to the speed of a fan.

Project and Environmental Conditions
Daylight

(1) Daylight Autonomy

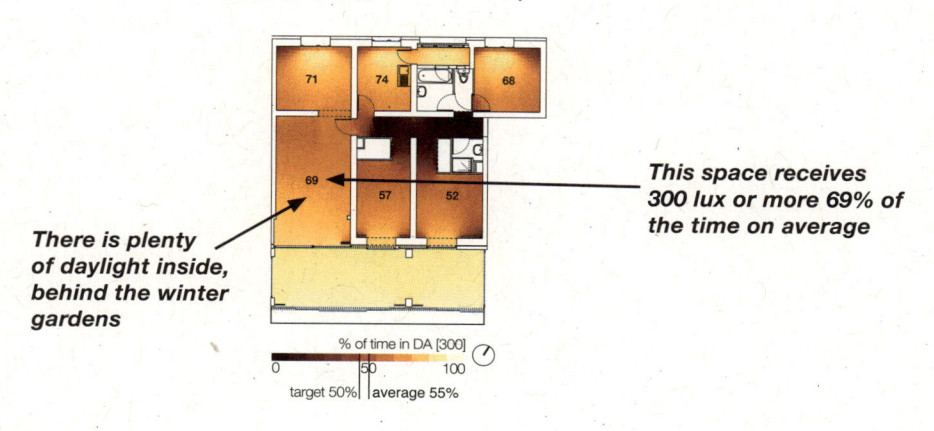

There is plenty of daylight inside, behind the winter gardens

This space receives 300 lux or more 69% of the time on average

% of time in DA [300]
target 50% | average 55%

(2) Space exceeding 50% of time with DA [300] (EN 17037)

reference plane: 50 cm off the walls from permanently occupied spaces

target 50% of space > 50% of time with DA [300]

Living Room	100%
Room S1	99%
Room S2	99%
Room N1	100%
Kitchen	100%
Room N2	100%
average	100%

At least 99% of all rooms have DA [300] more than 50% of the time, while the EN target is 50%

-> all the spaces largely exceed the recommendations of EN 17037

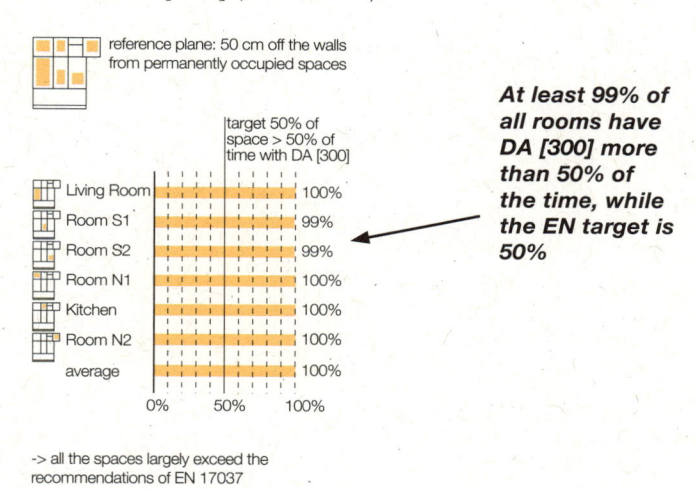

(1) Daylight Autonomy: Daylight inside the apartment is homogeneous and bright, with DA averages ranging from 52 to 69% in the main rooms behind the winter garden. Deeper rooms have larger openings, whereas shallower ones are lit with smaller openings.

(2) Space exceeding 50% of time with DA [300] (EN 17037): All the rooms largely surpass the EN criteria for a daylit apartment.

Case Study 3

Free-Running Mode Seasonal Performance

(1) Operative temperatures over the year

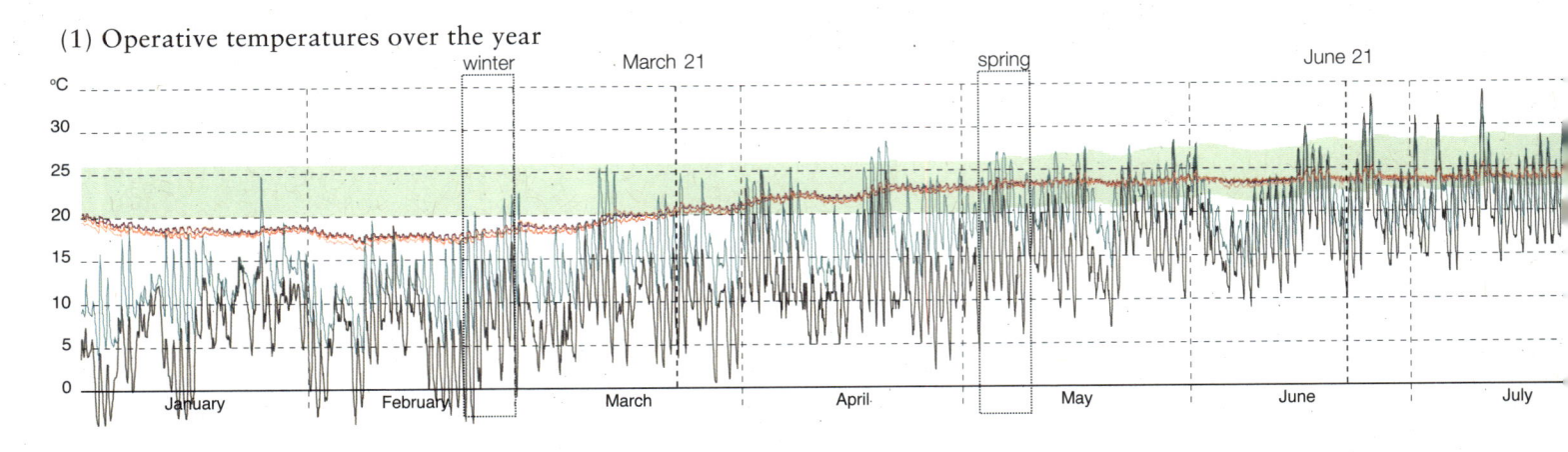

(2) Operative temperatures in winter

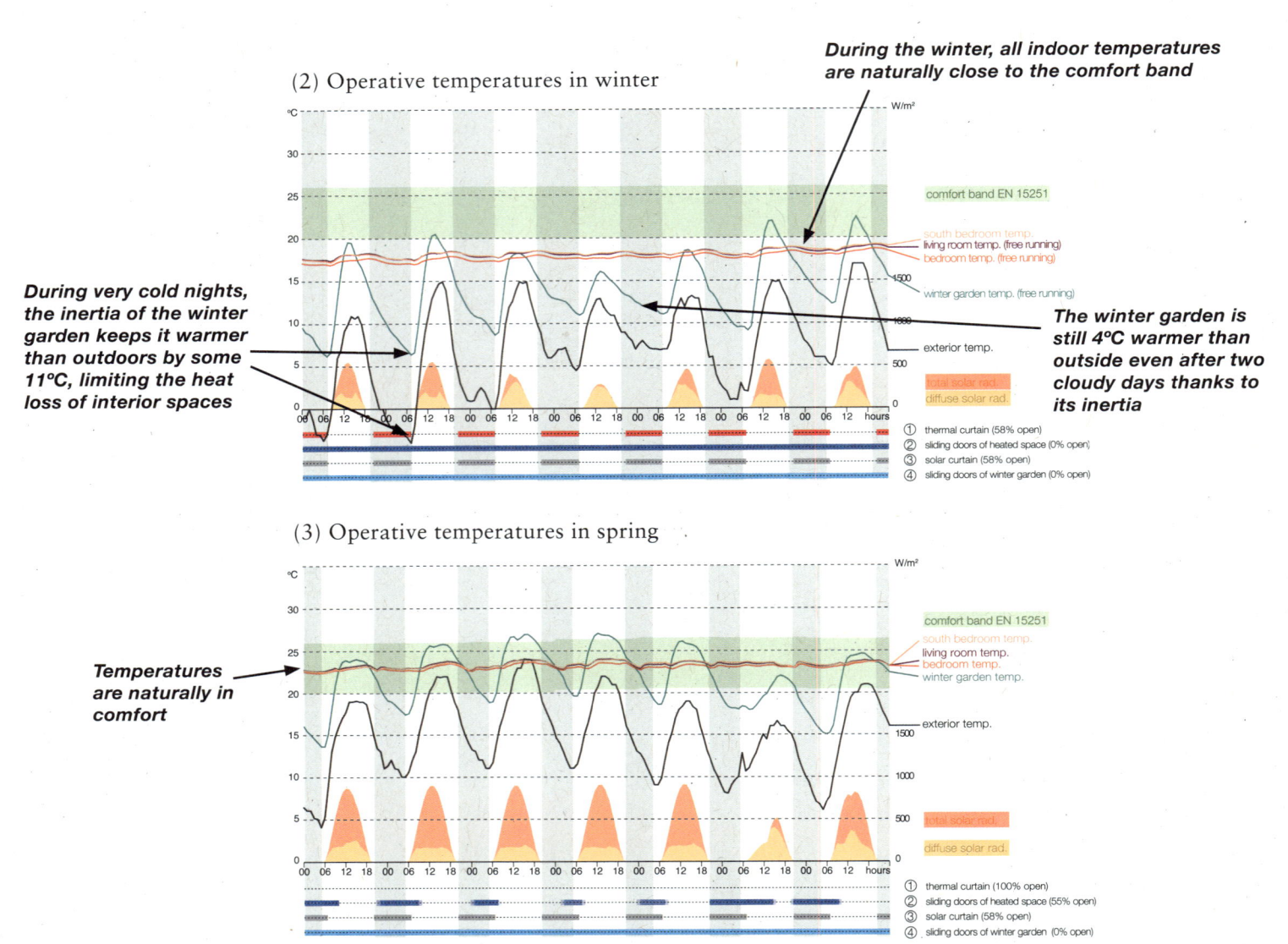

During the winter, all indoor temperatures are naturally close to the comfort band

During very cold nights, the inertia of the winter garden keeps it warmer than outdoors by some 11°C, limiting the heat loss of interior spaces

The winter garden is still 4°C warmer than outside even after two cloudy days thanks to its inertia

① thermal curtain (58% open)
② sliding doors of heated space (0% open)
③ solar curtain (58% open)
④ sliding doors of winter garden (0% open)

(3) Operative temperatures in spring

Temperatures are naturally in comfort

① thermal curtain (100% open)
② sliding doors of heated space (55% open)
③ solar curtain (58% open)
④ sliding doors of winter garden (0% open)

(1) Operative temperatures over the year: The simulation in free-running mode shows that indoor temperatures vary naturally from 16 to 26°C.

2) Operative temperatures in winter: During the winter, operative temperatures of the winter garden are 3–11°C warmer than outdoors. The narrower difference occurs during cloudy days, when the winter garden is only 3°C warmer. The sun increases temperatures by about 5–9°C. At night, the temperature difference with the outdoors is larger, as the concrete releases the heat that was stored during the day and increases temperatures. The operative temperature in free-running mode inside the apartment is very stable, with a variation of 1–2°C across the week. Both bedrooms and living room are almost inside the comfort band, around 17–19°C, due to the effect of the winter garden and the inertia of the concrete that further stabilizes the temperatures. The difference to be compensated by heating is therefore very small (1–3°C). The north bedroom temperature is slightly lower, around 0.5–1°C less, due to reduced solar gain.

3) Operative temperatures in spring: The winter garden has comfortable operative temperatures as an indoor space throughout the season, oscillating between the extremes of the comfort band (EN 15251), and can be used as an extension of the living space. It represents a temperature difference with the outdoors of 5 to 10°C. Indoor temperatures are very stable, around 23–24°C, and remain within the comfort band naturally. Opening and closing the sliding panels intuitively is enough to maintain comfortable temperatures inside. There is no need for heating throughout the spring—the heating period usually ends by the end of April.

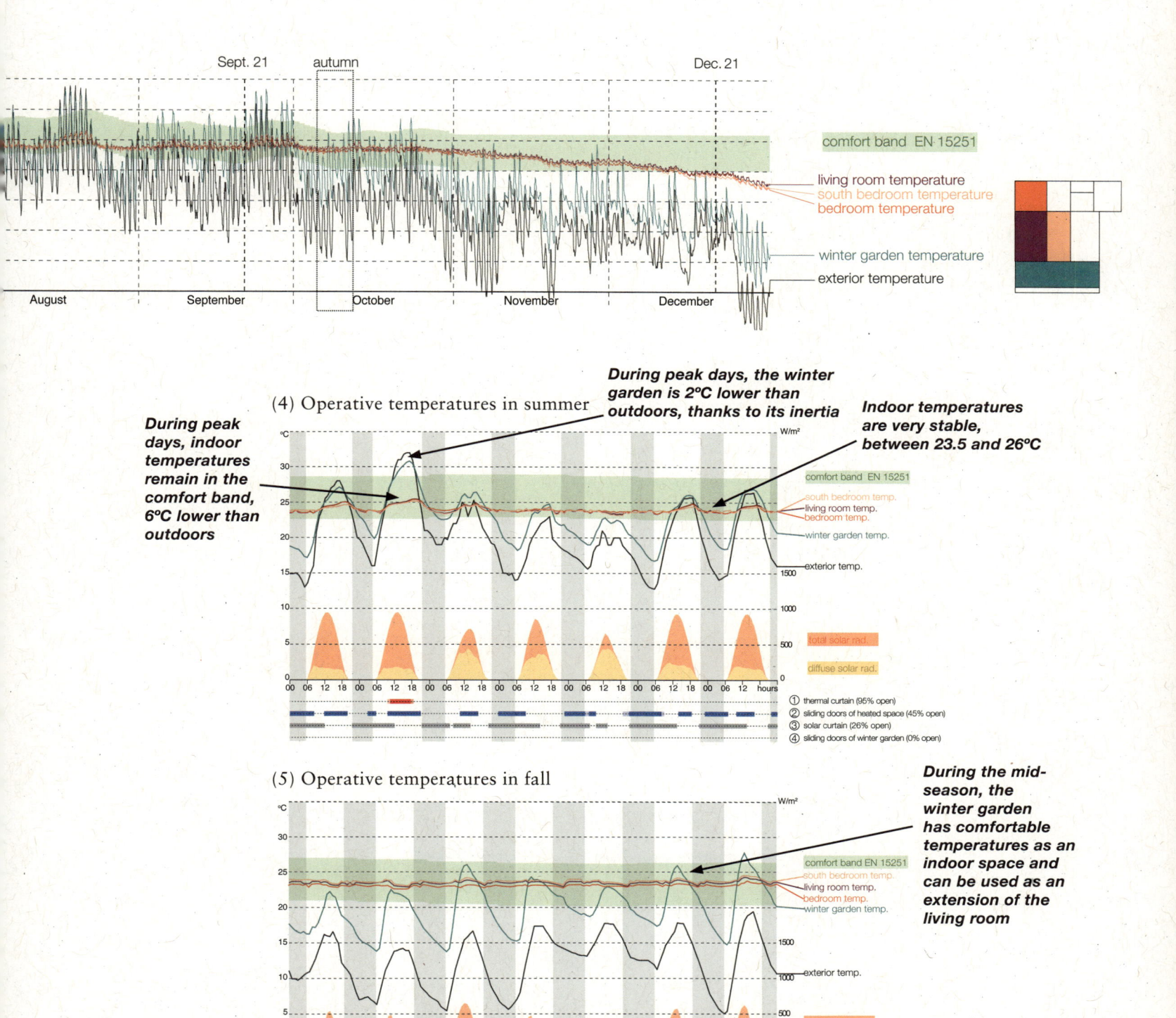

Case Study 3

(4) Operative temperatures in summer

During peak days, indoor temperatures remain in the comfort band, 6°C lower than outdoors

During peak days, the winter garden is 2°C lower than outdoors, thanks to its inertia

Indoor temperatures are very stable, between 23.5 and 26°C

① thermal curtain (95% open)
② sliding doors of heated space (45% open)
③ solar curtain (26% open)
④ sliding doors of winter garden (0% open)

(5) Operative temperatures in fall

During the mid-season, the winter garden has comfortable temperatures as an indoor space and can be used as an extension of the living room

① thermal curtain (58% open)
② sliding doors of heated space (40% open)
③ solar curtain (58% open)
④ sliding doors of winter garden (0% open)

4) Operative temperatures in summer: The operative temperature inside the apartment is remarkably stable, around 24–25°C, in the hot summers of Bordeaux, and remains far below outdoors during peak days. During peak days, when the outdoor temperature is above 32°C, drawing both curtains cuts the solar gain and, in combination with the thermal inertia, is sufficient to maintain indoor operative temperatures of around 25°C, which is 6–7°C cooler than outdoors. The operative temperature of the winter garden—which is fully open as a terrace—is generally 1–3°C higher than outdoors, except during the afternoons, where the difference is even smaller, almost close to 0°C. During peak days, the situation is inverted, and the winter garden remains 1–2°C fresher than outdoors due to the adequate shading and effect of thermal inertia of the concrete.

5) Operative temperatures in fall: The temperature of the winter garden (that remains closed) is 5–10°C warmer than outdoors even during cloudy days. During the daytime, operative temperatures reach the comfort band (EN 15251) and the space can be used as an extra indoor area. The indoor temperature is very stable and inside the comfort band around 23–24°C. There is almost no need for heating throughout the fall—the heating period usually starts in October.

Case Study 3

Free-Running Mode
Typical Days

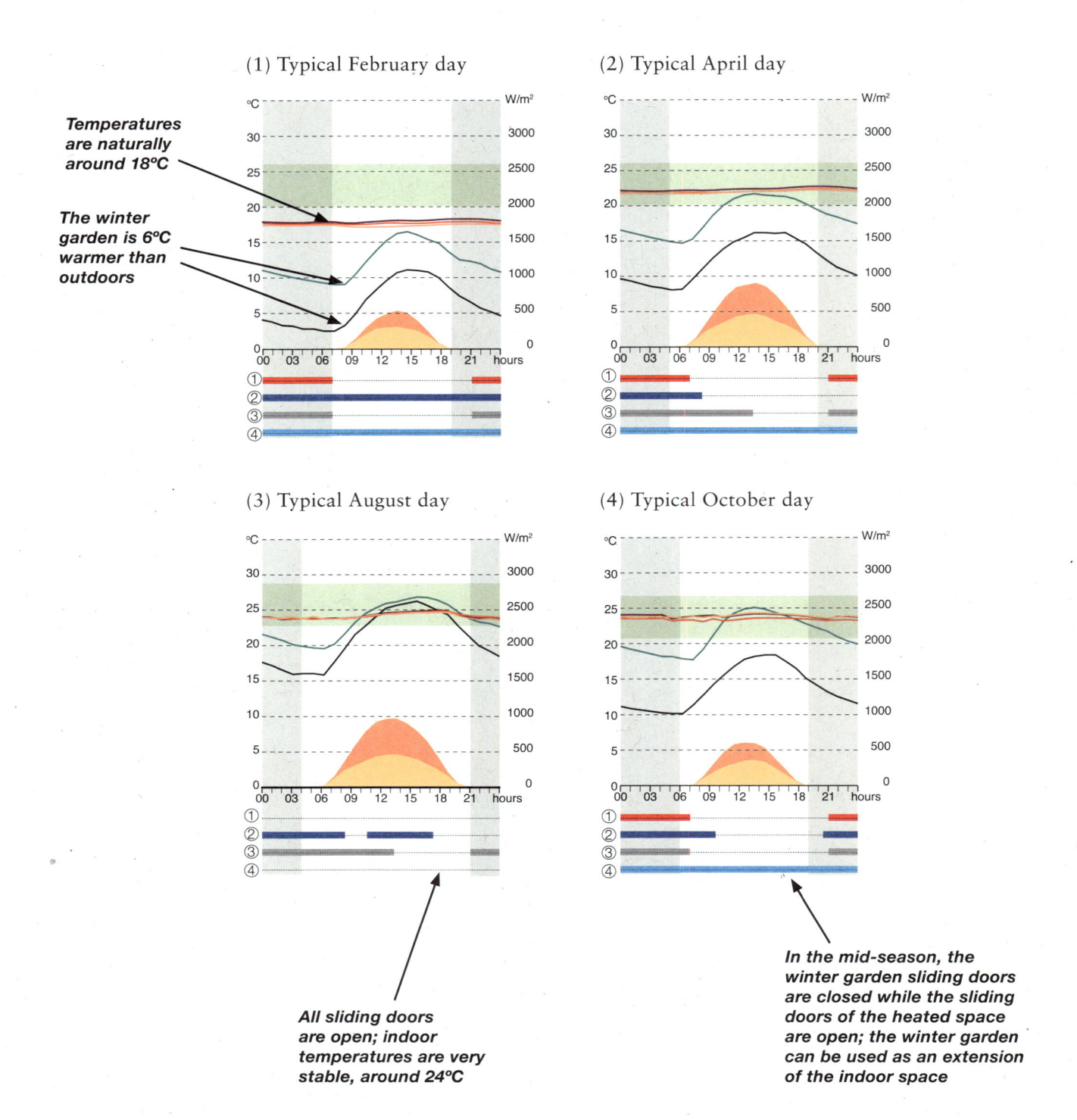

(1) Typical February day

Temperatures are naturally around 18°C

The winter garden is 6°C warmer than outdoors

(2) Typical April day

(3) Typical August day

All sliding doors are open; indoor temperatures are very stable, around 24°C

(4) Typical October day

In the mid-season, the winter garden sliding doors are closed while the sliding doors of the heated space are open; the winter garden can be used as an extension of the indoor space

(1) Typical February day: During a typical winter day, free-running operative temperatures inside the apartment are very stable, around 17–18°C. The inertia of the concrete helps to homogenize temperatures, even if the southern side receives more solar gains. The winter garden is consistently 6°C warmer than outdoors.

(3) Typical August day: During a typical summer day, internal room temperatures stay constant, around 24°C. Outdoor temperature peaks are barely noticeable indoors due to the inertia of the concrete and shading offered by the winter garden slabs. The temperature in the winter garden follows the outdoors closely, given its large operable area to allow natural ventilation.

(2)/(4) Typical spring and fall days: During a typical fall or spring day, indoor temperatures are stable within the comfort band ranging from 22 to 24°C. The operative temperature in the winter garden reaches indoor comfort temperatures during the central hours of the day, and some evening hours during the fall, and can be used as an extension of the living space.

Case Study 3

Free-Running Mode
Extreme Days

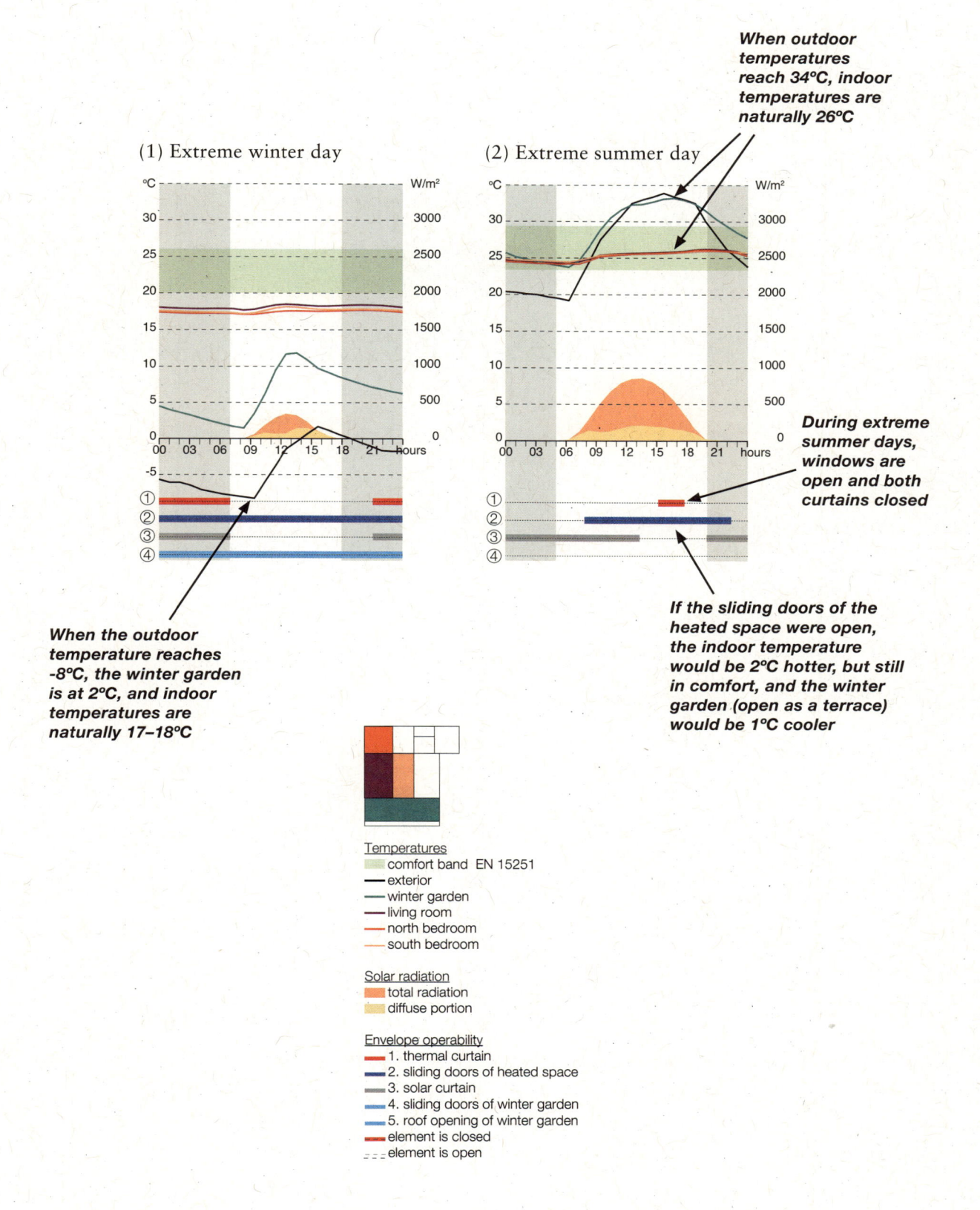

(1) Extreme winter day

(2) Extreme summer day

When outdoor temperatures reach 34°C, indoor temperatures are naturally 26°C

When the outdoor temperature reaches −8°C, the winter garden is at 2°C, and indoor temperatures are naturally 17–18°C

During extreme summer days, windows are open and both curtains closed

If the sliding doors of the heated space were open, the indoor temperature would be 2°C hotter, but still in comfort, and the winter garden (open as a terrace) would be 1°C cooler

Temperatures
- comfort band EN 15251
- exterior
- winter garden
- living room
- north bedroom
- south bedroom

Solar radiation
- total radiation
- diffuse portion

Envelope operability
- 1. thermal curtain
- 2. sliding doors of heated space
- 3. solar curtain
- 4. sliding doors of winter garden
- 5. roof opening of winter garden
- element is closed
- element is open

(1) Extreme winter day: During the coldest winter days, when the outdoor temperature remains below zero for most of the day, the winter garden operative temperature is around 10°C warmer, ranging from 1 to 12°C. It is to be noted that the coldest days are sunny, and thus the winter garden becomes most effective. Indoor operative temperatures are naturally around 17–18°C—without heating. The heating required to reach 20°C is therefore very low.

(2) Extreme summer day: During the hottest summer days, while the outdoor temperature peaks at 34°C, indoor operative temperatures remain within the comfort range of 25–27°C due to the effectiveness of the horizontal shading, the use of both solar and thermal curtains to block the lower sun, the presence of thermal inertia to stabilize temperatures, and the efficiency of the natural ventilation. Overall, indoor temperatures remain about 7°C below outdoors. The fully open winter garden's operative temperature also remains below outdoors by about 0.5°C.

Free-Running Mode
Thermal Comfort Conditions

(1) Resulting thermal comfort per room

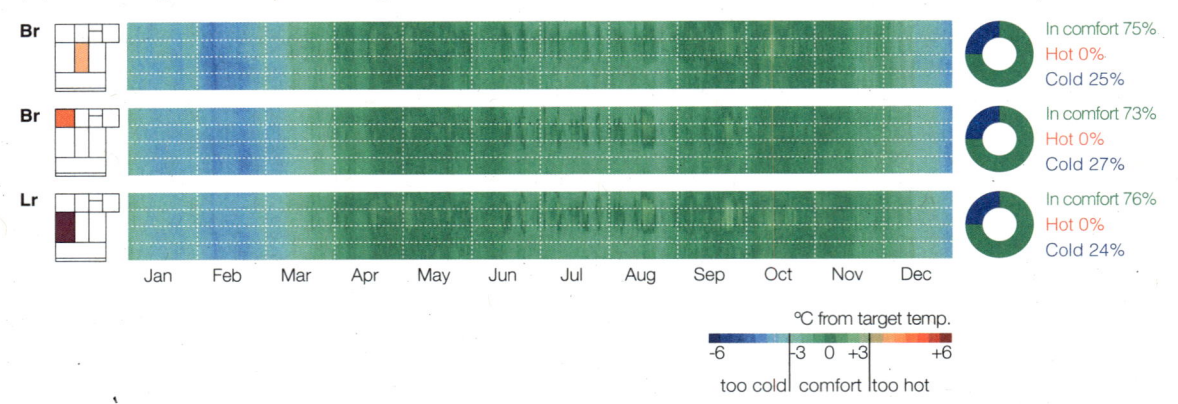

Br — In comfort 75% / Hot 0% / Cold 25%
Br — In comfort 73% / Hot 0% / Cold 27%
Lr — In comfort 76% / Hot 0% / Cold 24%

Jan Feb Mar Apr May Jun Jul Aug Sep Oct Nov Dec

°C from target temp.
-6   -3 0 +3   +6
too cold | comfort | too hot

(2) Operative temperatures indoors as a function of outdoors

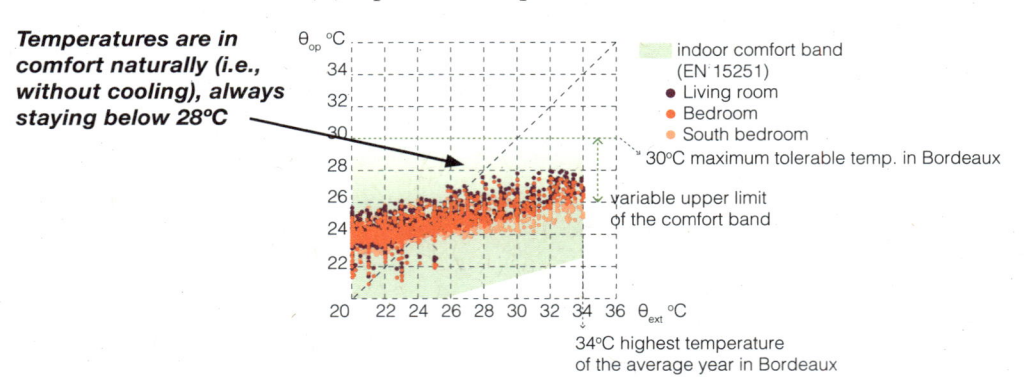

Temperatures are in comfort naturally (i.e., without cooling), always staying below 28°C

θ_{op} °C

- indoor comfort band (EN 15251)
- Living room
- Bedroom
- South bedroom

30°C maximum tolerable temp. in Bordeaux
variable upper limit of the comfort band

θ_{ext} °C

34°C highest temperature of the average year in Bordeaux

(3) Overheating evaluation

ideal target <350 °C·h   maximum tolerance

Living room   1
Bedroom   0
South bedroom 6
average   1

250 500 750 1000 1250 °C·h
350

- nighttime (22 to 7h): DH > 26°C
- daytime (7 to 22h): DH > EN 15251*
Comfort temperature is capped at 28°C

There is no overheating

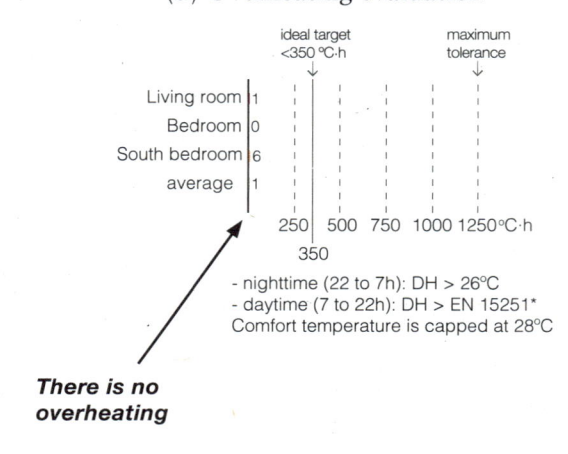

(1) Resulting thermal comfort per room: The apartment has indoor operative temperatures in comfort 75% of the time. The living room has comfortable temperatures 76% of the time. When it is cold, it is only by a small margin of around 2°C. Bedrooms, northwest-oriented, are within the comfort range 73% of the time. This facade does not benefit from the contribution of the winter garden but is insulated.

(2) Operative temperatures indoors as a function of outdoors: During the summer, indoor temperatures are within a small range and remain very stable, never surpassing 28°C. Even when it is 34°C outdoors, indoors temperatures are 25–28°C.

(3) Overheating evaluation: The unit has no overheating time or any degree hour above the comfort target, which is an optimal summer performance, especially considering this is the hottest climate of the case studies.

Case Study 3

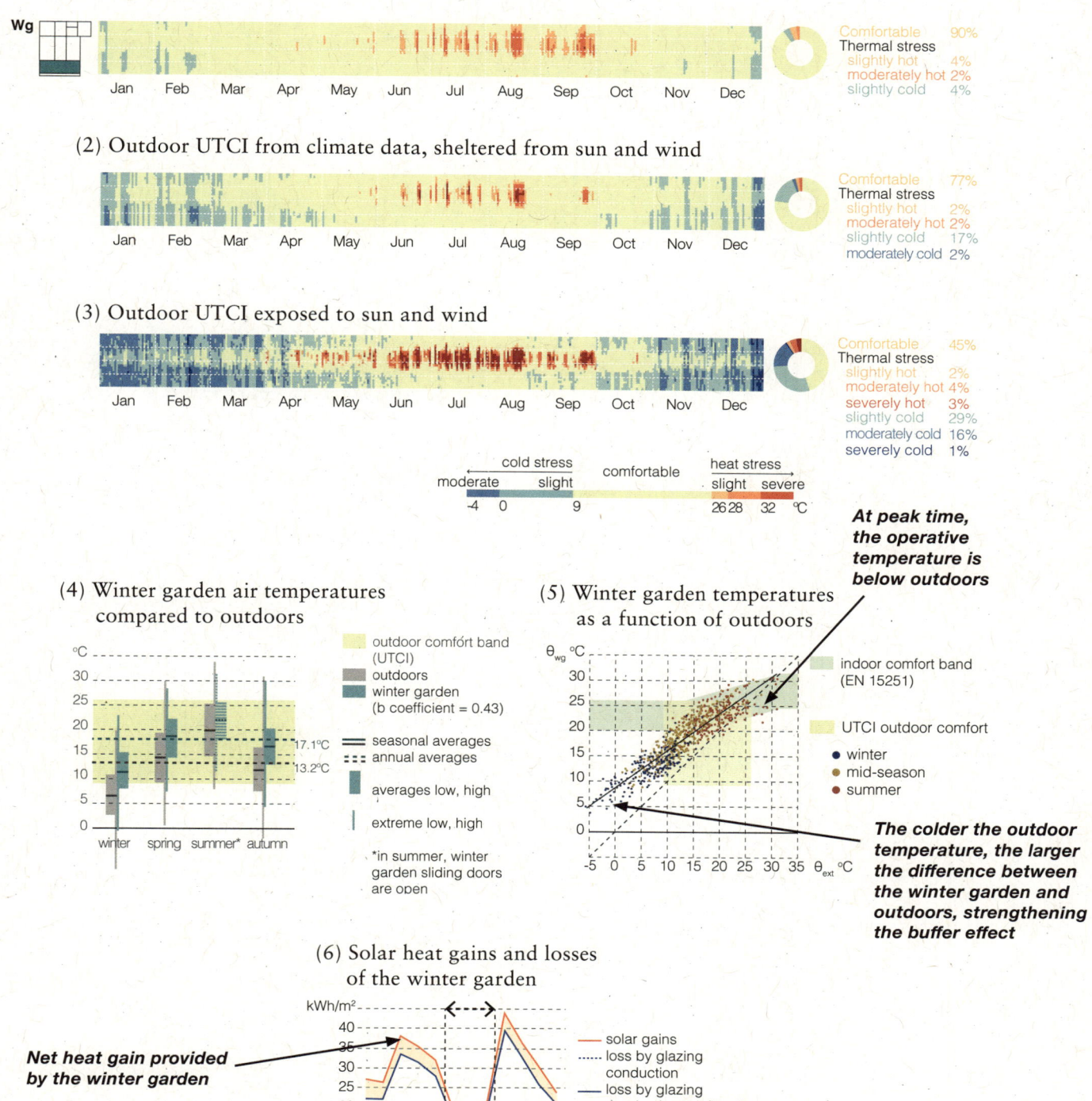

Free-Running Mode
Conditions inside the Winter Garden

(1) Winter garden UTCI (Universal Thermal Climate Index)

Comfortable 90%
Thermal stress
slightly hot 4%
moderately hot 2%
slightly cold 4%

(2) Outdoor UTCI from climate data, sheltered from sun and wind

Comfortable 77%
Thermal stress
slightly hot 2%
moderately hot 2%
slightly cold 17%
moderately cold 2%

(3) Outdoor UTCI exposed to sun and wind

Comfortable 45%
Thermal stress
slightly hot 2%
moderately hot 4%
severely hot 3%
slightly cold 29%
moderately cold 16%
severely cold 1%

cold stress	comfortable	heat stress
moderate slight		slight severe
-4 0	9	26 28 32 °C

(4) Winter garden air temperatures compared to outdoors

- outdoor comfort band (UTCI)
- outdoors
- winter garden (b coefficient = 0.43)
- seasonal averages
- annual averages
- averages low, high
- extreme low, high

17.1°C
13.2°C

*in summer, winter garden sliding doors are open

(5) Winter garden temperatures as a function of outdoors

At peak time, the operative temperature is below outdoors

- indoor comfort band (EN 15251)
- UTCI outdoor comfort
- winter
- mid-season
- summer

The colder the outdoor temperature, the larger the difference between the winter garden and outdoors, strengthening the buffer effect

(6) Solar heat gains and losses of the winter garden

Net heat gain provided by the winter garden

- solar gains
- loss by glazing conduction
- loss by glazing conduction + infiltration
- useful net heat gain
- ⟵⟶ winter garden sliding doors are open, no heat gain

---

(1)–(3) Winter garden and outdoor UTCI: These diagrams show how the winter garden improves outdoor comfort by comparing the UTCI inside with an exposed situation to sun and wind and to a sheltered situation (climate data). The winter garden has comfortable temperatures 90% of the time, which is double the time compared to an exposed situation, and 13% more than a sheltered situation. There is slight thermal stress during the coldest and hottest days of the year, but it is mitigated compared to outdoors.

(4) Winter garden air temperatures compared to outdoors: All the extremes from outdoors are more tempered in the winter garden thanks to the thermal inertia of the concrete. On average, air temperatures of the winter garden are 4°C higher than outdoors. During the winter, the increase is higher (5°C), whereas during the summer it is lower (2°C). The average high in summer is the same as outdoors, whereas the peaks are lower. The b coefficient is calculated following the European Norm (EN 13789) to calculate the reduction of heat losses of the heated envelope thanks to the effect of the winter garden. Here the result is 0.60, meaning that the winter garden reduces heat loss by 40%.

(5) Winter garden temperatures as a function of outdoors: During the summer, temperatures are mostly as comfortable as an indoor space, and during the peak days the temperature remains below outdoors. During the mid-season, the space is comfortable most of the time; it is even comfortable as an indoor space half of the time. During the winter, it mainly acts as a buffer space, with temperatures comfortable for an outdoor space (>9°C) most of the time. The colder the outdoor temperature, the larger the difference with the winter garden (up to 10°C), which shows its effectiveness.

(6) Solar heat gains and losses of the winter garden: The winter garden represents a net heat gain due to the solar contribution during the entire year. During the winter, the heat gain is at its maximum.

170 Case Study 3

Active Mode
Winter Air Temperatures and Heating Load

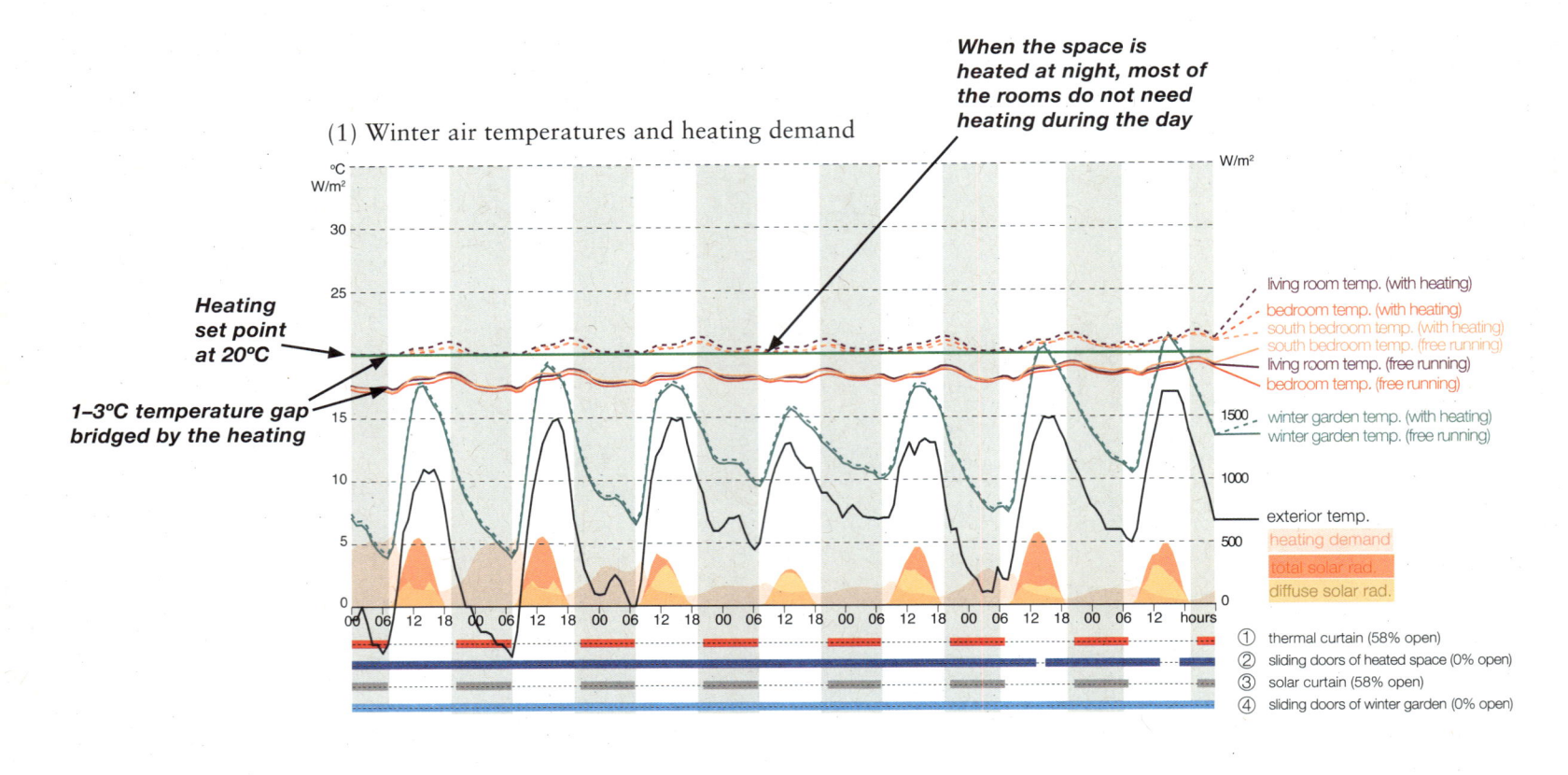

(1) Winter air temperatures and heating demand

When the space is heated at night, most of the rooms do not need heating during the day

Heating set point at 20°C

1–3°C temperature gap bridged by the heating

- living room temp. (with heating)
- bedroom temp. (with heating)
- south bedroom temp. (with heating)
- south bedroom temp. (free running)
- living room temp. (free running)
- bedroom temp. (free running)
- winter garden temp. (with heating)
- winter garden temp. (free running)
- exterior temp.
- heating demand
- total solar rad.
- diffuse solar rad.

① thermal curtain (58% open)
② sliding doors of heated space (0% open)
③ solar curtain (58% open)
④ sliding doors of winter garden (0% open)

(1) Winter air temperatures and heating demand: This graphic shows air temperature, rather than the operative ones of previous graphics, for heat-load evaluations. In free-running mode, both the living room and the bedrooms have temperatures between 17 and 19°C. The heating is required mostly at night and early in the morning. With a set point at 20°C, the spaces start the day warmer, and when the sun comes in, the temperatures raise to 21–22°C. The winter garden temperature is the same with or without indoor heating.

Case Study 3

Active Mode
Heating Demand

(1) Space heating demand

Heating demand is very low in the main spaces

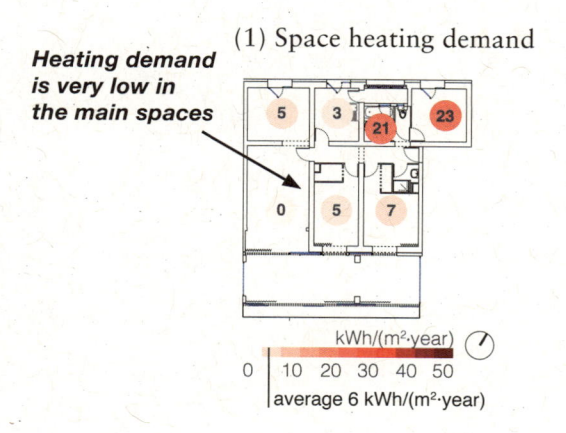

kWh/(m²·year)
0 | 10 20 30 40 50
average 6 kWh/(m²·year)

(2) Thermodynamic balance (November to March)

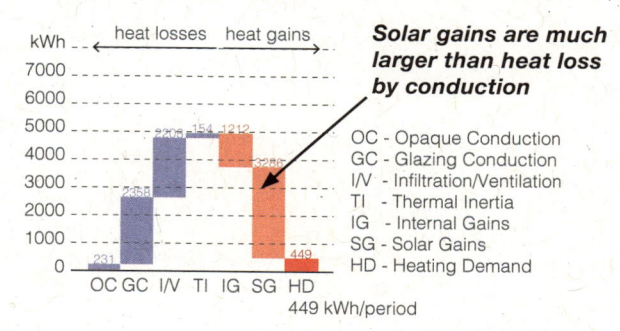

Solar gains are much larger than heat loss by conduction

kWh — heat losses   heat gains →

OC - Opaque Conduction
GC - Glazing Conduction
I/V - Infiltration/Ventilation
TI - Thermal Inertia
IG - Internal Gains
SG - Solar Gains
HD - Heating Demand

449 kWh/period

(3) Hourly heating demand

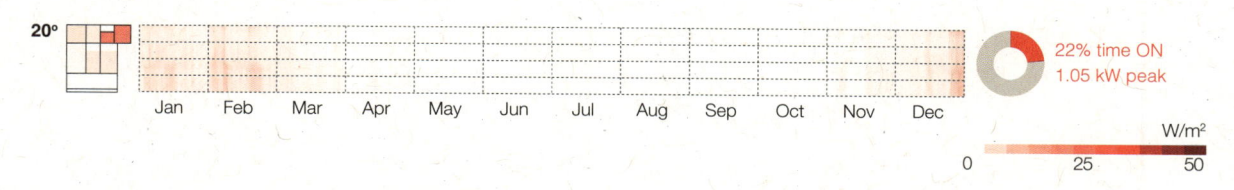

20°

Jan Feb Mar Apr May Jun Jul Aug Sep Oct Nov Dec

22% time ON
1.05 kW peak

W/m²
0   25   50

(4) Heating load monotone curve

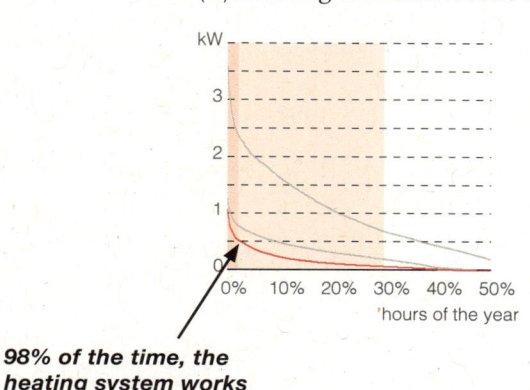

kW

0% 10% 20% 30% 40% 50%
hours of the year

98% of the time, the heating system works with less than 50% of its full power demand

(5) Heating demand variation

kWh/(m²·year)
0   5   10   15   20   25

according to number of occupants
2p
3p
4p
5p
6p

according to thermostat set point
17°C
18°C
regulations → 19°C
lower bound of → 20°C
comfort band   21°C
winter target temp. → 23°C
(EN 15251)
highest measured → 25°C
setpoint

according to floor height
14th floor
11th floor
8th floor

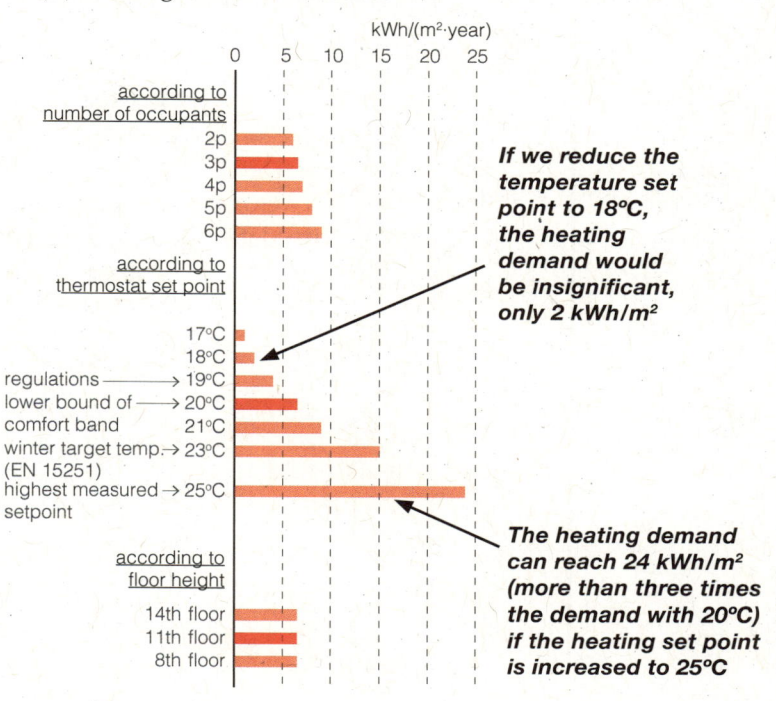

If we reduce the temperature set point to 18°C, the heating demand would be insignificant, only 2 kWh/m²

The heating demand can reach 24 kWh/m² (more than three times the demand with 20°C) if the heating set point is increased to 25°C

---

(1) Space heating demand: The heating demand is very low, around 6 kWh/(m²·year). The high comfort levels achieved in free-running mode translate in a shorter heating season and significantly reduce its intensity. One-third of the heating demand is concentrated in the bedroom that is disconnected from the apartment due to its northern orientation and its coupling with unheated spaces (circulation). This bedroom is only present in some units.

(2) Thermodynamic balance (November to March): Solar gains make the largest contribution to heating the space, representing almost three times more than internal gains and almost seven times more than heating itself. This ensures an adequate performance of the building, independently from how occupants use it. Heat is lost equally by glazing conduction and infiltration/hygienic ventilation. Thermal inertia is not a problem overall, as its balance during the cold months is almost neutral.

(3) Hourly heating demand: Heating is turned on between November and March, which amounts to 22% of the year.

(4) Heating load monotone curve: Peak demand is 1.05 kW, though it happens for only a few hours a year. 98% of the time, the heating system works with less than 50% of it full power demand.

(5) Heating demand variation: The heating demand with a thermostat at 20°C is very low. However, as thermostat temperature increases, so does the need for heating, which is also magnified by the need to heat the large mass of exposed concrete. A thermostat of 23°C doubles the demand, reaching 15 kWh/(m²·year) (which is still fairly low), and increasing it to 25°C brings heating up to 24 kWh/(m²·year). Reducing the set point reduces the demand significantly. At 18°C, the demand is already negligible.

Case Summary
Main Values

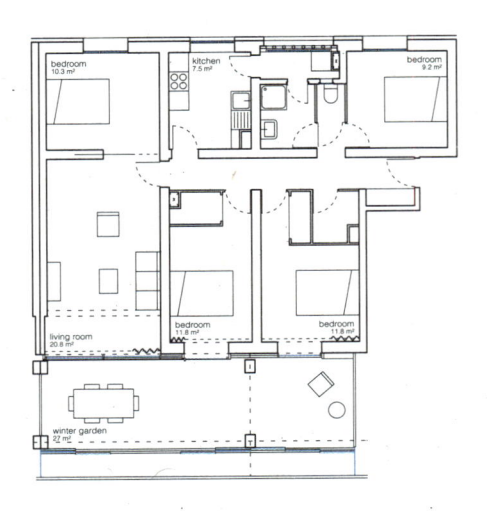

Daylight:
average daylight autonomy DA [300]: 55% of the time

all the spaces largely exceed the recommendations of EN 17037

Temperature and comfort in free-running mode:
above comfort: 0% of the time
within comfort: 72% of the time
below comfort: 28% of the time

average degree·hours
above comfort: 1°C·h

Solar gains and winter garden effect:
(temperature difference between the winter garden and outside)
winter: +3 to +8°C
mid-season: +2 to +10°C

Heating demand:
total: 6 kWh/(m²·year)
peak demand: 1.05 kW
Heating on:
1,814 / 8,760 hours per year
105 / 365 days per year

In the case of Grand Parc, the combination of the high thermal inertia of the original building and the deep winter garden results in optimal summer and winter performance. In summer, temperatures are never above 26°C, not even during peak days when the outdoor temperature reaches 34°C. This is an optimal summer performance, especially considering that Bordeaux has the hottest summer of all the case studies. During the winter, natural temperatures in the spaces never drop below 16.5°C, not even when it is below 0°C outdoors almost all day. This translates into a very low heating demand of 6 kWh/m², which is almost negligible. The apartments could be used without any heating. In the winter garden, temperatures are on average 4°C higher than outdoors. However, the difference is higher as the climate is cooler, reaching 10°C on peak cold days, and becomes smaller as the climate becomes hotter. During peak summer days, the inertia of the concrete helps to keep the winter garden cooler than outdoors. A north-facing winter garden for buildings H and I could further improve the performance. However, considering the already remarkable performance of the project, the investment may not be worthwhile from an energy-demand or embodied-carbon point of view. This case is first compared with the former state of the building, then with a standard refurbishment of the original state, and finally with building G, which is rotated 90° with mono-oriented units and a double winter garden.

Case Comparison 1
Modification: Former Building State

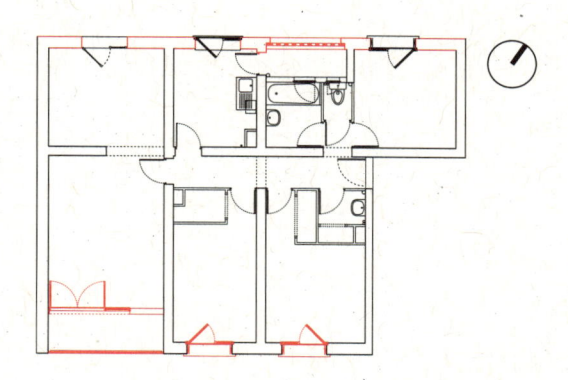

Daylight:
average daylight autonomy DA [300]: 60% (**+5%**) of the time

all the spaces largely exceed the recommendations of EN 17037

Temperature and comfort in free-running mode:
above comfort: 0% of the time
within comfort: 34% (**-38%**) of the time
below comfort: 66% (**+38%**) of the time

average degree·hours
above comfort: 73°C·h (**+72°C·h**)

Solar gains and winter garden effect:
(temperature difference between the winter garden and outside)
winter (with sunshine): -
mid-season: -

Heating demand:
total: 52 kWh/(m²·year) (**+46 kWh/(m²·year)**)
peak demand: 3.9 kW (**+2.85 kW**)
Heating on:
5,007 / 8,760 hours per year (**+3,193 h**)
262 / 365 days per year (**+157 d**)

Variation compared to the original project

Former state in detail:
Building in its former state, before refurbishment: no winter gardens, reduced window-to-floor ratio, reduced living room space, open laundry space, old double glazing
No wall insulation: U = 2.21 W/(m²·K)
Living room/bathroom: U = 4.20 W/(m²·K), SF = 0.6, VLT = 0.8
Bedrooms: U = 2.45 W/(m²·K), SF = 0.6, VLT = 0.6
Kitchen: U = 2.45 W/(m²·K), SF = 0.6, VLT = 0.8

To assess the achieved improvements, this scenario simulates the building in its former state, before the transformation: without the winter garden, with smaller and worse-performing windows on the south, less insulation, and the open laundry area. The original building had a very high heating demand, caused by the lack of insulation—both in the opaque walls and in the glazing—and not taking advantage of its solar exposure, as the south-facing windows were rather small. Winter temperatures in free-running mode were around 6°C lower and total heating demand was at 52 kWh/m², which is almost nine times more than after the transformation. In summer, temperatures were 1–2°C higher.

Case Comparison 1
Sun and Daylight

(1) Solar heat gains in winter

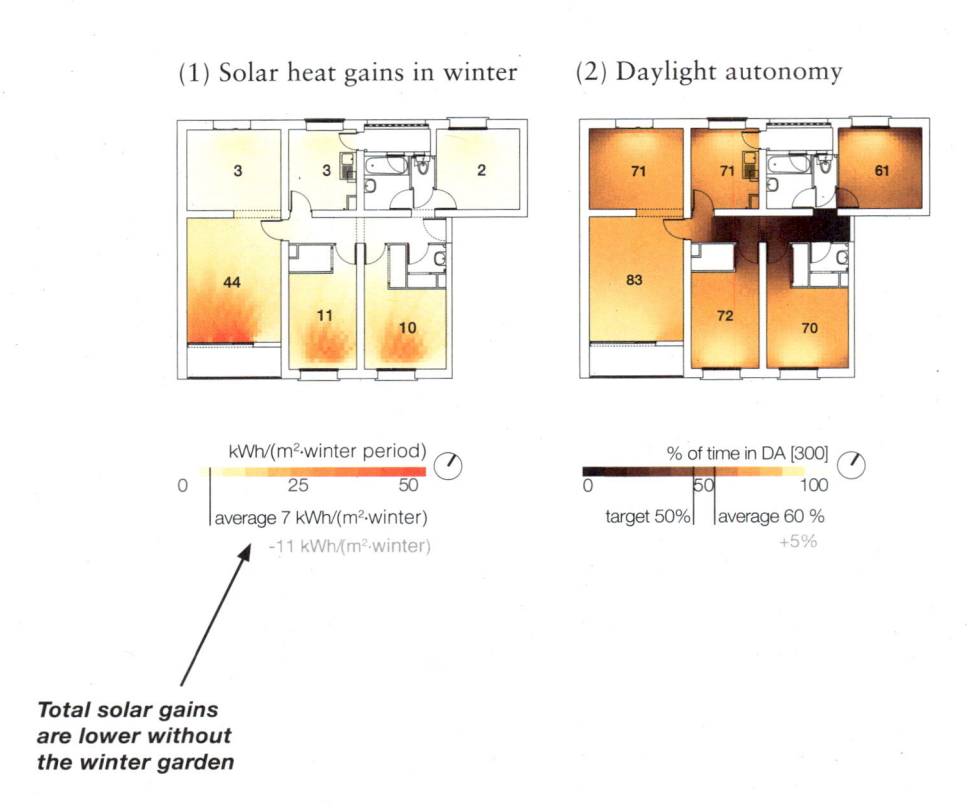

(2) Daylight autonomy

kWh/(m²·winter period)
0   25   50
average 7 kWh/(m²·winter)
−11 kWh/(m²·winter)

Total solar gains are lower without the winter garden

% of time in DA [300]
0   50   100
target 50%   average 60 %
+5%

(1) Solar heat gains in winter: Indoors solar gains were higher, as the sun directly entered the space. However, the winter garden captures considerably more heat, and the total solar heat is higher in the built renovation.

(2) Daylight autonomy: Daylight levels were sufficient, as the average daylight autonomy was 60%.

Case Study 3

Case Comparison 1
Typical Days

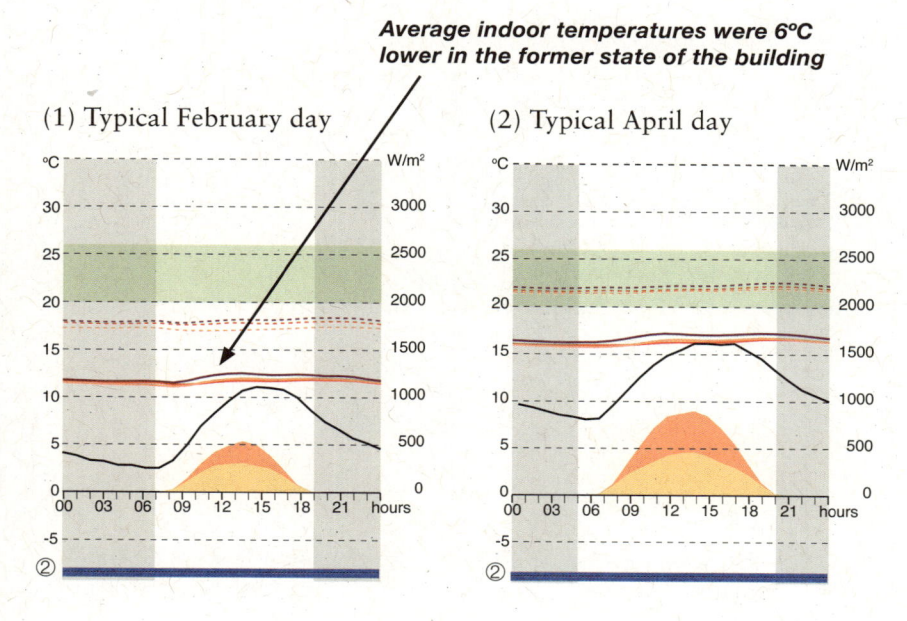

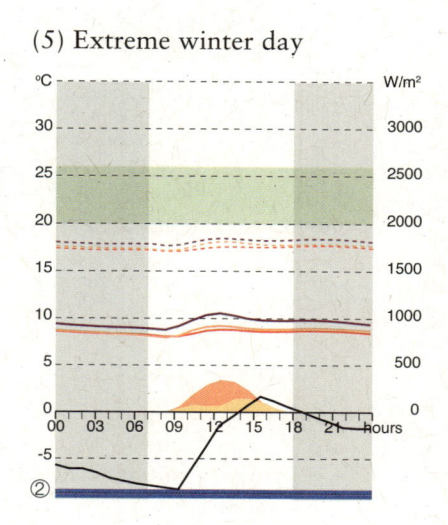

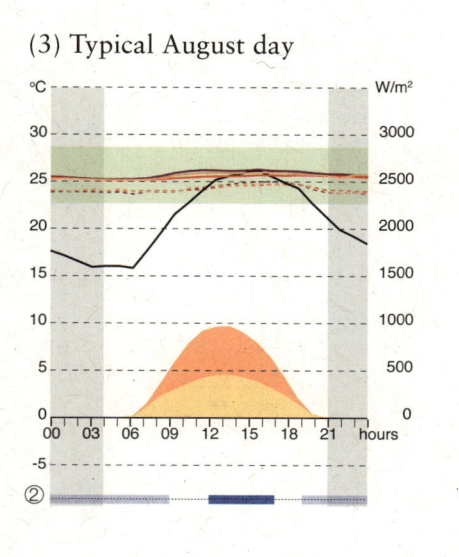

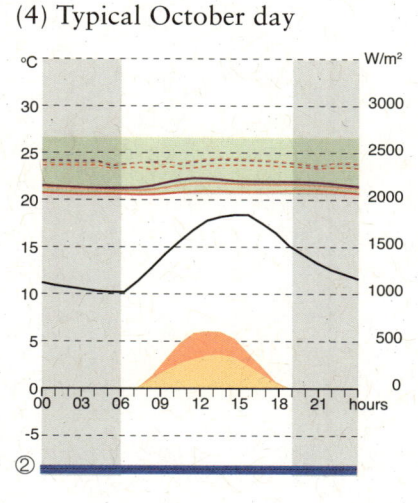

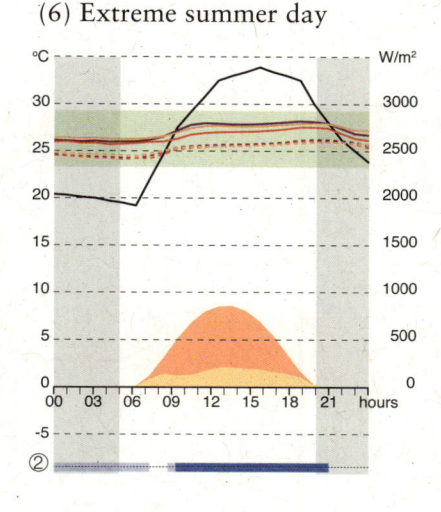

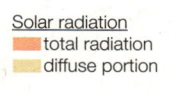

Average indoor temperatures were 6°C lower in the former state of the building

(1) Typical February day

(2) Typical April day

(5) Extreme winter day

(3) Typical August day

(4) Typical October day

(6) Extreme summer day

Temperatures
- comfort band EN 15251
- exterior
- living room
- bedroom

Solar radiation
- total radiation
- diffuse portion

(1) Typical February day: Indoor operative temperatures in free-running mode were cold, around 11–13°C. The project intervention raised the indoor temperatures by about 6°C.

(2) Typical April day: Passive temperatures of the apartment were still low, around 16–17°C for the living room. The refurbishment raised them around 6–7°C, bringing them into the comfort band. Capturing solar gains was key to increasing temperatures more than in winter.

(3) Typical August day: Operative temperatures in free-running mode were stable and within comfort, but about 1.5–2°C higher than in the actual project. The addition of the winter garden and insulation did not compromise summer comfort; on the contrary, it improved it.

(4) Typical October day: Indoor temperatures in free-running mode were already in comfort, around 20–21°C, thanks to the large inertia present in the structure. The renovation raised them to 23–24°C, closer to the target comfort temperature.

(5)/(6) Extreme days: During an extreme summer day, when outdoor temperatures peaked at around 34°C, the indoor temperature rose to 27–28°C and at night it remained at around 26°C. The performance is already acceptable (temperatures are always in comfort) due to the stability provided by the thermal inertia, but the improvements of the project reduced the temperature by 1–2.5°C overall. This is particularly relevant at night in the bedroom, as the temperature dropped to 24°C. During an extreme winter day, indoor temperatures were stable around 9°C in the bedroom and around 10°C in the living room. This is 8–9°C lower than in the actual project.

Case Comparison 1
Resulting Thermal Comfort and Active Mode

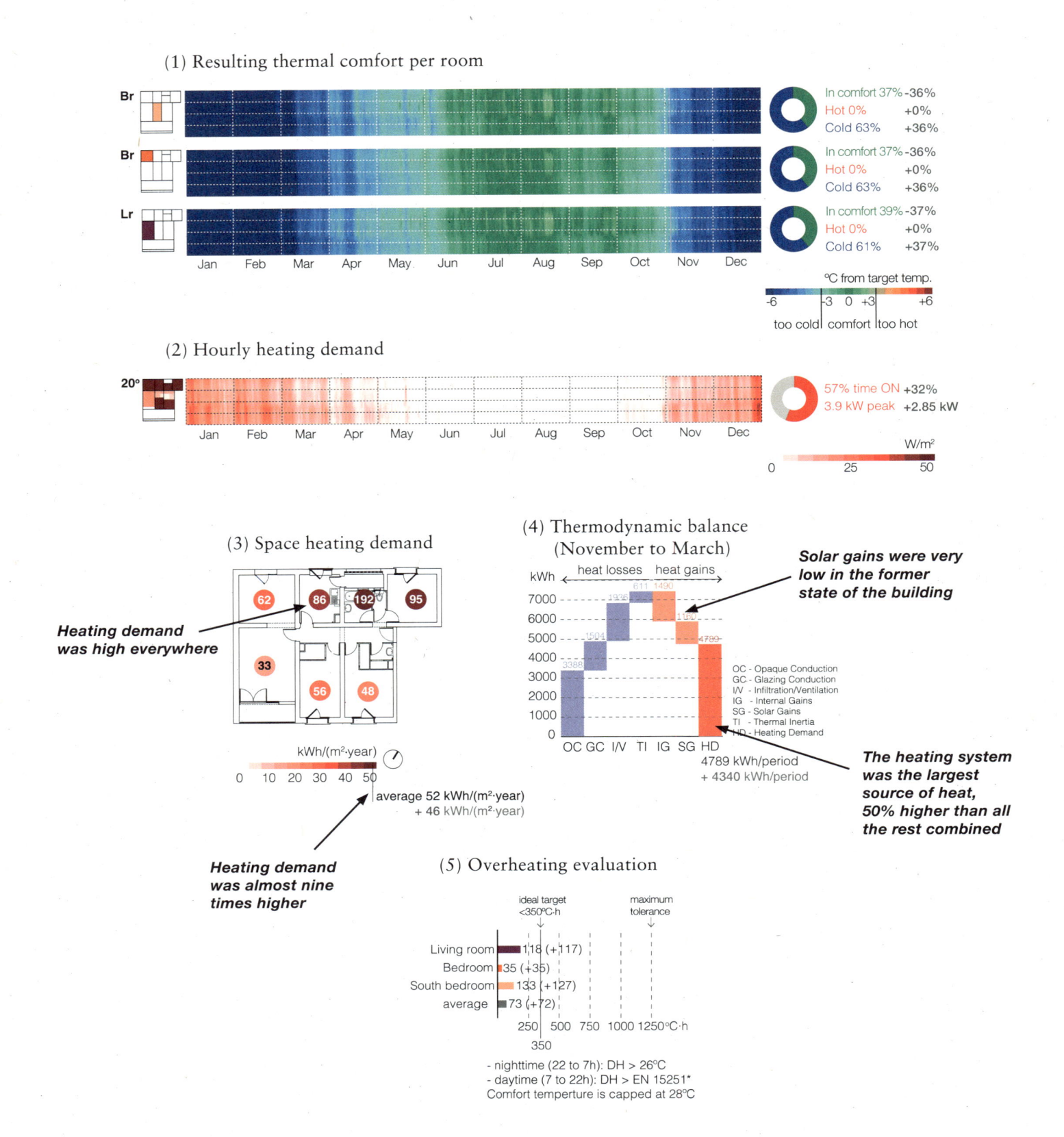

(1) Resulting thermal comfort per room

Br — In comfort 37% -36% / Hot 0% +0% / Cold 63% +36%
Br — In comfort 37% -36% / Hot 0% +0% / Cold 63% +36%
Lr — In comfort 39% -37% / Hot 0% +0% / Cold 61% +37%

°C from target temp.
-6 -3 0 +3 +6
too cold | comfort | too hot

(2) Hourly heating demand

57% time ON +32%
3.9 kW peak +2.85 kW

W/m²
0   25   50

(3) Space heating demand

62 86 192 95
33
56 48

Heating demand was high everywhere

kWh/(m²·year)
0 10 20 30 40 50

average 52 kWh/(m²·year)
+ 46 kWh/(m²·year)

Heating demand was almost nine times higher

(4) Thermodynamic balance (November to March)

kWh — heat losses ← → heat gains
7000 — 611 1490
6000 — 1938
5000 — 1504 1020
4000 — 3388   4789
3000
2000
1000
0
OC GC I/V TI IG SG HD

OC - Opaque Conduction
GC - Glazing Conduction
I/V - Infiltration/Ventilation
IG - Internal Gains
SG - Solar Gains
TI - Thermal Inertia
HD - Heating Demand

4789 kWh/period
+ 4340 kWh/period

Solar gains were very low in the former state of the building

The heating system was the largest source of heat, 50% higher than all the rest combined

(5) Overheating evaluation

ideal target <350°C·h   maximum tolerance

Living room — 118 (+117)
Bedroom — 35 (+35)
South bedroom — 133 (+127)
average — 73 (+72)

250 500 750 1000 1250 °C·h
350

- nighttime (22 to 7h): DH > 26°C
- daytime (7 to 22h): DH > EN 15251*
Comfort temperture is capped at 28°C

---

(1) Resulting thermal comfort per room: In the previous state of the building, the space was cold between November and May, amounting to 63% of the time; The bedrooms were in comfort only 39% of the time; the addition of insulation doubled the time in comfort. The living room used to be in comfort only 40% of the time. The winter garden addition increased this time to 76%, which is almost double.

(2)/(3) Heating demand: The heating demand used to be seven times higher, amounting to 52 kWh/(m²·year). Heating was required from the beginning of November until the end of April. The demand was too high in the northern bedrooms and very high in the southern ones, but not in the living room. Peak demand used to be 3.7 times higher, increasing equipment cost.

(4) Thermodynamic balance (November to March): The indoor temperature mainly relies on heating as its contribution is much higher than the addition of the rest. The lack of insulation and lack of solar gains were the cause for the high heating demand. With the refurbishment, the heat contribution of solar gains quadrupled.

(5) Overheating evaluation: All the spaces used to have considerably more hours above the overheating criteria, especially all the south spaces, as they reached 133°C·h above target. This still remains below the ideal target of 350°C·h. The overheating was already moderate due to the solar protection provided by the balcony and the presence of thermal inertia. However, the overheated hours happened mostly at night once the concrete collected all the heat, which makes sleeping more difficult in summer.

Case Comparison 2:
Standard Refurbishment

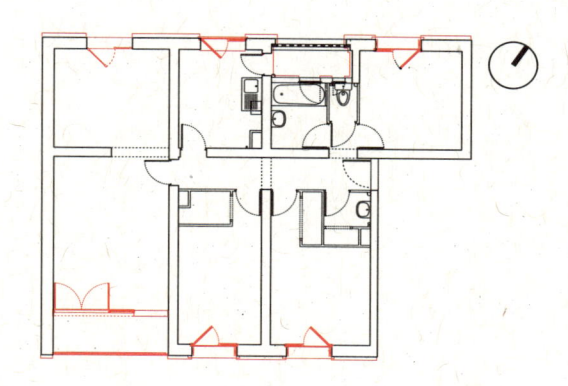

Daylight:
average daylight autonomy DA [300]: 61% (**+6%**) of the time

all the spaces largely exceed the recommendations of EN 17037

Temperature and comfort in free-running mode:
above comfort: 0% of the time
within comfort: 40% (**-32%**) of the time
below comfort: 60% (**+32%**) of the time

average degree·hours
above comfort: 38°C·h (**-37°C·h**)

Solar gains and winter garden effect:
(temperature difference between the winter garden and outside)
winter (with sunshine): -
mid-season: -

Heating demand:
total: 18 kWh/(m²·year) (**+12 kWh/(m²·year)**)
peak demand: 2.1 kW (**+1.05 kW**)
Heating on:
3,076 / 8,760 hours per year (**+1,262 h**)
149 / 365 days per year (**+44 d**)

Variation compared to the built case study

Modifications in detail:
Building in its former state, with a standard refurbishment, no winter gardens
Addition of insulation in opaque facade U = 0.26 W/(m²·K)
Improved double glazing U = 1.70 W/(m²·K), SF = 0.45, VLT = 0.75

In this scenario, a standard refurbishment was simulated, adding only insulation and replacing the windows with better-performing ones. This allows us to assess the impact of the winter gardens compared to what is usually carried out as a standard renovation in the industry. Although a standard refurbishment would reduce the heating demand to 18 kWh/m², this is still three times the demand of the project with the winter gardens. During the summer, the performance is similar. In this case, it wouldn't be possible to use the building without heating.

178 Case Study 3

Case Comparison 2
Sun and Daylight

(1) Solar heat gains in winter

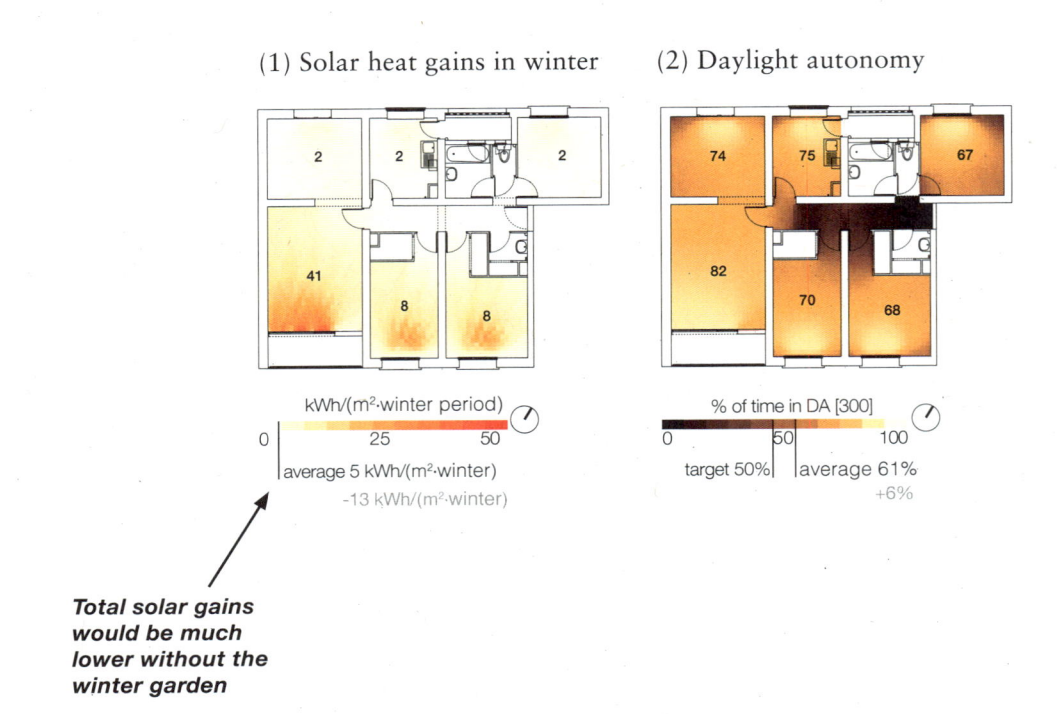

2	2		2
41	8		8

kWh/(m²·winter period)
0 — 25 — 50
average 5 kWh/(m²·winter)
-13 kWh/(m²·winter)

Total solar gains would be much lower without the winter garden

(2) Daylight autonomy

74	75		67
82	70		68

% of time in DA [300]
0 — 50 — 100
target 50%   average 61%
              +6%

(1) Solar heat gains in winter: In a standard refurbishment, the solar gains would be lower than in the former state, as better performing glazings are less transmissive. Still, they remain much lower than with the winter garden.

(2) Daylight Autonomy: A standard refurbishment would barely change daylight levels inside.

Case Study 3

Case Comparison 2
Typical Days

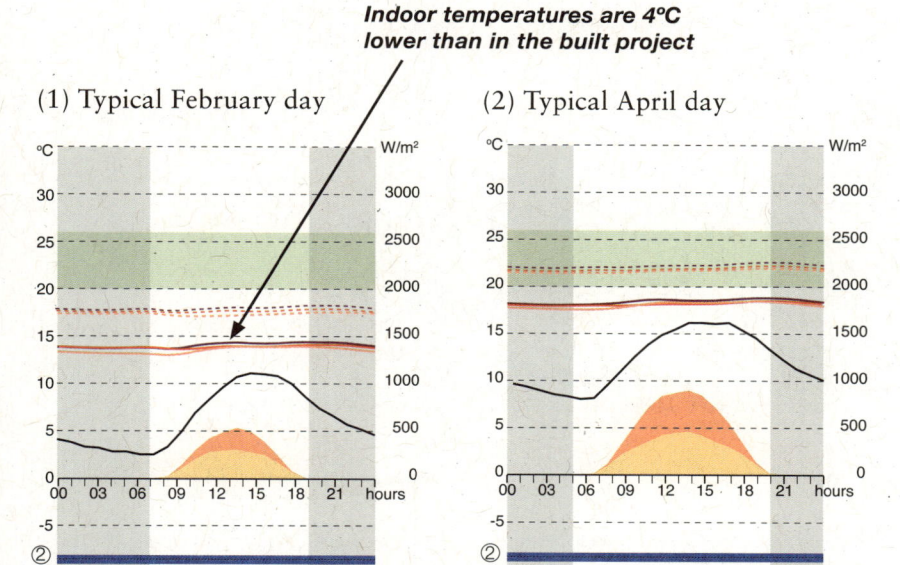

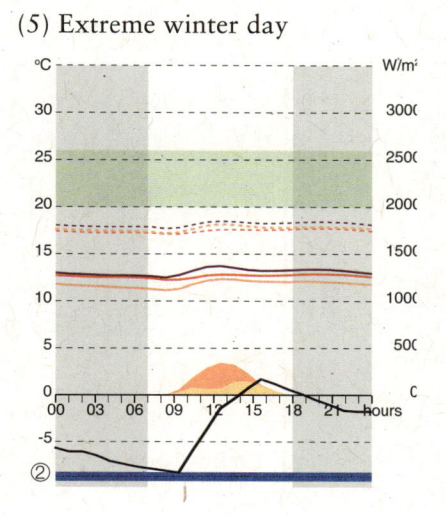

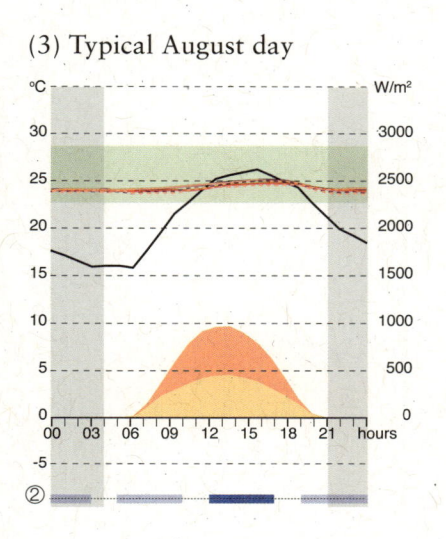

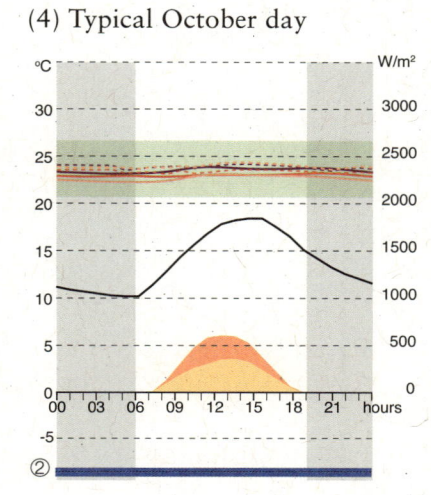

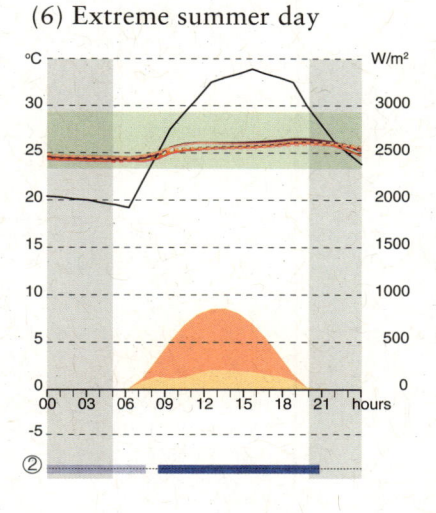

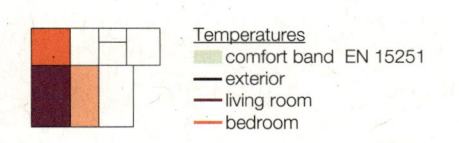

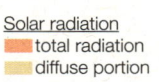

Indoor temperatures are 4°C lower than in the built project

(1) Typical February day

(2) Typical April day

(5) Extreme winter day

(3) Typical August day

(4) Typical October day

(6) Extreme summer day

Temperatures
- comfort band EN 15251
- exterior
- living room
- bedroom

Solar radiation
- total radiation
- diffuse portion

(1) Typical February day: Operative temperatures in free-running mode inside the apartment are low, around 14–15°C. These represent an increase of 2°C compared to the original state of the building. However, the project increased them by around 6°C, as it better captures the heat from the sun and the buffer effect of the winter garden avoids more heat losses. The difference with the built project is therefore around 4°C.

(2) Typical April day: Temperatures in the apartment remain low, around 17–18°C, again representing an increase of 1–2°C. The project actually raised them around 7°C, due to a better use of solar gains.

(3) Typical August day: Temperatures are stable and remain in comfort, similar to the actual built project.

(4) Typical October day: Temperatures are similar to the actual built project.

(5)/(6) Extreme days: During an extreme summer day, temperatures are similar to the actual project, as the thermal inertia keeps them stable in both cases. During an extreme winter day, temperatures remain at 11–14°C, which is about 5°C lower than the actual project.

Case Comparison 2
Resulting Thermal Comfort and Active Mode

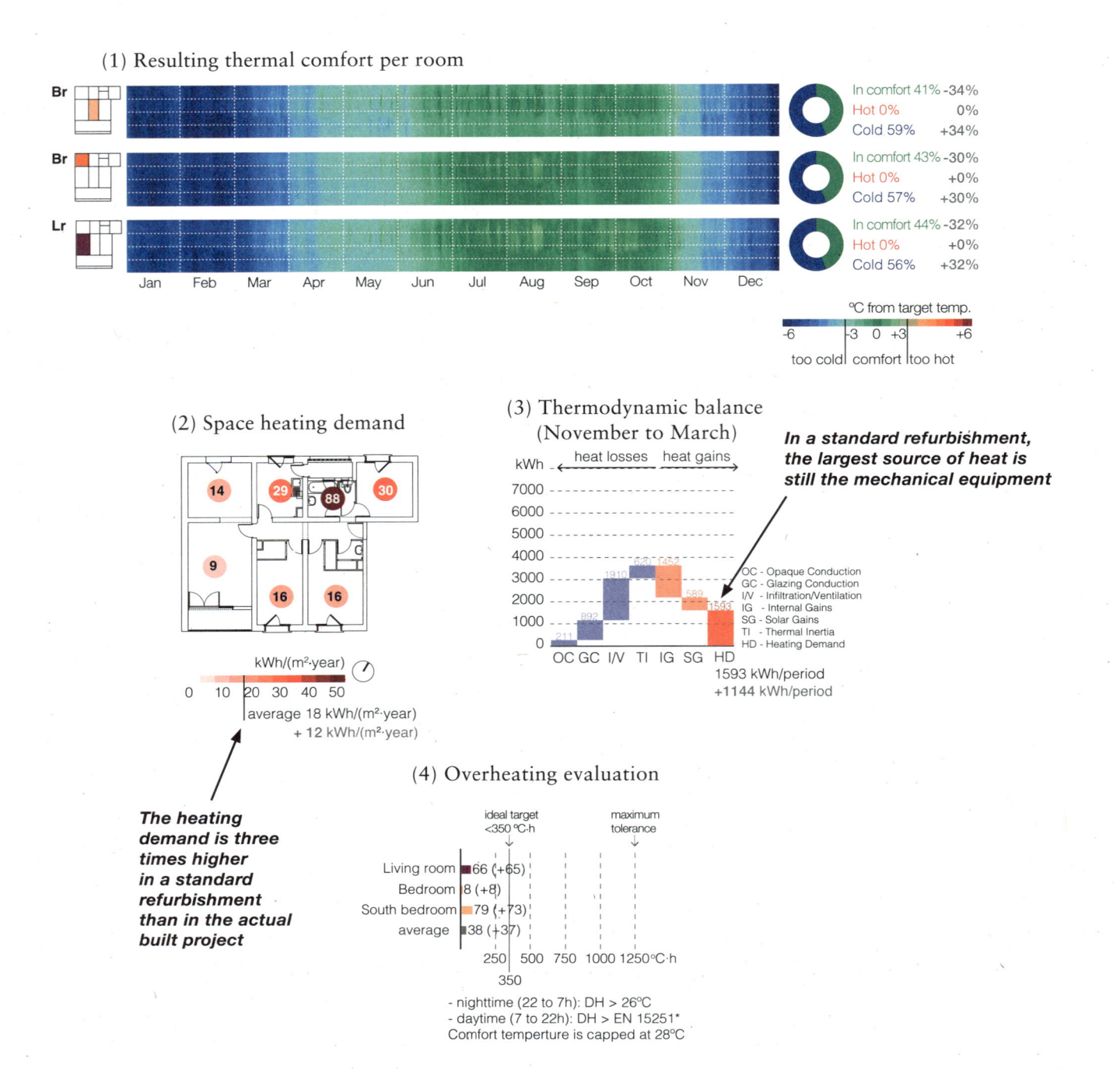

(1) Resulting thermal comfort per room

In comfort 41% −34%
Hot 0%   0%
Cold 59% +34%

In comfort 43% −30%
Hot 0%   +0%
Cold 57% +30%

In comfort 44% −32%
Hot 0%   +0%
Cold 56% +32%

°C from target temp.
−6 −3 0 +3 +6
too cold | comfort | too hot

(2) Space heating demand

kWh/(m²·year)
0 10 20 30 40 50
average 18 kWh/(m²·year)
+ 12 kWh/(m²·year)

The heating demand is three times higher in a standard refurbishment than in the actual built project

(3) Thermodynamic balance (November to March)

In a standard refurbishment, the largest source of heat is still the mechanical equipment

kWh ← heat losses | heat gains →

OC - Opaque Conduction
GC - Glazing Conduction
I/V - Infiltration/Ventilation
IG - Internal Gains
SG - Solar Gains
TI - Thermal Inertia
HD - Heating Demand

1593 kWh/period
+1144 kWh/period

(4) Overheating evaluation

ideal target <350 °C·h   maximum tolerance

Living room   66 (+65)
Bedroom   8 (+8)
South bedroom 79 (+73)
average   38 (+37)

250 500 750 1000 1250 °C·h
350

- nighttime (22 to 7h): DH > 26°C
- daytime (7 to 22h): DH > EN 15251*
Comfort temperature is capped at 28°C

(1) Resulting thermal comfort per room: On average, time in comfort barely increases with a standard refurbishment, as the comfortable hours of both the living room and bedrooms rise by 4–6%. The living room reaches 44% in comfort and the bedrooms 42% on average. This performance is considerably worse than the actual project, which reaches 76% comfort in the living room and 73% in the bedrooms. However, the severity of the cold is reduced during the entire winter period compared to the former state of the building.

(2) Space heating demand: A standard refurbishment focuses on reducing heat loss by improving envelope specifications. Even if time in comfort barely changes, heating demand is cut by almost two-thirds compared to the former state reaching 18 kWh/(m²·year). Compared to the built project, heating demand is still three times higher. Peak demand is reduced by more than half compared to the former state of the building reaching 2.1 kW, which is exactly double the peak demand of the actual project. Heating demand is significantly reduced in all spaces, as it remains below 30 kWh/(m²·year) (except the north bathroom). South-facing rooms have a lower demand due to the contribution of solar gains in these areas.

(3) Thermodynamic balance (November to March): The intervention significantly reduces the losses by glazing conduction and opaque conduction, shifting the main sources of heat loss to the ventilation and infiltration. It decreases the solar gain slightly. This happens because adding insulation is focused on reducing the losses and not capitalizing on gains. Mechanical heating is still the main source of heat, followed by the internal gains. Solar gains remain very low. This means that the unit depends on the internal equipment and loads and the machines to increase its temperature, instead of relying on the sun.

(4) Overheating evaluation: A standard renovation decreases the overheating hours by half, but remains well above the actual project. The hot hours still happen at night, making it difficult for people to sleep well.

Case Comparison 3
Building G

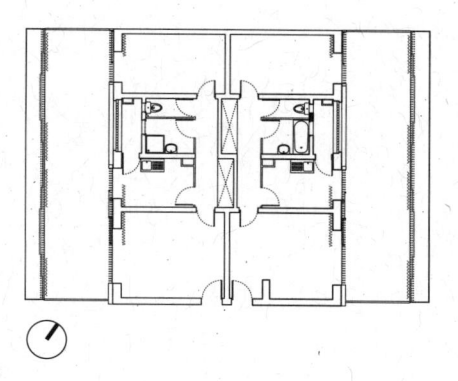

Daylight:
average daylight autonomy DA [300]: 48% (**-12%**) of the time

The east-facing apartment largely exceeds the recommendations of EN 17037, whereas there is only one room in this apartment with only 31% of the space receiving 300 lux at least 50% of the time

Temperature and comfort in free-running mode:
above comfort: 0% of the time
within comfort: 67% (**-5%**) of the time
below comfort: 33% (**+5%**) of the time

average degree·hours
above comfort: 37°C·h (**+36°C·h**)

Solar gains and winter garden effect:
(temperature difference between the winter garden and outside)
winter: east +4°C, west +6°C
mid-season: east +7°C, west +8°C

Heating demand:
total: 14 kWh/(m²·year) (**+8 kWh/(m²·year)**)
peak demand: 2.9 kW (**+1.85 kW**)
Heating on:
2,906 / 8,760 hours per year (**-1,092 h**)
122 / 365 days per year (**+17 d**)

Modifications in detail:
Study of the block G, as built in the project
Southwest- and northeast-facing units, 6th floor, 93.5 m²

The building G has a very similar structure and organization as buildings H and I. However, it is smaller and oriented 90° with respect to buildings H and I. This results in units oriented toward the southwest/northeast instead of southeast/northwest. Apartments are also smaller and mono-oriented instead of the dual aspect units of the buildings H and I. These conditions bring slight disadvantages to the units: In the southwest orientation, the heat in winter arrives in the afternoon and accumulates slightly less than when it arrives in the morning. In summer, the southwest orientation is more prone to overheating. The mono orientation prevents cross ventilation but also prevents the north units from benefiting from the mixing of air from the south. Also, in the case of buildings H and I, the rooms facing south are bigger than the ones facing north, which can accumulate more heat from the sun and further increase temperatures. This results in an overall performance that is slightly worse for building G, as temperatures in summer are in general a bit higher, especially in the afternoon. In winter, all temperatures are slightly lower, which results in a higher heating demand (double), but one that still remains very low.

Case Comparison 3
Sun and Daylight

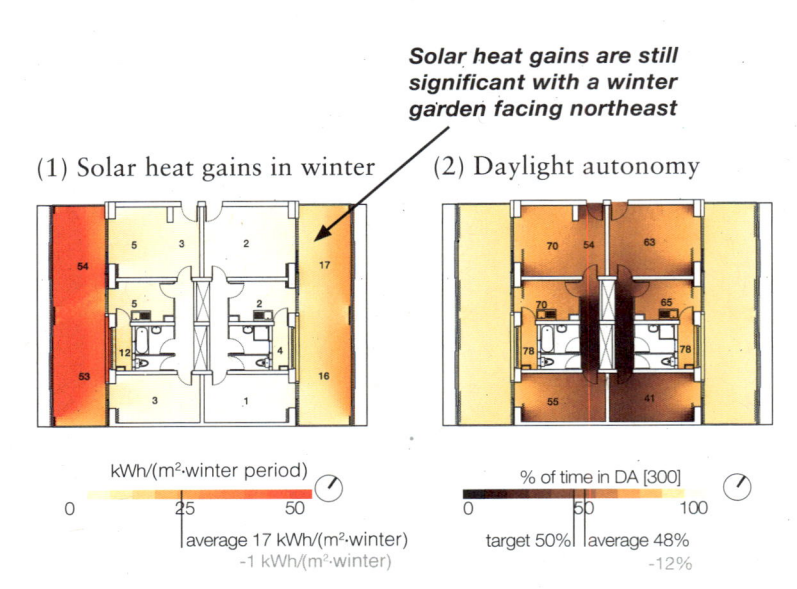

(1) Solar heat gains in winter   (2) Daylight autonomy

Solar heat gains are still significant with a winter garden facing northeast

kWh/(m²·winter period)

0   25   50

average 17 kWh/(m²·winter)
−1 kWh/(m²·winter)

% of time in DA [300]

0   50   100

target 50% average 48%
−12%

(1) Solar heat gains in winter: As all the buildings are oriented 45° with respect to the north, the total solar gain is very similar. Winter gardens oriented toward the southeast gained 59 kWh/m² of solar heat in winter whereas the ones oriented toward the southwest gained 54 kWh/m². However, the heat is not received at the same time of the day, and the accumulation happens in a different way. The winter gardens facing northeast still receive a significant amount of heat in winter, with a total of 17 kWh/m².

(2) Daylight Autonomy: Daylight provision is very similar in both cases where there is the winter garden, as daylight levels don't depend on orientation, but on sky view. All three buildings are in a park and are not obstructed, and therefore allow sky views. In building G there is less light due to the double winter garden and the higher compartmentalization of the space.

Case Comparison 3
Typical Days

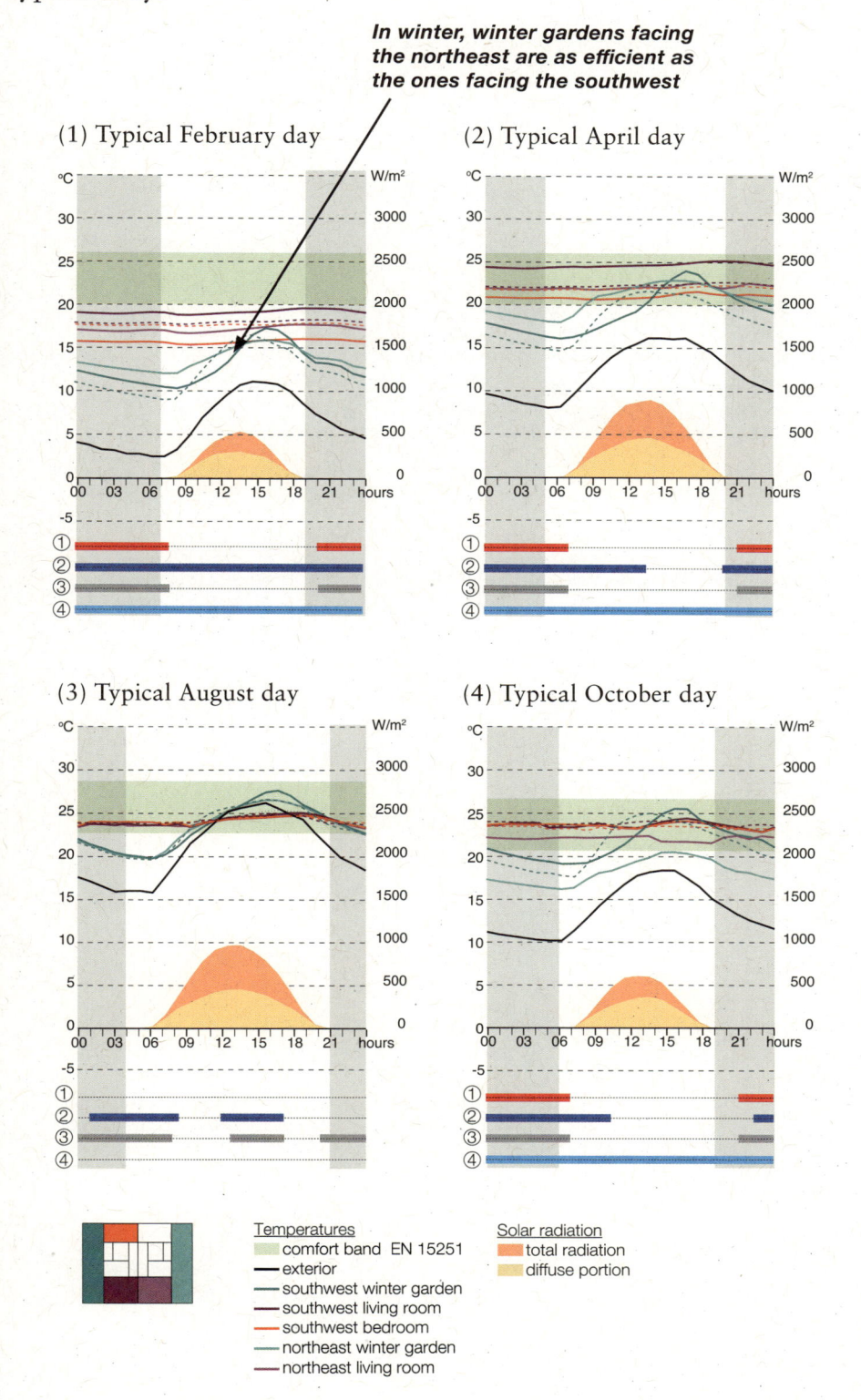

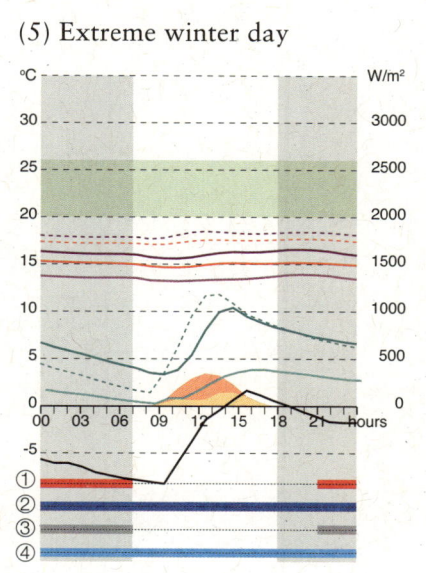

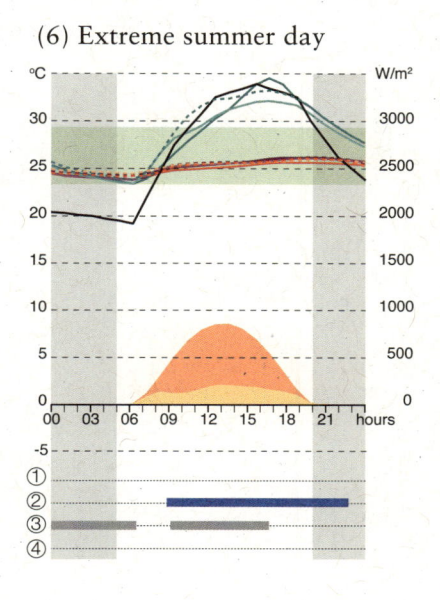

In winter, winter gardens facing the northeast are as efficient as the ones facing the southwest

(1) Typical February day

(2) Typical April day

(5) Extreme winter day

(3) Typical August day

(4) Typical October day

(6) Extreme summer day

Temperatures
- comfort band EN 15251
- exterior
- southwest winter garden
- southwest living room
- southwest bedroom
- northeast winter garden
- northeast living room

Solar radiation
- total radiation
- diffuse portion

(1) Typical February day: In winter, all winter gardens (southeast, southwest, and northeast) have similar temperatures—about 5–6°C more than outdoors—which proves their effectiveness in all orientations. Indoor temperatures are slightly lower in the northeast apartments and slightly higher in the southwest ones. Temperatures are higher in the southwest apartments because the same amount of solar gains in the glazed surface is divided into a greater usable area.

(2) Typical April day: All indoor temperatures are stable and within the comfort band naturally, from 21 to 25°C. Winter garden temperatures are all similar, from 15 to 24°C. In spring, the sun hits in all orientations, which increases temperatures in all the winter gardens. The sliding doors of the heated space are open most of the day, as temperatures are within the indoor comfort band. The winter garden can be used as an additional indoor space in all orientations.

(3) Typical August day: All temperatures are very similar among the units and remain within the comfort band, at 24–25°C. The inertia of the concrete helps to create this stability. Whereas the winter garden to the northeast has similar temperatures to outdoors, the one to the southwest has higher temperatures in the afternoon. This happens because the sun hits when temperatures are already high.

(5) Extreme winter day: During an extreme winter day, indoor temperatures are 13 to 17°C naturally, a few degrees lower than in the buildings H and I. Temperatures in the southwest winter garden are about 2–4°C degrees lower during the morning, but still keep a difference with the outdoors of 8–13°C. In the northeast, winter garden temperatures are even lower and maintain a difference with the outdoors of 2–10°C, which is significant. When outdoor temperatures are below zero almost all day, inside the winter gardens the temperatures are always 0–10°C.

(6) Extreme summer day: During an extreme summer day, all temperatures are within comfort naturally, and are similar in all apartments. When it is too hot outside, the sliding doors of the heated space are closed to prevent ventilating at a higher temperature, and the thermal inertia keeps temperatures cool.

Case Comparison 3
Resulting Thermal Comfort and Active Mode

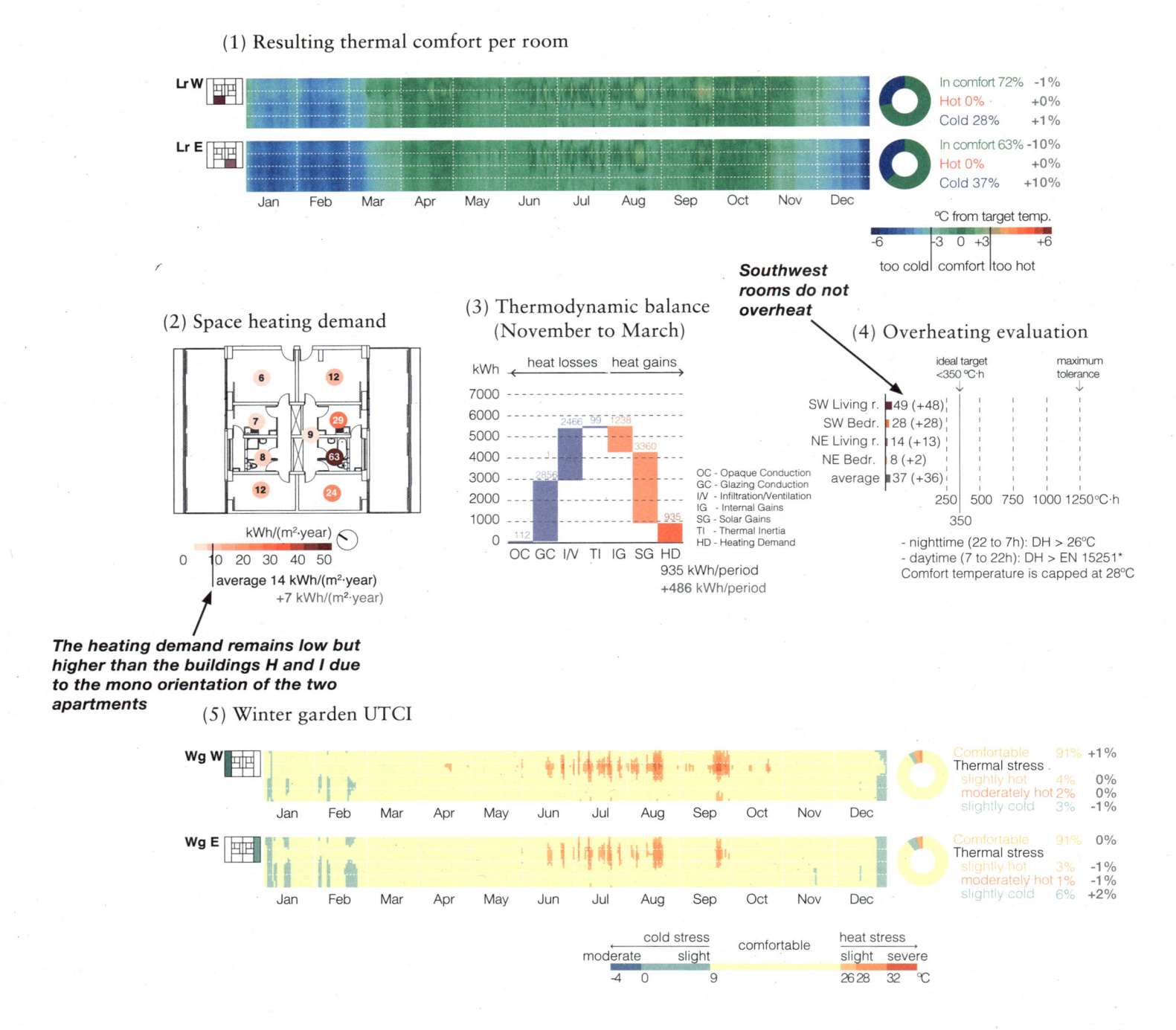

(1) Resulting thermal comfort per room

Lr W — In comfort 72% −1% / Hot 0% +0% / Cold 28% +1%
Lr E — In comfort 63% −10% / Hot 0% +0% / Cold 37% +10%

°C from target temp.
−6 −3 0 +3 +6
too cold | comfort | too hot

(2) Space heating demand

kWh/(m²·year)
0 10 20 30 40 50
average 14 kWh/(m²·year)
+7 kWh/(m²·year)

The heating demand remains low but higher than the buildings H and I due to the mono orientation of the two apartments

(3) Thermodynamic balance (November to March)

kWh — heat losses / heat gains
OC - Opaque Conduction
GC - Glazing Conduction
I/V - Infiltration/Ventilation
IG - Internal Gains
SG - Solar Gains
TI - Thermal Inertia
HD - Heating Demand

935 kWh/period
+486 kWh/period

Southwest rooms do not overheat

(4) Overheating evaluation

ideal target <350 °C·h   maximum tolerance
SW Living r. 49 (+48)
SW Bedr.   28 (+28)
NE Living r. 14 (+13)
NE Bedr.   8 (+2)
average   37 (+36)
             250 500 750 1000 1250 °C·h
             350

- nighttime (22 to 7h): DH > 26°C
- daytime (7 to 22h): DH > EN 15251*
Comfort temperature is capped at 28°C

(5) Winter garden UTCI

Wg W — Comfortable 91% +1% / Thermal stress / slightly hot 4% 0% / moderately hot 2% 0% / slightly cold 3% −1%

Wg E — Comfortable 91% 0% / Thermal stress / slightly hot 3% −1% / moderately hot 1% −1% / slightly cold 6% +2%

cold stress | comfortable | heat stress
moderate slight   slight severe
   −4   0   9   26 28   32 °C

---

(1) Resulting thermal comfort per room: In general, the passive performance of the southwest living room is very similar to the southeast one (in comfort 1% less of the time), whereas the northeast living room is in comfort 10% less of the time. None of the units spends time above comfort (EN 15251).

(2) Space heating demand: Heating demand is doubled compared to buildings H and I, as the northeast-facing area benefits much less from the sun. However, the demand remains very low (14 kWh/m²), and reaches a contemporary target of passive performance.

(3) Thermodynamic balance (November to March): In proportion, there are more exchanges by opaque conduction, glazing conduction, and solar gains in this case as there are winter gardens on both facades. Solar gains are still higher than losses by glazing conduction, and this diagram shows the interactions of the entire envelope.

(4) Overheating evaluation: All the rooms are considerably below the ideal target. Even southwest living rooms have very few hours above the overheating target.

(5) Winter garden UTCI: All winter gardens have similar conditions, as they reach 91% of the time without any thermal stress, which is double the amount compared to an exposed situation. The time in severe thermal stress is eliminated as well.

Case Study 4: Residential and Office Tower, Geneva, Switzerland

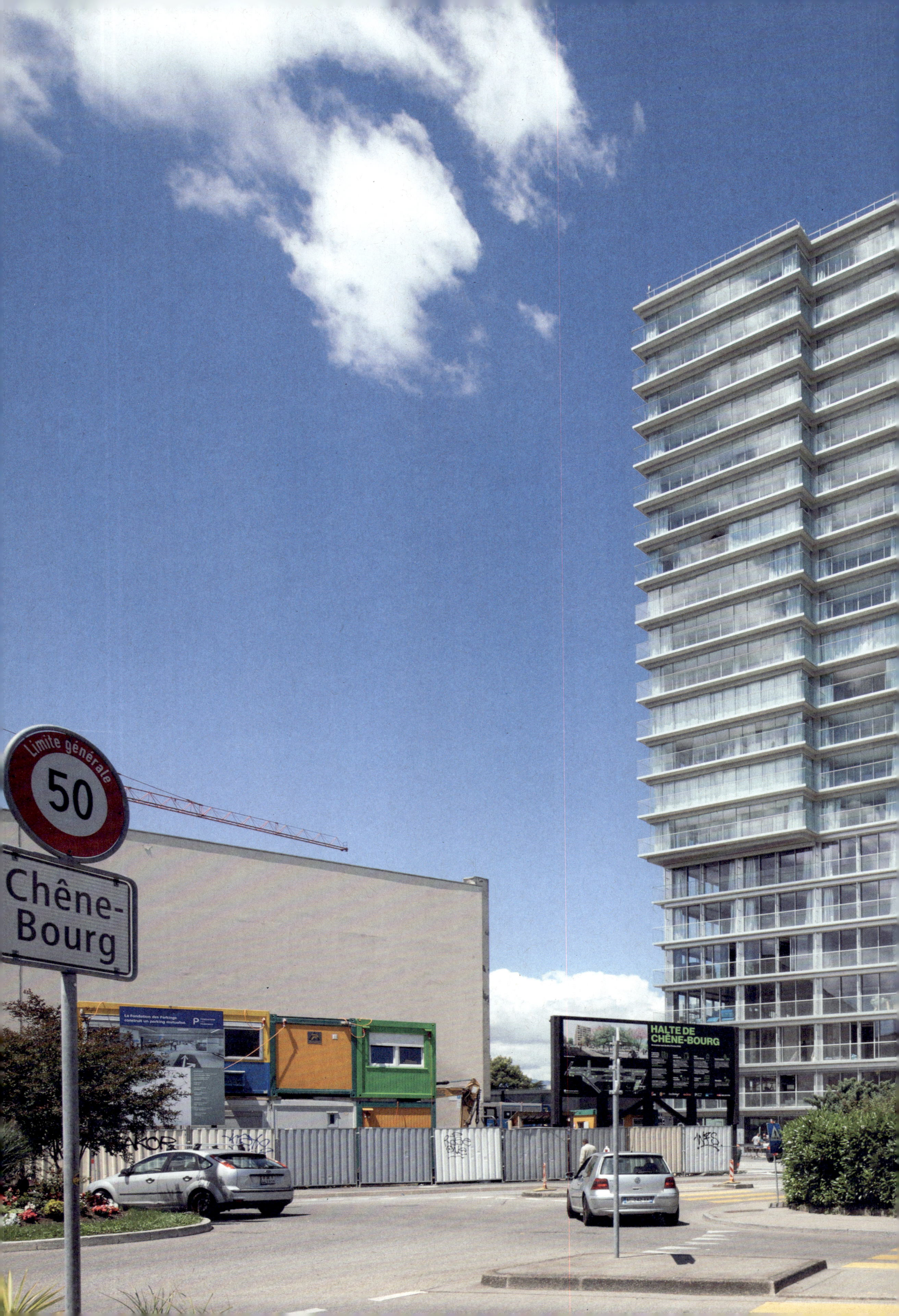
Limite générale
50
Chêne-
Bourg
HALTE DE
CHÊNE-BOURG

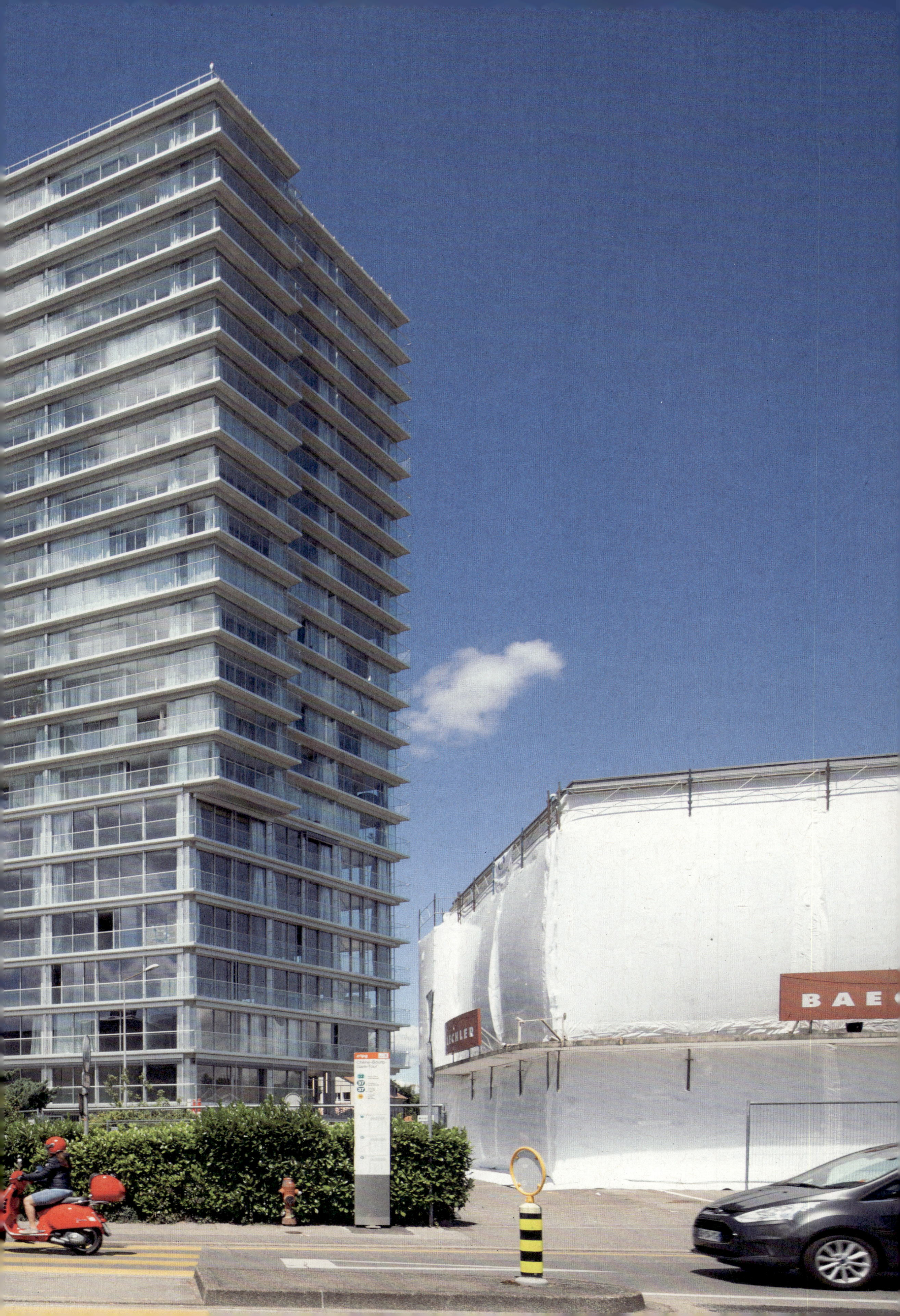
BAEC
BÄCHLER

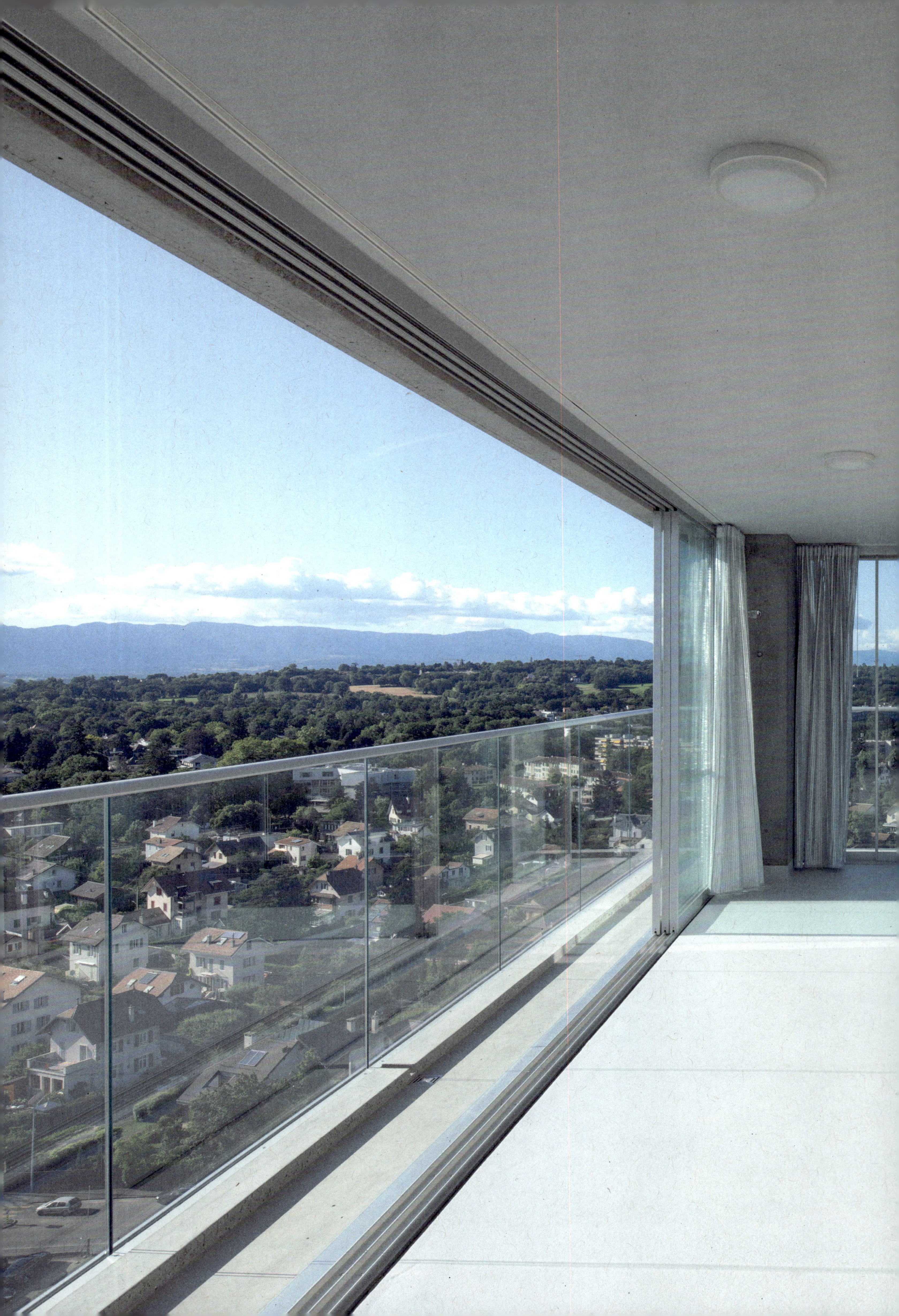

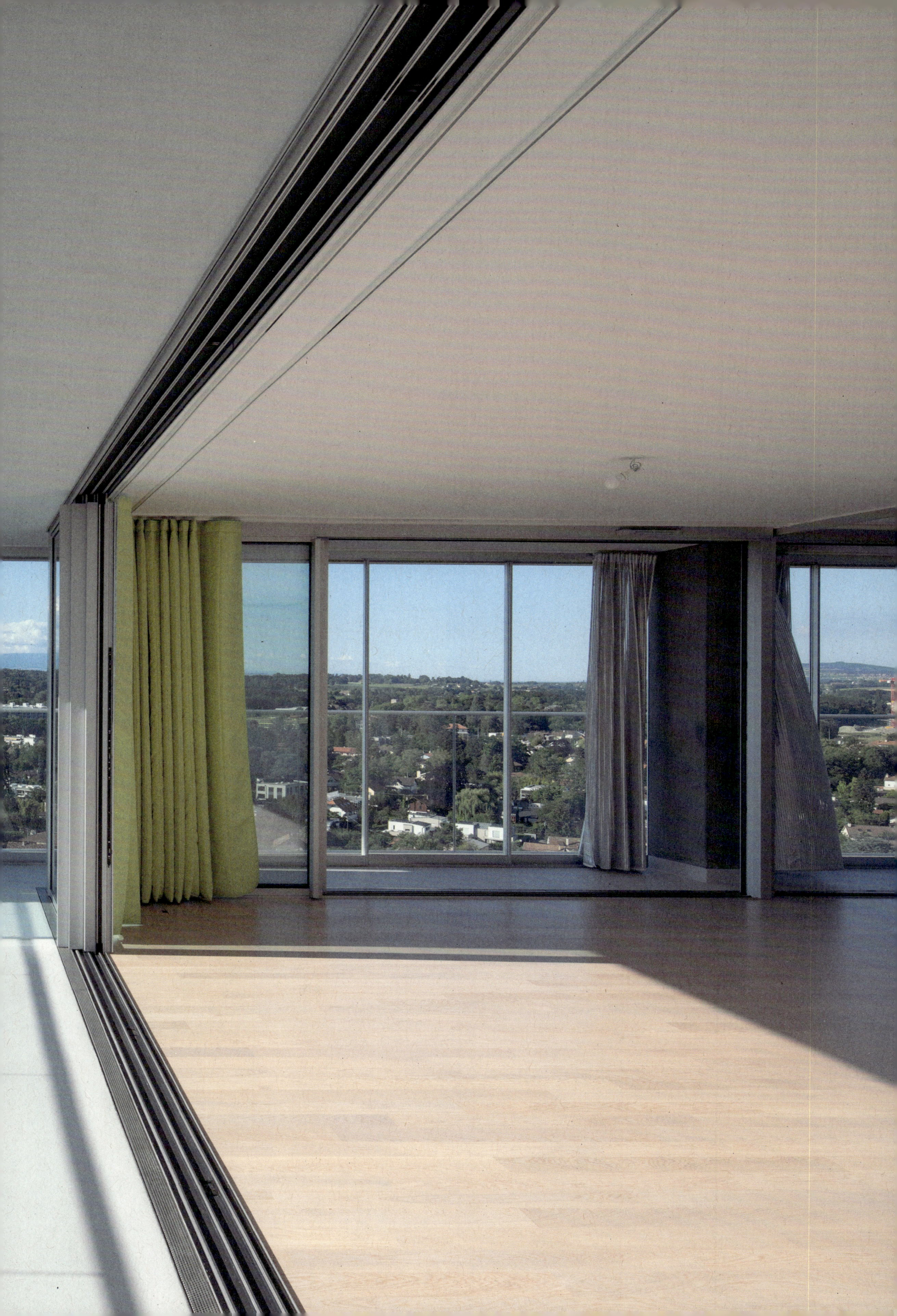

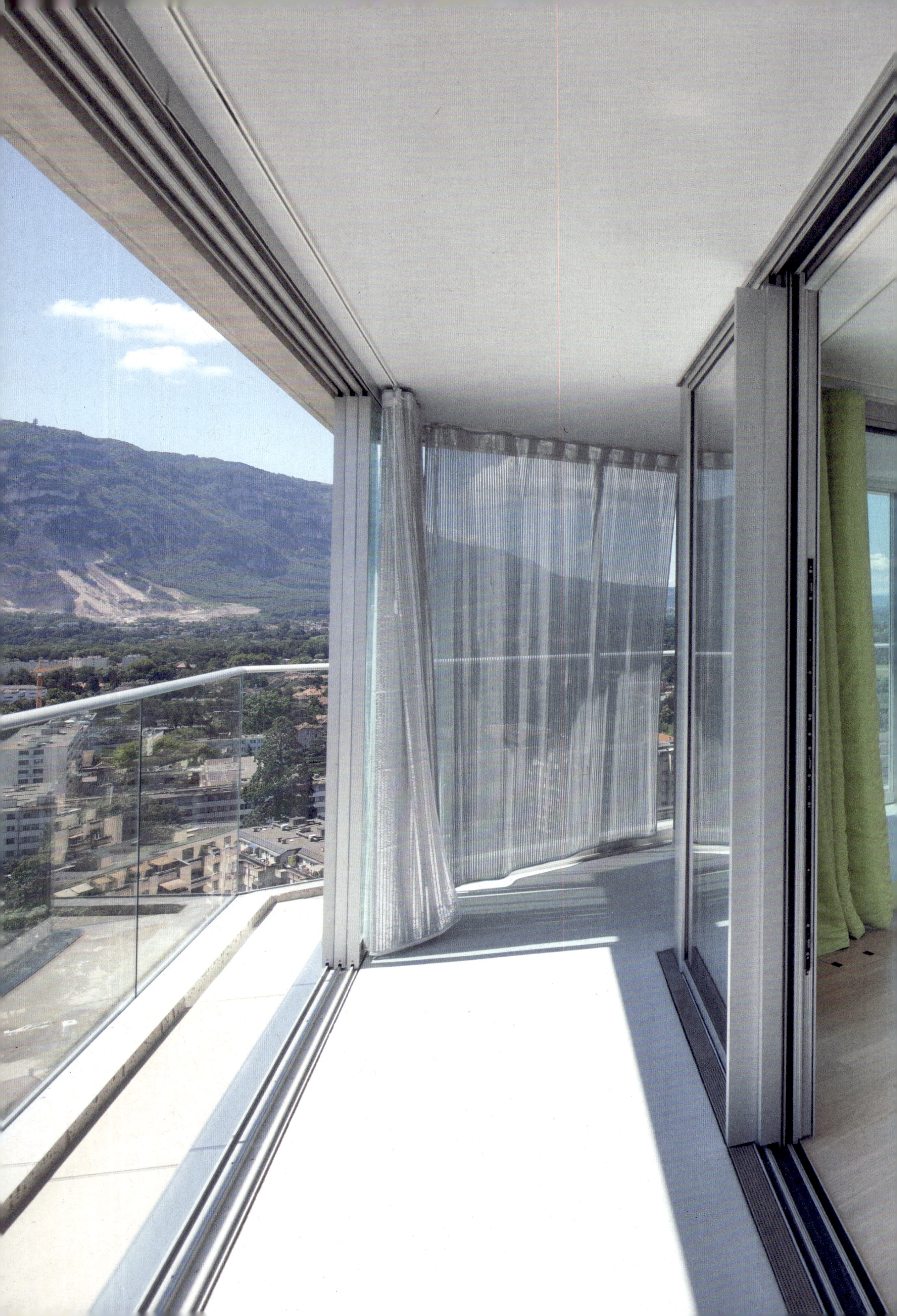

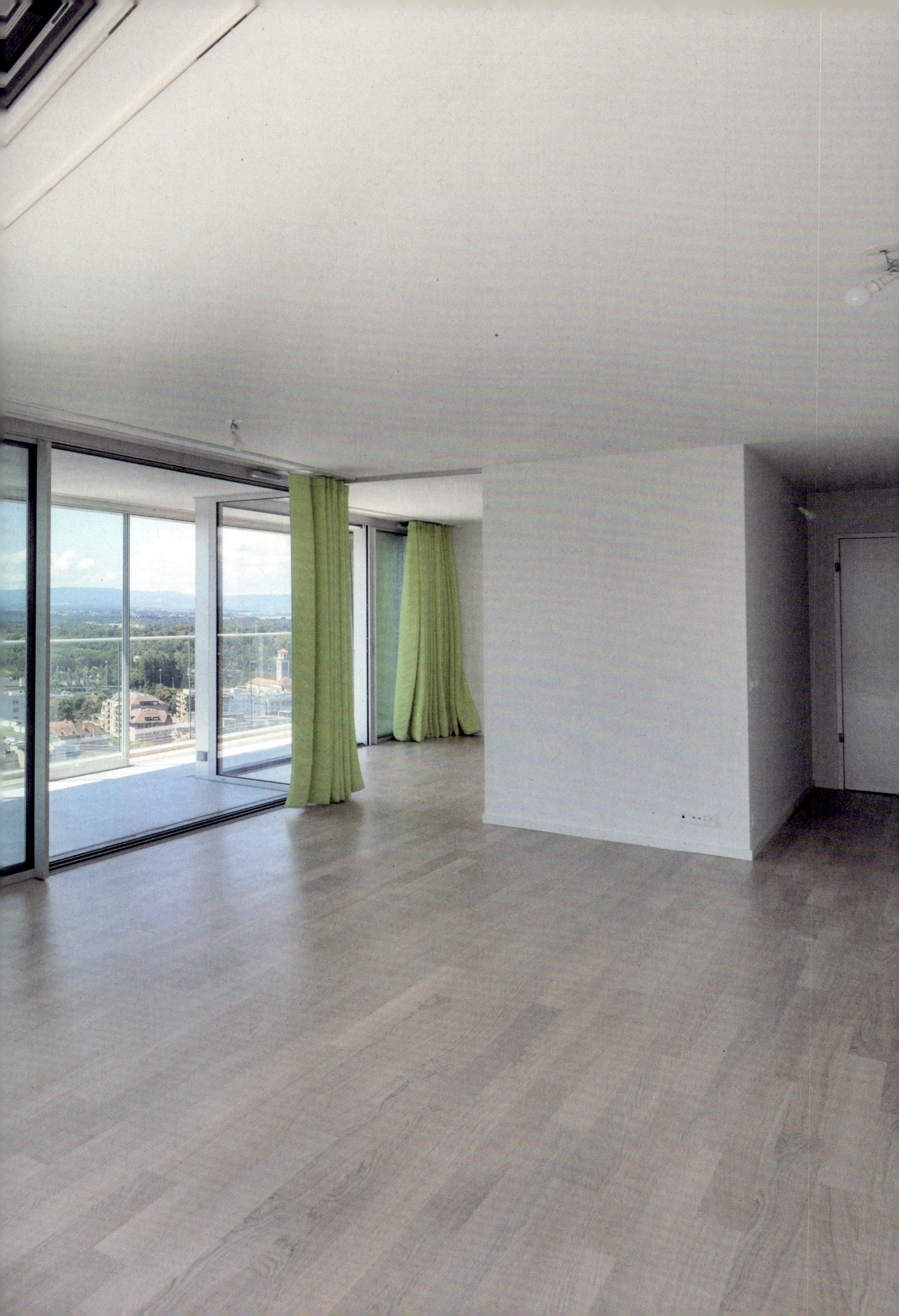

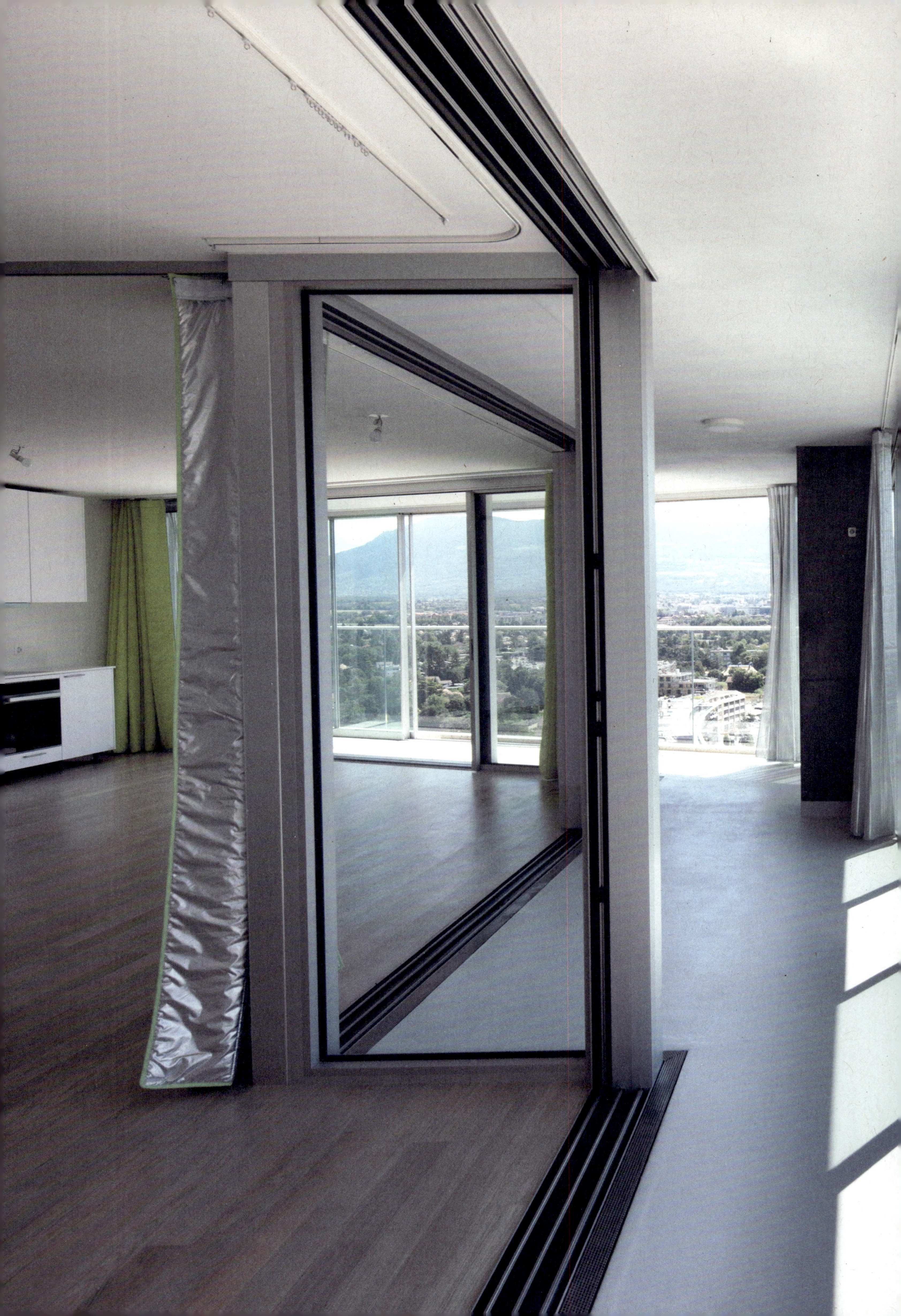

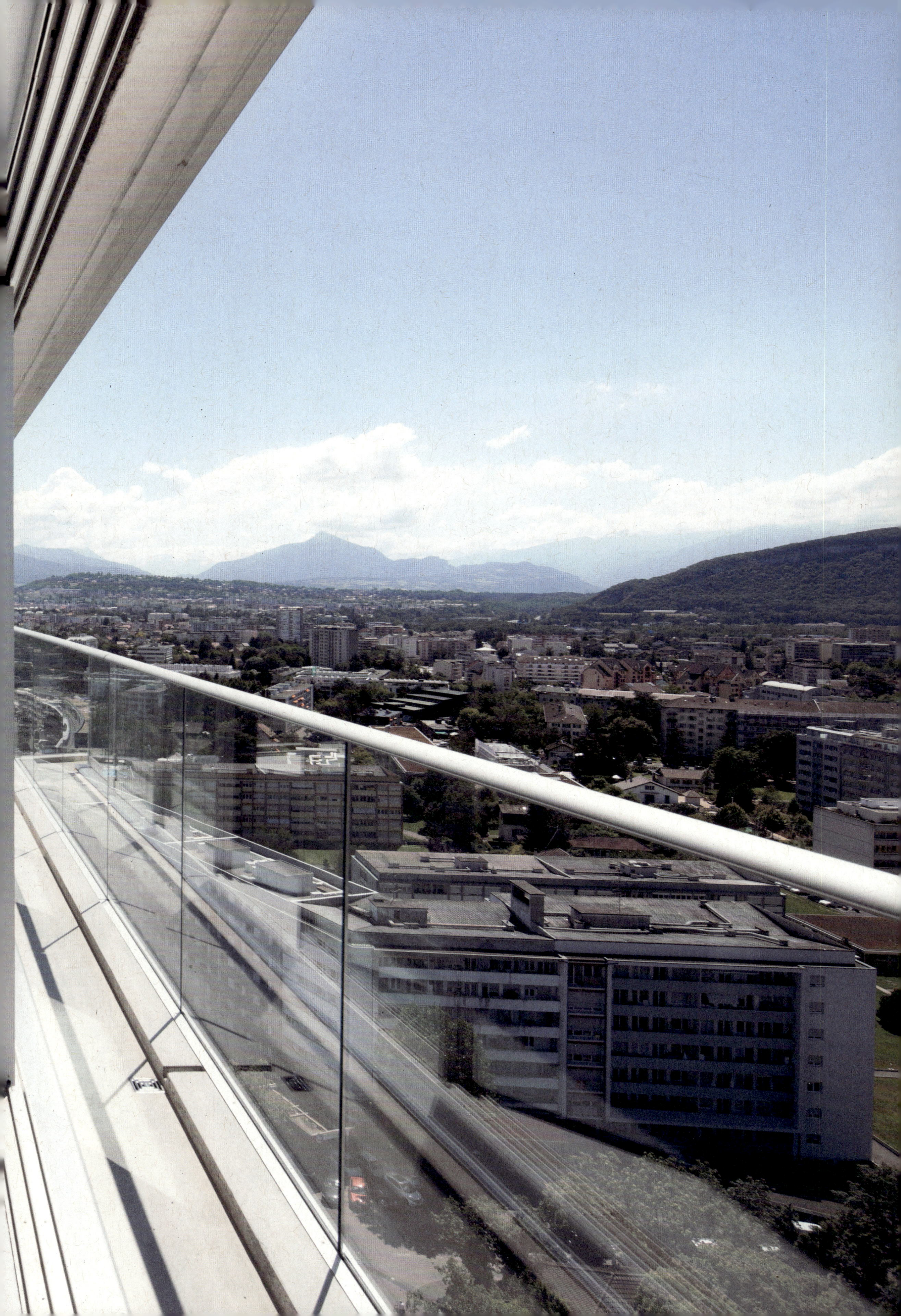

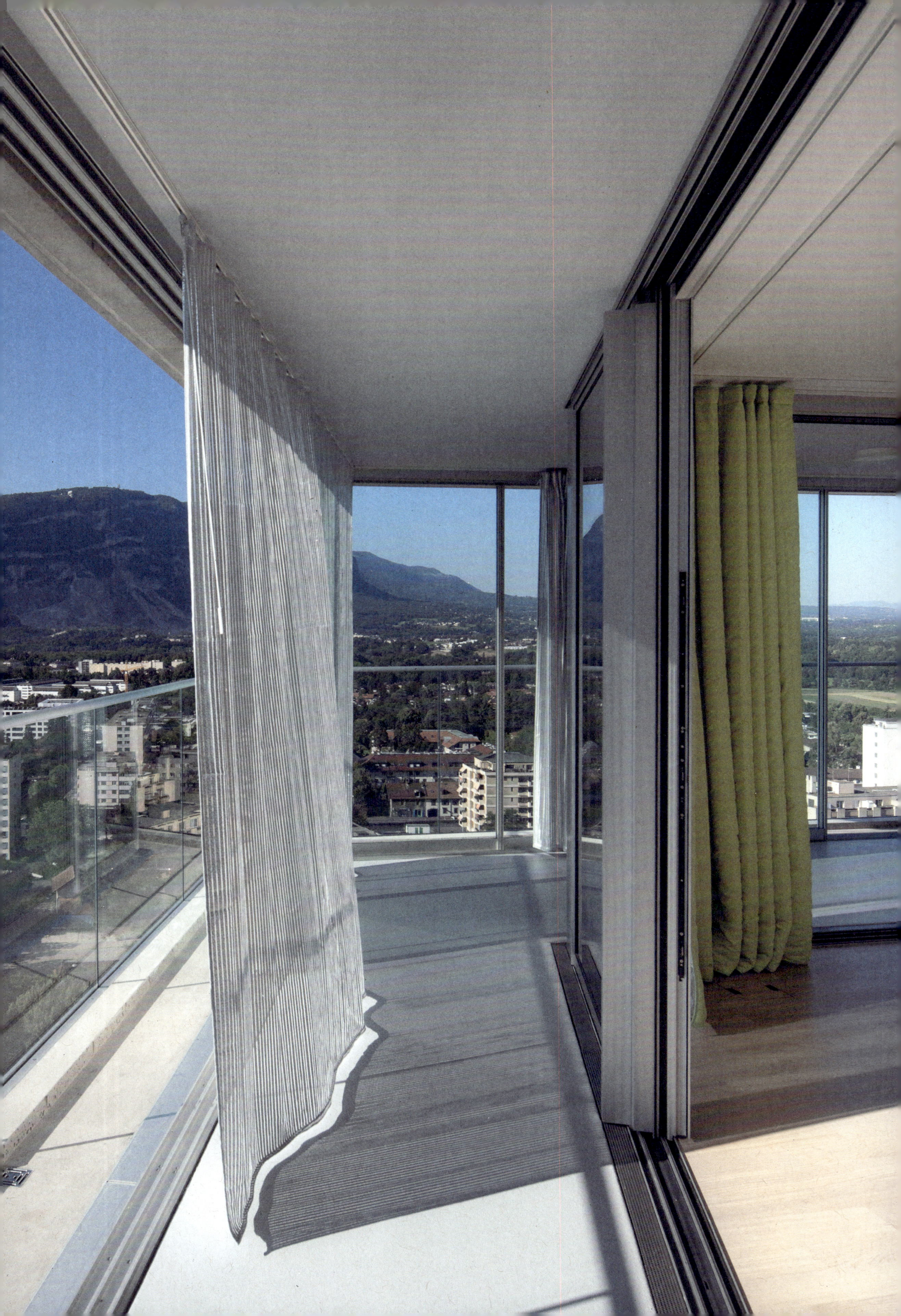

Residential and Office Tower

Geneva
Switzerland
2020

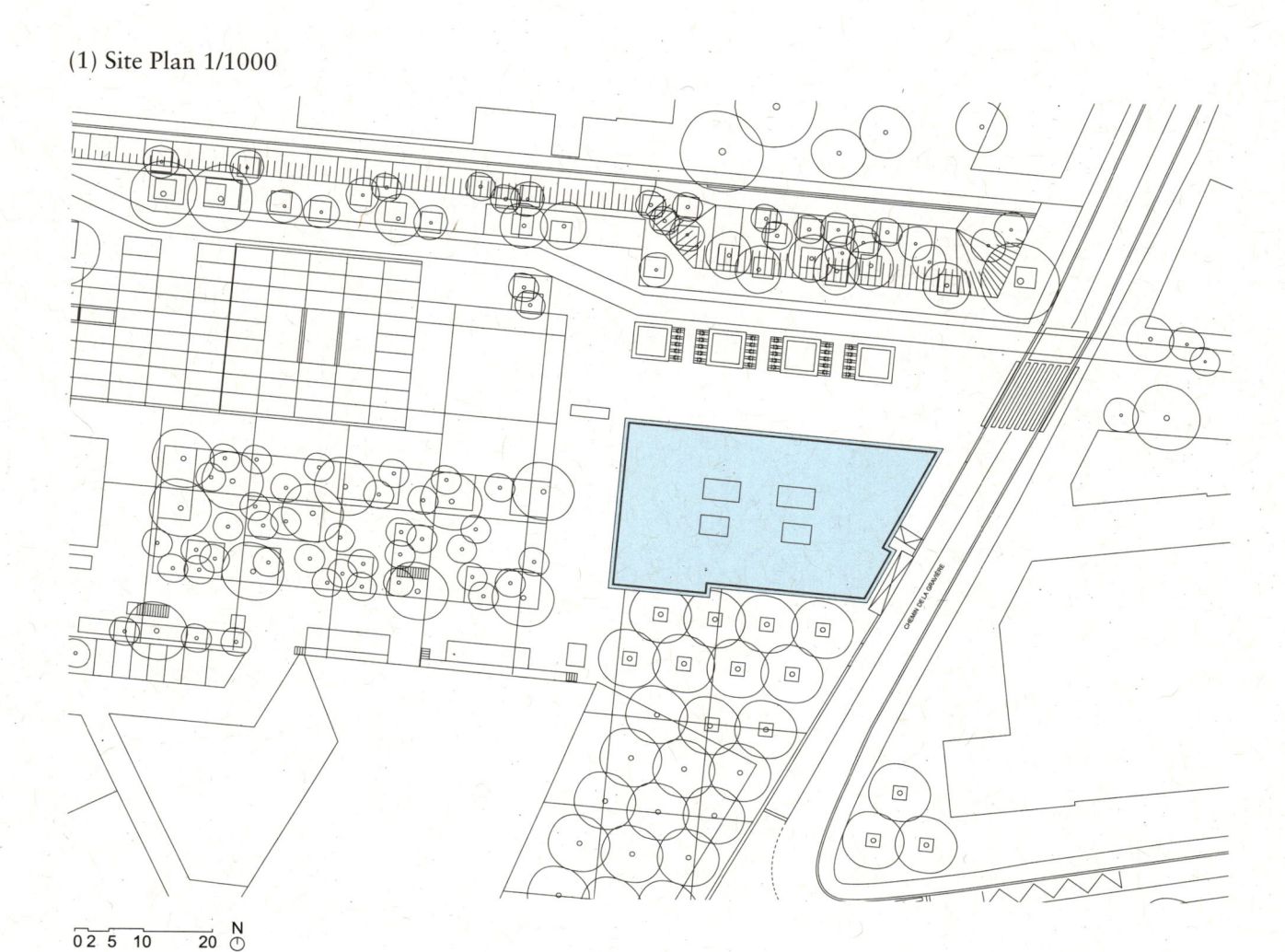

(1) Site Plan 1/1000

At the heart of the Chêne-Bourg district in the canton of Geneva, a new train station helped create a new center. A key element of the redeveloped area is this nineteen-story tower. The project optimizes the construction potential of the site to create 101 apartments on the upper fourteen floors, 5,000 m² of offices on the first five floors, and a commercial first floor above two basements dedicated to storerooms, collective laundry rooms, and technical spaces. The structural principle is simple and flexible, offering freedom of use in space and time. It is a skeleton system that allows for the creation of large spaces with little structural constraint. This completely clears the periphery of the floors, making it possible to freely construct the facades and allowing for a simple, long-term evolution of the program. Access to and circulation through the residential and commercial areas are independent from each other. The entrance to the apartments is located on the north facade, with two cores—elevators and staircases—avoiding a central distribution corridor on the floors and allowing apartments with multiple exposures. The offices are accessed by an entrance hall to the south and two elevators. The staircases are shared. The quality of space and freedom of use offered to the inhabitants, and the generosity of the living spaces, are the major objectives of the project. The five office floors are modular, available as one single space or divisible into two, three, or four independent units. The 101 apartments are spacious, pleasant, and well daylit, and they benefit from a variety of orientations, views, and direct sunlight in winter. Most of them are double-oriented, aiming to create the spatial qualities and character of a villa in the city. The tower is the first housing project where we created a double envelope and intermediate winter garden spaces around the entire periphery of the building and in all orientations.

Project and Environmental Conditions
Building

(1) Overall plan 1/400

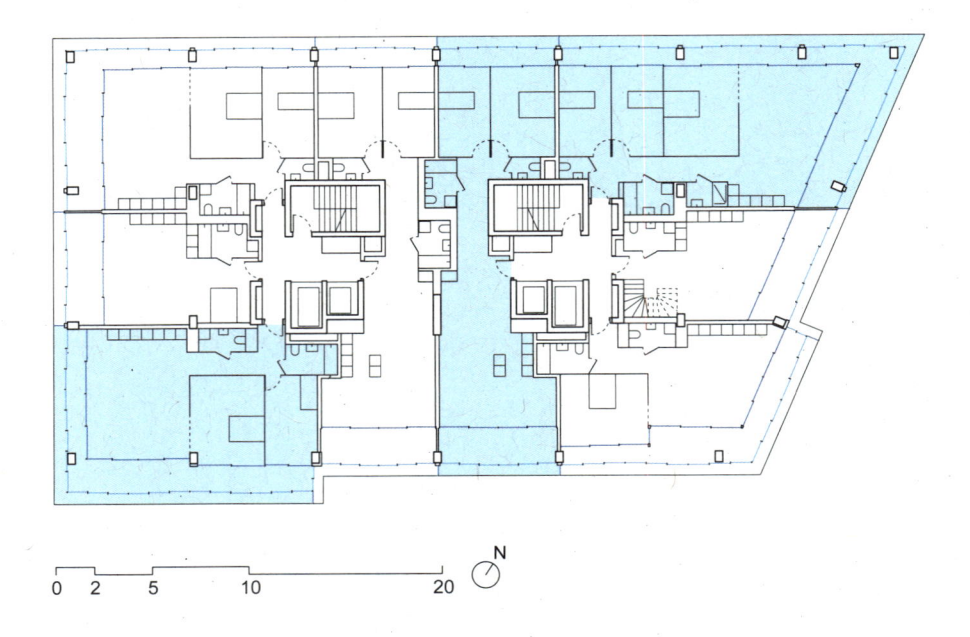

All the apartments have winter gardens and balconies that extend the interior space and offer a space for various uses, depending on the time of day, the season, or the inhabitants' wishes. The main rooms open onto these spaces through large floor-to-ceiling sliding glass doors, equipped with thermal curtains for comfort. The bioclimatic envelope, composed of the winter gardens, generously extends the use of interior space. Completely open in summer, the winter gardens become large shaded outdoor terraces that keep direct sunlight off the glass facades and thus avoid overheating. In winter, the glass facades of the winter gardens can be closed to create natural, protected intermediate spaces with climatic conditions that enhance solar gain and optimize energy savings. The office floors also have balconies that act as sunshades and allow for easy maintenance of the glass facades.

Case Study 4

Project and Environmental Conditions
Unit

(1) Analyzed unit 1:150

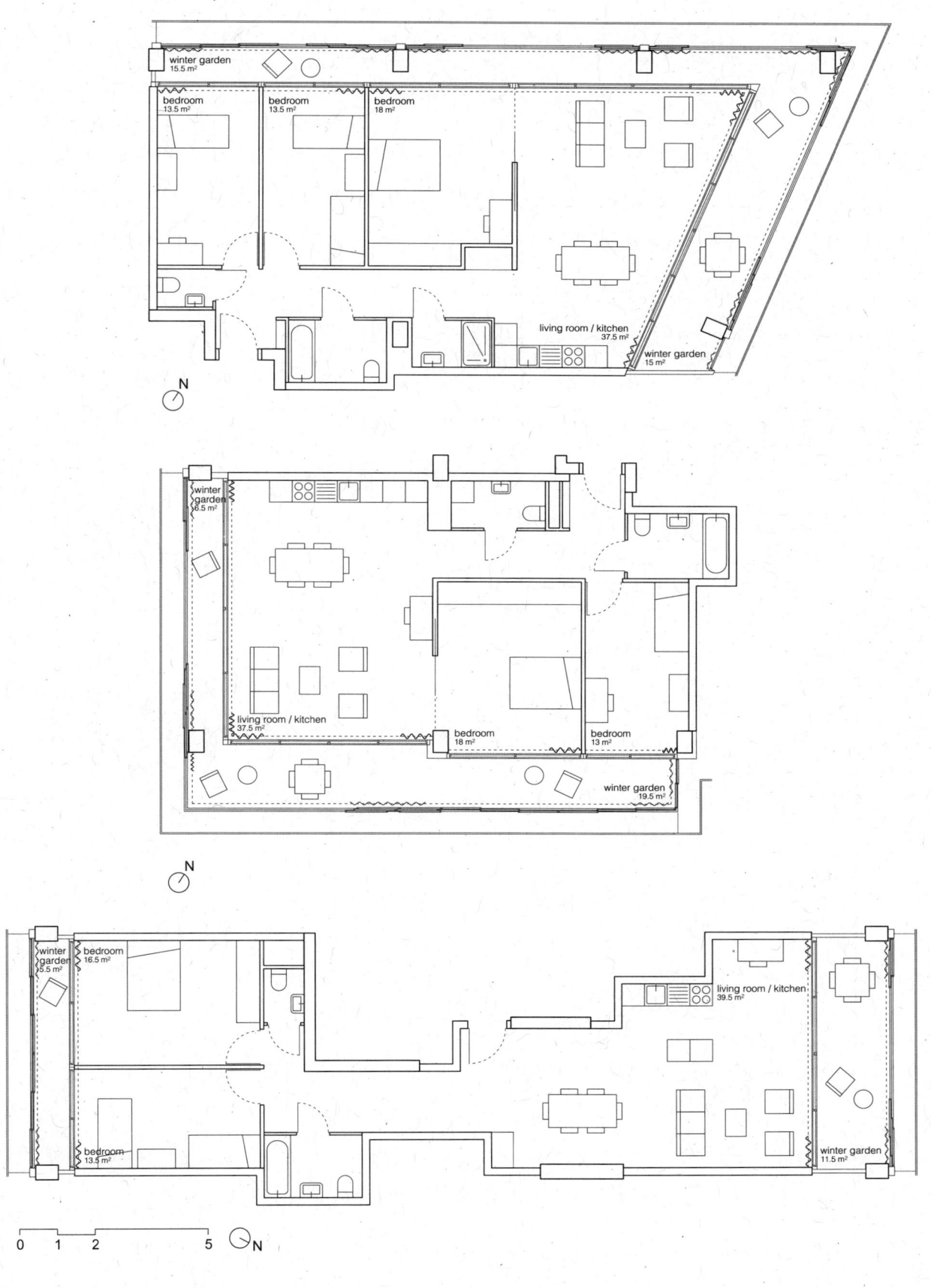

The unobstructed corners provide a focus for the apartment, allowing panoramic views of landscapes that are constantly changing with the weather and light. The living space extends without thresholds toward the adjacent room (separated by a sliding door) as well as the winter garden and the continuous balcony, which stretches along the unit's entire facade. This allows for fluent movement through all climatic layers and the dwelling's different spaces.

Case Study 4

Project and Environmental Conditions
Climate

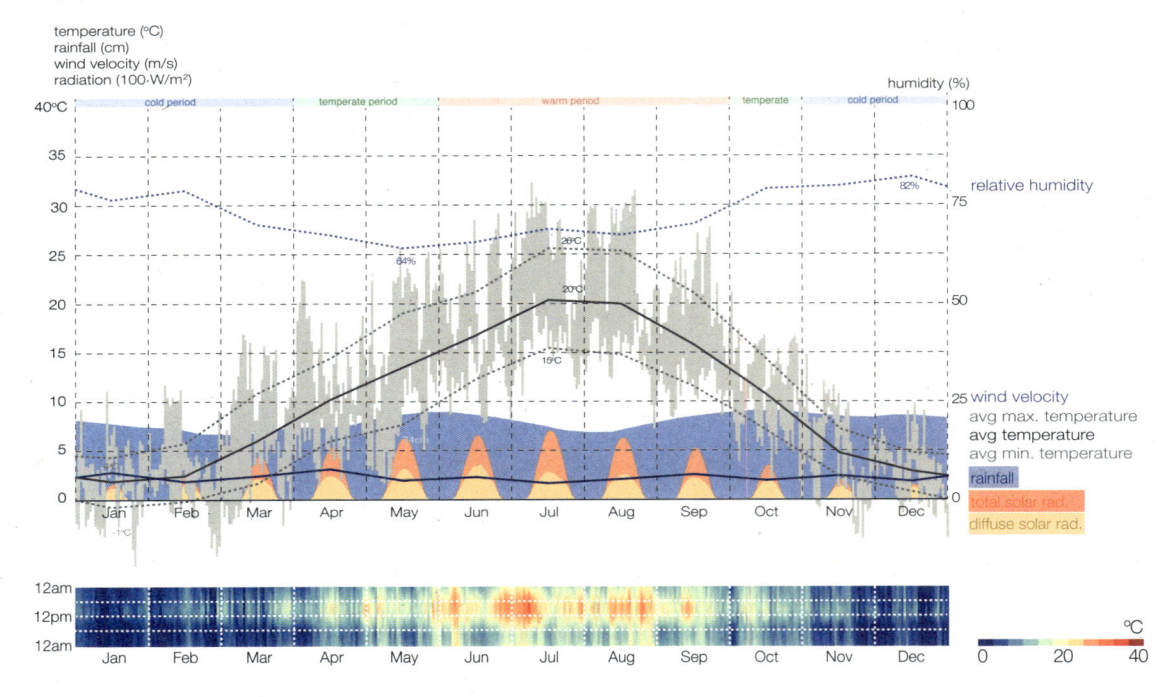

(1) Geneva climate summary

(2) Sky coverage in summer and winter

(3) Solar radiation in the sky vault in winter and summer

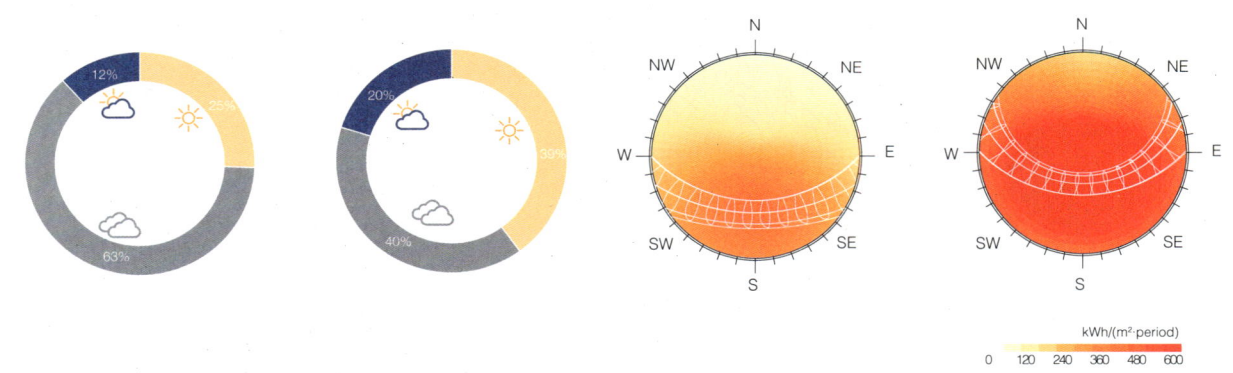

(4) Annual wind rose

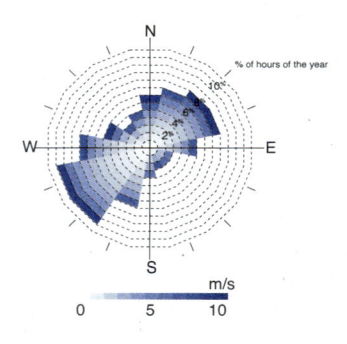

(1) Geneva climate summary: Geneva's climate is similar to Mulhouse's, but slightly less extreme. The sun is strong in summer, with a large proportion of direct radiation. In winter, it is low and mostly indirect due to the large proportion of cloudy days. During the hot period, the average high temperature is around 26°C, which is similar to other climates, but with fewer peak days, as temperatures rarely go beyond 30°C. The amplitude is large (9°C a day), which also calls for the use of thermal inertia to cool down the spaces naturally. During the cold period, the average temperature is only 4°C, and the average low is around -1°C, dropping below 0°C most of the winter.

(2)/(3) Sky coverage and solar radiation in the sky vault in winter and summer: During summer, the sky is very sunny, and radiation is higher on the horizontal surfaces. Among the vertical surfaces, the south, southwest, and southeast receive the largest amount of radiation, followed by the west and east. The northeast and northwest also receive a fair amount. During the coldest months, the sky is mostly cloudy, and radiation is higher on the south orientation, followed by the southwest and southeast.

(4) Annual wind rose: Wind blows predominantly and strongly from the southwest followed by the northeast.

Project and Environmental Conditions
Environmental Features

BUILDING
Year of delivery	2020
Type of delivery	New built
Type of building	Free-standing tower
Total amount of floors	19
Thermal regulation	Minergie SIA 380/1:2009

SIMULATED UNIT
Floor	11th
Heated surface	655 m²
Winter garden surface	188 m²
Balcony surface	81 m²
Ratio of extra space / heated surface	40%
Orientation	all
Ratio of exposed envelope that is winter garden	100%
Unit infiltration	0.17 air changes per hour
Total air renewal	60-90-120 m³/h, accounting 30 m³/(h·person)
Winter garden infiltration	5–10 ach

TECHNICAL SYSTEMS
Ventilation type	Centralized, humidity controlled exhaust ventilation
Heating system type	Centralized district heating
Heating regulation	Individual
Minergie limit value	37.8 kWh/(m²·year)
Project value	25.6 kWh/(m²·year)

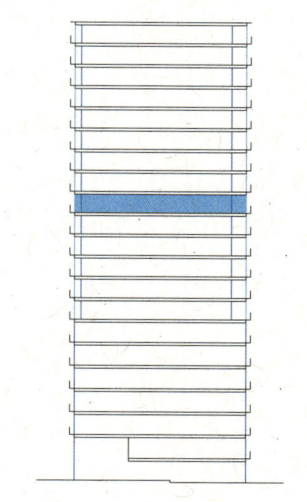

WINTER GARDEN

Orientation	Depth	Volume	Exposed facade area	Exposed concrete area	Total inertia (of winter garden)
South	1.4 m	72 m³	64 m²	132 m²	1.0 m²/m³, 318 kJ/(°K·m³)
North	0.7 m	57 m³	72 m²	86 m²	0.4 m²/m³, 48 kJ/(°K·m³)
East	1.4 m	50 m³	39 m²	83 m²	1.0 m²/m³, 318 kJ/(°K·m³)
West	1.4 m	46 m³	38 m²	75 m²	1.0 m²/m³, 318 kJ/(°K·m³)

	Element	Material	U-value W/(°K.m²)	SF	VLT	Reflectivity
①	Thermal curtain	Sheep's wool	2.17	0	0	0.9
②	Sliding doors of heated space	Double glazing	1.26	0.63	0.81	-
③	Solar curtain	Aluminum	-	0.38	0.38	0.6
④	Sliding doors of winter garden	Single glazing	6.0	0.92	0.86	-

* SF: Solar Factor; VLT: Visible Light Transmittance

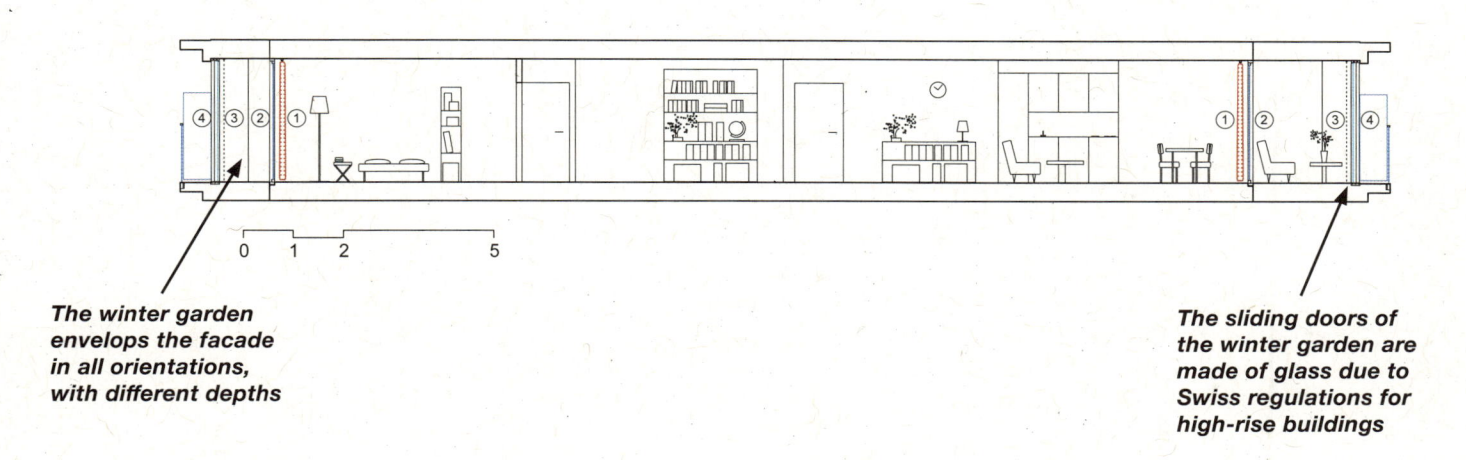

The winter garden envelops the facade in all orientations, with different depths

The sliding doors of the winter garden are made of glass due to Swiss regulations for high-rise buildings

In this case, the tower is covered by winter gardens on the full perimeter, with varying depths according to the orientation and construction rules. As in the previous examples, the living rooms are mainly facing south, or alternatively east and west, while nearly all bedrooms face north. Most of the units have double orientation to allow for cross ventilation. For the first time in the work of Lacaton & Vassal, the complete winter garden facade is made of glass. The winter gardens from the sixth to nineteenth floors serve as an effective windbreaker for the semi-exterior living extensions of the apartment. According to wind speed and direction, panels can be pushed into position in order to manipulate the amount of fresh air.

Case Study 4

Project and Environmental Conditions
Sun and Wind

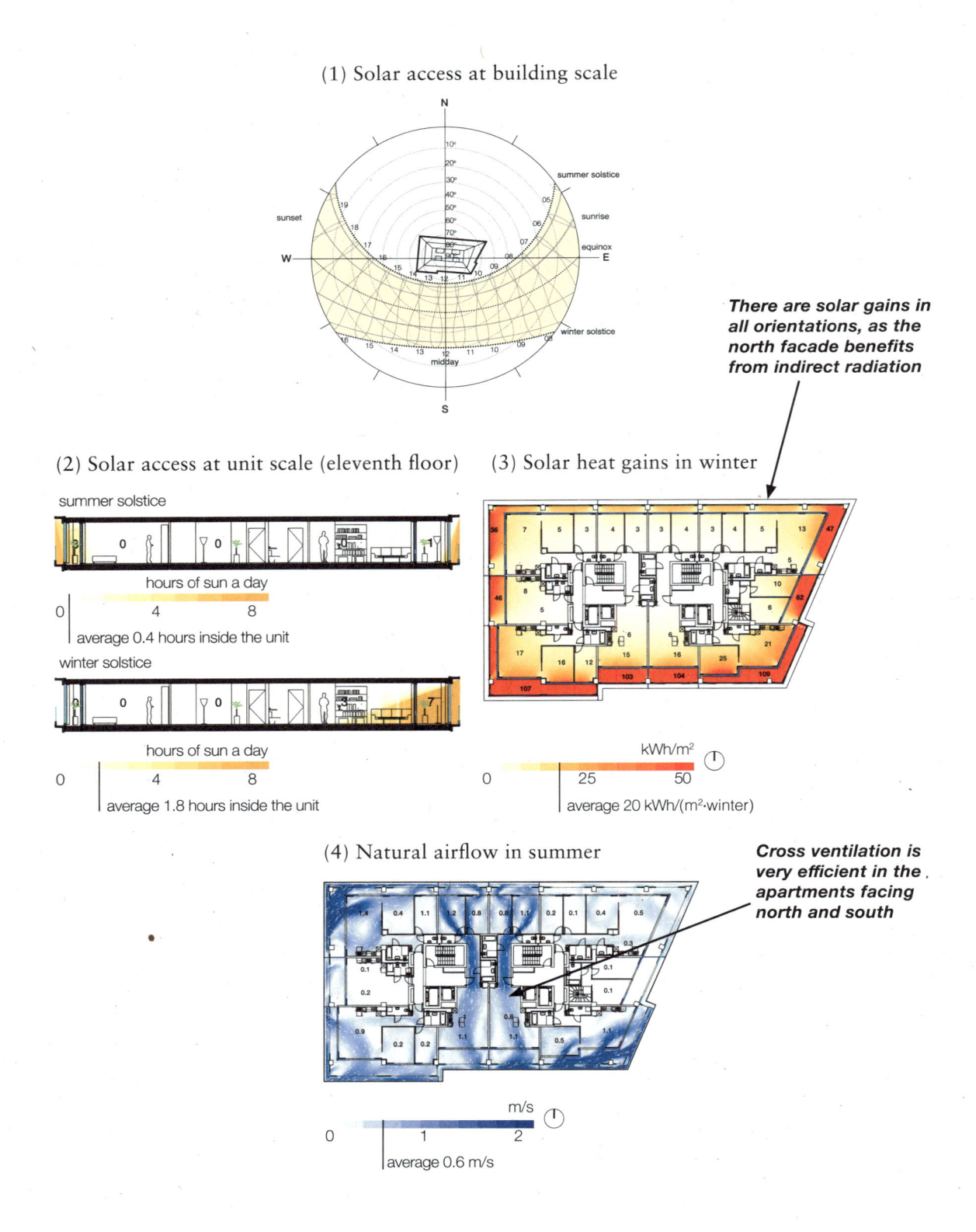

(1) Solar access at building scale

There are solar gains in all orientations, as the north facade benefits from indirect radiation

(2) Solar access at unit scale (eleventh floor)

summer solstice

hours of sun a day
average 0.4 hours inside the unit

winter solstice

hours of sun a day
average 1.8 hours inside the unit

(3) Solar heat gains in winter

kWh/m²
average 20 kWh/(m²·winter)

(4) Natural airflow in summer

Cross ventilation is very efficient in the apartments facing north and south

m/s
average 0.6 m/s

---

(1) Solar access at building scale: The surroundings of the building are rather low and there are no neighboring constructions that overshadow any of the residential levels. During the summer, the slab extensions cast shade on the internal facade. During the winter, the south, east, and west facades receive plenty of sun, which is converted into useful solar gains. All the units receive at least six hours of sun during the equinoxes, reaching the high solar access target of EN 17037.

(2)/(3) Solar access at unit scale (eleventh floor) and solar heat gains in winter: During the winter, the sun penetrates deeply and evenly into the south and east winter gardens. The west winter gardens also receive sun, though with less intensity. All south spaces receive high solar gains, and the east and west receive significant amounts. During the summer, due to the high solar angles and effectiveness of the shading depth, the sun barely reaches the interior glazing.

(4) Natural airflow in summer: Under average conditions and when all sliding panels are open, most of the units can effectively cross ventilate, as most of them have openings on two facades. The height of the tower and unobstructed surroundings allow the wind to flow rapidly. Regulating the openings can help diminish the air speed if necessary.

01 Case Study 4

Project and Environmental Conditions
Daylight

(1) Daylight Autonomy

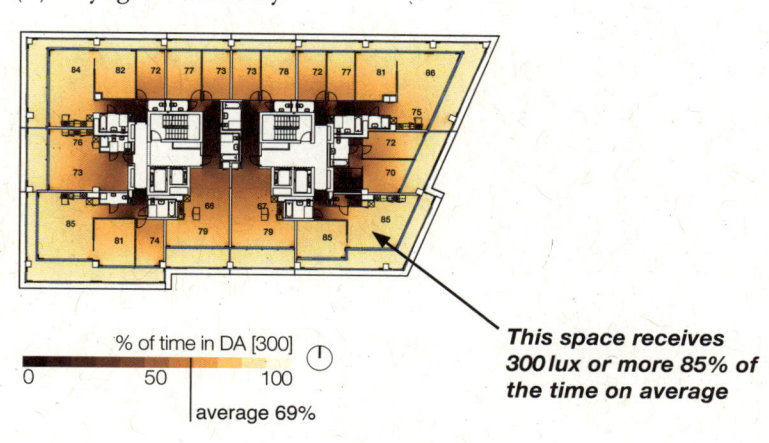

% of time in DA [300]
0   50   100
average 69%

This space receives 300 lux or more 85% of the time on average

(2) Space exceeding 50% of time with DA [300] (EN 17037)

reference plane: 50 cm off the walls from permanently occupied spaces

target 50% of space > 50% of time with DA [300]

Northwest lr	100%
North bedroom 1	100%
North bedroom 2	100%
North bedroom 3	99%
Northeast lr	100%
Southwest lr	100%
South living room	100%
South bedroom 1	100%
South bedroom 2	100%
Southeast lr	100%
West living room	100%
average	100%

-> all the spaces largely exceed the recommendations of EN 17037

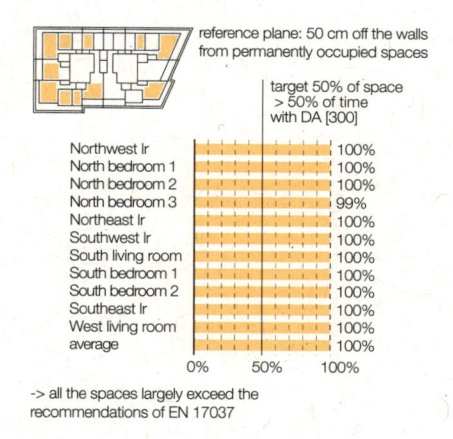

(1) Daylight Autonomy: All the rooms are in daylight autonomy, as the full glazed envelope allows plenty of daylight in. Living rooms have daylight averages ranging from 70 to 86%, which is high.

(2) Space exceeding 50% of time with DA [300] (EN 17037): Almost all the spaces have their entire area with DA [300] at least 50% of the time. Bedrooms have averages ranging from 72 to 82%. This performance largely exceeds the requirements of EN 17037.

Case Study 4

Free-Running Mode
Seasonal Performance of North–South Units

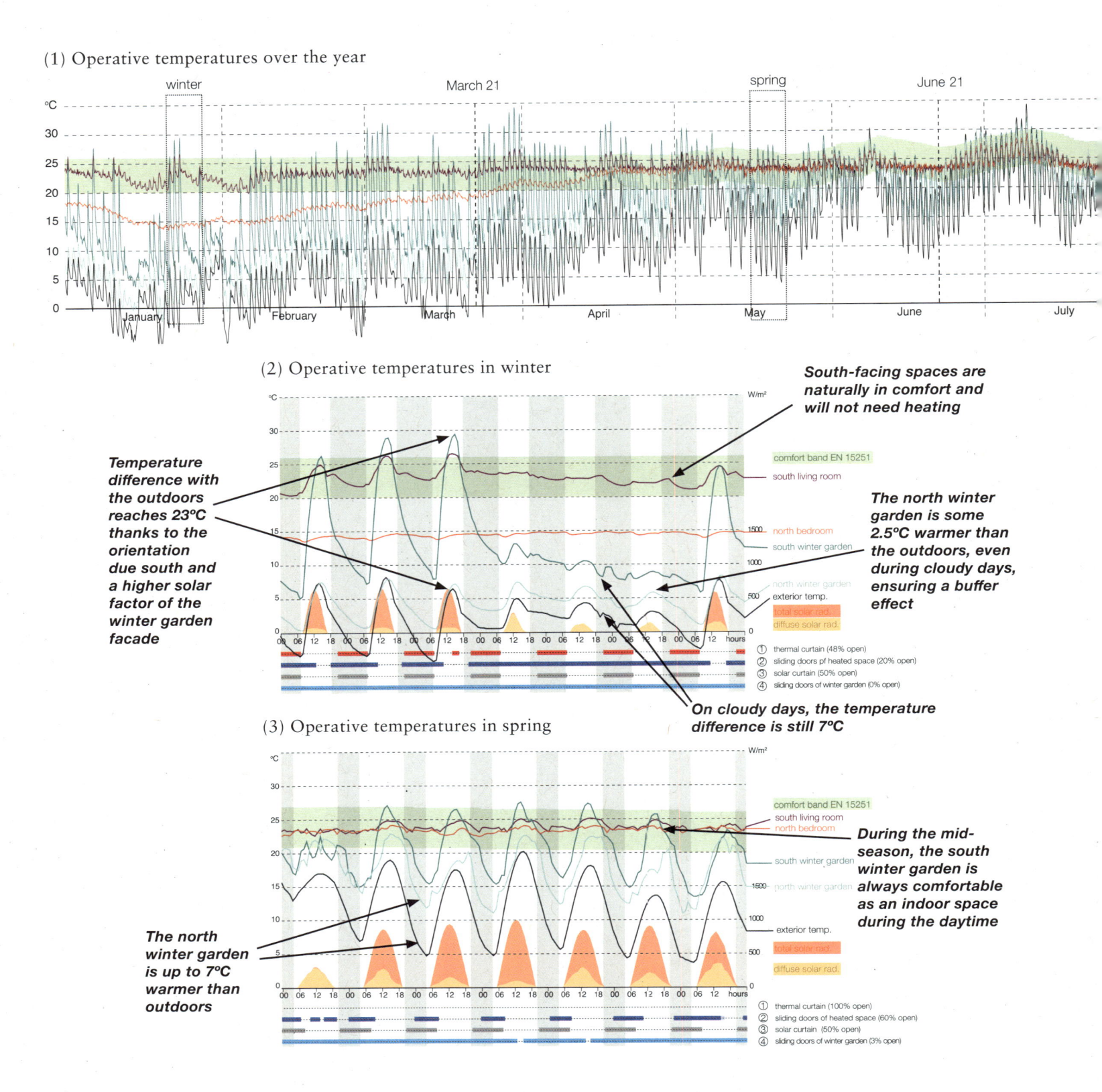

(1) Operative temperatures over the year

(2) Operative temperatures in winter

Temperature difference with the outdoors reaches 23°C thanks to the orientation due south and a higher solar factor of the winter garden facade

South-facing spaces are naturally in comfort and will not need heating

The north winter garden is some 2.5°C warmer than the outdoors, even during cloudy days, ensuring a buffer effect

On cloudy days, the temperature difference is still 7°C

① thermal curtain (48% open)
② sliding doors pf heated space (20% open)
③ solar curtain (50% open)
④ sliding doors of winter garden (0% open)

(3) Operative temperatures in spring

The north winter garden is up to 7°C warmer than outdoors

During the mid-season, the south winter garden is always comfortable as an indoor space during the daytime

① thermal curtain (100% open)
② sliding doors of heated space (60% open)
③ solar curtain (50% open)
④ sliding doors of winter garden (3% open)

---

(1) Operative temperatures over the year: The simulation in free-running mode shows that indoor temperatures vary naturally from 14 to 28°C.

(2) Operative temperatures in winter: Indoor operative temperatures in the living rooms are already in comfort—without the use of heating—varying between 22 and 26°C, depending on the sun, when the outdoors varies between -4 and 8°C. The north bedrooms have temperatures naturally around 15°C, and remain stable without the contribution of direct sunlight. The operative temperatures of the winter gardens facing south are 8–23°C warmer than outdoors during sunny days and about 7°C on cloudy ones. Winter gardens facing north are 0–5°C warmer than outdoors. During sunny mornings, the temperature is similar to outdoors as it rises very fast. In the afternoon, the heat accumulation starts to create a temperature difference that is maintained until the next morning, where the difference can be up to 5°C. During cloudy days, the heat is retained and the temperature difference with the outdoors is 2–3°C.

(3) Operative temperatures in spring: Indoor operative temperatures vary throughout the day and night within a close range of 2°C, and are always within comfort. South winter gardens have operative temperatures that are as comfortable as an indoor space (EN 15251) during the entire day, and remain above 15°C at night. North winter gardens are also as comfortable as an indoor space during sunny days, especially in the afternoon, and they can be used as an extension of the living spaces. At night, their operative temperature remains above 12°C, whereas outdoors falls around 5°C. The temperature difference between outdoors and the winter gardens is therefore between 3 and 12°C, depending on the sun and outdoor temperatures. The lower the outdoor temperatures, the greater the difference.

Case Study 4

(4) Operative temperatures in summer

All the indoor spaces are in comfort during summer

(5) Operative temperatures in fall

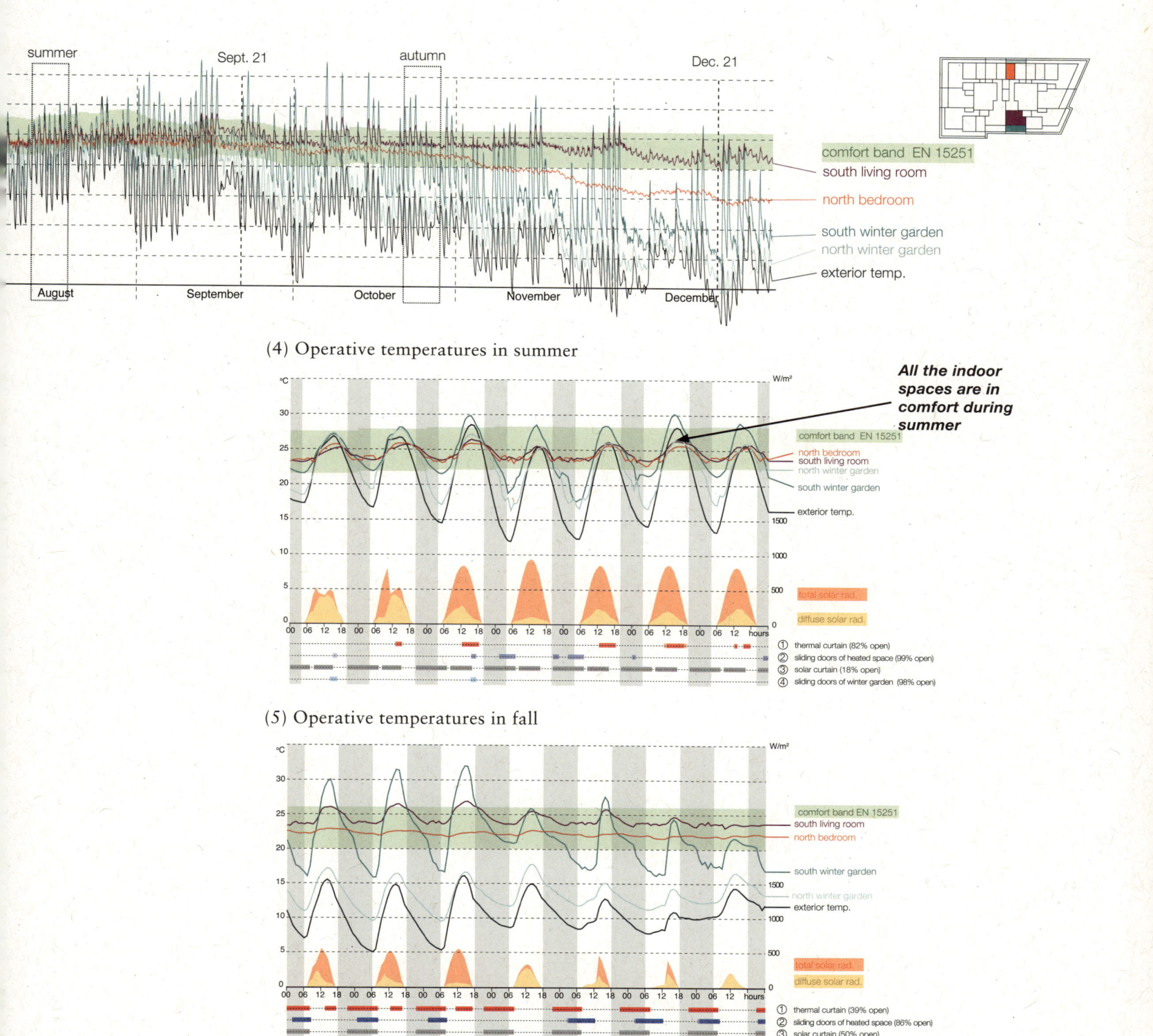

(4) Operative temperatures in summer: All the living spaces have operative temperatures inside the comfort band both day and night, without any overheating. The thermal inertia of the exposed concrete contains indoor temperatures during peak days, as they remain below the temperatures outdoors and in the winter gardens.

(5) Operative temperatures in fall: Indoor operative temperatures naturally vary throughout the day and night within a close range of 3°C, and are always within comfort. The living room is about 2–4°C warmer than the bedrooms due to the contribution of the sun. South winter gardens have operative temperatures that are as comfortable as an indoor space (EN 15251), though temperatures can peak very fast. These can be reduced by opening the winter garden sooner, and the space can be used as an extension of the indoors. At night, operative temperatures remain above 16°C, whereas outdoors it is 5–10°C. The temperature difference between the outdoors and the winter garden is 7–15°C, depending on the sun and outdoor temperatures. The winter garden heat accumulation during sunny days is enough for the apartment to be comfortable during cloudy days. The operative temperature of the north winter gardens is close to the temperatures outdoors, with a difference of 1–2°C during daytime and up to 5°C at night.

Free-Running Mode
Seasonal Performance of Corner Units

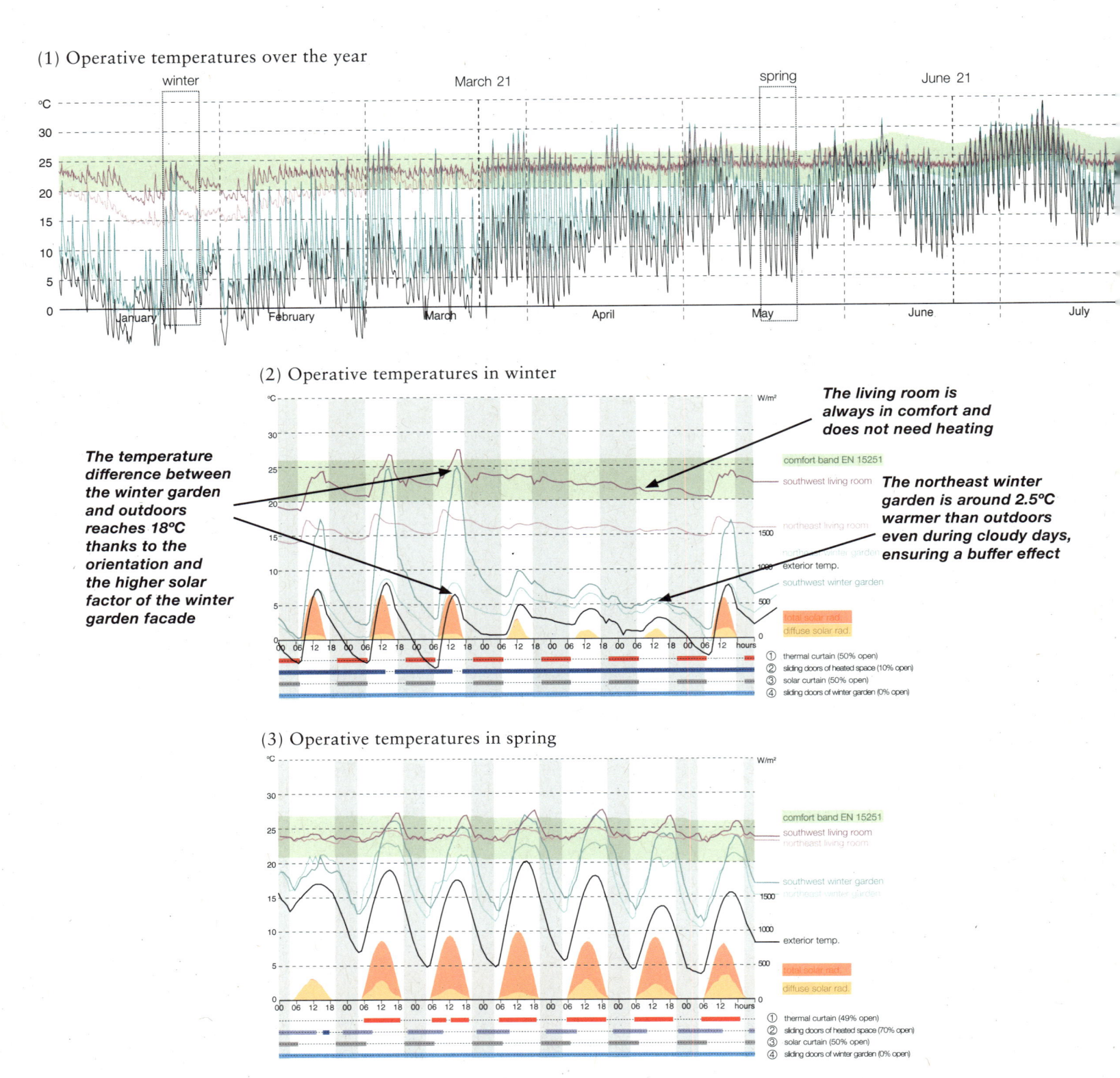

(1) Operative temperatures over the year

(2) Operative temperatures in winter

The temperature difference between the winter garden and outdoors reaches 18°C thanks to the orientation and the higher solar factor of the winter garden facade

The living room is always in comfort and does not need heating

The northeast winter garden is around 2.5°C warmer than outdoors even during cloudy days, ensuring a buffer effect

① thermal curtain (50% open)
② sliding doors of heated space (10% open)
③ solar curtain (50% open)
④ sliding doors of winter garden (0% open)

(3) Operative temperatures in spring

① thermal curtain (49% open)
② sliding doors of heated space (70% open)
③ solar curtain (50% open)
④ sliding doors of winter garden (0% open)

(1) Operative temperatures over the year: The simulation in free-running mode shows that indoor temperatures vary naturally from 14 to 32°C.

(2) Operative temperatures in winter: Indoor spaces on the south corners have operative temperatures within the comfort band in free-running mode due to the great quantity of solar gains captured by the winter garden, and their insulation effect. The northeast corner has operative temperatures varying from 15 to 18°C in free-running mode. During sunny days, the temperature rises quickly in the morning, reaching 17–18°C naturally, whereas at night or during cloudy days it drops to 15–16°C. The south winter garden's operative temperature can reach 25°C on sunny days, with a temperature difference with the outside of 10–19°C, whereas on cloudy days it is only 3–4°C higher. At night, temperatures drop but still maintain a difference of about 5°C with the outdoors due to the inertia of the concrete and the reduced air permeability. The north winter garden has an average operative temperature difference with the outdoors of 2–3°C.

(3) Operative temperatures in spring: Indoor operative temperatures are within comfort naturally. The simple handling of the elements guarantees a good performance: the sliding doors of the winter garden remain closed and the solar curtains are mostly open during the day. The sliding doors of the heated space are open most of the day, enlarging the living space, which also brings in the sun and heats up the interior space. Operative temperatures of the south winter garden are about 8°C above the outdoors during sunny days and about 3°C during cloudy ones. At night, the temperature difference observed during the day is maintained. The north winter garden has an operative temperature 3–6°C above the outdoors during the spring. At night, temperature differences are maintained thanks to the inertia of the concrete. The southwest living room is mostly in comfort except for some hours where temperature peaks (27–28°C) during sunny days. This could be reduced by opening the winter garden sliding doors wider.

Case Study 4

(4) Operative temperatures in summer

(5) Operative temperatures in fall

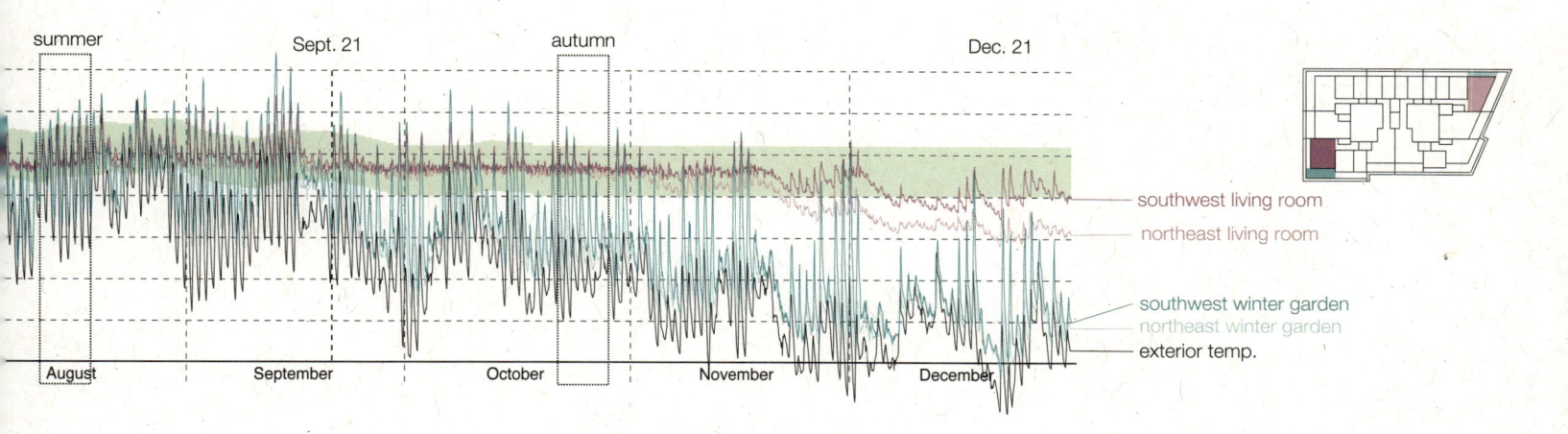

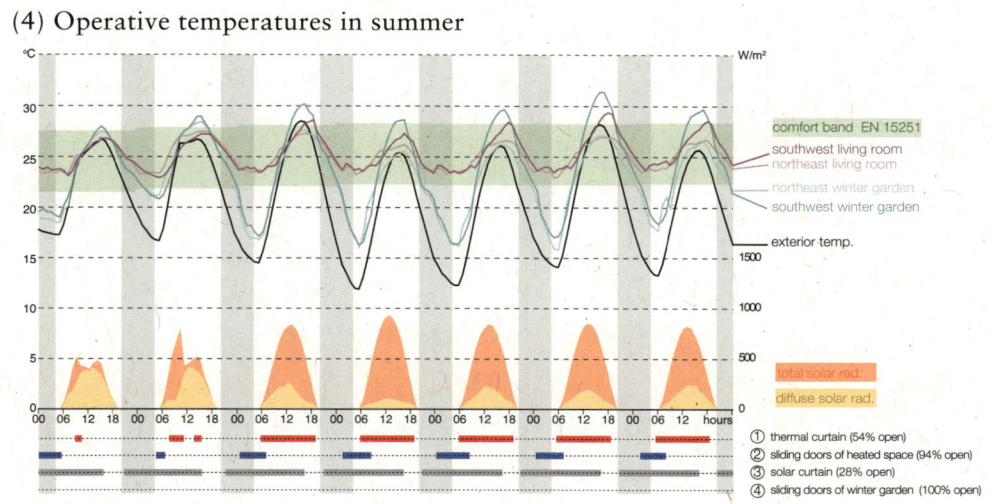

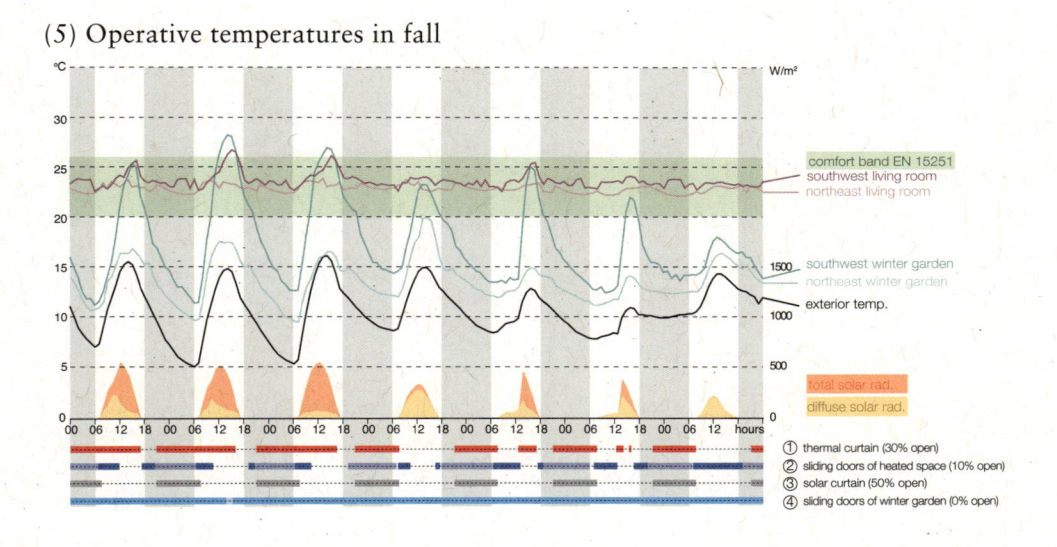

(4) Operative temperatures in summer: All the living spaces have operative temperatures within the comfort band day and night. Only during the hottest days, operative temperatures can be about 1–1.5°C above comfort in the southwest living room. The south winter garden, fully open as a terrace, is constantly about 2–3°C above outdoors, whereas the north one can have lower operative temperatures during peak days. During peak days, indoor operative temperatures on the east remain below both the outdoors and the winter gardens due to thermal inertia. In the southwest unit, operative temperatures are similar to outdoors or up to 1°C higher.

(5) Operative temperatures in fall: Indoor operative temperatures are naturally within comfort most of the time. The simple handling of the elements guarantees a good performance: the sliding doors remain closed and the solar and thermal curtains are open during the day. Only the southwest living room has operative temperatures above comfort for some hours of the day. This can be solved by opening the winter garden sliding doors. The south winter garden has operative temperatures that are as comfortable as an indoor space (EN 15251) on sunny days, as the temperature difference with outdoors reaches 8–13°C. At night, the difference can reach 4–5°C.

On cloudy days, the difference is smaller, about 3–4°C. The north winter garden's operative temperature is 2–5°C higher than outdoors due to the lower amount of radiation. At night, temperature differences are maintained thanks to the inertia of the concrete. Spaces are mostly open, which also brings in the sun and heats up the interior space. The thermal curtains need to be drawn to avoid overheating, as the sun is low and internal temperatures remain high.

Free-Running Mode
Typical Days in North–South Apartments

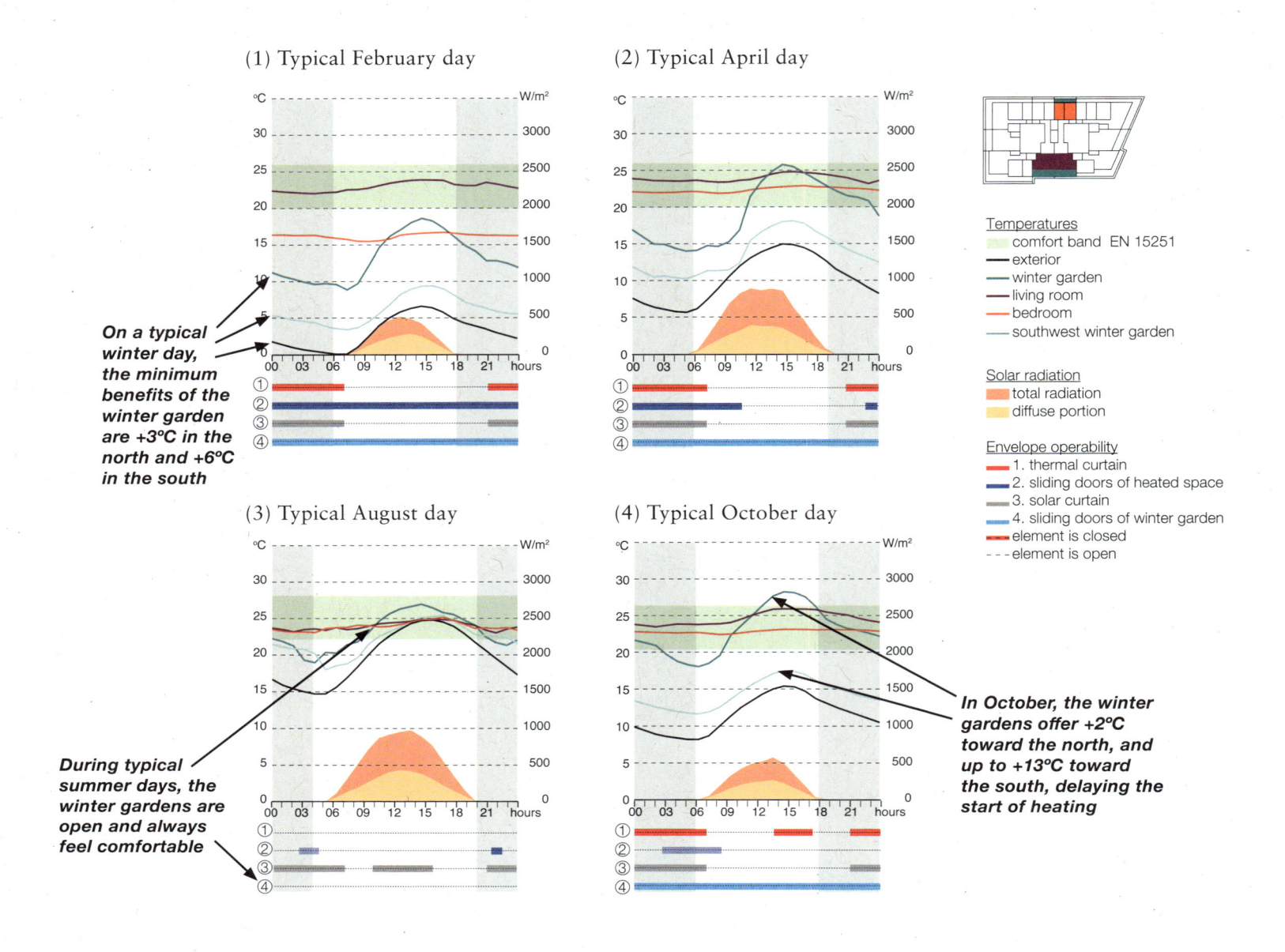

(1) Typical February day

On a typical winter day, the minimum benefits of the winter garden are +3°C in the north and +6°C in the south

(2) Typical April day

Temperatures
- comfort band EN 15251
- exterior
- winter garden
- living room
- bedroom
- southwest winter garden

Solar radiation
- total radiation
- diffuse portion

Envelope operability
- 1. thermal curtain
- 2. sliding doors of heated space
- 3. solar curtain
- 4. sliding doors of winter garden
- — element is closed
- --- element is open

(3) Typical August day

During typical summer days, the winter gardens are open and always feel comfortable

(4) Typical October day

In October, the winter gardens offer +2°C toward the north, and up to +13°C toward the south, delaying the start of heating

---

(1) Typical February day: Indoor operative temperatures vary significantly depending on orientation: while north-facing rooms have temperatures around 16°C, south-facing ones are around 22–24°C, which is within comfort naturally. The north winter gardens have on average an operative temperature 3–4°C higher than outdoors. The effect of the sun on the south ones raises it further by about 7°C on average, and up to 12°C during the sunnier hours.

(2)/(4) Typical mid-season day: Indoor operative temperatures remain within the comfort band throughout the mid-season, as adapting the envelope helps to adjust indoor conditions. Winter garden temperatures facing south have as comfortable temperatures as an indoor space during the day and drop below at nighttime. Winter gardens facing north are 2 to 5°C more than outdoors, depending on the time of the day.

(3) Typical August day: Indoor operative temperatures oscillate between 23 and 25°C and remain within the comfort band at all times. None of the spaces overheats, as the shading offered by the winter garden slabs and solar curtains protects the indoors from the sun. The operative temperature in the winter gardens, with the sliding doors fully open as an outdoor terrace, is 1–5°C more than outdoors. During the day, temperatures are as comfortable as indoors.

Case Study 4

Free-Running Mode
Typical Days in Corner Apartments

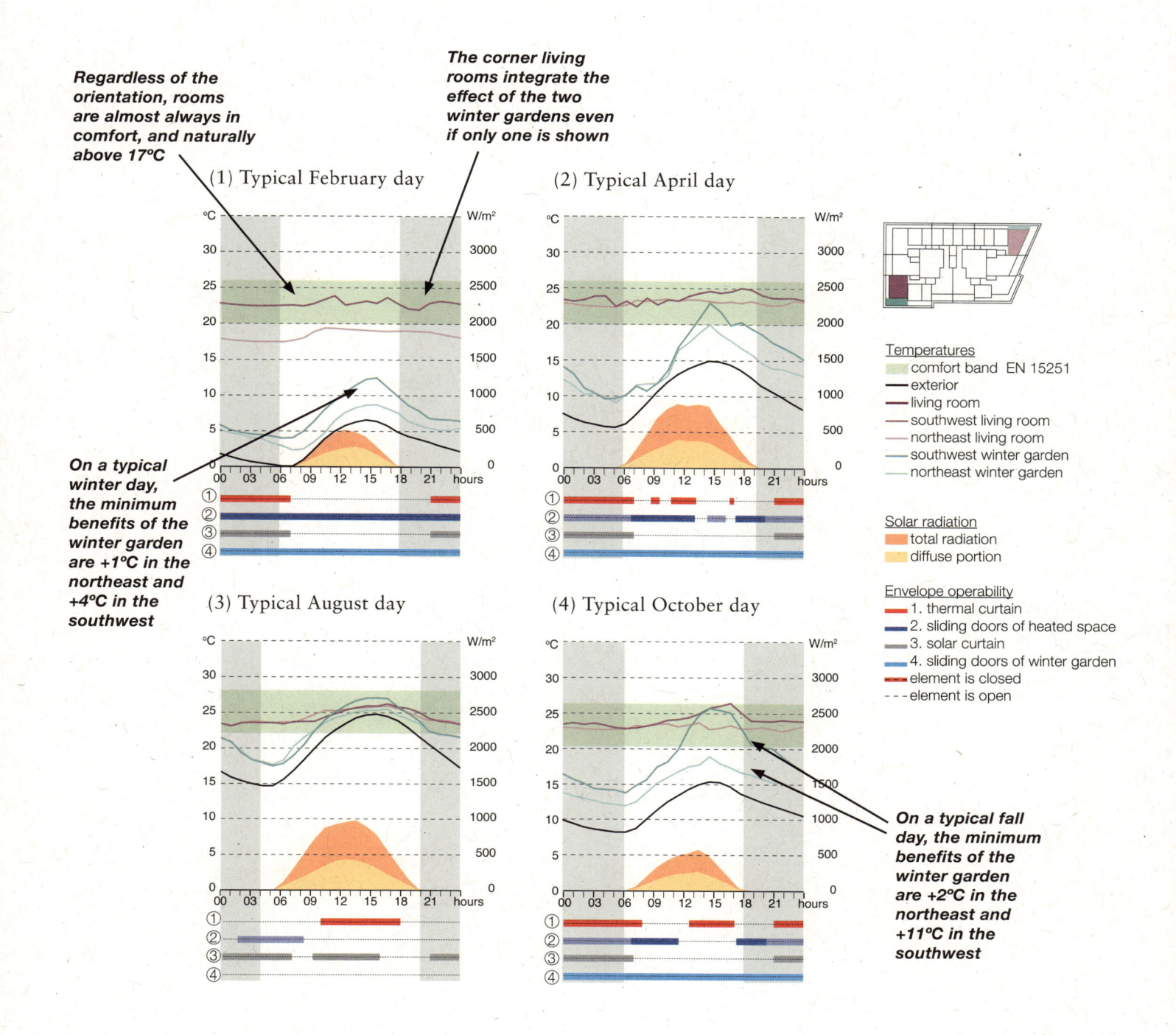

Regardless of the orientation, rooms are almost always in comfort, and naturally above 17°C

The corner living rooms integrate the effect of the two winter gardens even if only one is shown

(1) Typical February day

(2) Typical April day

On a typical winter day, the minimum benefits of the winter garden are +1°C in the northeast and +4°C in the southwest

(3) Typical August day

(4) Typical October day

Temperatures
- comfort band EN 15251
- exterior
- living room
- southwest living room
- northeast living room
- southwest winter garden
- northeast winter garden

Solar radiation
- total radiation
- diffuse portion

Envelope operability
- 1. thermal curtain
- 2. sliding doors of heated space
- 3. solar curtain
- 4. sliding doors of winter garden
- element is closed
- --- element is open

On a typical fall day, the minimum benefits of the winter garden are +2°C in the northeast and +11°C in the southwest

(1) Typical February day: The corner rooms have operative temperatures between the north–south facing ones and remain within 17 to 24°C naturally, depending on sun exposure. The northeast winter garden has slightly lower operative temperatures (3 to 9°C when outdoors is 0 to 7°C) than the northern one (4 to 10°C), as the greater exposed surface loses more heat than it gains from the sun in this orientation. The southwest winter garden also has a larger exposed area, but in this case, the solar contribution is enough to increase the operative temperature by 4–7°C compared to outdoors (4.5 to 12.5°C inside).

(2)/(4) Typical mid-season day: Indoor operative temperatures also remain within the comfort band throughout the mid-season, as adapting the envelope helps to adjust indoor conditions. Southwest-facing winter gardens have comfortable temperatures as an indoor space during the day and drop below comfort at night. Winter gardens facing the northeast are 3 to 5°C more than the outdoors, depending on the time of day.

(3) Typical August day: Indoor temperatures oscillate between 23.5 and 26.5°C and remain within the comfort band at all times. None of the spaces overheat, as the shading offered by the winter garden slabs and solar curtains protects the indoors from the sun. The operative temperature in the winter gardens, with the sliding doors fully open as an outdoor terrace, is 1–5°C more than outdoors. During the day, temperatures are comfortable as an indoor space.

Free-Running Mode Extreme Days

North–south apartments

(1) Extreme winter day

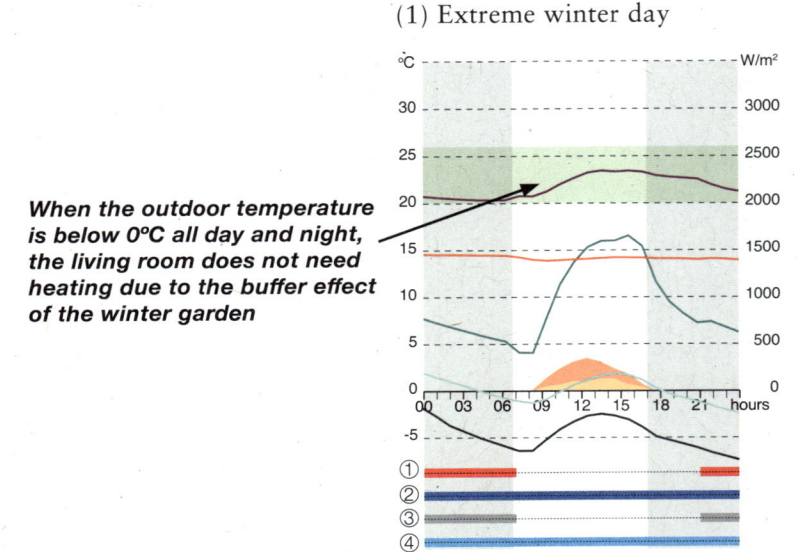

When the outdoor temperature is below 0°C all day and night, the living room does not need heating due to the buffer effect of the winter garden

(2) Extreme summer day

The peak in temperature early in the afternoon in the north winter garden and living room occur due to high wind speeds

At peak times, all the temperatures are lower than the outdoors; interior spaces remain in comfort

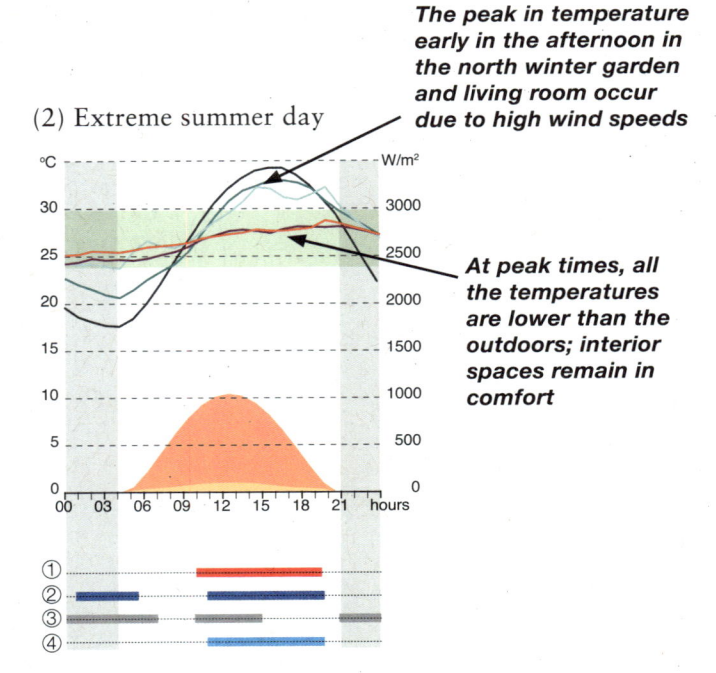

Corner apartments

(1) Extreme winter day

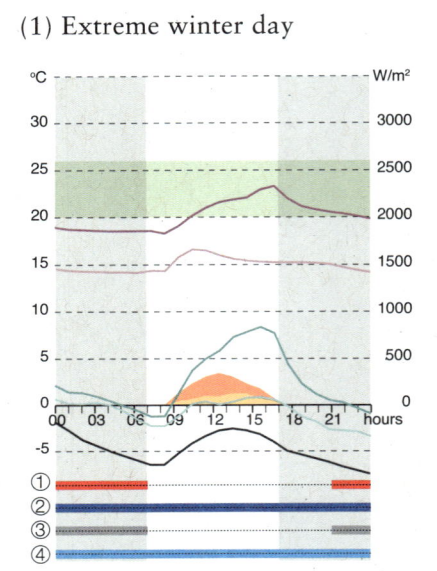

(2) Extreme summer day

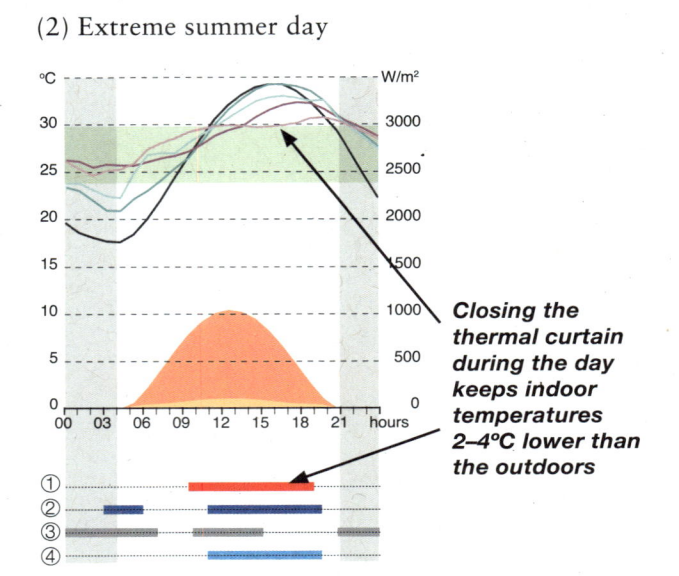

Closing the thermal curtain during the day keeps indoor temperatures 2–4°C lower than the outdoors

(1) Extreme winter day: When outdoor temperatures fall below zero during the day, indoor operative temperatures are naturally between 14°C for the north spaces and 23–24°C for the ones facing south. Winter gardens facing north have operative temperatures 3–5°C higher than outdoors, creating a milder environment between the north-facing rooms and outdoors. As the colder days are sunny, winter gardens facing south are 10–22°C warmer than outdoors, reaching 16°C during sunny hours for the ones facing south and 9°C for the ones of the southwest unit.

(2) Extreme summer day: When the outdoor temperature peaks at almost 35°C, indoor operative temperatures remain cooler by about 2–4°C for the corner units and about 6°C for the north–south units, which remain within comfort. The adequate shading avoids a larger increase in the southern rooms; closing the sliding doors of the heated space prevents the hot air from entering indoors, and the thermal inertia of the concrete helps to stabilize and lag the peaks. Whereas outdoor temperatures peak at around 4 pm, the hottest operative temperature indoors is at 6 pm. A simple fan would help to lower temperatures to within the comfort band in the corner units. Winter garden operative temperatures remain below those outdoors at peak time due to the shading and the inertia of the concrete.

Free-Running Mode
Thermal Comfort Conditions

(1) Resulting thermal comfort per room

Br N — In comfort 62% / Hot 0% / Cold 38%
Lr S — In comfort 98% / Hot 2% / Cold 0%

°C from target temp.
-6 … -3 … 0 … +3 … +6
too cold | comfort | too hot

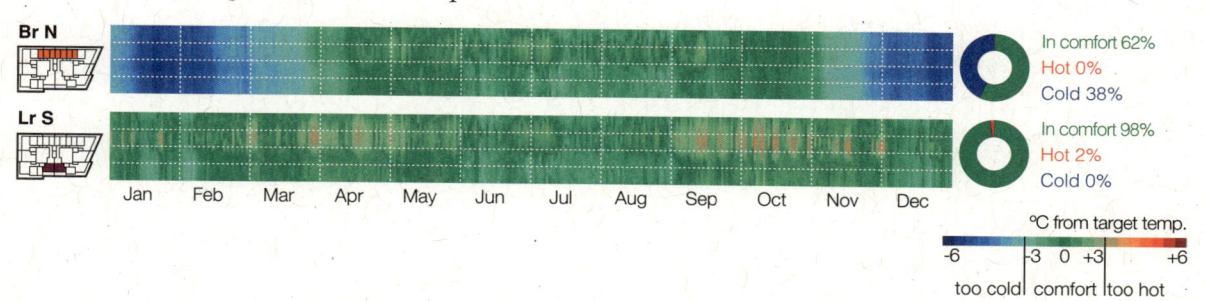

(2) Operative temeperatures indoors as a function of outdoors

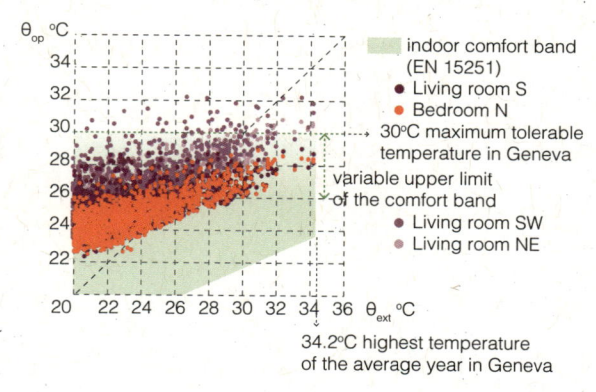

θ_{op} °C vs θ_{ext} °C

- indoor comfort band (EN 15251)
- Living room S
- Bedroom N
- 30°C maximum tolerable temperature in Geneva
- variable upper limit of the comfort band
- Living room SW
- Living room NE

34.2°C highest temperature of the average year in Geneva

(3) Overheating evaluation

ideal target <350°C·h | maximum tolerance

- Living room S — 119
- Bedroom N — 14
- Living room SW — 427 / 732
- Living room NE — 176
- weighted average — 142 / 275

250 | 500 | 750 | 1000 | 1250 °C·h
350

- nighttime (22 to 7h): DH > 26°C
- daytime (7 to 22h): DH > EN 15251
Comfort temperature is capped at 28°C
*the different values correspond to closing thermal curtains 50% and 75%

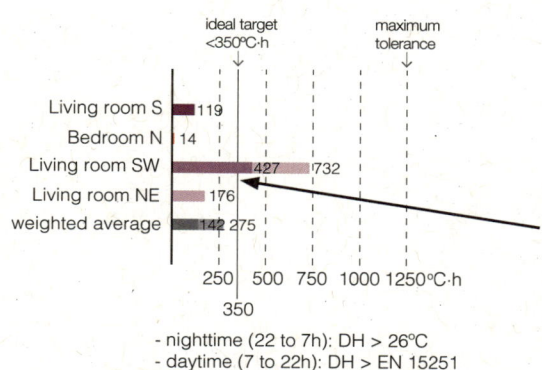

All the rooms, except the southwest living rooms, are under the ideal target of overheating. For the southwest orientation, which receives the critical sun, curtains need to be fully closed when the sun hits the facade.

---

(1) Resulting thermal comfort per room: Rooms facing south are in thermal autonomy as time in comfort rises to 98%. They do not require heating. The hours above comfort (2% for the southern rooms above EN 15251) during the mid-season (March to April and September to November) can be offset by further opening the exterior winter garden sliding doors. Rooms facing north are in comfort approximately 62% of the time, from early April until the end of October.

(2) Operative temperatures indoors as a function of outdoors: In the apartments facing north–south, temperatures are quite stable, independent from outdoor temperatures, and almost never surpass 29°C, even when the outdoors reaches 34°C. The northeast and southwest living rooms have much more variable conditions, as they have two exposed facades. This increases the time when the sun hits the space, but also increases heat loss. Sometimes, the southwest living room has temperatures between 30 and 32°C, which can be lowered by further closing the thermal curtain and using fans.

(3) Overheating evaluation: Most of the spaces do not overheat and their degree hours above comfort (and above 26°C at night) remain below the ideal target of 350°C·h, especially the north- and south-oriented ones. Some of the west-facing spaces surpass the ideal target but remain within a reasonable range of hours. These calculations have been done considering that the occupants close the thermal curtains by 50% only when its above 26°C indoors. If the occupants would fully close the curtains at 23°C, the overheating hours on the west-facing spaces would be cut in half. In this case, the average of the floor would be around 142°C·h.

Case Study 4

Free-Running Mode
Conditions inside the Winter Gardens

North-facing winter gardens

(1) Winter garden air temperatures compared to outdoors

(b coefficient = 0.64)

14.2°C
11°C

winter spring summer* autumn

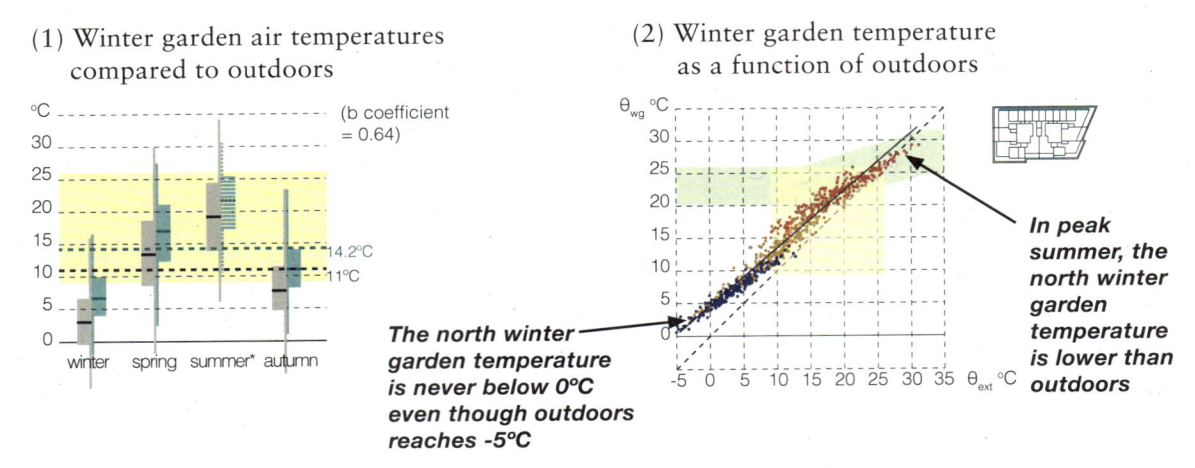

(2) Winter garden temperature as a function of outdoors

The north winter garden temperature is never below 0°C even though outdoors reaches -5°C

In peak summer, the north winter garden temperature is lower than outdoors

South-facing winter gardens

(3) Winter garden air temperature compared to outdoors

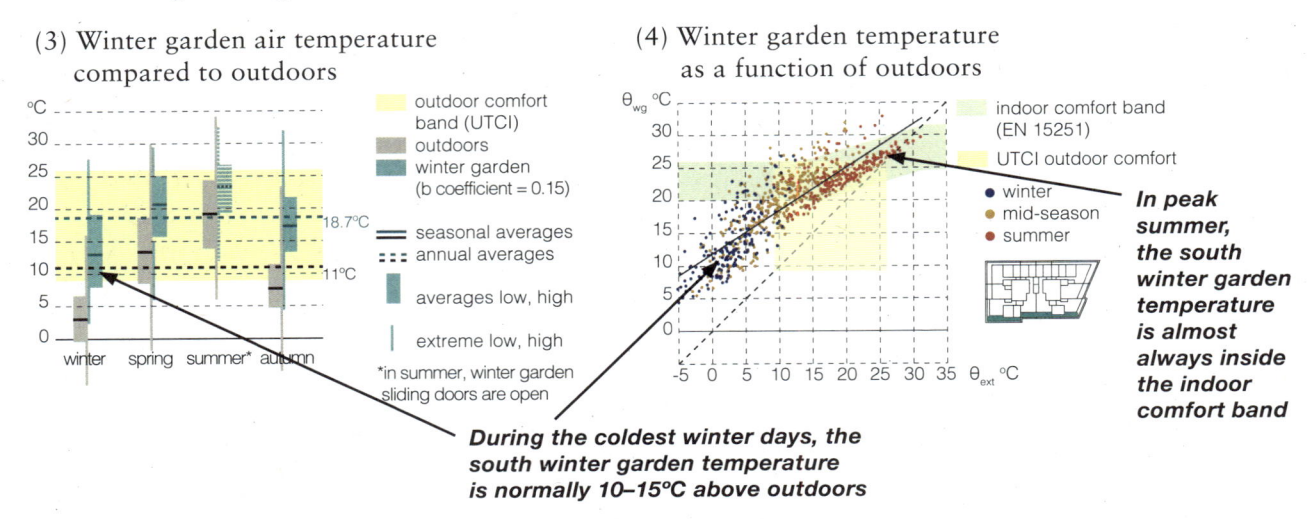

- outdoor comfort band (UTCI)
- outdoors
- winter garden (b coefficient = 0.15)
- seasonal averages
- annual averages
- averages low, high
- extreme low, high

*in summer, winter garden sliding doors are open

18.7°C
11°C

winter spring summer* autumn

During the coldest winter days, the south winter garden temperature is normally 10–15°C above outdoors

(4) Winter garden temperature as a function of outdoors

- indoor comfort band (EN 15251)
- UTCI outdoor comfort
- winter
- mid-season
- summer

In peak summer, the south winter garden temperature is almost always inside the indoor comfort band

(5) Solar heat gains and losses of the winter garden

In March, there are 22 kWh/m² of net heat gain

- solar gains
- loss by glazing conduction
- loss by glazing conduction + infiltration
- useful net heat gain
- ←--→ winter garden is open, no heat gain

J F M A M J J A S O N D

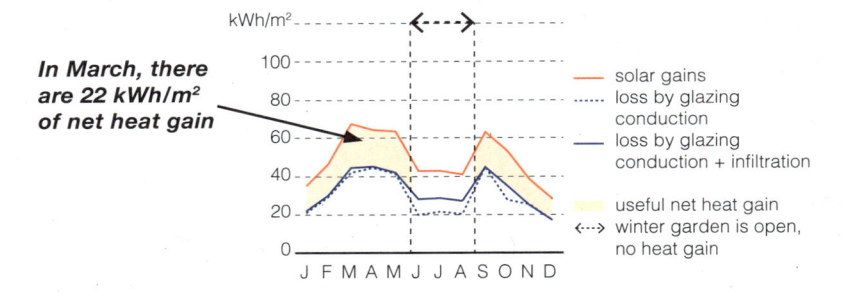

(1)/(3) Winter garden air temperatures compared to outdoors: All winter gardens have higher temperatures than outdoors throughout the year, except during the hottest hours, where winter garden temperatures are cooler thanks to their thermal inertia. The south winter garden has an average temperature difference with the outdoors of 7.7°C whereas the north one has an average difference of 3.2°C. The b coefficient is calculated following the European Norm (EN 13789) to calculate the reduction of heat losses of the heated envelope thanks to the effect of the winter garden. The b coefficient of the north winter garden is 0.64, which represents a reduction of heat loss of the main facade of 36%. For the south winter garden, the b coefficient is 0.15, representing an 85% reduction of heat loss.

(2)/(4) Winter garden temperature as a function of outdoors: The difference between the winter garden and outdoors is higher when temperatures are at their lowest, as it reaches at least 6°C in the north winter garden and 13°C in the south ones. In the south winter garden, the temperature difference can reach 17–18°C due to the effect of the sun. Winter garden temperatures almost never rise above the indoor comfort limit, and when they do, it is only by a low margin. During peak summertime, winter garden temperatures are below outdoors due to the inertia of the concrete.

(5) Solar heat gains and losses of the winter garden: The winter garden full envelope is a net heat gain for the interior spaces of 10 kWh/m² during the coldest months and of 20 kWh/m² during the mid-season.

Case Study 4

Free-Running Mode
Conditions inside the Winter Gardens

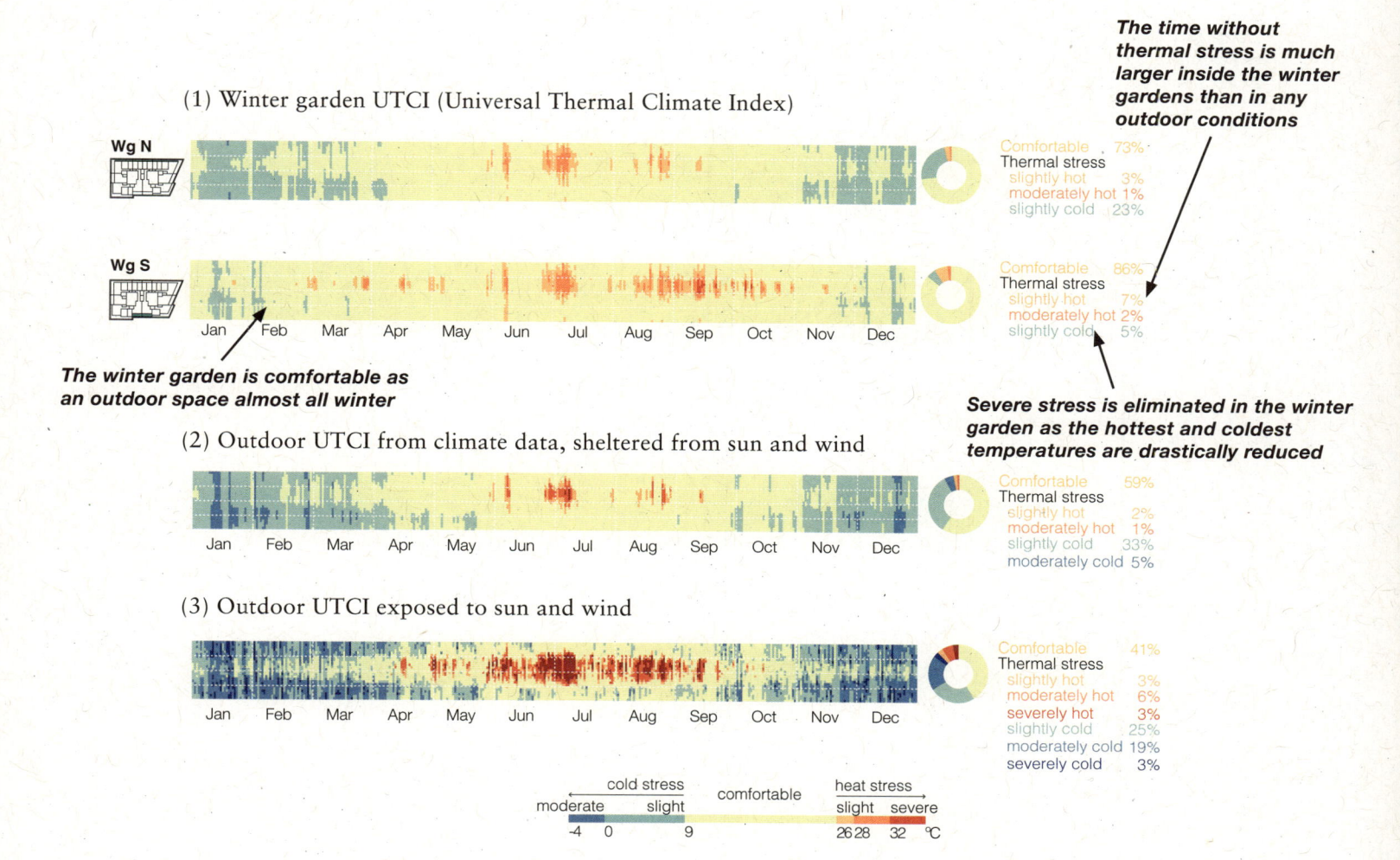

(1) Winter garden UTCI (Universal Thermal Climate Index)

Wg N

Comfortable 73%
Thermal stress
slightly hot 3%
moderately hot 1%
slightly cold 23%

The time without thermal stress is much larger inside the winter gardens than in any outdoor conditions

Wg S

Jan Feb Mar Apr May Jun Jul Aug Sep Oct Nov Dec

Comfortable 86%
Thermal stress
slightly hot 7%
moderately hot 2%
slightly cold 5%

The winter garden is comfortable as an outdoor space almost all winter

(2) Outdoor UTCI from climate data, sheltered from sun and wind

Jan Feb Mar Apr May Jun Jul Aug Sep Oct Nov Dec

Comfortable 59%
Thermal stress
slightly hot 2%
moderately hot 1%
slightly cold 33%
moderately cold 5%

Severe stress is eliminated in the winter garden as the hottest and coldest temperatures are drastically reduced

(3) Outdoor UTCI exposed to sun and wind

Jan Feb Mar Apr May Jun Jul Aug Sep Oct Nov Dec

Comfortable 41%
Thermal stress
slightly hot 3%
moderately hot 6%
severely hot 3%
slightly cold 25%
moderately cold 19%
severely cold 3%

```
        cold stress           comfortable        heat stress
moderate        slight                        slight    severe
   -4        0            9                 26 28    32   °C
```

(1)–(3) Winter garden and outdoor UTCI (Universal Thermal Climate Index): These diagrams show the efficiency of the winter garden compared to the real UTCI outdoor conditions with sun and wind as well as a sheltered outside. The south winter garden is without thermal stress most of the year (UTCI in comfort 86% of the time). It is slightly cold only 5% of the time, which occurs mostly at night. The heat stress is also light, as 98% of the year its UTCI remains below 28°C. The north winter garden is without thermal stress 73% of the time (UTCI), which is quite high for a space that barely receives sun. During the winter, and especially at night, the winter garden is colder. However, its thermal inertia maintains its temperatures always above 0°C. The heat stress is moderate, as its UTCI remains below 28°C 99% of the year. Compared to outdoor conditions, the winter gardens remain without thermal stress for a much larger portion of time. Severe stress is eliminated in the winter garden as the hottest temperatures are drastically reduced and the coldest ones drastically raised.

Active Mode
Winter Air Temperatures and Heating Load

(1) Winter air temperatures and heating demand in the north–south apartments

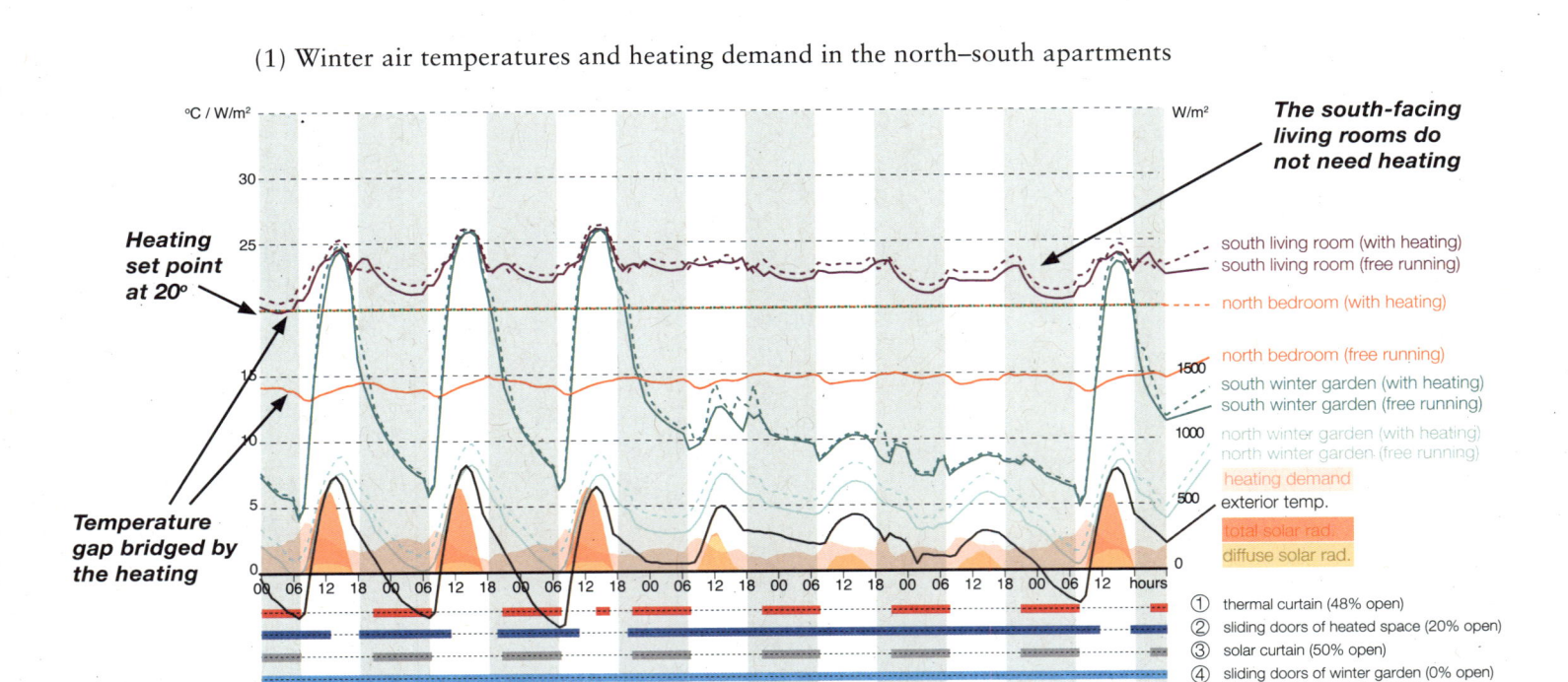

The south-facing living rooms do not need heating

Heating set point at 20°

Temperature gap bridged by the heating

- south living room (with heating)
- south living room (free running)
- north bedroom (with heating)
- north bedroom (free running)
- south winter garden (with heating)
- south winter garden (free running)
- north winter garden (with heating)
- north winter garden (free running)
- heating demand
- exterior temp.
- total solar rad.
- diffuse solar rad.

① thermal curtain (48% open)
② sliding doors of heated space (20% open)
③ solar curtain (50% open)
④ sliding doors of winter garden (0% open)

(2) Winter air temperatures and heating demand in the corner apartments

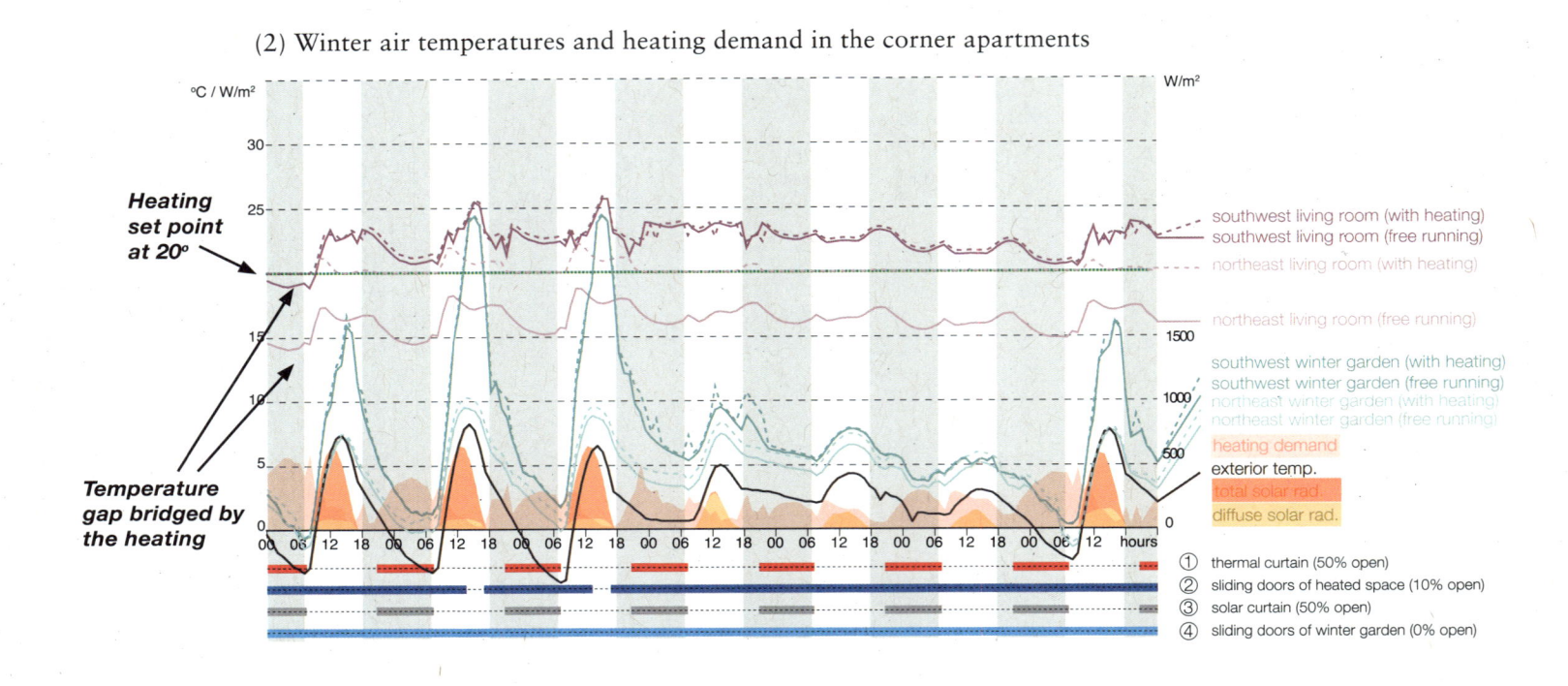

Heating set point at 20°

Temperature gap bridged by the heating

- southwest living room (with heating)
- southwest living room (free running)
- northeast living room (with heating)
- northeast living room (free running)
- southwest winter garden (with heating)
- southwest winter garden (free running)
- northeast winter garden (with heating)
- northeast winter garden (free running)
- heating demand
- exterior temp.
- total solar rad.
- diffuse solar rad.

① thermal curtain (50% open)
② sliding doors of heated space (10% open)
③ solar curtain (50% open)
④ sliding doors of winter garden (0% open)

(1)/(2) Winter air temperatures and heating demand: This graphic shows air temperature—rather than the operative temperatures of previous graphics—for heat-load evaluations. In the north–south units, living rooms have temperatures above 20°C naturally (between 20 and 26°C), and they require no heating. The bedrooms' temperatures are 14–15°C naturally and require heating to reach 20°C day and night. In the corner units, the south-facing living rooms have temperatures above 20°C naturally most of the time (19–26°C), which results in a very low heating load. The northeast living room has temperatures naturally between 15 and 18.5°C, and they require heating most of the time. However, when heating is on at night, and the space starts the day already at 20°C, when the sun comes in the temperature is raised to 22–22.5°C. The south winter garden's temperature is unchanged with and without indoor heating. The north winter gardens collect some of the interior heat, as their temperature is 1–1.5°C higher when heating is turned on inside.

Case Study 4

Active Mode
Heating Demand

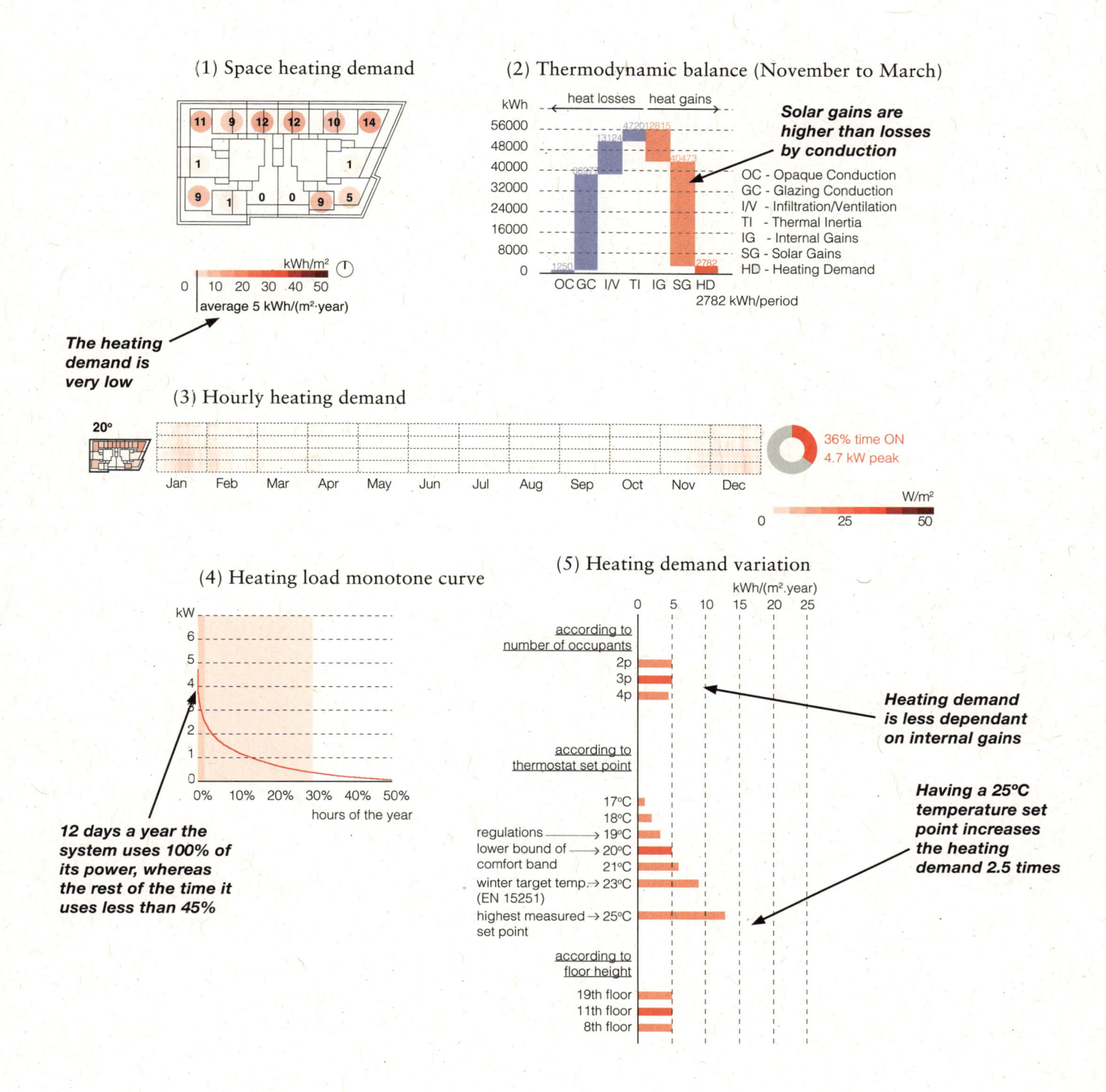

(1) Space heating demand

average 5 kWh/(m²·year)

The heating demand is very low

(2) Thermodynamic balance (November to March)

- OC - Opaque Conduction
- GC - Glazing Conduction
- I/V - Infiltration/Ventilation
- TI - Thermal Inertia
- IG - Internal Gains
- SG - Solar Gains
- HD - Heating Demand

2782 kWh/period

Solar gains are higher than losses by conduction

(3) Hourly heating demand

36% time ON
4.7 kW peak

(4) Heating load monotone curve

12 days a year the system uses 100% of its power, whereas the rest of the time it uses less than 45%

(5) Heating demand variation

according to number of occupants: 2p, 3p, 4p

Heating demand is less dependant on internal gains

according to thermostat set point:
- 17°C
- 18°C
- regulations → 19°C
- lower bound of comfort band → 20°C
- 21°C
- winter target temp. → 23°C (EN 15251)
- highest measured set point → 25°C

Having a 25°C temperature set point increases the heating demand 2.5 times

according to floor height:
- 19th floor
- 11th floor
- 8th floor

---

(1) Space heating demand: The average heating load of the entire floor is 5 kWh/(m²·year), which is almost negligible. The demand is concentrated in the bedrooms, which require about 12 kWh/(m²·year)—a very low demand—whereas the south living rooms have almost no energy demand. Northern bedrooms represent half of the total demand of the floor.

(2) Thermodynamic balance (November to March): The thermodynamic balance shows that solar gains are the main source of heat, accounting for more than fourteen times the amount of the heating load and more than three times the internal gains. Solar gains are also higher than all losses by glazing conduction.

(3) Hourly heating demand: The heating season is short. It occurs from late November to the end of March and is concentrated in all spaces facing north and the corner living rooms.

(4) Heating load monotone curve: Whereas heating can be used up to 36% of the time, the full power is only required during a very short amount of time (six days a year on average), and more than 65% of the full power is used for only twelve days. This provides room to require less equipment.

(5) Heating demand variation: The number of occupants barely changes the heating load, which shows the resiliency of the envelope as changes in indoor conditions slightly modify the heating demand. Raising the thermostat temperature increases the demand: a set point at 25°C doubles the demand though remains low (13 kWh/[m²·year]). Reducing the thermostat to 17 or 18°C almost suppresses the need for any heating, as demand is reduced to 2 or 3 kWh/(m²·year), respectively.

Case Summary
Main Values

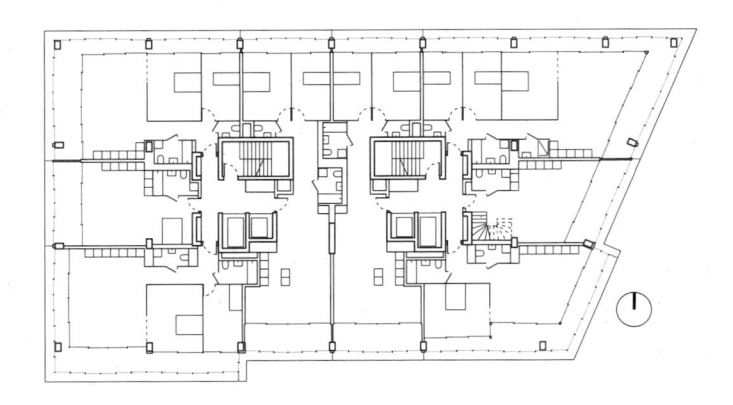

Daylight:
average daylight autonomy DA [300]: 69% of the time

all the spaces largely exceed the recommendations of EN 17037

Temperature and comfort in free-running mode:
above comfort: 3% of the time
within comfort: 81% of the time
below comfort: 16% of the time

average degree·hours
above comfort: 142°C·h

Solar gains and winter garden effect:
(temperature difference between the winter garden and outside)
winter: south +3 to +23°C, north up to +3°C
mid-season: south +2 to +17°C, north up to +5°C

Heating demand:
total: 5 kWh/(m²·year)
peak demand: 4.7 kW
Heating on:
3,148 / 8,760 hours per year
176 / 365 days per year

The winter garden around the entire perimeter of the building leads to an optimal winter performance, as the heating demand is the lowest of the case studies (5 kWh/m²) and rooms are very bright. Daylight levels are very high, as on average spaces reach 69% daylight autonomy. In free-running mode, average comfort levels reach an average of 80% in the entire floor plan, which is very high. Whereas the south-facing rooms never require heating, the north bedrooms are in comfort 62% of the time. Indoors, the temperature never drops below 14°C in any space, not even when outdoor temperatures fall below zero all day and night. In the north winter gardens, the temperature difference with the outdoors can reach 3°C, whereas the south ones can be up to 23°C higher than outdoors. During the summer, most of the spaces reach an optimal performance, with very few hours above comfort. Only the southwest-facing spaces show some overheating, which can be reduced by further closing the thermal curtains. To highlight the effect of the winter gardens, a variant of the project was studied with triple glazing instead of the double envelope.

Case Comparison
Modification: Triple Glazing Instead of Winter Garden

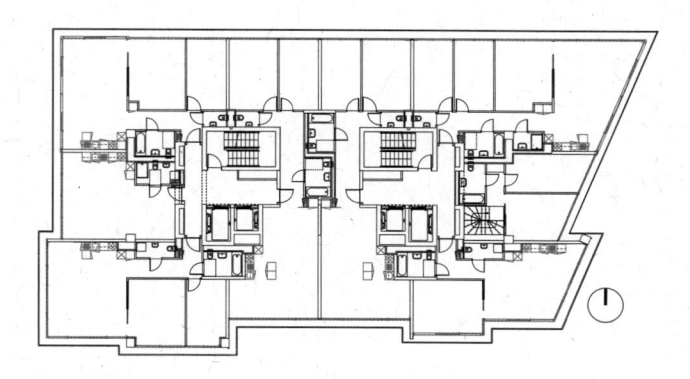

Daylight:
average daylight autonomy DA [300]: 73% (**+4%**) of the time

all the spaces largely exceed the recommendations of EN 17037

Temperature and comfort in free-running mode:
above comfort: 1% (**-2%**) of the time
within comfort: 69% (**-12%**) of the time
below comfort: 30% (**+14%**) of the time

average degree·hours
above comfort: 72°C·h (**-70**)

Solar gains and winter garden effect:
(temperature difference between the winter garden and outside)
winter: -
mid-season: -

Heating demand:
total: 10 kWh/(m²·year) (**+5 kWh/(m²·year)**)
peak demand: 8.7 kW (**+4 kW**)
Heating on:
3,262 / 8,760 hours per year (**+114 h**)
151 / 365 days per year (**-25 d**)

Modifications in detail:
Winter gardens are replaced by a full height window system:
triple glazing U=0.785 W/m²K, SF=0.35, VLT=0.66
light-color curtain SF=0.35, reflectivity=0.6

In this scenario, a version of the project was studied with triple glazing instead of winter gardens in order to identify the efficiency of the latter. This modification doubles the heating demand, which is a high relative difference, though the demand remains low in absolute values. The contribution of the solar gains decreases to one-third even if the facade is fully glazed, as solar-control glazing is required to cope with the high solar gains during the summer. Even if the units do not overheat, the bedrooms are too hot at night. The triple glazing performs well overall but fails to provide resiliency during peak days, as the built project adapts better to extremes.

Case Study 4

Case Comparison
Sun and Daylight

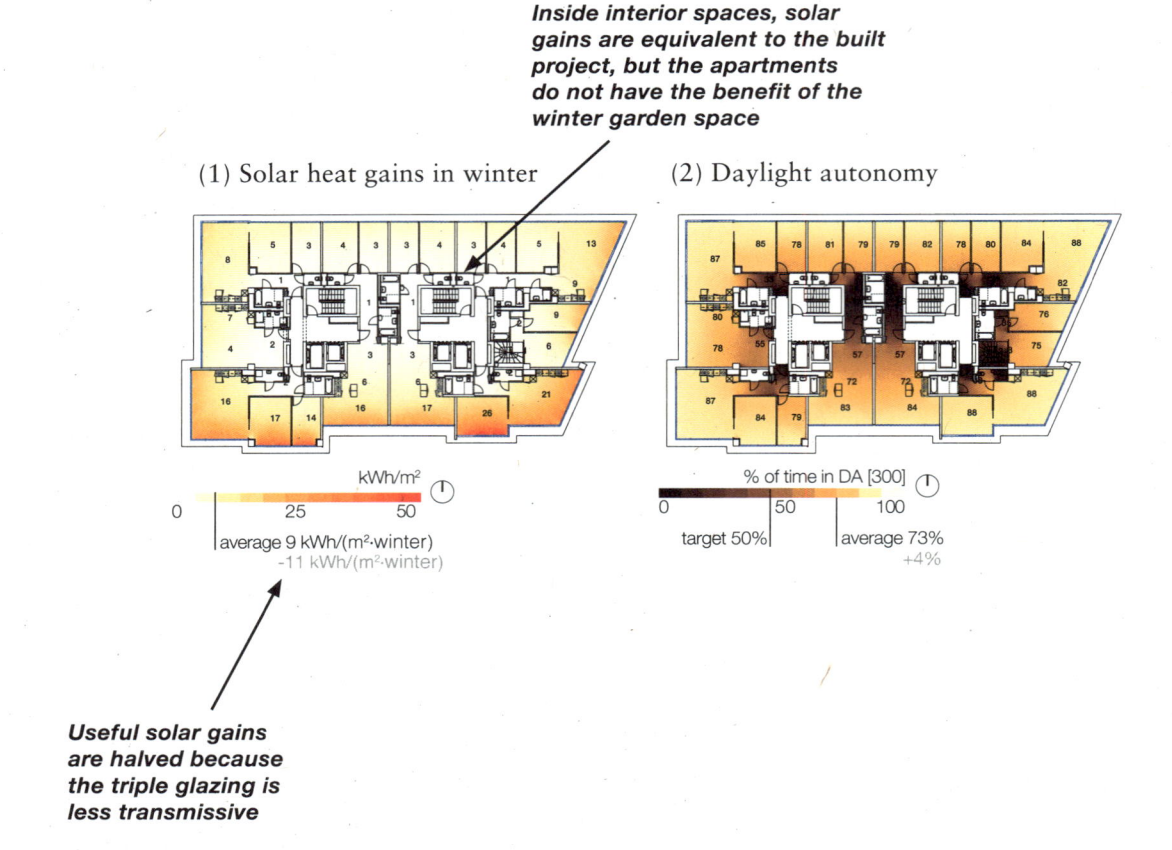

(1) Solar heat gains in winter

(2) Daylight autonomy

Inside interior spaces, solar gains are equivalent to the built project, but the apartments do not have the benefit of the winter garden space

kWh/m²
0   25   50
average 9 kWh/(m²·winter)
-11 kWh/(m²·winter)

% of time in DA [300]
0   50   100
target 50%   average 73%
+4%

Useful solar gains are halved because the triple glazing is less transmissive

(1) Solar heat gains in winter: During the winter, on average, the conventional solution with triple glazing capitalizes on half the solar gains. The south rooms receive large amounts of direct radiation as the sun reaches directly indoors, followed by the east and west rooms. Toward the south and north, the reduced solar factor evens out the presence of the winter garden (in the case of the built project) as absolute values inside the rooms are very similar. In the case of the east and west rooms, the winter gardens allow more sun inside than the triple glazing with the reduced solar factor. During the summer, interior radiation in all the south, east, and west rooms is high, as they all receive 12–23 kWh/(m²·year). The total amount of radiation is doubled compared to the actual project. On the north side, the difference is even higher. All in all, the interior spaces with the winter gardens receive the same heat gains in winter but less in summer. The winter garden helps to capitalize better on solar gains, and the total gains in winter are double.

(2) Daylight Autonomy: The case with triple glazing allows slightly more light in (4% more on average). However, in this case the curtains will need to be drawn for a longer period, as there is no winter garden slab to block the high sun. This would result in a reduction of the daylight availability in reality.

Case Study 4

Case Comparison
Typical Days

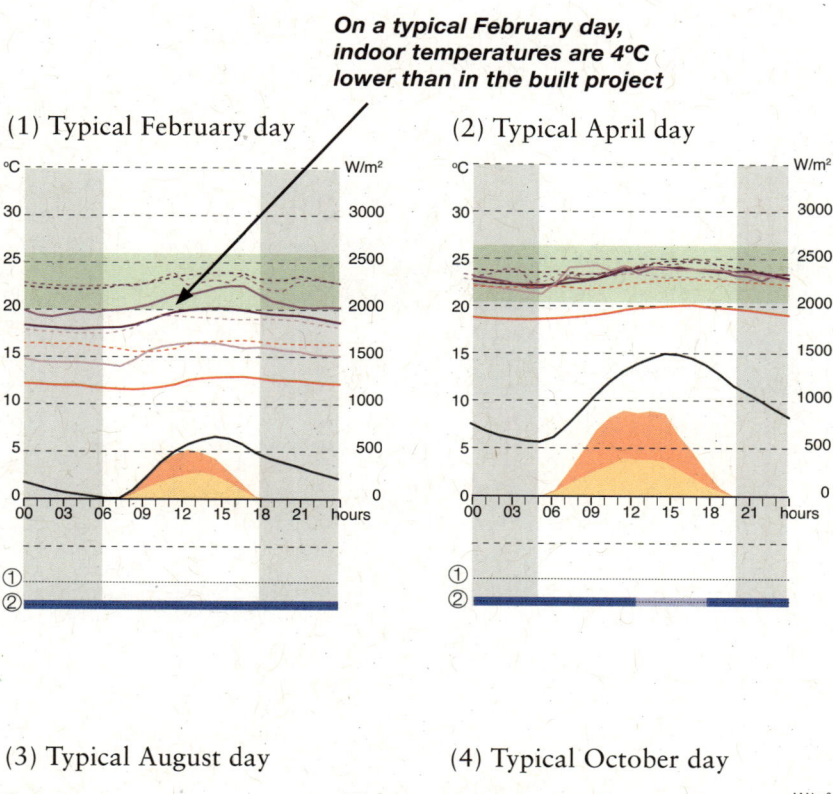

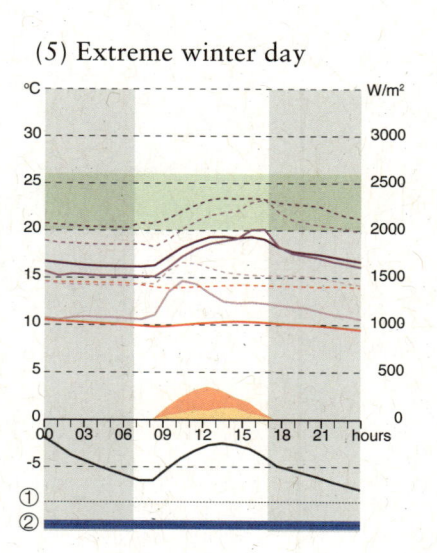

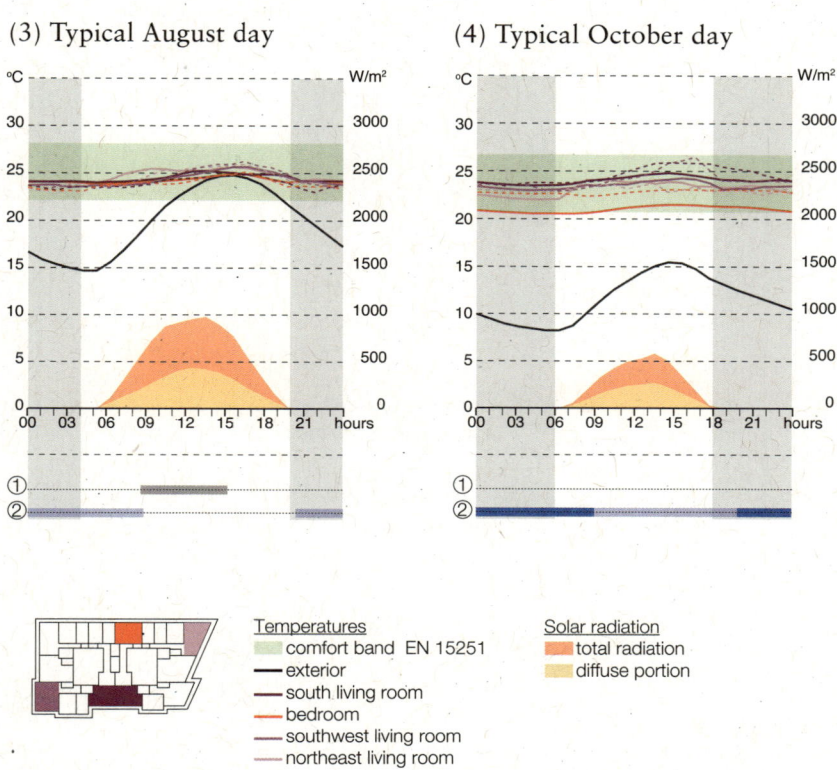

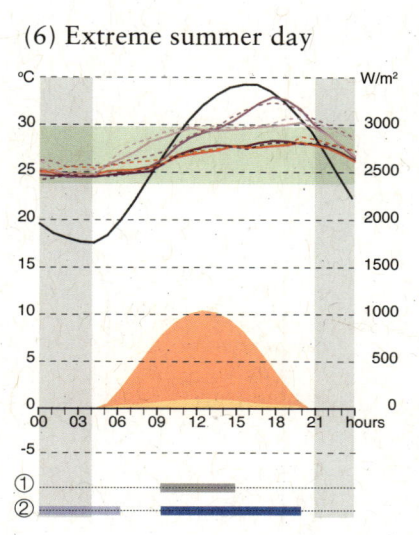

On a typical February day, indoor temperatures are 4°C lower than in the built project

(1) Typical February day
(2) Typical April day
(5) Extreme winter day
(3) Typical August day
(4) Typical October day
(6) Extreme summer day

Temperatures
- comfort band EN 15251
- exterior
- south living room
- bedroom
- southwest living room
- northeast living room

Solar radiation
- total radiation
- diffuse portion

(1) Typical February day: In winter, operative temperatures in free-running mode are about 3–4°C lower in the case with triple glazing. Only the southwest living room has temperatures that are 1–3°C lower. The buffer effect of the winter garden is more effective than the solar gains combined with a very insulated envelope. The difference is particularly relevant in the north bedrooms, as in the case with triple glazing indoor temperatures are 12–13°C.

(2) Typical April day: Most of the temperatures are similar in both cases, except the north bedrooms with triple glazing that are 3–4°C lower, falling below the comfort band (even if it is by a small margin).

(3) Typical August day: All the temperatures are very similar in both cases.

(4) Typical October day: All temperatures are very similar and remain within the comfort band naturally. The north bedroom is again slightly cooler.

(5)/(6) Extreme days: During an extreme summer day, all temperatures are very similar in both cases. During an extreme winter day, temperatures in the north–south units are 4°C lower in the case with triple glazing. In the corner units, the difference is slightly lower, 2–4°C. The colder the weather, the more effective the winter gardens become.

Case Study 4

Case Comparison
Resulting Thermal Comfort and Active Mode

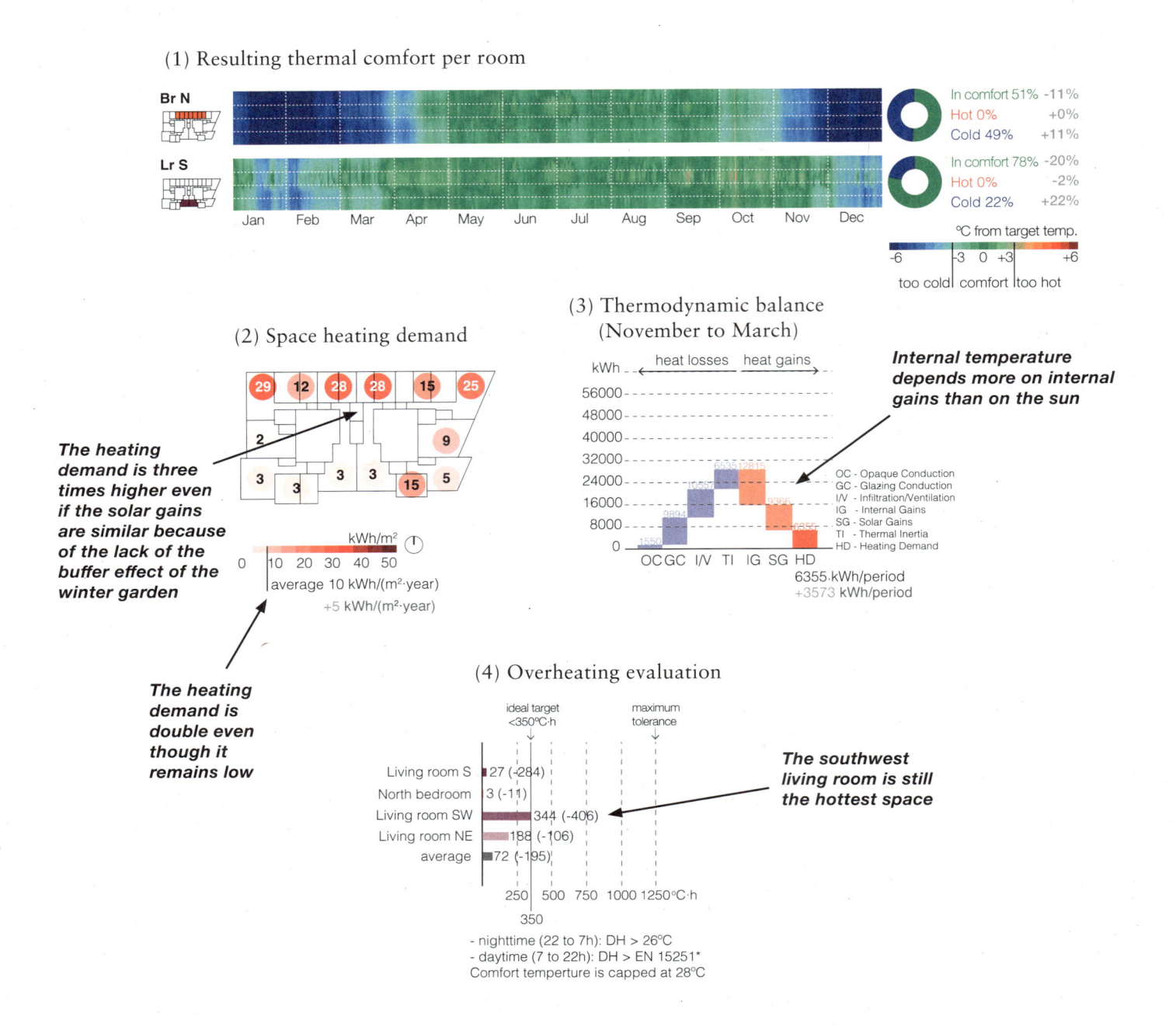

(1) Resulting thermal comfort per room

Br N
- In comfort 51% -11%
- Hot 0% +0%
- Cold 49% +11%

Lr S
- In comfort 78% -20%
- Hot 0% -2%
- Cold 22% +22%

°C from target temp.
-6 -3 0 +3 +6
too cold | comfort | too hot

(2) Space heating demand

29, 12, 28, 28, 15, 25
2, 9
3, 3, 3, 15, 5

The heating demand is three times higher even if the solar gains are similar because of the lack of the buffer effect of the winter garden

kWh/m²
0 10 20 30 40 50
average 10 kWh/(m²·year)
+5 kWh/(m²·year)

The heating demand is double even though it remains low

(3) Thermodynamic balance (November to March)

kWh — heat losses — heat gains

Internal temperature depends more on internal gains than on the sun

- OC - Opaque Conduction
- GC - Glazing Conduction
- I/V - Infiltration/Ventilation
- IG - Internal Gains
- SG - Solar Gains
- TI - Thermal Inertia
- HD - Heating Demand

OC GC I/V TI IG SG HD
6355 kWh/period
+3573 kWh/period

(4) Overheating evaluation

ideal target <350°C·h | maximum tolerance

- Living room S: 27 (-284)
- North bedroom: 3 (-11)
- Living room SW: 344 (-406)
- Living room NE: 188 (-106)
- average: 72 (-195)

250 500 750 1000 1250 °C·h
350

- nighttime (22 to 7h): DH > 26°C
- daytime (7 to 22h): DH > EN 15251*
Comfort temperature is capped at 28°C

The southwest living room is still the hottest space

---

(1) Resulting thermal comfort per room: Rooms facing south are only in comfort 78% of the time compared to 98% in the actual project. However, the margin by which comfort is not met is very small throughout the winter. Rooms facing north are only in comfort 51% of the time, compared to 62% in the actual project. The margin by which comfort is not met is much larger, with most of December, January, and February with temperatures 6°C below the comfort band.

(2) Space heating demand: The average heating load of the entire floor is 10 kWh/(m²·year), which is very low but still almost double the case with winter gardens. The demand occurs during a similar period but with more intensity, and the heating season extends until April. North bedrooms hold most of the demand, which is higher than in the case with winter gardens (even if the time below comfort is lower). This indicates that the cold severity is higher than in the case with winter gardens. Peak demand is 8.7 kW, which is 85% higher than the case with winter gardens.

(3) Thermodynamic balance (November to March): The total amount of losses is similar in both cases, which highlights the effect of the winter garden as buffer space and proves it is similarly effective as triple glazing. In this case, solar gains are actually lower during the heating period, and there is a greater dependence on internal gains and mechanical heating.

(4) Overheating evaluation: Overheating is controlled, as across the units only 0–1% of the time is above comfort, and all rooms remain below the ideal target of 350°C·h above comfort (and above 26°C at night). However, the bedrooms are too hot at night. The triple glazing performs well overall in summer but fails to provide resiliency during peak days. This issue will become more relevant as the climate gets hotter.

Summary of the Case Studies

Atmos Lab

The results of the case studies show that winter gardens offer numerous environmental advantages for their parent buildings. They provide the benefits of a transparent envelope while delivering exemplary levels of thermal performance and energy savings throughout the year in heating-dominated climates with mild summers. Their adaptive potential transforms the characteristics of the envelope according to the season and time of day: at night it can become opaque and more insulated, whereas during the day it is fully transparent with strategic shading for warmer days. The spaces adjacent to the winter garden benefit from its adaptability and are generally well daylit, thermally comfortable, and require little to no energy to operate in winter.

Apartment Configuration

The configuration of the apartments and the careful composition of the layers of the winter garden prove effective at regulating indoor conditions, thus achieving an optimal free-running performance. The depth of the winter garden slab and balcony is calibrated according to its orientation to provide shading to the interior spaces during summer; in fact, none of the winter gardens receives significant radiation in this period (except Cité Manifeste). However, during winter, the lower sun angles are not blocked and radiation heats the spaces effectively. Openings in facades with different orientations allow cross ventilation, as all interior spaces can regulate interior airflow from 0 to 2 m/s. This helps to aerate sufficiently, cool the space, and reduce the perceived temperature. A transparent envelope brings generous levels of daylight into the interior spaces, which creates well-daylit areas for the users. Daylight-Autonomy levels range from 61 to 73% (except Cité Manifeste, which has 45% DA, but different light ambiences); all units exceed the requirements of EN 17037, and all exceed its minimum threshold. The transparent envelope also allows close contact with the outdoors while regulating privacy through the different curtains.

Conditions in the Winter Garden

The winter garden is an effective climatic buffer space throughout the year no matter where it is oriented, as its temperature is consistently warmer than outdoors, except in summer. The temperature difference with the outdoors depends on the design of the space, climate conditions, orientation, and layer adjustment. However, in all case studies the temperature difference is greater when it is cooler outdoors, which means that on the coldest days the winter gardens are much warmer than outdoors, and on milder days the winter gardens have a similar temperature to outdoors. The difference flips during the hottest summer days, as the temperature inside the winter garden falls below the outdoor temperature because of its thermal inertia. The design of the winter garden allows its occupants to open and gradually close its layers and therefore adjust the envelope, which modifies its thermodynamic response according to the seasons.

During the winter, winter gardens exposed to the south capture sunrays, which helps heat indoor spaces naturally. On a sunny or partially sunny day, temperatures vary from 14 to 24°C across projects, which represents 7–20°C more than outdoors. At night or on cloudy days, they act as buffers that reduce heat loss from indoor spaces, as the insulation provided by the intermediate air volume, the thermal curtains, the low U-value of internal glazing, and the presence of the outer envelope all increase temperature some 2–10°C. The more concrete there is in the winter garden, the greater the thermal inertia, which maintains higher temperatures once the sun sets or is covered. The night temperatures of the winter gardens in Cité Manifeste are only 1–2°C above the outdoor temperature; for Ourcq-Jaurès and the Geneva tower the difference is 3–6°C above outdoors, and for Grand Parc it's normally 5–10°C. On the coldest days, the winter garden is even more effective: the lower the temperature outdoors, the greater the difference (8–14°C on the coldest day for Ourcq-Jaurès, Grand Parc, and the Geneva tower). These extremely cold days are normally sunny, and solar heat gains raise winter garden temperatures, which intensifies the buffering effect and reduces heat loss by infiltration, ventilation, and conduction. North-facing winter gardens are also effective as buffers in winter, with temperatures 2–5°C higher than outdoors in Geneva and in the Ourcq-Jaurès units with winter gardens on both sides. Moreover, the temperature difference is greater on peak days—in Geneva it can reach 5°C.

During the mid-season, when the exterior envelope is closed, the winter garden is mild in temperature, allowing its use as an additional indoor space that enlarges the living room. The milder the outdoor temperature and the sunnier the sky, the easier it is to passively reach a comfortable temperature during the central hours of the day. The indoor temperature reaches 17–26°C during the daytime, which represents 2–13°C more than outdoors. Great hourly and daily fluctuations of climatic conditions and user preferences make this season the most variable in terms of the winter garden's configuration: from tightly shut on colder nights to mostly open on sunnier days.

During the summer, the outer envelope of the winter garden remains fully open, and the space becomes a terrace protected from the sun by the reflective curtain. The balcony outside the winter garden blocks the high sun and keeps the space of the winter garden in the shade. When the sun is lower, the solar curtain shades the space even further. All these elements provide sufficient protection to the inner envelope. The temperature inside the winter garden is similar to outdoors because of the adequate shading, effective cross ventilation, and thermal inertia. The latter is particularly beneficial during peak days, as it further stabilizes temperatures that might be 1–2°C below outdoors.

The higher thermal inertia and greater depth of the winter gardens in Bordeaux is favorable to the hotter summers in the region, as they help stabilize temperatures. The configuration of the Geneva tower, with winter gardens on all sides, improves the building's performance in the winter, as the heating loads are minimal when it is very cold. The design of Cité Manifeste, Lacaton & Vassal's first social housing project, completed in 2005, is least optimal. Its exposed roof captures excessive solar heat in summer and loses heat excessively in winter, resulting in the least stable conditions compared to the other cases. However, since the apartments here exceed the standard size for social housing, there is more room for choice and the residents do not need to occupy the winter garden during the hottest summer days. Looking at the other projects, one can see the improvements made through accumulated knowledge and experience over the years.

Indoor Conditions

Indoor temperatures are naturally comfortable and relatively stable during the summer and the mid-season and near comfortable in winter.

In winter, the winter garden's insulation, combined with solar gains, raises temperatures to near-comfortable levels in free-running mode. Grand Parc maintains the most stable temperatures (16–19°C), followed by Ourcq-Jaurès, where there is a difference of 3–4°C between southeast-facing living rooms (16–19°C) and northwest-facing bedrooms (13–16°C). The Geneva tower maintains the highest temperatures (17–23°C), despite experiencing one of the coldest winters, thanks to the protection provided by the winter gardens on all orientations. Cité Manifeste experiences the lowest and most fluctuating indoor temperatures (12–18°C) due to the exposure of the roof (of the house and winter gardens) to the outdoors and the lack of insulation toward the ground.

During the mid-season, intuitive adjustments to the envelope aid in maintaining comfortable and stable indoor temperatures ranging from 21 to 26°C, according to the case-study findings. Ourcq-Jaurès and Grand Parc exhibit the most stable temperatures (22–25°C), while the Geneva tower experiences slightly higher and more variable temperatures (23–26°C) due to its exposure and multiple openings in various orientations. Cité Manifeste records the lowest and most variable temperatures (13–26°C) due to its exposed roof, ground floor, and winter gardens.

During the summer, the combination of opaque horizontal shading from the winter garden floor slab, vertical reflective shading, natural ventilation through the opening of both glazing layers, and the cooling effect of thermal inertia largely maintains indoor temperatures within a range of 24–27°C. As a result, none of the spaces experiences overheating, with only two exceptions: the upper living room of Cité Manifeste, where temperatures can reach 31°C on hot summer days due to the transmissive horizontal shading and lack of vertical shading; and in the Geneva tower, one of the eight living rooms that faces southwest. The ground floor of Cité Manifeste and the entire apartment of Grand Parc (where summers are the hottest) have a remarkable performance, as they have zero hours above the overheating target. Compared to standard solutions, such as a facade with a reduced window-to-wall ratio (as seen in case comparison of Grand Parc) or triple glazing instead of winter gardens (as seen in Geneva), the winter garden solution demonstrates more resilience to future climates, as indoor radiation is significantly reduced (by one-fourth to one-half in most cases) due to effective shading. As temperatures increase, standard solutions face greater challenges in preventing overheating.

Heating Demand, Equipment Size, and Mechanical Ventilation

A strong performance in free-running mode results in minimal heating demand across all case studies, with most maintaining a heating load below the threshold of 15 kWh/(m²·year). Notably, the transformation of building blocks in Grand Parc and the Geneva tower reaches 5–6 kWh/(m²·year). Within the units, heating demand approaches zero in the rooms adjacent to sun-exposed winter gardens but is higher in the north-facing bedrooms. Cité Manifeste, the first project with a row-house typology, exhibits the highest demand at 33 kWh/(m²·year), as it is more susceptible to heat loss than apartments. Furthermore, its location experiences one of the coldest winters of the case studies, and regulations regarding envelope performance were not as strict at the time of construction. Ourcq-Jaurès and the upgraded version of Cité Manifeste reach 15 kWh/(m²·year), which today lies within the targets of passive housing. The heating set points of the simulations are entered at 20°C, but bedrooms can be kept cooler at night while occupants sleep, further reducing the heating demand to negligible levels in many cases. The preheating of the air provided by winter gardens not only keeps annual demand and peak loads low but also obviates the need for a supply mechanical system, where air renewal is mechanically introduced and preheated via a system of air recirculation. Overall, both energy demand and embodied carbon footprint remain low.

Compared to standard solutions, the winter garden has demonstrated greater effectiveness in reducing both the annual heating load and the peak load, which determines the size of mechanical equipment, as its efficiency improves on the coldest days. The standard solution for the Geneva tower—triple glazing—requires approximately double the amount of heating (though it remains low), while the standard refurbishment at Grand Parc—adding insulation and improved U-values to the old building configuration—demands three times more heating than the actual transformation with the winter gardens. These examples yield a peak load double that of projects featuring winter gardens. In summary, the winter garden enables the parent building to reduce energy usage throughout the year, necessitate smaller equipment, and circumvent the need for supply mechanical systems, even in locales with cold winters like Geneva.

The winter garden enhances resilience for the parent buildings during winter by relying on the sun, which provides 50–75% of their total heat input—far exceeding internal gains or mechanical heating. Internal gains are based on typical appliance usage, and the occupancy schedule also matches that of a standard dwelling. However, as appliances become more efficient and release less heat in the future, and if occupants' habits change, temperatures in standard cases may decline, while those with winter gardens will maintain warmer temperatures due to solar reliance.

It is pertinent to recall that interviews with occupants have corroborated the simulation results. The testimonies not only affirm how the projects deliver low-energy housing in heating-dominated climates, they also convey the inhabitants' satisfaction.

Conclusion

The integration of winter gardens in Lacaton & Vassal's residential designs effectively regulates indoor conditions. The combination of the properties of a greenhouse—a structure that naturally captures solar radiation to generate heat—with the thermal inertia of concrete—a material that stores heat as it stabilizes temperatures—is an optimal way to passively heat indoor spaces. This approach significantly reduces the need for mechanical heating, the main energy demand of dwellings in the climates studied, by harnessing the winter garden's heat output.

Key design parameters such as location, orientation, composition, depth, and technical specifications influence the winter garden's environmental performance, which has evolved over time. The winter gardens in the first projects resembled actual greenhouses, and subsequent projects presented an opportunity to improve the system according to the local climate. Most recently, the properties have been adapted to specific conditions and orientations. The adaptable envelope returns control of indoor comfort to occupants, enabling them to tailor the space to their evolving needs and preferences.

Winter gardens not only provide more light and space but also offer greater energy efficiency and reduced reliance on mechanical equipment compared to standard procedures. More sustainable and less carbon intensive, they will be particularly resilient and beneficial for mitigating the extreme temperature challenges of the future.

From Intuition to Project:
For a Paradigm Shift

Anne Lacaton and Jean-Philippe Vassal

Understanding the history of the winter garden in the architecture we produce allows us to look back at all the projects we've worked on since we started our practice and understand that each operation carries all the experiences that preceded it. These crossed, intertwined, and assembled experiences bring together our research, of course, but also that of other professionals we have collaborated with, as well as the experience of the inhabitants. The winter garden is in no way a simple recipe, but a continuous, surprising, and evolving work process.

Based on a culture of observation and trust in intuition as a fundamental approach to the project, this history of the winter garden constitutes, in a way, a history of transparency, freedom, and escape—three important notions in the conception of our projects.

A Greenhouse in Front of a Home:
The Possibility of the Marvelous

At the beginning of the 2000s, for the Cité Manifeste, we had been in long-term discussions with manufacturers of horticultural greenhouses. It was a matter of continuing the maximum exploration of the greenhouse space and its climatic potential, which we had already begun to study and use for the Latapie and Coutras projects. For the first Latapie house design, we imagined a concrete structure topped by a greenhouse. In the end, the project's design evolved into a housing block on two floors adjacent to a greenhouse space with a height of more than six meters. As for the individual house project in Coutras, we coupled two greenhouse structures side by side, one containing an insulated wooden box—housing two bedrooms, an office, a bathroom, and a living room—and the other left as a completely empty greenhouse. Through these first two experiments, we understood that the combination of a horticultural greenhouse and an insulated and heated volume made it possible to create a new system of habitat, in terms of use and relation to the environment.

These first two projects mark the beginning of the use of the greenhouse as a kind of double envelope: What would be the benefit of putting the typical living cell in relation to another envelope, and how would that affect comfort—temperature regulation, acoustic insula-

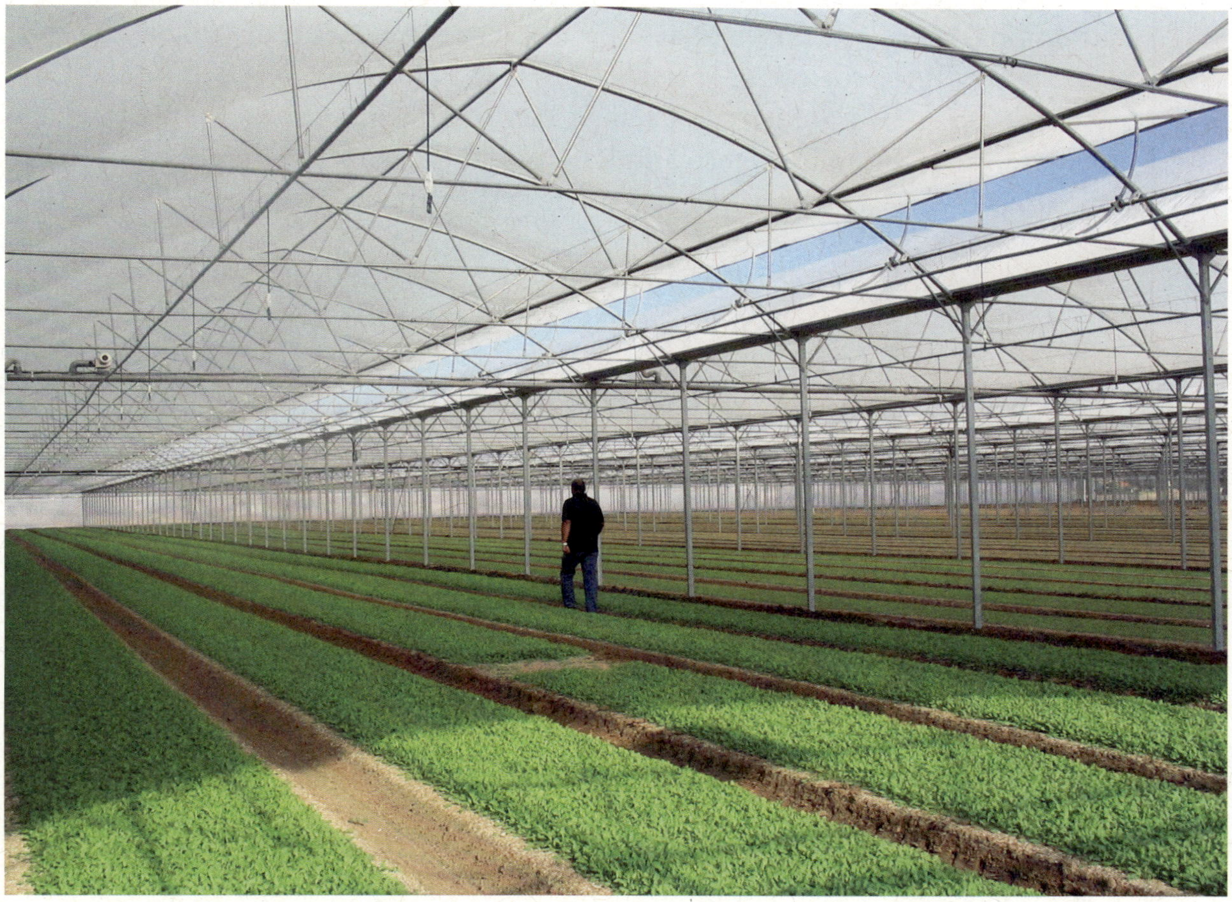

tion, and heating? In this combination, we observed that the climate produced by the greenhouse means the insulated part of the dwelling has direct contact not with the outside but with an intermediate climate. This idea comes from the observation that the greenhouses themselves produce a variation of climate in relation to the outside. When closed, the greenhouse can produce heat, or when everything is open, as in summer, ventilation and air cooling. After testing, we came to understand that the greenhouse attached to the habitat could function as a kind of thermal buffer and at the same time produce an additional space: a wonderful area in which one can expect anything. These founding projects were essential in helping us show it is preferable to create a productive exchange between the habitat and the climate, as we think of it, instead of an insulation. This idea, forged by observation, was deepened and supported by these experiences.

In the Beginning, a Generous, Usable, and Comfortable Space

The Cité Manifeste is a direct result of the first two experiments, the Latapie and Coutras houses. We had to think about adapting them to the context of collective housing, which obviously made things more complex: we had to prove to the relevant authorities that they met the thermal regulations then in place.

How could we ensure that the notion would hold up in a multi-family housing context while providing the generous spaces and the climatic benefits? The economic constraints—there was a very tight budget—were again unavoidable.

We followed the same reasoning that we used for the design of the architecture school in Nantes a few years later: to not initially worry about the requested program, but to try to build the maximum possible volume on a given plot of land, and to create a climate within it. Once this capacity is maximized in terms of cubic meters, floors, and climate, you can then install the program inside—be it a house or an architecture school.

So we first sought to make this large volume a qualified and efficient space with a great capacity for comfort. For the realization of the fourteen apartments of Cité Manifeste, the superposition of professional horticultural greenhouses on a kind of concrete table—made of concrete posts, beams, and slabs—created quite differentiated spaces, depending on whether one is at ground level or upstairs. Each apartment benefited from the qualities of each of the components of this system: views to the north, south, and east, a small garden, a door on one side, and a greenhouse on the first floor.

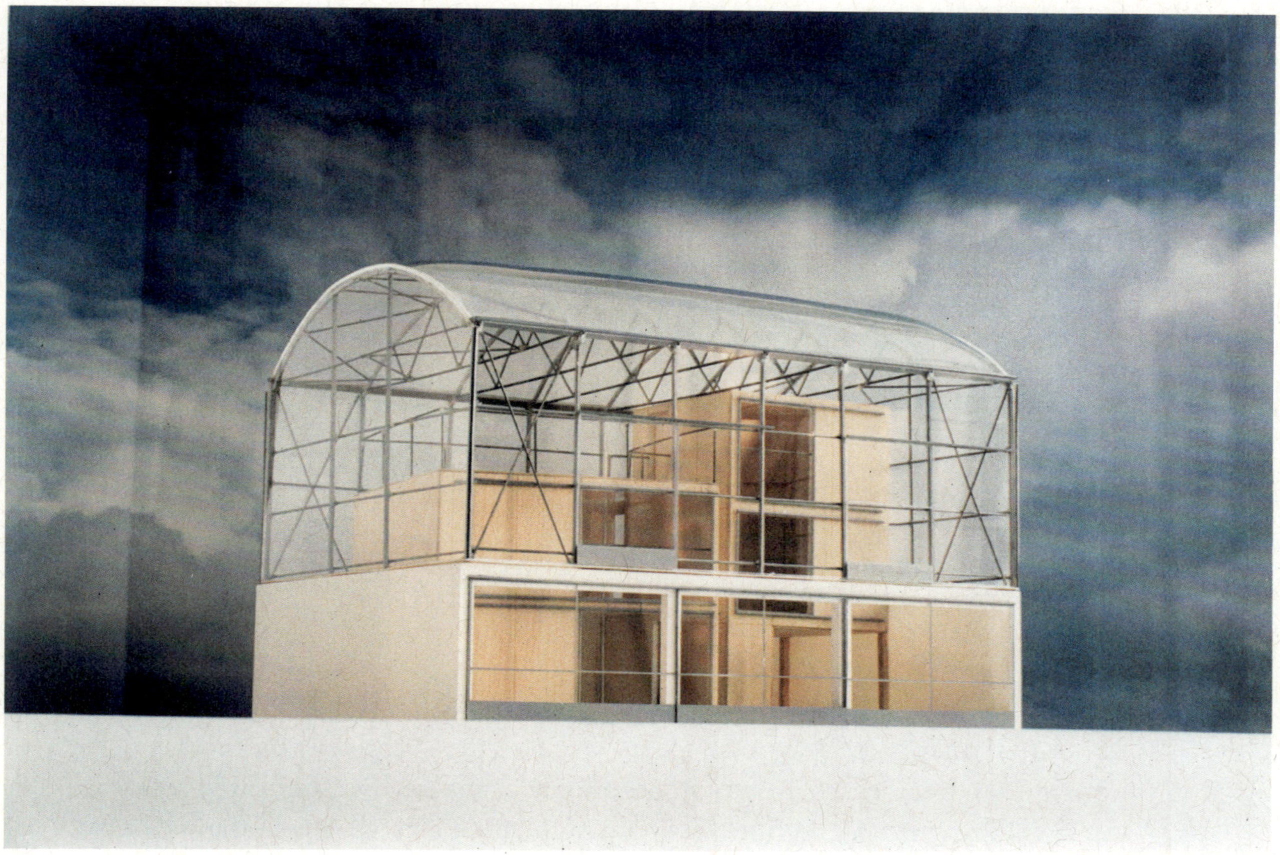

The Addition of a Horticultural Greenhouse
to Double the Living Area and
Create a Comfortable Natural Climate

When we built the Coutras house, we realized that we had to use standard horticultural greenhouses mass-produced for agriculture. They perfectly met the desired climate-management and budget constraints, and given that the project was very small (compared to the large quantities they normally build) we could not afford to ask the manufacturer to change the dimensions. For Cité Manifeste, we therefore used the standard dimensions of horticultural greenhouses to determine the size of the concrete structure. On top of this table, at a height of three meters, we placed three greenhouses, each 6.40 m wide, for a total of 19.20 m, and the entire construction was 60 m long. Since the dwellings are located transversally, this width of 19.20 m became the depth of each dwelling—far exceeding the conventional 12 m. For us, this represented not a constraint but an interesting opportunity to experiment with the quality of a deeper space.

On each end, behind the facades, there was a well-lit space of six meters. That left us with the remaining 7.20 m in the center, creating atypical interior spaces. Upstairs, the greenhouses covering the insulated volumes of habitable rooms create a climate that's naturally protected from the outside.

This solution fulfilled our desire to generate a system as flexible as possible while meeting the goal we had set for ourselves: to build apartments that were twice as large as the standard for social housing, and to create a passive bioclimatic system by combining the dwelling with a greenhouse space. On this basis we presented our project to the contracting authority.

For our argument, we relied on several elements: our observations of horticultural greenhouses—transparency as a solar collector, combined with curtains, openings, and insulation—and technical references from the agricultural field and the Latapie and Coutras projects. We also used photos and feedback from inhabitants that evoked the pleasure of living in these spaces. And of course we cited the great economic interest of building usable and livable spaces with great thermal efficiency. We also went to visit Latapie and Coutras with Pierre Zemp, the director of SOMCO, the contracting authority. On the thermal question, he was convinced, though a little unnerved by the freedom granted to the inhabitant! But he was willing … and the project began on the basis that we proposed.

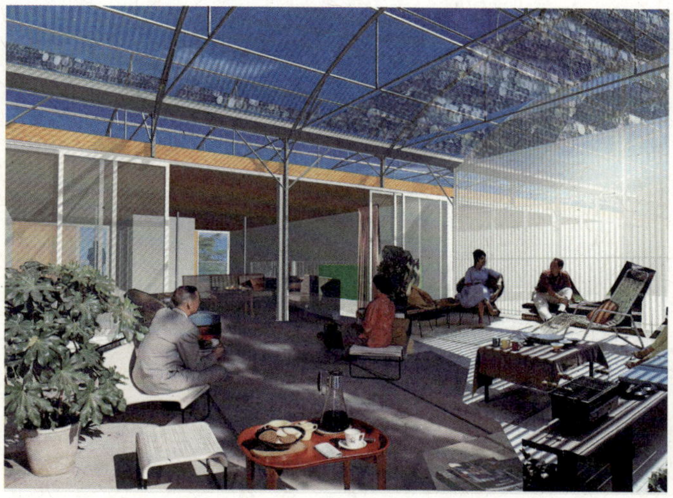
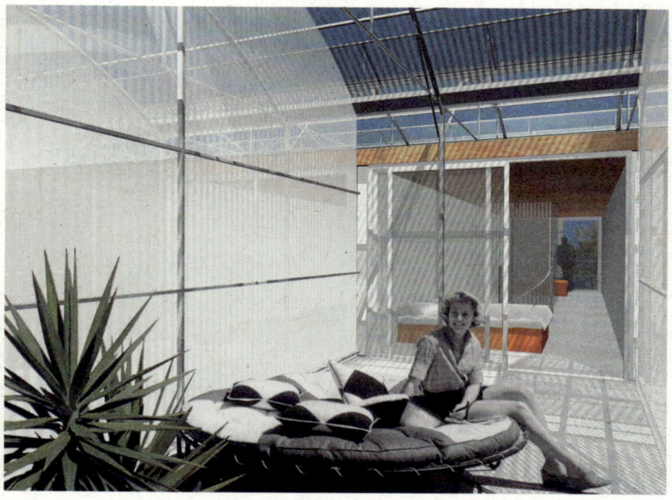
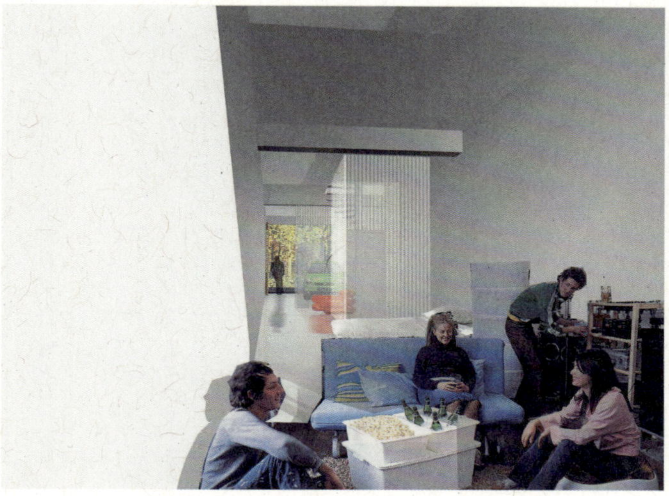
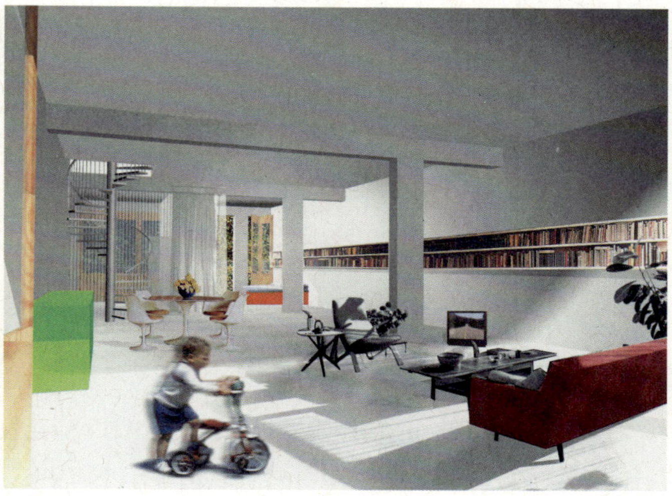

Intuition and Field Experience as Project Drivers

At a crucial moment in the project phase of Cité Manifeste, the climate engineering firm we were working with quit, saying the project wouldn't meet local or national regulations. But of course, for the client to obtain state subsidies we needed an assessment of the thermal efficiency of the greenhouses in order to prove the project corresponded to regulations. So we and the client decided to consult the Ministry of Housing and defend our project ourselves to request an exemption. To everyone's surprise, that was received warmly. The Ministry's commission confirmed that the project fulfilled—and in some respects even exceeded—the regulatory requirements. This confirmed our approach and our reasoning. We simply needed to make the calculations for this specific type of project. It was at this point that we met Christian, a thermal engineer and member of the commission. He took an interest in the project and advised us, producing the calculations proving that we met the objectives of RT 2000, the national guidelines on thermal performance. Since that time, Christian has collaborated on almost all our projects.

This moment in the history of our work shows that our intuition, observations, analysis, and reasoning have always been the triggers of our projects. That's where we started—not with calculations and data, which we applied only later. Without this prior intuition and the argumentation that followed, projects like the Latapie house or Cité Manifeste would never have been built. No conventional calculation would have validated the development of the project. And yet the feedback, the measurements, and the simulations carried out after the fact with more developed calculation tools have always confirmed the thermal performance of the projects. This is important because nowadays the opposite occurs. Only calculations are admitted for the project's validation. And the models for those calculations, created for standard situations, aren't suitable for atypical projects!

For building the greenhouses, we asked an industrial manufacturer, and we were always amazed by the professionalism of the greenhouse fitters. To see them working on a regular construction site with such precision was incredible. They needed just three weeks to assemble the three greenhouses for Cité Manifeste. Although it was far from their usual field of work, they were very engaged in the realization of the project. Since greenhouses are agricultural products, the construction methods had to meet the rules for housing, which are different from those for agriculture. Similarly, we needed to devise a system for fixing the greenhouses to the concrete floor, because normally they are anchored in the earth with small foundations. The structural steel engineer we collaborate with for most of the projects helped a lot, working with the greenhouse manufacturer and their own design offices to adapt all the calculation models for agricultural constructions to the norms for housing.

It was also the first time we used thermal curtains on a larger scale than a single-family home. Until then, we had worked with a tailor who made the curtains to measure. They were made of an insulating fabric (like what's used in ski parkas) sandwiched between layers of aluminum fabric.

We needed to quickly obtain these curtains in large quantities. That meant working with a manufacturer that could produce them industrially, delivering a material that could be guaranteed and which met the performance requirements for a public housing project.

We found a company that produced thin insulating material for cold rooms and related products such as insulated curtains for the small windows of travel caravans. They were interested in developing such curtains on a larger scale and finding new markets for their use, and Cité Manifeste presented a good opportunity to do that. This was the first project where thermal curtains were implemented as a building element—part of the basic infrastructure, just like the facade or load-bearing structure—and should not be removed, which implied new definitions in terms of maintenance, responsibilities, leases, and so forth.

To determine the thermal performance, Christian, the thermal engineer, considered the various layers as a single element: the interior curtain, the space between it and the glass doors, the space behind them, the greenhouse facade, and the shade curtain. For his calculations, he treated the space in the conservatory as a single material. All these approaches—from the design offices of the industrial world, those of the building world, ours, the manufacturers'—came together and were nourished by everyone's previous experiences. We discussed everything. We debated all the elements proving the efficiency because it was important to demonstrate that it complied with the regulations' objectives. It was not a question of escaping thermal regulations in the name of experimentation. Over the course of the projects, we managed to refine the performance evaluation of greenhouses, winter gardens, and thermal curtains. Manufacturers have developed studies that facilitate validation and inclusion in proving thermal efficiency. This is the case for thermal curtains, for example, which now can be included in regulatory calculations.

The Multiplied Performance of Two Combined Devices:
Greenhouses and Insulated Space

We spoke with a company that had installed greenhouses in climates similar to Mulhouse, and compared our intuition about their behavior. Given the economic considerations at play, greenhouse builders take a lot of measurements in order to do a detailed evaluation, and they're always searching for ways to improve performance. For Cité Manifeste, they helped us build a very precise argumentation tailored to Mulhouse's climate—cold in winter and hot in summer. This made us realize that the so-called standard horticultural greenhouse is not a generic product but a set of parts that can be adapted to various climates, sometimes with extremes of hot or cold. It's a product that's been in constant evolution for fifty years.

By creating a climate in which plants from different continents can grow, a greenhouse evokes the idea of acclimatization. The conditions required for human life are extremely precise. Just as for flowers, these conditions must be adapted to residents with delicacy. We thought about this a lot with the Latapie house. We pondered how to design a house that allows people to create the climate they want, and we achieved this with a pair of systems that work in harmony.

On one side, there is the greenhouse, which on its own isn't suited for human habitation. On the other side, there is the insulated box. The greenhouse is transparent and air-permeable. The insulated box is more stable and airtight. The relationship and the exchanges between the two entities create a protected place with incredible sensations. We have always avoided making bubbles. We try to build envelopes in relation with the outside that adapt to its variations. The facade is like a garment that can be put on or taken off.

This combination of the insulated system with the greenhouse space allows us to create a large volume, produce a pleasant climate, and save energy. All this is very simple and very trivial. But brought together, the two devices blend and produce something wonderful that allows creative input from the inhabitants. Based on the ease of the exchange, this assembly also makes it easy to create a free ground plan. We always prefer to avoid building walls; our instinct is to open rather than divide, to unite spaces by a sliding door rather than separate them with a solid one. This merging of two worlds that never intersect—of housing construction and of greenhouse makers—pushed us to question what is really effective. On our side, we know that the definition of the performance (regarding thermal comfort) is much larger than what is usually defined) Indeed, a

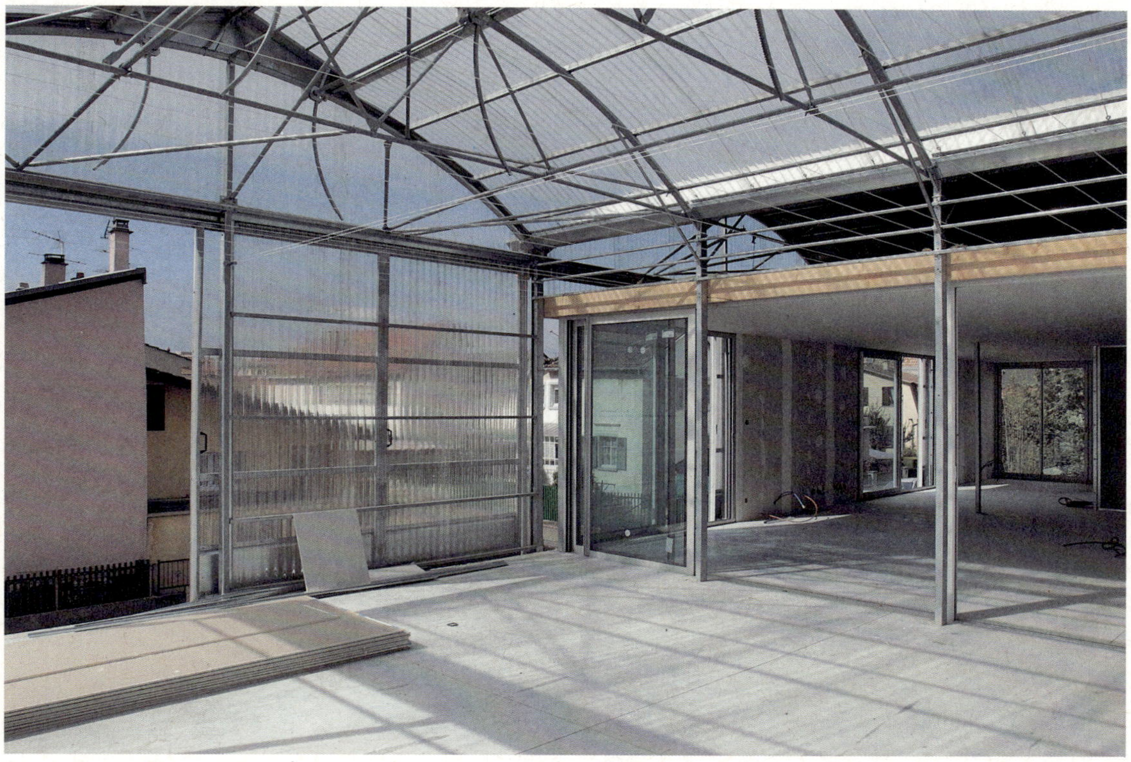

greenhouse captures, enhances, and amplifies climatic resources, radiation, and air. Unlike a building that is insulated to create constant and uniform conditions, it doesn't create a barrier from the outdoors.

The same is true for structural performance. Industrial systems are more efficient than ordinary building methods. Optimizing performance involves stepping outside of one's field of practice and what we are used to looking at. We don't always find it where we think it is.

From the Horticultural Greenhouse to the Winter Garden:
A Response to Verticality and Density

After completing Cité Manifeste, we had the feeling that the system was a bit limited, so we wanted to study the possibility of using greenhouses for a multistory apartment building. A project of 23 collective housing units in Trignac—which included triplexes and two floors with a greenhouse on the roof—gave us that chance. Then we did something similar with a project that included 53 housing units in Saint-Nazaire.

This was when we moved from the idea of a greenhouse superimposed on an insulated space to that of a winter garden placed in front of a home. At about the same time, as we worked on the transformation of the 100 apartments of the Bois-le-Prêtre tower in Paris, we developed the principle of adding winter gardens to apartments by extending the original facade.

The move from the greenhouse to the winter garden is typically linked to a superimposition of living spaces. With their transparent roofs, greenhouses work well when placed atop a structure to take advantage of the light flooding in from above. The greenhouses must be high—typically more than four meters—to ensure the proper functioning of vents in the roof, which release hot air that accumulates and rises to the top of the space. This is how the idea of the winter garden came about in cities, where the experience of the greenhouse and its climatic efficiency can be adapted to the context of height and density.

In taller buildings, the sun collector is no longer the roof but the facade, whose surface is much larger. In winter, with the sun relatively low on the horizon, a vertical wall can capture more heat than a horizontal one. In summer, by contrast, the horizontal floor slabs and the balcony overhangs become the most important element in the system by producing shade.

Variations in use and climate then come from the depth of the winter garden, which can range from 80 cm, as in our last project in Geneva, to the four meters we used in the transformation of the Cité du Grand Parc in Bordeaux. In a winter garden, the functionality of the greenhouse effectively shifts from the horizontal to the vertical.

In winter, the building's facade must be as close as possible to the exterior to capture the maximum amount of radiation, so the winter garden remains closed. In summer, the facade must retreat deeper into the shade. In this context, the winter garden—completely open—functions as a shaded terrace thanks to the upper floor slab. A fixed facade with triple glazing doesn't allow for these variations.

In our first projects, we considered winter gardens to be a solution for increasing comfort in the colder months, as they helped reduce the energy needed for heating. This performance has long been verified and confirmed. Today, the issue has shifted to summer comfort, which has become much more crucial. And we can now see that the winter garden is as effective in summer as it is in winter. It is an alternative to insulation. In the summer, it is no longer a winter garden, but a terrace that provides shade and protection from the direct sunlight hitting the facade. With the shade curtains, this can create a cooler and more comfortable climate inside.

The Fundamental Necessity of Transparency

Our first intuition was that transparency is absolutely necessary.

For us, it is essential that our buildings be totally glazed in order to maximize solar gain and natural light and to offer a continuity between interior and exterior.

Without a winter garden, we could not meet thermal regulations, or we would need triple glazing everywhere. So the winter garden offers an efficient solution, allowing us to comply with regulations, maintain 100% transparency, and provide extra living space.

Being transparent allows everything. It can be opaque if you want, using blackout curtains or furniture to create divisions, or it can be completely open. Transparency offers the possibility of giving inhabitants the freedom to choose how they want to live. It is the opposite of a framed window.

A floor-to-ceiling window represents maximum freedom and view. With the absence of a wall and the continuity of the floor, it offers the sense of living at ground level even when you're on a higher floor. You can create varying configurations, retracting the facade to expand your living space. This brings us back to the genesis of the construction principle. We prefer post-and-beam systems that free up space between floors rather than load-bearing walls. That creates the possibility of floor-to-ceiling openings for the facade, allowing seamless passage from the inside to outside—unlike windows, which are just a hole in an opaque wall. We usually use sliding glass panels over the entire height of that floor of the building.

Thanks to this system, two spaces can become one. The floor can continue without obstacles, and the sliding panel creates a new space. This system makes the limits vanish and, taking advantage of full-height glazing, creates the conditions for escape and freedom. The more any visible, solid frame disappears, the more the limits evaporate, the greater the possibility of escape.

The Winter Garden:
A Space of Uses and Climates

In all the winter gardens we've built, the inhabitants speak of climate when discussing the ways they use the space. That varies according to the season, the time of the day, sunlight, the breeze. The interior climate of the complex is a catalyst for modifying and adapting their usage. Many things in daily life are defined by the climate.

In Geneva, where we recently delivered a 101-unit tower, we placed winter gardens all around the building. Their depth varies. The winter gardens adjacent to the bedrooms are quite narrow, about 80 cm, allowing for the storage of plants or the placement of an armchair. Others, connected to the living rooms, are deeper. Placed on the corners and with all four exposures, the winter gardens offer different forms of mobility, as in a villa. It is not a tower but a sum of houses, a superposition of grounds. As with each project, the tower in Geneva allowed us to explore and analyze the particularities and benefits of a new configuration of the winter garden—in this case all orientations and variable depths.

These operations have given us a very precise knowledge of the climatic functioning of winter gardens and their thermal efficiency. They have taught us that this space is climatically as effective in winter as in summer in its ability to create comfort. And we've discovered that the winter garden is not only effective with a southern exposure in winter as a heat collector. In reality, it serves an important function of insulation even toward the north. It's possible

(1) Existing

apartment 1 – living room   apartment 2 – living room

(2) Transformation

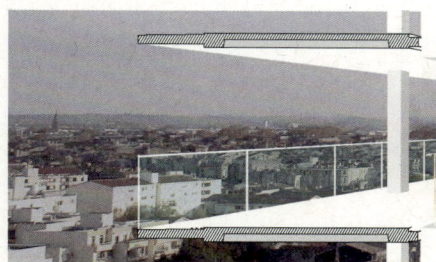

extension 3.80 m   extension 3.80 m
winter garden + balcony   winter garden + balcony

(3) New Apartments

balcony   winter garden   apartment 1 – living room   apartment 2 – living room   winter garden   balcony

to achieve two different and interesting efficiencies. The variation in depth was also interesting for us. The winter garden maintained its full functionality even when its surface was variable, for example with the narrower space on the bedroom side and the wider ones on the living-room side. In Geneva, we found that it allows other uses while maintaining energy efficiency.

Through all our projects and the evolution of winter and summer gardens, we have observed that this space always brings something. There's not a single typical benefit. The winter gardens always work, allowing more usable space where residents can invent new uses, increasing the quality of living even in the most constrained situations.

Beyond the climatic function, the winter garden can be transformed into terraces in the summer. It allows circulation, entry and exit, access to neighboring rooms in various ways, and serves to extend and multiply the inhabited space and offer freedom.

All Situations Can Spur Metamorphosis

In 2017, we completed the transformation of 530 social housing units in the Cité du Grand Parc in Bordeaux with Frédéric Druot and Christophe Hutin. For the project—three modernist buildings from the 1970s that had escaped demolition—we had to respond to regulatory, energy, and technical issues in a mass-production context. Without displacing any of the inhabitants during the construction, we gave the buildings a new spatial and climatic quality by placing four-meter-deep winter gardens in front of all the dwellings. The space constitutes a radical change in circulation, use, views, and comfort due to its great depth. But it's also because the winter gardens create something that didn't exist before: transparency and light, whereas the original interior spaces only had small windows. Adding winter gardens to an existing structure in this way is particularly effective where the initial quality of the housing is not so good. This demonstrates that even a low-quality building can be transformed by the addition of winter gardens. And the energy performance can be improved as efficiently as it can by other standard insulation materials. It creates usable space and a new sustainable life cycle, which creates long-term added value and a new status to the buildings as well as a much more pleasant living experience for their inhabitants.

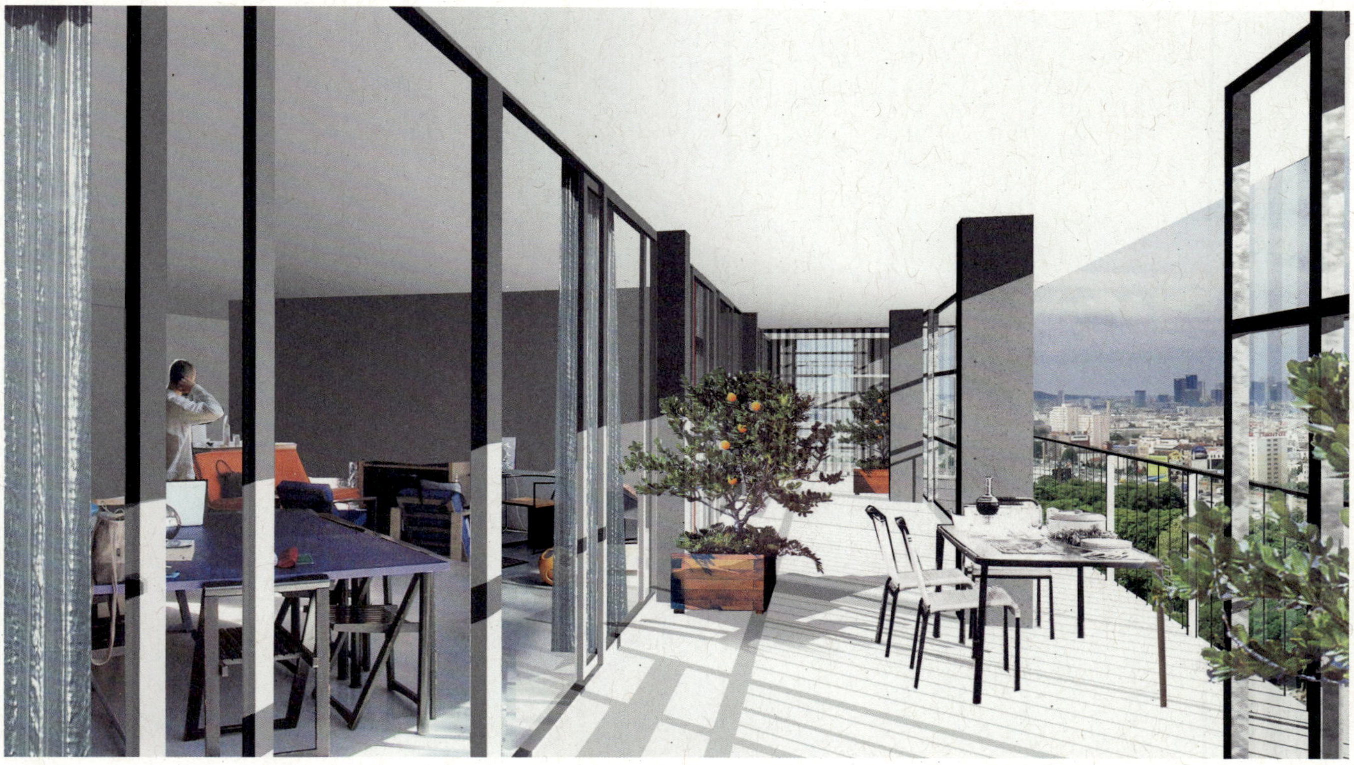

*In the winter garden,
I feel very free ...*

Aurélia Ramos, Grand Parc, Bordeaux

Annex: Research Methodology

For a Precise Understanding of Micro-climatic Conditions and Resulting Thermal and Visual Comfort

Atmos Lab

I. Introduction

When Lacaton & Vassal started to work with winter gardens in the early 1990s, they combined the available knowledge on greenhouse technology, solar principles, and heat-loss calculations as well as common sense and their own experience of climate and its effect on the human body and psyche. At that time, the existing regulatory requirements only related to heat loss. However, Lacaton & Vassal were mindful of the importance of the resource economy and providing a pleasant atmosphere and climatic experience for people in their homes. Their designs were confirmed while evolving over time, as new knowledge, technology, and evaluation methods became available.

Nowadays, developments in these fields have peaked: technological progress has enabled the interaction between global climate data and computer models; computational fluid dynamics, ray tracing, and thermodynamic simulations have become more accessible; most of the real interactions between climate, buildings, and users can be mimicked; and a consensus was reached in Europe about the standards defining thermal and visual comfort. Now, environmental performance can be assessed from a holistic perspective with a strict methodological approach.

Recently, the industry's focus has shifted to the carbon emissions generated by buildings. The emphasis has been on solar panels, the efficiency of the equipment, and the materiality of the constructions, particularly for wooden buildings—all of which relate to what can be seen in and on the building without tackling the demand to reduce energy. According to the UN Global Status Report from 2023, the building industry is responsible for 37% of the carbon emissions related to energy consumption, 10% of which is because of the embodied energy of materials, and the rest is related to the operational emissions, meaning the energy the building uses during its lifetime.[1] The Intergovernmental Panel on Climate Change reports that in 2019, buildings accounted for 31% of total CO_2 emissions, 31% of global energy demand, and 18% of global electricity demand[2]. The report also introduces a plan to reduce the impact and cost of constructing and using buildings without reducing the level of comfort of the occupant. Called the SER framework, it is composed of three stages:

1. S (sufficiency): tackles the causes of environmental impact by avoiding the demand for energy and materials

2. E (efficiency): tackles the symptoms by improving energy and material intensities

3. R (renewables): tackles the consequences by reducing the carbon intensity of energy supply

Bioclimatic design—as Lacaton & Vassal are developing it—deals with the sufficiency stage. The immaterial qualities of the building—air and light—are shaped by the properties of the architecture. The energy demand decreases, which in turn reduces the total emissions of the building industry.

II. The Case Studies

The case studies show the environmental benefits associated with the design and operation of winter gardens. However, winter gardens are not a closed system but always function in conjunction with the living spaces. Most of the dwellings designed by Lacaton & Vassal are oriented in two directions to allow for cross ventilation. Living areas are systematically oriented toward the south or southeast, depending on the plot, to take advantage of the warmth of the sun. Winter gardens always attach to living areas, therefore receiving the sun in the morning, and sometimes early afternoon, year-round. Bedrooms are located in the northern or northwestern quadrants, as they require less heat and do not necessarily have winter gardens. There are no divisions, or minimal ones inside the apartment to allow uninterrupted airflow during the summer. If there are doors, they are usually sliding, to increase the size of the openings and reduce the obstruction of airflow. The winter garden can only be accessed from the apartment—it is a private space for the occupants and cannot be entered from the outside.

The case-study buildings present a diverse range of typologies in various climates for which winter gardens are suited. The addition of the winter gardens is possible only in climates in which shelter from cold is the main priority but summers are still warm, and where there is sufficient solar radiation throughout the year. According to the Köppen-Geiger system (1), all the case studies are located in the climate region classified as Cfb, which is described as "temperate oceanic, with no dry season and warm summers." More precisely, the coldest month averages above 0°C, all months have average temperatures below 22°C, and at least four months average above 10°C, and there is no significant precipitation difference between seasons. The annual sum of global horizontal irradiation map (2) shows that this region receives between 1100 and 1400 kWh/m² a year; it encompasses the north of Spain, most of France and Switzerland, Belgium, the Netherlands, a large part of Germany, and the south of England.

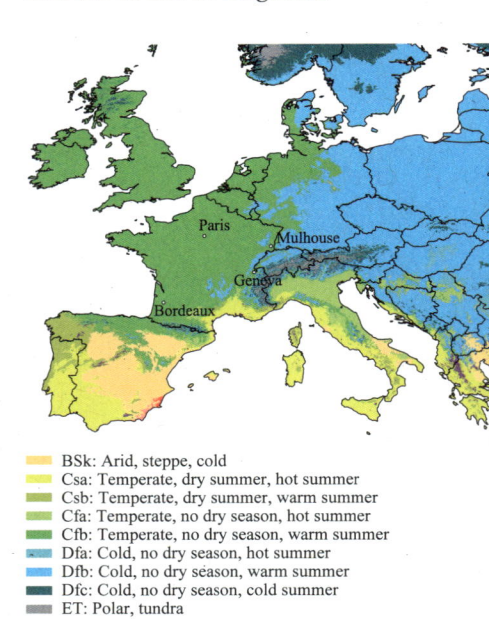

BSk: Arid, steppe, cold
Csa: Temperate, dry summer, hot summer
Csb: Temperate, dry summer, warm summer
Cfa: Temperate, no dry season, hot summer
Cfb: Temperate, no dry season, warm summer
Dfa: Cold, no dry season, hot summer
Dfb: Cold, no dry season, warm summer
Dfc: Cold, no dry season, cold summer
ET: Polar, tundra

1) Climate classification of western Europe (Köppen-Geiger), after Beck et al.[3]

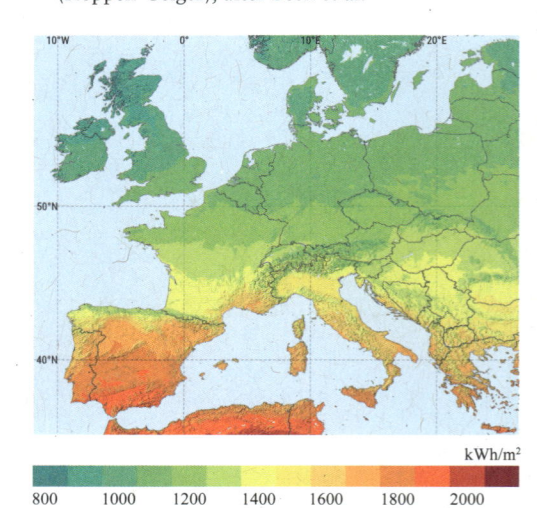

2) Average annual sum of global horizontal irradiation (1994–2016), after Uyan and Dogmus[4]

3) Data-logger location for temperature monitoring

- exterior
- winter garden
- living room
- bedroom

The characteristics of this climatic region make it suitable for winter gardens. However, it shows slight variations, especially during peak conditions. Paris has the mildest climate, with shorter and less frequent peaks in summer and lows in winter, the smallest daily amplitude overall, and the smallest amount of radiation in winter. Bordeaux has the hottest summer, both on average and in number of peaks. Geneva has the coldest winters on average, though temperatures can reach the lowest in Mulhouse. Sky conditions also differ: whereas summers are sunny only 14% of the time in Paris, Geneva has clear skies 25% of the summer. Geneva and Bordeaux have more radiation throughout the year than Paris and Mulhouse. The general prevailing wind direction is to the southwest. The French climates have more homogeneous wind in all directions, while the wind in Geneva travels on a clear southwest–northeast axis. In Bordeaux, the wind mainly comes from the west.

The analysis of this sequence of projects from 2005 to 2020 traces the evolution of the design of the winter garden in Lacaton & Vassal's housing projects and sets out potential further improvements. The study aims to validate the architects' reasoning during the design process, which predicted the performance of buildings with winter gardens. These buildings' performance is thoroughly investigated to grasp the influence of architectural design, climate, location, and occupant behavior. Conclusions are drawn from information provided by the architects as well as interviews, observations, temperature monitoring, and environmental simulations.

III. Research Methodology

1. Selection of the Case Studies and Individual Units

The case studies were chosen to cover the different typologies of residential buildings with winter gardens. For each case study, a typical unit located on a middle floor was studied to represent average conditions. The only exception was the tower in Geneva, where an entire floor was studied to understand the effect of the winter garden as an overall double envelope.

2. Climates

The weather data used for this publication was obtained from Meteonorm 7.3, with datasets recorded from 2000 to 2009 (the most updated ones at the time of the research) from the weather station closest to each case study:

for Mulhouse, the Bale/Mulhouse station (WMO id 72990);

for Paris, the Paris-Montsouris station (WMO id 71560);

for Bordeaux, the Bordeaux station (WMO id 75100);

for Geneva, the Geneve/Cointrin station (WMO id 67000).[5]

3. Fieldwork and Monitoring

The objective of the fieldwork was to understand how the spaces perform in reality. It consisted of on-site measurements of temperature and humidity and short interviews and surveys with the buildings' inhabitants, some of whom have been there over a decade.

For the monitoring, data loggers (Testo 174H) were used to record temperature and humidity on a fifteen-minute interval. Data was recorded in at least three locations inside one residential unit per building and in one location in the immediate surroundings for outdoor temperature (3). These readings exposed dynamic temperature differences between the outdoors and the winter gardens as well as indoor set points for heating and interaction with the winter gardens (4–7). The sub-hourly datasets were used to calibrate subsequent computer models, reduce the uncertainty surrounding occupant behavior, and inform their respective analysis. Additional weather data regarding solar radiation and wind for the period was retrieved from a representative local weather station. The interviews were aimed at understanding envelope use and occupant satisfaction. They consisted of questions about how much and for what purpose occupants use the adaptive elements and questions about thermal perception, where occupants had to express their vote in the scale of thermal sensation of ASHRAE and thermal preference (8–10). It is important to point out that all the occupants use the envelope layers efficiently, either from intuition or following the recommendations from the architects for an optimal use, and none has installed heating in the winter garden.

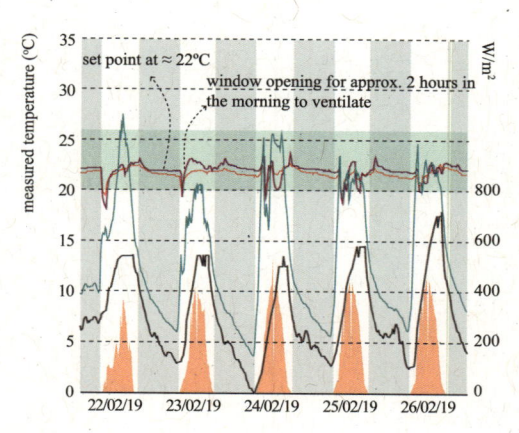

4) Temperature recording, Cité Manifeste

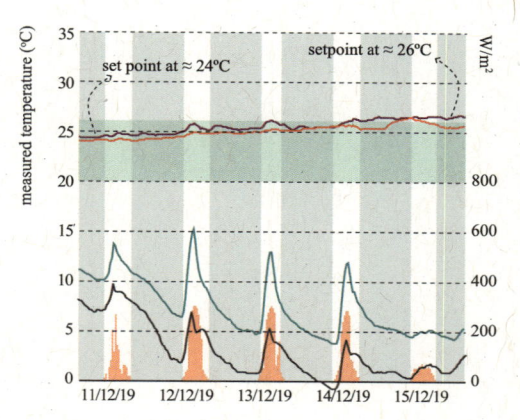

5) Temperature recording, Ourcq-Jaurès

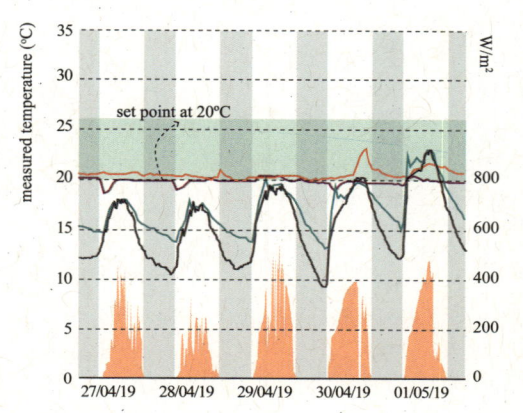

6) Temperature recording, Grand Parc

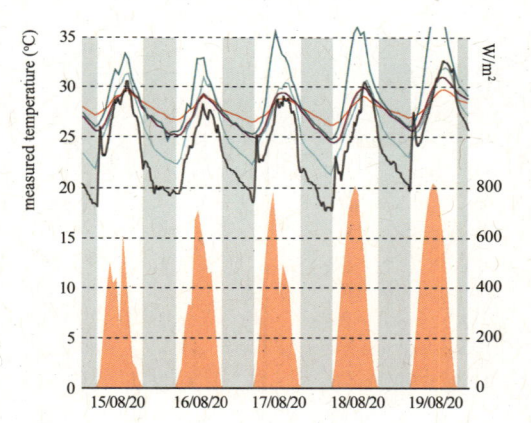

7) Temperature recording, Geneva tower

This points to the fact that everyone understands the space to be a buffer space and not an indoor one, which is fundamental to its effectiveness. One of the key points of the interviews was to understand when the users felt it was time to open the interior sliding doors, as there was no existing data or surveys covering that topic. The most common reply was: "As soon as the weather's nice."

The monitoring of Cité Manifeste, Ourcq-Jaurès, and Grand Parc was

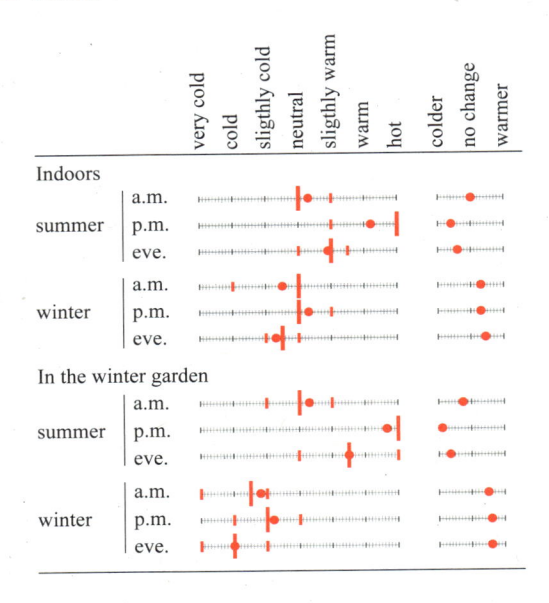

8) Thermal votes for Cité Manifeste (10 interviews)

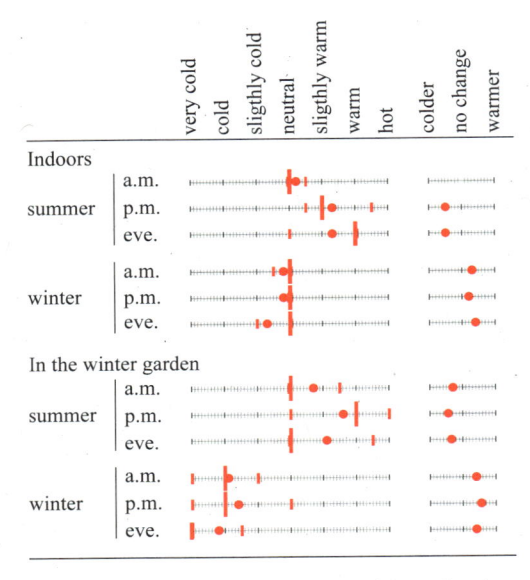

9) Thermal votes for Ourcq-Jaurès (10 interviews)

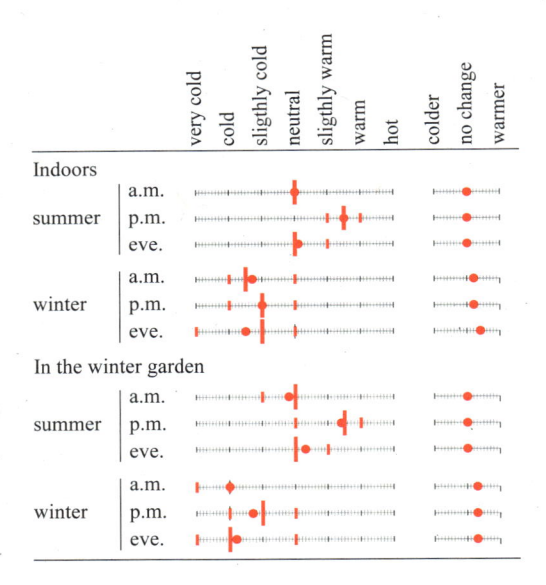

10) Thermal votes for Grand Parc (11 interviews)

conducted in winter and with the building in use, while the fieldwork in Geneva was conducted in summer and before occupants moved in.

In the case of Cité Manifeste (4), temperatures in the winter garden are 3–5°C warmer than outdoors during the night and 5–13°C warmer during the day when the sun is shining. Winter garden temperature generally peaks in the range of 21°C, when the top window is set to open automatically, while the roof shading was always deployed. Indoors, the occupant mentioned setting the heating thermostat to 22°C, which can be seen throughout the day and night, and ventilating for around an hour every morning. When the occupant did so, the temperature dropped as low as 19°C. In general, all occupants use the elements to protect from either the sun, heat, or cold. The inhabitants' awareness of the benefits of the thermal mass was remarkable, and some even mentioned how nice it was to be barefoot on winter afternoons because of the heat released by the concrete. In winter, temperatures in the house seem to be mild and in the winter garden rather cold. What the inhabitants expressed confirms the variations, atmospheres, and climatic changes highlighted in the study (both in the winter garden and indoors).

The Ourcq-Jaurès student and social housing (5), which was also monitored in winter, has central heating, and the residents don't seem to know that they can regulate it. The set point was around 24.5°C for the first few days, then increased to 26°C when the outside temperature dropped below zero, and decreased to 25°C when the temperature rose back to 8–10°C.

The lack of control by the occupants resulted in higher heating consumption and a lower use of the regulating elements, since the occupants themselves had to be less active. This is particularly true for the thermal curtains, which are used by only 33% of the residents. The buffering effect of the winter garden is obvious, as it is always 2–8°C above the outside temperature. On sunny days, the temperature rises quickly, reaching differences of 6–8°C. This is particularly effective on very cold sunny days.

The effect of inertia becomes apparent in the measurements from December 15: after three sunny days and one cloudy day, the temperature difference is still 4°C. On the second cloudy day, the difference is reduced to 2°C. On cloudy days, the winter garden is still a buffer space. The thermal sensation described by the users shows consistent comfort results indoors. The only issue mentioned by the occupants is that the bedrooms are too hot during the summer afternoons/evenings, as the low summer sun directly hits the glazed surfaces, which lack sun protection from the northwest.

In the case of Grand Parc (6), the temperature of the winter garden is very close to the outside temperature during the day because the occupant has left it open. At night, however, the difference with the outside temperature is 3 to 4°C, mainly due to the inertia of the concrete, which releases heat at night that is absorbed during the day. Indoor temperatures are very stable, around 20°C.

The heating in the living room was set to 20°C, which was particularly noticeable in the first three days. If the winter garden had been closed, the buffer effect would have been sufficient to maintain the same temperatures passively. The residents stated that they were very satisfied with the thermal

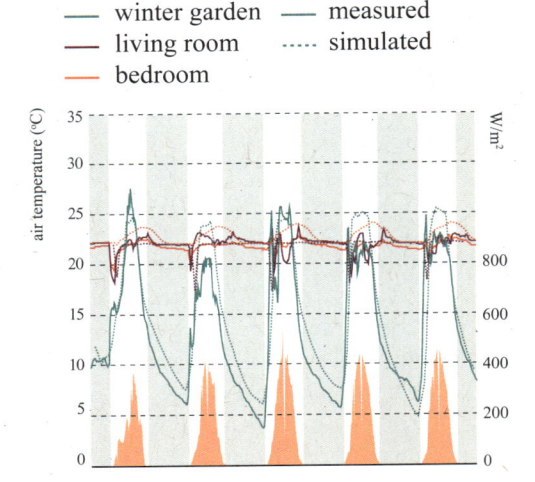

11) Calibration results for Cité Manifeste

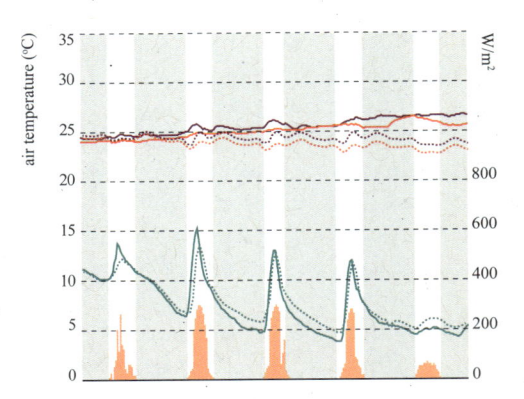

12) Calibration results for Ourcq-Jaurès

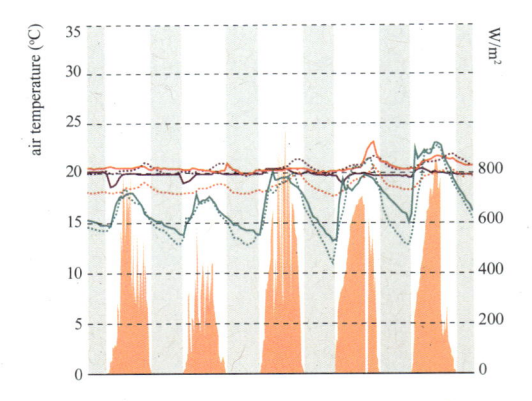

13) Calibration results for Grand Parc

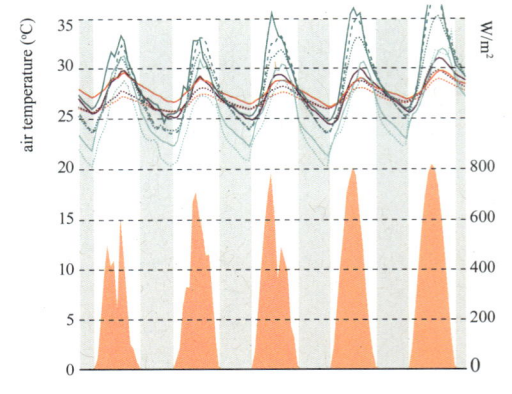

14) Calibration results for the Geneva tower

performance of the unit, the temperatures both indoors and in the winter garden. In summer, the satisfaction is remarkable, as there were no complaints about the heat, and no one indicated a preference for cooler temperatures in any of the rooms, even though this climate has the warmest summer of all the case studies. This is mainly due to the high thermal inertia of the structure. Even though people find the space a little cold in winter, they hardly expressed a preference for warmer conditions.

At the time of this research, the office and residential tower in Geneva (7) was completed but not yet occupied, so there was no feedback from the occupants, nor were there any users operating the envelope elements. All intermediate openings and the north winter garden were left closed, while the south winter garden was left about 35 cm open. Solar curtains were mostly open. This explains the high temperatures measured in all rooms and in the winter garden, all of which had very limited ventilation. Temperatures in the north winter garden are similar to those outside, while they are 2–6°C higher in the south winter garden.

4. Calibration Process

The process of calibration refers to the adjustment of a building's real properties in a simulation model to increase the model's accuracy. The aim is to mimic the real measured temperature by fine-tuning the envelope and material properties in the computational model so the simulation results approximate reality as much as possible.

After setting up the initial thermal model, each case study was simulated under the specific weather data collected during the fieldwork. A site- and period-specific weather file was created using the software Elements, with measured humidity and outdoor temperature along with wind (direction and velocity) and solar radiation data retrieved from a local weather station (Wunderground, https://www.wunderground.com/, or Solcast, https://solcast.com). Elements derives the remaining variables required for simulation and ensures consistency across them, and approximates the breakdown of direct or diffuse solar radiation. Heating set points and operable elements were also adjusted to match those of reality. Resulting indoor temperatures were compared with site measurements hour by hour and the input parameters adjusted accordingly until the temperature matched (11–14).

In this research, it was important to adjust the thermal inertia and air changes of the winter garden. As it has little internal gains and a highly variable temperature (compared to indoors), it is particularly relevant to calibrate these

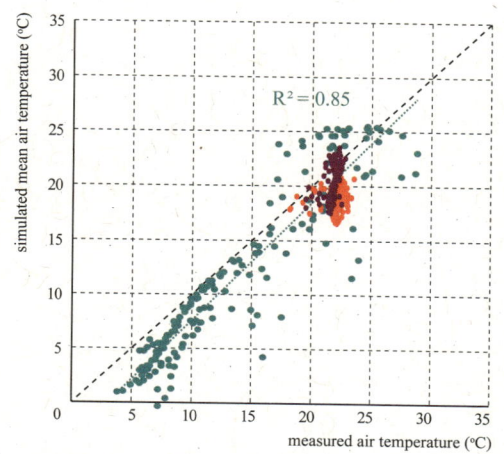

15) Correlation between simulated and measured air temperature for Cité Manifeste

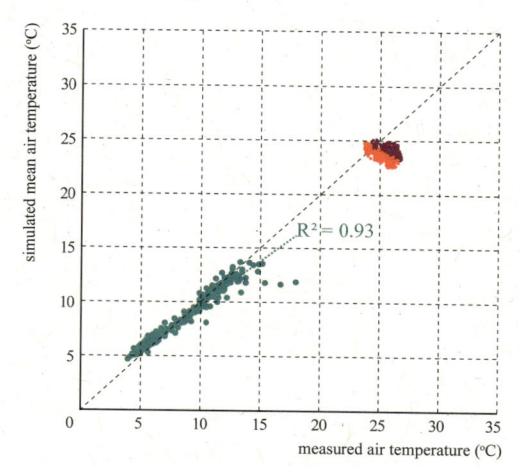

16) Correlation between simulated and measured air temperature for Ourcq-Jaurès

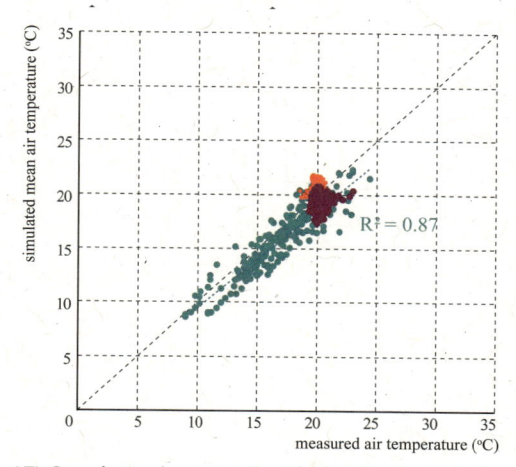

17) Correlation between simulated and measured air temperature for Grand Parc

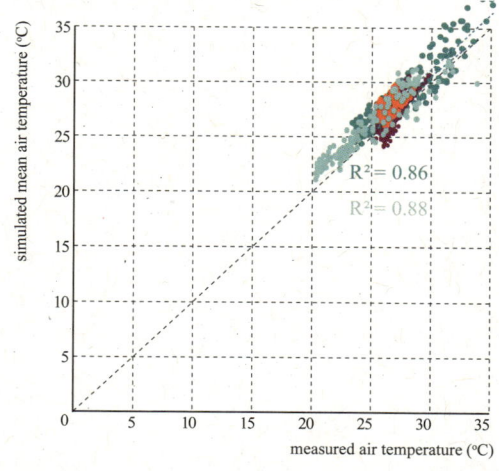

18) Correlation between simulated and measured air temperature for the Geneva tower

spaces. In turn, indoor temperatures normally vary within a closer range and are sometimes biased by number of occupants, cooking, or other activities. The average temperature difference between the measured indoor curves and the simulated ones is 1°C, whereas the largest difference is around 3°C. The winter garden temperatures match closely since they depend on envelope and material properties, whereas cooking or number of people present influence the indoor temperature. Regression analyses (15–18) indicate that the models are calibrated to be closely correlated to reality. R^2 range 0.85–0.93, which could be translated into models that are 85–93% accurate.

In Cité Manifeste (15), the R^2 of the winter garden is 0.85. Indoor temperatures are driven by the heating set point, though it can be observed that the stability of the temperature is similar (barely unaffected by solar gains in both cases), and when opening and closing the windows, the temperature of the house picks up at a similar speed. The specific location of the data logger and thermal results (always on the centroid of the zone) also explain the slight differences.

Ourcq-Jaurès (12) was calibrated for an intermediate heating set point of 23.5°C, as it can be seen at the beginning and the end of the selected period. The set point was not increased with the outside temperature as in reality. However, the difference between the rooms is accurate, as are the internal variations due to the sun or appliances. For the winter garden, the regression curve is 0.93 (16), which is the highest accuracy obtained: the average temperature difference is <0.5°C. The peak value on the eighth day is not matched in the simulation, which is probably due to the different weather conditions on-site and the location where the climate data was retrieved (e.g., localized clouds).

In Grand Parc (13), temperatures have a close match and a similar variation, especially the living room. The regression plot of the winter garden temperature is 0.87 (17), which also indicates a close correlation. The largest differences occur when the sun reaches the data logger and there are small high peaks.

For the Geneva tower (14), the interior calibration was focused on the last days of measurement, as the heat inertia contained in the building was more difficult to estimate during the first ones. The calibration shows both the curve of simulated air and the operative temperature. The relation of measured to simulated temperatures is closer to the operative results, as some solar rays coming through the curtains paired with the radiation from the glass slightly affected the data-logger readings. Regression analysis shows a high correlation between measured and simulated, with R^2 values at 0.86 and 0.88 (15–18).

5. Analytic Tools

State-of-the-art technology was used to mimic real building performance to the best extent possible, with reasonable skill, care, and diligence. All the analyses have been conducted with the Ladybug Tools plug-ins for Grasshopper on Rhinoceros, namely Ladybug, Honeybee, and Butterfly.[6] Simulations of the different environmental variables were run on industry-standard validated engines. Climate files used were .epw from Meteonorm 7.3. Indoor solar simulations and daylight simulations were conducted using Radiance for ray tracing.[7] Simulations of natural airflow were conducted through Computational Fluid Dynamics using Butterfly and Open FOAM.[8] Thermodynamic simulations were carried out using the EnergyPlus engine because of its capacity to simulate most of the thermodynamic phenomena.[9]

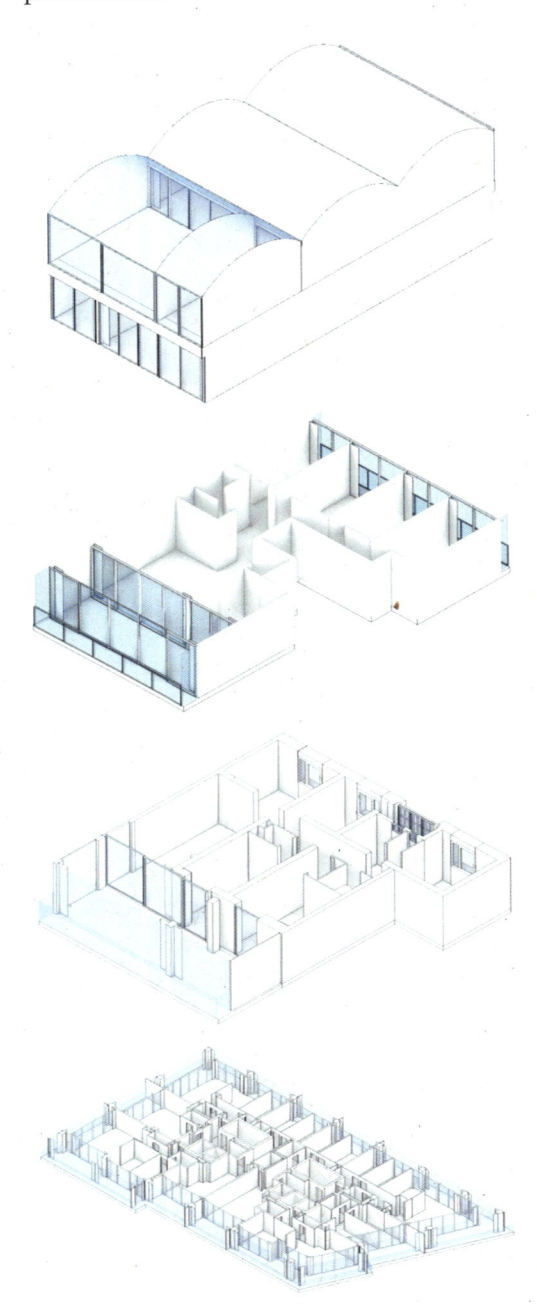

Solar simulations revealed the amount of sun each space receives at different times of the year and the potential for heat gain in winter. Airflow simulations revealed the potential for ventilation under typical wind conditions. Ray-tracing simulations were carried out to show the potential for daylight provision in each climate. Annual simulations were performed with dynamic thermal models evaluating each scheme under the same parameters to determine their performance. The parameters were defined according to built specifications, national regulations, and European standards.

The results are presented in comprehensible color scales, which become the tool for performance analysis. All color scales shown in this publication are "perceptually uniform," which means that the color difference between each step is uniform and the color variation in each drawing is accurate to the physical variable it represents.

6. Defining the Computer Models and Input Data

Three-dimensional models were reconstructed in Rhino based on the project drawings (19). The detailed version was used for solar, wind, and daylight analysis, whereas the thermal model requires a definition of thermal zones and some simplifications of geometric inputs. The same context was used in all studies for solar, daylight, and radiative obstruction purposes (20). All parameters mentioned in this section were applied to all case studies following the same principles and according to local regulations or European norms.

6.1. Daylight and Indoor Solar Simulations

All calculations of annual daylight levels (lux) or solar radiation levels (Wh/m^2) were carried out in Radiance via Honeybee, based on the daylight coefficient method. Material properties (reflectivity, transmissivity, specularity, and roughness) were estimated to match the ones found in the spectrophotometric database Lighting Materials.[10] In general, all walls are considered white with a reflectance of 0.81, ceilings are set as either polished gray concrete at 0.24 or white at 0.87 reflectance, floorings are polished concrete with a reflectance varying from 0.24 to 0.5, window frames are set as aluminum at 0.78, and context with a generic reflectance of 0.3. Glazing properties are specified for each case study, but generally visible light transmittance ranges from 0.6 to 0.8 for the intermediate openings and around 0.9 for the winter garden opening. For the solar simulations, the solar factor was used instead.

Solar simulations were calculated during key days (summer solstice, winter solstice, and spring and fall equinox) and during the winter period (December 21–March 21) to allow for comparison among the cases. The solar-access simulations show the location of the sun at different moments of the year and the hours of sunlight for those days. Solar-radiation simulations show the potential

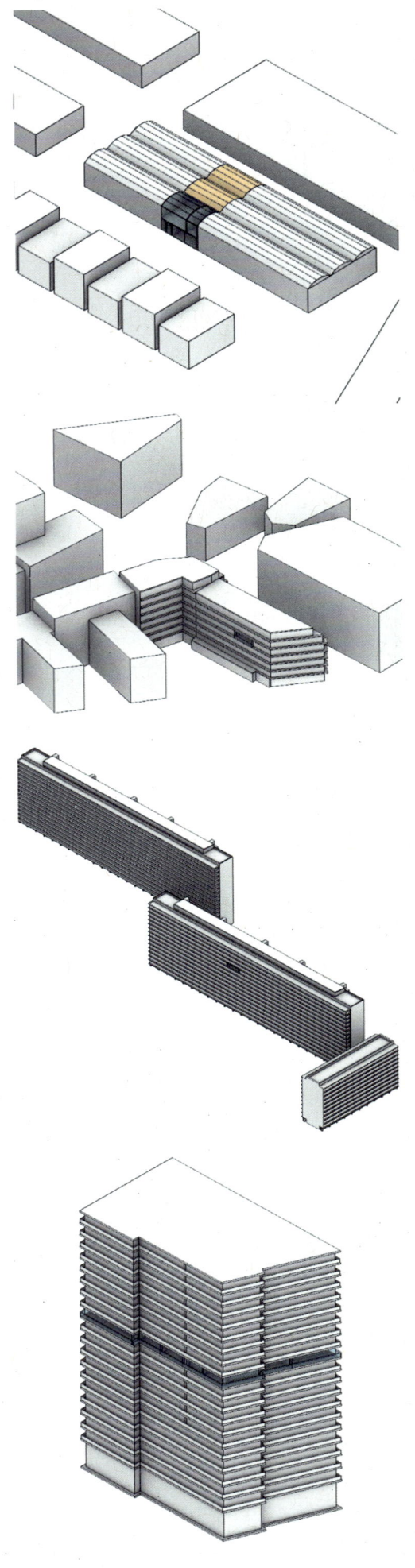

19) Detailed three-dimensional models

20) Three-dimensional model of surroundings and context

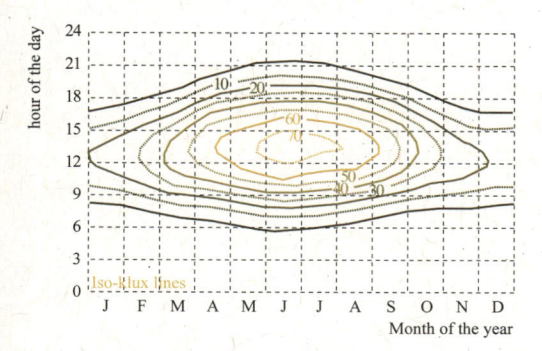

21) Daylight availability in Mulhouse

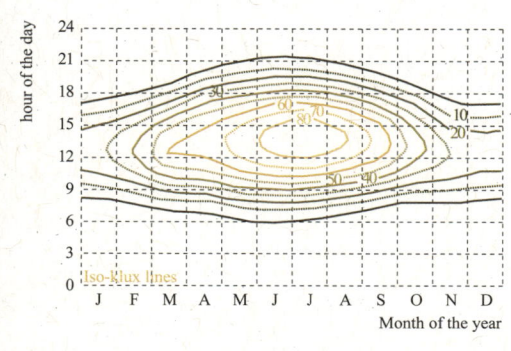

22) Daylight availability in Bordeaux

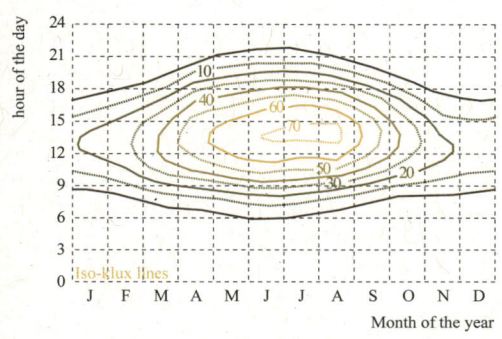

23) Daylight availability in Paris

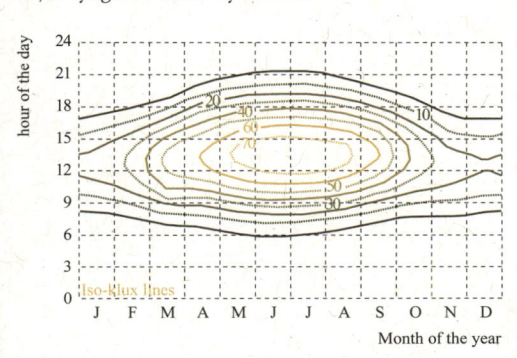

24) Daylight availability in Geneva

heat gain. Simulations were carried out without shading, sliding panels closed and thermal curtains fully open, though the stack back of the curtain was left opaque. They depict the apartment's maximum heat gain. If the user wishes less heat, the operable elements provide adaptive opportunities.

The simulations of daylight autonomy were carried out as specified in the EN 17037 climate-based method. The amount of light the sky has in each corresponds to the statistical data. The annual daylight availability of each climate is shown in figures 21–24. Simulation parameters were set to high complexity to capture illuminance entirely and ensure accurate spatial distribution. (Ambient bounce, 6; ambient division, 25,000; ambient sampling, 4,096; ambient resolution, 128; ambient accuracy, 0.1.)

6.2. Natural Airflow Simulations

Airflow simulations were carried out in OpenFOAM, which is the most rigorously validated open-source computational fluid dynamics (CFD) engine. The pressure-driven simulations conducted in the studies are based on steady-state solvers for incompressible flows. Predominant wind directions at each project location and their respective average velocities were derived from the local weather data. For each case, an initial outdoor simulation including the surrounding urban context and the facade was carried out to calculate the wind-pressure levels. Pressure-difference data between openings were entered into a subsequent indoor simulation to calculate the airflow through the unit. All sliding panels and doors were considered open, as the simulation intends to show the maximum airflow potential for each unit. All simulations were considered a steady state and based on the Reynolds-averaged Navier-Stokes equations to evaluate pressure-driven flows while including turbulence.[11] The computational domains were defined according to best practice guidelines—REHVA No. 10 and COST Action 732—to ensure a good quality of meshing and to limit calculation errors, and for the fluids to develop more naturally.[12]

6.3. Thermodynamic Simulations

All thermodynamic simulations (free-running mode and active mode) were carried out in EnergyPlus (9.1). The software works by enacting a mathematical model that provides an approximate representation of the building, broken down into smaller computational domains called thermal zones. The model is then subjected to dynamic heat-transfer mechanisms induced by the local climate, and the results of one time step become the initial conditions for the next one. It calculates surface temperatures, thermal comfort, and condensation based on the heat-balance-based solution of radiant and convective effects; accounts for air movement between zones; supports advanced fenestration models (including controllable window shades and layer-by-layer heat balances that calculate solar energy absorbed by windowpanes); features an internal programming language (EMS) to incorporate additional control algorithms; includes a ground heat transfer pre-processor; and calculates the transmission of solar energy through thermal zones. Results are as precise as the inputs provided for the model. For each case, the following parameters were considered:

Site Information:
Longitude and latitude, orientation of the building, context, and ground properties (for the case of Cité Manifeste, the only one in contact with the ground, the "ground heat transfer" was specifically modeled to consider accurate monthly average ground temperatures. These were precalculated via EnergyPlus slab preprocessor and set as boundary condition).

Geometry:
Building shape including envelope, openings, and room-by-room breakdown of thermal zones. A thermal zone corresponds to a volume of air in a building at a uniform temperature, as specified in the Energy Plus manual. All thermal zones are shown in figure 25.

Constructions:
A detailed layer-by-layer input of material thermal properties and thickness, according to construction details. Table 26 shows a summary of the main opaque elements. Glazed elements are shown in each case study.

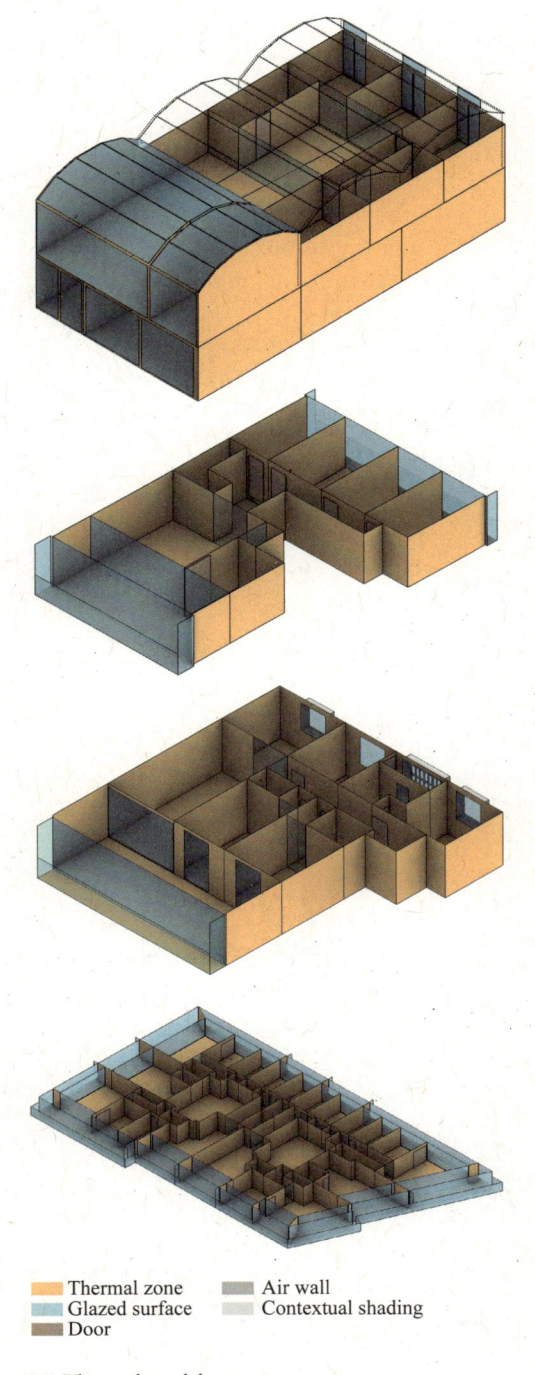

Thermal zone — Air wall
Glazed surface — Contextual shading
Door

25) Thermal models

Internal Gains:
Occupant density was determined according to the number of bedrooms per case. Lights and equipment loads were entered as specified in EN 15251 where possible.[13] At the time of this research, the new EN 16978, which holds the schedules, did not exist.[14] Instead, schedules from the national database of the US Department of Energy were introduced (27).[15] For appliances, peak load in the kitchen is 10 W/m², and in the living room 3.5 W/m²; bedrooms, halls, and toilets do not have appliances. For lighting, peak load in the kitchen is 5 W/m², and in all the other rooms 2.5 W/m² (except the halls that do not have lighting gains).

Occupants:
According to the number of bedrooms per case.

Fresh Air:
30 m³/(h·person) (EN 15251 – Cat I–II, EN 13779 – IDA 3).[13, 16]

Infiltration and Fresh Air Supply:
Infiltration was estimated according to French regulations by case (RT 2012).[17] If the resulting air renewal was sufficient to supply the demand of fresh air for the occupants, no more fresh air was introduced. If the demand was not met, additional fresh air was introduced to reach the desired target, with the same schedule as occupancy patterns. The air renewal of the winter gardens was estimated through calibration:

- indoor infiltration of new constructions (after 2012): 1.0 m³/h·m²

- indoor infiltration of constructions prior to 2012 and renovations (Grand Parc and Cité Manifeste): 1.7 m³/h·m²

- winter garden infiltration: calibrated according to real measurements (Cité Manifeste = 0.3–0.8 ach, Grand Parc = 3.6–5.1 ach, Ourcq-Jaurès = 6–8.2 ach, Geneva = 1–3.3 ach)

Ventilation:
The opening characteristics of each window are defined through its discharge coefficient and openable ratio. Discharge coefficients numerically represent the efficiency of an opening to allow airflow when open. It depends on the window type—projecting, sliding, or pivoting—and its geometry. Input discharge coefficients range from 0.4 for sliding windows to 0.75 for pivoting windows.

Envelope Control:
Window opening, shading, and thermal-curtain activation and winter garden operability are controlled through conditional statements. The elements of the envelope are operated according to fieldwork outcomes, logic patterns, optimal behavior, and user descriptions based on a set of conditions using indoor and winter garden temperatures, sunny or cloudy conditions, incident sun on windows, and night privacy. The resulting operability of the elements is as follows:

1. Thermal curtains are used to insulate during cold nights as well as for privacy and summer solar protection.

– Closed at night (9 pm–7:30 am) during the fall and winter and closed during the day in summer if t_{int} > 26°C and it's sunny (direct solar radiation > 250 W/m² was used as a basis, > 100 W/m² was used for Cité Manifeste, and > 150 W/m² for the Geneva tower, as those units were more exposed).

2. Sliding doors of the heated space: it is opened "as soon as the weather's nice."

– Open when t_{int} > 20°C and t_{wg} > 20.5°C, or t_{int} > 24°C.

3. Solar curtains are closed to avoid too much sun in the winter gardens during the summer and for privacy at night.

– Closed when it's sunny (direct radiation > 150W), during the summer, and at night throughout the year.

4. Sliding doors of the winter garden are open when it's hot.

– Open fully during summer months and when t_{wg} > 26°C and t_{ext} < t_{wg}.

5. Roof openings (Cité Manifeste only) are automatized, as in greenhouses.

– Open when t_{wg} > 21°C.

6. Roof shading (Cité Manifeste only).

– Closed during winter nights (9 pm–7:30 am) or when t_{wg} > 25.5°C during the day, and always closed during the summer and mid-season (April–October).

Note: The elements are operated both during the day and at night to avoid setting a time when occupants go to bed, and because it's not uncommon for people to wake up and open or close windows if the indoor temperature isn't comfortable.

Note 2: Even though EnergyPlus has one of the most detailed databases for input control, the four layers of the winter gardens did not fit within the standard inputs and had to be coded with advanced control algorithms and incorporated into the model via the Energy Management System (EMS).

HVAC (heating, ventilation, and air conditioning) set-point temperature:

– Heating was set at 20°C, corresponding to the lower bound of the comfort band (EN 15251) in winter and to the minimum measured set point while doing fieldwork. Even if French regulations recommend 19°C, common practice is to set the indoor temperature at 20°C.
– There was no cooling set point, as buildings do not have a cooling system and they are intended to work passively during the summer.
– Ventilation: Fresh air provision is met partially with infiltration of the envelope. When this is not sufficient, the extraction system of the humid rooms is activated. The air inlets are slits above the windows that allow in air based on moisture content. If more fresh air is required, simply opening the windows should suffice.

Note: When studying the environmental performance of the building, all the values related to heating correspond to space demand—the energy input required for a space to be maintained at the target temperature. HVAC properties are not defined—they would need to be factored in to calculate real energy consumption. This research project aims to verify the

U-Values (W/m²K)	CM	OJ	GP	GT
Internal slab	0.41	2.65	1.97	0.7
Ground slab	2.7/0.41	-	-	-
Opaque facade	0.33/0.37	-	0.24/1.78	0.2
Roof	0.19	-	-	-

26) U-values of opaque elements

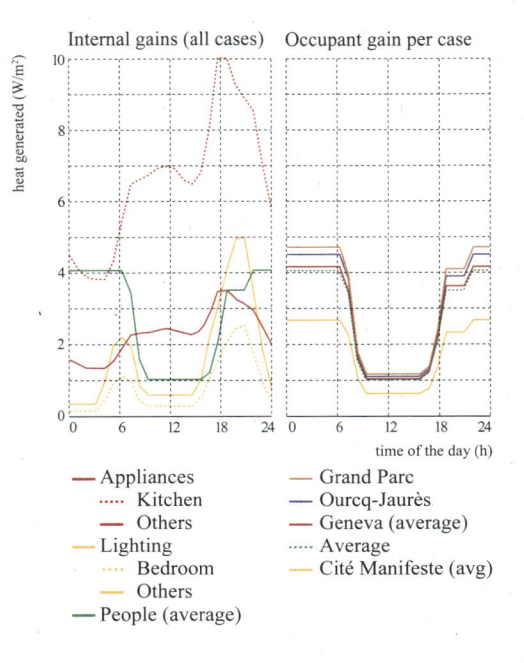

27) Internal heat gains

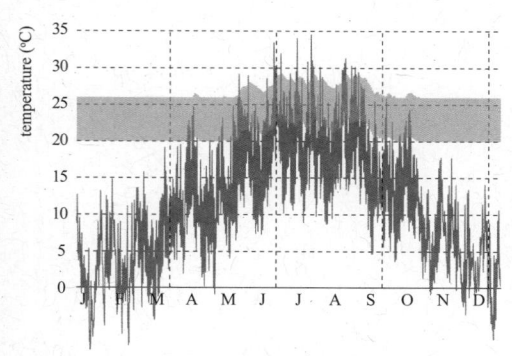

28) Indoor thermal comfort band based on outdoor temperature, for Mulhouse

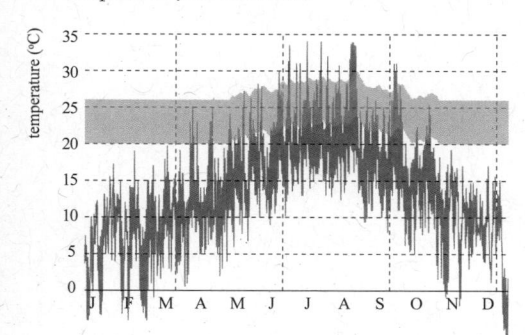

29) Indoor thermal comfort band based on outdoor temperature, for Paris

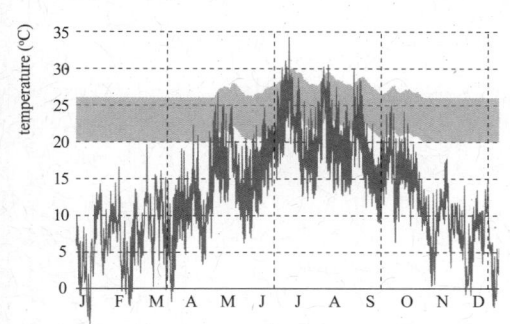

30) Indoor thermal comfort band based on outdoor temperature, for Bordeaux

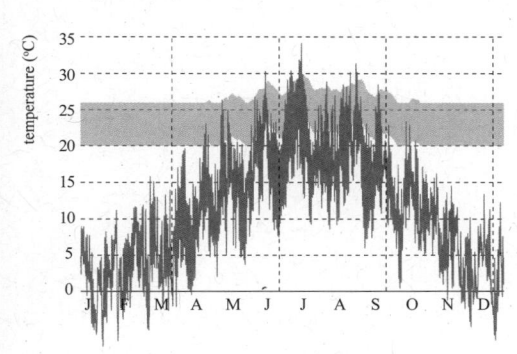

31) Indoor thermal comfort band based on outdoor temperature, for Geneva

performance of the architectural projects and the effect of their winter gardens in reducing spatial demand. Any spatial demand can be met with a varying range of HVAC systems with different efficiencies.

7. Outputs, Benchmarks, and Comparisons

To evaluate thermal and visual comfort, the European Norms guidelines were used, as they are the most up-to-date documents in the field and are applied in the climatic and cultural context of the case studies. More details about the norms can be found in the next chapter.

For visual comfort, lux levels at each point in space and time were evaluated with the criteria provided in EN 17037 for daylight provision.[18] Daylight autonomy is visualized as the percentage of time that a point in space receives 300 lux or more. Each space of the unit is then evaluated with the percentage of space exceeding 50% of time with DA [300] (target 50% according to EN 17037), and the percentage of space exceeding 50% of time with DA [100] (target 95% according to EN 17037).

Daylight availability in each climate is shown in figures 21–24. For calculating annual climate-based metrics, EN 17037 considers the 4,380 "most daylit hours" of the year to evaluate the daylight potential of the spaces to reach adequate illuminance levels. Summer hours are likely to be included more than winter ones. Note that Bordeaux has the brightest sky, especially during the summer, followed by Geneva. Paris and Mulhouse have the darkest skies.

Thermal performance was analyzed under free-running conditions (i.e., no mechanical control on indoor temperature, always shown first in the section "Free-Running Mode") as well as with thermostatic control to predict space-heating loads (shown in the "Heating Demand" section of each case study). The behavior of the buildings was tested for a full year with typical meteorological conditions. The output of thermal simulations in free-running mode is the hourly operative temperature in each thermal zone. Annual graphs are provided for each case, from which four typical weeks of each season are extracted. These typical weeks indicate daily variations through different climate conditions and daily cycles as they represent typical conditions during each season: they were selected so that average dry-bulb temperature and the breakdown of sunny and cloudy days correspond to those of each season. The regime of seasons was maintained (instead of using "hot period" and "cold period") to allow for comparison. Typical days are simulated independently, as they correspond to the average conditions of an entire month. For each hour of the day, temperature, direct and indirect solar radiation, and wind speed are averaged and introduced as an altered day inside the year .epw (format of the weather file). For extreme days, the hottest and coldest day of the .epw was selected in each case. To determine the probability of thermal comfort, the resulting hourly operative temperature of each space was evaluated against the comfort band determined in EN 15251 Category II (new buildings and renovations), and defined as:

– upper limit: $\Theta_{i\,max} = 0.33\,T_{RM} + 18.8 + 3$

– lower limit: $\Theta_{i\,min} = 0.33\,T_{RM} + 18.8 - 3$

T_{RM} makes reference to the Running Mean Temperature and the way the previous days are weighted on average. The comfort band of each climate is plotted together with outdoor temperature in figures 28–31. Note that the comfort bands span 20–26°C during the coldest half of the year and rise as a function of the outdoor temperature during the warmer half. For the studied climates, the peak of the comfort band reaches 29.5°C on the hottest summer days. Grand Parc in Bordeaux has the hottest summer, both on average and in the number of peaks, which explains why the comfort band is higher and more constant in that climate.

The results of the simulations in free-running mode show the percentage of time that each space has its temperature inside the comfort band, indicating how much time that space can function without the need of mechanical equipment. As for the time outside it, most happens below (cold hours) either at night, when the heating need is reduced as occupants are in bed, or during the day, which is offset by turning on the heating. Temperatures above the comfort band should be limited as much as possible to avoid creating the need for refrigeration equipment (which isn't required in these climates). Some hours are acceptable and by a small margin, as simple fans can be used, a soft solution that is significantly less energy intensive than refrigeration equipment. Tolerance above comfort is set as follows, based on the French regulation RE 2020 (which was partially published during this research):[19]

– Maximum percentage of overheating time: 3% of occupied hours.

– Degree hours above the threshold temperature: The ideal target is below 350°C·h (the room will not need mechanical cooling), though tolerance goes to 1250°C·h.

– At night (10 pm–7 am) it is considered above 26°C.

– During the day (7 am–10 pm) the adaptive comfort band EN 15251 is considered, but capped at 28°C.

All other outputs are extracted from the simulations with the ideal loads on (heating only). The heating set point of 20°C for air temperature throughout the day for all studies corresponds to the lower bound of the comfort band of EN 15251 and fits the lowest set point measured during fieldwork. An initial temperature graph of a typical winter week is provided, as heating operates based on air temperature. Calculations with other set points are provided to set anchor points toward regulations or other parameters regarding variation in the heating load:

Mulhouse

Bordeaux

Paris

Geneva

Universal Thermal Climate Index
— exterior temperature
Thermal stress

- >32°C, severe heat
- 28–32°C, moderate heat
- 26–28°C, slight heat
- 9–26°C, no stress
- 0–9°C, slight cold
- -13–0°C, moderate cold

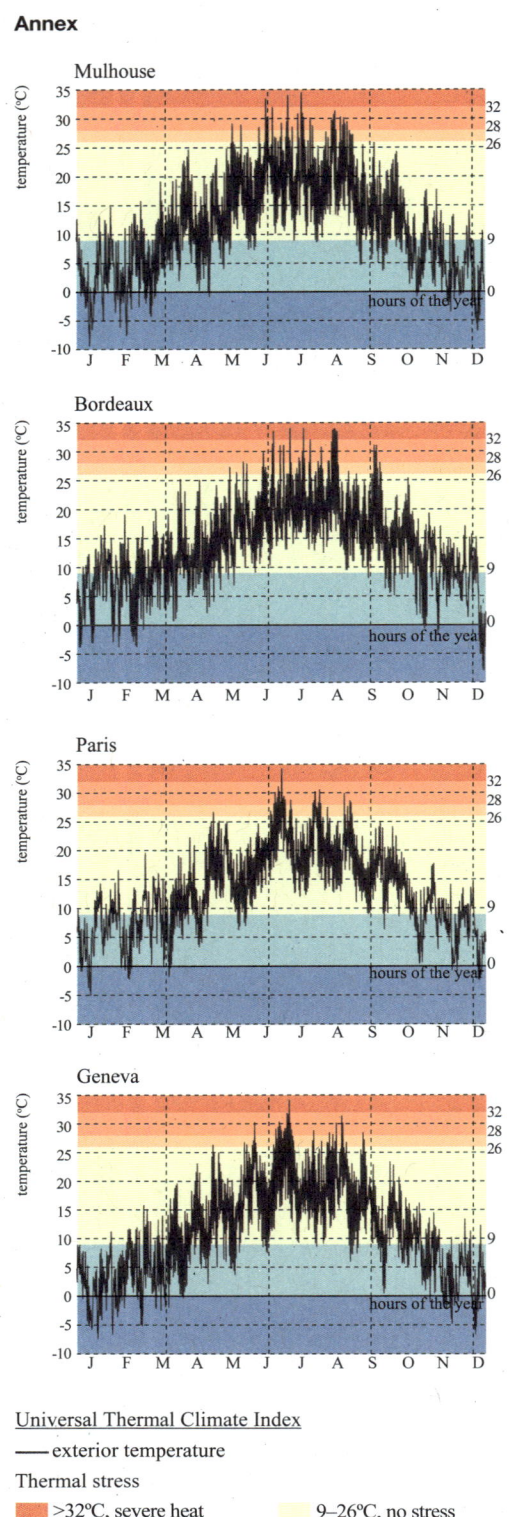

32) UTCI thermal stress bands and outdoor temperature per climate

19°C corresponds to the maximum set point allowed in France by regulations.

23°C corresponds to the target temperature in winter (center of the comfort band), according to EN 15251.

25°C corresponds to the highest measured set point during fieldwork.

When central heating is installed and regulation is done manually according to outdoor temperature, it is common practice (unfortunately) to have 25°C indoors (which was the case in Ourcq-Jaurès).

Other common factors that produce a variation in the heating load are the floor level and the number of people indoors. The floor is impacted by the surrounding context and therefore affects solar obstruction as well as sky radiative cooling at night (the more obstructed the environment, the less sky radiative cooling available). To perform the calculations, an average floor was selected. More occupants provide more internal heat gain but also require a higher amount of fresh air, which has a higher impact on the energy balance: more occupants therefore require more heating. For the general calculation, occupation was determined according to apartment size. The thermodynamic balance shows the breakdown of heat gain and heat loss of the entire apartment, including the winter garden, and its corresponding effect. Lastly, the heat-load duration curve is used to understand how much time a year equipment is used in its full potential, and allows us to question whether such large equipment is really needed.

Thermal conditions in the winter gardens are assessed with the Universal Thermal Climate Index (UTCI), a metric proposed by the International Society of Biometeorology and developed by the EU group COST Action 730 to evaluate thermal comfort conditions in outdoor environments.[20] It enables the calculation of a single "feels like" temperature accounting for air temperature, mean radiant temperature, air velocity, and humidity, and includes the variation of people's clothing under different weather conditions. The indicator, UTCI temperature, is compared with a reference scale from extreme to slight cold stress on the cold side, no thermal stress in the middle, and from moderate to extreme heat stress on the heat side (32).[21]

No specific benchmark is required in this index, as it only describes outdoor conditions. In this research, the objective is to compare the amount of thermal stress to determine how much nicer conditions in the winter garden are compared to outdoors. Two outdoor settings are provided for comparison: the resulting temperature in a sheltered condition (no sun and no wind, which reflects the climate data), and the resulting temperature in a fully exposed condition (with sun and wind).

All other infographics are based on the same criteria. Comparisons provide a benchmark to assess the performance of a project compared to previous states of the building, standard procedures, or improved specifications. In order to draw meaningful conclusions, all the parameters are equal to the base case, except when stated otherwise.

Note: Temperature variations are measured in kelvins, a unit defined by the international system that equates to a degree Celsius in relative terms. In absolute terms, 0°C equals 273.15 K. Although scientifically inaccurate, this publication measures temperature variations in degrees Celsius to facilitate understanding by a nontechnical audience.

7. About "Perceptually Uniform Colors"

Results are visualized using a set of color gradients which are "the interface between data and the brain." These were carefully defined to represent the environmental data accurately, as interpolations to create color gradients were done in a perceptually uniform color space (CAM02–UCS).[22] Perceptually uniform color spaces were designed to address the drawbacks of commonly used color spaces such as RGB or CMYK, to ensure that the variation in numerical data is represented accurately to our eyes; in other words, a variation in air movement of 0.5 m/s is perceived equally whether it happens in a still room with light shades of blue and results between 0.5 and 1 m/s, or a windy area with darker tones and results between 2.0 and 2.5 m/s.

IV. The Science behind the Definition of Thermal and Visual Comfort

There are many approaches to low energy housing today. The main objective in the European context (especially in the climates studied) is to reduce both the duration and the intensity of heating periods and to maintain acceptable temperatures in summer (without the need for cooling systems) and maximize daylighting (thus minimizing electric lighting). It is now widely assumed that "best practice" for a sustainable building is to minimize the exchange with the outside, to insulate and seal as much as possible, which has made highly insulated envelopes and triple-glazed windows almost the new normal. The resulting buildings rely primarily on efficient mechanical equipment to control temperature and provide fresh air, and any natural exchange with the outside climate is interpreted as a drawback. Another approach is "smart buildings" with automated envelopes, where the exchange with the outside climate is controlled by digital technology. However, these solutions are often nonintuitive, prone to malfunctioning, and take away control from the occupant: they have become a threat to the building's performance.

The approach proposed in the buildings by Lacaton & Vassal is to solve energy efficiency and thermal and visual comfort by the means of architecture through controlled interactions with the climate. The control over the building envelope is given back to the occupants, who regulate the interaction with the outdoor climate through the different layers of the double envelope: maximal exchange when it is pleasant, and gradually reducing the exchange as outdoor weather gets colder. The flexibility and ease of use of the envelope allow users to adapt their indoor spaces and control the relation with the climate to suit their needs passively (33). The research approach of this book is based on a very precise consideration of building physics, local climate variables, physiological responses, adaptive opportunities, and state-of-the art targets. Daylight and temperature can be predicted with a high degree of accuracy and thermal and visual comfort can be quantified. Achieving an adequate passive performance (requiring a minimum heating load, minimum electric light, and no cooling) that is solved by the means of architecture depends on the careful manipulation of these variables, as every aspect of the building design influences environmental performance. The work of this research builds on academic knowledge and best practice methodologies to inspect thoroughly the relation of architecture with climate and the role of its inhabitants. The following pages present a brief explanation of the scientific basis of the building physics as well as the targets employed through this research and their origins. The latter are all based on state-of-the-art European Norms.

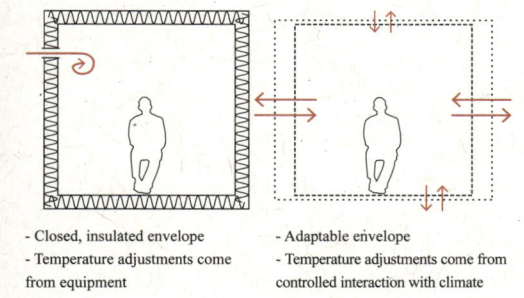

- Closed, insulated envelope
- Temperature adjustments come from equipment

- Adaptable envelope
- Temperature adjustments come from controlled interaction with climate

33) Strategies to adjust temperature inside a space

1. Visual Comfort: Measuring Daylight

Humans are highly sensitive to daylight, as they have evolved in outdoor environments. Exposure to light regulates circadian rhythms, which is the internal clock that synchronizes physiological functions and keeps the body's hormones and bodily processes on a roughly 24-hour cycle, even in continuous darkness. Light is the most important cue to align our daily routines to the solar day (WELL Standard),[23] having an influence on sleep patterns, brain activity, metabolism, hormonal production, and behavior. The clearest example is the sleep-wake cycle, which is controlled by the melatonin hormone (34). High melatonin levels make us feel drowsy and contribute to a restorative sleep.[25] Light triggers its suppression in the body, which causes humans to feel awake. Daylight has also been largely

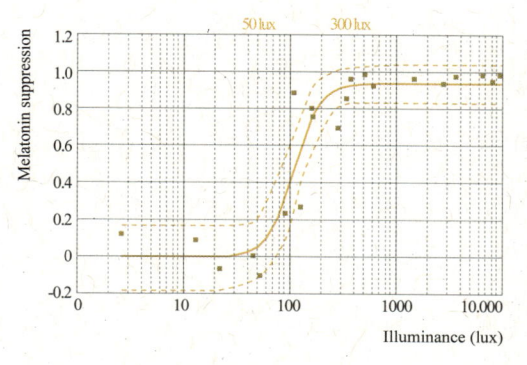

34) Light needed to trigger circadian responses, after Zeitzer et al.[24]

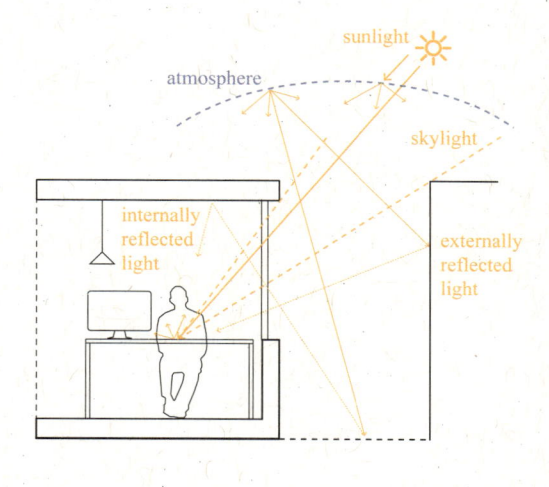

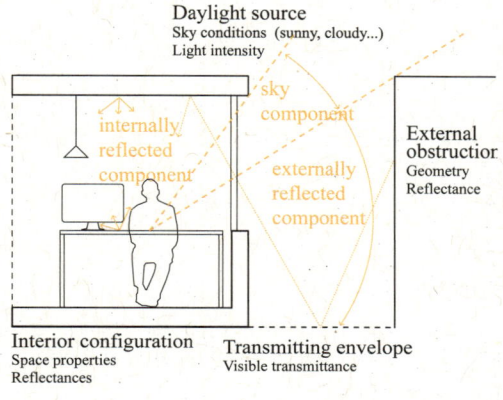

35) Components and parameters of daylight in buildings

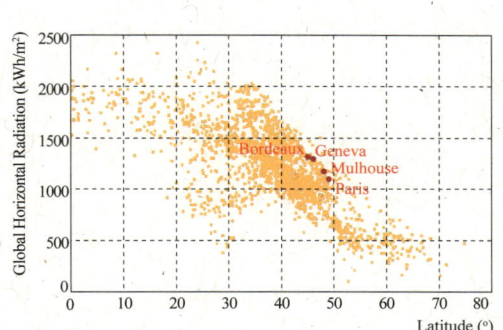

36) Annual solar radiation values for 2,000 locations worldwide, after Reinhart 2014[27]

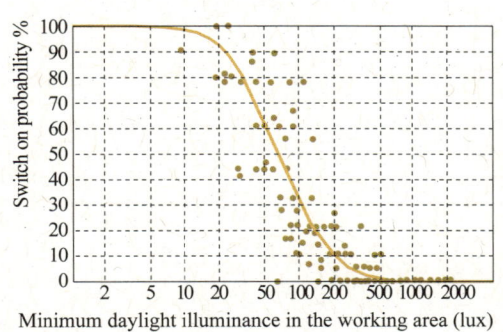

37) Probability of someone turning artificial lighting on in a daylit space, after Hunt[33]

linked to well-being, a healthier life, a better mood, and more productivity. Direct sunlight has been linked to health since the times of the ancient Greeks, and particularly picked up on modern architecture as a means to create healthier environments, as one of the ways to cure tuberculosis.

Note: Light comes directly from the sun, which is referred to as sunlight, or is diffused by the atmosphere. In technical language, the term daylight refers only to the diffused light coming from the sky hemisphere.[26]

The building scientist C. Reinhart defines a daylit space as primarily lit by natural light, which combines overall user satisfaction regarding their thermal and visual comfort with low energy use.[27] Daylight provision of a space depends first on the availability of daylight outside: diffuse horizontal illuminance and global horizontal illuminance, which in its turn depend on the project's latitude on earth and local sky conditions (the average total solar radiation reaching the top of the atmosphere being constant at 1367 W/m^2); external surroundings creating obstructions and their corresponding reflectances; space properties, such as room configuration, depth, opening size and height, internal partitions, external overhangs or balconies; transmissivity of the openings, such as materiality and visible light transmittance; and internal reflections (indoor surfaces, fixed objects) that depend on color, texture, and materiality (EN 17037) (35).

When measuring daylight in a building, two aspects can be considered: one is the daylight performance, which can be referred to as "the maximum displacement of artificial lighting for the minimum of unwanted thermal effects—eg. heat loss, solar gain";[28] and the other one is visual comfort, which was recently defined by the European Norms with specific targets. They consider that visual comfort is linked not only to the amount of daylight received but also to the connection with the exterior, in terms of views and sunlight exposure (EN 17037).

1.1. How to Measure Daylight: Daylight Factor vs. Climate-Based Daylight Modeling

One of the first metrics developed to study daylight in buildings was the Daylight Factor,[29] and even today it still stands as the most common metric used. It corresponds to the percentage of outdoor light that reaches a given point indoors. It was developed for the climate of the UK, as it considers an overcast sky and uniform conditions. However, daylight availability varies significantly with latitude and location (21–24), and sun reflections can play a major role in increasing light inside a space.

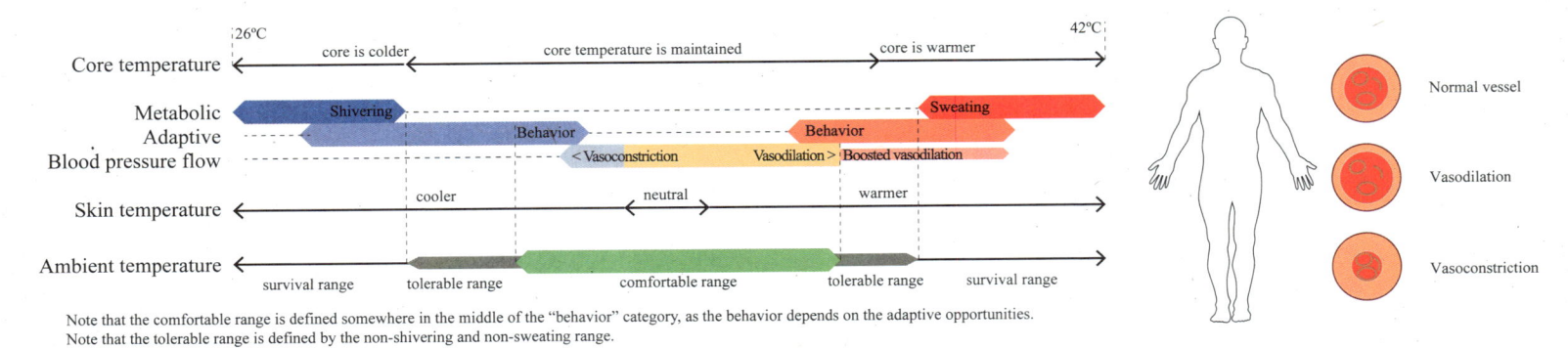

38) Body mechanisms to regulate temperature

Climate-based daylight modeling allows simulating light conditions according to the local climate, accounting for variations over time such as cloud coverage and solar incidence.[30] Figure 36 shows the annual solar radiation values for 2,000 locations worldwide. Note that the locations of the projects are particularly sunny for their latitude and have a greater daylight availability than other cities of the world at the same latitude. This type of simulation allows to predict illuminance inside a space, a unit that is easily measured physically (lux) and can therefore be linked to studies of other fields (perception, physiology, triggering of switch-on light, etc.). In this research, the method of climate-based daylight modeling was employed to simulate daylight.

1.2. A Definition of Visual Comfort: EN 17037

EN 17037 is the European Norm that refers to daylight in buildings. It has been the reference used to quantify the quality of light across this research. It specifies "elements for achieving, by means of natural light, an adequate subjective impression of lightness indoors, and for providing an adequate view out. In addition, recommendations for the duration of sunshine exposure within occupied rooms are given."

Regarding daylight provision, the norm states: "A space is considered to provide adequate daylight if a target illuminance level is achieved across a fraction of the reference plane within a space for at least half of the daylight hours."

As for the target illuminance level, a "well-daylit space" may be perceived as subjective. However, several field studies have proven that the limits are still quantifiable. The norm considers the target of 300 lux as the minimum level. The choice of this value corresponds to what was evaluated as a "well-daylit space" for most of building users,[27] as an optimal light level for working,[31, 32] and also to a very low probability of "switch-on" electric lighting (37).[33] Finally, looking at the light needed to trigger circadian responses,[24] 300 lux corresponds to almost the maximum level of melatonin suppression (34).

This target of 300 lux is also used in the US.[27, 34]

As for the "fraction of the reference plane within the space," the norm identifies three categories based on the median daylight levels of the space:

– Minimum
  [50% of area above 300 lux] and
  [95% of area above 100 lux]

– Medium
  [50% of area above 500 lux] and
  [95% of area above 300 lux]

– High
  [50% of area above 750 lux] and
  [95% of area above 500 lux]

Half of the daylight hours is considered as the analysis period. The norm defines it as the 4,380 hours of the year with more outdoor daylight.

Regarding sunlight exposure, the norm states that in dwellings, at least one habitable space should be provided with a minimum sunlight exposure. This translates into a minimum number of hours that one space receives direct sun across one day. That day should be selected between February 1 and March 21. Three categories are again identified depending on the number of hours:

– Minimum: 1.5 h
– Medium: 3.0 h
– High: 4.0 h

Throughout this research, daylight has been evaluated with daylight autonomy, and a target of 300 lux, following the norm. Each case study also has a reference to the amount of sun hours the units receive, in line with the recommendations of EN 17037.

2. Thermal Comfort: Measuring Felt Temperature

2.1. Physiology of the Human Body

The temperature of the human body at the core is around 37°C, which needs to be maintained within close limits for survival, whereas skin temperature normally ranges from 31 to 34°C.[35] As explained by Simos Yannas, founder and director of the MSc/MArch Sustainable Environmental Design (AA SED) at the Architectural Association since 1980, our body "has its own mechanism for heat production. The heat generated by metabolic activity greatly exceeds that required to maintain deep body temperature at its normal level […]; the principal physiological requirement for thermal comfort is to discharge the excess heat. In order to do this, however, we require surroundings that will allow us to keep cooling without stress: the body's cooling processes are suppressed under very hot or humid conditions and exaggerated when we are too cool, dry or draughty. Between such extremes is a range of conditions perceived as comfortable or unstressful."[36]

When the core temperature starts to deviate from its thermal neutrality, the body produces internal physiological reactions to regulate the temperature, that are more or less perceptible, and that increase with the severity of the heat or the cold (38). The first line of defense, which is imperceptible, is a change in the blood-pressure flow, meaning that when the body temperature starts to drop, vasoconstriction begins, followed by a reduction of blood circulation to the extremities of the body. This helps to keep the valuable heat at the core and maintain its temperature. If the body temperature drops further, some body tissues increase the burning of brown fats (non-shivering thermogenesis), which creates more heat inside. After this, if the core temperature still drops, muscles increase their activity (shivering thermogenesis), and the body shivers.[37] On the side of heat, when body temperature starts to rise vasodilation begins, which boosts blood circulation to the extremities of the body. This reaction increases the skin temperature, which

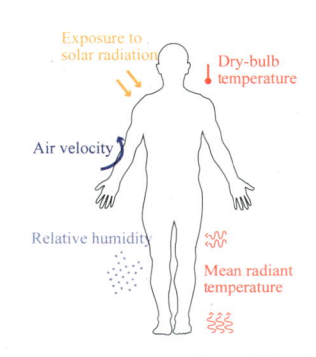

39) Environmental variables affecting thermal comfort

further increases the heat-loss rate of the body. If the core temperature still rises, the body sweats to increase heat loss, as water in the skin is evaporated. The range between shivering and sweating is the tolerable range of the body. When the core temperature reaches 42°C, the body experiences a heat stroke, and when it reaches 35°C, the body starts to suffer from hypothermia, though the survival range can extend to 25°C.

Thermal stress is therefore a "warning that environmental conditions are not conducive to long-term survival." However, as explained in a physiological study, in between the imperceptible change in the blood-pressure flow and the metabolic reactions of shivering and sweating, people recruit a wide range of behavioral adaptations to avoid the thermal stress, from changing clothing, moving, performing activities, opening the window, or drinking water.[38] Both the physiological responses (autonomic) and behavioral adaptations are called thermoeffectors, and the order of recruitment depends on the relative physiological cost. Thermal comfort (or lack of thermal stress) is a fundamental requirement for the body and is linked to avoiding those physiological responses. As expressed by ASHRAE, "Thermal comfort is the condition of mind that expresses satisfaction with the thermal environment and is assessed by subjective evaluation."[39] It can also be defined as "the range of ambient temperatures, associated with specified mean radiant temperature, humidity, and air movement, within which a human in specified clothing expresses indifference to the thermal environment for an indefinite period."

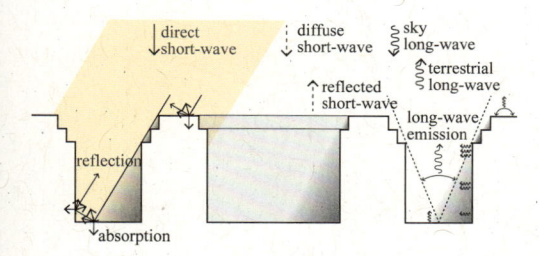

40) Radiative exchanges in an urban environment, after Erell et al.[40]

2.2. Parameters Affecting the Felt Temperature of the Body

The temperature that the body actually perceives (felt temperature) is affected by different environmental variables (39). In an indoor environment, the variables that intervene are air temperature (dry-bulb temperature), the temperature of surrounding surfaces (radiant temperature), air movement, and humidity. According to Yannas, "Air temperature and air movement affect the rate of heat dissipation by convection from the human body. Surface temperatures affect thermal exchanges by radiation and conduction. Humidity affects the rate of evaporation. Solar radiation affects both the surface and air temperature of a space. Direct exposure to solar radiation, either indoors or out, causes a sensation of warmth: the radiation absorbed by clothing or skin is converted to heat and perceived as a higher temperature."[36] In an outdoor environment, more environmental variables intervene, such as the reflected shortwave radiation from the sun by surrounding surfaces, and long-wave radiation (infrared) to and from the sky (40).

The clothing level and metabolic rate (depending on activity) will also impact the felt temperature, but that depends on each individual variation. These are not considered in this research, as the focus remains on architecture and how buildings impact thermal comfort. A thermally comfortable environment is therefore different indoors and outdoors, which entails different calculation methods and different ways of defining thermal comfort.

2.3. Perceived Temperature in an Indoor Space

In order to determine the perceived temperature in an indoor environment, some approximations can be done:

– The effect of the sun is only considered through the effect it has on air and surfaces, as the impact on the body changes according to the particular location of the person (41).

– Air movement generally barely affects the felt temperature indoors (especially if the windows are closed) and is also accounted for through the air changes of the room as the impact on the body also depends on location. The effect of air movement when indoor air speed is at or below 0.1 m/s (normal air speed indoors, with windows closed) is negligible (42).[39, 41, 42]

– The effect of humidity is minimal indoors (in the European context) and can be disregarded to calculate the felt temperature.[42]

– Even if the body heat exchange mechanism varies according to temperature, in an indoor environment, the range is much narrower than outdoors, and these factors can be disregarded (43).

As a consequence, the felt temperature inside a space can be approximated through the combined effect of air and radiant temperature. Air temperature is affected by natural ventilation and infiltration, internal heat gains, and air heat gain or loss by convection from enclosed surfaces. Radiant temperature is in turn influenced by solar gains, internal heat gains, long-wave radiation between internal surfaces, long-wave radiation from external surfaces to the sky/surrounding buildings, surface heat gain/loss by conduction to the outside or to adjacent rooms, surface heat gain/loss by convection, and heat exchanged with the air. "For occupants engaged in near sedentary physical activity (with metabolic rates between 1.0 and 1.3 met), not in direct sunlight, and not exposed to air velocities greater than 0.20 m/s (40 fpm), it is acceptable to approximate the relationship [between air and radiant temperature] with acceptable accuracy by [their average]." The resulting temperature is called the operative temperature.[39, 41, 42]

2.4. Controlling the Operative Temperature of a Space

The operative temperature of a space depends on the specific microclimate of the context (44), envelope interactions (solar gains, infiltration, exchange by conduction, fresh air provision), internal gains (lights, equipment, and occupants),

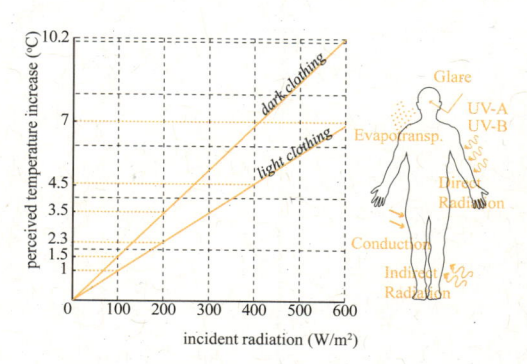

41) Warming effect of solar radiation, after CIBSE Guide A (2015)[41]

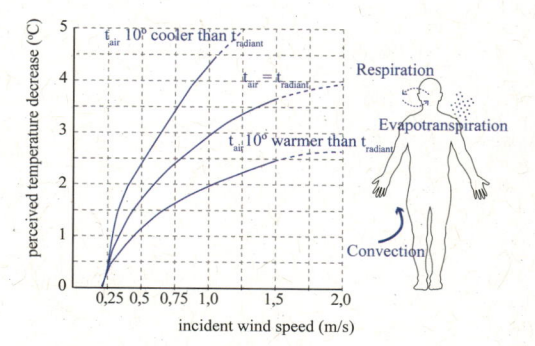

42) Wind chill effect, after ISO 7730[43]

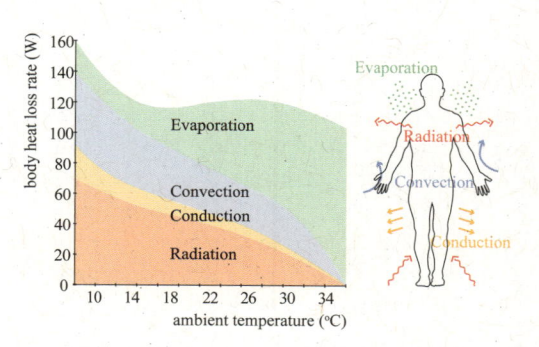

43) Body heat exchange type according to temperature, after Yannas 1994[36]

and the amount of thermal inertia (45). According to Yannas,[36] if a building did not have heat gains, its temperature would closely follow that of outside, with slightly more stability depending on the amount of thermal inertia of its components. With outdoor temperatures most of the time below the comfortable or unstressful range, in principle additional heat sources are needed to heat up spaces. These heat sources come from:

- solar radiation admitted through the transparent parts of the envelope and retained within the building fabric (passive solar heating);

- occupant activity, equipment, lights, referred to as internal gains;

- heating appliances.

All of these sources raise air and surface temperatures of any given interior space. "The effect of any source heat inside a building is to raise the temperature of room surfaces and air above that outdoors. A difference is then established between inside and outside temperatures. This drives a process of heat flow away from the building, a heat loss. [...] Heat is also stored within the building structure and released after a period of time, often several hours."[36]

Most heat loss depends on the properties of the building fabric and not on indoor conditions, except for fresh air provision. The human body requires oxygen to breath and releases CO_2, which is why air renewal is necessary. Also, indoor air can be up to five times more polluted than outside,[44] as indoor activities and building materials release volatile organic compounds (VOCs), which need to be evacuated. The industry standard is that each person requires some 25 to 36 m³/h of fresh air to evacuate breath-related CO_2 levels, and in most programs this air rate is enough to evacuate VOCs from other pollutants to acceptable levels.[13] Throughout this research, a widely accepted intermediate value of 30 m³/h person was considered.[13]

In a residential context, fresh air provision can be partially met with infiltration through the envelope. Alternatively, simple systems of moisture regulation through openings can complete the provision, sometimes coupled with air extraction through humid rooms (simple flux systems). If more fresh air is required, simply opening the windows should suffice. This fresh air can introduce more heat loss, which can slightly increase the heating load. "Controlling a building's heat loss rate and matching it, where possible, with heat gains from the sun, occupancy, and other ambient sources, are the main architectural and constructional strategies for displacing conventional heating, thus saving energy as well as reducing emissions of greenhouse gases."[36]

For the warm periods of the year, the objective is to minimize heat gains (mainly solar radiation) and lose sufficient heat to avoid raising too much indoor temperatures. This can be achieved by increasing the air exchanges with outdoors through openings. When temperatures are even higher, natural ventilation can increase physiological cooling if openings are large enough. Ultimately, only the presence of thermal inertia in the components of the building can stabilize temperatures during peak hours of the hottest days. In the climates of this research, summers are mild, even if some days can be very hot. Conventional cooling should not be needed in residential buildings in this context, as night temperatures allow for night cooling, and passive strategies should be sufficient to cool down spaces.

Each of the parameters mentioned above are "a function of, and an opportunity for design."[25] Keeping indoor temperatures inside the comfortable range by the means of architecture is achievable with precise work. The definition of the "comfortable or unstressful range" and the method through which "comfort" is evaluated have far-reaching consequences.

2.5. Toward a Definition of Thermal Comfort: Steady-State vs. Adaptive Comfort

The notion of thermal comfort has for a long time (since the second half of the twentieth century) been linked to mechanically controlled spaces with

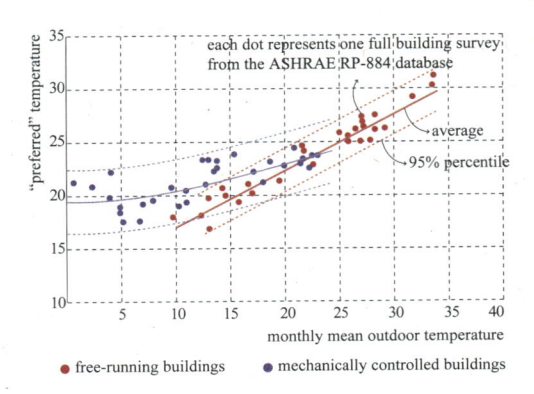

46) Preferred temperature in relation to outdoors, after Humphreys 1978[51]

fixed temperatures, as air conditioning companies marketed their equipment as "providers of comfort." The responsibility of thermal comfort was naturally transferred to equipment and engineers. While Le Corbusier called for a constant use of mechanical equipment, "the buildings of Russia, Paris, Suez or Buenos Aires, the steamer crossing the Equator, will be hermetically closed. In winter warmed, in summer cooled, which means that pure controlled air at 18°C circulates within forever."[45] Reyner Banham declared "this book need never have been written, because those services in buildings that provide for the comfort and well-being of humans would have always have been part of the history of architecture," in his book *The Architecture of the Well-Tempered Environment*.[46] Until very recently, target temperature in a building was determined under this philosophy, with fixed set points following Fanger's steady-state comfort model,[47] which was based on heat-balance equations and studies carried out with test subjects in a climate chamber. The latter involved 1,296 students with a similar profile, dressed in similar clothing, sitting in a room with no windows and within a controlled environment. The subjects were meant to emit a vote in the ASHRAE scale based on their thermal perception. This "steady-state" model takes for granted the use of air conditioning and is only applicable in such controlled atmospheres, where no adaptation is possible, and the subjects are constantly seeking any slight discomfort. Following these studies, the PMV/PPD method was created, which set the narrow comfort criteria used to justify energy-intense equipment and strict temperature set points. Although it has opened the field of thermal comfort and has been the basis for decades, the Fanger model has not proven to be successful in predicting thermal comfort when comparison was drawn from a large comfort-survey database. The accuracy of the model was only 34%, as subjects were a lot more tolerant than predicted from Fanger's heat-balance theory.[48] Standard ISO 7730 (2005) is based on the PMV/PPD model.[43] The

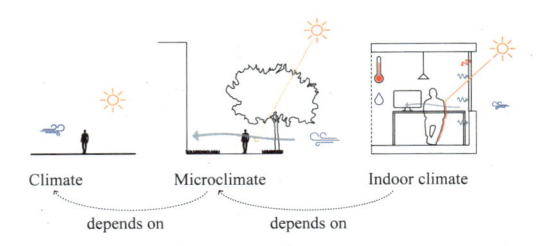

44) External conditions affecting indoor temperature

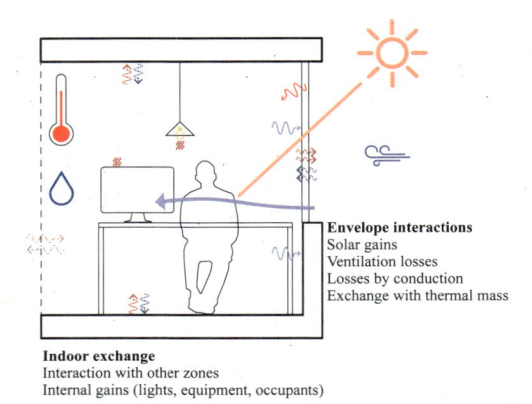

45) Building parameters affecting indoor temperature

Envelope interactions
Solar gains
Ventilation losses
Losses by conduction
Exchange with thermal mass

Indoor exchange
Interaction with other zones
Internal gains (lights, equipment, occupants)

current context of the climate crisis calls for a different approach of architecture toward the means to provide thermally comfortable environments and energy demand, and a more scientific view of the thermal needs of the human body.

In the late 1970s, Humphreys introduced the adaptive comfort theory, challenging Fanger's approach: "If building occupants are allowed to adapt to their environment, either by adjusting clothing, controls or location, then they could tolerate environmental conditions outside those recommended by the 'steady-state' theories."[49] When there is the possibility of choice or adaptation, tolerance can be higher, as the brain knows that the current situation does not present a danger. Examples of "adaptive behavior" can be opening the windows, the use of blinds, the use of fans, local heating, a relatively short distance to windows, flexibility of choice inside the space, freedom of clothing choice. However, when there are no adaptation possibilities, the brain is less tolerant and the only way to reduce discomfort is to modify the temperature through machines. Examples of nonadaptive environments can be deep plans, lack of flexibility of choice in the space, dense occupation, central controls, not being able to open the windows, not being able to choose clothing.[50] Buildings can therefore provide more or less adaptive opportunities, more or less layers to interact, which in turn impacts occupants' tolerance.

The adaptive comfort theory was in turn derived from field surveys in real settings (46). Humphreys observed that the "preferred temperature" in a free-running building was linearly related to the monthly mean outdoor temperature, whereas the "preferred temperature" in a conditioned building followed a different curve. These observations were confirmed with a larger database in later studies (47–48).[51, 52]

2.6. A Contemporary Definition of Thermal Comfort: EN 15251

The European standard EN 15251 provides, among other parameters, the adaptive comfort algorithm (ACA) that defines "comfort temperatures" in the European context.[13] This algorithm was the result of a large research project funded by the EU and was based on Humphrey's adaptive comfort theory.[51] Starting from the notion that "the optimum internal temperature for a building, i.e. the temperature at which most people will report comfort, could be related to the external temperature at that location over a considerable range," the initial equation took the form of

$T_{RMn} = c.T_{RMn-1} + (1-c).T_{DMn-1}$

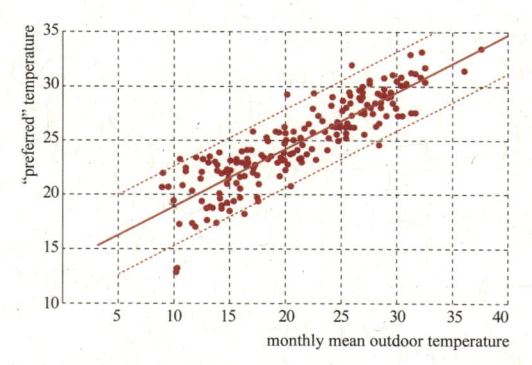

47) Preferred temperature in free-running buildings, after Humphreys et al. 1978–2010[51]

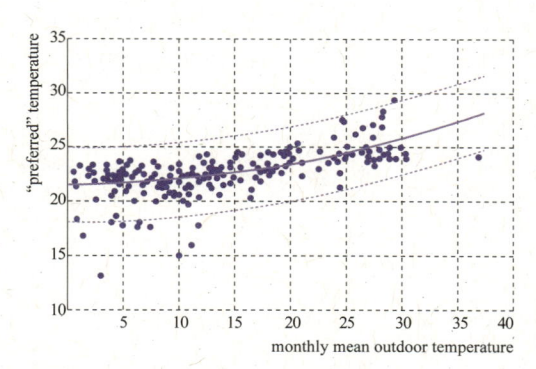

48) Preferred temperature in mechanically conditioned buildings, after Humphreys et al. 1978–2010[51]

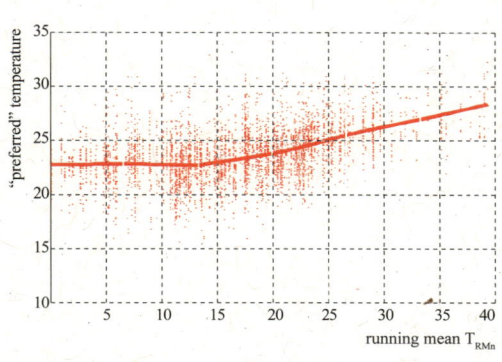

49) Studies for the adaptive comfort algorithm, after McCartney and Nicol 2002[52]

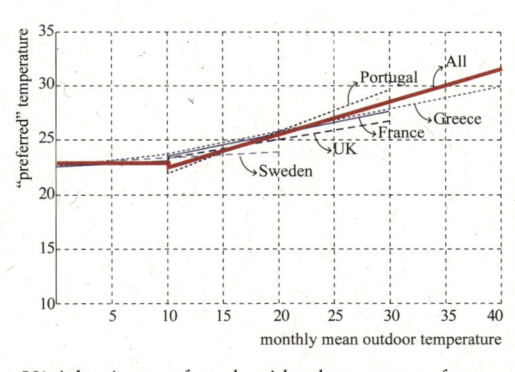

50) Adaptive comfort algorithm by country, after McCartney and Nicol 2002[52]

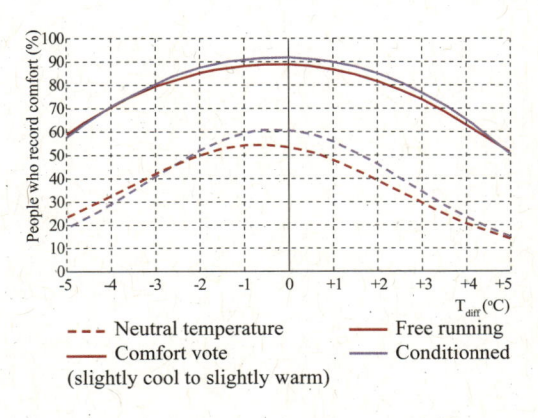

51) Studies on comfort and deviation from neutral temperature, after Humphreys et al. 2010[42]

However, this form of the equation resulted in interior temperatures that are too low when it is cold outside, and a lower limit of T_{RMn} was specified. The final form resulted as follows:

$T_C = d.T_{RMn} + e; T_{RM} > f$ °C and

$T_C = g; T_{RMn} < f$ °C

where d, e, f, g are constants.

The field studies aimed to find those constants through the analysis of empirical field data and verify the resulting methodology in practice (49). Surveys were made on 25 buildings in five countries—the UK, France, Sweden, Greece, and Portugal—considering a variety of types, building construction, sizes, and use (50). They consisted of longitudinal and transversal questionnaires to determine the "comfort temperature" while monitoring air temperature, globe temperature, relative humidity, air velocity, CO_2 concentration, illuminance at working plane, and background noise level. Comfort temperature was defined as "the indoor operative temperature at which an average subject will vote comfortable (or neutral) on the ASHRAE scale." Results helped to specify those constants using regression analysis on data obtained. The final form of the equations are as follows:

$T_C = 0.33\ T_{RM80} + 18.8$ if

$T_{RM80} > 10$°C

$T_C = 22.88$ °C, if

$T_{RM80} < 10$°C

All other parameters aside from the weighted mean outside temperature were found to be negligible for an indoor study in the European context. The correlation between field data and the ACA was the highest ($r^2 = 0.38$) among several comfort methods (for instance, Fanger's method was 0.25).

The acceptable deviation from the neutral temperature was also explored, based on the field studies, to determine a "comfort range" (51).[42] It was concluded that the "proportion comfortable decreases little within 2°C of the neutral temperature. At 3°C, the risk of discomfort increases to 25%," and is therefore used as the limit for most of the buildings. In EN 15251, the comfort range varies according to the building category, depending on the levels of expectations: category I (±2°C) is for buildings occupied with very sensitive or fragile people (disabled, sick, babies, elderly); category II (±3°C) is for normal levels of expectation; and category III (±4°C) is for existing buildings. In this publication, category II was used to enable comparison. The resulting limits of the comfort band were used to evaluate the free-running mode of all case studies:

Upper limit:
$\Theta_{i\,max} = 0.33\,T_{RM80} + 18.8 + 3$

Lower limit:
$\Theta_{i\,min} = 0.33\,T_{RM80} + 18.8 - 3$

Note: EN 15251 has already been superseded by EN 16798. At the time of this research, EN 16798 did not exist, and all studies were carried out under EN 15251. The comfort algorithm in both standards is very similar, though the new one has more tolerance in the low bound (1°C) during the warmer parts of the year.

2.7. Defining Outdoor Comfort: UTCI

For outdoor comfort, the Universal Thermal Climate Index by COST Action 730 takes a multidimensional set of environmental variables and calculates a single indicator, similar to a feels-like temperature: the temperature under reference conditions that produces an physiological response equivalent to the given combination of environmental variables.[53] The resulting equivalent temperature is categorized into ten categories according to the responses of the human body.[21,54] Its authors developed it based on a detailed multi-node model of the human body (Fiala model),[55] together with a bespoke adaptive clothing algorithm that considers the behavioral adaptation observed in the general population, the unequal clothing distribution over the body, and its thermal and evapotranspiration insulation properties.[54] Throughout this research, the UTCI has been employed to assess outdoor comfort.

– Extreme heat stress [UTCI above 46°C]: steep increase in sweat rate and decrease in total net heat loss.

– Very strong heat stress [UTCI 38–46°C]: core to skin temperature difference below 1°C after 30 min.

– Strong heat stress [UTCI 32–38°C]: medium sweat rate.

– Moderate heat stress [UTCI 26–32°C]: steep increase in skin wettedness and occurrence of sweating at 30 min.

– No thermal stress [UTCI 9–26°C].

– Slight cold stress [UTCI 0–9°C]: local minimum temperature on hands.

– Moderate cold stress [UTCI -13–0°C]: decreased blood flow after 120 min., vasoconstriction, decrease in face temperature (pain).

– Strong cold stress [UTCI -13– -27°C]: increase in core/skin temperature gradient, face skin temperature below 7°C (numbness).

– Very strong cold stress [UTCI -27– -40°C]: shivering and high risk of frostbite on face skin.

– Extreme cold stress [UTCI below -40°C]: frostbite on face skin.

1. United Nations Environment Programme and Global Alliance for Buildings and Construction, Global Status Report for Buildings and Construction - Beyond foundations: Mainstreaming sustainable solutions to cut emissions from the buildings sector. [online]. Available: https://wedocs.unep.org/20.500.11822/45095. [Accessed: Sept. 12, 2024].

2. IPCC, 2022: Climate Change 2022: Mitigation of Climate Change. Contribution of Working Group III to the Sixth Assessment Report of the Intergovernmental Panel on Climate Change [P.R. Shukla, J. Skea, R. Slade, A. Al Khourdajie, R. van Diemen, D. McCollum, M. Pathak, S. Some, P. Vyas, R. Fradera, M. Belkacemi, A. Hasija, G. Lisboa, S. Luz, J. Malley, (eds.)]. Cambridge University Press, Cambridge, UK and New York, NY, USA. doi: 10.1017/9781009157926

3. H. Beck et al., "Present and Future Köppen-Geiger Climate Classification Maps at 1-km Resolution," *Sci Data* 5 (2018), https://doi.org/10.1038/sdata.2018.214.

4. M. Uyan and O. L. Dogmus, "An Integrated GIS-Based ANP Analysis for Selecting Solar Farm Installation Locations: Case Study in Cumra Region, Turkey," *Environ Model Assess* 28 (2023): 105–119, https://doi.org/10.1007/s10666-022-09870-1.

5. Meteotest AG, "Meteonorm Software," 1994, accessed 2019, https://meteonorm.com/en/.

6. M. S. Roudsari and M. Pak, "Ladybug: A Parametric Environmental Plugin for Grasshopper to Help Designers Create an Environmentally-Conscious Design," in *Proceedings of BS 2013: 13th Conference of the International Building Performance Simulation Association Proceedings of the 13th International IBPSA Conference* (2013): 3128–35.

7. G. Ward Larson and R. Shakespeare, *Rendering with Radiance: The Art and Science of Lighting Visualization* (San Francisco: Morgan Kaufmann Publishers, 1998).

8. H. Weller, G. Tabor, H. Jasak, and C. Fureby, "A Tensorial Approach to Computational Continuum Mechanics Using Object-Oriented Techniques," *Computers in Physics* 12, no. 6 (1998): 620–31.

9. US Department of Energy, "EnergyPlus Engineering Reference: The Reference to EnergyPlus Calculations. EnergyPlus Version 8.7," accessed 2019, https://energyplus.net/.

10. J. A. Jakubiec, "Lighting Materials," accessed 2019, http://www.lighting-materials.com/ (URL no longer active).

11. W. K. George, "Lectures in Turbulence for the 21st Century," January 16, 2013, "Lecture Notes at Chalmers University of Technology, Gothenburg, Sweden," 2013, http://www.turbulence-online.com/Publications/Lecture_Notes/Turbulence_Lille/TB_16January2013.pdf.

12. P. Nielsen, F. Allard, H. Awbi, L. Davidson, and A. Schälin, "Computational Fluid Dynamics in Ventilation Design," REHVA Guidebook No. 10, *International Journal of Ventilation* 6, no. 3 (2007): 291–94; J. Franke, A. Hellsten, H. Schlünzen, and B. Carissimo, eds., *Best Practice Guideline for the CFD Simulation of Flows in the Urban Environment: COST Action 732; Quality Assurance and Improvement of Microscale Meteorological Models* (Brussels: COST Office, 2007).

13. CEN, *EN 15251: Indoor Environmental Input Parameters for Design and Assessment of Energy Performance of Buildings Addressing Indoor Air Quality, Thermal Environment, Lighting and Acoustics* (Brussels: European Committee for Standardization, 2007).

14. CEN, *EN 16798-1: Energy Performance of Buildings. Ventilation for Buildings. Indoor Environmental Input Parameters for Design and Assessment of Energy Performance of Buildings Addressing Indoor Air Quality, Thermal Environment, Lighting and Acoustics* (Brussels: European Committee for Standardization, 2019).

15. M. Deru, K. Field, D. Studer, K. Benne, B. Griffith, P. Torcellini, B. Liu, M. Halverson, D. Winiarski, M. Rosenberg, M. Yazdanian, J. Huang, and D. Crawley, *U.S. Department of Energy Commercial Reference Building Models of the National Building Stock* (US Department of Energy, 2011), https://www.nrel.gov/docs/fy11osti/46861.pdf.

16. CEN, *EN 13779: Ventilation for Non-residential Buildings: Performance Requirements for Ventilation and Room-Conditioning Systems* (Brussels: European Committee for Standardization, 2007).

17. Ministère de la Transition Ecologique et de la Cohésion des territoires, Ministère de la Transition Ecologique et Solidaire (MTES), and Ministère de la Cohésion des Territoires et des Relations avec les Collectivités Territoriales (MCTRCT), "RT2012," https://rt-re-batiment.developpement-durable.gouv.fr/rt2012-r269.html?lang=fr.

18. CEN, *EN 17037: Daylight in Buildings* (Brussels: European Committee for Standardization, 2018).

19. Ministère de la Transition Ecologique, "Projets de décret et arrêtés relatifs aux exigences de performance énergétique et environnementale, et à la méthode de calcul associée, pour la réglementation environnementale 2020 (RE2020)," http://www.consultations-publiques.developpement-durable.gouv.fr/projets-de-decret-et-arretes-relatifs-aux-a2330.html.

20. European Cooperation in the Field of Scientific and Technical Research (COST), "COST Action 730 Executive Summary: The Universal Thermal Climate Index UTCI for Assessing the Thermal Environment of the Human Being," 2009, https://www.utci.org/cost.html.

21. P. Bröde, G. Jendritzky, D. Fiala, and G. Havenith, "The Universal Thermal Climate Index UTCI in Operational Use" (conference contribution, "Adapting to Change: New Thinking on Comfort," Cumberland Lodge, Windsor, 2010).

22. M. Ronnier Luo, Guihua Cui, and Changjun Li, "Uniform Colour Spaces Based on CIECAM02 Colour Appearance Model," *Color Research and Application* 31, no. 4 (2006): 320–30.

23. E. C. O. M. M. O. E. W. E. Lewis, "WELL Building Standard," 2018.

24. J. Zeitzer, D. Dijk, R. Kronauer, E. Brown, and C. Czeisler, "Sensitivity of the Human Circadian

Pacemaker to Nocturnal Light: Melatonin Phase Resetting and Suppression," *Journal of Physiology* 526 (2000): 695–702.

25. N. Baker and K. Steemers, *Healthy Homes: Designing with Light and Air for Sustainability and Wellbeing* (London: RIBA, 2019).

26. S. V. Szokolay, *Introduction to Architectural Science: The Basis of Sustainable Design* (Abingdon: Routledge, 2014).

27. C. Reinhart, *Daylighting Handbook Vol. 1* (Cambridge, MA: Building Technology Press, 2014).

28. N. Baker, "Daylighting," 2015, lecture at the MSc Program Sustainable Environmental Design at the Architectural Association, London.

29. P. Tregenza, "The Daylight Factor and Actual Illuminance Ratios," *Lighting Research and Technology* 1, no. 2 (1980).

30. J. Mardaljevic, "Examples of Climate-Based Daylight Modeling," Paper No. 67, CIBSE National Conference 2006: Engineering the Future, 2006.

31. CEN, *EN 12464-1: Light and Lighting. Lighting of Work Places. Indoor Work Places* (Brussels: European Committee for Standardization, 2011).

32. CIE, "Daylight," *International Commission on Illumination* (1970).

33. D. Hunt, "Predicting Artificial Lighting Use: A Method Based upon Observed Patterns of Behaviour," *Lighting Research & Technology* (1980).

34. M. S. Rea, *The IESNA Lighting Handbook: Reference & Application* (New York: Illuminating Engineering Society of North America, 2000).

35. A. Psikuta, D. Fiala, G. Laschewski, G. Jendritzky, M. Richards, K. Blazejcyk, I. Mek Javic, R. De Dear, G. Havenith, and H. Rintamäki, "Evaluation of the Fiala Multi-node Thermophysiological Model for UTCI Application," *International Journal of Biometeorology* 56, no. 3 (2012): 443–60.

36. S. Yannas, *Solar Energy and Housing Design: Principles, Objectives, Guidelines* (London: Architectural Association Publications, 1994).

37. F. Nicol, M. Humphreys, and S. Roaf, *Adaptive Thermal Comfort* (London: Routledge, 2012).

38. Z. J. Schlader and N. T. Vargas, "Regulation of Body Temperature by Autonomic and Behavioral Thermoeffectors," *Exercise and Sport Sciences Reviews* 47, no. 2 (2019): 116–26.

39. ASHRAE, "ASHRAE 55: Thermal Environmental Conditions for Human Occupancy," 2010, www.ashrae.org.

40. E. Erell, D. Pearlmutter, and T. J. Williamson, "Urban Microclimate: Designing the Spaces between Buildings," 2011.

41. CIBSE, *Guide A: Environmental Design* (Chartered Institution of Building Services Engineers, 2017).

42. F. Nicol and M. Humphreys, "Derivation of the Adaptive Equations for Thermal Comfort in Free-Running Buildings in European Standard EN 15251," *Building and Environment* 45 (2010): 11–17.

43. International Organization for Standardization, "ISO 7730:2005 – Ergonomics of the Thermal Environment," 2005.

44. U. E. P. Agency, "Indoor Air Quality," US Environmental Protection Agency, accessed 2019, https://www.epa.gov/report-environment/indoor-air-quality.

45. Le Corbusier, "Précisions," 1930.

46. R. Banham, *The Architecture of the Well-Tempered Environment* (City: Publisher, 1969).

47. O. Fanger, *Thermal Comfort* (Copenhagen: Danish Technical Press, 1970).

48. T. Cheung, S. Schiavon, T. Parkinson, P. Li, and G. Brager, "Analysis of the Accuracy on PMV–PPD Model Using the ASHRAE Global Thermal Comfort Database II," *Building and Environment* 153 (2019): 205–17.

49. M. A. Humphreys, "Outdoor Temperatures and Comfort Indoors," *Building Research and Practice (J CIB)* 6, no. 2 (1978): 92–105.

50. N. Baker, "Adaptive Thermal Comfort," 2015, lecture at the MSc Program Sustainable Environmental Design at the Architectural Association, London.

51. M. Humphreys, H. Rijal, and F. Nicol, "Examining and Developing the Adaptive Relation between Climate and Thermal Comfort Indoors," *Proceedings of Conference: Adapting to Change: New Thinking on Comfort* (2010).

52. K. McCartney and F. Nicol, "Developing an Adaptive Control Algorithm for Europe," *Energy and Buildings* 34 (2002): 623–35.

53. European Cooperation in the Field of Scientific and Technical Research (COST), "Memorandum of Understanding for the Implementation of a European Concerted Research Action Designated as COST Action 730: Towards a Universal Thermal Climate Index UTCI for Assessing the Thermal Environment of the Human Being," 2005.

54. K. Błażejczyk, G. Jendritzky, P. Bröde, D. Fiala, G. Havenith, Y. Epstein, A. Psikuta, and B. Kampmann, "An Introduction to the Universal Thermal Climate Index (UTCI)," *Geographia Polonica* 86, no. 1 (2013): 5–10.

55. D. Fiala, G. Havenith, P. Broede, B. Kampmann, and G. Jendritzky, "Utci-fiala Multi-node Model of Human Heat Transfer and Temperature Regulation," *International Journal of Biometeorology* 56 (2019): 429–41.

Image Credits:

p. 3: Guilhem Vellut, Creative Commons Attribution 2.0 generic license

pp. 5, 7, 79–81, 119–21, 195–97: © Lacaton & Vassal

Cover, pp. 12, 16, 19, 20, 22, 27, 28, 31, 32, 35, 37, 38, 41, 45, 46, 49, 50–52, 66–71, 78, 105–18, 140–56, 185–94, 231: © Philippe Ruault

pp. 15, 223, 225, 227: © Anne Lacaton & Jean-Philippe Vassal

pp. 24, 65, 72–77: © DP (David Pradel)

p. 42: © Elisa Murcia Artengo

pp. 235, 237: ©Frédéric Druot, Anne Lacaton & Jean-Philippe Vassal

pp. 55–64, 82–104, 122–39, 160–84, 198–218, 240–53: © Atmos Lab, if not stated otherwise

Colophon

Editors:
Anne Lacaton, Jean-Philippe Vassal

Analytic Studies:
Atmos Lab (Florencia Collo, Olivier Dambron, Rafael Alonso Candau)

Research Team: Anne Lacaton, Jean-Philippe Vassal, Florencia Collo, Olivier Dambron, Rafael Alonso Candau, Gaëtan Redelsperger

Project and Content Coordination, Documentation: Carina Sacher

Advisors: Christian Cardonnel, Julien Callot

Design: Something Fantastic

Graphic Production:
Julien Sage-Thomas,
Gaëtan Redelsperger

Photos: Philippe Ruault, Elisa Murcia Artengo, David Pradel, Lacaton & Vassal

Illustrations: Frédéric Druot, Lacaton & Vassal, David Pradel

Copy Editors: David Rocks, Max Bach

Proofreading: Max Bach

Typeface: Sabon LT Pro, Helvetica Neue
Paper: Enviro nature 90g
Lithography: Falk Flach / typegerecht
Printing and Binding: Gugler, Austria

The German National Library lists this publication in the Deutsche Nationalbibliografie. Detailed bibliographic data is available online at https://portal.dnb.de/opac.htm.

This work is subject to copyright. All rights are reserved, whether the whole or part of the material is concerned, specifically the rights of translation, reprinting, reuse of illustrations, recitation, broadcasting, reproduction on microfilms or in other ways, and storage in data banks. For any kind of use, permission of the copyright holder must be obtained.

© 2025 Ruby Press, Berlin
© The contributors for their texts and images

Every effort has been made to obtain proper credit information and permission. However, we have used a small number of images for which copyright holders could not be identified. It has been our assumption that such images belong to the public domain. If you claim ownership of any of the images presented here, and have not been properly identified, please notify Ruby Press and we will be happy to make an acknowledgment in future editions.

This publication was made possible by the generous support of:

DARCH   **ETH**zürich
Faculty of Architecture

Acknowledgments: Carina Sacher, Karine Dana, Christian Cardonnel, Gaëtan Redelsperger; Denis Gilloots, the greenhouse builder who agreed to adapt agricultural greenhouses to our architectural projects; Frédéric Druot, Christophe Hutin, and all the architects and collaborators of the office who contributed to the design and realization of the projects; and the residents who agreed to be interviewed and photographed and have sensors installed in their homes.

RUBY PRESS GmbH
Schönholzer Str. 11
10115 Berlin
Germany
www.ruby-press.com

Printed in Austria
ISBN 978-3-944074-37-5